Presented To:

_____

From:

_____

Date:

_____

THE

DIVINITY
CODE
TO UNDERSTANDING YOUR DREAMS AND VISIONS

THE

DIVINITY
CODE

TO UNDERSTANDING YOUR DREAMS AND VISIONS

Adam F. Thompson & Adrian Beale

DESTINY IMAGE® PUBLISHERS, INC.
P.O. Box 310, Shippensburg, PA 17257-0310
"Promoting Inspired Lives."

This book and all other Destiny Image, Revival Press, MercyPlace, Fresh Bread, Destiny Image Fiction, and Treasure House books are available at Christian bookstores and distributors worldwide.

For a U.S. bookstore nearest you, call 1-800-722-6774.
For more information on foreign distributors, call 717-532-3040.
Reach us on the Internet: www.destinyimage.com.

ISBN 13 TP: 978-0-7684-4090-4

ISBN 13 Ebook: 978-0-7684-8878-4

For Worldwide Distribution, Printed in the U.S.A.
10 / 18

DEDICATION

We would like to dedicate this book to all those who have gone before us, having heard God's voice through dreams and visions, who have been mocked and scorned for their belief.

Thanks to all those involved in proofreading this text: Andrew, Rhonda, Paula, Todd, Steve, Lesley, John, Vicki, Paul, Maureen, Jenny, Josie, and Karen.

Thanks to all those who made contributions through their dreams and visions, without which this text would not exist: Shane, Paula, Gretel, Lesley, Michael, Kirrily, Cathy, Katie, Jan, Rachel, Lois, and Casey.

Our greatest praise to the Holy Spirit for revealing and teaching us that which we are simply passing on.

ENDORSEMENTS

This is *by far* the most thorough and exhaustive manual on dreams, visions, symbolism, and dream interpretation that we have seen. We consider it a mandatory tool in our personal reference library. This is a must-have for every believer who wants to go farther and deeper into the seer realm

Jeff and Jan Jansen
Global Fire Ministries
Global Fire Church and World Miracle Center

Adam and Adrian have produced the most comprehensive book on dreams and interpretation I have ever seen!

Kathie Walters
www.kathiewaltersministry.com

The Divinity Code to Understanding Your Dreams and Visions is an excellent resource for all prophetic people. The depth of biblical theology and spiritual insight in this book will greatly aid all those who want to know more about the proper function of prophecy. This book also provides sound principals of how to interpret dreams and analyze biblical symbolism. I highly recommend it!"

Stacey Campbell
www.revivalnow.com

The Divinity Code to Understanding Your Dreams and Visions is quickly becoming the dream interpreters dream. I use is regularly to help confirm my dreams.

It's a masterpiece that will become part of your private library. Thank you Adrian and Adam for your dedication and sacrifice in producing this outstanding book —just what we all needed."

Chris Harvey
www.chrisharvey.org

Adam and Adrian have done what few in today's "microwave" culture are willing to do. They have painstakingly researched the topic of dream interpretation like no one else, to my knowledge, in history has. I believe this resource is a must have for every scholar or any person serious about understanding the way God speaks to us through dreams. Adam and Adrian, congratulations on a true masterpiece that I believe will stand the test of time throughout many generations.

David Tomberlin
David Tomberlin Ministries

Many times the Lord has spoken to us through dreams, but we would have difficulty knowing what the symbols mean to correctly interpret them. This carefully researched book has a full dictionary to help us interpret our dreams. *The Divinity Code to Understanding Your Dreams and Visions* is an incredible tool in showing us what God is speaking to us on a regular basis, and I would highly recommend it.

Jim Drown
Global Evangelistic Missions

A fellow pastor from Canada gave me a gift of *The Divinity Code to Understanding Your Dreams and Visions* by Adrian Beale and Adam F. Thompson of Australia. They, like myself, realized the importance of listening to the voice of God today through dreams and visions, but also like myself, were unable to obtain a textbook untainted apart from an occult background. God led them to prepare the above text over a four-year period, based on true Evangelical and Bible-grounded background, and made it available in 2008. Following a 10 chapter "help" in dream and vision interpretation, they have then added 101 Sample Dream and Vision Interpretations, based on a Metaphor Dictionary of some 2000 most common Biblically based Metaphors, and also a People and Place Name Dictionary.

I have very thoroughly studied the 10 initial chapters and spent some time also in their other helps. It is my conviction that God has raised up these two brothers in these last days for a most helpful enlargement upon the tribe of Zebulun and for evangelism strengthened by "signs following" through a correct method of interpreting dreams and visions. They like myself do not see *The Divinity Code to Understanding Your Dreams and Visions* alone as a cure-all. but as part of a package of a number of powerful Revival Principles.

Jim Watt
Last remaining elder from the 1948 Latter Rain Revival
Apostolic Teacher
Seattle, USA

This is an important book for the Body of Christ and has been a profound blessing both to me personally and to many in our church. It serves as a powerful key to a deeper level of relationship with God as it awakens a hunger to hear more from Him and opens a door to revelation previously ignored. I used to believe that I would hear from God in dreams only on relatively rare occasions, and this book has helped me realize how limited my awareness of God's voice in dreams has been. How wonderful to now recognize the voice of God, not only speaking prophetically to me, but revealing my heart and the mysteries of the Kingdom through my nightly dreams! The Scripture warns us to not to despise prophecy (see 1 Thess. 5:20), and this book is a valuable tool in helping the Body of Christ to actively value the voice of God.

Katherine Ruonala
Prophetic Evangelist
New Day Ministries

This is an *excellent* book. I can't praise it enough. It takes dream interpretation onto a whole new level. I use it everyday. I carry it all over the world with me. It makes dream and vision interpretation quick, simple, and accessible for all Christians.

The Metaphor Dictionary alone is worth its weight in gold. The absolute best I have ever seen. If you had offered me $10,000 or this book, I would have taken the book. It's that powerful.

For a prophetic person, this book is like being handed a speedboat in place of a canoe, a red Ferrari instead of a bicycle, a spanking new touch screen iPod instead of an old record collection. It's that good.

Please do yourself and the Body of Christ a favor. Buy a dozen copies, keep at least two, and give the rest away to family and friends and anyone who's ever had a dream. It'll change their lives. They will be eternally grateful.

I believe this book is God's gift to the prophetic community worldwide. I am excited at the powerful upgrade it brings to equipping the saints. Thank You, Jesus! Well done, Adrian and Adam!

Brendan McCauley
Irish prophet and author

Dear Adam, I am in Brisbane at the moment with our TV equipment suppliers. Your ministry was a blessing to my church during your recent visit to LAE.

I have been tremendously blessed by your short ministry. Susan always uses your Divinity Code book as a Kingdom tool to guide her as she interprets the dreams that she has. Our church people are still discussing the impact of your ministry with us. Some people who have been complacent and relaxed have been tremendously ignited in the Spirit to run the race. Spiritual hunger was imparted and the people want more of the things of the Spirit. They have come to understand clearly that God speaks to them through dreams and visions today.

The Divinity Code to Understanding Your Dreams and Visions is such a vital tool in the hands of the ordinary believer that the Holy Ghost can use to guide them as they interpret dreams. I would recommend this book to any believer who is moving into the supernatural as the Church is advancing into the apostolic era. This is one of the best books I have on my shelf. God speaks to people using dreams throughout the Scriptures. God speaks through seven channels including directly through the Bible, Gifts of the Spirit, Fivefold Ministry, Audible voice of the Spirit, Inward witness, Angelic messengers, and of course *dreams* and Visions. Therefore, *The Divinity Code to Understanding Your Dreams and Visions* is a must-read for those who thirst and hunger for the prophetic dreams that the Lord is speaking to His Church. As we read this book may we seek the God the Father who gives us His dreams.

The Late Joseph Kingal
PNG Tele-evangelist
LAE

If God used dreams and their interpretation to shape world superpowers through the likes of Joseph and Daniel, how much more today do we need to have understanding of such matters when He is pouring out His Spirit on all flesh through an abundance of dreams and visions. I believe that *The Divinity*

Code to Understanding Your Dreams and Visions is an invaluable resource in equipping us to decode our dreams while inspiring us to go deeper in the things of the Spirit.

This book has been a huge blessing to me and many in our church who have seen their lives impacted as they begin to unlock the things that God has been speaking to them, but previously did not understand. Dream interpretation is not a "spiritual fad" for I have personally witnessed the Holy Spirit use it to expose secrets of the heart, bring repentance and the resulting breakthroughs.

I have found it to be prophetic, inspiring, meticulously researched, and scripturally sound and would recommend it to anyone who is hungry to go deeper in their spiritual journey.

Todd Weatherly
Senior Pastor Field of Dreams Australia

I have been so very blessed through the book, *The Divinity Code to Understanding Your Dreams and Visions*. I have always been interested in how God speaks to us through dreams, but have rarely understood what He is saying to me personally through them. I have bought other dream books, but was frustrated at the limited symbol interpretation.

Since buying *The Divinity Code to Understanding Your Dreams and Visions*, I feel that a new realm of intimacy and communication has opened up to me—the comprehensive interpretations have opened up my dreams in an incredible way. I have been so encouraged by God, but also so blessed that He has warned me and shown me the error in some of my thinking. I encourage everyone to buy this book and especially to read the teachings before the actual dream symbol interpretations. The teachings on dreams is *excellent* and a valuable resource for us all. I love it that this book does not present itself as the ultimate authority, but stresses again and again that it is a resource to be used *always* with the help of the Holy Spirit.

My three favorite books—1. *The Bible*, 2. *My Concordance*, and 3. *The Divinity Code to Understanding Your Dreams and Visions* . . . . it's *that* good!"

Tess Bartsch
Beloved daughter of the King!

This practical tool is well thought out and reads with ease. From the very first sentence I was captivated as I was taken into another person's world and could relate to the very story being shared. The early chapters lay solid theological foundations into the realm of the Spirit and teaching on the "how to" of dream interpretation, giving the reader insight into many examples as they are shared throughout the book.

I have not found to date a tool that is so well referenced and utilized in my personal library on dream and vision interpretation. I use it almost on a daily basis as I am able to sit and write out my dreams and the dreams that others share with me in a sequenced fashion, allowing the Holy Spirit to show me the metaphorical or literal meaning to abstract aspects of my dreams, allowing a vivid and concise interpretation.

One such dream was one I had recurring as a child. After three decades, I now have some answers to questions that have been shelved in my memory bank. *The Divinity Code to Understanding Your Dreams and Visions* is a highly valuable tool and provides much insight into situations, releasing life to the hearer.

Well done to Adam and Adrian for your labor of love! I believe this book serves as a mighty weapon of discernment. The words are living and powerful and sharper than any two edged sword.

Super-Abounding Grace to you,

Veronica Kilrain
Wife, Mother, and Prophetic Intercessor
Western Australia

I think that I have not found two men that have ministered more to me in the area of dreams and visions than any other I have encountered in my 40 years of ministry. I recommend that you read their book, (a great resource for dreams and visions), and attend their conference. It will bring clarity and direction to all who walk with God.

Howard A. Robinson, Jr.
Chief Apostle/Presiding Bishop
Agape Christian Fellowship International

CONTENTS

FOREWORD

The realm of seeing into the mysteries of the Kingdom of God through dreams, visions, and revelations has been accelerated by the Holy Spirit in this generation. Although the aspect of God speaking to His people through dreams has been found all throughout Church and biblical history and is nothing new, we are witnessing an increase of individuals receiving God-inspired dreams. The Lord is definitely speaking through dreams today, and child and adult alike are enjoying profound insights into the heart of God, prophetic glimpses into the future, and clear direction for their lives through this avenue of revelation.

In *The Divinity Code To Understanding Your Dreams and Visions,* you will find practical teaching and understanding on the subject of dreams, their interpretation, and their possible applications. *The Divinity Code To Understanding Your Dreams and Visions* is not only a great book on the subject that offers knowledge, instruction, and encouragement to the reader, but it is an encyclopedia of knowledge and a handbook for symbolism that will benefit dreamers tremendously as they seek to accurately interpret and apply their dreams.

I met both Adrian and Adam while ministering at their church in Australia. They are humble and sincere men who long to see dreamers gain the understanding they need to accurately work with their dreams. They have helped many grow in dream interpretation. Through their teaching seminars and workshops, they have taught church congregations and hungry believers on the subject and have prayed for many to receive an increase of dreams, visions, and revelations. When I met Adam and discerned the authentic call on his life in the area of dreams, I had him pray for me. As a result, I am dreaming more and understanding more. He shared with me how many who attend their workshops or who read *The Divinity Code To Understanding Your Dreams and Visions* begin to dream and have supernatural interpretation after receiving instruction.

If you desire to dream or increase in your ability to interpret and apply them, I highly recommend *The Divinity Code To Understanding Your Dreams and Visions.* It is a reference book that you will want to keep in your study or library. It is a gift. So dream on dreamer; may you discover the voice of the Lord and the seer dimension in clearer ways than ever before.

Patricia King
XPmedia.com

Part I

Discovering Dreams and Visions

Chapter One

Dreams: a Controversial Subject
By Adrian Beale

Before writing this book I had the following dream:

I was wearing a blue shirt with a pen in the shirt pocket. The pen had leaked out dark-blue ink, causing a stain about the size of a quarter. A male friend pointed the stain out. The pen had leaked because the nib had not been retracted.

The interpretation of this dream was that I was going to write material that will offend some people because the subject would be highly controversial, and in writing, I would not hold back. The stain speaks of that offense. The dark blue coloration speaks of the inspiration of the Holy Spirit in what was to be written.

The book you are now holding in your hands is the result of that dream and four years of weekly fellowship with the co-author, Adam Thompson. The same dream was repeated six months later. In repeating the dream, God was reminding me of the importance of this message.

(An explanation of the metaphors used to interpret this dream is found in the sample dream and vision section of this book. See dream 34.)

An Important Preface

Before we endeavor to explore the subject of dreams and visions, I would like to preface our journey with a Scripture that was never more relevant, *"He who answers a matter before he hears it, it is folly and shame to him"* (Prov. 18:13).

21

If until this time you have held some preconceived opinions about the nature of dreams and visions, I would ask that you put these on hold and openly and humbly come to see what the Word of God has to say on the matter (see James 1:21) before you pass judgment. All of us need to be honest enough to admit that our different backgrounds and upbringings have built within us preconceptions and prejudices that potentially will keep us from moving into all that God has for us. This is why the apostle Paul pleads with us to be transformed by the renewing of our minds (see Rom. 12:2).

The Last Days

On the day of Pentecost, Peter aligned the outpouring of the Holy Spirit in Jerusalem with an earlier prophecy made by Joel the prophet (see Joel 2:28-32). In the midst of quoting Joel's words, Peter declared,

> *And it shall come to pass in the last days, says God, that I will pour out of My Spirit on all flesh; your sons and your daughters shall prophesy, your young men shall see visions, your old men shall dream dreams* (Acts 2:17; See Joel 2:28).

This verse proclaims that in the last days God will pour out His Spirit on all of humanity, and the result will be dreams, visions, and prophecy. In quoting Joel, Peter not only associated the events of Pentecost with Joel's earlier prophecy, he also confirmed it to be the fulfillment of Joel's prophecy. In doing that, he also indirectly announced that the "last days" commenced from that moment and will be completed when Christ returns. What that means is that we are in the last days. And we cannot get more last days than these days, right? And yet, if we are honest, as a whole the Body of Christ struggles with dreams (particularly) and visions as being from God and for us today. The message of this book is that God is speaking; He is speaking to believers and unbelievers alike by His Spirit, and this book is a wholesale call by the Spirit of God for the Body of Christ to awaken spiritually and tune in to what He is saying.

The Gospels record that Jesus came to the nation of Israel—who was to be God's chosen vessel to the world—and presented truths from the Father. He was God's representative, and His credentials of signs and wonders affirmed His ambassadorial authority. However, the scribes and Pharisees who claimed to have a relationship with God did not want anything to do with God the Son. Regardless of the signs that confirmed His message, they remained hard-hearted and missed the message He brought to the nation. For the scribes and Pharisees, Jesus was a thorn in their sides because He interfered with their political and selfish agendas and exposed their religious façades. So when they could ignore Him no longer, they killed Him.

Some of us today are like the Pharisees of Jesus' day. We claim to have a relationship with Jesus, yet ignore the current ambassador, the Holy Spirit. Just as they ignored Jesus, claiming to know the Father, we claim to know Jesus and ignore the Spirit!

Others are opting out of the spotlight of what God wants to do in this generation by choosing to live in the past or the future. It is an amazing thing that we can believe for yesterday, we can believe for tomorrow, yet we struggle with faith for today, and yet that is what faith is, *"**Now faith** is the substance of things hoped for, the evidence of things not seen"* (Heb.11:1). And further, it is meant to be our everyday experience, *". . . The just shall live by faith"* (Rom. 1:17).

However, if the truth were known, we do not like to live by faith. We would much prefer to have our security in front of us or in the bank. As a consequence, on the one hand, we have become like Gideon (see Judg. 6:13), looking at past events of the Bible and somehow accepting what happened in those times, but, so that it does not interfere with our reality today, we deal with it by putting it into some dispensational phase of what God was doing "back then." And on the other hand, we are also like Pharaoh who, when asked, "When do you want God to move?" said, "How about tomorrow" (see Exod. 8:9-10). In distancing ourselves in this way, we deny that we have ignored the Spirit of God, and we also pacify our consciences with the fact that some day in the future God will again move in power. For the most part, we don't deny God did what He did in the Bible, but what we struggle with is what He is doing today.

Therefore, unfortunately, we have positioned ourselves to be in much the same place as the Pharisees, who were not privy to the meanings behind Jesus' teachings through parables. We, like them, are missing truth from the Spirit of God through discrediting our dreams as not from God. We think, *Surely, God would speak more clearly and precisely than through those hazy ramblings we experience.* In doing so, we have shut ourselves off to God's voice through dreams and have become like hardened waysides, and as a consequence, *". . . the wicked one comes and snatches away what was sown . . ."* in our hearts (Matt. 13:19). A simple test to see whether this is the case would be to ask ourselves whether we can personally remember the last three dreams we have had?

In comparison, the proponents of the New Age and some schools of psycho-analysis have embraced dreams in their hunger for answers to life's questions. However, being without the Holy Spirit, who is the author (see Acts 2:17) and interpreter (see Gen. 40:8) of dreams, they are nonetheless still in the dark—blind leaders of the blind. Today, some churches are not even aware that God speaks through dreams. We obviously don't know the importance of dreams in the plans and purposes of God, and we have forgotten that the promise of the Holy Spirit brings with it God's prophetic guidance through dreams and visions. Sadly, we look at the equivalent of Nebuchadnezzar's magicians today and see them dabbling with dreams and interpretation and are turned off. We have thrown the baby out with the bathwater when God is calling for an army of Daniels to arise!

Listen to what the Bible says about prophets in the Old Testament,

> *Hear now My words: If there is a prophet among you, I, the Lord, make Myself known to him in a vision; I speak to him in a dream. Not so with My servant Moses; he is faithful in all My house. I speak with him face to face, even plainly, and not in dark sayings . . .* (Numbers 12:6-8).

In these verses God is making a point to Aaron and Miriam, who were complaining about Moses. God, in vindicating Moses before them, shows exactly how prophets other than Moses received their revelation. He says it comes to them in the dark sayings of a dream or vision. The word here for *dark sayings* is the Hebrew word *chidah*, which literally means "a puzzle, riddle, or parable." That God likes to communicate using parables is further displayed in His Word through Hosea, when He says,

> *I have also spoken to [you by] the prophets, and I have multiplied visions [for you] and [have appealed to you] through parables acted out by the prophets* (Hosea 12:10 AMP).

Not only did God speak to the prophets in the Old Testament using parables, He also spoke through the prophets by having them act out His Word using parable-type messages. For example, Hosea married a harlot to show Israel's unfaithfulness to God (see Hos. 1:2); Ezekiel had to dig through a wall in the sight of the house of Israel to convey that they would go into captivity (see Ezek. 12:5); and Jeremiah was to break an earthen flask in the sight of the elders of Jerusalem to show how God was going to break Jerusalem (see Jer. 19:10-13). Later we find in the Gospels that Jesus Himself used more than 50 parables to teach the truths of the Kingdom of God. In fact, parables were His preferred teaching method! Should it be a surprise to us that God is still using parables today?

The Bible says in the last days God will pour out His Spirit on all flesh, and the result of that outpouring is prophecy, visions, and dreams (see Acts 2:17). Those days did not cease with the death of the 12 apostles, as some think, and those days are not in the distant future. Those days are these days! God is speaking in dreams and visions today. The countless dreams and visions that God has allowed the authors to interpret are testament to this fact. The information and counsel disclosed in these dreams in most cases could only be from the Spirit of God.

Human beings know instinctively that God is a miracle-working God. And this is confirmed as we read the Bible. The Bible also says that God has not changed (see Mal. 3:6) and that He is the same today as He has ever been (see Heb. 13:8). But the truth we really need to take to heart is that He is still the miracle-working God for those who have ears to hear (see Matt. 13:9).

Are We Hearing What God Is Saying?

A pastor friend came to me with the following dream,

I saw some terrorists on a gallows about to be hung; at the same time I heard commentary about how these terrorists were planning to escape and then attack. I watched as one of the terrorists rolled off the platform with an accompanied explosion, and then I heard gun-fire. There were wounded soldiers sitting in pews looking on; then one of the soldiers (he had his hand in a sling) got up and fired his machine gun back at the terrorists above the heads of the soldiers in the pews. I had some concerns that he may have hit others in the pews because he was careless in shooting back.

This dream is a significant warning. It speaks of potential problems created by false converts (the terrorists) who do not truly come to the cross of Christ. The gallows represent the cross and avoidance of the hangman's noose says that they have not truly died at Calvary and thus avoid its demands on the human heart. These are seen as terrorists because they are used by the enemy to sow discord and strife in the Body of Christ. They are the equivalent to the tares in Christ's parable of the wheat and tares (see Matt. 13:25, 27-28).

The explosion speaks about an incident that is threatening to flare up, which will be followed by words fired back and forth. Soldiers in the pews show the Church as God's spiritual army. They are shown to be wounded because they have not fully dealt with the hurts and disappointments of the past.

The soldier with a sling firing back is possibly a picture of a leader who is not fully whole himself reacting to the words that follow the incident with the potential of hurting others within the ministry.

This is a warning to be aware of false converts, a reminder to work through past hurts, and also a caution not to react to everything that is said in and around the Church.

(An explanation of the metaphors used to interpret this dream is found in the dream and vision sample section of this book. See dream 43.)

If you are in leadership in the Body of Christ, chances are, because of your busy schedule, God will take the opportunity to speak to you during your down-time (sleep). Would you have missed this message from God? Thankfully the ministry involved in the above dream had ears to hear what the Holy Spirit was saying and was subsequently prepared for the potential danger.

Joseph and Daniel

It was the Holy Spirit who empowered Joseph to interpret Pharaoh's dreams, *"And Pharaoh said to his servants, 'Can we find such a one as this, a man in whom is the Spirit of God?'"* (Gen. 41:38). And it was the Holy Spirit, acknowledged by Nebuchadnezzar, who gave Daniel the incredible insight he possessed.

> *Belteshazzar* [Daniel], *chief of the magicians, because I know that the Spirit of the Holy God is in you, and no secret troubles you, explain to me the visions of my dream that I have seen, and its interpretation* (Daniel 4:9).

Joseph and Daniel were especially endowed with the Spirit of God. They were men God placed specifically at the right place and at the right time to be used through dreams, visions, and their interpretation. The beauty of Joel's prophecy in the opening verse of this chapter is that God is pouring out the same Spirit that Joseph and Daniel were partakers of, but in greater measure (see John 14:12) on you and me, today!

Therefore, if we are going to be used of God to the measure He has planned, we need to recognize that our dreams are deeply significant in the plan of God for our lives. Like He did with Daniel and Joseph, God, through dreams, is speaking and preparing us for what He has specifically brought us forth to accomplish at this time. I believe there is a mission for you and me that will not be fully realized unless we move on the instruction we receive through dreams. Likewise, if we are going to understand what God is saying to us in these dream messages, we need to repent of our insensitivity to the Holy Spirit and to cultivate a relationship with Him.

Jesus and Nicodemus

When Nicodemus visited Jesus, he had hardly gotten through his opening lines when Jesus nailed him! Nicodemus says, *"Rabbi, we know that You are a teacher come from God; for no one can do these signs that You do unless God is with him"* (John 3:2). Quick as a flash, Jesus replies, *"Truly, truly, I say to you, unless one is born again, he cannot **see** the kingdom of God"* (John 3:3 NASB).

If it seems to you that Jesus answered a different question than what Nicodemus was asking, you're on the ball. Actually Nicodemus hadn't even got to his question when—*wham!* Jesus goes to the heart of the matter. Nicodemus is a Jew of Jews and recognized by Jesus as *the* teacher of Israel (see John 3:10). The question on every true Jew's heart was, *When is the Messianic kingdom coming?* There is too much in Jesus' response to go into depth here, but let us just note a couple of things. First, He is speaking to someone who really knows the Old Testament, and second, He said you can only *see* the Kingdom if you are born again. Nicodemus is still not even on the same page because he replies, *"How can a man be born when he is old? Can he enter a second time into his mother's womb and be born?"* (John 3:4).

Jesus is speaking spiritually, and Nicodemus is thinking naturally. That is exactly what happens when God speaks to us in dreams and visions. God plumbs and divides our hearts or reveals Kingdom dynamics, and we are left thinking, *What was that about?* He speaks spiritually, and we tend to think naturally. This story goes further, as Jesus responds by saying, *"Truly, truly, I say to you, unless one is born of water and the Spirit, he cannot **enter** into the kingdom of God"* (John 3:5 NASB).

Here it is important to understand that now Jesus has moved beyond just *seeing* the Kingdom to *entering* it. Remember who Jesus is speaking to here: the teacher of Israel, a person soaked in the Old Testament. Who in the Old

Testament saw, but did not enter? That person would have to be Moses. Why didn't he enter? He wasn't able to enter because he was disobedient or insensitive to the Spirit of God at the waters of Meribah (see Num. 20:12). Who was allowed to enter? That would have to be Joshua and Caleb and a new generation not bound to Egypt (the world) in their thinking. Of Joshua, it is said that he was *"a man in whom is the Spirit"* (Num. 27:18). And of Caleb, the Bible records, *"he has a different spirit in him"* (Num. 14:24). Who else was unable to enter? All those who did not believe God after He had brought them out of Egypt and who continued only to see things in the natural (see Num. 13:33).

What is this saying? It is saying there is a generation of people who know the Word of God, who are born again, and who see God's Kingdom on the pages of the Bible, but who fail to enter what God has for them because they are only prepared to think naturally, or rather, not prepared to think spiritually (see Isa. 55:8-9; Rom. 8:5-6). Now we know this is not you, or you would not be reading this book. However, there is a group of people in danger of dying in the spiritual training ground that is designed to teach them Kingdom dynamics (see Deut. 8:2-3), unless they are prepared to be led by the Spirit of God into the Promised Land in the next phase of their journey. These are those still holding on to past tradition and religious practices. If we deny His leading, like Nicodemus, we will remain spiritual babes, regardless of our Bible knowledge or title within the Church (see Rom. 8:14).

Think about it. If the characters in the Bible had ignored the guidance they received specifically through dreams, there would be:

- No Isaac (see Gen 20:3, 6-7)
- No Israel (see Gen 41:37-41; 45:5; 50:20)
- No Solomon's kingdom (see 1 Kings 3:5-15)
- Less understanding of future world events (see Dan 2; 4)
- No Jesus (see Matt 1:20-24; 2:13,22)

Now, if there had been no Jesus, there would be no salvation through His death upon the cross. If there had been no salvation, there would be no release of the Holy Spirit. If there is no means of salvation and no release of the Holy Spirit, humankind is without eternal life and we are forever doomed to be permanently separated from the Presence of God. Aren't you glad that someone took dreams seriously?

Old and Young Men?

Doubt about whether we are supposed to receive dreams may be created by the age criteria in Joel's prophecy. So it would be useful to clarify that question and at the same time present what is perhaps the key reason we ignore the Holy Spirit's guidance through dreams. When the Bible says, *" . . . Your young men shall see visions, your old men shall dream dreams"* (Acts 2:17), it is not talking about natural age. It is speaking spiritually, just as Jesus did with Nicodemus. Dreams occur when we are asleep. In spiritual terms, *sleep* is the same as *death*.

Do you remember when Jesus went to resurrect Lazarus? He said, *"Our friend Lazarus sleeps, but I go that I may wake him up"* (John 11:11). When the disciples heard these words, they thought He was speaking naturally. They said, *"Lord, if he sleeps he will get well"* (John 11:12). Jesus had to spell it out for them, "Lazarus is dead" (see John 11:13). Jesus was talking about cold, hard physical death, but He called it *sleep*.

Now to turn this around; when we have dreams, we are asleep. That is, we are, spiritually speaking, as dead people. To put it another way, a dream comes to us in the soulish faculties of our minds, and that is, spiritually speaking, to the "old self" (see Rom. 6:6)—the "old men" of this prophecy. Now the old self is dead to the things of God. This is why this chapter begins with the acknowledgement that believers and unbelievers alike receive dreams from the Spirit of God. Both believers and unbelievers receive dreams from God through their "old self." (Many versions of the Bible use "old man," but that term is not intended as gender specific.) The fact that it is the old self, or our soul, that receives the dreams we dream is perhaps the main reason we deny the dreams we experience as being from God. Think about it. Dreams relate what is happening in the spirit realm to the natural person. They can only be interpreted if the spiritual person is tuned in to the Spirit of God!

Visions, on the other hand, are direct communications to the regenerated spirit of people and, as such, are only for believers. The text calls them "young men," those who are hungry to do God's will and who are consequently empowered by the Spirit of God. Let us confirm this scripturally. David the psalmist writes, *"Who satisfies your mouth with good things, so that your youth is renewed like the eagle's"* (Ps. 103:5). Why does David make reference to the eagle here? He does so because he is not talking about natural sustenance. He is saying that when we are hungry for God, He supplies us with the living Word of God, and in receiving that, our spiritual selves (the eagle) are rejuvenated. Therefore, our spirit self is the "young man."

Remember what the apostle Paul said about conversion? He said, *"Therefore if any one is in Christ, he is a new creation; old things have passed away; behold, all things have become new"* (2 Cor. 5:17). Here both the *old* and the *new* self are contrasted for us. The *old* refers to our spiritually dead existence prior to coming to the cross of Christ, and the *new* talks about the birthing of our spirit person. Jesus said it like this, *"Truly, truly, I say to you, unless one is born again, he cannot **see** the kingdom of God"* (John 3:3 NASB). In a discussion about those who receive visions, this Scripture alone is very pointed. Jesus Himself says we have to be "born again" to see!

Now, that baby spirit has to grow, and it grows by hungering for God's will and by imbibing the Word of God. Over a period of time, by applying what it takes in, it becomes a "young man." As John the apostle confirms, *". . . I have written to you, young men, because you are strong, and the word of God abides in you . . ."* (1 John 2:14). Finally, the apostle Paul removes any ambiguity that it is the spirit person that is growing within us by saying, *". . . Even though our outward man is perishing, yet the inward man is being renewed day by day"* (2 Cor. 4:16).

So we can openly see that physical age has nothing to do with the reception of dreams or visions. It is all about the receptivity and development of the spirit person. Dreams come to everyone—Christian and non-Christian alike. How they are understood depends on whether the spirit person is "switched on." Visions, on the other hand, are only for believers hungering after God's will and applying His Word.

What about unbelievers who receive visions? I believe that unbelievers who receive visions do so through occultic means, such as drugs and divination. I know people who have had extensive visions under the influence of drugs. Drug use opens people up to the spirit realm of demonic deception. In fact, when you dig beneath the English translation of the Scriptures to the original languages, you discover that drug use is directly linked to witchcraft. The word *sorceries* in Revelation 9:21 is the Greek word, *pharmakeia*. This is the word from which we get the word *pharmacy*. *Pharmakeia* is translated as "witchcraft" in Paul's list of works of the flesh to the Galatian church (see Gal. 5:20).

The Bible also shows that those operating under the influence of familiar spirits are empowered to see in the spirit realm. This is evident when Paul and

Silas are thrown into prison for casting out a spirit of divination from a fortune-telling slave-girl in the Book of Acts. Luke, the writer of Acts says,

> *Now it happened, as we went to prayer, that a certain slave girl possessed with a spirit of divination met us, who brought her masters much profit by fortune-telling. This girl followed Paul and us, and cried out, saying, "These men are the servants of the Most High God, who proclaim to us the way of salvation." And this she did for many days. But Paul, greatly annoyed, turned and said to the spirit, "I command you in the name of Jesus Christ to come out of her." And he came out that very hour* (Acts 16:16-18).

After Paul had commanded the spirit to come out, the Scripture says,

> *But when her masters saw that their hope of profit was gone, they seized Paul and Silas and dragged them into the marketplace to the authorities* (Acts 16:19).

It is pretty obvious that it was the spirit within the slave-girl that gave her the ability to see in the spirit realm, and once he was removed, she was no longer able to receive her spiritual visions. This explanation adequately accounts for the reaction of the slave-girl's masters, whose hope for further profit was taken away when the spirit was cast out of her.

Dreams Are Controversial

Yes, the subject of dreams and dream interpretation is one of great controversy within the Body of Christ. And some may fear that if we open ourselves to this method of guidance from God, it will put us into a position to be easily misled down some sidetrack away from the fundamental teachings of the Bible. However, it is both of the authors' experience that the opposite is the truth. If the Church is going to embrace the Holy Spirit's voice through dreams, it also has to be totally soaked in the Scriptures. It takes a balanced view of the whole of Scripture to interpret correctly, and therefore, the people who want to improve their interpretation skills have to be disciplined in Bible reading. They also have to believe and apply what they are reading. Rather than being led astray, embracing dreams as messages from God actually leads us deeper into the ways of God. This is because, through dreams, the Holy Spirit teaches the application of the principal of referencing (or linking truth with truth), as outlined within the Scriptures, "*. . . the Holy Spirit teaches, comparing spiritual things with spiritual*" (1 Cor. 2:13b).

Therefore, without a solid grounding in the Word of God, you cannot possibly know that what you are receiving is from God, let alone understand what it means. The Holy Spirit will only endorse God's Word further through His voice in the night. If you hear anything contrary to God's written Word, then it is not God who is speaking!

The Real Reason Dreams Are a Threat

The real basis of this controversy is the devil's doing. The devil does not want the empowerment of God's people through this channel of communication. He is always attempting to thwart the purposes of God. Listen to his voice through Peter as Jesus begins to reveal spiritual truth incomprehensible to the natural mind,

> From that time Jesus began to show to His disciples that He must go to Jerusalem, and suffer many things from the elders and chief priests and scribes, and be killed, and be raised the third day. Then Peter took Him aside and began to rebuke Him, saying, "Far be it from You, Lord; this shall not happen to You!" But He turned and said to Peter, "Get behind Me, Satan! You are an offense to Me, for you are not mindful of the things of God, but the things of men" (Matthew 16:21-23).

Just as the devil used Peter's personal agenda and limited outlook to challenge Christ, he still is using those whose security is not truly in God in an attempt to stifle God's plans. If we have our security in anything other than Christ alone—position, money, power, recognition, religion, intellect, or acceptance—then the old self will come out fighting as soon as a spiritual truth is declared that threatens that security, "For the flesh lusts against the Spirit . . . and these are contrary to one another" (Gal. 5:17).

As in Peter's case, often it is spiritual pride through which the devil is allowed to enter and attempt to coerce the Body of Christ away from God's intended path. Moments before this rebuke, Peter had received the revelation that Jesus was "the Christ, the Son of the living God" (Matt. 16:16-19). And following that gem from the Father, he was commended by Jesus as being blessed, told that he would be pivotal to the coming Kingdom and that he would be endowed with authority. What a promise! However, it was all too much for the would-be apostle. The devil had an entry point—Peter's pride—and in the next breath, Peter takes it upon himself to correct Jesus.

If the devil can keep us blind to the fact that God is actually speaking through dreams, then he has effectively cut off one of the main channels of communication God has used for more than 4000 years to mobilize His troops. Doesn't it seem strange to you that we would think that God, who has communicated for such a long time using dreams, would pull the plug on this means of communication, especially when He promised He would do it more?

Summary: Chapter 1

- Hold off on making a judgment about dreams and visions until you've heard what the Bible has to say on the matter.

- We are standing in the last days, which are marked by an outpouring of God's Spirit.

- The outpouring of the Spirit includes prophecy through dreams and visions.

- The Holy Spirit is the current representative of the Godhead on earth today.

- We can have a propensity to live in the past or in the future to avoid exercising faith today.

- The call to live by faith is a call to hear what God is saying today.

- As Christians, we are prone to "throw the baby out with the bathwater" because we see the New Age movement and psychoanalysis embrace dream interpretation for guidance.

- Old Testament prophets heard God's Word, as we do, through parable-type dreams and visions.

- Jesus' preferred teaching method was to use parables.

- Christian leaders, because of their busyness, can expect God to speak to them in their down-time (sleep) through dreams and visions.

- We will miss the current outpouring of the Spirit if we don't have ears to hear.

- Nicodemus shows us our own tendency to think naturally when God is speaking to us spiritually.

- We will miss the voice of God for this generation if we, like Nicodemus, are only prepared to think naturally and miss the need to "listen" spiritually.

- Dreams are for both the Christian and non-Christian; visions, on the other hand, are the domain of the believer.

- The Holy Spirit teaches relating spiritual things with spiritual. Therefore, a solid understanding of the Bible is a prerequisite for accurate interpretation.
- The devil uses the threat to personal agendas to cause the flesh to rise up and thwart the work of God.
- God has used dreams and visions for more than 4,000 years as a means of guidance, so why should He stop now when He has said that He would do it more?

Chapter 2

Why Dreams Are So Important
By Adrian Beale

A Hidden Truth

Having laid a brief foundation in the previous chapter, we need to now expand upon that and explain why dreams are so important in the purposes of God before we can consider their individual functions. What I am about to share will initially challenge many Christians because it is a truth which is not commonly taught from our pulpits. What I ask you to do is be noble like the Bereans (see Acts 17:11) and go to your Bible and search to see what it says on the matter.

Let me set the scene and present my case scripturally. When Joseph, Jacob's son, was 17 years of age, he dreamed two dreams which declared that his brothers and his parents would someday bow to him (see Gen. 37:5-11). His prideful boasting of this revelation, together with his father's favoritism toward him, put him at enmity with his brothers who, as a consequence, sold him down the river to Egypt. The dreams that Joseph had dreamed lay dormant as he served as a slave and prisoner within Egypt.

In case you are unfamiliar with the story, here's a brief recap. Joseph was eventually used to interpret two dreams that Pharaoh had dreamed. These showed that the nation of Egypt would experience seven years of plenty followed by seven years of the most severe famine (see Gen. 41:17-31). When Pharaoh heard Joseph's interpretation and his advice in how to counter this forthcoming blight, he set Joseph as prime minister over the nation. And yes, you guessed it, his brothers came to Egypt to buy food and found themselves bowing unknowingly to the one they conspired against, just as it had been foretold in Joseph's original dreams some 20 or so years earlier. Now what is remarkable about this incident is the way that it is recorded in the book of Psalms,

> *Moreover He called for a famine in the land; He destroyed all the provision of bread. He sent a man before them—Joseph—who was sold as a slave. They hurt his feet with fetters, he was laid in irons. Until the time that **his word** came to pass, the word of the Lord tested him (Psalm 105:16-19).*

Notice that it says that he was kept in prison *"until the time that **his word** came to pass."* What was Joseph's word? His word was the dream he had received as a 17-year-old boy! Let me put that another way: Joseph's dream was God's word for him! *Whoa!*

Going Deeper

Now if we do our homework on this psalm, we will find out that two different Hebrew words are used in place of the English word *word:*

> *Until the time that his **word** [davar[1]] came to pass, The **word** [emrah[2]] of the Lord tested him (Psalm 105:19).*

However, if we dig a little deeper, we find that both of these words are used interchangeably for God's Word throughout the Old Testament. There are numerous examples, but primarily using Psalm 119 I would like to show just a few to confirm what I am saying,

> *Thou art my portion, O Lord: I have said that I would keep Thy **words** [davar]. I intreated Thy favor with my whole heart: be merciful unto me according to Thy **word** [emrah] (Psalm 119:57-58 KJV).*

> *My soul fainteth for Thy salvation: but I hope in Thy **word** [davar]. Mine eyes fail for Thy **word** [emrah], saying, When wilt Thou comfort me? (Psalm 119:81-82 KJV)*

> *Princes have persecuted me without a cause: but my heart standeth in awe of Thy **word** [davar]. I rejoice at Thy **word** [emrah], as one that findeth great spoil (Psalm 119:161-162 KJV).*

We also find that *davar,* the particular word used to describe God's Word to Joseph, is used when describing the Ten Commandments, *"... He wrote on the tablets the **words** [davar] of the covenant, the Ten **Commandments** [davar] (Exod. 34:28b).*

Therefore, what I am suggesting is that dreams are part of God's ongoing word to us. They are not the whole picture, but they accompany and augment what God is saying to us through His written word and prayer.

Let me now confirm what I am saying from another account within Scripture. When Jacob was fleeing because of death threats from his brother, Esau, he had an encounter with God at Bethel. The Bible records,

> *Then he dreamed, and behold, a ladder was set up on the earth, and its top reached to heaven; and there the angels of God were ascending and descending on it. And behold, the Lord stood above it, and said:*
>
> *"I am the Lord God of Abraham your father, and the God of Isaac; the land on which you lie I will give to you and your descendants. Also your descendants shall be as the dust of the earth; you shall spread abroad to the west and the east, to the north and the south; and in you and in your seed all the families of the earth shall be blessed. Behold, I am with you and will keep you wherever you go, and will bring you back to this land; for **I will not leave you until I have done what I have spoken to you**"* (Genesis 28:12-15).

What a fantastic encouragement this dream must have been to the anxious traveler, Jacob, heading to an unfamiliar destination. When God is rounding off this encounter with Jacob, He promises that He will not leave him until He has completed what He has *"spoken to"* him. To put that another way, He says He will not leave him until He has completed *"His word"* to him. And what was His word to Jacob? It was the dream he had just been given.

So impacting was this word on Jacob that the marginal rendering of Genesis 29:1 in the King James Version, says, *"Then Jacob lifted up his feet, and came to the land of the people of the East"* (Gen. 29:1 KJV). The heaviness with which he left home had been completely stripped from him because he had a word from God. He didn't think, *I shouldn't have eaten that pizza last night.* No, he recognized God's word when it came to him!

Dreams Teach

In Matthew 5–7, Jesus delivers what is called the Sermon on the Mount. Many regard this passage of Scripture as the Magna Carta of Kingdom living. In the midst of this passage, there is a well-known verse which says, *"But seek first the kingdom of God and His righteousness, and all these things shall be added to you"* (Matt. 6:33).

This verse speaks about getting things right in our hearts and allowing God to rule and reign there, and it promises that if we do so, God will provide for our needs. This is a challenging verse, particularly when the world and circumstance can be yelling for us to seek security everywhere else but in God.

Have you ever wondered, *Where did Jesus gain such insight?* Most of us forget that He had to learn spiritual truth like we do. The Bible reveals prophetically that He had a daily reading plan,

> *[The Servant of God says] The Lord God has given Me the tongue of a disciple and of one who is taught, that I should know how to speak a word in season to him who is weary. He wakens Me morning by morning, He wakens My ear to hear as a disciple [as one who is taught]* (Isaiah 50:4 AMP).

The basis of Jesus' teaching in Matthew, which is a pillar for the Kingdom of God, is actually a dream, a dream that Solomon had over 950 years earlier,

> *At Gibeon the Lord appeared to Solomon in a dream by night; and God said, "Ask! What shall I give you?" . . . **Therefore give to Your servant an understanding heart** to judge Your people, that I may discern between good and evil. For who is able to judge this great people of Yours?" The speech pleased the Lord, that Solomon had asked this thing. Then God said to him: "Because you have asked this thing, and have not asked long life for yourself, nor have asked riches for yourself, nor have asked the life of your enemies, but have asked for yourself understanding to discern justice, behold, I have done according to your words; see, I have given you a wise and understanding heart, so that there has not been anyone like you before you, nor shall any like you arise after you. **And I have also given you what you have not asked: both riches and honor**, so that there shall not be anyone like you among the kings all your days"* (1 Kings 3:5, 9-13).

We discover here that dreams have a capacity to teach at a number of levels. It is not just the recipient of the dream that benefits from it. Solomon's dream here is literal, in the sense that he doesn't have to decode the message. And Jesus' teaching based on this dream is a great example of succinctly relating the truth outlined in a dream. However, the majority of dreams are metaphors, parables, and riddles. Therefore, someone has to interpret them. If that person is not the recipient of the dream, then he or she also learns from the spiritual truth taught through the dream, as do all those who are subsequently exposed to its teaching. When interpreting dreams, Adam (co-author) and I have both been convicted about things needing to be addressed in our own lives that God has pinpointed through dreams given to others.

Joseph

The classic example of this in Scripture is in the life of Joseph. Most people read the life of Joseph at a very superficial level, colored by the Children's Bible account of this "perfect" specimen of the human race. Joseph was just like you and me; he was not superhuman, without weaknesses. In some things Joseph was exemplary, like when he flees the temptation presented by Potiphar's wife. However, just like us, he had issues that needed addressing. God was purifying him in prison, as we read earlier, *"The word of the Lord tested him"* (Ps. 105:19). The word *tested* used here is the Hebrew word *tsaraph*, which means, "literally or figuratively to refine (as gold and silver is refined by fire) in order to separate it from the impurities within." If Joseph was perfect, then why did he need refining?

While Joseph was in prison, he interpreted the dreams of Pharaoh's butler and baker. Hopefully you are familiar with the story. The butler began,

> *Behold, in my dream a vine was before me, and in the vine were three branches; it was as though it budded, its blossoms shot forth, and its clusters brought forth ripe grapes. Then Pharaoh's cup was in my hand; and I took the grapes and pressed them into Pharaoh's cup, and placed the cup in Pharaoh's hand* (Genesis 40:9-11).

Joseph interpreted the dream, saying,

> *The three branches are three days. Now within three days Pharaoh will lift up your head and restore you to your place, and you will put Pharaoh's cup in his hand according to the former manner, when you were his butler* (Genesis 40:12-13).

The baker thought that sounded pretty good so he likewise offloaded his dream for interpretation. He said,

> *I also was in my dream, and there were three white baskets on my head. In the uppermost basket were all kinds of baked goods for Pharaoh, and the birds ate them out of the basket on my head* (Genesis 40:16-17).

And Joseph interpreted his dream, saying,

The three baskets are three days. Within three days Pharaoh will lift off your head from you and hang you on a tree; and the birds will eat your flesh from you (Genesis 40:18-19).

And sure enough, three days later it happened just as the dreams had prophesied. The butler was restored, and the baker was hanged. You would think that was enough to get Joseph out of confinement; after all he now has an ally in Pharaoh's household. But that wasn't to be the case. Why? Simply because God wasn't through purifying him yet. The next thing we read is, *"Then it came to pass, at the end of two full years, that Pharaoh had a dream . . ."* (Gen. 41:1).

In the Book of Genesis, nothing is recorded about those two years. And as is often the case, the Bible speaks the loudest when it says nothing at all. What does it say? It says in which year Joseph was resurrected. That must have been the third year. In Hebrew understanding, there is a week of days, there is a week of weeks, there is a week of months—the seventh month is a month of feasts—and there is a week of years. The seventh year is a year of rest or Sabbath for the land (see Lev. 25:4). Therefore, Joseph was resurrected on the equivalent of day three. This of course, in some measure parallels the resurrection of Christ and is one reason why the number *three* is often interpreted as "resurrection." The story doesn't end there because this is where it gets exciting.

What does a bewildered Joseph think after correctly interpreting Pharaoh's servants' dreams and yet still finding himself behind bars? For a little while he is hopeful that the butler will mention him, and then he gets to the stage where he is annoyed and frustrated. Then, perhaps he remembers a principle his father taught him as a lad, that when God seems to go quiet on you, you need to go back to your last revelation. Or perhaps he started thinking how good it was to deliver those interpretations, or simply the Holy Spirit took him there. Whatever the route, he begins thinking through the dreams and their interpretation for the butler and the baker.

And what does he discover? By meditating on the dreams, he discovers that it is faith (fruit) that is blessed, whereas works (baked goods) are cursed and put to death. He discovers the person seeking his own glory (the baker) is judged by God (Pharaoh in this story). While the person willing to lay down his life for the one he serves (the butler) is resurrected. The baker's dream describes him as carrying three baskets of baked goods. (Can't you just smell that fresh bread and see those plaited loaves or coffee scrolls or whatever it was that Pharaoh's household was into?) Why, if the baker knew there were birds, didn't he keep them covered? He didn't keep them covered because he wanted to gain glory by letting everyone see his handiwork! The basis of whatever he was hung for is found here as his heart is revealed. He is a person seeking his own glory.

Now as Joseph meditates on this revelation, God shows him his own heart. Let me walk you through it progressively. When Joseph had his first dream, well the first one recorded in Scripture, what does he say? He says, *"Please hear this dream which **I** have dreamed"* (Gen. 37:6). Who is claiming the glory here? Joseph is! At the next landmark, before he interprets the butler and baker's dreams, he says, *"Do not interpretations belong to God? Tell them to **me**, please"* (Gen. 40:8).

Now we are beginning to see the humbling of Joseph having an effect. He has been a slave in Egypt for around ten years at this point. But he is not at the place where God can use him to the extent of what He has in store. Notice in his declaration to the butler and baker that he puts God first, but he still wants a measure of the glory. This is further revealed in what he blurts out between interpreting the butler and baker's dream. He says,

> But remember **me** when it is well with you, and please show kindness to **me**; make mention of **me** to Pharaoh, and get **me** out of this house. For indeed **I** was stolen away from the land of the Hebrews; and also **I** have done nothing here that they should put **me** into the dungeon (Genesis 40:14-15).

Have you ever opened your mouth and then thought, *Oops, I never knew that was there?* I believe, on reflection, that is what happens to Joseph here. If you count the number of personal pronouns—*me* and *I*—you will find that there are seven of them. Seven is representative of divine perfection, but in this case, it is revealing that though he is growing in God; he still has too much focus on self. Another way of saying this is that, even though he says the right words, his heart is not fully given over to God. He is not resting in God. Whose works is he expecting will get him out of this confinement? His own. At this point, he is more like the baker than the butler.

What is holding him back is also revealed in the above statement to the butler. There are some areas of his heart not yet yielded to God. From his statement in verse 15, we know who he holds responsible for putting him in this predicament. Look at his words, *"and also I have done nothing here that they . . . ."* His words reveal that in his heart he holds his brothers and Potiphar's wife responsible. He is saying, "I'm not responsible; they are." It sounds pretty much like he thinks they owe him. Therefore, he is harbouring a debt, and that debt is unforgiveness (see Matt. 18:21-35). Where there is unforgiveness there is most certainly an area of one's heart not yet yielded to God.

At the same time as God shows him this, the clock is running. God's perfect timing is being displayed. Joseph is coming to the third day (year), the day of resurrection, but before he can experience resurrection, he has to experience death. You cannot have a resurrection unless you first put something to death! What did he have to crucify? He had to crucify sin—the very thing that put Jesus upon the cross. Joseph had to bury his unforgiveness toward those who had abused him; otherwise the Spirit of God could not raise him from the pit. This is confirmed in Scripture when it is recorded of Joseph that prior to his audience before Pharaoh the, *"Lord was with him"* (Gen. 39:2, 21, 23). However, after his death and resurrection experience, Pharaoh, when speaking about Joseph declares, *"Can we find such a one as this, a man **in whom** is the Spirit of God?"* (Gen. 41:38).

At this point, God can take up full residence. He no longer is looking on from the outside. Now that the rubbish has been dealt with, He is on the inside directing and leading Joseph. Now Joseph, at long last, is like the butler who takes the grapes, crushes them, and places the cup into Pharaoh's hand. He is now truly able to give God all the glory. If we compare Joseph's earlier declaration about his dream to his brothers and also his confession before the butler and baker with what he now says to Pharaoh, we see a vast change has taken place. He says, "... ***It is not in me;*** *God will give Pharaoh an answer of peace"* (Gen. 41:16). Joseph is at last truly ready for what God has for him because he is now prepared to give God all the glory.

The truth of this incident is that the butler and the baker are in all of us. And it was the teaching within the dreams of the butler and baker that discerned the thoughts and intents of Joseph's heart and brought about the necessary adjustment for him to be used of God "... .*to save many people alive"* (Gen. 50:20b).

Now put this understanding into Psalm 105, where we read earlier, *"Until the time that his **word** [davar] came to pass, the **word** [emrah] of the Lord tested him"* (Ps. 105:19). What is important to understand is that it was the word of God in the butler and baker's dreams that purified Joseph over that three year period while he waited for the prophetic word of his own dream to come to pass.

Dividing Between Soul and Spirit

What we have just witnessed in the life of Joseph is that dreams have the power to divide between soul and spirit and act as a discloser of the thoughts and intents of the heart. The writer to the Hebrews captures this when he says,

> *For the word of God is living and powerful, and sharper than any two-edged sword, piercing even to the division of soul and spirit, and of joints and marrow, and is a discerner of the thoughts and intents of the heart* (Hebrews 4:12).

The hidden truth the Bible reveals is that dreams have the power to divide between soul and spirit because they are a deposit of God's living Word to us today! To some, that will be a pretty radical thought, and I hear many asking, "Are you suggesting we should endorse extra-biblical revelation?" No! What I am saying is that God is still speaking and that He didn't cease speaking at the completion of the canonical books of the Bible. The Book of Acts is an open-ended book, and it is still being written today. However, let me reiterate that what He says today has to be in line with what He has said in the past (see Heb. 13:8). This is why the metaphors that fill this book are based primarily on Scripture.

We cannot afford to be like the Pharisees and teachers of the law who sat insensitively in the presence of Jesus, inwardly criticizing His every word and consequently failing to receive what God had for them even though "*. . . the power of the Lord was present to heal them*" (Luke 5:17). If that is our attitude, then it will be someone else who will break through the roof we have placed ourselves under and by faith grab a hold of what God had originally planned for us (see Luke 5:19-20).

Dreams divide between soul and spirit, not just in the individual, but also at the family, church, business, national, and Kingdom levels. The authors have people approach them with dreams to interpret on a regular basis. However, often what people think a dream means and what it turns out to say can be radically different. Acting like Nathan's parable to David (see 2 Sam. 12:1-13), dreams and their correct interpretations bypass the heart's natural defense mechanisms and allow the Holy Spirit to bring conviction and correction.

The Hands-on-Throat Dream

A great example of this ability to discern and disclose hearts happened as I was writing this material. One morning I was sharing with a group of people a couple of directive dreams God had given me. During our discussion, a young man asked what would it mean in a dream if he had his hand on his ex-partner's throat? I asked him about the context of the dream and whether he had ever threatened her. He said, to his recollection of things, he had not openly threatened her, though she may feel threatened by him. He also explained that the night before he had gone to hear someone preaching. The sermon touched on forgiveness. He explained that before he went to bed he had verbally forgiven his ex-partner.

Hmm . . .hand on someone's throat? I said, "You don't really have to be a rocket scientist to say it doesn't really sound good." But I wasn't sure yet on the exact interpretation. That afternoon as I sat meditating on the dream, I did a quick search on an electronic pocket Bible Adam (co-author) and I both carry for such occasions. I punched in the words *hand* and *throat,* and began a search. Immediately two options came up. One reference was in the Old Testament and one in the New. In the Old Testament reference, the words *hand* and *throat* were not connected so I ignored that reference. As I brought up the New Testament verse, *Wham!* The New Testament verse read,

> *But that servant went out and found one of his fellow servants who owed him a hundred denarii; and he laid **hands** on him and took him by the **throat**, saying, "Pay me what you owe!"* (Matthew 18:28).

As the context of this verse is talking about forgiveness, I knew instantly what God was saying. As I shared the essence of what God was saying, the Holy Spirit powerfully witnessed and brought conviction. The young man was blown away that God, through a dream, was able to pinpoint the true state of his heart. Through the dream, God was showing him that he had not really forgiven his ex-partner from his heart, that he still held her responsible and was expecting an apology from her. This is not only a great example of God's ability to divide hearts through dreams, but it also emphasizes the importance of using the Bible to find the interpretation. This method is particularly useful if the metaphor dictionary does not have an entry that seems to fit the context of the dream.

Entering the Kingdom

This experience reinforces a truth that Israel was meant to learn before they entered the Promised Land and that all of us, likewise, have to learn before we are able to move fully-fledged into the Kingdom. As Jesus, quoting Moses, puts it, *"Man shall not live by bread alone, but by every word that **proceeds** from the mouth of God"* (Matt. 4:4).

In fact, entering the Kingdom is dependent on this truth. Notice that this Scripture says that it is by every word that "proceeds" and not "proceeded." One is present tense; the other is past tense. We cannot move into the spiritual promises of God on yesterday's manna. We need a living Word today. Of course, the devil wants to shut this down because dreams have the capacity to provide a major component of what God is saying to us today. He knows that once this truth is out, the Church is once again on the move and closer to the Book of Acts!

Don't Dreams Come by Much Activity?

Even now I hear some say, "But doesn't the Bible say that a dream comes about by much activity?" Yes, it does, well, something along those lines. But where does it say that in the Bible? It says it in the Book of Ecclesiastes, *"For a dream comes through much activity, and a fool's voice is known by his many words"* (Eccl. 5:3).

What is the perspective of this book written by Solomon? It is a pessimistic look at "life under the sun." (See Ecclesiastes 1:3, along with 30 other occurrences.) Therefore, the book, for the most part, is a secular and non-believing look at a world without God. And what this verse actually says is, *"The world says a dream comes by much activity."* (Ecc. 5:3) Is that the correct perspective? It is the non-spiritual one.

Alternatively, this verse can also be understood to say, "While a fool is babbling on, the only way to get to your dream (goal) is by actively pursuing it." Interpreted either way, this verse limits us to the physical domain outside of God and is, therefore, an empty defence against the truth revealed here.

Uniting the Word and the Spirit

A well-known British author and teacher who recently visited Australia says that God is about to bring together a generation where the proponents of the

Word (those strong in Bible teaching) come together with those who claim to be Spirit-led (of Charismatic persuasion). The acceptance of dreams as messages from God can and will only take place among those with this balance. Recognition of that fact has us poised at the door of the next tipping-point[3] in God. Will we step through?

If, as you have read these first two chapters, you find yourself saying, "I want to be a part of that generation that unites the Word and the Spirit," but also find yourself admitting, "Well, God doesn't speak to me in dreams," then you need to consider what you have done in the past when He has spoken to you in a dream. Think about it; if you were speaking to someone and they continually ignored you, would you keep speaking to them? No, you wouldn't. The Bible says, "*. . .For with the same measure that you use, it will be measured back to you*" (Luke 6:38b).

God is not like Robin Hood, who takes from the rich to give to the poor. He takes from the poor and gives to the rich! If you don't believe me, read Matthew 25:14-30. If this is you right now, stop reading and apologize to the Holy Spirit for grieving Him with your insensitivity. Ask that He cleanse you of any sin in your heart under the precious blood of Christ and also cry unto Him to give you an understanding (receptive) heart. Finally say, "Lord, speak, for your servant is listening."

Summary: Chapter Two

- A detailed study of the life of Joseph reveals that dreams are part of God's living Word. They augment what He is saying to us through the written word and prayer.

- Jesus taught principles from a dream Solomon had 950 years earlier.

- According to a contextual understanding of Psalm 105:17-19, Joseph was refined through the dreams of the butler and baker of Pharaoh. These dreams refined him while he waited for the *word* of his own dreams to be fulfilled.

- Dreams and their correct interpretation bypass the heart's natural defence mechanisms and allow the Holy Spirit to bring conviction and correction.

- Dreams have the power to divide between soul and spirit and act as a discloser of the thoughts and intents of the heart.

- The Kingdom of God is gained by receiving the ongoing *"word that proceeds from the mouth of God."* Dreams are a major component of that *proceeding* word.

- The natural person (world) thinks dreams come through much activity.
- There is a need to repent and apologize to the Holy Spirit for our insensitivity and ignorance of His voice to us in the night.

Endnotes

1. Sames Strong, *Strong's Exhaustive Concordance of the Bible,* Hebrew #1697.
2. *Ibid.,* Hebrew #565.
3. For our purposes, a "tipping-point" is a point in time when a revelation, person, or church suddenly breaks through into a new level in God and opens the way for others to follow. Roger Bannister provides a good example in the sporting arena. Before Roger Bannister broke the four-minute mile in 1954, everyone thought the human body was not capable of sustaining such rigorous exercise. This thinking effectively created a mental barrier that kept runners at bay. However, after Roger Bannister broke through this psychological barrier, others followed in rapid succession.

Chapter Three

The Purpose of Dreams and Visions
By Adrian Beale

In Romans 10:17, it says, *"So then faith comes by hearing, and hearing by the* **word** *of God."* In this passage, the Greek word *rhema* has simply been translated "word." *Rhema* actually means the "spoken word" and denotes "that which is spoken, what is uttered in speech or writing."[1] In classical Greek, it may be considered the term for a message. It is not the Greek word used to describe the entire Bible, for that, another Greek word, *logos,* is used. It is this spoken word or message that proceeds from the mouth of God (see Matt. 4:4). And it is this spoken word or message that is *"the sword of the Spirit, which is the word* [rhema] *of God"* (Eph. 6:17).

As dreams and visions are two of the ways we receive this spoken word or message from God, their main purpose is to create, build, and strengthen faith. As the sword of the Spirit, they also divide between soul and spirit, joints and marrow, and are used by the Holy Spirit to disclose the thoughts and intents of the heart. Further to this, in providing illumination on a personal level, they are consistently employed to confirm direction.

Building Faith

The story of Gideon in the Bible (see Judg. 6–8) provides a good example of how a dream can strengthen faith. In this passage of Scripture, the story is told of how God visited and encouraged a man who was a self-confessed "weakest of the weak" (see Judg. 6:15) to take on and defeat an innumerable Midianite army.

If you are aware of the story, you will know that God progressively built faith in Gideon through a series of confirming events. The final tool used to make the fearful Gideon resolute in faith was a dream! It was not a dream Gideon had, but a dream that one of the enemy soldiers had and retold in Gideon's hearing. The Scriptures describe the final scene before Gideon leads his carefully selected army against Israel's opponents,

> And when Gideon had come, there was a man telling a dream to his companion. He said, "I have had a dream: To my surprise, a loaf of barley bread tumbled into the camp of Midian; it came to a tent and struck it so that it fell and overturned, and the tent collapsed." Then his companion answered and said, "This is nothing else but the sword of Gideon the son of Joash, a man of Israel! Into his hand God has delivered Midian and the whole camp" (Judges 7:13-14).

The sudden barley loaf tumbling into the camp of Midian is a classic example of how metaphors are used in dreams today. Compared to wheat, barley is an inferior grain; its head contains fewer grains, it is more susceptible to loss through windstorms, and it is not as hard. The dream begins with the words, *"To my surprise a loaf of barley bread tumbled into the camp . . ."* (Judg. 7:13).

This describes for us not only the element of surprise employed by Gideon—He gets his men to conceal lamps in earthen vessels, which when broken and accompanied with the blast of trumpets supply the shock tactics needed to rout the enemy—but also provides a cleverly chosen image of Gideon and his unified and comparatively inferior entourage of followers (see Judg. 6:16). Gideon was encouraged, or rather had his faith strengthened, through hearing a message from God given through a dream shared between two enemy soldiers.

Faith for Healing

The book *Even Greater,* by Reinhard Bonnke,[2] tells of a current-day example of how a dream was used to build faith for healing.

By 1988, a pain-wracked and wheelchair-bound English woman, Jean Neil, had undergone several unsuccessful spinal operations, the last of which had left her in a plaster cast for six months. Emerging from that cast, Jean was told she would never walk again, but was given a 50-50 chance of a better lifestyle if she were to undergo a risky operation to reconstruct her spine. While she weighed the risk of the operation against the constant daily pain she experienced, Jean received two dreams in the same night. In the first dream, she saw herself undergoing the operation and dying on the operating table. In the second dream, she saw herself in a huge room with at least 12 other people who were also in wheelchairs. She heard a man speaking with a foreign accent and noted the color of the carpet and the seats that filled that room. She saw the speaker (whom she later discovered to be Reinhard Bonnke) go to the first wheelchair and pray for a woman sitting in it. The woman got up and then slumped back into the chair in utter defeat. The speaker then came and prayed for Jean, and she saw herself take off running from her wheelchair—totally healed!

The dreams told Jean two things. First, it was clear that God, through a literal dream, was warning her not to undergo surgery. The second dream also declared that God had another plan. Two weeks after this revelation, Jean traveled to hear Reinhard Bonnke speak at a youth convention in Birmingham, England. At this stage, Jean had not seen Reinhard in real-life. She had heard only that he was an evangelist and that when he ministered it was not unusual for the miraculous to take place. She was hopeful. That afternoon as Reinhard entered the stage, Jean thought he looked somewhat like the man in her dream. However, when he opened his mouth to speak, her faith began to rise as his tone and accent were identical to the man in her dream. When the events of that afternoon unraveled as Jean had dreamed them, including the color of the seats and carpet, and the woman in the first wheelchair failing to receive her healing, Jean was full of faith to receive her healing, and the rest is well-documented history.

Jean Neil was filled with faith and received her healing because God, in a dream, allowed her to preview a future event with incredible accuracy. This is an example of a dream dividing between joints and marrow and bringing healing through the faith it inspired. This incredible miracle from God is also documented on the DVD *M.S.I.* (Miracle Scene Investigation) by Full Flame Asia Pty. Ltd.[3]

Revealing Secrets and Answering Questions

Last year my eldest daughter, who like most teenagers talks to her friends over the Internet, received a series of e-mails from someone who used the title, "Your Secret Admirer." After a couple of these e-mails she came to her mother and me and disclosed the content of these messages, asking for some advice on what she should do in this situation. The nature of the communication was courteous and succinct and was not in any way rude or intrusive. All the same, we encouraged her to be polite, but to discourage this person by explaining our (mom and dad's) views on dating. The comments made through the e-mails suggested that the person involved was a Christian, nevertheless, given that this was not a face-to-face conversation, and the age of our daughter, our resolve was firm. The last communication from the secret admirer was that he would disclose himself in time to me (dad) and ask permission to proceed in asking her out.

While we were taking a short weekend away to relax as a family, God showed me in a dream one night who the secret admirer was. I saw him literally in front of me and knew in my spirit the message God was conveying to me. I shot upright in bed and said to my wife, "The secret admirer is so and so!" To which my wife said something like, "I could have told you that." Talk about having your bubble burst!

Anyway, a few weeks later, I was observing this person after church. Eventually, when our eyes met, he obviously sensed that there was an opportunity to speak to me and came toward me. He opened the conversation by saying, "I would like to speak to you . . ." I was able to say, "I know. God has revealed to me that you are the secret admirer, but our daughter is a little too young and this is how it is . . ." (I hold this young man and his family in high regard today for their commitment to Christ. The objection was not to him, but to our daughter's age.) God answered the question on our hearts at that time through a message delivered in visual form. And in doing so, He was able to allay any fears we held over this incident.

There was a time in Israel's history when King Saul was looking for guidance because a large Philistine army was parked on his doorstep. Unfortunately, Saul had gone off the rails in his walk with God because of his jealousy of David. Samuel, the nation's prophet, was dead, so Saul, in trepidation, approached God. The Scripture says, *"And when Saul inquired of the Lord, the Lord did not answer him, either by dreams or by Urim, or by the prophets"* (1 Sam. 28:6).

Though Saul did not receive the revelation he was looking for in this situation, it is evident from Scripture that dreams were a regular way in which God answered questions (see Dan. 2:29). He is still using the same method today, as is apparent above.

Warning and Guidance

One of my friends came to me recently with the following dream for interpretation. He said,

> I saw two cars heading straight toward each other like they were going to have a head-on crash. The two drivers were young and seemed to be playing chicken with each other. I saw the two cars crash, and I also saw and recognized the driver that got hurt.

This dream was a warning from God. In the circumstance in which it was given, it means that two departments (vehicles) of the ministry in which the dreamer is involved will come to a place where there will be one department set against the other. Due to spiritual immaturity, neither will be willing to yield to the other, and the dream showed which department will be hurt. The Scripture that instantly came to mind was Genesis 13:7-9. Therefore, meekness and trust in God was called for at that time. (An explanation of the metaphors used to interpret this dream is found in the dream and vision sample section of this book. See dream 51.)

God gave this dream so that an impending tragedy could be averted. It is a good thing that the leadership of this ministry was open to this word from God. And I am relieved to say that, just as the "cars" were sizing each other up, God, through this dream, disarmed the situation.

Similarly, there are many accounts within Scripture where dreams were God's method of warning their recipients. After the wise men had found Jesus as a young child, God warned them about Herod's evil intensions. The Bible says, *"Then, being divinely warned in a dream that they should not return to Herod, they departed for their own country another way"* (Matt. 2:12).

And again in the next verse, Joseph, Mary's husband, was warned and given a similar message to move location because Herod saw Christ as a threat and wanted to destroy Him. The Scripture states,

> *Now when they had departed, behold, an angel of the Lord appeared to Joseph in a dream, saying, "Arise, take the young Child and His mother, flee to Egypt, and stay there until I bring you word; for Herod will seek the young Child to destroy Him"* (Matthew 2:13).

So urgent was this warning that Joseph responded straight away. As is recorded, *"When he arose, he took the young Child and His mother by night and departed for Egypt"* (Matt. 2:14).

After a brief stay in Egypt, God brought Joseph and his little family back into Israel through additional guidance given in a dream (see Matt. 2:19-20). The story doesn't end there, as he is further warned in another dream (see Matt. 2:22). That is four dreams, all recorded in Matthew 2, to protect the coming Promise of God.

I have deliberately referred to the young Child as the Promise of God, firstly because that's how our promises may appear in a dream (as babies) and also to alert us to the fact that the devil is still playing the same game today. Whenever God births His promises, the devil will try and abort them. The Book of Revelation recounts the spiritual perspective of that threat on the young child Jesus with the following words,

> *Now a great sign appeared in heaven: a woman clothed with the sun, with the moon under her feet, and on her head a garland of twelve stars. Then being with child, she cried out in labor and in pain to give birth. And another sign appeared in heaven: behold, a great, fiery red dragon having seven heads and ten horns, and seven diadems on his heads. His tail drew a third of the stars of heaven and threw them to the earth. And the dragon stood before the woman who was ready to give birth, to devour her Child as soon as it was born* (Revelation 12:1-4).

This heavenly insight provides us with a principle as true today as it was 2000 years ago. If we are about to do something new in God, we need to be open to receive guidance from the Holy Spirit through dreams, because for every promise birthed, there is a scheme of the enemy to abort it! This threat is very real, as the following dream portrays:

I was with a young couple in a fern-house/tent type structure outside their home. The roof of the fern house caught on fire as the woman brought a flame into it. We tried to put it out, not knowing till later that the fire had spread to the house and killed their young child in the upstairs bedroom.

In this dream, I believe God is warning that gossip could destroy the new ministry venture being embarked on. The woman possibly represents the church or its leadership (or the dreamer's wife) as the instigators who try to stop what God is birthing. Note also that the baby is upstairs; this says that what is being birthed is from God. (An explanation of the metaphors used to interpret this dream is found in the dream and vision sample section of this book. See dream 21.)

Correction

Appreciating the nature of people's hearts (see Jer. 17:9.) and given the power of God's Word to divide and discern the hearts of people means that a common purpose of dreams is correction. We saw this beautifully portrayed in the previous chapter concerning Joseph, and it is poetically documented in the oldest book in the Bible, Job, where Elihu states,

> *For God may speak one way, or in another, yet man does not perceive it. In a dream, in a vision of the night, when deep sleep falls upon men, while slumbering on their beds, then He opens the ears of men, and seals their instruction.* **In order to turn man from his deed** *(Job. 33:14-17a).*

We see that God will bring instruction through a dream that is intended to correct a faulty determination within the heart. Often, as it does here, correction comes with a warning, *"He keeps back his soul from the pit, and his life from passing over into Sheol"* (Job 33:18 NASB).

If someone denies that correction is needed or enjoys doing what God is trying to correct, God will persevere in His longsuffering love to bring that person around, often graciously repeating a dream to do so. However, there will come a time when His patience will be balanced with judgment. Recently, I interpreted one such dream that I am not at liberty to share here. What I can share is the Scriptures that instantly came to my spirit,

> *For you know that afterward, when he wanted to inherit the blessing, he was rejected, for he found no place for repentance, though he sought it diligently with tears* (Hebrews 12:17).

After explaining the dream, I pleaded earnestly that the person concerned would understand the gravity of the situation. Thankfully, I have not been exposed to many such situations. That situation was a sobering reminder that God is both a God of love and also a consuming fire (see Heb. 12:29).

There are not too many of us who appreciate correction. The Scripture captures this truth well when it says,

> *Now no chastening seems to be joyful for the present, but painful; nevertheless, afterward it yields the peaceable fruit of righteousness to those who have been trained by it* (Hebrews 12:11).

We have to keep in mind that it is due to the goodness of God that we are alive at all (see Acts 17:28). And it is certainly by the grace of God that we may be saved through the death of His dear Son Jesus Christ (see Eph. 2:8-9). Therefore, when a dream shows an area needing change, it is important that the people concerned understand that it is God's triple-fold goodness that is bringing this area into the spotlight. What it says is that God cares enough about them individually that He doesn't want them to get hurt. And they will get hurt if they continue without change in this particular area, though at times (due to our limited perspective) it may not feel, appear, or sound like that is the case. At these times, the call upon us is to trust Him, for He sees beyond the moment and knows what awaits us around the corner. As a God of love, He is always moving with our best interests at heart.

The Prophetic

Nothing strengthens faith like a prophetic word. For this reason, the word of God, through dreams, is often loaded with promises for the future. Operating in this way, a dream brings Heaven to earth in an instant and opens new frontiers and opportunities not thought of by the dreamer. Through prophetic dreams, God is able to encourage, prepare, marshal, and direct His troops for the expansion of the Kingdom. It is the same today as it was in the dream revealed to Gideon (see Judg. 7:13-14), in the promise to Jacob (see Gen. 28:12-15), and in the dreams of Pharaoh (see Gen. 41:1-7).

Through a prophetic dream, God may open His ministers to be led more by the Spirit, as the following dream shows,

I saw a river running diagonally through what was currently the church congregation's sitting area. It ran between the pulpit and the congregation. At the back of the church were huge stands—like in a football stadium. When I awoke, I was concerned because I thought that the river separated the speaker from the audience.

I believe the river in this dream represents the flow of the Holy Spirit. The fact that the river flowed in front of the speaker is a good thing as it means that the preacher is putting the Spirit before himself. When this is done, God will draw crowds of people—the stands. The concern about the river in front of the speaker indicates that moving in the Spirit is not something the speaker is comfortable with at this stage and says that God is challenging the dreamer in this area. (An explanation of the metaphors used to interpret this dream is found in the dream and vision sample section of this book. See dream 2.)

Through a prophetic promise given in a dream, God may also remind those with the call of God on their lives that the gifts and callings of God are without repentance (see Rom. 11:29). This is what He does in this example, forwarded by a male friend,

> I was with a friend who I went to Bible College with some years earlier. He and I were in the ministry together. We were at post-boxes collecting our mail. I opened my box, and it was literally jammed-packed with letters. There were so many letters that it took me some time to "jimmy" a couple of envelopes free before the rest could be emptied out of the box.

The person who had this dream was no longer in a recognized ministry position. This dream indicates that he will once again take up a ministry position, as seen by the fact that he is with someone with ministry status. The many envelopes indicate invitations to speak and also seems to indicate that his ministry will be itinerant. God is encouraging and directing him into an itinerant ministry with this prophetic-futuristic dream. (An explanation of the metaphors used to interpret this dream is found in the dream and vision sample section of this book. See dream 3.)

Disclosure

Dreams may foretell things that are going to happen tomorrow, or they may foretell something that is going to happen 20 years from now. It is not always possible to clearly define the timeline in which God is operating. For this reason, unlike Joseph (see Gen. 37:5-7), it is wise not to share everything revealed with everyone. It is better to be like Mary, who "... *kept all these things and pondered them in her heart*" (Luke 2:19).

When Israel was about to go out to battle, God told them that they were to separate from their ranks those who were fearful (see Deut. 20:8). These were those without faith for the situation. God had them remove the spirit of fear because it has an incredible ability to be transferred. In the same way, Jesus removed the doubters when He was about to resurrect Jairus' daughter from the dead (see Matt. 9:18-26). Similarly, it is wise to be very selective about to whom you reveal what God is promising you. Not everyone knows or appreciates the call of God upon your life, and if you share or surround yourself with people who are not able to see you in the Spirit (see 2 Cor. 5:16), their doubt may undermine your faith and begin a decay of the promise within you.

Salvation

The story of Joseph in the previous chapter shows that God used dreams to save not only the nation of Egypt, but also the would-be nation of Israel. One of the reasons that this incident is recorded is so that the Church would join the dots and see the spiritual parallel it is meant to convey. Many will know that Joseph is a picture of Jesus in more than 100 ways (see Appendix A). He is hated by his brethren, he is sold by Judah (Judas) for silver, he is thrown into a pit (hell), he is resurrected, he is glorified, he is revealed to his brethren the second time, and he distributes the life-giving seed, to name a few parallels between the two. As impressive as that may be, a more liberating truth is that it was the Holy Spirit who raised Joseph up after He had brought conviction and repentance through the interpretation of two deeply symbolic dreams while he was in prison.

In the same way, God wants to release the prisoners of satan today and bring them into God's courts. Everyone who does not know Christ—rich or poor, educated or untaught, successful or failure, whether they realize it or not—is a slave of satan. Stop and think about that for a while; it puts things back into correct perspective. This truth is outlined by Paul in his instruction to Timothy,

> *In meekness instructing those that oppose themselves; if God peradventure will give them repentance to the acknowledging of the truth; and **that they may recover themselves out of the snare of the devil, who are taken captive by him at his will*** (2 Timothy 2:25-26 KJV).

These verses not only point out, as highlighted, that the people of the world are satan's captives, but they also say that people of the world *"oppose themselves."* This is because, in resisting the Gospel, people are not so much opposing the Church or the Gospel, but are in fact, keeping themselves bound under satan's jurisdiction and hence really opposing themselves. They want to experience freedom, but in its place they have captivity!

This spiritual reality is reinforced as believers are encouraged to give thanks for our arrival into the Kingdom of God and also our liberation from satan's shackles. As is stated in Colossians,

*Giving thanks to the Father, who has qualified and made us fit to share the portion which is the inheritance of the saints (God's holy people) in the Light. [The Father] has delivered and **drawn us to Himself out of the control and the dominion of darkness** and has transferred us into the kingdom of the Son of His love* (Colossians 1:12-13 AMP).

God is in the immigration business. He is continually looking for opportunities to draw people into His Kingdom and release them from satan's clutches because His prime concern is humankind's eternal destiny.

For this reason, God will continually reach out to them, even in their sleep. Let's refer once again to the passage we read earlier, in Job, where Elihu said,

*Indeed God speaks once, or twice, yet no one notices it. In a dream, a vision of the night, when sound sleep falls on men, while they slumber in their beds, then He opens the ears of men, and seals their instruction, that He may turn man aside from his conduct, and keep man from pride; **He keeps back his soul from the pit, and his life from passing over into Sheol*** (Job 33:14-18 NASB).

We see that God speaks to the unsaved at least twice through dreams during their lifetime to get them saved! So passionate is He that they spend eternity with Him. He has made provision through His own death[4] upon the cross that no one need go to hell. The passage above records that they don't understand what they have received in their dreams due to the veil upon their hearts. They desperately need someone with the Spirit of God to enlighten them.

Regularly, friends ask me about dreams that unsaved people they interact with have been having. Like the nurse whose patient repeatedly dreamed of compulsive cleaning, the father who continually dreamed of falling, the young man struggling to get the manhole hatch into the ceiling open, or the mature lady who repeatedly saw herself running down a hallway to get away from the fire that was chasing her. All of these dreams are God speaking to these people about their need for salvation. Dreams and their interpretations are an untapped reservoir of opportunities. If we lift our eyes and learn to interpret, then there is truly a white harvest field of souls before us (see John 4:35).

Our neighbors, friends, workmates, and clients may never come to church, but they all dream, and God has provided a priceless outreach tool in the interpretation of their dreams. Start asking them humbly about their dreams, and they will begin to open to our message as God proves Himself by disclosing their hearts and their futures.

If as you have read these pages, you are acutely aware that you are not presently right with God, please turn to Appendix B at the rear of this book right now before proceeding further.

Summary: Chapter Three

- Dreams and visions are *rhema* words from God to build and strengthen faith.
- You can be strengthened in faith by hearing the dreams of others, like Gideon, who was strengthened in faith by hearing two enemy soldiers sharing a dream.
- God uses dreams to prepare people for healing, as He did with Jean Neil.
- Dreams and visions reveal secrets and answer questions on people's hearts.
- Dreams are a powerful vehicle for God to warn and guide His people. This is particularly true for those who are embarking on new ventures in God because the enemy is constant in his endeavors to abort the promises of God.
- Dreams are used to correct, as is shown in the Book of Job, where God uses dreams to *"turn man from his deed."*
- The prophetic nature of many dreams strengthens faith and endurance.
- It is not wise to disclose every dream or vision you receive because many people will not appreciate or understand the call of God upon your life. Your listener's doubt is like fear, which has the potential to begin a decay of the promise of God within you.
- Dreams are a regular means by which God communicates to non-Christians their need for salvation.
- Everyone who has not come to the cross of Christ is a prisoner of satan.
- According to Job, God is so passionate about people's souls that He uses dreams at least twice during their lifetime to prevent them from going to hell.
- Everyone dreams; therefore, skills developed in dream interpretation create new harvest field opportunities.
- If you are not currently in right relationship with God, please read Appendix B at the rear of this book.

Endnotes

1. W.E. Vine, M.F. Unger, and W. White Jr., *Vine's Complete Expository Dictionary of Old and New Testament Words* (Nashville, TN: Thomas Nelson, 1985). Used by Permission.

2. Reinhard Bonnke, *Even Greater* (Orlando: Full Flame LLC, 2004).

3. See www.e-r-productions.com for a comprehensive list of Reinhard Bonnke's publications.

4. Sadly, many people do not realize who it was who died for them. When we see Jesus dying upon the cross, we are looking at the incarnation of God Himself taking our place and receiving the judgment we rightly deserve for our sin. Jesus said, *" . . . If you believe not that **I am**, ye shall die in your sins"* (John 8:24 literal translation). Here He identifies Himself with the One who met Moses at the burning bush (see Exod. 3:14) and puts Himself under threat of stoning by declaring it (see John 8:58-59). He is also called *Immanuel*—God with us (see Isa. 7:14) and the *Everlasting Father* (see Isa. 9:6). The Book of Colossians declares this truth a mystery, *" . . . to the knowledge of the mystery of God, both of the Father and of Christ"* (Col. 2:2). Can we comprehend it? No! But it is a mystery nonetheless revealed in the New Testament. Comparing Revelation 1:8 with Revelation 22:12-16, we discover that the Alpha and Omega, the First and the Last, is none other than Jesus, who is Almighty God! It was Almighty God who died on the cross for you and me. This surely amplifies the words of the writer to the Hebrews when he says, *"How shall we escape if we neglect so great a salvation . . ."* (Heb. 2:3).

Chapter Four

Are All Dreams From God? (Part 1)
By Adam F. Thompson

Are all dreams from God? This is a common question I am asked. A lot of dreams do not make sense; they come across as completely strange. You may have heard many people say, "I had a really weird dream last night; it made no sense at all." The truth is, God is trying to communicate with us, and He speaks to us daily in and through dreams—every dream.

Nightmares

You may be thinking to yourself, *What if I have a nightmare? Is that from God? Or if I have a demonic attack in my dream, is that from God?* The truth is, as Christians, even when we are awake, the enemy is looking for opportunities to attack us and bring us down. Also, while we are sleeping, our spiritual senses can pick up spiritual warfare or demonic oppression (in the heavenlies) which may be occurring in the area. It is important to remember that Jesus has defeated the enemy (see Col. 2:15). The Bible also declares that we have been given the authority to trample on snakes and scorpions and over all the powers of the evil one (see Luke 10:19). Praise God!

Primarily a nightmare is a signal. It is the cry of a heart carrying an unresolved issue and needing attention. Now generally, if Christians are walking in the Spirit and living in the counsel of the Lord, they do not have nightmares. However, if as a Christian, you do have constant nightmares, there is definitely a heart issue needing to be resolved.

Some prophetic dreams and visions may come across as nightmares because of the enormity of the events shown in them. These are normally received by those with a strong prophetic calling. Daniel experienced this type of nightmare while lying on his bed (see Dan. 4:5).

Constant nightmares would probably mean that there is an oppression operating in your life. This may indicate that you are being harassed by an oppressing spirit. Oppression is not possession, but rather harassment. If this is the case, you will require some counseling and ministry of the Holy Spirit under the guidance of a discerning and trusted mature believer. In the main, this occurs when there is a stronghold in your mind or heart due to something that has happened in the past that has affected you deeply, such as an abuse or trauma of some kind. Ultimately, what we look for in these situations is the legal ground on which the enemy is allowed to gain access. This is explained further below.

Another such occurrence is when, as Christians, we sin with our mouths. I am not talking about the attributes of sin, such as drinking, smoking, sexual immorality, theft, and so on. I am talking about sinning with our mouths without being consciously aware of it. What I am referring to is either when we curse ourselves or others by labeling ourselves or others as "idiots" or something similar. This can also happen if we keep making negative confessions with our mouths, such as, "I must be going crazy." Similarly, we may be guilty of openly confessing doubt or fear, which likewise gives the enemy the right to harass and torment us. Cursing ourselves and denying the Word of God like this grieves the Holy Spirit and gives a foothold to the enemy (see Eph. 4:27-30). We need to be ever aware that "*. . .we do not wrestle against flesh and blood, but against principalities, against powers. . .in the heavenly places*" (Eph. 6:12).

As Christians, we must be very careful what we say and confess with our mouths. The Book of Proverbs says we have power in our tongues to speak words of life or death (see Prov.18:21). This is not an empty platitude that we can choose to ignore; this is a living reality we need to take to heart. Therefore, it is really important to always speak as if we are speaking the very words of God and to have our vocabulary lined up with the Word of God, because this empowers us to receive the promises of God. When we align our speech with God's Word in this way, we frustrate the enemy because God's Word cannot be broken (see John 10:35). Jesus said that "*Heaven and earth will pass away, but My words will by no means pass away*" (Matt. 24:35).

Angels and demons constantly hear every word we say. If we start speaking the Word of God and our vocabulary is in agreement with the Word of God, it activates the power of God and empowers the angels to encamp around us and to prepare the way for the destiny that God has for us. When we start speaking death, curses, or doubt, it empowers demons to respond and gives them the right to bring havoc into our lives, to strike us and steer us off God's path. Our victory is in being in harmony with God's Word.

The Scriptures further say the devil roams around like a roaring lion, looking to devour us. If as Christians we are having nightmares and are under constant attack by the enemy, God is allowing this so that we can learn to overcome with the blood of the Lamb and by the word of our testimony (see Rev. 12:11). It is important to understand that there is a difference between allowing something to happen and being the perpetrator of that horror. The Bible says, *"Let no one say when he is tempted, 'I am tempted by God'; for God cannot be tempted by evil, nor does He Himself tempt anyone"* (James 1:13).

Temptation

It is evident from Scripture that God allows the enemy access to us to test or prove us. Though He was without sin, Jesus was tempted by the devil in the wilderness (see Luke 4:1-13). This temptation may come in the form of a dream or a vision, as it did with Christ. Luke's Gospel records, *"Then the devil, taking Him up on a high mountain, showed Him all the kingdoms of the world in a moment of time"* (Luke 4:5). The fact that the devil was able to show Jesus all the kingdoms of the world *"in a moment of time"* suggests that this temptation came in the form of a vision.

Why would God allow the enemy to tempt us? The answer to that question is twofold. If we fail the test, it acts like a refining fire by bringing what is truly in our hearts to the surface so that we deal with it. It thus produces a humbler and holier disciple.

A good example of this is when God withdrew from Hezekiah. Hezekiah had previously shown Babylonian envoys all the wealth and treasures of his kingdom (see 2 Kings 20:12-13). In response to Hezekiah's proud and impetuous act, the Bible records,

> *Howbeit in the business of the ambassadors of the princes of Babylon, who sent unto him to enquire of the wonder that was done in the land,* **God**

left him, to try him, that he might know all that was in his heart (2 Chronicles 32:31 KJV).

God withdrew from Hezekiah so that he would see the pride of his own heart, repent, and not suffer eternally for it. In allowing Hezekiah to be tested, God was working in the king's best interests.

God also allows us to undergo temptation so that, when we have come through the temptation victoriously, we are aware that we have grown stronger in God and moved to another spiritual level. For Christ, graduation through His wilderness temptations meant that He was now ready for ministry,

> *Then Jesus returned in the power of the Spirit to Galilee, and news of Him went out through all the surrounding region. And He taught in their synagogues, being glorified by all* (Luke 4:14-15).

Learning From Job

Reading the Book of Job, we find that he was a righteous man. There was no one like him on the earth, and he was righteous to the point where God proclaimed his righteousness. The devil came to God, and God asked him where he had been, to which he answered, *"From going to and fro on the earth . . ."* (Job 1:7). He was looking to find legal grounds to enter the lives of men and women on earth, particularly those who were in relationship with God, which at the time included Job. That didn't just happen to Job without reason. I believe that this passage of Scripture is there to show us potentially what can happen to all saints. In the spirit realm, there is a constant battle going on, and the enemy is on the prowl, looking to devour and constantly accusing believers before God (see 1 Pet. 5:8). The Bible records that he does not let up, but is constantly leveling accusations to God about believers, day and night (see Rev. 12:10). The devil is vigilant in his quest for a foothold into believers' lives.

God did not allow satan to attack Job's life or touch him without consent. In fact, the devil can do nothing without God's consent. This is why Paul can say that *"all things work together for good . . ."* (Rom. 8:28). The Lord said to satan, *"Behold, all that he has is in your power; only do not lay a hand on his person"* (Job 1:12).

Then satan went out from God's presence to bring calamity to Job. The encouraging thing in the Book of Job is that all the hardship and all the attacks of the enemy purged him and caused him to be stronger, wiser, and more faithful to the Lord, even though at one point he seemed to be weak in his faith. Job was not suffering because of sin, but God in His foresight knew that in suffering Job would sin. It was God's wisdom at work, because He hadn't finished with Job. God wanted him to come to the fullness He had for him. This attack on Job's life included experiencing nightmares. Job himself said, *"Then You scare me with dreams, and terrify me with visions"* (Job 7:14).

Job attributed the nightmares to God. It appears he experienced them because God allowed the devil access to him. God took down the hedge of protection around Job (see Job 1:10), a spiritual hedge that we likewise are protected by if we are born again and living rightly before God (see Ps. 34:7; Isa. 5:1-2). Job's protection was removed ultimately for his benefit and to show us what happens in the spirit realm. I don't believe that God freely gives evil spirits access to our lives today without them having some legal right to do so. These situations happen if there are unresolved issues that give the enemy legal grounds to come into God's Kingdom—you (see Luke 17:21).

If we are experiencing nightmares, then the enemy has a legal right to enter. We need to ask the Holy Spirit to help us identify the grounds on which the enemy is getting in. The common grounds on which the enemy gains access are:

- Unforgiveness related to some form of abuse or trauma (see Matt. 18:21-35)
- Rebellion and unrepentant sin (see Prov. 17:11)
- Witchcraft and divination (see 1 Sam. 15:23; 16:14)
- Generational curses (see Exod. 20:4-5; Deut. 5:9)
- Wrong confession with our mouths (see Eph. 4:25-27)
- Extreme jealousy, envy, or rage (see Eph. 4:25-27)
- Strongholds: defiant mental attitudes contrary to the Word of God (see 1 Sam. 15:23; Prov. 17:11)

Pornographic Dreams

If we are experiencing pornographic dreams, then there is generally a core issue as outlined above—often having more than one strand and manifesting itself as lust in our lives. The devil has been known to build a stronghold of lust around a three-fold cord of jealousy, unforgiveness, and mental strongholds. I have also seen a spirit of perversion operating over people's lives among pornographic nightmare sufferers. This means that when dealing with this problem, it is necessary to address more than just the manifesting problem of lust. The pornographic nightmare sufferer needs to come clean with heart issues through confession and repentance, giving the enemy no legal ground for entry before a prayer identifying and severing spiritual bonds or soul-ties is declared in authority over the believer. It is important that this problem is not further fed by the dreamer—by looking at other people or media with lust—because that gives the enemy further ground on which to enter. Like Job, all believers need to make a covenant with their eyes (see Job 31:1) when thoughts stray beyond pure relationships, particularly when battling with lust.

In Job's case, we find at the end of the book that he was blessed with a double-portion of what he had in the beginning. His experience humbled him and gave him insight and wisdom. It gave him the humility and love to pray for those who rose up against him, which is a display of the same nature as Jesus Christ.

At times God will also directly trouble our souls through a nightmare to direct and warn us. These dreams may manifest as a fear of the Lord in regard to pending judgment. This was the case with Pilate's wife (see Matt. 27:19), Abimelech (see Gen. 20:3-7), Pharaoh (see Gen. 41:8), and Nebuchadnezzar (see Dan. 2:1; 4:5).

So God both indirectly allows enemy access to torment us (see Matt. 18:34; Prov. 17:11) and directly gives nightmares, but always with a beneficial intention. These come if we are not fully grown in the Lord and are holding certain issues contrary to the Word of God in our hearts, so that we can grow, pinpoint the issues, and overcome the enemy. Ours is not to hide these dreams, but to find a trustful, mature believer and work through the issues the dreams identify.

With Job, even though he was initially considered righteous, the trials and tribulations brought on by the attack of the enemy exposed certain issues he held deep in his heart. There was some resentment he held and some things that he cried out to the Lord which weren't right (see Job 38:1-2; 42:3), which when confessed and repented of gave him a greater revelation of God. So God wants us to live in the fullness of what He has for us, and at times, He uses adversity to refine us. This is so that when we stand before Him on the Day of Judgment we can have confidence without suffering any loss and can take our place holding our head high with full assurance, knowing we have completely fulfilled His divine plan for our lives.

Wisdom Found in Parables

Yes, the days of thinking we had a weird dream because we ate too much pizza are over. That one-liner is peddled way too often. I believe that all dreams are communications from God. Weird dreams that do not seem to make sense are not meaningless or without purpose. Actually, they are all significant. We need to always keep in mind that when God speaks to us in dreams He does it primarily through metaphors and symbols. As He has said in His Word, *"I will open My mouth in a parable, I will utter dark sayings of old"* (Ps. 78:2).

That prophecy was not just fulfilled in Jesus' teaching, but it continues as He speaks to us in dreams and visions today. We discover in Scripture that the Proverbs were written so the understanding person *". . .will attain wise counsel, to understand a proverb and an enigma* [parable], *the words of the wise and their riddles"* (Prov. 1:5b-6).

Just as His wisdom is conveyed through proverbs, God also communicates to us using parables in dreams to bring us His wisdom. Just as Jesus spoke in parables, talking about seed-sowing to the farmer (see Matt. 13:3-9), about fishing to fishermen (see Matt. 4:19), and about finance to stewards (see Matt. 25:14-30), so He speaks to us in allegorical dreams today. It's clear that God speaks to us in riddle-like dreams, and we need the Holy Spirit to give us the spiritual insight to interpret these parables and riddles.

When Jesus explained the parable saying that what comes out of the mouth comes directly from the heart, Peter came up to Him and petitioned, *"Explain this parable to us."* Jesus said in response, *"Are you also still without understanding?"* (Matt. 15:15-16). Even though he was awake and in the physical presence of Jesus, it is obvious that Peter still didn't understand the parable and needed to have it explained or interpreted for him. We likewise experience parable-type communication from God through our dreams and equally need them interpreted if we are going to understand them.

When we stop and think about it, Jesus Christ is the best communicator the world has ever known because He relates to all people at their level and on their wavelength through everyday realities and experiences. He did it when He was physically here on earth, and He is still doing it through our dreams by His Spirit while He is with the Father.

Why Metaphors?

Why does God speak to us in metaphors? God uses metaphors because images are very powerful. God created our minds to relate to and remember images and sounds quicker and more readily than written words. For example, when we drive along in our cars and see a "School Crossing" sign, we see more than just the words *School Crossing.* We see a symbol, a silhouette of a woman holding the hand of a child crossing the road.

This is because, though our verbal thoughts can be very fast, visual images received by our brains are much faster. Compared to the visual, trying to take information in by reading is much slower. When we read, we have to comprehend it. While reading, we have to process the information in our minds and try to imagine what we are reading. We read it first and then have to create the image. On the other hand, seeing an image or hearing a sound has the potential to go straight into our minds and our spirits.

Another illustration of the power of images is found on most computer desktops. When you look for the trashcan, do you look for the word *trashcan*, or do you look for the image of the little trashcan? Everybody responds to the icon quicker than they do to the words.

In business education circles today, the inherent power of metaphors as advanced communication tools and vehicles for change is being widely recognized. Francesco Sofo[1] notes that "metaphors can refocus the familiar and show it in a new light," "provoke a vivid image which make future actions more tangible," and "connote meanings on a cognitive, emotional, and behavioral level in a holistic way." He says further that "the metaphor makes messages highly memorable and facilitates the reframing of views and mental sets. . . ." Brink[2] has outlined that metaphors are more easily heard than rational explanations and, therefore, encourage listening, and because the symbolism is creative, they have the power to stimulate reflection and action. Broussine and Vince[3] state that metaphors have the power to promote engagement and through engagement, change. And finally, Bennis[4] found that successful leaders have an ability to use metaphors to make their vision clear to others. Wow, today's cutting-edge business educators are promoting the power of teaching methodologies utilized by Christ 2,000 years ago!

This should be no real surprise to us. After all, Jesus knows what works. He made us (see John 1:1-3; Col. 1:16). It is also little wonder that Jesus is still using this most powerful of teaching methods in our dreams and visions today.

This is why the Internet, television, and radio, and media like them, are very influential forms of communication. The Internet is very powerful because it is full of images and has tremendous potential to be used for good or for evil. I am not saying the Internet is wrong; it is just a means of communication and can be a great source of information. My own children use it regularly for study and good purposes. Unfortunately, this so-called information highway is also being used to flood and corrode our society with a plethora of pornographic, occultic, and other ungodly information.

I personally make a habit of listening to the Word of God over and over because faith comes from *hearing* the Word (see Rom. 10:17). If we listen to the Word of God over and over again, it gives our inner ear greater opportunity to *hear* (see Ezek. 3:10). When I was a child, I struggled with dyslexia. Nowadays, by listening to dramatized versions of the Word of God on my iPod, I am able to visualize and retain more of what I hear. In a similar way, God not only gives us mental images in dreams, but also at times provides an emphasis-adding audible "voice-over" as well. This is in line with the fact that our minds give priority to images and audio over-and-above mere written words.

God also uses parables because He knows that we will be hungry to know what the dreams mean. I have found that, as soon as we understand that God speaks to us this way, we get even hungrier to know what He is saying. As the Scripture has it, *"It is the glory of God to conceal a thing: but the honour of kings is to search out a matter"* (Prov. 25:2 KJV).

It is inherent in us to search for the answer to the code—the Divinity Code—He has set before us. Indeed, there is a blessing for those with this hunger, because the Bible declares that there is fulfillment in *asking, seeking, and knocking* (see Matt. 7:7).

Finally, God uses parables because they have an inherent ability to bypass the heart's natural defense mechanisms. We witness this in the correction of David after he commits adultery with Bathsheba (see 2 Sam. 12:1-15). Nathan, the prophet, comes to David and relates a parable of a rich man stealing a poor man's one and only ewe lamb. David makes a judgment concerning the rich man, and the prophet reveals the hidden truth behind the parable—David is that rich man! He is convicted and repents of his actions.

So God speaks to us in parables because they relate to us, and have greater potential to be anchored in our minds, just as Jesus' disciples remembered His teachings and, later, wrote the Gospels. He also encodes His wisdom using metaphors because they are more readily received, they create a hunger in us for the interpretation, and they bypass our heart's natural self-protective tendencies.

Summary: Chapter Four

- Every dream is communication from God.
- Some prophetic dreams come across as nightmares because of the enormity of the events they portray.
- Constant nightmares point to an oppression operating in the life of the dreamer.
- Negative confession may give the enemy ground on which to harass us.
- It is important to have our vocabulary line up with the Word of God.
- Our victory over principalities and powers is in being in harmony with God's Word.
- God allows demonic harassment so that we learn to overcome through the blood of the Lamb and the word of our testimony.
- We are particularly susceptible to temptation in our dreams. These refine or approve us.
- The Book of Job provides insight into the spirit realm. The devil is constantly seeking permission to enter the lives of people. He cannot do anything without legal grounds, which he presents to God to gain access.
- The common grounds on which the enemy gains access are:
  - Unforgiveness
  - Rebellion
  - Witchcraft
  - Generational curses
  - Wrong confession
  - Extreme jealousy, envy, and rage
  - Strongholds
- Pornographic nightmares may indicate a multi-stranded stronghold which manifests and operates as lust.

- Spirit-sensitive counseling is suggested for nightmare and pornographic dream sufferers.
- God uses adversity to refine us.
- Dreams may appear weird because God uses parables to communicate to us.
- Jesus is the best communicator the world has ever known because He employs parables using everyday realities to speak to every person at their level and on their wavelength.
- God uses metaphors because:
  - They create a more memorable message.
  - They are more readily heard.
  - They stimulate reflection and action.
  - They readily convey vision.
  - They refocus the familiar in a new light.
  - They bypass the heart's self-protective mechanisms.

Endnotes

1. F. Sofo, *Human Resource Development* (Woodslane, Warriewood, NSW. Australia, 1999).

2. T.L. Brink, "Metaphor as data in the study of organizations," *Journal of Management Inquiry* (1993) 2.4, 366-371.

3. M. Broussine and R. Vince, "Working with metaphor towards organizational change," *Organizational Development: Metaphoric explorations* (London: Pitman Publishing, 1996).

4. W. Bennis, "The four competencies of leadership," *Training & Development Journal* (1984), 38.8, 14-19.

Chapter Five

Are All Dreams From God? (Part 2)
By Adrian Beale

Because of the nature of some of their dreams, many people think that God is not the author of all dreams. The authors believe that God speaks to us through every dream, but is He the author of every dream? Yes and No. The vast majority of our dreams are God speaking directly to us. However, the Scriptures also seem to indicate that the enemy has an ability to provide visionary experiences, and we ourselves are able to influence what God reveals through our dreams.

Dreams From the Enemy

Consider the enemy for a moment. When Jesus was led by the Spirit into the wilderness to be tempted by the devil, the devil was able to manifest a vision of the future. The Bible records, *"Then the devil, taking Him up on a high mountain, showed Him all the kingdoms of the world in a moment of time"* (Luke 4:5).

Note that the devil was able in some way to provide a vision of future kingdoms. Who led Jesus into this situation to be tempted? God—the Spirit—did (see Luke 4:1). God was always in control. He knew the enemy's abilities and allowed it. Who authored the vision? On one level, the devil did, but on a far superior level, God did because He had foreknowledge of the devil's plan, permitted it, and used it in accordance with His will and purpose. We must always remember that the enemy can only do what God permits. For this reason, we should not be too quick to ignore or discredit any dream on the grounds that "It is not from God."

Biased Dreams

It also appears that God will reveal the agendas on our hearts through our dreams. This seems to be the essence of God's communication through Jeremiah,

> For thus says the Lord of hosts, the God of Israel: Do not let your prophets and your diviners who are in your midst deceive you, **nor listen to your dreams which you cause to be dreamed** (Jeremiah 29:8).

It may be that this text does not refer so much to a "self-generated" dream, but rather that it is potentially explained by another Scripture,

> Therefore speak to them, and say to them, "Thus says the Lord God: 'Everyone of the house of Israel **who sets up his idols in his heart**, and puts before him what causes him to stumble into iniquity, and then comes to the prophet, **I the Lord will answer him who comes, according to the multitude of his idols**'" (Ezekiel 14:4).

This says that if we come to God with preconceived plans (our idols), then God will answer us (in this case, in a dream) according to that which is in our hearts. God causes the dreamer to dream a dream that reveals the idolatry within the heart. In terms of God's statement to Jeremiah, these are the dreams *"you cause to be dreamed."*

The dream is a message from God to show dreamers the states of their hearts and is designed to bring them back to God. This is why Ezekiel continues to say, *"that I may seize the house of Israel by their heart. . ."* (Ezek. 14:5).

Balaam

Balaam went through a similar situation. He was initially told not to go with the messengers of Balak the king of Moab who wanted him to curse Israel (see Num. 22:12). However, when the next envoy came to Balaam with the promise of greater reward, we find God apparently changing his mind and telling Balaam to go with them (see Num. 22:20). In the morning, as Balaam sets out on his journey to Balak's camp, we find out that God is angry with Balaam (see Num. 22:22). Why? Balaam was going against the purposes and command of God by going with Balak's men.

How can that be the case when the Bible records that it was God who told Balaam to go the second time? *"And God came to Balaam at night and said to him, 'If the men come to call you, rise and go with them. . .'"* (Num. 22:20). God spoke to Balaam what he wanted to hear. In Balaam's case, it was his greed that allowed his heart to be seduced. Similarly, God will speak to us in dreams that our hearts "cause us" to dream because of the idolatry there.

Discrediting God

It is really important that we do not move too quickly to discredit the source and, therefore, the veracity of our dreams. Let me give you a couple of examples. While I was working in a teaching role at a Christian rehabilitation program, one of my students had a dream that he was injecting his own neck with a syringe. Now this was something that he had never done in real life. On similar occasions other Christian teachers had told me that, "God would never remind a person of where they've come from." They would try to further discredit the dream by saying, "That's sick; that's from the enemy!" But on this occasion, I simply asked the dreamer, "Are you seeking a quick fix here? For this is the interpretation of your dream." As I asked this question, you could see the conviction of the Holy Spirit on the person's face as his heart was revealed. That student did not want to fully embrace Christianity, but was undergoing the program with an ulterior motive, and God revealed the motivation of the heart.

Another example that is not uncommon is when a married man or woman may dream of having sex with someone other than their partner. Don't be too quick to write these dreams off because of the pangs of guilt. This is particularly important if there is no sexual arousal in the dream. (Sexual arousal generally indicates a lust or temptation issue is involved.) Sure enough, in the natural, this does not sound like a work of God. However, when we consider that one of the metaphors for sexual intimacy is "union" with another, and if we understand that kissing may be interpreted as "embracing" or "seduction," we learn not to write off these messages so quickly. So, a man being kissed by a woman in black may be God saying we are being seduced by death! And we need to consider the name of the person (if that person is known to us) kissing us in the dream. Being kissed by "Linda," for example, may say that we are embracing the enemy. *Linda* means "one who comes with wisdom," but its German root *lindi* means "serpent" or "snake-like." These are serious warnings that we would be wise to heed.

Dreams: The Product of Brain Chemistry or Conditioning?

Some may even believe that dreams are merely the product of brain chemistry or conditioning. If that is the case, how would you explain two people getting exactly the same dream? Honestly, what are the chances? Yet this has been recorded on several occasions, but I will cite only two readily-available and documented accounts to confirm my point.

Firstly, in Reinhard Bonnke's book, *Even Greater,* Reinhard details the story of how he and his brother, Jurgen, had the same dream, though thousands of miles apart and living very different lives. The dream showed Jurgen crossing a suspension bridge and falling into an abyss. After this dream, Jurgen asked God to confirm that it was indeed a warning from Him by verifying it in some way through his brother. When Reinhard wrote to Jurgen detailing exactly the same dream, the witness of the two dreams led Jurgen to receive Christ as his personal Savior![1]

Secondly, in the book, *India: One Act of Kindness,* by Brendan McCauley, God gave two sisters—Bini and Beena Thampy—the same dream of the Second Coming of Christ on the same night to encourage them and their family in their dedication to the Lord's work in India.[2] If you want to feed your faith, both of these books—which are present-day accounts of the Acts of the Apostles—are well worth the investment.

Take Them All Seriously

Finally, if we believe that God is only the author of some dreams, and if we discredit the weird ones as either from the enemy or as figments of our own imagination, we have become like those who rule out unpalatable passages of Scripture as uninspired. I like that dream, but I don't like that one. So all the nice dreams are from God, and all the others—corrective and disciplinary ones—are from the enemy. When we pick and choose which dreams are inspired and which are not, we close ourselves off from the full counsel of God. The ultimate consequence of this is spiritual insensitivity, leading to an imbalanced and powerless Christian walk.

Rather than ignoring them, we are to realize that dreams are dealing with real heart issues. Consider how much of the problem of our heart's insensitivity or bias is addressed when we begin to see that God is communicating through *all* dreams and start to take them *all* seriously.

Summary: Chapter Five

- God speaks through every dream.
- God, the devil, and our own hearts influence the dreams we dream.
- Beware of idols in your heart because God will answer you according to your idols.
- God responded to Balaam's inquiry with what he wanted to hear.
- Go slow in discrediting dreams on the basis of their apparent source.
- Two people having exactly the same dream may answer the question of whether brain chemistry or conditioning are responsible for our dreams.
- Don't pick and choose which dreams are inspired.
- Take all dreams seriously.

Endnotes

1. Reinhard Bonnke, *Even Greater* (Orlando: Full Flame LLC, 2004).
2. Brendan McCauley, *India: One Act of Kindness* (Oklahoma City: Tate Publishing, 2004).

Chapter Six

Visions
By Adam F. Thompson

Step Into It and Grow

I have learned over the years that walking in the Spirit and moving in the prophetic is something in which we grow. Why is that relevant in a book on dreams and visions? To understand, we need to reconsider God's message through Joel. He says,

> . . . *I will pour out My Spirit on all flesh; your sons and your daughters shall prophesy, your young men shall see visions, your old men shall dream dreams* (Acts 2:17; Joel 2:28).

This passage points out that there is a link between prophecy and dreams and visions. In reality, dreams and visions are a vehicle to bring us into the prophetic. That is not to say that we are all prophets in the five-fold ministry sense of the word (see Eph. 4:11). However, dreams and visions are one of the primary ways in which God communicates to His prophets. This is confirmed as God says through Moses, " . . . *If there is a prophet among you, I, the Lord, make Myself known to him in a vision; I speak to him in a dream*" (Num. 12:6).

Therefore, in pouring out His Spirit, God has equipped all of us with the ability to prophesy. That should get us excited and expectant. Just as God told Israel to begin to possess the land inhabited by the enemy as they moved from the wilderness into the Promised Land, so God tells us to spiritually step into what He has for us today (see Deut. 2:24, 31). As with Israel, God is encouraging us to begin possessing what belongs to us, because without the understanding that it is ours, we lack the faith to step into it.

Having been stirred to move in the spiritual gifts, such as prophecy, we need to understand that God doesn't just wave a wand and give us them overnight. It is a gradual thing. There will be times when we make mistakes. When I first started moving in the prophetic, I became discouraged if I made an error. I thought that perhaps I had misunderstood God and that He didn't really want me to move in the gifts. However, I have discovered that it doesn't matter if we make mistakes. The Lord will help us to grow while learning from our mistakes. This is one of the reasons why the Bible sets forth that we are to judge prophecy—including the interpretation of a dream—(see 1 John 4:1) and also explains the need for the schools of the prophets during the ministry of Elijah (see 2 Kings 2).

Sensitivity Required

A person might have a powerful spiritual gift of seeing in the Spirit as a seer (one who has visions), prophesying, or even interpreting dreams, but it is another thing to have the sensitivity of heart to know if, when, and how to deliver what that person is shown. The prophetic is as much about knowing *what to do with* what God shows you as it is about having the discernment of heart to *receive* what He shows you. At times, God will simply give people spiritual insight so that they can pray for those to whom the revelation relates, often without those it concerns knowing it. We always need to ask the Holy Spirit for wisdom to match the gift, because although our hearts may be zealous, the Holy Spirit helps us to be effective.

Getting visions is common among prophetic people or those who are baptized in the Holy Spirit and moving in spiritual gifts. A vision can come either while we are awake or when we are asleep. Often visions come and we are not even aware that we have received one. I personally have found that two of our most receptive times to receive visions are just before we fall asleep or, conversely, just as we are stirring to consciousness, but not yet awake. At these times, because of our insensitivity to the voice of the Spirit, we are prone to miss what God is saying, as "*. . .the natural man does not receive the things of the Spirit of God, for they are foolishness to him*" (1 Cor. 2:14a).

As explained earlier, a vision is a revelation straight to the human spirit, a deposit from God injected into our spirits that interrupts soulish or conscious activity. However, without spiritual discernment, our natural inclination is to dismiss and ignore such revelations as vacant meanderings of our own mind.

I often get visions when I pray for people. It is very much like having a dream while being awake. These visions are mostly metaphoric or symbolic in nature. However, they can also be literal. When God gives me the interpretation of the vision, much like He would a dream, and I speak it out, it becomes a powerful prophecy in the lives of those with whom I am praying.

I remember once praying for a young man, and as I prayed, God gave me a vision of him working at a tire business. In the vision, he was working at a blue bench, and in front of him was a windowsill which had a potted plant on it. I saw him looking out the window dreaming about the desires of his heart. As I described the scene, he told me that I had described his workplace with incredible detail. He said he actually did look out the window and daydream about the things he wanted. The vision and prophecy that went with it encouraged him in the Lord and revealed that God cared about him individually and had a plan for his life.

Joel's prophecy says that *"your young men shall have visions"* (Joel 2:28). From the material presented in this book, it should be evident that this means that God has made a way for every believer to operate in this spiritual gift today, just as Jesus did. When Jesus was introduced to Nathaniel, He said, *"Behold, an Israelite indeed, in whom is no deceit"* (John 1:47). There's a depth revealed in this declaration, not evident to those who did not know Nathaniel personally. An Israelite *with* deceit would have been a fleshly man, a Jacob, or a grabber. Nathaniel, on the other hand, is a very devout Jew—an apparent rarity in Jesus' day. Therefore, he naturally responded by asking, *"How do You know me?"* to which Jesus replied, *"Before Philip called you, when you were under the fig tree, I saw you"* (John. 1:48).

Now it was obvious that Jesus was not there physically to see Nathaniel under the fig tree. I believe that Jesus had a vision and had seen in the Spirit that Nathaniel was alone by the fig tree prior to Philip calling him. Sometimes the metaphoric and literal natures of visions run simultaneously, as they do here. When Jesus saw Nathaniel by the fig tree, where I believe he was praying, He was provided with a metaphor of him being a true Israelite because the fig tree represents Israel, and his act of praying was a literal confirmation of that metaphor. Jesus' vision was the faith-generating foundation to the power of this encounter. In revealing Nathaniel's heart, it opened him to see Jesus as the Son of God.

Vision Leading to Renewal

Recently while waiting upon God when I was ministering in India, I received a vision of a pergola that was half covered (an outside wooden structure with only half a roof). Immediately I sensed God saying to me, "What do you see?" So I said, "I see a half-covered pergola." In my spirit He said, "Half of My people here are not under My covering. Half are still serving the gods of their fathers. They are serving two masters." Instantly a Scripture came into my spirit. It was,

> *I will also destroy the idols, and cause the images to cease from Noph; there shall no longer be princes from the land of Egypt; I will put fear in the land of Egypt* (Ezekiel 30:13).

I knew that God was asking me to preach about pending judgment on the nation of India, particularly warning Christians against walking a dual path. Those under Christ would be protected, whereas those living a syncretized lifestyle would receive judgment. As you can imagine, this was not a message that was going to tickle ears, but because I have vowed to preach what He gives me, regardless of politics and the fear of people, I shared this message in several meetings in and around Pithapuram. Sure enough, some people walked out of those gatherings, but in every church where I preached this message, 20-30 percent of the congregation came forward to rededicate their lives to Christ! At one church of around 300 people, the pastor's daughter came forward, repented, and rededicated her life to Christ. Can I suggest that for her to do that would have taken true Holy Spirit conviction because of the politics and cultural influences involved? Visions are an extremely powerful vehicle of communication from God to which everyone needs to be open and attuned.

Hunger to Hear and Do the Will of God

The question you may be asking yourself is, "How can I experience visions?" Well, it is simple! Visions are just one of the ways God's Word is communicated to us when we earnestly desire to hear and fulfill God's will. God uses visions from cover to cover of the Bible to communicate with humankind. He used a vision to speak to Abram, *"After these things the word of the Lord came to Abram in a vision. . ."* (Gen. 15:1). And He used visions in giving the apostle John the Book of Revelation, *". . I heard the number of them. And thus I saw the horses in the vision"* (Rev. 9:16b-17a).

Peter captures the hunger required as he speaks about the Old Testament prophets and their desire to know about the coming of Christ,

> . . . *the prophets have inquired and* **searched carefully**, *who prophesied of the grace that would come to you, searching what, or what manner of time, the Spirit of Christ who was in them was indicating when He testified* . . .**To them it was revealed**. . . (1 Peter 1:10-12a).

Notice that the nation's "watchmen" (the prophets) hungered or, as the text puts it, *"searched carefully"* and that *"it was revealed"* to them as a result of that hunger. The fact that God brings revelation in response to our hunger to hear and fulfill God's will can be seen as we consider a few Scriptures.

Beginning with Moses' words to Israel about the purpose of the wilderness wanderings, we read,

> *And you shall remember that the Lord your God led you all the way these forty years in the wilderness. . . So He humbled you, allowed you to hunger, and fed you with manna which you did not know nor did your fathers know, that He might make you know that man shall not live by bread alone; but man lives by every word that proceeds from the mouth of the Lord* (Deuteronomy 8:2-3).

Here God wants us to see the parallel between physical hunger and its spiritual counterpart. Whilst not denying our physical need (*"man shall not live by bread alone"*), the emphasis is on understanding that our greatest need is spiritual food, *" . . .but man lives by every word that proceeds from the mouth of the Lord"* (Deut. 8:3).

How important is this? In case we miss it, as the Israelites did in the wilderness, Jesus comes to our rescue in the New Testament by restating these exact words in response to temptation to meet His physical hunger (see Matt. 4:4; Luke 4:4). Jesus graduates where Israel failed because He was hungrier for God's Word than for physical food! Job brings us this same truth as he says, *" . . .I have treasured the words of His mouth more than my necessary food"* (Job 23:12).

By allowing Jesus to complete the picture for us in John's Gospel (when speaking to His disciples about the Samaritan harvest), God links the fulfillment of His will with food. When Jesus' disciples requested that He eat, Jesus responded by saying, *"I have food to eat of which you do not know"* (John 4:32).

When they missed the point He was making, He spelled it out for them, *"My food is to do the will of Him who sent Me, and to finish His work"* (John 4:34).

It is little wonder, in Jesus' encounter with the woman at the well (which precedes these verses), that so much was revealed to Him about her personal life. When we hunger to know God's Word and fulfill His will with similar fervency, we can be sure He will communicate to us, and one of His main methods will be visions.

A Personal Hunger Rewarded

Several years ago the Lord gave me a desire and a passion to pray in the Holy Spirit for long periods of time. At the time, as the owner of an advertising agency, I had the opportunity to do just that. God allocated the time; two hours in the morning before work, two hours at lunch time and two hours in the evening praying in the Holy Spirit. I did that, six hours a day, five days a week for two years. As you can imagine, some people thought I had "lost it." But, as I walked and prayed, the Holy Spirit started to do things in my life. A lot of the issues and the flaws in my life and some of the major strongholds (like the deceitfulness of riches and the cares of the world and the lust of the flesh) started to break off my life.

The Bible says, *". . . Whatever a man sows, that he will also reap"* (Gal. 6:7). This is a universal truth. If you sow righteousness, you will reap righteousness. If you sow sin, you will reap sin. When it comes to sowing into prayer and having a passion to seek God for periods of time, you will reap the rewards. God has also promised that He is a rewarder of those who diligently seek Him (see Heb. 11:6). My current ministry is testimony to the Lord's faithfulness to honor His Word, for I have been blessed with visions, the gift of interpreting dreams, and the witness of seeing signs and wonders following the preaching of the Gospel.

The Anointing Breaks the Yoke

While I was ministering in Pakistan recently, the Lord gave me a vision. I was looking out at the audience when the Lord showed me that a particular woman had pain associated with one of her legs. Now this woman was wearing a long gown down to the ground, so that you could not see her legs with the naked eye. However, what I saw in the Spirit was some kind of infection on her leg. I declared what God was showing me and asked her through an interpreter whether she could confirm my words. Did she indeed have pain in that particular leg? When she confirmed what God had shown me, I then called her forward for prayer. I have found that when you are seeing in the Spirit and declare what you see, it builds faith in those involved. I prayed for healing of her leg and then continued ministering in the gifts and preaching the Word. I gave it no further thought. However, a week later I was again in the area where this gathering had been held, and the people were abuzz with excitement and expectancy because the woman had been healed of leprosy in her leg! All glory to God!

On the same trip I was on my way to catch the plane home and somewhat pressed for time. We called in at a particular pastor's home to say a brief farewell. As we entered the home, there was an air of grief about the place because the pastor's father had had a major heart attack and was lying on a bed on the floor. The family did not know whether their father would make it through the night. I offered to pray for him, and as I did, the Lord showed me the man on his feet and doing things with a smile on his face. I once again declared what the Lord had shown me and that this sickness was not unto death. About a week later, I was back home at my desk when I received a phone call from the pastor whose father had been on that deathbed. He was rejoicing because his father was up and about, smiling exactly as the Lord had shown me. Praise God!

Similarly, a couple of years ago, I visited a family to give God's interpretation of a dream. As I sat with the husband and wife interpreting their dream, I received several visions. In one I saw a car at the front of their home with a man in it with a young lady. The Holy Spirit laid upon my heart that there was a sex predator around their daughter. I asked about their daughter and if she was involved with a man who wasn't a Christian. It turned out that this vision was literal. The couple was very concerned about their daughter. A relationship had developed which included parking outside their home prior to dropping her off at night.

As we were speaking, I had another vision of their daughter standing in a clothes shop with a man behind her. I wasn't quite sure what it meant, so I described what I saw. This time the vision was a metaphor. The mother said that they were having considerable debate about their daughter's choice of clothing. The daughter was wearing revealing clothes, which was a concern to her parents because she dressed in a way that would attract and cause men to stumble. There had been extensive disputes and arguments about her dress code. After our discussion, we prayed, and as I was prophesying into their lives, the Holy Spirit broke something very powerful over the family. The next night when the daughter came home, she told her mom that God had spoken to her. She wanted to apologize and get back to serving God. The daughter went on to say that her parents were right and that she wanted to change her life and do what God wanted her to do. The parents were in awe of what God had done in that one brief encounter when we prayed and broke the demonic yoke that was over their family. This is a great example of how visions release faith that enables people to powerfully receive from God and break the enemy's yoke.

I believe that this is the way that God wants us to minister. There is nothing like being led by the Holy Spirit. It is just like Jesus with the woman at the well (see John 4). He knew that she had had five husbands, and it opened her up to receive what Jesus was saying to her and led her to gather the townsfolk, which set the scene so that revival could break out. If we claim to know Jesus, the Bible says we will walk the way He walked (see 1 John 2:6). And Jesus walked in this way. He was the prophet of all prophets. He did not need any promotion. He did not need any publicists. The power of the Holy Spirit was His herald, drawing crowds through signs and wonders. Visions are a major key for the Holy Spirit to prepare the ground, open people, and build faith for that which is to follow. Even now you may be receiving things in the Spirit, but not understand them. God could be revealing to you the future plans of the enemy operating in the second heaven (the spiritual realm) so that you can prepare for spiritual warfare, or He could be showing you the third heaven (where He dwells) and its storehouse of miracles. These spiritual downloads empower us to *call things that are not as though they are*" (Rom 4:17) and see them manifest into the natural realm. I trust the few experiences I have related here will inspire you to step out with what you receive.

Deception Revealed

As mentioned earlier, sometimes we receive visions when we are falling asleep. You know that time when you are not fully asleep, but in that zone just before falling asleep. Someone may be reading this right now and saying, "Yes, I get that!" Well, at one of those times I had a vision, a vivid vision of the *Mona Lisa*. It was so vivid and real that it quickly brought me back to consciousness. I came to myself thinking, *Why did I have a vision of the Mona Lisa?* I told my wife about it and the next day began some research on the *Mona Lisa*. However, it took about eight months for true understanding to be revealed. At times, God doesn't give the interpretation of a dream or vision straight away. I found out that this famous painting has been associated with mystery and intrigue. The experts are not sure why she was painted or if she was even a real person. The consensus of opinion was that she was not an upright woman. Apparently, in 16th century Italy, if a woman wore her hair down, she was classed as a "loose" woman. However, eight months after I had the vision, the National Research Council of Canada announced that new 3-D imagery technology had revealed that the subject of the painting originally had her hair up in a bun.[1] After all this time, it was finally settled that she was a woman of high moral standing. In terms of a metaphor, the *Mona Lisa* signifies mystery and deception.

Now, to carry this thought a little farther, if we get a dream or vision about a woman, it can represent the Church. If we see the woman as a businesswoman, it can represent the Church becoming a marketplace. God revealed to me that the vision of the *Mona Lisa* is a metaphor of what the Church has become in the world's eyes. While the true Church of God is a woman of high stature and moral reputation (see Eph. 5:27), the enemy has painted the Church to look like a woman of low moral standing. The media particularly takes great pleasure in exposing any loss of her virtue.

When the movie *The Da Vinci Code* was released, it came with its worldwide platform of media hype and promotion. Even 6 to 12 months after the movie, the marketing paraphernalia still filled the stores. Though merely a novel, Dan Brown's book had some advocates believing it to be a true story. The enemy gained ground from it because those living in darkness want to believe the lie and quell their troubled consciences. But when the dust settles, like the painting that was a pivotal part of the novel, like the picture painted of the Church by the devil, and like the movie taken from Dan Brown's novel, all we've seen is deception.

When God doesn't immediately provide an interpretation for a dream or vision, like the *Mona Lisa* vision, it may be that He has a deeper revelation to bring (see John 11:6, 25). It may also be that God uses the timing of the interpretation to develop patience (see James 1:3), create greater faith (see Heb. 11:9-10), or profoundly strengthen the inner self by causing us to wait upon God with greater desire (see Isa. 40:31). Sometimes one dream or vision may not give enough of the message for it to be firmly interpreted. In this case, further revelations—in visions and dreams—will give direction to the interpretation.

Finally, it is possible that the delay between the revelation and its interpretation is designed to prevent human effort from sabotaging God's purpose. Whatever the reason, whenever we receive a dream or vision, we should always wait upon the Holy Spirit to provide the interpretation. However, if one is not immediately forthcoming, we can rest assured God will always bring forth an answer to the genuine enquirer in His time and with our best interests at heart.

Summary: Chapter Six

- According to Acts 2:17, dreams and visions bring us into the realm of the prophetic.
- We grow in the prophetic, learning from our mistakes.
- The prophetic is as much about knowing what to do with what God shows us as it is about having the discernment of heart to receive what He shows us.
- Two very receptive times to receive visions are, firstly, just when we are falling asleep, and secondly, just as we are stirring from sleep.
- Metaphoric and literal elements can be combined in dreams and visions.
- Visions are just one of the ways God's Word is communicated to us when we earnestly desire to hear and fulfill God's will.
- We are to hunger for God's Word and the fulfillment of His will more than we do for our natural sustenance.
- If we sow in prayer, we will reap His answers.
- Visions are a major key for the Holy Spirit to prepare the ground, open people, and build faith for that which is to follow.
- Like the *Mona Lisa,* the true Church of God is a woman of high stature and moral reputation which the enemy takes particular delight in painting as a woman of low moral standing.
- When an interpretation for a vision or dream is not immediately forthcoming, we can be sure that God will bring an interpretation to the genuine enquirer in His time and with our best interests at heart.

Endnote

1. M. Comte, "The Mona Lisa Masterpiece," *The Advertiser* (September 28, 2006), 33.

Chapter Seven

Counterfeit Interpretations by the Occult
By Adam F. Thompson

The Source of Interpretations

As established in the first chapter, God has poured out His Spirit on all flesh in accordance with the prophecy of Joel,

> *And it shall come to pass in the last days, says God, that I will pour out My Spirit on all flesh; your sons and your daughters shall prophesy, your young men shall see visions, your old men shall dream dreams* (Acts 2:17; Joel 2:28).

It should also be evident, after reading the opening chapters, that it is God's will for us, through the Holy Spirit, to prophesy and to have dreams and visions. However, it is one thing to have dreams and visions; where we go to obtain their interpretation is an entirely different matter. Many unknowingly turn to the occult in their desire for answers.

At this point, it is important to understand that the devil is not a part of the Godhead. He is actually a fallen angel, a created being, and he cannot create anything but mayhem. While it is impossible for him to constructively create, he is the master of imitation and deception. As *the* thief (see John 10:10) he will, through imitation, attempt to steal the glory that rightly belongs to God and rob the inheritance that belongs to the saints. Consequently, when we look at those who dabble in occult practices, such as tarot cards, astrology, palm-reading (even interpreting dreams), what we see is the devil imitating and perverting what God has for the saints. Likewise, when people go to clairvoyants, they are visiting counterfeit prophets and seers. Clairvoyants have an inherent sensitivity to the spirit realm and most likely have familiar spirits operating in their lives (see Acts 16:16; 1 Sam. 28:7). Having bought the devil's lie—that they are clairvoyant—they enter the heavenlies illegally and assist the devil in seizing what God has for the saints.

Once we understand that God is the Creator and the devil is the imitator, we don't have to fear that Christian dream interpretation or the gifts of the Spirit are vehicles to bring us into the occult (see 1 Cor. 12). God initiated our spirituality, not the devil. The occult is a mutation of what God had originally planned for us. Consider that a counterfeit Picasso painting has no value unless there is an original. Operating in the image of God as spiritual beings simply moves us into God's original plan. The fall of humanity robbed us of this primary calling to walk and talk with God as fellow spirit-beings (see Gen. 3). However, it was not the plan of God that we should remain without a spiritual dimension. And so, through His death upon the Cross, Jesus once again made a way for us to fulfill our true spiritual nature. Born-again believers have been re-created to become the Spirit-led people God intended them to be (see 2 Cor. 5:17)—able to prophesy, move in the gifts of the Spirit, and interpret dreams and visions. This is nothing new. It is what we were created to do. Jesus did not die for us that we would merely be saved, but that we would be saved, filled, and empowered by His Holy Spirit and fulfill the perfect plan that He has for us. Those who enter the heavenly realms using occult practices are doing so illegally according to the Word of God, and place themselves under a curse and at enmity with God (see Lev. 20:6; Deut. 18:11-12; 1 Chron. 10:13).

The Danger of Half Truths

Jesus told His disciples, "...*when He, the Spirit of truth, has come, He will guide you into all truth...*" (John 16:13). Jesus said that the Holy Spirit will reveal, *"all truth,"* that is the whole truth and nothing but the truth. The devil, on the other hand, likes to feed us partial truths. You may be thinking to yourself right now, *What does that mean?* The devil knows that half-truths are more destructive, addictive, and convincing than blatant lies. Being deceived and anesthetized by a half-truth often keeps us away from the whole truth. How blatantly real this is! The devil has effectively swamped the spiritual arena with many half-truths, making it harder for the righteous to make it through unscathed. Every weekend we witness religious door-knockers sincerely pounding their beats trying to coerce others into their organizational web of half-truths. If you have ever tried to converse with those believing a half-truth, then you have experienced the ensnarement of half-truths and the associated difficulty of breaking the mental strongholds they create.

Similarly, at the Fall, satan said to Eve, *"You will not surely die. For God knows that in the day you eat of it your eyes will be opened, and you will be like God"* (Gen. 3:4-5). Now while that is partially true, it is not the whole truth. The devil, acting like the slick salesman he is, peels off all the benefits, but conveniently omits to tell the shortcomings or consequences of his proposal. It was true that humankind would become like God in one dimension (choosing between good and evil), but he did not tell them that their disobedience would bring human-kind into sin, suffering separation from Almighty God.

This reminds me of an incident that happened about 20 years ago. A fe-male friend got saved and was born-again. However, being a young Christian, she was very ignorant about the Word of God and what was right and wrong. After her conversion, the grace of God was fully on her life, yet she was robbed spiritually due to her lack of knowledge. She had arranged to be baptized, but in the week prior, she went to a clairvoyant, one whom she had been consult-ing regularly before her salvation. The clairvoyant did not know she was going to get baptized, but as he was giving his prophecy into her life, he told her he sensed she was going to go near water. She said, "Yes, that's true," and it drew her in. The clairvoyant said, "If you are going near water, that is dangerous. You must stay away from water." That really confused her and brought fear into her, and unfortunately she did not get baptized, but went back into the world. This is a classic example of how the enemy can reveal some truth to deceive us.

A similar thing happened when Jesus went into the desert after His baptism. The devil tried these same tactics of half-truths on the Messiah. Praise God, Jesus overcame the devil! The devil threw truth at Jesus, even using Scripture to try and deceive Him. However, as the Word of God personified (see John 1:14), Jesus, pulsing with Spirit and Life (see John 6:63), was able to outmaneuver and humiliate the enemy. Though Jesus was at the end of a 40-day fast, it was the devil who withdrew, needing respite after this encounter (see Luke 4:13).

Jesus defeated the devil on the same grounds that you and I do, through liv-ing the Word. Notice that I did not say, "By quoting the Word of God." Many people can quote the Word of God, but fewer are living it! Our victory is not in knowing the Word of God, but in Jesus (the Word of God) knowing us (see Matt. 7:22-23). We are to so absorb the Word of God that it is no longer we who live, but He who lives in us (see Gal. 2:20). God is still empowering the "Word become flesh" today, by His Spirit.

Jesus not only won the opening round, He went on to win the ultimate victory at Calvary. The Father raised Him from the dead and seated Him in heavenly places. The Bible says that we share in that victory. Paul states that God has "*. . .raised us up together, and made us sit together in the heavenly places in Christ Jesus*" (Eph. 2:6).

This means that, in Christ, we also have overcome the world—with its lusts—and are victoriously seated, by faith, in Heaven. The Holy Spirit has also given us discernment and spiritual gifts to hear from God so that we understand all the truth (see John 16:13). When we know truth, anything short of it sets alarm bells ringing. As believers, we have a responsibility to be immersed or baptized in the Word—through study and application—so that we can detect the faintest hint of falsity. We need not turn to the occult or the New Age for interpretation, because the interpreter is "on-board" within us, and He will draw from the deposit of the Word within us to bring the interpretation.

Summary: Chapter Seven

- Where we go to get our dreams and visions interpreted is important. Many turn to the occult in their desire for answers, not realizing the consequences of their actions—placing themselves under a curse and at enmity with God.

- The devil is the master of imitation and deception.

- As *the* thief, the devil steals the glory due to God and the inheritance that is rightly the saints'.

- Going to clairvoyants or palm readers or using tarot cards, astrology, and New Age dream interpretation materials is effectively opening oneself up to counterfeit prophecy and deception.

- Jesus did not die for us that we would merely be saved. God also made provision with the infilling of the Holy Spirit for His children to live as the true spirit beings they were destined to be. Dream and vision interpretation is just exercising our spiritual senses in the Holy Spirit so we go on to receive our God-given inheritance.

- The devil likes to feed us half-truths. These not only deceive us, but also keep us from exploring the whole truth.

- Half-truths create mental strongholds that have the potential to rob us spiritually.

- Our victory over the devil is not in merely quoting the Word of God, but in Jesus (the Word of God) knowing us!

- When we know truth, anything short of it sets alarm bells ringing. Therefore, we have a responsibility to be immersed in the Scriptures through study and application.

Chapter Eight

Beyond Dreams and Visions
By Adrian Beale

A Statement of Doubt and Unbelief

Near to my home is a church with a notice board which at this very moment reads, "The gifts of the Holy Spirit are not available today." What a statement of doubt and unbelief! This billboard is an announcement that what goes on behind those doors is merely intellectual and dead religion. A denial of the gifts of the Holy Spirit is a blatant denial of the Word of God and is a prime example of those who claim it is possible to know God apart from His Spirit.

In building a scriptural response to such a declaration, let us consider a few points. In 21 chapters, the apostle John outlines the life of Jesus as God become man. Of those 21 chapters, which span a period of three years, almost a quarter of the book (chapters 13—17) is allocated to the upper room discourse, which took only a few hours. This stark contrast of content allocation against time says that the communion around the Last Supper is vitally important and is not captured without purpose. Prior to His departure, in the midst of that intimacy with His disciples, Jesus promised that He would send His replacement. He said, *"And I will pray the Father, and He will give you **another** Helper, that He may abide with you **forever**"* (John 14:16).

Take note how long Jesus said His replacement would be with us. He said *forever!* Now, considering in greater depth the words Jesus used here, we also discover that the word *another* is the Greek word *allos,* which means "another of the same quality." There is a Greek word which describes "another of different quality." That word is, *heteros.*[1] Let me illustrate this. If I gave you a tennis ball and then said, "I will give you another ball" and proceeded to give you a golf ball, I will have given you another (*heteros*) ball of a different kind. If I am to give you another (*allos*) of the same kind, I would have to give you another tennis ball. Therefore, in choosing to use the word *allos,* Jesus meant that He would send someone exactly the same as Himself. This means that we cannot only be sure that the Holy Spirit has come, but also that He is of the same essence and quality as Jesus and that He is here forever. It is also not unreasonable to expect, because they are the same, that the replacement would have a ministry like the One He replaces.

If at this point we add Peter's declaration that the Holy Spirit—the Promise of the Father (see Luke 24:49)—is available *"to all who are afar off"* (Acts 2:39), we immediately recognize that the statement on the billboard is in violation of Scripture. Peter's pronouncement not only confirms Jesus' promise that this gift is not limited by time, but also confidently asserts that it is not restricted by distance either. Are we distant in distance or time? Then it is for us!

Our current common understanding of the word *helper* (see John 14:16) is also far from its biblical usage. The word *helper* is the Greek word *parakletos,* which comes from a word which means "to speak to" and "to encourage." It describes someone who is a legal advisor or advocate.[2] This is why Jesus says in the previous verse, *"If you love Me, keep My commandments"* (John 14:15). When we are legally right with God by keeping His Word, the Holy Spirit (as the *Parakletos*) comes forward as the representative of Christ and is empowered to undertake for us while Jesus is absent from the world. The Holy Spirit will only undertake in line with the Word.

Finally, take note of the words Luke uses to open the Book of Acts. *"The former account I made, O Theophilus, of all that Jesus* **began** *both to* **do** *and* **teach**" (Acts 1:1). Does Luke say, "all that Jesus completed"? No! He deliberately says that his former work—the Book of Luke—only portrays what Jesus *began* to do and teach. That beginning, as seen in the ministry of Christ, is continued because the Holy Spirit is poured out so that all believers are empowered to do even greater works (see John 14:12). In using the words, *do* and *teach,* Luke also silences any ambiguity about Jesus' continued ministry through the Holy Spirit. We can be sure that if there is proper teaching there will also be *doing* to confirm that Word (see Mark 16:20). The Book of Acts is then a confirmation and proof that Jesus has not finished, that He has not packed up shop and gone home, but that He is still continuing both in doing and teaching today by His Spirit. To say that the gifts of the Spirit are not for today is a statement inspired by the devil, propagated by those who seek to strengthen their own religious position (see Matt. 12:24) and who are mindful only of the things of people (see Matt. 16:23).

While most churches would not make a blatant confession like the one this chapter opens with, the obvious lack of the gifts of the Spirit flowing in the Church today may indicate that we are settling for such a belief in our hearts.

God Awaits an Invitation

God is the Master Craftsman. He is capable of engineering the events in people's lives with incredible precision. The Bible is full of examples of what may look like just a random sequence of events that then turn out to prefigure events in the life of Christ. Some examples are the life of Joseph (as discussed earlier), Abraham's offering up of Isaac on Mount Moriah (see 2 Sam. 12:1-15), and the death and resurrection of Jonah, to name a few. One such sequence in the life of Christ reveals truth about the Holy Spirit that I would like to share now. We are likely to miss this gem without the opportunity provided by this longitudinal preview.

John's Gospel records that after He had fed the five thousand, Jesus perceived that the people would come and take Him by force and make Him king (see John 6:15). This same Scripture says that when Jesus saw what was about to happen, He departed alone to the mountain. This is very significant.

There was to be a day when Jesus would accept the people's accolades as their king, but this was not it. That day was yet to come and was manifest as the day of His triumphant entry into Jerusalem (see Luke 19:37-40). The prophet Daniel records that day in prophecy with pinpoint accuracy. He says that recognition of *Meshiach Nagid* (Messiah King) would take place 173,880 days[3] from the date of the decree to rebuild Jerusalem (see Dan. 9:25-26). On the exact day prophesied by Daniel, Jesus entered Jerusalem, accepted recognition as their king, and was subsequently executed as the nation's substitutionary sacrifice. This is all recorded in Daniel's prophecy.

Therefore, when John records that Jesus went up the mountain alone, he is showing us something deeper. In Mark's account of this episode, he tells us that

Jesus made His disciples get into the boat and go before Him to the other side, and then He went up the mountain to pray (see Mark 6:45-46). John adds, *"Now when evening came, His disciples went down to the sea"* (John 6:16).

If we make a parallel between going up the mount and Jesus entering Heaven (see Heb. 8:5), recognize that *evening* is a metaphor for Jesus' departure (see John 9:4-5), and also note that Jesus is praying for His disciples in Heaven (see Heb. 7:25-26; Rom. 8:34), an incredible insight is revealed to us.

In outline, what we see is:

- Jesus broken as the Bread of Life (see John 6:35)
- Feeding an innumerable number of people
- Being proclaimed king
- Rising up into Heaven
- His physical absence from the earth
- Praying for His disciples
- The disciples making their way across the sea of humanity.

Hopefully you can appreciate that what we are seeing outworked here is a prophetic prefiguring of what was about to happen.

Therefore, when Jesus comes down to His disciples and observes their struggle rowing (see Mark 6:48), we see His current response to our own need when we are likewise working in our own strength. As eye-opening as that may be, what is even more remarkable is what Mark next records. *"Now about the fourth watch of the night He came to them, walking on the sea, and would have passed them by"* (Mark 6:48b). Did you see that? Jesus sees their struggle *"and would have passed them by."* What was He doing? Couldn't He see their need? What was He waiting for?

Before we offer an answer, let's consider also how He appeared to them on the sea. Mark says, *"But when they saw him walking upon the sea, they supposed it had been **a spirit**, and cried out"* (Mark 6:49 KJV). They perceived Jesus as a spirit, a point echoed in Matthew's Gospel, but they were mistaken because Jesus was physically walking on the water. It is no coincidence that their misconception is recorded because this is how Jesus passes by us today, as the Holy Spirit. Stop and think about that for a moment. What is He waiting for? He is waiting for a faith-filled invitation (see Matt. 14:28) and a ceasing from our own works of the flesh (see John 6:21) before He enters into our boat.

Jesus reinforces this truth when He appears, unexpected and unrecognized, after His death, to two disciples on their way to Emmaus (see Luke 24:13-31). The Bible records,

> *Then they drew near to the village where they were going, and He indicated that He would have gone farther. But they constrained Him, saying, "Abide with us, for it is toward evening, and the day is far spent." And He went in to stay with them* (Luke 24:28-29).

How amazing! After achieving the greatest victory in the history of humankind—resurrection from the dead—here is Jesus awaiting an invitation before entering into communion with His disciples. Only in the light of the forthcoming ministry of the Holy Spirit can we fully explain this anomaly. It illustrates the disciples' ignorance *and* emphasizes their need for sensitivity. The truth here is that although the Holy Spirit is incredibly powerful, we are in need of heightened spiritual awareness to commune with Him.

An Awakening to Relationship

This is a lesson that is seen in the life of Elijah. Elijah had a tremendous victory on Mount Carmel, a victory that included calling down fire, killing 450 false prophets, breaking a three-year drought through prayer, and outrunning the king's chariot (see 1 Kings 18:19-46). Yet, in the very next chapter, we see God contrasting power with the inner voice of the Holy Spirit to break a wrong mindset within Elijah. The Scripture records,

> *Then He said, "Go out, and stand on the mountain before the Lord." And behold, the Lord passed by, and a great and strong wind tore into the mountains and broke the rocks in pieces before the Lord, but the Lord was not in the wind; and after the wind an earthquake, but the Lord was not in the earthquake; and after the earthquake a fire, but the Lord was not in the fire; and after the fire a still small voice* (1 Kings 19:11-12).

Like Elijah, we can be so caught up with the ministry or the manifestation of God's power that we miss the need for relationship with Him. As in all relationships, it is only in heart-to-heart communication that we truly hear what the other is saying. Sensitivity to the Holy Spirit is developed when there is less room in our own hearts for self. Elijah had a fixation that he was the last godly man standing (see 1 Kings 19:10,14). This was a wrong mindset, brought to the surface by Jezebel's death-threat, which took advantage of burnout due to his overwork in the ministry. God's mighty demonstration of power to Elijah highlights the need to appreciate the distinction between a manifestation of God and God Himself. In the light of this, we are always to remember that visions and dreams—as a manifestation of the power of God—are not an end in themselves and, though they lead us in the purposes of God, they are ultimately to direct us deeper in our relationship with the Holy Spirit.

Following this object lesson, God commissions Elijah to anoint two kings and Elisha. It is interesting to see that Elijah caught what God was trying to convey because, like Enoch before him, he was taken up as one who walked with God (see Gen. 5:24). Perhaps more revealing is the fact that Elijah did not personally anoint the two kings, Hazael and Jehu, as he was commissioned by God to do, but that Elisha, his understudy, did (see 2 Kings 8:13-15; 9:1-3). What does that say? It says that, in getting closer to God, Elijah lay down his life by pouring it into his successor. In doing that, he created and developed an unquenchable hunger and sensitivity for the Holy Spirit in Elisha. This hunger was openly displayed on the day in which Elijah was taken up. (If you haven't read Second Kings 2:1-14 recently, please stop here and take the time to familiarize yourself with its contents.[4])

This was an appetite that would not stop for repeated offers of rest or be dissuaded by the voice of his peers (see 2 Kings 2:2-6). He would not settle for conversion (symbolized by *Gilgal*) nor be content at coming into the House of God (symbolized by *Bethel*). Under Elijah's training, Elisha developed such hunger that he would not be satisfied merely with a demonstration of God's power (symbolized by their trip to *Jericho*). He was prepared to lay down his life (*Jordan*, which means "descender" or "death") and was rewarded with a double portion of the Holy Spirit!

Have We Forgotten the Cost?

Somehow, we read about the great exploits of Old and New Testament saints and even of Christ Himself, and yet we forget the cost. Considering Jesus for a moment, whilst we recognize and reverence Him as the God-Man, it is important to remember that He did not perform His miracles as God, but as a man. The miracles He worked were those of a man empowered by the Holy Spirit, to show us how it is done. Yes, that's right. He was as totally reliant upon the Holy

Spirit for ministry as we are. Why else did He need to be anointed? As Luke records,

> *The Spirit of the Lord is upon Me, because He has anointed Me to preach the gospel to the poor; He has sent Me to heal the brokenhearted, to proclaim liberty to the captives and recovery of sight to the blind, to set at liberty those who are oppressed; to proclaim the acceptable year of the Lord* (Luke 4:18-19).

And elsewhere it says,

> *How God anointed Jesus of Nazareth with the Holy Spirit and with power, who went about doing good and healing all who were oppressed by the devil, for God was with Him* (Acts 10:38).

It is easy to lose sight of the fact that as a man (like all the Old Testament greats before Him), Jesus needed an anointing of the Holy Spirit to minister— an anointing birthed and renewed in prayer. Again, in Luke, the Gospel that speaks about Jesus as a man, we read,

> *When all the people were baptized, it came to pass that Jesus also was baptized; and while He prayed, the heaven was opened. And the Holy Spirit descended. . .* (Luke 3:21-22).

The anointing is poured out in prayerful relationship. It is no coincidence that we see Jesus in prayer—in the wilderness (see Luke 5:16), before He chose His disciples (see Luke 6:12), before Peter's confession of faith (see Luke 9:18), at the transfiguration (see Luke 9:28-29), before teaching His disciples to pray (see Luke 11:1), and after feeding the 5,000 (see Matt. 14:23)—and it should be noted that on the night of Jesus' betrayal that Judas knew where to find Him because He often withdrew to that place to pray (see Luke 22:39; John 18:2). It was not so much that He went to prayer because He was about to minister, but rather that His ministry flowed out of His relationship with God, as marked by prayer.

Not only does the Bible record that He prayed, but it also captures His desire for prayer, *"Now in the morning, having risen a long while before daylight, He went out and departed to a solitary place; and there He prayed"* (Mark 1:35). And on another occasion He *"continued all night in prayer to God"* (Luke 6:12). Jesus was passionate about prayer. It was like oxygen to Him.

Sadly, we lack that fervency today. Many mistakenly believe that it was different for Jesus and that we could never attain to His level of ministry. That is a lie that hampers our spiritual progress. For the most part, we are like the disciples in the garden of Gethsemane; our spirits are willing, but the flesh is weak.

When you meet someone genuinely passionate for the things of God, it is truly inspirational. I have been fortunate to work with such a person on this project. In more than 20 years of ministry, I have not met another person who has the ability to consistently move in the gifts of the Holy Spirit like my co-author. It is not surprising that the unction with which he moves has come at tremendous personal cost. Though he has already shared about his two-year investment praying in the Spirit, he hasn't told you about the 40-day fasts, or the countless nights on his face before God in prayer, or his prayer-partnership with his best friend, Todd. It shouldn't be any surprise, then, that his unquenchable passion for souls and obedience to God will cause him to leave his office to minister to a dying soul on the other side of the city or to openly preach the Gospel on the city streets. It has also led him to encounter typhoons in the Philippines, to be eaten by fire ants in the jungles of Southern Mindanao, and to cause the churches in which he was ministering in India to be "stoned" by Hindu fundamentalists.

So far in this chapter, we have confirmed the presence of the Holy Spirit with us today. We have discussed the need for increased sensitivity to commune with Him, and we have seen the difference between a manifestation of God and God Himself. We have also explored how this revelation comes with a call to a deeper personal relationship with God. This led us to recognize the cost of prayerful relationship for the anointing we seek.

Seeing Ourselves in the Mirror

It has been long said that *the New Testament is in the Old Testament concealed, and the Old Testament is in the New Testament revealed.* The premise on which this is based is that the New Testament opens Old Testament truth that was previously hidden from human understanding. While this is true, it is also worth noting that the Old Testament in its physical and positional "types" opens to us deeper understanding of our spiritual standing in the New Testament. So that we can take this discussion farther, it is worth looking at two very revealing parallels in the Old Testament to appreciate where we stand in the plan and purposes of God today.

1: Moses, Joshua, and Judges

Moses led the people of Israel out of Egypt, but it was Joshua who led them into the Promised Land. Though Joshua began to clear Canaan of opposition forces, the Bible also records that,

> . . .*the children of Manasseh **could not drive out the inhabitants of those cities**, but the Canaanites were determined to dwell in that land. And it happened, when the children of Israel grew strong, that they put the Canaanites to forced labor, **but did not utterly drive them out*** (Joshua 17:12-13).

The Book of Judges follows Joshua and describes this same inability to push home the advantage gained through Joshua's invasion. We read,

> *But the children of **Benjamin did not drive out** the Jebusites who inhabited Jerusalem; so the Jebusites dwell with the children of Benjamin in Jerusalem to this day* (Judges 1:21).

The first chapter of the Book of Judges records this failure to drive out the inhabitants by the respective tribes: Ephraim, Zebulun, Asher, Naphtali, and Dan (see Judg. 1:29-34). Why did they fail to take hold of all that God had promised them? In the next chapter we read,

> *"And you shall make no covenant with the inhabitants of this land; you shall tear down their altars." But you have not obeyed My voice. Why have you done this? Therefore I also said, "I will not drive them out before you; but they shall be thorns in your side, and their gods shall be a snare to you"* (Judges 2:2-3).

The reason that Israel failed in their conquest was that they began to settle down and relax when the job was only half done. They embraced the values of the society around them and consequently paid dearly for their spiritual apathy.

2: Elijah, Elisha, and Gehazi

As we have already discussed, Elijah passed on the mantle to Elisha, who received a double-portion of the Spirit that was upon his mentor. Elisha had someone who he was likewise preparing to pass on the baton to. His servant and understudy was Gehazi. However, after God had healed Namaan the leper through the ministry of Elisha, Gehazi went after Namaan to receive the reward his master had turned down (see 2 Kings 5:20-27). On Gehazi's return to Elisha, his master's words to him are particularly enlightening. Elisha says,

Did not my heart go with you when the man turned back from his chariot to meet you? Is it time to receive money and to receive clothing, olive groves and vineyards, sheep and oxen, male and female servants? (2 Kings 5:26)

As is indicated by the words, *"Is it time,"* Gehazi had no idea where he stood in the purposes of God. He also had no appreciation of the anointing he would have received if only he had not sought material security.

3: John the Baptist, Jesus, and. . . ?

Now, to bring this closer to home, Jesus said that the ministry of John the Baptist was a parallel to that of Elijah. Speaking of John, Jesus said, *"And if you are willing to receive it, he is Elijah who is to come"* (Matt. 11:14). And He also said,

But I say to you that Elijah has come already, and they did not know him. . . Then the disciples understood that He spoke to them of John the Baptist (Matthew 17:12-13).

So John held a parallel spiritual role to that of Elijah. It was not by chance that Jesus' baptism took place in the Jordan, the same place where Elijah passed the mantle on to Elisha. And the Jordan was also the place through which Joshua would lead the children of Israel so that they could enter their Promised Land. Like Moses before him, John prepared the people by leading them in renewal in the wilderness so that they, likewise, could come into the Kingdom being opened by Christ (see Matt. 4:17, 12:28). It is no coincidence that the name *Joshua* is the Old Testament equivalent of the name *Jesus* in the New Testament. Are you getting this? Moses and Elijah are a type of John the Baptist. Joshua and Elisha were foreshadows of Jesus. Gehazi holds the same position as the children of Israel in the Book of Judges, but who holds this position today? Who did Jesus pass the mantle on to? Answer: the Church. Whoa!

Table of Parallel Roles

Exit	Entry	Conquest
Moses	Joshua	Judges
Elijah	Elisha	Gehazi
John the Baptist	Jesus	The Church

Could it be that God was forewarning us that the Church, like the children of Israel, would be prone to embrace the world and stop short of God's intended goal?

Entry Versus Conquest

I hear some say, "But didn't Jesus do it all for us?" To answer that question, let's go back to Joshua's crossing of the Jordan River for a moment. The Scripture records that Joshua said, *"Behold, the ark of the covenant of the Lord of all the earth is crossing over before you into the Jordan"* (Josh. 3:11).

What does the ark represent? Well, what did it have in it? It had the two tablets of stone containing the Ten Commandments, Aaron's rod that budded, and a piece of the manna from the wilderness. The tablets represent the Word of God, Aaron's rod represents resurrection, and the manna represents the bread of the wilderness. Who is the Word of God, the Resurrection, and the Bread of Life? Jesus is all three! So the ark here represents Jesus. What does *Jordan* mean? *Jordan* means "descender" or "death." So the ark entering into the Jordan represents Jesus passing into death. What happened when the feet of those who bore the ark touched the waters of the Jordan? The Bible says, when the feet of the priests touched the water,

> *That the waters which came down from upstream stood still, and rose in a heap **very far away [all the way back to] Adam**, the city that is beside Zaretan. So the waters that went down into the Sea of the Arabah, the Salt Sea, failed, and were cut off; and the people crossed over opposite Jericho* (Joshua 3:16).

When the anointed bearers of the Ark entered the river, the water retreated all the way back to a town called Adam. If we recognize that *"the wages of sin is death. . ."* (Rom. 6:23) and that it is no coincidence that the town was called Adam, we will realize that we are foreseeing physically a spiritual truth yet to happen in Christ's death upon the cross. When Jesus entered into death (the Jordan), the flow of sin was rolled back to Adam. Hallelujah! The children of Israel subsequently built a memorial with 12 stones, which represent the 12 apostles (see Matt. 16:18), and then symbolically cut off the flesh through circumcision before proceeding to take the Promised Land. Was the Promised Land given to them through the ark causing them to cross over on dry ground? Yes and No. Yes, God had made a way, and no, they had to clear the land as they were led by God (see

Josh. 5:14-15). As we have already seen in the Book of Judges, Israel failed to press home their advantage. Flanked by fear, they chose rather to embrace the society they were sent to conquer. Today, we can see whether Jesus has done it all for us by looking at the equivalent of land clearing and simply asking ourselves a rhetorical question: Are there still those oppressed of the devil and unsaved in our world?

Jesus would have passed the disciples by, and likewise the Holy Spirit is walking past our boat right now. But could it be that, like Gehazi, we are prone to miss where we stand on God's timeline and find ourselves clamoring for superficial security in our homes, cars, and retirement plans?

Like Elisha before us, we cannot afford to be content to just arrive at conversion (Gilgal) or to stop at the house of God (Bethel) or be satisfied by a display of God's power (Jericho). Let us rather cut off the flesh (crossing over the Jordan) and push in to receive all of the Spirit that Jesus has for us! Let us not forget that Jesus has said,

> *Most assuredly, I say to you, he who believes in Me, the works that I do he will do also; and greater works than these he will do, because I go to My Father* (John 14:12).

In these words, He is promising us a double-portion of His Spirit. Are we as hungry for the Spirit of our Master as Elisha was? Are we prepared like Elisha for the tests of perseverance? Or are we comfortable just to adopt the fatalistic stance of our peers?

We can and should get excited about dreams and visions, but we are not to settle here. God has so much more for us than we could ever imagine. Dreams and visions are but a catalyst to awaken and revitalize a sensitivity and hunger within us for the Holy Spirit. Lifting our spiritual eyes, we see that there is a Kingdom to be won and the offer of a double-portion anointing to lead us into complete victory. If this book does anything, let it create within you a passion for the Holy Spirit that will not be satisfied with anything less than the fullness of God!

Summary: Chapter Eight

- The Holy Spirit is exactly like Jesus and comes to complete the work that Jesus began.
- The Promise of the Father (the Holy Spirit) is available to everyone independent of distance and time.

- Wherever there is correct *teaching*, there will be accompanied *doing* of the works of Christ. The Book of Acts is confirmation that Jesus has not finished His ministry.

- The ministry of Christ outlines the ministry of the Holy Spirit today.

- One such series of events sets out:

  - Jesus broken as the Bread of Life

  - Feeding an innumerable group of people

  - Being proclaimed King

  - Going into Heaven

  - His physical absence from the earth

  - Praying for His disciples

  - The disciples struggling in their own strength across the sea of humanity

  - Christ coming to them as the Holy Spirit

  - The need for increased sensitivity in dealing with the Holy Spirit

- Although the Holy Spirit is incredibly powerful, we are in need of increased sensitivity to commune with Him.

- The life of Elijah illustrated the importance of making the distinction between a manifestation of God and God Himself.

- Dreams and visions are manifestations of God; they are not an end in themselves. They are to direct us into a deeper relationship with God.

- The miracles Jesus performed were of a man anointed by the Holy Spirit, to show us how it is done.

- The anointing is poured out in prayerful relationship.

- Moses led the children of Israel out of Egypt. Joshua led them into the Promised Land. The Book of Judges shows us that Israel failed to take all of the land because they embraced the world they were supposed to conquer.

- Elijah passed the anointing on to Elisha. However, Elisha's servant and would-be replacement—Gehazi—failed to understand his time by clamoring after material security.

- John the Baptist led the people out in preparation for Jesus' ministry. Jesus led the people into the Promised Land and in turn passed the baton on to the Church. The Church, like its predecessors—Judges and Gehazi—has stopped short of what God intended for her!

- There is still a job to be done; people are still going to hell! We cannot camp on Jesus' accomplishments. The Holy Spirit wants to lead us into more so that we can complete the work. We are not to get hung up on dreams and visions; they are but a means to help us complete the conquest of bringing the Promised Land to others.

Endnotes

1. Blue Letter Bible. "Dictionary and Word Search for *heteros (Strong's 2087)*". Blue Letter Bible. 1996-2011. 30 Aug 2011. < http:// www.blueletterbible.org/lang/lexicon/lexicon.cfm?strongs=G2087&t=KJV&page=4 >

2. Merriam-Webster Dictionary. http://www.merriam-webster.com/dictionary/helper

3. In working through Daniel's prophecy (see Dan. 9:25-26) we need to consider that:
   - All the ancient calendars were based on a 360-day year.
   - 69 weeks speaks of 69 weeks of years. The Hebrews had a week of days, a week of weeks, a week of months, and a week of years (Lev.25:1-22; 26:33-35).
   - Therefore, 69 weeks = 69 X 7 X 360 = 173,880 days.
   - For a complete breakdown of Daniel's prophecy, see Chuck Missler, *Cosmic Codes* (Idaho: Koinonia House, 2004), 235f.

4. *Gilgal* means "circle of stones" and was the first camp of Israel after crossing the Jordan River (see Josh. 4:19-20). It is the place where Joshua renewed the rite of covenant by circumcising all the males born in the wilderness and thus *"rolled away the reproach of Egypt"* (Josh. 5:2-9). Gilgal, therefore, symbolizes the rolling away of the heart of stone and the beginning of the life of faith. *Bethel* means "House of God" and symbolizes the new home in which we have been adopted as heirs. Jericho is the place of Israel's first victory in Canaan and is also known as the City of Palms (see Deut. 34:3). It, therefore, symbolizes the victory we come into by exercising the Word of God (see Rev. 12:11). *Jordan* means "descender" or "death." The journey Gilgal>Bethel>Jericho>Jordan, therefore, depicts the walk of faith from the new birth to glory. The fact that Elisha receives a double portion anointing suggests that this is also a depiction of his path to maturity in the Spirit!

Chapter Nine

The Language of Dreams:
The Principles of Interpretation
By Adrian Beale

It is important to point out that there is no formula for interpreting dreams. It is more about cultivating a relationship with the Holy Spirit than applying a series of rules for interpreting. This is because God the Holy Spirit is the author of dreams:

> . . .*God has shown Pharaoh* [through his dreams] *what He is about to do* (Genesis 41:28).

> *And the dream. . .is established by God, and God will shortly bring it to pass* (Genesis 41:32).

> *For God may speak in one way, or in another, yet man does not perceive it. In a dream, in a vision of the night, when deep sleep falls upon men, while slumbering on their beds* (Job 33:14-15).

> *Then, being divinely warned in a dream. . .* (Matthew 2:12).

> *. . .And being warned by God in a dream. . .* (Matthew 2:22).

He is also the interpreter of dreams:

> *But there is a God in heaven who reveals secrets, and He has made known. . .your dream, and the visions of your head upon your bed. . .* (Daniel 2:28).

Do not interpretations belong to God. . . (Genesis 40:8).

. . .Because I know that the Spirit of the Holy God is in you, and no secret troubles you, explain to me the visions of my dream that I have seen, and its interpretation (Daniel 4:9).

However, having established this truth (and that a person wanting to interpret needs to have a foundation in the Scriptures), there are some individual principles to assist in opening God's messages through dreams.

Before delving into these principles, two Kingdom truths that strengthen us in the Word and the Spirit need to be unfurled. The first of these is that spiritual understanding is not a mental faculty; it is a dimension of the heart. This is highlighted when Jesus explains the parable of the sower. He says,

*When any one hears the word of the kingdom, and does not **understand it**, then the wicked one comes and snatches away what was **sown in his heart**. This is he who received seed by the wayside* (Matthew 13:19).

Here Jesus links the heart with understanding, explaining that a heart that lacks understanding is vulnerable to becoming unproductive. Jesus further explains two other soil types—stony and thorn-ridden—and then says,

But he who received seed on the good ground is he who hears the word and understands it, who indeed bears fruit and produces: some a hundredfold, some sixty, some thirty (Matthew 13:23).

Notice that both the unproductive and productive soil-types hear the Word. The difference is in the understanding. The understanding spoken of here is the application of the Word on a person's heart. To put it another way, understanding comes when someone is "under-standing" (or under the authority of) the Word of God. This verse says that we will only bear fruit when we are applying the Word of God to our lives. And since the gift of the Holy Spirit is conditional on obedience (see John 14:15-16), we are not going to be able to interpret fruitfully without applying the Word to our hearts.

The second principle is this. We who consider ourselves Spirit-filled—those who are baptized in the Holy Spirit with the evidence of speaking in tongues—must not be merely Pentecostal by name, but also by nature. It is not enough to speak in tongues in public church life; it must become a key and substantial part of our everyday life. The apostle Paul said,

But now, brethren, if I come to you speaking with tongues, what shall I profit you unless I speak to you either by revelation, by knowledge, by prophesying, or by teaching? (1 Corinthians 14:6).

What is he saying? He is saying that speaking in tongues is the avenue for growing in sensitivity to the Holy Spirit. Why else would Paul pray in tongues more than everybody else? (See 1 Corinthians 14:18.) Perhaps, like Paul, you do a lot of traveling—riding on a bus, driving a truck, or walking to school; all of these are opportunities for you to exercise your spirit person by praying in tongues.

In developing our inner selves through speaking in tongues (see Jude 20), we open our hearts as receptors of Holy Spirit revelation, knowledge, prophecy, and doctrine. If we are serious about entering the spiritual Promised Land, we must also be like Israel (see Josh. 6:8-10) by firstly shutting down the doubt-ridden natural mind and then placing the spiritual trumpet to our lips to see the barriers come down.

Dreams Recorded in the Bible

No	Person	Ref.	M/L*	Nature	Comments
1	Abimelech	Gen. 20:3-7	L	Warning	Protecting Sarah Threat of death
2	Jacob	Gen. 28:12-15	M	Promise	Ladder (See John 1:51) Land, descendants, Presence of God, fulfill Word
3	Jacob	Gen. 31:10-13	L	Directive	Confirmed current situation, then gave direction to go to Canaan
4	Laban	Gen. 31:24	L	Warning	God protecting Jacob
5	Joseph	Gen. 37:5-7	M	Promise	Leadership over brothers
6	Joseph	Gen. 37:9	M	Promise	Leadership over family
7	Butler	Gen. 40:9-11	M	Promise	Resurrection promise (faith)
8	Baker	Gen. 40:16-17	M	Judgment	Judgment promise (works)

9	Pharaoh	Gen. 41:1-7	M	Forewarning	Two angles of same situation (see Gen. 41:25)
10	Midianite	Judg. 7:13-14	M	Forewarning	Weakened recipients, strengthened faith in Gideon
11	Solomon	1 Kings 3:5-15	L	Promise	Requested a hearing heart
12	Nebuchadnezzar	Dan. 2:31-35	M	Future Events	Forgot dream (see Dan. 2:5)
13	Nebuchadnezzar	Dan. 4:10-18	M	Warning	Judgment for pride—seven years; God rules and gives to whomever He wills
14	Daniel	Dan. 7:1-14	M	Future Events	Wrote the dream (see Dan. 7:1)
15	Joseph	Matt. 1:20-23	L	Directive	To marry Mary
16	Wise Men	Matt. 2:12	M	Directive	Warning about Herod's jealousy and to return home another way
17	Joseph	Matt. 2:13	L	Directive	Angel warns about Herod's attempt to kill Jesus and directs to Egypt
18	Joseph	Matt. 2:19-20	L	Directive	Angel directs to Israel
19	Joseph	Matt. 2:22	L	Directive	Warning to go into Galilee
20	Pilate's Wife	Matt. 27:19	M	Warning	Warned of suffering because of their part in judgment of Jesus

*M/L = Metaphor or literal dream, Table B

Metaphor or Literal

It is imperative to recognize that the vast majority of dreams are metaphors. They come as parables, riddles, and puzzles to be decoded. Of the 20 dreams recorded in Scripture, 12 of them are symbolic in nature. That is, 60 percent are metaphors, compared with 40 percent that are literal (see Table B above). Literal dreams do not require interpretation because they do not consist of symbolic images. In our experience, the percentage of parable-type dreams is higher today than that of Scripture. This is probably because the Holy Spirit has been poured out and the Bible is more readily available.

As the majority of dreams come as parables, a very common mistake is to disregard such dreams because they utilize elements of something to which we have recently been exposed. Say, for example, I find a bee floating in the dishwater in the kitchen sink, and that night I dream about a swarm of bees. If I wake and say to myself, "I had that dream because of that bee in the sink last night" and then dismiss it as nonsense, I have missed God's voice. This is because God takes the opportunity to use the images to which we have been freshly exposed to give us new perspectives on our spiritual walk. Just as Jesus related to fishermen with net casting (see Matt. 4:19), to farmers with seed sowing (see Matt. 13:1-9), and to a strongly relational society with scenes of marriage (see Matt. 22:37-39), so the Holy Spirit loves to use images fresh in our memories, often throwing in abstract elements and people we know to convey truth.

I experienced one such dream after watching a war movie with my wife. That night I had the following dream,

A foreign army was invading, and I saw them at the base of a huge rock that went down into the sea. I and others were positioned somewhere higher on the rock looking down at their landing. I ran to get rifles and ammunition to shoot at them. To do so, I had to crawl through the entrance of a narrow sandy cave about one foot high. There was something like a dozen orange candles on the base of this sandy entrance which led down deeper into the cave where it opened up. The candles were all at different stages of dying out. The majority were just wax mounds where once there had stood a candle. At this point in the dream, I had the revelation that this was only a dream, and yet the scene was so vivid and real I could practically smell the wax and the cool sand. Down beyond the entrance were two of my compatriots—one male, one female. The entrance was so narrow I thought that the roof could collapse on me at any minute and I would die here. I realized that it did not matter if I died here because if I didn't get through, I would die anyway when the enemy overran the place. I realized that I must not give up and that there was something greater at stake here. I made my way through the narrow entrance and down into the cave where the male person (who reminded me of actor Mel Gibson) took me through a different exit to a powerful dune buggy-type vehicle, and we went to get the arms we were after. In the next scene we had the arms (rifles and ammunition) and were on our way back, and I was conscious that the enemy were infiltrating. Mel showed me on a plan how he had worked out to get us back to the hotspot. He, as the driver, was going to jump the car onto the roof of a fortress-type structure and again jump it onto the top of a wall that ran toward where we needed to go. It looked pretty spectacular and exciting, but I was confident in his ability to get us to the hotspot. I was also aware that we would be shot at on the way.

My natural man was saying, "What a ridiculous dream!" Yet, here is its interpretation.

The invasion speaks of a subtle, evil plan of the enemy (see Gen. 3:1; Acts 13:10). I have nothing against foreigners; the Spirit of God is just using them as a parallel from the past to show a deeper spiritual truth today. Their invasion speaks about the infiltration and subtle influence of technology leading the Church away and captive (addicted) to entertainment. The cave speaks about the Church hiding. This is the female deep in the cave. The narrow sandy entrance says two things. First, that the way is going to be under pressure (see Matt. 7:13-14). Second, it says that we, the Church, are toying with the Word of God. The orange candles are a warning about the state of the Church and its fading apostolic mandate (see Matt. 28:19; Luke 11:33; Acts 1:8). For the most part, the Western Church is being drawn into a flesh-comforting, entertainment-rich lifestyle. As a consequence, we have become spectators expecting people to come to us instead of going out and carrying the message we have been given.

The fear of death I experienced on crawling through this narrow opening represents the fear of ridicule I feel I will experience for sharing this revelation. The realization that something greater is at stake says that I will proceed with this because I realize if I don't, the Church is in jeopardy. The awareness that what I was experiencing was a dream, and yet it appeared so real, says that even though it was just a dream, it is a certain spiritual reality.

Mel means, "chief" (see Eph. 2:20; 1 Pet. 5:4), and therefore, Mel Gibson in this dream represents Jesus Christ, who has been taken into hiding by the

Church (the female). The dune buggy symbolizes a powerful ministry driven by Jesus Christ who will carry this message onto a preaching platform (see Matt. 10:27) and over the obstacles and barriers (walls) that would otherwise prevent it. The rifles are willing hearts (launching pads) for words, and the munitions are those words. Being shot at speaks of "friendly-fire" from people within the Church for carrying this message.

Is the Western Church being lulled into a false security? (See Revelation 3:17-18.) Have we gradually become spectators of the Gospel instead of bearers of its life-giving message? Are we worshipping God or the riffs and melodies of the music we have created to do so? Don't misunderstand what I am saying; I am not saying we should get rid of all electronic devices, but that we should all examine our hearts to make sure that it is indeed God we are worshipping. If these questions and issues raise concerns within us, then it is evident that we need a new level of sensitivity to the Spirit of God and His Word, especially as they come to us in dreams.

God is waiting for the Church to reawaken spiritual sensitivity so that He can give the world dreams for Him to interpret through us, dreams that will confirm His reality. There is, therefore, a need for a "School of the Prophets" in which to grow and develop that spiritual sensitivity. Sadly, without a prophetic edge, we continually revert to the systems of people to build the Church.

Now, back to the dream. Does it sound weird? I think it does! But perhaps it is no weirder than seven emaciated cows coming up out of a river and eating seven fat cows (see Gen. 41:10) or a man's heart being ripped out and being replaced by an animal's heart (see Dan. 4:16). What does the Spirit of God tell you about it? Does He say, "Too much pizza!" or "There's truth in these words." So many dreams that the Holy Spirit has allowed Adam (my co-author) and I to interpret are introduced to us by people saying, "I had a really weird dream. . .." Don't disregard any dream, no matter how bizarre. It is God speaking to you. (An explanation of the metaphors used to interpret this dream is found in the dream and vision sample section of this book. See dream 53.)

Speaking again in general, about symbolic or metaphoric dreams, a few years ago, I dreamed that I saw one of my daughters was taken by a great white shark. At the time, the image put a fear in me that my child would be taken while at a family outing to the beach. Today I would know that this type of dream is more likely to be a warning from God of a predatory person. This is a warning to be vigilant in the area of childhood associations and friendships. If my daughter were older, it could be a warning of sexual, financial, or contractual predatory behavior.

As the majority of our dreams are metaphors, they are more likely to convey a spiritual parallel. A bush fire is more likely to indicate judgment, and a car accident is probably a warning of a potential family, ministry, or business mishap. At this point, however, it is really important to see that a potential spiritual catastrophe should be treated with the same urgency that its physical counterpart would be treated with. This is because the spiritual well-being of a person, city, or nation is more important than their physical welfare (see Matt. 16:26). The reason I say that is because we are talking about the contrast of a brief physical life compared to eternity. And there is no comparison.

Context

Just as it is important to consider the context of Scripture when putting meaning to it, so it is equally true that dreams need to be interpreted with consideration for the environment in which they occur. I will occasionally get phone calls or SMS messages asking for the meaning of one element of a dream. Unfortunately, without the rest of the dream and a measure of understanding of the circumstances surrounding the dreamer, an accurate picture is unlikely.

Let's consider a Biblical example. Suppose we are considering the meaning of a particular character in a Scripture, let's say, Jacob. When Jacob is on his way back into Canaan, just before he meets his brother Esau, he has an encounter with God at Peniel (see Gen. 32:22-32). God wrestles with Jacob to get a confession from, and a revelation to, him. A pivotal point comes in this encounter and is recorded in this way, *"So He said to him, 'What is your name?' He said, 'Jacob.' And He said, 'Your name shall no longer be called Jacob, but Israel. . .'"* (Gen. 32:27-28a).

Jacob has to come to understand who he is. His name literally means "Grabber, swindler, or supplanter"; it describes someone who is only out for himself. This picture is confirmed in Scripture as he steals both the birthright and the blessing from his brother Esau. It continues as we see him working as hard as he can to cheat a bigger swindler, Laban, when Laban's flocks are conceiving (see Gen. 30:37-42).

Now if it was God with whom Jacob was wrestling, why did God ask him his name? Surely He already knew! He asked him his name so that Jacob would make a confession and receive a revelation. This is the same confession you and I need to make to come to God. We first need to see ourselves as sinners. Sin has its root in selfishness, so sins are the things we do without consideration of others (see Isa. 53:6). In saying his name, Jacob says, "I'm out only for myself!" After that confession, God through His grace says, you shall no longer be called "Swindler," but "Israel," which means "a Prince with God." Jacob is a picture of the fleshly person—the old self—who is only out for himself despite any self-righteous acts he may perform. When God said he will be called Israel, God was calling him to live according to the spiritual person. From this point on, whenever we see Jacob and Israel mentioned, Jacob represents the fleshly person in action, and Israel the spiritual person.

We see this in the very next chapter of Genesis after Jacob has met his brother Esau. He agrees to meet his brother at Mount Seir, but because of fear—the fleshly person in operation—he goes in a totally different direction and finds himself at Shechem (see Gen. 33:14-18). This is where his daughter Dinah gets raped (see Gen. 34:2). God has to remind him that his name is Israel and no longer Jacob (see Gen. 35:10). We might think this would clinch it for him, but no, we find Jacob still in there wanting to run the show, but losing the battle against the spiritual person right up until his death in chapter 49 of Genesis. The study of the use of the two names through these chapters is worth investing an hour or two.

With that insight, we might think that every time we see Jacob (and its derivatives, James, Jamie, Jackie, Jake) in the Word (Scripture and dreams), we are seeing the fleshly person. However, this is not always the case. It is true when we see Jacob and Israel together, but when the name Jacob appears with Esau, then it is a different matter. Compared to Esau, Jacob is the spiritual person and Esau the fleshly person. This truth is what is behind the following Scripture, *"As it is written, 'Jacob I have loved, but Esau I have hated'"* (Rom. 9:13; see also Obad. 1:18; Mal. 1:2-3)

Just as the meaning of *Jacob* is dependent on who he is mentioned with in Scripture, so the meaning of an element of a dream is dependent on its surroundings. The principle of considering the context, therefore, teaches us that the elements of interpretation of one dream are not necessarily transferable to another. The context of the dream will influence the meaning. What is going on in the life of the dreamer also needs to be considered as context.

The Ping Pong (Table Tennis) Dream

A good example of the importance of context is shown in a dream I had while preparing this material. This occasion was unique for a number of reasons. Firstly, before I went to bed that night, I heard in my spirit very faintly the sound my cell phone makes when it receives an SMS message. I gauged from this that God was going to speak to me through a dream that night. Early the next morning, sure enough, I awoke to a dream.

In the dream I was playing table tennis with my daughter's ex-basketball coach, Glenn. The ball was solid rubber. When Glenn served, it was in such a way that the ball hit the table without any bounce and rolled off the table. It was impossible for me to play a shot. I said to Glenn, "I will continue to play this way, but you are not giving me a chance to play the ball!"

I roused myself and, in the dark, wrote the outline of the dream down on the 8" x 5" notepad on my bedside cabinet. As I lay there thinking through what the dream could mean, I was vacantly looking at the clock also on the cabinet, when the Holy Spirit told me to note the numbers on the clock face. The clock read, 3:46: Now, that hadn't happened before; neither has it happened since then.

What did this dream mean? To understand the dream, you would need to appreciate what was happening in my life at the time (i.e. the context of my life). That day my wife and I had gone shopping. As we were coming out of a store, my wife was crying. I said to her, "Are you alright?"

She said something like, "I'm OK." It was evident that she was not, but that was not the time nor the place to pursue the matter.

Just to back-track a little, that particular week my family had arranged to go on holidays with their cousins to a seaside location. While they—my wife and children—were away, I was to stay home so that I could get some of this material written. This arrangement had been in place for three weeks, and I thought that my absence from them was understood and agreed upon. However, the day before our shopping trip, my wife asked me why I wasn't coming with them. I said, "I thought we had arranged for me to write some of the book while you are away," to which there was no reply.

After a few minutes meditating on the dream, I knew what God was saying. I could tell my wife was also awake. So I turned to her and said, "Are you awake? God has just spoken to me in a dream. Do you want to talk?"

She said, "Yes, OK."

So, I told her the dream. And then I said, "This is what I believe God is saying. *Glenn* means, 'Lives in the valley.'" I went on gently, and I said, "Honey that is you; you are feeling down at the moment. The ball represents words. You are not saying anything, and you are not allowing me to speak." I paused, then continued, "The numbers on the clock say that you have allowed a resurrection (three) of the rule (four) of man (six) in our relationship."

My wife started crying as the Holy Spirit plumbed her heart. Then she explained that she had received a couple of phone calls that week from friends asking her why I wasn't going away with the family. This had the detrimental effect of causing her to reevaluate and misconstrue my absence and internalize her hurt. The dream helped her identify the root of the problem. We re-established my need for space so that I could work on the book and resolved the issue. After a time of prayer, my wife and children left for their holiday with harmony back in our relationship.

Though personal, this dream shows how important it is to have an understanding of the events in the life of the dreamer (its context) for correct interpretation to take place. For this reason, when interpreting for a third party, you will most likely have to ask some questions to complete the picture of its context.

A few years ago, I would have totally missed what God was saying through this dream. It would have been nonsense, perhaps associated with the curry or the late night I had the night before.

Meditate on a Dream as a Whole Before Offering an Interpretation

Following on from this is the need to take one's time, particularly with longer dreams, before venturing an interpretation. Daniel applied this principle when interpreting Nebuchadnezzar's dreams. As the following Scripture shows,

"This dream I, King Nebuchadnezzar, have seen. Now you, Belteshazzar, declare its interpretation, since all the wise men of my kingdom are not able to make known to me the interpretation; but you are able, for the Spirit of the Holy God is in you." Then Daniel, whose name was Belteshazzar, was astonished for a time, and his thoughts troubled him. . . (Daniel 4:18-19).

There are at least three good reasons for taking our time with an interpretation. Firstly, we need to see the overall image God is conveying in the dream. We may have individual elements pegged for certain parts of the dream, but until we can see the overview, we will not know how they fit what God has mapped out. It is easy to be led into false interpretation as we move from the elements to the whole (overview). We must also consider how the whole affects the elements if we are to get a true interpretation.

Secondly, we must take our time to "see" the dream. What I am trying to relate is that we need to look through, or past, the scenes and actions of the dream to gain understanding. For example, Jeremiah was directed to view the potter before God had him deliver His message to Israel. As the Scripture outlines,

> *The word which came to Jeremiah from the Lord, saying: "Arise and go down to the potter's house, and there I will cause you to hear My words." Then I went down to the potter's house, and there he was, making something at the wheel. And the vessel that he made of clay was marred in the hand of the potter; so he made it again into another vessel, as it seemed good to the potter to make. Then the word of the Lord came to me, saying, "O house of Israel, can I not do with you as this potter?" says the Lord. "Look, as the clay is in the potter's hand, so are you in My hand, O house of Israel"* (Jeremiah 18:1-6).

Just as Jeremiah gained an increased understanding of God's desired message to Israel through observing the potter, so we need to look beyond the mere words of the dream to "see" what message God is conveying through all the scenes.

The third reason to take our time is so that we can seek God's wisdom in knowing how to deliver the interpretation to the dreamer. It is one thing to have an interpretation; it is another to know what action the dreamer should take from the interpretation and how to convey that.

Joseph, when giving the interpretation of Pharaoh's dreams, is the classic example. Filled with the Spirit of God, he said,

> *Now therefore, let Pharaoh select a discerning and wise man, and set him over the land of Egypt. Let Pharaoh do this, and let him appoint officers over the land, to collect one-fifth of the produce of the land of Egypt in the seven plentiful years. And let them gather all the food of those good years that are coming, and store up grain under the authority of Pharaoh, and let*

them keep food in the cities. Then that food shall be as a reserve for the land for the seven years of famine which shall be in the land of Egypt, that the land may not perish during the famine (Genesis 41:33-36).

Pharaoh then acknowledged before his servants, *"Can we find such a one as this, a man in whom is the Spirit of God?"* He continued by saying to Joseph, *"Inasmuch as God has shown you all this, there is no one as discerning and wise as you"* (Gen. 41:38-39).

The key to knowing how to deliver an interpretation (and indeed how to interpret the dreams we are given) is to have receptive hearts toward the Holy Spirit. Notice that Joseph no longer is clamoring to be released, as we saw in Chapter 2. He has now dealt with the past, is filled with the Spirit of God, and is, therefore, at peace with God and within himself. This also illustrates the truth that we cannot interpret at our best when we are not in the Spirit because of overwork or stress.

Sequence Importance

Closely relating to the last two major points is the importance of the sequence or order of the dream. We not only need to get the context and the overview; we also need an accurate sequence or order. Sequence relates strongly to seeing through the scenes in the dream. If, for some reason, the person who has had the dream has recorded information out of order, it can throw the intended meaning into disarray. Make sure things happened in the order they are described by listing the main points of the dream before writing up the final draft of the dream.

Past, Present, and Future

Not all dreams relate to the future. At times, God will pick up a scene from the past to set the context and build faith by revealing something only you and He know, then show where you are today before moving on to where He is directing you in the future. In these dreams, the opening scene may hint of a journey. These types of dreams are relatively long and may begin in, or center on, a vessel or vehicle (see Dream Samples 28 and 48) or a hallway or corridor.

Very often dreams reveal the state of the local church or people's hearts. These dreams are those where God discerns and discloses truth that only He and those concerned know. In disclosing this insight, He is bringing that which is not even conscious to the fore so that the individual, church, or ministry can see and address issues. When these dreams are experienced by a third party, the dreamer needs tremendous wisdom and an awareness of the timing of God to know if and when they are to deliver the dream or its interpretation to those it concerns.

Not all dreams and interpretations need to be revealed. At times, some dreams are just informing you how something looks spiritually or what is happening spiritually in a situation. At other times, they are a call to prayer.

Repeat Dreams

When God repeats a matter, it is a sign of confirmation, importance, imminence, or urgency. A repeat dream says you weren't listening the first time. If we experience repeated dreams, we need to take note because God wants us to act on the message. When addressing Pharaoh, Joseph said, *"And the dream was repeated to Pharaoh twice because the thing is established by God, and God will shortly bring it to pass"* (Gen. 41:32).

Here Joseph explained that the repeated dream confirmed God was speaking to Pharaoh and that what was revealed was about to happen. In Pharaoh's case, the two dreams were not identical, but were two powerful views of the same impending issue (see Gen. 41:17-25). In the original manuscripts of the Book of John, Jesus sometimes began by saying, *"Truly, Truly"* (John 1:51, among other occurrences). Each time, Jesus firmly captured His disciples' attention before imparting powerful spiritual truth. In much the same way today, the Holy Spirit attempts to gain our attention through a repeated dream to impart spiritual truth.

When Abraham was about to sacrifice his own son in obedience to God, God caught his attention by repeating his name (see Gen. 22:11). Abraham was so intent on obedience that God had to repeat his name to break that focus and prevent the sacrifice. Likewise today, God will break a wrong or intense focus and also impart urgency through a repeated dream.

God, in His grace, many times gives unbelievers repeat dreams concerning their eternal spiritual welfare. Dreams of people falling, washing, toileting, flying in fear, or of dark figures around the bed are strong calls for people to get things right with God so that their spiritual person has an eternal future in God's presence.

Feelings

The feelings of the dreamer are indicative of much of the meaning conveyed in the scenes of a dream. Even when the visual elements of two dreams are the same, the feelings of the dreamers may be vastly different. It is therefore important, where possible, to describe the feelings associated with a given situation. Anger, fear, confidence, or anxiety in a particular scene conveys just as much meaning as the visual images.

For example, flying in a dream can be either an exhilarating or terrifying experience. Both scenes describe life in the Spirit. The one accompanied with exhilaration will generally convey moving in the gifts or flowing with the Spirit of God. The scene that is enjoined with fear says something is not right spiritually and carries with it a warning of danger.

Gender

When we see someone in a dream as a male or female, it is no assurance that they portray someone of that gender in real life. In many aspects of heavenly thinking, both male and female are related as humankind. Speaking to wives, Peter says,

> *Likewise, ye wives, be in subjection to your own husbands; that, if any obey not the word, they also may without the word be won by the conversation of the wives; while they behold your chaste conversation coupled with fear. Whose adorning let it not be that outward adorning of plaiting the hair, and of wearing of gold, or of putting on of apparel;* **but let it be the hidden man of the heart**, *in that which is not corruptible, even the ornament of a meek and quiet spirit, which is in the sight of God of great price* (1 Peter 3:1-4 KJV).

Peter, in addressing wives, speaks of them adorning the *"hidden man of the heart."* This non-gender aspect is also evidence that both male and female are included in Scriptures that talk about the man of the flesh. Paul to the Romans states,

> *Knowing this, that* **our old man** *was crucified with Him, that the body of sin might be done away with, that we should no longer be slaves of sin* (Romans 6:6).

It should be obvious that both male and female are included in this address to live as dead to sin. For this reason, an old man in a female's dream can represent her "man of the flesh," that is, that aspect of her that is opposed to the Spirit.

Finally, it should be noted that the man of Macedonia who appeared to Paul in a vision of the night beckoning him to come to Europe (see Acts 16:9-10) turned out to be a woman (see Acts 16:13-15).

Alternatively, it is also worth noting that a woman in a dream may also be representative of the Church (see Eph. 5:25). Often she (the Church) may be portrayed as a person's mother, sister, or even a young girl, because these may represent aspects of her (the Church) spiritually.

Names

The names of places and people in dreams are very significant. Sometimes the people in dreams represent themselves, and at other times, the meaning of names is a major key to dream interpretation. Or the presence of someone you know in a dream may instead point to their chief characteristic or what they represent to you. Once again, the key is to look at the dream as a whole before assuming that the dream literally refers to that person or the meaning of their name. However, when it comes to name meanings, the dream with Mel Gibson, earlier in this chapter, is a fair example of how a name meaning assists in opening up a dream for interpretation.

People in dreams may represent:

- Themselves
- Their character
- Their position, role, or what they represent to the dreamer
- The organization or church they represent
- The meaning of their names.

The name dictionary included in this book provides more than a 1,200 meanings for common place and people names. However, if you anticipate doing a lot of dream interpretation, you may consider investing further by purchasing a comprehensive book of name meanings. I chose the one I use because it was relatively economical and provides more than 50,000 name meanings.

Search engines on the Internet are also a good resource for further name definitions, but be aware that many baby-name internet sites have links to gambling and pornography. Due to variations in the agreed etymological roots of a name, it is a good idea to look at a couple of sources before accepting a name meaning as final.

Numbers

Numbers always provide something of significance to a dream interpretation. The implication of numbers in a dream is best shown through an example. The following dream is particularly rich in numerical significance,

> In my dream I had someone whom I loved a great deal, but I hardly ever saw him. We both had a set of numbers, and the numbers were a matching set. My numbers were six, seven, eight, and his were something that went with them, but I can't remember them. So what I was going to do was to post or display my numbers so that he would see them when he went a certain way. I was going to put them up at the corner of Reservoir Road and Smart Road at the roundabout.

This dream relates to a relationship between husband and wife. A husband and wife are to complement one another. It appears that this couple does not spend enough time together. It also appears that God is communicating to the husband through this dream. The wife's numbers are six, seven, and eight. These particular numbers in this order are a good combination for they say that she is progressing spiritually. They say that she was in the flesh (six), is moving to Divine perfection (seven), and is ready for a new beginning (eight) spiritually. What they spell out is a code for the husband to decipher.

It is possible that the husband's numbers are four, three and two which would be the complementary numbers to complete the order or round to ten. This combination, in this context, would mean that he now has rule (four) and will experience resurrection (three) through her unity (two) in the home. The corner of Reservoir and Smart roads is also significant because it says shortly (corner) she will get to the wisdom (smart) of God (reservoir) and turn around (roundabout).

This is an absolute gem of a dream. Not only does it beautifully relate the use of numbers in a dream, but also ingeniously employs road names as well.

The metaphor dictionary also shows that a number may equate with its face value. For example, a three in a dream may mean exactly that. As you look at the interpretation of individual elements, be sensitive to the inner voice of the Holy Spirit while you consider which interpretation for a number is the correct one. When you have the right interpretation, there will be an inner knowing or confirmatory "witness," and the message of the dream as a whole will be made apparent.

Local, National, and Cultural Idiosyncrasies

The dictionary of metaphors in this book is based on a generally white and Western outlook. At times this will not be able to convey local community knowledge or the cultural perspective of a given situation.

For example, I was talking to Adam (my co-author) one day when he instantly received a vision of a bunch of bananas being cut in half while they were being held in someone's hand. That may not mean much to you unless you knew that at that time the northern parts of Australia (the country in which we both live) had experienced a cyclone which decimated the banana growing regions. This meant that bananas now sold for up to $15.00 a kilogram, which is very expensive in our part of the country. Therefore, the vision said that something of value is going to be cut in a certain ministry situation relating to me.

When you find something not mentioned in the dictionary, or a listing that does not convey your understanding of a subject, look up any relevant Bible verses relating to that subject and also write down the alternatives of what that person, place, or thing means to you and see which interpretation best fits the overall message conveyed in the dream.

At times Adam and I have had to go to sleep not knowing a particular element within a dream only to have the Holy Spirit give us understanding in the night. For this reason, I keep a notepad next to my bed. If you get a deposit of gold given to you in the night, make sure you write it down straightaway because, chances are, you will not remember it in the morning.

Also realize that at times God will stretch your spiritual understanding through the dreams He gives you. You will not always get an instant interpretation. In fact, you may have to wait days, weeks, or months before you fully understand what it was He was saying, but when the fulfillment comes, you can be sure your faith will be lifted.

Practical Advice

If you are going to take dreams and their interpretation seriously, then I recommend that you establish a dream log. Mine is simply an exercise book in which I write and date the dream. Depending on the size of the dream, I leave room either underneath the dream or on the opposite page for its interpretation.

I also keep a notepad (8" x 5") by my bed. I used to use a smaller one, but this larger size allows me to write in the dark and not disturb my wife by putting the light on, and at the same time gives me room to be a bit messy in my writing without continually running off the page. I usually only write a few salient points in the dark, just enough to refresh my memory for when I am fully awake. If you choose to follow this technique, make sure that you test your pen before putting the light out and laying your head on that pillow. I have learned this the hard way. There is nothing worse than waking to find that what you thought you wrote is not on the page because the pen wasn't working.

In the morning, I bullet-point the dream so that I maintain the correct order of events, and then, when I am happy I have extracted all the details, I write it up in the exercise book. In this way, I have a permanent record of what God has been speaking to me about over a period of time.

Reading through the dreams is a faith-building exercise as I am able to see the things God has completed or confirmed in the past and at the same time look to where He is directing me in the future. My dream log also provides me with things to pray about, and in praying through it, I can confidently bring Heaven to earth (see Matt. 6:10).

Summary: Chapter Nine

- There is no formula for interpreting dreams. It is more about cultivating a relationship with the Holy Spirit. He is the author and interpreter of dreams.
- Understanding comes when a person is "under-standing" (or under the authority of) the Word of God. Therefore, interpretation is dependent on obedience.
- Use every opportunity to pray in tongues, particularly while traveling, as it is the vehicle for revelation, teaching, and prophecy.
- As the majority of dreams are metaphoric in nature, we should not disregard a dream because it contains "weird" or recently experienced events in our lives.

- Catastrophic dreams are most likely to convey a spiritual parallel.
- Dreams need to be interpreted in context. This refers not only to interpreting elements against other elements in the same dream; it also means knowing what is going on in the life of the dreamer.
- We need to take our time interpreting, particularly with long dreams, because:
  - We need to see the overall image God is conveying. Here we need to confirm our interpretation of the individual elements by ensuring the whole dream makes sense.
  - Time is needed to see past the individual scenes to the overall message being conveyed.
  - Wisdom is needed in knowing how to deliver the interpretation.
- Not all dreams relate a future scene. They may show past, present, future, or all three.
- Not all dreams need to be revealed to the parties concerned. At times, some dreams are just informing us how something looks spiritually or what is going on spiritually. At other times, they are a call to prayer.
- Repeat dreams are a sign of importance, confirmation, imminence, or urgency. They say we weren't listening the first time.
- Many times God, in His grace, repeats dreams to unbelievers concerning their eternal spiritual destinies. Falling, washing, flying in fear, and dark figures around the bed are all calls to get right with God.
- Feelings can convey much of the meaning of a dream. Similar scenes can be vastly different in interpretation, dependent on the feelings experienced by the dreamer.
- Gender is not fixed in dreams. A woman may be representative of a man and vice versa. Very often the meaning of the names of people in a dream will assist in crossing this divide.
- Name meanings of people and places are very significant in dreams.
- People in dreams may represent:
  - Themselves
  - Their character
  - Their position, role, or what they represent to the dreamer
  - The organization or church they represent
  - The meaning of their names.

- Numbers always lend significant meaning to the interpretation of dreams and visions.

- There will be times when the Metaphor Dictionary does not provide a relevant local or national cultural understanding of a particular dream or vision element. If this new understanding for a particular element fits in the overall context of the dream or vision, then feel free to use it.

Chapter Ten

Before Using the Dictionary
By Adrian Beale and Adam F. Thompson

Is Interpretation a Gift, or Is It Developed?

The Bible relates that some people are particularly gifted in the interpretation of dreams and visions. Daniel and Joseph are two such examples. Of Daniel, the Bible records, "*. . .And Daniel had understanding in all visions and dreams*" (Dan. 1:17). This is most definitely a God-given ability, but it is also a God-given ability in which a person can grow.

When Elijah was about to hand the baton over to Elisha on the last day of his earthly ministry, he told Elisha that he would receive his request for a double portion of the Spirit if he saw Elijah taken. The Bible records the incident like this,

> *And so it was, when they had crossed over, that Elijah said to Elisha, "Ask! What may I do for you, before I am taken away from you?" Elisha said, "Please let a double portion of your spirit be upon me." So he said, "You have asked a hard thing. Nevertheless, if you **see** me when I am taken from you, it shall be so for you; but if not, it shall not be so"* (2 Kings 2:9-10).

The endowment of a double anointing was conditional on Elisha's ability to *see* in the spirit realm. Most will know the rest of the story. Elisha saw an angelic chariot come and take his master away (see 2 Kings 2:11, 6:16-17). As we read the Bible account, the whole scene seems to move so quickly that we easily miss the condition required for the fulfillment of Elisha's request. He had to be able to *see* in the spirit realm to be able to fulfill the call upon his life. Stop and think about that. The fact that this episode happens at the culmination of a progression that depicts the Christian path to maturity—Gilgal>Bethel>Jericho>Jordan (see 2 Kings 2:1-6)—is strongly suggestive that seeing in the Spirit is something in which we grow. However, Elijah also suggests that it is a divine endowment by the fact that he doesn't confirm or deny the impartation of the gift upon Elisha, but allows God to confirm its impartation by its operation.

The writer to the Hebrews confirms that we grow in spiritual sensitivity when he says, *"But solid food belongs to those who are of full age, that is, **those who by reason of use have their senses exercised** to discern both good and evil"* (Heb. 5:14). In short, this verse says that our spiritual senses are developed as they are exercised. Just as the would-be prophet, Samuel, initially did not recognize God's voice (see 1 Sam. 3:4-9), we likewise will develop our spirit senses by being attuned through frequency of practice. And just as in the case of Samuel, God initiates the call.

Is interpretation a gift, or is it developed? It is both! Having said that, our experience is that those with a prophetic calling are more spiritually inclined to see what a dream or vision is saying. However, those with a gifting in this area will only fully reach their potential if they are prepared to invest time in developing it.

How to Interpret: Joining the Dots

How do you interpret dreams and visions? Well at one time, I helped my young daughter to color in a picture, but first we had to join the dots so that we could see what it was that we were actually looking at. This simple illustration is a powerful blueprint of how a dream is interpreted. Each metaphoric element in a dream is like a dot, like a peg, and once the Holy Spirit helps us to join them together—giving us the meaning behind each element of the dream—it becomes a picture and a story that we are not likely to forget, a story that will be burned in our memory.

Start by prayerfully looking at each element of the dream. The metaphoric dictionary in this book has been designed to help you look at alternatives for each element of a dream. Remember that it is more about your relationship with God than a formula to be followed. It is the Holy Spirit who will witness with your heart about the suitability and correctness of each element of the dream, and it is the Holy Spirit who will piece them together.

> *But the anointing which you have received from Him abides in you, and you do not need that anyone teach you; but as the same anointing teaches you concerning all things. . .* (1 John 2:27).

It is also the Holy Spirit who will bring to your remembrance any Scriptures that fit or depict the dream.

How do you know which interpretation for an element is the correct one? Again it is dependence on the Holy Spirit that is the key. Spirit thoughts often come "out of the blue," bypassing the natural thinking process. Often a Scripture will jump to mind. Look at the options presented in the metaphor dictionary, and as you do, consider the context of the dream. By that I mean, look at how the interpretation of one element affects other elements of the dream and the overall purpose of the dream. This method is particularly important when the metaphor dictionary presents many options for a given dream element. At other times, you will have an inner understanding of what is meant by a particular element within a dream or vision and then, when you look it up in the metaphor dictionary, you will get a confirmation as the elements paint a picture of what God is saying. At other times, thoughts will bubble up as you pray in the Spirit while looking over an outline of the dream.

The method used to interpret the "Hands on Throat Dream" (see page 27-28) spoken about earlier is also a vitally important one. This is particularly useful when the metaphor dictionary doesn't have an entry that seems to fit the context of the dream. In these situations, simply search the Bible for combinations of elements using a pocket Bible, PDA, on-line Bible, or Bible program on your computer.

At times the Bible will not contain the exact word that you may be looking for. In these situations, you will need to think laterally and conduct a search using related subjects. For example, the word *steam* does not appear in the Bible, but the words *water* and *boil* do. In these situations you will need to conduct your search whilst thinking beyond the confines of the key word.

Find the Subject of the Dream

After you have some elements pegged, start looking for the subject of the dream. By *subject* I mean, what is the dream about? In our experience, at least 90 percent of dreams are about the dreamer. Dreams will address the concerns of your heart. They will also raise heart purification issues (sanctification). They will relate to questions for which you are looking for answers. They will focus on the big issues in your life—body health issues and family and relationship issues—as well as ministry or working environment matters. What are the issues weighing heavily on your heart? Your dreams will center on you and the people over which you have influence and also will show people and organizations that have influence over you. This means that if you are in ministry, your dreams will also address leadership, congregational, denominational, and other related concerns.

The emotions felt during a dream are an excellent pointer to help identify the subject of the dream. Simply asking where you are experiencing the emotions portrayed in the dream will often pinpoint the subject. Likewise, the action symbolized in a dream is also a good indicator of a dream's subject. As you would with emotions, ask yourself where in your life you are experiencing actions similar to those symbolized in the dream. For example, if in a dream you are taking off a coat, ask yourself where you are giving up authority. If in a dream, you are in a bus queue, ask yourself in what part of your life are you waiting. And if in a dream you are pruning a tree, consider where in your life you are applying discipline.

What Is the Theme?

We must also remember that in every dream that God gives us to interpret, there will be a theme which will carry us to a purpose. All dreams and visions are a means to an end. Every dream sets forth a hope and a future produced by the interpretation, and it is moving by faith on that hope that bears fruit in people's lives. Without that, it is meaningless. God always speaks with purpose. As the interpretation comes to light, ask yourself what the purpose of the dream is. This is its theme. The purpose or theme of a dream may take the form of: a faith-building encouragement, the reassurance of His love, an answer to a question, a secret revealed or a warning, His guidance or direction, a correction, a prophetic promise, or an invitation to salvation.

Dreams About Others

Our experience has been that the more prophetic the calling on your life, the more likely you are to receive dreams and visions about others. It appears that for five-fold prophetic ministries (see Eph. 4:11), the greater the responsibility, the broader afield the prophet will dream. This means that as well as dreaming on a personal level, the prophet will dream on a congregational, city, national, and international level, dependent on that prophet's calling.

However, before presuming the dream is about others, be aware that many times God uses other people you know as symbols of whatever that person represents to you. Ask yourself how you see that person. What position does that person hold? What is that person's personality type and spiritual gift? Does that person represent a business or ministry? The "boss" may represent Jesus Christ. A person with a known ministry gift may represent a person in your life with a similar gifting, and a person you see as shy may speak of an area where you are not forthright enough. A dream with your brother or sister in it is just as likely to be an issue relating to a fellow believer (who is scripturally a "brother") as it is to actually relate to your family. Finally, consider the meaning of the name of the person in your dream before presuming the dream is actually about somebody else.

Having said that, dependent on your ministry role, God will give insights for counseling purposes into the spiritual well-being of others over whom you have responsibility or influence. For example, while working at a Christian rehabilitation program, I was given the following dreams about students.

In the first dream, Debra had stolen a ship. She had stealthily stolen away in the night to sail the ship solo. I was looking across the top of a line of trees expecting to see a sail. What I saw was a chimney and smoke above the tree-line. Someone said, "If she got to Boston Bay, they wouldn't be able to catch her." Talking the dream over with Debra, I found that she had been very tempted that particular week to leave the program because of family issues. The fact that the dream portrayed smoke and not a sail was indicating that she would be doing so under her "own steam" and without the unction of the Holy Spirit (see 1 John 2:20; John 3:8).

In another dream, I saw myself digging a burrow for Bobby the cat with my right arm. This dream suggests that in Bible teaching (my strength and calling) I was giving Bobby a place to hide. This insight enabled staff to address the student each time he used Scripture as a smoke screen to avoid dealing with his own heart issues. I could quite easily have missed the instruction of this dream because, two years earlier, my family had experienced the death of our cat whose name was Bobby.

Problems of Subjectivity

It is often difficult to see what is being said immediately after a dream or vision because you are so close to it. It takes practice to be able to see the dream or vision objectively. You really have to see the initial imagery on another level. When you have difficulty doing this, write it down and come away from it. Seek the Lord in prayer, and as you do, He will drop fresh insights into your heart that will open up a new perspective from which to view the message. Getting someone else who is open to receive from God through dreams (and is also growing in the gift of interpretation) to view the dream or vision is also a good method of dealing with any problems of subjectivity. Your ability to hear the interpretation from God will improve with practice. Many times you will find yourself saying, "What could that possibly be about?" As you acknowledge your own inability, suddenly the Holy Spirit will drop a thought into your heart that will crack the code, and the whole thing will be revealed before your eyes.

Idols in Your Heart

Here is a word of warning. It is very dangerous to come before God seeking an interpretation whilst holding a preconceived agenda in your heart. If you do this, the Bible declares that God will give you what you want to hear. God warns Israel of this very thing through Ezekiel by stating,

> . . .*Everyone of the house of Israel who sets up his idols in his heart, and puts before him what causes him to stumble into iniquity, and then comes to the prophet, I the Lord will answer him who comes, according to the multitude of his idols* (Ezekiel 14:4).

When coming before God for any form of guidance, we need to put our hearts into neutral before looking for an interpretation. That is not to say that we should blindly accept everything that someone puts forth as an interpretation of a dream or vision (see the section "Judge All Interpretations" later in this chapter). What it does say is that if we do hear the voice of God through an interpretation, then we need to be obedient to it. If we come prepared to hear only what we want to hear, then that is what we will hear, and that is dangerous.

Not a Forgone Conclusion!

Another vitally important point to remember is that when God gives a dream or vision, He does so with our best interests at heart. Dreams and visions often show potential outcomes—either good or bad—but the outcome is not *a fait accompli* (a done deal). Without that understanding, we may become philosophical, fatalistic, or defeatist in our outlook, doing nothing to avoid a negative scenario. God may show a problem, risk, or hazard so that we may avert the danger. We can take steps to put things right before they go awry. When Nebuchadnezzar dreamed of a tree cut down and someone treated as an animal, Daniel foresaw that God was warning Nebuchadnezzar to humble himself or be taken from the throne. It seems that Daniel did not believe it was an accomplished fact because he tried to prevent the dream's fulfillment by pleading with Nebuchadnezzar to change. He said,

> *Therefore, O king, let my advice be acceptable to you; break off your sins by being righteous, and your iniquities by showing mercy to the poor. Perhaps there may be a lengthening of your prosperity* (Daniel 4:27).

Daniel was giving Nebuchadnezzar the steps to avert the pending judgment of God. However, Nebuchadnezzar did not listen and was duly humbled in accordance with the dream (see Dan. 4:28-33). On the other hand, when Pharaoh dreamed of an imminent famine, he listened to Joseph's interpretation and advice, and the potential catastrophe was avoided (see Gen. 41:26-43).

We are also not to use a dream or vision interpretation as an excuse to do what we want to do contrary to the Word of God. For example, a dream about a potential homosexual relationship or a marriage breakdown is not justification for us to pursue these avenues of thought as our unalterable fate. No! These dreams are warnings about the state of our hearts so that we take steps to avoid these outcomes.

Judge All Interpretations

The importance of judging what is said in the interpretation of a dream or vision cannot be overstated. In Chapter 1, we discovered that dreams and visions were two of the main methods used by God to speak to His prophets (see Num. 12:6-8). We have also seen that the receiving of dreams and visions and their consequent interpretation and declaration constitutes prophetic ministry (in a limited sense).

In regard to prophetic ministry, Paul advised the Corinthian congregation to evaluate, or weigh up, what was said. He said, *"Let two or three prophets speak, and let the others judge"* (1 Cor. 14:29). When writing to the Thessalonian church, Paul also said, *"Do not despise prophecies. Test all things; hold fast what is good"* (1 Thess. 5:20-21).

Paul is saying that when someone is operating in the prophetic, there is need for evaluation or judgment of what is said. This takes into account that we deliver God's treasure through earthen vessels and also acknowledges that none of us has arrived yet. We are all in the process of growing in the things of the Spirit. As dreams, visions, and their interpretations equate to prophecy, they need to be judged and evaluated. When judging an interpretation, you might consider the following questions:

- Is it in line with Scripture?
- If what is being said is corrective, is it free of condemnation?
- Does the prophecy provide a future and a hope?
- Is there an inner witness or conviction that what is being said is truth?
- Does the prophecy meet a heart need?
- Does what is being said line up with what God has been saying through other avenues of guidance?

A negative response to one of these would put what is being said in question. At the very least, it should cause us to put whatever is said "on the shelf" until confirmation is received. A negative response to two or more of these questions would seriously put the prophecy in doubt. At such times, it is best to come away from interpreting until a later date. Often, future revelation will shed light on questionable interpretations.

The Metaphor Dictionary

The metaphor dictionary provides a comprehensive list of dream and vision metaphors. However, due to the creativity of God, the individuality of our personal makeup, and cultural differences, there will be occasions when an entry does not provide an accurate interpretation for a dream or vision element. On these occasions, you may know instinctively what is meant by an element in your dream, and if that is correct, there will be a fit with the rest of the interpretation. If you are unsure of the interpretation, you may need to research a subject, animal, or person to find what facet or characteristic of it God is communicating to you. This is very important when animals and birds are involved.

For example, if you see a particular breed of parrot in a dream and happen to know that this particular species has only one partner for life, it may be that aspect God is communicating to you rather than the metaphor dictionary listing of "gossip." Don't be afraid to research the characteristics of a particular species beyond what is listed here. If God has given you a dream, don't be lazy, He knows what resources are available to you. Also, don't overlook the simplest interpretation. A cat may simply represent curiosity, as in "curiosity killed the cat." A bull may simply portray heavy-handedness, as in "a bull in a china shop." Have fun decoding the messages God is giving you, and don't be afraid to think outside the box.

God bless,

Adrian and Adam

Summary: Chapter Ten

- Dream and vision interpretation is a God-given gift, but it is a God-given gift in which a person can grow.

- Spiritual senses are developed as they are exercised.

- Each element in a metaphoric dream is like a dot in a dot-painting that, once joined, becomes a story we are not likely to forget.

- It is the Holy Spirit who will witness with our hearts about the suitability and correctness of each element of the dream, and it is the Holy Spirit who will piece them together.

- From our experience, about 90 percent of dreams are about the dreamer.

- Dreams most often address the concerns that are weighing heavily upon the dreamer's heart.

- Asking ourselves where we are experiencing the emotions and actions similar to those portrayed in a dream is a good indicator of a dream's subject.

- Every dream has a purpose.

- God will often give dreams to those in ministry that are about the spiritual well-being of those for whom they are accountable.

- When we are experiencing difficulty interpreting a dream, we can write it down in sequence using dot points.

- When approaching God for an interpretation, we must be sure to put our hearts in neutral. The Bible warns about coming to God for guidance with idols (preconceived preferences) in our hearts.

- Dreams and visions show potential outcomes—either good or bad—but the outcomes are not *a fait accompli* (a done deal).
- God shows problems, risks, and hazards so that we may take steps to put things right before they go awry.
- We are not to use a dream or vision interpretation as an excuse to act and live contrary to the Word of God.
- As dreams and visions constitute prophetic ministry, their interpretation needs to be judged according to Scripture.

Making a Start

- Recognize that God uses dreams as a vital means of communication.
- Write the dream out immediately on awakening.
- Record any feelings associated with the dream.
- Ask God to help you both recall and interpret the dream.
- Put the dream into its correct sequence.
- Note any Scriptures that come to mind.
- Write out any "instant" thoughts on the meaning of the elements of the dream.
- Look up the metaphor dictionary for individual element interpretations.
- Allow the Holy Spirit to piece the message together.
- Identify the subject of the dream by considering the feelings and action in the dream.
- Ask yourself where in your life you feel this way.
- Ask yourself, "What are the current concerns of my heart?"
- Identify the theme or overall purpose of the dream by looking at it as a whole.
- Ask yourself whether the dream deals with past, present, or future? Or all three?
- If there are hidden elements not yet revealed, hold off on the interpretation.
- Once you have an interpretation, "judge" the interpretation against the questions listed earlier.
- If you are able to positively identify the dream's message, move on it.
- If the dream is genuinely about another person, begin praying for them.
- Thank God for His care and concern for you.

Part II

Dream Dictionaries

101 Sample Dream and Vision Interpretations
Actual dreams and visions with names changed for privacy

1. Flying Dream

River, Flying, Daughter, Running, Waterfall, Tricks, Riverbank

I was running along a riverbank. My youngest daughter was running ahead of me. I had trouble keeping up until I remembered that I could fly. I started flying over the river and overtook my daughter. It was amazing as I flew over a waterfall and continued down the river before I turned around to find her. I saw myself do a few tricks flying in front of a group of people on the bank.

Interpretation:

The river is the river of the Holy Spirit (see *River*). Your youngest daughter represents your offspring or future running ahead of you (see *Daughter*). Flying over the river means moving in a supernatural gift of the Holy Spirit (see *Flying*). God is also warning you when you start to move more in the Spirit to watch out for self-glory (see *Tricks*). The waterfall suggests that you will be part of an outpouring of the Spirit of God (see *Waterfall*). The people you are doing tricks in front of are not yet in the river (see *Bank*).

2. River in Church Dream

River, Church, Pulpit, Congregation, Stands

I saw a river running diagonally through what was currently the church congregation's sitting area. It ran between the pulpit and the congregation. At the back of the church were huge stands—like in a football stadium. I was concerned because I thought that the river separated the speaker from the audience.

Interpretation:

The river is the flow of the Holy Spirit (see *River*). The fact that the river flowed in front of the speaker is a good thing. It means that the preacher is putting the Spirit before himself (see *Pulpit* and *Congregation*). When this is done, God will draw crowds of people—the stands.

3. Letter Box Dream

Letterbox, Mail, Abundance

I was with a friend who I went to Bible College with some years earlier. He and I were in the ministry together. We were at post-boxes collecting our mail. I opened my box, and it was literally jammed-packed with letters. There were so many letters that it took me some time to jimmy a couple of envelopes free before the rest could be emptied out of the box.

Interpretation:

(The person who had this dream was no longer in a recognized ministry position.) This dream indicates that you will once again take up a ministry position as seen by the fact that you are with someone with ministry status. The many envelopes indicate invitations to speak (see *Letters*) and could also indicate that your ministry will be itinerant (see *Mailbox*). God is encouraging you with this prophetic-futuristic dream.

4. Plaques Dream

Plaques, Screws, Codes

I saw several plaques (shields) on which were words. I knew instinctively that the screws that were to hold them in place were positioned in such a way as to decode the messages on the plaques. Some screws were in the corners, which indicated that the corner words were the message. Some screws were in the middle, which indicated that the words in the same position (i.e. in the middle) were the words to take note of.

Interpretation:

The plaques are messages from God that you will share publicly (see *Plaque*). This dream is to show that the deposits of revelation (encoded words) you have received are from Him (see *Codes* and *Screws*). The instinct you speak of is guidance by the Spirit of God (an inward knowing). This is an encouragement dream showing that what you are receiving is from God. Keep doing what you are doing.

5. Hotel Foyer Dream

Hotel Foyer/Reception

I dreamt I was in a hotel foyer/reception area.

Interpretation:

(The recipient of this dream was asked whether there was some uncertainty about their tenure in their current employment position. He confirmed that finances were tight at work.) With that information, it is indicative that God is showing that you are about to check out of your current work situation and/or check into something new (see *Hotel Reception*).

6. Coach, Baggage, and Margaret Dream

Interstate Coach, Bus Stop, Baggage, Daughter, Taxi, Cost, Margaret

I got off the interstate coach I was traveling on to talk to someone, and when I returned, the coach was gone. I walked (with others) toward the next stop because my bags were still on the coach. I realized that if I didn't get to the set-down point before the bus departed, my baggage would go on with the coach. I thought of phoning (via cell phone) Margaret (who was on the bus) to ask her to offload my bags at the next stop. My daughter was in there somewhere. I thought of getting a taxi, but I realized that would cost me.

Interpretation:

The bus is the ministry in which you currently work (see *Bus*). The bus going on before you indicates that there is concern that you will leave your current position having not dealt with baggage from that position (see *Bag*). The baggage is most probably unforgiveness (feeling like they owe you). *Margaret* means "pearl." This is a reference to Jesus as the pearl of great price (see *Pearl*).

The reference to the taxi costing you means that if you don't deal with this baggage by taking it to Jesus, then it will cost you (you will not reach your God-given potential).

We recommend you approach whoever it is within your ministry with whom you have the unresolved issue and ask for forgiveness for harboring resentment and bitterness toward them. Your daughter's presence indicates that this concerns your future (see *Daughter*).

7. Laundry Anointing Dream

Laundry, Modern House, Younger, Parents, Wardrobes, Clothes, Air-Freshener, Fragrance

I was in the laundry of a modern house, which was well-appointed with good cupboards and doors. In the dream, I was a young girl (a daughter) and I could hear my parents saying nice things to each other through the wall (they were in the next room). There were wardrobes in the laundry, and I understood that they had clothes in them. There was also an air-freshening device in the laundry. I pressed it and a little sprayed in my face. I couldn't turn it off, so I opened the door. The scent went throughout the house into the air conditioner and filled the house with the fragrance.

Interpretation:

The new house speaks of your new, transformed, and well-fitted house as a Christian (see *House*). The fact that you are in the laundry suggests that you have just undergone a cleansing process (see *Laundry*). This is reinforced by the clothes in the cupboards. These are what you put on when you are clean. The Scripture that comes to mind is Zechariah 3:4-5.

Seeing yourself as the daughter refers to you being younger, which is often a characteristic of the spirit person (see *Younger*). A daughter is also a daughter of God. Your parents saying nice things to each other in the next room is representative of you being in harmony and intimate with Christ in the secret place. The air-freshener is the anointing (see *Air Freshener*), and getting some on your face means your heart has been anointed (see *Face*). Once this has been touched, the fragrance of Christ fills your whole being (house).

This is a great dream. Be encouraged. The previous pruning (cleansing) you have recently undergone has brought you to this place.

8. New Irrigation and Roof Dream

Dining Table, Parents, Dressing Gowns, Expecting Someone, Upstairs, Sleep, Roof Tiles, Front Yard, Irrigation, Grass, Quickly

I was sitting at the dining table talking to my parents. We were organizing something and sitting in dressing gowns. I was the daughter, but we were in the house I live in now. We were expecting someone. Someone came to the door, and my parents answered it. I went upstairs to sleep.

Workmen started working in the front yard, so I thought I would sleep. But then they also started working on the roof tiles just outside the upstairs window. I looked down, and they were replacing all the irrigation in the front yard. The workmen had diggers and excavating machines taking the dirt out and digging trenches. They were going to replace the irrigation pipes and relay them and put in new grass finishing the job that same day! It was a challenge to get it all done, but they were confident it could be completed.

Interpretation:

The dining table speaks of intimacy and unity with Jesus (see *Table*). This is reinforced by the wearing of dressing gowns, symbolizing a just cleansed and relaxed atmosphere (see *Dressing Gown*).

Going upstairs refers to going to God for rest (see *Upstairs*).

This dream deals with the external aspect of God's mantle upon you. God is mantling you with His power (see *Mantle*). He is placing the anointing upon the flesh (see *Grass*). At the same time, He is making adjustments to your authority and covering (see *Roof*). It should be evident that the dream also indicates a quick work will be done.

9. Train Station Dream

Railway Station, Train Departure, Spokesman, Platform, Curved, 400, Anxious

I was at a railway station awaiting the departure of a train. I was with a party or group of people. I was not the spokesman, and I got rapped over the knuckles for speaking about an incident when I shouldn't have. The platform was curved like a gentle S. A train pulled in; it was the final train, the "400." I didn't think I was meant to be on this train because I couldn't see other members of my group on it. I was anxiously looking to see whether people I knew were on it, having the thought that if this was the final train, and this wasn't the one I was meant to be on, then what then?

Interpretation:

The railway station says you are awaiting ministry (see *Railway Station*). The fact that you are not the spokesman refers to the fact that you are currently under another ministry without a pulpit profile. Getting disciplined for speaking means that you have said something that your current leadership does not like, and therefore, they are holding the pulpit from you.

The curved platform (gentle S) means that you are currently bound in the Spirit and are about to be released (see *Curved*).

The final train being the 400 means the spiritual train that you are really awaiting is just around the corner (see *Four*). Israel was in Egypt 400 years, and after the 400 years, they were delivered. This suggests that there is a spiritual time-lock at work in your situation (see *Watch*). You are experiencing anxiety because a ministry opportunity is closing (the 400 train leaving), and your next ministry opportunity (train) has not yet apparently arrived.

This is an encouraging dream. It lets you know that God is aware of your situation. You have no need to fear; when the 400 train departs (it appears your dream ends before it does), God's train will come. Though He may appear later than you would like, He will come!

10. Overtaking Dream and Auto Accident Dream

Passenger, Automobile, Father, Overtaking, Dirt Road, Blind Corner, Not Wanting To Be There

I was traveling with another passenger in a car that my father was driving. Our car was behind another car, and I knew dad wanted to overtake the car in front. Down the straight road ahead, I could see a car coming off a dirt road. It was coming in our direction. Dad nosed the car out to have a look and saw the other car and pulled back in behind the car ahead of us. We went round a sweeping left-hand bend, and then my father overtook on a blind right-hand bend with a bit of a crest. It was the sort of maneuver that if you had been in the car, you would not want to ride with that driver again.

Interpretation:

Your father represents leadership of the ministry in which you are currently involved (see *Father*). The ministry is the car (see *Automobile*).

Seeing down the straight road ahead refers to having spiritual vision (see *Straight* and *Window*). The fact that you avoided a head-on with an on-coming vehicle (coming off a dirt road) suggests that because of spiritual vision you have avoided confrontation and potential catastrophe with someone doing their own thing or a country ministry (see *Dirt Road* and *Auto Accident*).

The fact that your father did not wait for a clear road before attempting to overtake suggests that leadership is in a hurry to make a decision (see *Overtaking*). The driver overtaking on a blind corner means that the decision which is about to be made is spiritually blind. You did not collide with any other vehicle, but you and the other passenger will have second thoughts about traveling with that leadership again.

11. Slate Tile Platform and Roof Dream

Slate Tiles, Step, Roof, Platform, Length, House

I saw slate tiles suspended by cables between the ground and the roof of my house. The slate tiles created a platform to step up onto the roof. The platform that the tiles provided was two tiles wide and ran the length of the house.

Interpretation:

The slate tiles represent writing (see *Slate*). You are going to write material that will give you the opportunity to step into the pulpit (see *Roof*). As the slate tiles ran the whole length of the house, it appears that there will be many books to follow or the influence of your book (or books, as there were two tiles) will be ongoing, and it may also be that you use this platform to introduce others to the platform.

12. Property with a View Dream

House, View, Buy, 100,000

I bought a property (house) with a view. It was situated high, and you could see a long way into the distance. It cost $100,000.00.

Interpretation:

The property says that you are moving into a prophetic office (see *View*) by laying down your life (see *Buying*).

One hundred means "whole" and a *thousand* means "ever increasing." This suggests that it is purchased by your growth in the Spirit (see *Hundred* and *Thousand*).

13. Closing Window Dream

CD Installation, Computer, Young Adults, Different Rooms, Closing Window, Noise, Joking

I had gone to someone's home to let them install a CD I had on their computer. My wife had loaded the CD, so I wasn't familiar with the contents on it. There were three to five young adults, aged in their late teens to early twenties, living in the home. One of the girls whom I knew was named Ann.

I went into one room, and they into another. We spoke through a window which was horizontally long and narrow. At the same time as they were installing the CD in the other room, there was a lot of noise filling the house, and because of the noise, the window between us was being closed (in an attempt to cut out the noise).

There was a problem installing the CD, I joked about not hearing correctly. I was unable to help because I was not familiar with the material on the CD.

Interpretation:

Ann means "favored graciously". Knowing that one of your daughters is named Hannah, which is the root for Ann, it is evident that this is your children in the dream.

The CD loaded by your wife suggests that your wife has been the primary input into your children's lives in their developmental stages (see *Computer CD*). The dream suggests that as maturing youth/young adults, your children are now entering their own independent stage of life by going into other rooms. Your input into their lives is being drowned out by the noise of your children's interests and the world (see *Noise*).

The window closing says that the opportunity to input is narrowing (see *Window*). The noise is also hindering any programming you are attempting at the moment. This is a problem amplified by the fact that you are not as personal or intimate with them as your wife. The joking may refer to not taking the situation seriously (see *Joking*).

14. Miniature Cricket Bat Dream

Cricket Bat, Childhood, Blue, Green, Bigger, Carved, Countries

I bought an ornamental miniature cricket bat (sporting memorabilia). It was signed by players of the village in which I was raised as a child in England.

When it was brought out of the trader's display cabinet, it was blue and green in color. It was bigger than I thought, and it had the players' names and initials carved into the front face of the bat.

On the back of the bat were multiple country stamps where it had been. I can remember seeing Spain and Brazil and many others. This seemed a little strange to me because of the insignificant team it represented.

Interpretation:

A cricket side has twelve players (11+1), which reminds us of the apostles. Note that it is a miniature bat; this is because it is not in fact a bat, but rather a baton. It is blue-green in color because it carries with it influence in Heaven (blue) and earth (green) (see *Blue* and *Green*).

Your childhood village in England is mentioned because God has had this call on your life from before your birth (see Gal. 1:15).

The names are carved into the bat and not merely signed for two reasons. Firstly, it is because the bearers of this bat (baton) are those for whom the cost is their lives, and secondly, because they made their mark (see *Carved*)!

It is bigger than you thought because what is being presented to you (in the display cabinet) is a more significant calling than you thought. This is in line with the country stamps on the back of the bat of where it has been taken thus far (see *Country*).

The Lord has used a cricket bat to show you that when you get the call to bat, it is time for your innings to take up an apostolic and international ministry (see *Cricket Bat*).

15. The Flying Bible Dream

Bible, Falling, Automobile, Highway

My Bible fell out of my car as I went around a slipway (curved feeder road) onto a highway.

Interpretation:

In this dream, the highway is the commercial world (see *Highway*). What God is saying is that it would be a mistake for you to take a secular job because you will lose the call on your life (see *Bible*).

16. Money Given Into Your Hand Dream

Money, Suit, Insincere, Dark Blue, Dropping, Picking Up, Coins, Scrunched Up

I was in a foyer speaking to someone. An insincere man, wearing a dark blue suit, came up to me and unexpectedly gave me some money.

There were two fifty dollar notes and some coins all scrunched up together. I dropped some of the coins as they rolled out of the notes. I bent over and picked it up.

Interpretation:

(When asked whether this person knows anyone who wears a dark blue suit, it was discovered that he wears a dark blue suit when he does a specific contract job. At this time, this work had ceased for more than six months. Asked how the person felt about this work, it was evident that his heart was not in it. He had let some opportunities for more of this work drop by not attending an annual workshop.) This suggests that the insincere man is you when you are doing this work. With that information, it is evident that God is showing you there is going to be an unexpected and brief increase in this line of work (see *Dropping*), brief because only a small amount of money is involved.

Also note that you dropped the coins and picked them up. This is a picture of letting this work slip by not attending the workshop and then taking it up again. God is encouraging you to take this opportunity when it comes, as shown by picking up the coins (see *Lifting*).

17. Lift Dream

Lift, Women, Black, Kill, Comb, Words, Entrapment

Two women dressed in black were trying to kill me in a lift, and I had the sense that this would continue afterward. One had a comb with a long steel hilt, and she was trying to stab me with it. The other woman was trying to catch or entrap me in my words.

Interpretation:

This is a warning from God. It applies from the point where you are moving in the Spirit (being elevated) and from thereon (see *Lift*). The two women are two subtle demonic forces (see *Woman* and *Black*).

The first is using the trap of pride, i.e. trying to get you to make yourself look good (see *Comb*).

The second is the trap of wanting to speak what people want to hear rather than what God wants you to speak (see *Entrapment* and *Fear of Man*).

18. Marathon Race Dream

Running, Race, Old Man, Grey-Haired, Rerun, Champion, Timing, Crowd, Excitement, Briefcase, Carrying

I was running in a long race. I was behind in the pack of runners. We had just completed running around a looped section of the track when an old, grey-haired man took me from running in the pack to catch up with the leaders. Though I had run around the looped section of the track, when he led me to the front of the pack, he took me over a section of the track I had already run over. So I had to rerun over ground I had covered before.

The elderly man was a known champion who had previously won this race. As we ran, he took hold of my briefcase and carried it for me. I was aware that the timing of this man's runs was always perfect—he was the type of runner who measured to perfection his energy levels and would be increasing speed at the end of the race when others were spent. I was also aware that the crowd (spectators) were aware of his reputation to run through the pack, and it brought excitement to the crowd.

Interpretation:

This is a very encouraging dream. The race is the race of faith (see *Race*). God is going to take you in the Spirit from being in the congregation up to the front as a leader (see *Front*). In the dream you rerun over past ground; this is symbolic of going over some things that need to be dealt with from the past (see *Rerun*).

I believe the elderly man symbolizes the mantle of an apostle (like Paul, see 2 Tim. 4:7). He carries your briefcase, which symbolizes your teaching, and he has run this race of faith (see *Briefcase*). This is in line with your consciousness of crowd excitement (see *Crowd*).

The fact that he times his runs to perfection is evidence that the old man is Pauline in nature. This also suggests that the latter part of your life will be more productive than the former. This is seen in the old man speeding up to the finish line.

19. Opening a Bedroom Into a Lounge Dream

Visitors, Expectation, Opening Doors, Bedroom, Lounge

I knew we were expecting visitors. I had a sense of joyful expectation. To accommodate the guests, I was opening a set of double doors (that don't actually exist) between my daughter's bedroom and the lounge area.

Interpretation:

Joyful expectation is a good sign. God is showing you that what He has given you in privacy is going to become positively public (see *Bedroom* and *Living Room*). You can also expect more opportunities, interest, and traffic as a result of the inner changes (see *Door*).

20. High Speed Over Water Dream

High Speed, Water, Sundown, South, North, Trees, Gum Trees, Channel, Deep Water, Shallow, Destination, Left, Somebody Else, Soaring, Gulf Stream

I was traveling at high speed over water just before sundown. Though I have never been to New Zealand, I was aware that I was traveling from the South Island to the North Island of that country.

There were lots of trees (big gum trees) in the water to my left (a north-westerly direction). I was also aware that I was following the deep water channel (heading north-easterly) and not being taken (I was not driving the boat) across the shallow water to my left in which the big gum trees stood. The more direct route to my destination would have had me naturally steer between the gum trees. However, whoever was driving my boat was heading on a tangent or at right angles to a path through the gum trees.

I was conscious that I was somebody else, and that the boat wasn't actually in the water. I also had understanding that at the end of the channel on which my boat was traveling was a Gulf Stream that would automatically speed my delivery to my destination.

Interpretation:

This is an encouraging dream from God showing where you are currently in the Spirit. You are traveling from south to north; this is toward God and the spiritual inheritance He has for you (see *North* and *Northward*).

The big gum trees are prominent church leaders (see *Big Tree*). It is tempting in the natural to look for a short-cut to your destination by appealing to these leaders for recognition. It may also be that prominent leaders befriend you and ask you to join their ministry.

The Holy Spirit, your unknown pilot, is taking you via the deep water of the Spirit to your destination (see *Unseen Accomplice*). Though it appears a more indirect route to what He has for you, when you clear the channel, things will accelerate in the Spiritual Gulf Stream.

You are conscious that you are someone else because it is the spiritual person undergoing this journey (see *Unrecognized*).

The fact that the boat you are in is not actually in the water says two things. Firstly, you are in the Spirit (see *Flying*). Secondly, it suggests that you are heading away from the gum trees, not so much because of the shallow water, but because entanglement with them will actually slow your journey.

21. Warning of Death of a Ministry

Young Couple, Roof, Fire, Baby, Young Child, Flame, Fire, Kill

I was with a young couple in a fern house/tent type structure outside their home. The roof of the fern house caught on fire as the woman brought a flame into it. We tried to put it out, not knowing till later that the fire had spread to the house and killed their young child in the upstairs bedroom.

Interpretation:

This is a warning that gossip (see *Fire*) could destroy the new ministry venture (see *Baby*) you are embarking on. The woman may represent the church or its leadership as the instigators who try and stop what God has put on your heart (see *Woman*). Note also that the baby is upstairs; this says that what you have is from God (see *Upstairs*).

22. Black Plastic Under Skin Dream

Black, Plastic, Tweezers, Under Skin

I had a piece of black plastic under my skin, and I needed tweezers to remove it.

Interpretation:

This dream suggests that someone superficial (see *Plastic*) and without the light of the Spirit (see *Black*) is annoying you (see *Under*). God is also telling you to be careful (see *Tweezers*) in how you deal with the situation.

23. Seeing and Hearing Something Different

Rye Loaf, Sugar-Coated Candy, Seeing vs. Hearing

I heard someone describing a loaf of rye bread and going into what goodness it contained. However, what I saw was a sugar-coated candy.

Interpretation:

In this dream God is showing you that what someone is professing to present to you is not what it is claimed to be. It is suggested in the dream that someone is claiming to provide real sustenance—a hearty loaf—yet in reality it is empty calories (see *Candy*). It appears, in short, that this dream says you are not getting real meat, but rather ear tickling (candy) in what is dished up to you (see Heb. 5:12; 2 Tim. 4:3-4).

24. Washing in Front of People Dream

Washing, In Front of, Group, Unashamed, Enjoyment

I saw myself washing in front of a group of people and unashamedly enjoying it.

Interpretation:

This dream shows you applying the Word of God in front of a congregation or classroom of people (see *Washing*). It also suggests that there is confession and honesty as you do. Finally, it says that you are being cleaned up as you prepare and deliver the Word of God (see *Water*).

25. Buying a Four-Wheel Drive

Four-Wheel Drive, Buying

I saw my dad buy a four-wheel drive vehicle from his close Christian friend.

Interpretation:

This dream suggests that because of the influence of your father's close Christian friend, your father will enter into itinerant ministry (see *Four-Wheel Drive*). Buying here relates to laying down one's life: That is giving up your agenda for God's (see *Buying*).

26. Reinhard Bonnke in a Dream

Famous Person, River, Reserve, Speedboat, Rifle, Telescopic Sights, Gunfire

I saw Reinhardt Bonnke (the famous evangelist) enjoying fellowship with his family on a reserve or park area alongside a river. Two speedboats came along; the people on them pulled out rifles with telescopic sights and shot at him. He was able to duck for cover, and others in his party returned gunfire.

Interpretation:

(When asked whether the person who dreamed this dream had an acquaintance with an apostolic figure, it was confirmed that they did [see *Famous People*]). God is showing you that this apostolic figure will experience critical words (see *Bow*) from powerful ministries (see *Speedboat*) at a distance (see *Telescope*).

This is a warning that friends or staff of the apostolic figure will return harsh words. God says, "Vengeance is Mine" (see Rom. 12:19; Heb. 10:30).

27. Wheat Container Dream

Daughter, Back Verandah, Stick, Spider, Spider Web, Weevils, Container

In my dream, I was with my daughter and we were out on the back verandah. We were cleaning and looking in some wheat containers we have there.

My daughter had a stick and I said, "Check this one." She put the stick in, and when she pulled it out, it had spider webs on it. We looked in the container to see if there were any weevils in it, and we saw a spider in the container. I said, "Put the lid on and leave the container," and I thought, *I will get some dry ice and kill the lot* (spiders and weevils).

Interpretation:

The back verandah is that which is private, hidden, and undercover (see *Back Yard* and *Verandah*).

The wheat containers represent people (see *Sack*). They are bearers of the Word (*wheat*, see Matt. 13:18-19). See also the sacks in Genesis 42:25ff. The stick is discipline (either correction and/or the discipline of Bible devotions) (see *Sticks*). What you are seeing is inside your daughter.

The spider represents an issue which, when touched, causes a reaction and threat from her (see *Spider*). The spider and weevils also represent what is sown in with the Word. Think about what weevils do to wheat for a moment—they destroy the wheat! Weevils are destructive insects that secretly corrupt the Word within an individual (see *Weevils*). Cobwebs speak of deception (see *Web*). It could be that something is being kept from you or that your daughter is not dealing with an issue which has her in deception.

You saying to leave the container and deal with it later shows you have a propensity to avoid confrontation and not deal with issues because of the threat it raises. This is a warning from God to deal with issues as they surface or you will suffer the consequences later.

28. Old House Dream

Daughter, Camp, Rooms, Old House, Left, Door Ajar, Living Room, Alex, Friend, Playing, Chairs, Lectern, Game Console, Big Screen, Bedroom, Bedtime, Toilet, Office, Clean, Safe, Quiet

In my dream I was staying with my youngest daughter at some sort of camp. We were in an old house with many rooms. I walked down the corridor. There were a lot of doorways to my left, slightly ajar, but I had no interest in them. I only noticed them.

My daughter and I went into a room which was like a common or living room. Alex and a friend were playing there. There were no chairs in the room, only a lectern with a game console and, on the wall, a big screen.

My daughter and I went through the room up to the bedroom to get a game to play. I was wondering if we could play and whether Alex would mind. When we got back to the common room, Alex didn't mind, so we played a game which was called "Funny Home Videos."

Later, it was bedtime; the children went to bed. I had to go to the toilet. I had to go through my daughter's room, which led into the office, and Alex was sleeping in the office, and there was a toilet next to the office, which I went to because it was clean and safe and quiet.

Interpretation:

The old house is the past (see *Old House*). The corridor represents your journey through your husband's backslidden time (see *Corridor*). The doors left ajar on the left suggest that you were tempted to join him, but didn't (see *Door* and *Left*). This is a good thing, and God recognizes this!

However, you have now come to a room with a lectern in it. This represents your husband's pulpit ministry (see *Pulpit*). Notice that there are no chairs there. This means that he does not currently have an audience, which makes recognition of the call on his life harder for you to see.

In coming into the living room, you have come to the place of the fulfillment and promise, which scripturally is the place of rest—and there are no chairs (see *Living Room*). There are no chairs because entertainment and pleasure are getting in the way. It seems you are not taking the call on your husband's life—pulpit ministry—seriously.

Your daughter, whose name is Ann, is the grace of God that has been traveling with you through the journey, and Alex is Christ (the Protector of people). God has been protecting you and even now protects the business represented by the office (see *Office*).

Your going to the toilet represents repentance once you recognize the situation, which God has displayed through your daughter's room or through the grace of God (see *Toilet*).

29. Spider Dream

Kitchen, Spider, Leaf, Woman, Web, Ornament, Curtain Rail, Toilet, Killed, Purse, Money

I was in the kitchen, and I saw something run across the ceiling. I thought it was a spider; then I thought it was a leaf; then I realized it was a spider covered by a leaf.

A woman was there. She was smartly dressed and had long, straight blonde hair. She caught the spider and hung it up by a thin web as an ornament on the curtain rail and said, "Would you look after this for me?"

She went to the toilet (I think). I looked at the spider and thought, *I don't want that in here,* and squashed it. She came back, and my husband said to her, "She's killed it!" Then the woman took out her purse and opened it and said, "I was going to offer you money to look after that for me."

Interpretation:

The kitchen is your heart (see *Kitchen*). The spider is a stronghold and is covered or hiding (see *Spider*). The fact that it walks across the ceiling suggests that it has a tenacity to cling (see Prov. 30:28) and is in rule (see *Ceiling*).

The woman relates to the spider. The woman gives the spider the right to be in the home. A spider, when threatened, will rear up and lash out. The woman is Jezebel; she is an unclean spirit who likes to control and manipulate (see *Woman*).

The leaf speaks of prosperity, and as the spider is under the leaf, this indicates that the stronghold (spider) is hiding under the guise of abundant life (see *Leaf*). The dining room speaks of the place where you are fed spiritually. And when the spider is hung on the curtain rail as an ornament, it says that there is an association between Heaven and prosperity (see *Curtain*). Note that there is a real connection between Heaven and prosperity. However, one of the greatest traps today is to have our primary focus on money, rather than the Gospel, when Scripture tells us to do the reverse (see Matt. 6:33).

The woman goes to the toilet, which means you detox and get rid of it—note that at the same time you deal with the spider! This is a good thing, for it means you recognize the power money has over your heart and break its influence in your life by examination of your heart, confession, and repentance (see *Toilet*).

However, the woman returns (this is its clinging tenacity). Your husband's statement, *"She killed it!"* is a declaration, as the authority in the home, that *Jezebel has no right to be in this home!*

The woman's action of taking out the purse, opening it, and offering money reinforces that this was the stronghold (see *Wallet*). I perceive in the spirit that you are at a crossroad (it is decision time) at which you must choose between the need for prosperity and security through money and the need to give God your heart with no strings attached. You have a fear in your heart of letting go. When the woman comes back, she is feeding you a demonic lie that you would have been prosperous and getting rid of this earning power has cost you.

This is a good dream as it shows you a foundational problem that needs to be dealt with. The dream also shows you that the woman will try to come back, but God's revelation through the dream prepares you for this before it happens.

30. University Dream

University, Lunch, Outdoor Table, Lawn, Platter, Finger-Food, Aris, Joke, Sister, Face Away, Friendship, Relationship, Bored

I was sitting at an outdoor table eating lunch with a boy named Aris I liked in grade seven. The table looked across the lawn to the Barr-Smith Library (Adelaide University). Our lunch was a platter of finger-food, and we were sharing the one plate.

We were friends, but it was as if there was awkwardness, or perhaps we were going to be more than friends. I turned to ask him what his sisters were doing now, and I unintentionally brushed against him. He made a joke about his sisters' having finished Uni a couple of times and that they were practicing being wives now. I turned my face away, and he gently stroked my hand. I thought, *We are not good at having a relationship (that is more than friendship),* and I also thought, *Are we bored with studying and we need a bit of excitement?*

Interpretation:

Sitting at an outdoor table suggests the revealing (exposure) of your relationship, fellowship, and communion (see *Table* and *Outside*). The boy's name is *Aris*, which means "best" and this ties in with the number seven (see *Seven*). What it suggests is that this is not you and this boy, but rather you and your husband. You want your marriage relationship to be the best, and God wants it to be divinely perfect. There may be similarities between your husband and Aris that you have subconsciously picked up. God is revealing your heart.

The Spirit is showing me that you love picnics and walks in the park, botanic gardens, and the like. God is showing you an up-and-coming awkwardness between you and your husband.

Asking Aris about his sisters is, in effect, asking your husband what the churches are doing (see *Sister*). The unintentional brush against him is either a misunderstanding between you or perceived misunderstanding between you.

His joke about his sisters suggests that you are not taking the move of the churches seriously. The reference to University and having done it a couple times is a reference to over-emphasis of intellect in the church (see *University*).

When you turn away, it means that you have turned your heart away from either God's call upon your husband or the church (see *Turning*). It may be that you have lost confidence in the church. Your boredom suggests that you are currently undergoing a midlife crisis. You are at the crossroads and have to choose between security for your future and Jesus' need for first love.

31. Old Men Dream

Outdoor Parade, Tent, Feet, Shoes, Cold, Bare, Tip-Toes, Old Man

My family and I were going to some sort of an outdoor parade or performance. We were all going as a family. We came up to a small, oblong tent shelter. I looked down at my feet and thought, *Why didn't I wear any shoes?* as the ground was a bit cold and my feet were bare.

We went into the shelter and had to sort of stand on tip-toes to see whatever we had come to see. In the tent there were at least two older gentlemen, probably in their 70s—John and Harry—that I recognized. We acknowledged each other, and I thought, *What are they doing here?*

Interpretation:

This seems to relate to your move to another church. The outdoor arena suggests exposure or revealing of issues (see *Outside*). The oblong tent shelter is a gathering place (church) and says that in your heart you see this move as a temporary arrangement (see *Tent*).

When you look down at your feet, you notice you have no shoes on. No shoes may suggest a lack of preparation (see *Shoes* and *Shoes Off*). The ground is cold because you have "cold feet" over this move (see *Cold*).

The fact that you have to stand on tip-toes to see says that you are trying to see what you are there for by sight, not by faith. If you are going to see what you are there for, you need to be in the Spirit (see *Toes*).

It could be that you find it threatening to be exposed as associated with this type of church in front of these men. The two older men equally represent the "old man" (see Rom. 6:6) strongholds in your heart (see *Old Man*). The two men you see probably characterize the strongholds of your old self (pre-Christian life), and also being in their 70s may suggest release from Babylon and being set for increase (see *Seventy*). Your husband has suggested that John has a very definite money-security issue. Given your dreams previously interpreted, I would guess that Harry has a control issue. Either his wife runs the home or he is a leader/controller. Please prayerfully consider whether your discomfort in the move and before the two men perhaps suggests that you are looking to the world (success in worldly terms tied to money) and have an authority issue.

32. Old Man Dream

Can't Sleep, Upstairs, Window, Corner, House, Ambulance, Car, Walk, Tree, Front Door, Lady, Sitting, Step, Bent Over, Grief, Wife, Left, Grey, Early Morning, Lawn, Street, Dressing Gowns, Mouth, Shaving Cream, Masking Tape, Turn, Cardboard, Socks, Five, Six, Blue, Black, Business, Main Road

I can't sleep and it is about 3 A.M., I think. I look out my upstairs window across to the corner house. I see an ambulance and a small car screech up and pull up in front of the corner house. I think that there is something wrong with the lady of the house.

I decide to go for a walk. As I walk, I watch the man on the corner house walk behind a tree and toward his front door. As I come in view of his front door, I see him sitting on a step near the front door. He is faced toward the door, and he is bent over and is sobbing with grief. I think that something has happened to his wife. I think I will go and comfort him, but I go on turning the corner to the left.

It is now the grey of early morning, and I am in a street more like a street near where I lived as a young person. I look across the street and see three men in old-type dressing gowns in a row on the front lawn. I go to pass them, and I see that the first man has something across his mouth. First, I think it is masking tape in an X and then I think it is shaving cream. I am a little frightened, and I start to run, but then I realize that they only want to encourage me. I turn around, and they have crossed the street to give me a hug and encourage me.

I go on to the next corner. As I turn left around the corner, I see two men across the street under the cover of the trees so I don't see them clearly. But they give me two thick pieces of cardboard, and when I open them, I see that they have given me two pairs of socks. One pair is navy and one pair is black. I think one was size 6 and one was size 5, but I'm not sure. But what I thought was, *It is good you get things while you're out walking at this time of the morning,* and I thought, *I wonder if these will fit anyone in my family?*

Then as I came to the end of that street, I came out to a main road something like Port Wakefield Road, and there were businesses, and I wasn't where I expected I would be.

Interpretation:

Waking up says that you are currently experiencing unrest. You go out to see what is going on. The ambulance and small car screeching up to the house says that this is an emergency and that the issues to be dealt with require urgency (see *Ambulance*).

Christ is the man (see *Man*). You are wondering whether He is in this? He walks behind a tree; this represents life (He is behind it) (see *Tree*). The woman is both you and the Church (see *Woman*). He doesn't go to comfort His wife (Church) because she is unwell. The ambulance suggests she is on the brink of death (see *Ambulance*). Not going to Him as He sobs suggests that you are not intimate with Him. Christ outside the house also represents He is outside your heart. He is outside and wants to commune with you (see *Outside*). You are looking at having your needs met from your husband, not from God. You turn left (and not right) (left=flesh, right=Spirit) and go into your past (see *Left* and *Right*). What this says is that past issues make you turn from Christ. You are struggling to be intimate with Christ because of the past.

The "grey of early" morning suggests that you are lukewarm in your walk and uncertain in your heart (see *Grey*). Could it be that your heart desire is not to be in want?

The three old men on the front lawn are three strongholds in your old life, which cause the old self to rise up (see *Old Man*). The lawn represents the flesh and says that you are not mindful of the things of God (see *Grass*). I am not quite sure, but would suggest that the man with the X on his mouth represents that you have to watch what you say. The shaving cream would indicate you need to clean up what comes out of your mouth—speaking life rather than death—as your confession of faith. It may also refer to speaking in tongues. It represents the fact that you in some way cannot see the purpose, have shut it down, doubt its validity, or in some way feel it is unclean or foreign. I would suggest that your church upbringing is behind this. The Jezebel spirit doesn't like the freedom of the Spirit; it tells you it is wrong or has no purpose.

The two other men (also appearing in dream 31) are probably money and control. You run from them, knowing it is wrong. However, they operate in conjunction with a seductive/deceptive spirit that says it only wants to help.

Each corner is decision time (see *Corner*). The two men under the trees represent the religious and the spiritual paths (Cain and Abel, Jacob and Israel, Simon and Peter, and so forth) (see *Two* and *Man*). They appear unclear because you are not walking in the Spirit (you are making left turns).

They offer you two pieces of thick cardboard, which speaks about not knowing what you are getting until it is unwrapped. Even then, a person needs spiritual insight to discern what is on offer. The two pairs of socks talks about clothing for your feet for different paths (see *Socks*). The blue pair is heavenly (Spirit-given), the black pair is lacking light (religious/sin) (see *Blue* and *Black*). This is also suggested by their sizes: size 5 (grace/favor) and size 6 (man/sin) (see *Five* and *Six*).

God is telling you that you have to make a decision. I am picking up in the Spirit that you don't make decisions easily and will often let things ride because you do not want to decide either way. This is suggested by the fact that you did not put either pair on. You intend bringing home the socks and are not aware what you are bringing in. You don't put either pair on, and end up not where you expected. Port Wakefield Road is a busy road (everybody's on it, see Matt. 7:13) (see *Highway*). God is challenging you to make a decision to choose His way or you will end up on the busy-ness treadmill like everyone else without Him.

You need to get back to first love with Christ. Again, as mentioned earlier, you also need to be praying in the Spirit. The absence of exercise here is why you are lacking spiritual discernment and clarity. You are currently double-minded. This is because when the heat is on, the yeast of the Pharisees (religious doctrines from the past) puffs up and corrupts everything in your heart (see Matt. 16:6). Past doctrines have sown seeds that manifest when pressure comes. The Scripture I am also strongly getting is John 21:18.

> *Most assuredly, I say to you, when you were younger, you girded yourself and walked where you wished; but when you are old, you will stretch out your hands, and another will gird you and carry you where you do not wish.*

You are clothing yourself and ending up at Port Wakefield Road. You need to die to self and walk by faith, allowing God to carry you where He wishes.

33. People Running a Race Carrying Ladders

Running, Race, Ladder, Horses, Elephant, Tracks, Hill, Finish Line, Unseen Friend

I was standing on some sort of athletic track, and I saw people in teams of differing sizes (some on their own, others in groups of twos, threes, and fours and more) in a race running on individual tracks carrying ladders and heading for what I imagined must have been a finish line. I knew some of the people who were running. At first there was one or two who came into view over the brow of a small hill, and then more and more came running, or more like charging, for the finish line. As I watched, I saw some coming over the hill on horses, and finally one came over the hill straight toward me on an elephant. It was a little bit daunting watching this big elephant charging straight for me. It stopped just before getting to me. I knew someone was with me, though I didn't see him.

Interpretation:

The people are running in the race of faith (see *Race* and *Running*). The different sized groups represent families, individuals, and congregations. The ladder they are all carrying represents Jesus Christ and the Cross (see *Ladder*).

The people on horses could represent those who have elements of the world in their Christian walk (see *Horse*), but they are more likely to symbolize those strong in faith (see *Horse*). The brow of the hill from which the runners come into view represents the place of revelation and strength without which these runners would not be able to charge to the finish line (see *Hill*).

The elephant which was on your track is representative of the large or high-profile ministry God has destined for you (see *Elephant*). The sense of foreboding you experienced means that in the natural this would not be possible. However, your unseen accomplice is the Holy Spirit, He is the one who is orchestrating this dream and is also in it with you. He will be with you (see *Unseen Accomplice*).

34. Pen in Pocket Dream

Pen, Ink, Stain, Dark Blue, Blue, Leak, Repeat Dream

I was wearing a blue shirt with a pen in the shirt pocket. The pen had leaked out dark blue ink causing a stain about the size of quarter (Aus: twenty cent piece). A male friend had pointed the stain out. The pen had leaked because the nib had not been retracted. I have had this dream twice with six months to a year in between dreams.

Interpretation:

You are going to write material that will offend because you are not going to hold back (see *Ink*). The stain speaks of the offense (see *Stain*). The dark blue speaks of the inspiration of the Holy Spirit in what you write (see *Blue*). The dream is repeated twice as a sign of urgency and a confirmation of the message you are to write (see *Repeated Dream*).

35. Person Tossed Off of a Rock

Rock, Wall, Fall, Toss, Brett, Toes, Legs. Pain, Groaning

I saw George get tossed off of the rock on which he was standing by another man named Brett. He hit a rock wall and fell down onto another rock, hurting his toes and legs. He was groaning in pain.

Interpretation:

Brett means "Brittany," an area in France that was so named because it retained its British flavor (see *Brett* in Name and Place Dictionary). Therefore, George being tossed by Brett means that George has been removed because of the lack of change.

Hitting the wall of rock and falling onto the rock speaks of brokenness (see Matt. 22:42-44) (see *Rock*). It also says that George has been taken from his place of prominence and security.

Hurting one's legs speaks of losing one's strength. Hurting the toes in this situation speaks of having a serious affect on the walk of George's spiritual children—the littlest members (see *Legs* and *Toes*). Groaning speaks of release of the spirit through death (see *Groaning*).

36. Floating Dream

Room, Float, Window, Haze, Left, Eye, Hall, Cracked, Glass, Tripping, Floor, Tent, Mom, Dad, Zipper, Shut, Could Not Get In

I was in a room, a big room. I started to float across the room saying, "God is in the house!" I was in front of a large window with shut curtains, which were purple in color. The Presence of God fell on me. Then I started to go across the other side of the room. It was blurry; I saw a white haze in front of me. I reached out with my arms into the haze trying to touch the Presence there. The Presence was stronger.

I started to leave the room down the hall. Seeing through my left eye was like looking through a cracked glass window. As I went down the hall, fear came over me, and I was afraid of tripping over things on the floor because I could not see very well.

I finally came to a tent, I was aware my mom and dad were inside. The zipper was shut, I could not get in. The dream ended. I woke up, and Psalm 22 and Jeremiah 8 came to mind.

Interpretation:

The Lord is showing you that you are a heavenly house of God (see *House*). Later this is contrasted with your parents, who by comparison are earthly tents (see *Tents*). The window speaks about "an opportunity" and "the eyes of your soul" (see *Window*). The purple curtain is Jesus (see *Purple*).

The anointing brings up a past issue (your parents). Your relationship with your parents causes you to stumble when you look through your natural eyes (see *Left, Corridor,* and *Father*).

It appears you have trouble relating to your parents. There is no familiar ground, and their presence intimidates you. The Lord is warning you that this is a potential stumbling block and that it quenches the anointing and Presence of God in you.

Your parents are not saved (earthly tents). In the natural (left eye), it looks like your parents will not be open (zipper stuck) to you, God, and the Gospel (see *Zipper*). This has the potential to seriously affect your walk with God.

You want a deeper love relationship with your parents, but when you go to your parents, it sucks the anointing out of you, like a bucket of water has been thrown over you. It's like every time you connect with family, it's in the flesh and you lose focus (even when you try to talk about the things of God), and you go away grieving.

God is showing you that you are not to look at them in the natural, but look at them through God's eyes—His glory (the haze). You are to stay in the Spirit, to see them as God sees them, and in doing so, you will become Jesus around them, and you will see them open up (see *Cloud*).

37. Stone Wall Dream

Living Wall

I saw something like a stone wall, only it was soft and alive. Words really cannot describe it. The stones were soft and interacting with each other. The wall was vibrant, pulsing, and alive. I thought how incredible and beautifully engaging the wall was, and I really wanted to keep looking at it.

Interpretation:

This wall is you (see *Wall*). The stones in the wall represent the deposits God has placed within you (see *Stones*). People will marvel at the anointing upon you.

38. Frog and Take-Away Dream

Drive-Through, Car, Frog, Hobbling, Drain, Chicken Leg, Strapped, Tree, Hopped, Black, Birds of Prey, Ripped, Weird

I was driving through a take-away (drive-through) place in the car that I'd been given by a lady from church (this lady has a reputation of not being reliable). I saw a frog or toad hobbling along a drain culvert (with small holes in it) on the ground. I thought, *OK. . . ?*

Then I noticed its legs were tied together. It had a piece of uncooked skinless chicken leg strapped to its back. It hopped up a tree, and a flock of birds attacked it (big black birds of prey—crows, ravens, and so forth) and ripped it to pieces. Then I drove off thinking, *Well, that's a bit weird!!* And I woke up!

Interpretation:

The drive-through is really what is happening in your life. You are getting in your car to get fed, and you are unaware of what is going on. God is showing you via this everyday situation (you may regularly eat take-away) what is going on spiritually (see *Automobile*). In short, it appears you are looking for ministry as your source of being fed by God. The car going through the drive-through represents a commercial quick-fix mindset (see *Drive-Through*). You are rushing things and not meditating in the Word or seeking God (see Heb. 5:14). Be careful not to put ministry before your relationship with Jesus.

When you see the frog, God is showing you what is really happening. The *frog* represents two things:

1. Deception (a lying spirit) or you have bought a deception (see *Frog*).

2. A stronghold with influence over your life. The stronghold is looking to a human father-figure as your source instead of God. The broken promises you experienced from your earthly father cause you to look to other men as a substitute. The Lord doesn't want this to repeat in your life in the later days, because God is your heavenly Daddy. He will never break His promises to you.

The blessing of the Lord makes one rich, and He adds no sorrow with it (Proverbs 10:22).

People's promises are not always what they appear. Many promises appear very attractive, yet they come with troubles.

The fact that the car is meant to come from a Christian lady (as you described her) represents a ministry promised to you from an unreliable source. The promised car parallels the promised ministry you are expecting. Both are deception (the frog).

You need to be fed and well established before you go into ministry. God, not people, gives ministry. Once you are established in Christ and know who you are, with a full appreciation of your giftings and empowered by the Holy Spirit, you can minister out of overflow.

The fact that the frog is bound means it is losing its power, hold, influence over your life (see *Bound*). However, though you think you have moved on from past disappointment (from false promises), God is warning you that this could possibly surface again. The fact that the frog's legs are bound means that it is partially dealt with, not fully dealt with. Hobbling along the drain represents a barren place, not being effective, no anointing (see *Drain*).

The chicken leg strapped to the frog indicates food or being fed. Uncooked means it is not yet ready for consumption (see *Uncooked*). It has not yet passed through the fire of testing.

The birds being black means they are demonic (see *Birds*). Should you climb too early into ministry, God is showing you your vulnerability and what the devil will do (see *Tree*). It could also represent the devil waiting till you are at the peak of your ministry before bringing you down.

This is a warning from God. It is a good dream. It shows that God is concerned for your welfare, and He doesn't want His plan for your life jeopardized or derailed because of your childhood disappointments (see Jer. 29:11). You are vulnerable to men (father-figures) who make empty promises and cause you to suffer the heartache of disappointment.

He wants you to slow down in your aspirations for ministry. To rush ahead of God and His plans for your life will lead to catastrophe as the enemy will have a field day/feast. God does not want you to step into a role beyond your depth. When the timing is right, He will open the door, and His timing is perfect.

Please do not be fearful, for God has not given us a spirit of fear. For through this, God will give you the gift of discernment and wisdom.

39. Roofing Dream

Floor, Sitting, Chair, Playing, Toys, Roof, Leaking, Dripping, Doing Nothing, Water, Upset, Anger, Cleaning, Gutter, Dry Grass, Dirt, Muck, Hole, Flowing Water, Living Room

I was in the living room at my friend Tom's house. Tom was sitting on the floor. Jean (his wife) was sitting on a lounge chair. Caleb (their son) was playing. There were other people in the room in the background (X4). I don't know who they were. I was playing with Caleb. He showed me his room full of toys. Then I looked at Tom; the roof was leaking with water. It was dripping on Tom. He sat there and did nothing about it. I looked over at Jean in the chair. She looked upset and angry.

In the next scene, I went onto the roof of the house. I was cleaning the gutter. It had dry grass, dirt and muck in it. I cleaned it and discovered water flowing over a big hole, which led into the living room.

Interpretation:

The picture given by this dream shows Tom on the floor and Jean in the lounge chair. This seems to indicate that Tom is not in the place of authority at home. Jean is in authority and possibly puts Tom down (see *Sitting*). This wrongful authority structure is choking the Holy Spirit and blocking His flow into the household.

The Holy Spirit is coming in, but not correctly, which should be via the door. There are blockages in Tom. He is stumbling, perhaps due to strongholds—self-esteem, unworthiness—which may be blocking him because of past failure. It appears Jean doesn't have respect or trust in him (because of past sin/failure?). Jean may need to forgive Tom for something so that Tom can walk in his God-given authority. Tom will also then be released from a burden which keeps him from taking his rightful role.

Caleb playing with a room full of toys seems to indicate that he is spoiled (see *Toys*). His future is at risk because he is not really learning the ways of God from Tom.

The leak suggests that the Holy Spirit is coming in via a wrong way, and Jean finds this offensive (see *Water*). This may be because Jean sees a character flaw in Tom, which he appears to be doing nothing about, thus discrediting him in her eyes. The fact that this has been revealed to you means that there is a lesson here for you. It may also be true that Tom has a blind spot and cannot see it. Tom may be able to take this revelation from you (please pray for receptivity). [This dream has application in all households, particularly where the husband is more spiritual than the wife. If the man does not provide security through leadership and finances, he can be despised in his wife's eyes, especially if his emphasis is the spiritual over the practical.]

Tom may need to deal with some wood, hay, and stubble (the grass, dirt, and muck in the dream) to make himself a better husband (see 1 Cor. 3:12). We can be anointed to help others and not help ourselves or deal with ourselves. A bad leak is created through our flaws.

God's grace has revealed this, so that means God wants to bring His plans to fruition. Tom is praying about his calling and a door to open, which is God's answer. God is saying that Tom needs to rectify things at home before other ministry will open to him. God doesn't want Tom to come unstuck later because of a faulty home structure.

40. Two Pairs of Shoes Dream

Shoes

I saw two pairs of shoes. One pair were the shoes I wear to work (in Christian ministry); the other the shoes I wear around home.

Interpretation:

God is telling you not to have two different walks. He is saying what you do at work in the ministry should be the same at home (see *Shoes*).

41. Spider in the Slippers Dream

Slippers, Dark Blue, Floor, Spider

My husband is away a lot preaching the Gospel. I saw his dark blue slippers on the floor, and a spider crawled into one of them.

Interpretation:

This is a warning that when your husband is away (empty slippers) the enemy is going to try and hinder his effectiveness of moving in the Holy Spirit by attacking the home (his foundation). The Scripture that comes to mind is First Samuel 30:1-6 (see *Slippers, Spider, Floor,* and *Blue*).

There is an additional warning that, when your husband returns from ministry, the enemy will try to attack him in the home.

42. Burning Wallet Dream

Wallet, Fire, Friend, Fence, Death, Corner, North

I set fire to my wallet. I was with a friend (though I didn't see him). My wallet was suspended on a post and wire fence. I had the knowledge that I was doing it in respect of a friend who had died. I was on the corner of Smith Road and the Main North Road. I was worried afterward that all my identification details were destroyed.

Interpretation:

Your friend is Christ (see *Friend*). The fence is a demarcation point; it is the separation between the old self and the new self (see *Fence*). This is reinforced by the fact that you were burning the wallet in respect of a friend who had died (see *Wallet*). That friend was your old self (see *Friend*).

You happen to be on the corner of Smith and Main North Roads, which indicates you will soon be moving around the corner from being lost in the crowd (Smith) to taking a closer walk with Christ who resides in the sides of the north (see *North* and *Corner*). The fact that it is not about money, but rather about identity is again reinforced by your concern for your identity details and not the loss of your money after the event. However, it is fair to say that this transition will cost you everything.

43. Terrorist Dream

Terrorists, Gallows, Hanging, Soldiers, Machine Gun, Wounded, Bullets

I saw some terrorists on a gallows about to be hung. At the same time, I heard commentary about how these terrorists were planning to escape and then attack. I watched as one of the terrorists rolled off the platform with an accompanied explosion, and then I heard gun fire. There were wounded soldiers sitting in pews looking on; then one of the soldiers (he had his hand in a sling) got up and fired his machine gun back at the terrorists above the heads of the soldiers in the pews. I had some concerns that he may have hit others in the pews because he was careless in shooting back.

Interpretation:

This dream is a significant warning. It speaks of potential problems created by false converts (the terrorists), who do not truly come to the cross of Christ. The gallows represent the cross and avoidance of the hangman's noose says that they have not truly died at Calvary and thus avoid its demands on the human heart (see *Hanging*). These are seen as terrorists because they are used by the enemy to sow discord and strife in the Body of Christ (see *Terrorists*). They are the equivalent to the tares in Christ's parable of the wheat and tares (see Matt. 13:25, 27-28).

The explosion speaks about an incident that is threatening to flare up, which will be followed by words fired back and forth (see *Explosion* and *Shooting*). Soldiers in the pews show the Church as God's spiritual army (see *Soldier*). They are shown to be wounded because they have not fully dealt with the hurts and disappointments of the past (see *Wound*).

Wounded people are more susceptible to the attacks of the enemy and are prone to react without due regard for the welfare of the rest of the Body of Christ.

The soldier with a sling firing back is possibly a picture of a leader who is not fully whole himself reacting to the words that follow the incident; this has potential to hurt others within the ministry.

This is a warning to be aware of false converts, a reminder to work through past hurts, and also a caution not to react to everything that is said in and around the church.

44. Coded Numbers Message Dream

Code, Numbers, Two, Three, Four, Six, Seven, Eight, Display, Corner, Reservoir, Smart, Roundabout

In my dream I had someone whom I loved a great deal, but whom I hardly ever saw. We both had a set of numbers and the numbers were a matching set. My numbers were six, seven, eight, and his were something that went with them, but I can't remember them. So what I was going to do was to post/display my numbers so that he would see them when he went on a certain road. I was going to put them up at the corner of Reservoir Road and Smart Road at the roundabout.

Interpretation:

This dream relates to your relationship with your husband. You complement one another. It appears that you and your husband do not spend enough time together. It also appears that God is communicating to your husband through this dream. Your numbers are six, seven, and eight. These particular numbers in this order are a good combination for they say that you are progressing spiritually. They say that you were in the flesh (six), are moving to Divine perfection (seven), and are ready for a new beginning (eight) spiritually (see *Six, Seven,* and *Eight*). What they spell out is a code for your husband to decipher.

It is possible that your husband's numbers are four, three, and two which would be the complementary numbers to complete the order, or round to ten.

This combination, in this context, would mean that he now has rule (four) and will experience resurrection (three) through your unity (two) (see *Two, Three,* and *Four*).

The corner of Reservoir and Smart Roads is also significant because it says shortly (corner) you will get to the wisdom (smart) of God (reservoir) and turn around (roundabout) (see *Reservoir, Corner,* and *Roundabout*). This is a fantastic dream!

45. Shoplifter Dream

Shoplifter, Vase, Service Clerk, Supermarket

I saw someone stealing vases in a supermarket. He picked up a vase and put it upside down in a carry-bag. I could see four vases in the bag. He then ducked down in the queue at the checkout, and when no one was watching, he made his way through the checkout undetected. Once outside the supermarket, the shoplifter gave the bag to another man waiting outside in the mall.

I spoke to the store clerk about what I had seen, and he said they needed evidence. He then said he didn't mind if I raised the alarm because any attention given to the would-be shoplifters would give him a break from serving when the crowd came to watch what was going on.

Interpretation:

The shoplifter is the devil (see *Thief*). The vases are people—potential bearers of the glory of God (see *Vase*). They are turned upside down because now they no longer are able to be used to carry the Spirit of God.

The supermarket is the church, and the store clerk is the shepherd of that flock (see *Shop* and *Store Clerk*). Unfortunately, this shepherd appears to be a hireling (one that is there for the pay only) because he does not carry genuine concern for the welfare of those for whom he is responsible (see John 10:12-13). The person in the mall is a religious spirit.

This dream is a picture of how the cults are used by the devil to rob God of His servants by luring them away from truth. The problem is that the members do not have a solid foundation in the Word of God and, therefore, are unable to discern truth from error. The cults typically have a distorted view of the deity of Christ, the Trinity, the devil, and hell, and they also discount the power of the Holy Spirit for today.

46. Dry and Hard Pizza Dream

Pizza, Dry, Cooking, Lady, Red, Wife, Fighting, Red-headed girl, Scratched Face, Wrestling, Kicking

I ordered a pizza. Although it took a long time to cook (about an hour and a half), I waited patiently. When it was ready, it looked dry and hard. I said to the lady politely that I didn't want the pizza. She was very rude, so I threatened to throw the pizza at her. Then I made a complaint in private to my senior pastor. He said he would look after it. He went away and came back with the same pizza. I was upset and then walked out of the room (I believe it was red).

Then, I saw my wife fighting with a red-headed girl where I had ordered the pizza (I believe in the front foyer). My wife's face was scratched. Then, I found myself on the floor wrestling and trying to hit her (the red-headed girl). She was trying to avoid me by kicking me with her feet.

Interpretation:

This dream relates to your relationship with your church. The lady is the church (see *Woman*). It looks like you are waiting to complete the will of God (food, pizza), and you don't get what you expected dished up (see *Food*). This could refer to your area of involvement or the role you are expecting because you appear to wait patiently for it. What you do get is without life, hard, dry, and perhaps a religious mindset—you know, the "this is the way things operate around here" attitude. This is seen in the speed to cook the pizza, which is equivalent to a "slow to respond to needs" attitude. Cooking also speaks of works of the flesh (see *Cook*).

When you are disgruntled and say something about what is dished up, it appears the church turns on you. You don't agree with something that is said or the way things are done and you tell someone (this is the threat of throwing the pizza away). This could also be a threat to leave the church.

This brings you in front of the senior pastor. The senior pastor listens to your case, but is powerless to offer you more. He really only wants to keep the peace and will side with those who have been longer in the church. The red room is an angry or passionate situation in which the flesh rises up (see *Red*).

In the midst of this, your wife is hurt (a scratched face means a hurt heart) and intimidated by an evil spirit that threatens to expose (in the foyer) some issue (see *Face*, *Scratch*, and *Foyer*).

The dream closes with you in spiritual warfare with this evil spirit. It appears that it is fearful of you (avoiding you), but lashing out when it has the opportunity. I am also reminded of Genesis 25:25-27 (see *Red-Headed Woman*).

47. Harlot Church Dream

Door, Mirrors, Elevators, Left-hand, Beautiful, Room, Old People, Man, Harlot

I was walking around the city; don't know which city. Then I saw a church. I was looking down. There were two big doors. One of the doors opened; the one on my left-hand side, it closed. I saw two smaller doors within the two bigger doors. I went through them to a lobby. It was beautiful inside, full of shiny metal mirrors.

Then I saw lifts (elevators), and I went in one. I looked on my left-hand side whilst in the elevator and saw another elevator, which was open. I debated whether I should go into that elevator. I was concerned I might get lost, so I stayed where I was and turned to the control panel. It looked a bit like an H. I knew this was a picture of the two lifts and that I was in the left hand column. I pressed up, and it took me to another beautiful room.

There were elderly people around, and I found myself talking to a man who was large in stature. I asked if he was a Christian. He acknowledged and said, "Yes." Then I asked if he believed in what the Bible says, he said, "Yes." Then, I asked again, "Do you believe in the whole Bible?" and he said, "Most of it." Then, it was like I went into preach mode, telling him he must believe all of it. Then, I realized I had no shoes on at that time.

Then, the man was gone and a lady in her mid- to late 50s wearing a red skirt, white shirt, and red blazer was on the same chair the man had been on. She was lying there on the chair. I asked her if she spoke in tongues, and she said, "Yes." I started telling her it's the only way to keep yourself in the love of God. You can't do it in your own strength. I also told her I was concerned and that's why I was telling her all this. I didn't want her to go to hell. I said, "I better go now."

Grabbing her on the leg, I got a bit aroused—I had the thought to take her or ask her if she would like to go to her room. I knew it was wrong to do such a thing, but instead I got up and began to leave. Then she said, "Don't go. I want to hear more . . . ."

Interpretation:

You have entered into salvation (the narrow road, see Matt. 7:13-14) in a place where others have entered via the broad road (the big doors), which open for others to enter (see *Doors*). This took place at a time when you were depressed (looking down, see *Down*). The doors opening (prior to entering via the little doors) suggests that you were offered religion before you found Christ. You are also coming to an understanding that the real Church is within the church (door within a door).

Now that you have entered, you have begun to see beyond the shiny façade (an outward show with little substance behind it). The mirrors probably refer to smoke and mirrors (deception), vanity, or a preoccupation with self (see *Mirrors*). Having entered, you want to progress upward or grow spiritually. The elevator in the dream is the vehicle for spiritual progress (see *Lift*). However, you entered into the left-hand elevator. *Left* in this situation represents the fleshly, self-righteous, religious, unbelief, cursed, judged, death path attempt to get to God (see *Left* and *Right*).

Your concern about getting lost if you go into the other elevator may be a concern you have that if you go into the right elevator (God's way), you may lose friendships you value (see *Right*).

You went up and arrived at what appeared to be a beautiful room (remember that the temptation fruit looked appealing to the eyes, see Gen. 3:6; 13:10). Seeing the old people means you are seeing the past. These people once experienced a move of God (see *Old Man*).

You speak to a man who is large in stature (see *Tall*). He represents the earthly authority in the church. You find out that he doesn't believe in all of the Bible when you press him harder for truth. You also find you have no shoes on, which probably means that you have been stripped of authority to speak to him (see *Shoes*). Naturally, when people have no shoes on, they are cautious where they tread and cannot freely conduct warfare (here, warfare means witnessing or evangelism). The reason you have had your shoes taken from you is because, though there is a man in apparent authority, there is also a spiritual force behind him—the woman. She is lying on the chair. The chair is the seat of authority. She is a harlot—dressed in red—covering a white shirt (there was once a move of God in this place, but it has been prostituted and is covered by red [see *Harlot*]). The harlot says, "Yes," to your questions to stall for time. This is lip service to buy more time to try and seduce you.

Though you apparently made the first move by touching her leg, she is seductive and is a master at presenting herself in an appealing way (see Prov. 6:25-26; 7:10-18). She wants you to feel you instigated the sexual arousal (she knows men's hearts), but you remained faithful. Get out of there (see 2 Tim. 2:22)!

48. In the Army Looking for Part of the Platoon

Army, School, Bus, Garage, Hospital, Outside, Ballet

I'm in the army on a cruise ship. We land in an unknown city and are billeted in a school. A previous senior pastor of mine is our commander. I went looking for part of the platoon in a coach (bus). I went into the school garages, but couldn't find the coach.

As I went further, the school led into a children's hospital. I stepped outside through one door to see three people talking. One of them started to fall off a balcony-type area. I reached out and stopped her falling.

I went back inside and the rooms and corridors were like a maze. I came out into a large recreation-mall type area. I saw one child tied down and understood that he had a mental condition. I went past this person, and I saw people running to secure table-tennis tables so that they could play in their lunch break.

I went outside and got caught up with the crowds walking on the sidewalk. I stopped to put on one ballet slipper.

I was concerned because I wanted to get back to the school where I was billeted. I was unsure in which direction to go. Last thing I recall was I was going down some side street on a water ride like at a theme park.

Interpretation:

The cruise ship suggests that this dream outlines something of your Christian journey. What we are seeing is the period of time from when you were under that previous senior pastor.

The school represents learning through life (see *School*). When you are looking for the coach, it says you are looking for ministry (see *Bus*). The garage speaks of the need of organizational repair (see *Garage*).

You are next in a children's hospital, and this could suggest that you were working with sick and immature Christians and perhaps are in need of personal repair yourself (see *Hospital*).

You step outside through one door, which is stepping outside of Christ. Outside you did have influence in stopping someone falling away (see *Outside*).

You stepped back into Christ. And what you have experienced has been like an ever-changing blockade in your attempt to make it through (see *Maze*). When you moved into the large recreation area, you noticed the neglect of those with mental issues, and instead of communion, found false love (table tennis) and games-playing. You step outside the system and are moved by the mass of humanity lost and going nowhere. At this time you stop to put on one ballet slipper, which speaks of God's grace balancing you with the love of God (see *Ballet*).

Wanting to get back to the school where you were billeted may speak about an attitude ingrained within you of wanting to re-establish yourself within the organizational structure in which you were schooled. However, though you appear to go through a period of uncertainty, you find yourself being led by the Spirit (the water ride). This promises to be both a mixture of fun and uncertainty, taking you to places you have never been before (see John 21:18).

You need to put to death the desire to go back, which is looking for security in the old system. This will take some cutting of emotional soul-ties. In doing so, you will find the freedom of the Spirit and the ministry (coach) you are looking for.

49. Parrot Dream

Parrot, Multi-colored, White, Feeding

I saw a multi-colored parrot pretending to be a cockatoo (white parrot), and I was feeding it.

Interpretation:

A parrot is a gossip (see *Parrot*). This one claims to be righteous, but it is not what it claims to be (see *White*). The fact that you are feeding it means you are giving the gossip fuel to pass on to others (see *Feeding*).

50. Flood Dream

Village, Straight Road, Old Houses, Middle, Mucky Water, Women, Flood, Staircase, Foundation, Pregnant, Wood, Stairs, Old Man

There was this rural community like a village. In this community there was this straight road in the middle, and on both sides of the road were old houses and buildings.

Then I saw myself standing in the middle of the road, and I could see this water gushing up the road from one direction. The water was mucky. There were two or three women on that road who said, "We will still go through the flood anyway as it is not that deep." But as they went through the flood, the water started gushing through really fast and deeper.

While I was watching them, I made the decision to go in a different direction, and I saw myself climbing to this one solid cement post that was standing still. This post was a part of the staircase (and a part of the foundation), so if you think about it, it followed the risers and steps.

As I was hanging on the post and feeling uncomfortable because I am pregnant, I looked around and saw this old house just three feet away. This house had a proper wooden staircase at the front, and I saw this couple with a young child on top of the staircase just feeling comfortable and safe where they were. And I said, "I could have gone to that staircase, which would have been a lot easier for me."

Not long after that, the water subsided, and I got down from the post. An old man was watching me. I'm not sure what happened to those people who went through the gushing water.

Interpretation:

The rural community is your church; you may even think of it as such. The straight road is the way of the righteous and what lies ahead (see *Straight* and *Road*). The old houses and buildings represent those who are not changing. They are those who have a form of godliness, but are not applying the Word of God to their lives (see *Old House*). This may not yet be apparent to you. They have settled into life as Christians living in the flesh rather than in the Spirit. It is important to note that these people look and act like Christians, but God is showing you what they really look like.

While you are contemplating a major decision (standing in the middle of the road), a flood of muck or torrent of unearthing words (muck raking) comes gushing in (this may include lies) (see *Road*). It appears that these words affect many churches and not just yours (see *Mucky*).

It seems that God is going to allow some rather unsavory things to be revealed about leadership in the Church in general that will rock it and test its foundation. Some information gets unearthed, and this will promote a further flood of information probably as the media or one particular person sets about digging for more dirt to feed on.

The women that you saw on the road are churches (Christ's Bride, see Eph. 5:25). The churches that attempt to make it through in their own strength will be swept away. These are the woman who said they can make it through because it is not too deep. You choose to go in the right direction (as you call it, "another direction"). That direction is seeking Christ in the Spirit. He is the only One who can save us in such a predicament (see Isa. 59:19b). He is the standard. He is the staircase (see Gen. 28:12; John 1:51), the foundation (see 1 Cor. 3:11), and the Word. And the Cross is the post (or pole, see John 3:14) on which you cling (see *Steps, Foundation,* and *Pole*).

I think your pregnancy helps us put a time on this event, and I would suggest, because you have less than six months left, we are looking at something within that time frame, although we always need to be wary of putting time-frames on God. Your pregnancy also says you are carrying a promise from God, possibly a prophecy over your lives (see *Pregnancy*).

Looking over at the old house with the wooden staircase symbolizes looking at the past (see *Old House*). It looks comfortable, but this is deception. The couple you are looking at is actually you looking to get back to the good life of your comfortable past. We need to be mindful that Jesus said, *"No man, having put his hand to the plow, and looking back, is fit for the kingdom of God"* (Luke 9:62). However, though they look comfortable, the wooden staircase means that what this couple has built is of wood (flesh) and not the Spirit (see 1 Cor. 3:12-13), and again, it is old and therefore unchanged (see *Wood*).

You even think about leaving because it is particularly uncomfortable. But before you can make this decision, the torrent will cease.

On getting down the pole, an old man is looking at you. This old man is your past looking at you (see *Old Man*). You are going to be tempted to go back to the past comfort you once had. God is bringing you to the place where you are at peace. You can enter into the secret place that Jacob couldn't (see Gen. 28:12ff). God is calling you to get back into the Spirit and be more mindful of spiritual things. You are currently experiencing anxiety and must be more in the Spirit to birth the promise you are now carrying. There is also a soul-tie of the fear of poverty from the distant past that is causing you concern.

You are uncertain what has become of those who tried to make it through in their own strength. They are those who did not have the right foundation. When the flood came, they were swept away because they were moved by circumstance rather than by the Word of God (see Matt. 7:24-27).

It is important for you to understand that God is using this torrent of muck to His own ends. He is cleaning up the church before revival. It is interesting that when the Israelites crossed the Jordan to enter the Promised Land, the Jordan was in flood, but this is also the time of harvest (see Josh. 3:15).

God is giving you this dream to prepare you for what lies ahead. I believe that you are being measured in your faith. God is saying to get in the Spirit. Be led by the Spirit, because it is in the Spirit that we birth God's promises and become fruitful. It is our fruit (and seeing the fulfillment of His promises) that will shine when we stand before Him at the completion of the race. All that is of the flesh—wood, hay, stubble—will be destroyed.

51. Head-on Crash Dream

Cars, Crash, Drivers, Hurt

I saw two cars heading straight toward each other like they were going to have a head-on crash. The two drivers were young and seemed to be playing chicken with each other. I saw the two cars crash, and I also saw and recognized the driver who got hurt.

Interpretation:

This dream is a warning from God (see *Auto Accident*). In the circumstance in which it was given, it means that two departments (vehicles) of the ministry in which the dreamer is involved will come to a place where there will be one department set against the other (see *Automobile*).

Due to spiritual immaturity, neither will be willing to yield to the other, and if that is the case, then the dream shows the department that will get hurt. The Scripture that instantly came to mind is Genesis 13:7-9. Therefore, meekness and trust in God are called for at this time.

52. The White Hearse Vision

White, Hearse, Women, Passenger

I saw a white hearse with John (one of my congregation members) in the passenger seat. Someone else was driving, and there were two women in the back seat.

Interpretation:

The white hearse symbolizes the burial of an offense (see *Hearse*). The offense is identified by the two women in the back seat. One woman symbolizes an issue concerning John's estranged wife, and the other the church at which John experienced betrayal by the pastor in a marriage counseling session (see *Woman*).

53. Foreign Invasion Dream

Foreign, Army, Invading, Rock, Sea, Rifle, Sand, Cave, Candles, Orange, Mel, Dune Buggy, Roof, Wall

A foreign army was invading, and I saw them at the base of a huge rock that went down into the sea. I and others were positioned somewhere higher on the rock looking down at their landing. I ran to get rifles and ammunition to shoot at them.

To do so, I had to crawl through the entrance of a narrow sandy cave about one foot high. There was something like a dozen orange candles on the base of this sandy entrance which led down deeper into the cave where it opened up. The candles were all at different stages of dying out. The majority were just wax mounds where once there had stood a candle.

At this point in the dream I had the revelation that it was only a dream, and yet the scene was so vivid and real, I could practically smell the wax and cool sand. Down beyond the entrance were two people—my compatriots—one male, one female. The entrance was so narrow I thought that the roof could collapse on me at any minute and I would die here. I realized that it did not matter if I died here because if I didn't get through I would die anyway when the enemy overran the place. I realized that I must not give up and that there was something greater at stake here.

I made my way through the narrow entrance and down into the cave where the male person, who reminded me of actor Mel Gibson took me through a different exit to a powerful dune buggy type vehicle, and we went and got the arms we were after.

In the next scene, we had the arms (rifles and ammunition), and were on our way back, and I was conscious that the enemy was infiltrating. Mel showed me on a map how he had worked out to get us back to the hotspot. He, as the driver, was going to jump the car onto the roof of a fortress type structure and again jump it onto the top of a wall that ran toward where we needed to go. It looked pretty spectacular and exciting, but I was confident in his ability to get us to the hotspot. I was also aware that we would be shot at on the way.

Interpretation:

The invasion speaks about the infiltration and subtle influence of technology, which is leading the Church away and captive (addicted) to entertainment.

The cave speaks about the Church hiding (see *Cave*); this is the female deep in the cave (see *Woman*). The narrow sandy entrance says two things. Firstly, it says that the way is going to be under pressure. Secondly, it says that the Church is for the most part merely toying with the Word of God (see Matt. 7:26) (see *Narrow*). The orange candles are a warning about the state of the Church and its fading apostolic mandate (see Matt. 28:19-20). We, the Western Church, are being drawn into a flesh-comforting entertainment-rich lifestyle and, as a consequence, have become spectators. We expect people to come to us instead of going out carrying the message we have been given.

The fear of death I experienced on crawling through this narrow opening represents the fear of ridicule I feel I will experience for sharing this revelation. The realization that something greater is at stake says that I will proceed with this because I realize the Church is in jeopardy. The awareness that what I was experiencing was a dream and yet it appeared so real says that even though it was just a dream it is a certain spiritual reality.

Mel means "chief," and therefore, Mel Gibson in this dream represents Jesus Christ, who has been taken into hiding by the Church (see *Woman* and *Chief*).

The dune buggy symbolizes a powerful ministry (see *Dune Buggy*) driven by Jesus Christ, who will carry this message onto a preaching platform (see *Roof*) and over the obstacles and barriers (walls) that would otherwise prevent it (see *Walls*). The rifles are willing hearts (launching pads) for words, and the munitions are those words (see *Bullets*).

Being shot at speaks of "friendly fire" from people within the Church for carrying this message.

54. New House and Goldie Dream

New Home, Gold, Five, Identification

I came home to a new home. The house was bigger than usual and everything was like new inside. As I went in, I saw Goldie was inside. She said, "It's only me; it's not a burglar or anything." Goldie was going through my things, picking out five things that identified me. She had a photo and a hat and three other things.

Interpretation:

The new house is the promise of spiritual growth and fulfilment (see *House* and *New*).

The name *Goldie* means "a precious yellow metal" (see *Goldie* in Name and Place Dictionary). It represents money and relates to your spiritual growth and the prosperity that is associated with it. This is a warning from God that when you come into your spiritual inheritance to beware of money's subtle power to steal away who you are in Christ (your identity). In the dream, Goldie says, "It's only me; it's not a burglar. ..." This is a mark of the apparent friendship between you and her. However, she (money) is stealing your identity in Christ. She is attempting to take the grace and favor of God which identifies you (see *Five*). Beware, you cannot afford to lose who you are in Christ. Jesus says that you can gain the whole world and lose your soul (see Matt. 16:26). This is the danger here (see Deut. 8:7-11, 18).

55. Climbing out of Window Dream

Storm, Window, Upstairs, Roof, North

I knew that a really high wind storm was coming. I told my husband, and he tried to see it out the window.

In the next scene, we were upstairs, and he said, "I'll have a look." My husband stepped straight through the window and onto the roof and walked easily to the gutter and looked north to view the approaching storm. I was looking at his feet, thinking he wouldn't normally do that, because a person would be cautious on the roof, but he stepped out confidently, like it wasn't an issue.

Interpretation:

A wind storm coming from the north is indicative of the pending judgment of God (see *North* and *Storm*). Taking a look speaks of prophetic insight (see *Lookout*). Going upstairs represents going into the Presence of God (see *Upstairs*).

Stepping through the window says that your husband is stepping into the prophetic promises of God (see *Stepping*). He is going beyond merely seeing and is moving into place (see John 3:3-5). Confidently walking on the roof represents moving in faith on a preaching platform, and it appears part of his message may be judgment (see *Roof*).

56. Skateboard Dream

Skateboard, Tricks, Wheels, New

I was on a skateboard, and as I was riding it, I was doing some tricks. The tricks were basically kicking the back of the board to get it to slide out. I picked up the board when I had finished, and there was another young person with me. I looked at my wheels, and they were all worn out. His wheels were brand new.

Interpretation:

The skateboard speaks of youth ministry (see *Skateboard*). Doing tricks represents moving in the gifts of the Holy Spirit (see *Trick*). Wheels are representative of your spirit; having worn-out wheels means that you are not replenishing yourself in God after ministering (see *Wheel*). Seeing his wheels are brand new says that the other person is spending time with God to renew his spirit (see Isa. 40:30-31).

57. Looking at Mushrooms Dream

Table, Jamie, Right, Mushrooms

I walked up to a table. Jamie, an old friend, was with me on my right. I looked down on the table, and there were assorted mushrooms on the table. I had to choose the one I wanted.

Interpretation:

The table is the decision-making process, and choosing the mushroom says that you are allowing the decision-makers to keep you in the dark (see *Table* and *Mushroom*).

Jamie on the right means that the flesh is in control and, therefore, you are not seeing what is going on spiritually (see *Jamie* in Name and Place Dictionary). Like Jacob, you need to wrestle with God for His promises and not rely on people or ministries for your promotion in God (see Gen. 32:22-32).

58. The Flying Bus Dream

Flying, Bus, Butterfly, Carolyn, Seat, Coat, Cold, View, Coastline, Home

I was on board a flying bus called "The Butterfly." Carolyn said the ride wasn't the best (she had been on it before). I thought it was great! Inside was bigger than a normal bus, more like a 747 interior. We were coming back from a day trip.

I moved seats to be with someone else. I left my coat in the other seat. It was a little cold, but OK. I was concerned that perhaps my other seat would rob someone of a seat (that it wouldn't be filled). We didn't realize that the bus flew until we started to see from the air. There was a great view along a coastline. We were free of traffic, and there were great views. We were relaxed and having fun on our way home.

Interpretation:

The Butterfly speaks of a ministry in the Spirit (see *Butterfly*). The butterfly is contrasted with the earth-bound caterpillar as being free from limitations.

Carolyn means "woman" (see *Carolyn* in Name and Place Dictionary). In this situation, it is a reference to a woman in your life who is not comfortable walking by faith (in the Spirit). A day trip is a reference to ministry in Christ (see *Day*).

Moving seats is a change of role and authority (see *Sitting*). This is reinforced by the fact that you left your coat in the other seat (see *Coat*). It appears that in changing roles you are concerned that your former position be filled. The slight cold you felt seems to indicate a cold reception of the decision to change roles (see *Cold*).

Seeing from the air refers to being in the Spirit and moving in the prophetic (see *Seeing*). The coastline is the border between the spiritual and natural realms (the boundary of faith) (see *Coastline*).

Being free of traffic refers to being free of the commercial systems of people. Being relaxed on your way home refers to making your way to Heaven (see *Home*), and not being caught up in traffic is a reference to being free of political or religious competition.

59. Water Flying Over Keyboard Vision

Water, Flying, Computer

I saw water flying in slow motion over my laptop.

Interpretation:

The water flying over the keyboard speaks of an anointing over what you are writing (see *Water* and *Computer*). It is moving in slow motion because what is being written is taking time to come together (see *Slow Motion*).

60. Screws in Head and Cheek

Son, Screws, Head, Cheek

My son had a screw in his head and one in his cheek. I offered to take them out with a battery-powered drill I held in my hand. He wouldn't let me. He came back a while later and said, "I got them out myself."

Interpretation:

The screws represent strongholds (see *Screw*). This dream shows that your son has two strongholds; one is a mental attitude, and the other is cheekiness.

His refusal to allow you to take them out indicates that he needs to be instrumental in removing them. Though he currently needs to deal with these two areas, it appears in the right environment that he will. The battery-powered drill in your hand symbolizes the Holy Spirit in your heart (see *Battery* and *Hands*). Don't push the issue to force their extraction. Keep doing what you are doing, and God will lead him to deal with them.

61. Tennis Player Smuggling Cheese Dream

Cheese, Smuggling, Television, Law

I dreamed that a prominent woman tennis player was caught smuggling cheese. I could see the shape of the cheese; it looked like mozzarella. The tennis player was in a lot of trouble because of the smuggling offense. It seemed a silly law, but it was the law, and there were serious consequences.

Interpretation:

(Asked about her relationship with tennis, the dreamer revealed that she used to play competition tennis and that more recently she had spent a fair amount of time watching the Australian Open on television.) With this information, it appears that God is showing that you are having your Christian maturity (cheese), or opportunity for Christian maturity, stolen or smuggled from you by television watching, as evidenced by your television watching of this event (see *Cheese*).

Though the television watching seems harmless (silly), it will have spiritual ramifications. This is a serious warning that if this continues, it will lead to problems because the call upon your life is going to require considerable Christian maturity.

62. Shower of Gold Dream

Gold, Shower

In my dream, I saw a shower (like a rain shower), but it was of gold particles.

Interpretation:

As this dream was experienced by a Bible teacher (its context), it is likely to be about an outpouring of powerful teaching (see *Shower* and *Gold*).

63. Wife Holding Calculator Dream

Calculator, Dad, Wife

I saw my wife holding a calculator because her dad was not there.

Interpretation:

This dream suggests that the wife is concerned about her financial security instead of trusting God (her true Father) for her security (see *Calculator* and *Father*).

64. Three Long-Sleeve T-Shirts Dream

Clothes, Blue, Grey, Famous Person, Reporter, Mother-in-Law

I had been given three long-sleeve T-shirts in different colors: dark blue, grey, and light blue. Each shirt had been written on by the hand of someone famous.

A female reporter was at my home looking at two of the shirts and transcribing some of the writings. My wife's mother had called in the reporter.

Interpretation:

The long-sleeved T-shirts represent ministry roles. The various colors say that the three shirts are three roles (see *Clothing*). It could be that this is past, present, and future. Light blue speaks about your spirit, grey about a period of uncertainty, and the dark blue a ministry in the Holy Spirit (see *Blue* and *Grey*).

The famous person is Christ (see *Famous Person*). I believe that those who are written on are pillar-like ministries within the Church (see Rev. 3:12).

This suggests that God is calling you to an apostolic role and that your work will become part of church history (the reporter commissioned by your mother-in-law) (see *Reporter* and *Mother-in-Law*).

65. Supermarket with no Meat Dream

Supermarket, Meat, Box, Backdoor, Vacuum Cleaner

I went into a supermarket with a group of people. I couldn't find much of a selection of meat. Instead of coming out the front door, I went around the back and climbed over boxes. Three vacuum cleaner boxes fell down in the warehouse.

Interpretation:

The supermarket represents a commercial church (see *Shop*). The lack of meat means that there is a scarcity of Bible truth being preached (see Heb. 5:12-14) (see *Meat*). Not going out the front door possibly suggests that you are leaving this church unofficially (see *Backdoor*). The three vacuum cleaner boxes say that the fullness of the Spirit has been denied and also explains the lack of solid Bible teaching (see *Vacuum Cleaner, Box,* and *Three*).

66. Friend Chris Sinking in Sand Dream

Sand

My friend Chris was at the beach up to his waist in sand.

Interpretation:

In the context in which it was given, this dream suggests that Chris (a recent convert), is sinking back into the world after his conversion because he has no foundation in the Word of God (see *Sand*).

67. Swapping Sunglasses Dream

Sunglasses, Kym

In my dream, my friend Kym swapped sunglasses with me. He gave me his sunglasses, and then in return, I gave him my own.

Interpretation:

This dream says that you will be given Christ's perspective, and in return, you surrender your own. Kym is Christ because *Kym* means "chief" or "ruler" (see *Sunglasses*; see *Kym* in Name and Place Dictionary).

68. Fox Dream

Fox, Field

I saw a fox leaving a field.

Interpretation:

The fox represents a political person or spirit who is harming the sheep (by tearing them apart) leaving a congregation (see *Fox* and *Field*). This is a good dream as it says that a divisive person is leaving the church.

69. Five Computer Disks Dream

Five, Computer CD

I had a set of computer files on five disks (I felt like I have had this dream before). I kept them in that group because I didn't understand them; they were too hard. I discussed this with someone. I looked through them again; they still seemed a puzzle. I didn't understand them.

Interpretation:

This dream seems to refer to your thoughts about the grace of God given through faith. Five is the number of grace and favor of God (see *Five*). That grace and favor is accessed by faith.

The CDs represent your thoughts (see *Computer CD*). What this says is that you find it hard to understand salvation through grace rather than works. It may be that you have had this dream before or more likely that you have been asked to walk by faith in God's grace before and found it equally discomforting. You may have previously felt that you have earned your right for approval by God.

70. Sleeping Baby Dream

Bench, Baby, Sleep, Pram, Heavy, Bed, Table, Sheet, Center

We were, as a family, sitting on a bench in front of a building. I was holding a baby, and the baby went to sleep. As we didn't have a pram with us, and I thought the baby would get heavy, we went to some friends' place to see if we could lay the baby on a bed.

Their house had only one room with the bed in the center. The table was in the corner. They had been decorating, but had not finished yet. I lay the baby on the bed. Then I noticed a few marks on the sheet, so I was careful where I lay the baby. I gently pulled the quilt around the baby.

Interpretation:

Sitting on a bench as a family speaks of unity in your relationship. The bench refers to being on the sidelines or awaiting ministry (see *Bench*). Being in front of a building refers to a time before the establishment of your promise. The baby is that promise of God (see *Baby*). The fact that it is asleep means that it is resting and being strengthened in private before it awakens to a public life (see *Sleeping*).

The heaviness refers to the weight of expectancy/responsibility and going to your friend's home suggests that you want to share your promise with them (see *Heavy*). A pram is a ministry to carry a promise, and the absence of a pram means that you do not currently have a public ministry that can carry the promise for you (see *Pram*).

A one-roomed house points to the fact that your friends are perhaps undeveloped spiritually (see *House*). Your desire to put the baby in their bed talks of a desire to share your promise with them and for there to be an agreement or alignment with them (see *Bed*).

The bed in the center speaks of thoughts or the flesh running the home, and the table in the corner says that their communion with you is not central or on the same wavelength (see *Table*). It also says that Christ is not truly central in this home. This is perhaps reinforced by them decorating, which may say that they are into superficial things.

The marks on the sheets speak of wrong thoughts toward the revealing of the promise (see *Sheet*). When your friends say something that showed they weren't at your faith level, you closed in to protect the promise. Pulling the quilt around the baby says you chose to protect the promise.

71. Tracksuit Pants

White, Stripe, Tracksuit Pants

I was wearing a white pair of tracksuit pants with a red stripe down the side.

Interpretation:

This suggests that you have come into a righteous walk because you have been purified by Christ's blood (see *Legs*, *White*, and *Stripes*). It also speaks of strength, grace, and boldness in your walk of faith.

72. Spiders Crawled Behind the Desk Dream

Desk, Spiders

I went into a room with someone to do some work at a desk. As we approached the desk, black spiders of various sizes went scurrying for cover behind the desk. I thought first to spray them with insect killer spray, but then realized if I did that they would crawl back out again and that would present a greater threat than if I left them alone until I was leaving the room. When I left, I could leave a spider bomb (a can of insect killer that empties itself, killing all the spiders over a period of an hour or two).

Interpretation:

This dream speaks of a desire not to confront issues (the spiders) with a student (suggested by the desk) because of the threat that it would raise (see *Spider* and *Desk*). It also says that you would prefer to leave the need to deal with threatening issues till later.

This dream is a correction for you not to hesitate about dealing with issues. You are going to have to confront issues as they come up in the future.

73. Playing Lead Guitar With Brian Dream

Guitar, Brian, Angel

I was playing lead guitar with a competent guitarist named Brian. I was playing way beyond my own ability and at the same time singing the song, "Heaven must be missing an angel."

Interpretation:

Brian means "hill" or "strength" and is a picture of the Holy Spirit because He is the source of our strength (see Eph. 3:16) (see *Brian* in Name and Place Dictionary).

As angels worship in the Presence of God, and you were playing guitar singing about angels on earth, the dream is suggestive that you will lead people into true worship (see *Angel*).

74. Tire Tracks on a Wet Field Vision

Water, Automobile, Field, Tire Tracks, Color

I saw four sets of different colored tire tracks in a wet field.

Interpretation:

This is a retake of the parable of the sower and the seed (see Matt. 13:3-9, 18-23). The wet field is a picture of the Word of God being preached (see *Water*) in the world (see *Field*).

The different color tire tracks represent the individual responses to that Word (see *Automobile*). This is a reminder that not everyone will respond the same way. There will be heart issues that stop the Word from truly being rooted in a person's heart, and there likewise will be people who are distracted by the cares of the world. These issues will stop the Word of God from having full impact in the life of the individuals to whom you are ministering.

Your job is to preach the Word, and the hearers will choose their own paths and thus declare in their actions whether they are true or false believers.

75. Last Person on a Bus

Bus, Country Town, Related

I was on a bus to a country town. While travelling, I related with and was friendly to people on the bus. Everyone got off the bus progressively until I was the last person on the bus. I had the understanding that those who were getting off were catching connecting buses to other destinations.

Interpretation:

The country-bound bus is a country church you are currently attending (see *Bus*). In this dream, God is preparing you for His timing in coming to where He wants you. He is directing you not to look at others because what He has for them is different than what He has for you. It appears you will be in the place where you may become frustrated or anxious when it appears others are being fulfilled and you are not. That is because God has a special assignment for you.

I would recommend that you meditate on Christ's 30 years of preparation, John the Baptist's years in the desert, and Joseph's confinement in Egypt. The degree to which God wants to use you is displayed proportionally in the number of years of preparation you have to undergo to get there (see Isa. 49:2).

76. Preaching Platform in Car Park Vision

Car Park, Platform

I saw a preaching platform with a handrail on the up-ramp to a several story car park.

Interpretation:

This vision says that you will have an invitation to preach in churches that are filled with people who are going nowhere spiritually (see *Platform* and *Car Park*). Parked ministries have no destiny in God.

77. Baldness Dream

Baldness

I was looking at my head and face from the front and saw that I had lost a lot more hair than I had previously noticed. There was hardly any hair on the top of my head, and I had this mane along my back neckline. I was initially surprised and yet settled that this was how things were.

Interpretation:

I believe this a sign of the humbling of God and the cutting away of the flesh that you are currently undergoing (see *Baldness*).

78. Trucks Over the Railway Tracks Dream

Train Tracks, Truck, Earthmover

I saw several train tracks—perhaps a dozen—as you would see in a rail yard, and there were trucks and earthmovers driving over the tracks, damaging the tracks.

Interpretation:

What you are seeing is leadership being insensitive to the plans and purposes of God (see *Truck* and *Railway Tracks*). It appears those in leadership (in this situation, the husband of the dreamer) are working at cross-purposes to the things of God. Earthmoving signifies working in the flesh.

79. New Cell Phone Dream

Dad, Three, Cell Phone, Code, Sim Card, Collingwood, MP3 Tunes, Recharge

My dad and I went to a mobile phone shop. They polished and fixed my scratched cell phone. I received a code and a new sim card for the phone. They also gave me a Collingwood (Australian football team, they are black and white and also known as the Magpies) phone cover. They copied dad's MP3 tunes and also gave me several games and a $30 recharge. (A 9-year-old boy had this dream.)

Interpretation:

Dad represents God (see *Father*). The three phone shop signifies fullness of communication with God (see *Three* and *Telephone*). Fixing or repairing a scratched cell phone refers to renewing one's spirit or correcting your prayer life. This is reinforced by the issuing of a new sim card, which is the heart of the phone (see *Sim Card*) with the ability of praying in the Holy Spirit. Praying in the Spirit is a direct line to the Father. The code refers to unlocking mysteries through praying in the Spirit (see *Code*).

The Collingwood phone cover is reference to being clothed as a hero. The tunes are worship songs from the heart of God, and the games are the gifts of the Spirit. The $30 recharge is showing this will happen at the right time (see *Thirty*). God is reassuring the parent that there will be a point of time when the son will be baptized in the Spirit and used of God.

80. Eaten by the Devil Dream

Eating, Devil

In my dream, I was eaten by the devil

Interpretation:

The teenage girl who had this dream was about to have her weekend off after four months at a live-in Christian rehabilitation program, traveling 500 kilometers to stay with her parents.

The interpretation of this dream is best seen in the following Scripture,

> *Be sober, be vigilant; because your adversary the devil walks about like a roaring lion, seeking whom he may devour* (1 Peter 5:8).

This Scripture depicts the devil as a lion roaring causing the fearful to run so that he may devour them. If you read the context of this Scripture (see 1 Pet. 5:5-9), you discover that this advice is given in reference to young-old relationships. Therefore, the dream is a warning from God that the devil is going to threaten and try to provoke you, the teenager, in an attempt to get you to go into the flesh at home with your parents when you are on leave from the rehab program. There is probably an existing rift in the parent-child relationship that the devil is going to play on.

The solution in this situation is to maintain humility, which is also provided in these Scriptures (see 1 Pet. 5:5). Remember that we do not battle against flesh and blood (see Eph. 6:12). The devil always tries to get us to go into the flesh by reacting when provoked. It is important to understand that love and humility are the solid foundations for conducting spiritual warfare. By staying in the Spirit, clothed in the armor of God (see Eph. 6:11-18), a person resists the devil and he will flee.

81. Shooting at Clock Dream

Shooting, Clock, Shane, House, Bullets, Paneled Wall, Evidence, Closing Blind, Kissing

Someone was shooting at a clock. Shane and I were inside the house. The bullets were hitting the wood-paneled wall. We were trying to work out why he was shooting at the clock. It came to us that it was because the clock contained evidence. We pulled the blind down so that whoever it was doing the shooting was not able to destroy it. I kissed Shane.

Interpretation:

This dream is a warning about a spiritual attack. Shooting at the clock represents trying to end a person's life by stopping time with damaging words (see *Shooting* and *Clock*). Bullets hitting the paneled wall say that the enemy is taking shots at your health (see *Wall*). Trying to work out why the clock is being shot at speaks of waking up to this spiritual attack of the enemy. The evidence is the testimony you are carrying (see *Evidence*).

Shane is representative of the Grace of God (see *Shane* in Name and Place Dictionary). Pulling the blind down with Shane speaks of God's grace protecting you in this attack (see Ps. 84:11). Ordinarily, pulling blinds down could represent death. However, because pulling the blind down means guarding your heart, which stops the clock's destruction, and this is followed by you embracing God's grace (kissing Shane), it appears that there is a new level and balance attained in your relationship with God (see Ps. 85:10).

82. Jets and Pilots Scrambling Dream

Jet Pilots, Aircraft

I saw military aircrews scrambling (pilots running in combat conditions) to get to their aircraft. This was followed by scenes of a sky full of planes dogfighting with freeze-frames of two individual aircraft. It was action-packed, similar to recruitment advertising.

Interpretation:

I believe this dream in its context is a warning of spiritual warfare taking place in your life. It is a call to prayer and intercession.

83. Seduced by a Female in Black Dream

Seduced, Kiss, Spitting, Black

In my dream, a female dressed in black seduced and kissed me; then I spat it out.

Interpretation:

This is a warning dream. The woman in black is a spirit of death (see *Woman*). Being kissed says that you have embraced a lie from the enemy (see

Kiss). Spitting it out says that you recognize the lie and reject it (see *Spit/ting*). This dream was one of a series (also see Dreams 81, 82, and 84). Therefore, in its context, it suggests that the lie relates to a health issue (death), and the person concerned was encouraged to stand by faith against the enemy's lies.

84. Crooks Caught Moving Goods Dream

Gang, Crooks, Gun, Pistol, Telescope, Police, Jenny, Blanket, Chocolate

A gang of crooks were moving goods at my home. We caught them and grabbed their gun, which the leader was holding. The leader went into another room to get another gun. I caught him putting it together and disarmed him. Both guns were pistols, though quite unusual was the fact that both had telescopic sights.

We were holding the leader of the gang until the police came. I went outside with Jenny and a car pulled up across from our house. It was invisible and the people in it were invisible also, though I could see the car's and the occupants' outline somehow.

We had the gang leader under a blanket on the floor. He was eating some form of chocolate-coated sweets that were scattered on the floor.

Interpretation:

This is an insightful warning. The gang of crooks are evil spirits and their leader a principality or power (see *Gang*). The gun speaks of the enemy using words against you (see *Gun*). The leader going into another room speaks about a two-fold attack (two incidents or two areas of attack) (see *Rooms*). The fact that the pistols had telescopic sights suggests that the attack is close range (see *Pistol*) and at the same time spiritual (from the second heaven—the spiritual realm) (see *Telescope*).

The police speak of angels (see *Police*). Also see Daniel 10:13. Going outside with Jenny talks about the Holy Spirit (see *Jenny* in Name and Place Dictionary) opening your spiritual eyes (see 2 Kings 6:17).

Having the gang leader under a blanket says that you have the principality under the authority of God's Word. The chocolate represents the Word of God (see *Chocolate*).

85. Long-legged Spider on Back Dream

Spider, Long-legged, Back, Wife

I had a long-legged spider on my back. My wife had to knock it off.

Interpretation:

A spider is an issue or stronghold in your life. This one is long-legged, which means that it is long-standing (i.e. you have had it for a while) (see *Spider*). This is reinforced by the fact that it is on your back, which means it comes from your past and is steering your life (see *Back*).

Your wife having to knock it off suggests that the Body of Christ will be used to deal with a long-standing issue in your life (see *Wife*). I believe this is most likely spiritual pride, which could also be suggested by the long-legs.

86. Firing an Arrow Into a Flock of Sheep Dream

Neighbor, Cliff, Arrow, Sheep, Evidence

I was on a cliff overlooking my neighbor's flock of sheep standing in water below. I fired an arrow at the flock of sheep. The arrow scared the ones close to it as it skimmed across the water, but it really didn't make the distance. I was concerned that my arrow was floating in the water as evidence.

Interpretation:

This is a warning against saying something wrong about another church (see *Neighbor*). Your neighbor's flock of sheep is another church (see *Sheep*). Overlooking speaks of having prophetic insight (see *Cliff*). Firing the arrow suggests that you are in danger of saying something against another church (see *Arrow*). Though what you said doesn't carry too far, you are concerned about reprisal for your lack of wisdom in speaking as you did (see *Evidence*).

87. Snake Dream

Bed, Snake, Leaves, Holes

My husband and I were fast asleep, and in my dream we were sleeping on soft leaves that are neatly matted together—it looked like it was comfortable to sleep on. Then all of a sudden, I was woken up. I felt something slithering in between us. I knew straight away that it was a snake, so I thought to myself not to move or else I will get bitten.

My husband was fast asleep, not knowing what was going on. I couldn't really wake him up, and I was very cautious not to move. As I was lying and watching the snake slithering in between us, I saw the tail curl with a hissing sound. Just after the snake had gone past, I felt another one crawling under the matted leaves where we were lying. This one was a lot bigger than the other one—about four or five times bigger.

As the snake was crawling underneath, I could feel it under my ribs, and it felt a bit ticklish, so I tried to control myself not to move. The next morning I saw the trail and the holes (like a tube) underneath the matted leaves where the snake had gone through, and I was showing the trails to someone and asking for wisdom or maybe interpretation of what happened that night.

Interpretation:

A bed is symbolic of your agreement, alignment, or unity (see Isa. 57:8). The bed of leaves represents the righteous life of your marriage (ordained by God) and the positive words you have built your relationship on (as in leaves of a book, see Jer. 36:23). However, the snake represents poisonous words that have been spoken recently between you which act as a trouble-maker. The fact that it crawls between you is indicating a desire to divide you through misunderstanding. Not moving refers to not responding to the poisonous words.

The larger snake is the devil, who is lurking in the background testing your relationship looking for ground on which to get in (see Eph. 4:25-27). I believe the ribs refer to your heart and the tickling is trying to woo you and find entry. This reminds us of the garden where the devil got in through the woman who was created from Adam's rib. Not moving displays the faithfulness of your heart. Beware of a lying spirit at work in the background of your thoughts.

I think the trail is evidence that the enemy has been at work, and the holes represent the devil trying to undermine your unity. A request for wisdom is a request for *how to* deal with this issue, and interpretation is a request for *understanding* of what is going on.

I think the dream is God's warning to you both of what is going on. The way to deal with this is always to be undergirded by humility and love. As well as repentance for what has been said, you both need to seek the Holy Spirit for wisdom on how to address this issue. The big snake in the background is a real warning to take seriously a threat to your marriage.

88. Wearing Shoes in Bed Vision

Shoes, Bed

I was wearing shoes in bed.

Interpretation:

This signifies that you are being lazy with the Gospel (see *Bed* and *Shoe*).

89. Reinhard Bonnke in Hotel Dream

Famous Person, Hotel, Woman

I saw Reinhard Bonnke in a hotel with lots of people. He was restricted in preaching by a woman wearing a red corporate suit (uniform). She escorted him when he went into the different areas of the hotel, restricting him and his ability to speak freely to the unsaved. The woman was employed by the hotel chain.

Interpretation:

Reinhard Bonnke represents the evangelist and his message of salvation (see *Famous Person*). The woman is the corporate Church (see *Woman*). The hotel chain represents the church denominations at rest (see *Hotel*). The business-like nature of the church is stopping the flow of the Spirit of God and His ability to reach the unsaved.

90. Termites in the Water Meter Dream

Termites, Water Meter

There were termites in the water meter.

Interpretation:

This dream, which is apparently nonsense, actually refers to something destructive robbing a person of the anointing. The water meter symbolizes measuring the anointing (see *Water Meter*). The termites represent people undermining you because of the effectiveness of the anointing (see *Termites*).

91. Kicking a Ball Into the Queen Dream

Ball, Kicking ball, Left, Right, Group, Queen, Shoulder

I kicked a football with my left foot into a group of people, intending to pass it to a person on the right of the group. However, it hit the queen in the back shoulder blade. Someone said, "What a shot!" (I recently was kicking a football around with some friends and did use my left foot when I was playing more casually).

Interpretation:

Kicking a football speaks of speaking or releasing words with power (see *Ball* [*Kicking Ball*] and *Legs*). Passing the ball to the person on the right of the group speaks of wanting to pass on revelation to those who are really living for God with all their hearts (see *Right*). The group speaks of the Body of Christ.

Your casual kick is saying that though you innocently pass the Word on, it becomes a burden for the religious church (see *Queen* and *Shoulder*). This is because it will expose both their religiosity and the superficial nature of their belief. Someone saying "What a shot!" says that a more deliberately planned scheme to expose the false church could not have been developed. It also says that what you are saying is from the Spirit of God for this particular purpose.

92. Stepping in Dog Poop Dream

Dog Poop, Odor

My children were telling me, "Dad, you've stepped in it!" referring to dog poop.

Interpretation:

This is a reference to offending your children. As the offense is depicted as odorous, it suggests that you have addressed something in their lives in the wrong spirit (see *Odor* and *Dog Poop*).

93. Alternative Therapist Dream

Queue, Alternative Therapist, Fat

I was in a queue to see an alternative therapist. I was conscious that I did not need to be there. I looked up at the list of services provided by the therapist and the only one I could identify as being of any benefit to me was, 'Calculating your fat index'.

Interpretation:

Being in a queue says that you are waiting for ministry (see *Queue*). The alternative therapist says that while you are waiting, you find yourself attending an unconventional (not usual) medical practitioner. This equates to going to a "faith" church (see *Alternative Therapist*). "Calculating your fat index" is reference to recognizing the measure of the anointing you currently carry and adjusting your spiritual diet to increase it (See [+] entry under *Fat*).

94. Purchasing Chairs Dream

Buying, Outside/Outdoors, Chairs, Table

We were one of two couples who bought a pair of outside chairs with a table between them.

Interpretation:

Buying an outside chair says that you are laying your life down for an independent work which carries authority (See *Buying, Outside/Outdoor,* and *Sit/ting*). The table says that this is God's provision for you (see *Table*). As you are one of two couples, it appears that you share the work with another couple.

95. Sister Taking Dad's Shoes Dream

Sister, Dad, Shoes

I saw my older sister picking up my dad's shoes. I said, "Put them back; don't take dad's shoes!" My sister ran off with the shoes.

Interpretation:

In its context, this dream says that dad has lost his peace because of a breakdown in the relationship between himself and his teenage daughter through rebellion (see *Shoes*). There is also a warning of jeopardizing dad's future ministry (see 1 Tim. 3:4).

96. Face Cut Vision

Face, Cut, Light, Laser, Machine gun

I saw a face being cut on the cheeks. It could have been torture. Then light broke through a crack in the head. It became a laser machine gun.

Interpretation:

The face being cut speaks of cutting away the flesh from the heart (see *Cut* and *Face*). This leads to the heart being a true vessel for the glory of God, which becomes a powerful and focused force (through words) for God (see *Light* and *Machine Gun*). See Judges 6:16 (note "as one man"); 7:16-21.

97. Rocket Firing in the Distance Dream

Horizon, Water, Rocket, Sky

I was sitting on a bank with a group of people when I saw what looked like a rocket being launched on the horizon from Iraq. It looked like a firework—the trail—going into the sky. The rocket split into two missiles. One of the missiles came down, just missing me and the group of people I was with. It went over a body of water, causing a bow wave as the water was sucked up in the wake. It hit an embankment and failed to detonate or explode.

Interpretation:

This dream is a warning of spiritual warfare ahead. It appears you have been targeted by the enemy. The rocket is that attack being launched, and it is on the horizon because it is in the foreseeable future (see *Horizon*). The rocket is launched from Iraq, which depicts the enemy. It appears that you are not the only target of the enemy because the rocket has two warheads. The body of water speaks about your heart (see *Deep*). Though it initially moves your heart—the bow wave—it fails to detonate, which means it doesn't have lasting impact. The water is also representing the Holy Spirit, and it appears that He has deflected the attack and protected you.

98. Wife With Tattoos on Her Body Dream

Wife, Tattoos, Body, Lake, Daughter, Truck, Water

My wife had tattoos all over her body. She unashamedly took her clothes off and was next to a lake about to go in. It surprised me. One of the tattoos was like a chessboard. The tattoos in some way represented the teachings of her father. My daughter was also there. I said, "Be careful" and stepped between my wife and a truck (which had two workmen in it) that pulled up in the next field. My wife didn't care. There were things stored in and around the lake. I saw a stack of face towels under the water.

Interpretation:

Your wife represents the Church (see *Wife*). The tattoos symbolize the teachings of God (her Father). Your daughter being present says that this is a future event (see *Daughter*).

When you step between your wife and a truck with workmen in it, you are moving to protect the Church from big ministries, or leadership, that are in the flesh (see *Truck*). Your wife entering the lake speaks of the Church being cleaned up. This is reinforced by the face towels under the water (see *Water*).

99. Stretching Legs Dream

Legs, Stretching

I saw myself stretching my legs and exercising.

Interpretation:

This dream speaks of preparation and strengthening prior to the ministry that God has for you (see *Legs* and *Stretching*). I foresee the need for more time praying in the Spirit (see Jude 20).

100. Rebuilding a Light-Fitting Dream

Light-Fitting, Tank, Enemy, River, Supervisor, Rendezvous

I was rebuilding a light fitting for a tank (army), which was floating on a pontoon in readiness for a landing. An enemy soldier kicked the fitting into the river. I reported the incident to my supervisor. We were getting ready, counting down time to be ready to go to a rendezvous.

Interpretation:

Rebuilding a light-fitting speaks about preparing your heart as the place where the light or glory of God is to reside (see *Light-Fitting*).

The fact that the light is part of a tank says that your ministry will be powerful and impacting (see *Tank [Army]*). The enemy is a spiritual foe, and his opposition to slow you down actually causes your heart to be immersed in the Spirit (see *River*). Your supervisor is the Holy Spirit (see *Supervisor*).

The landing and rendezvous is a preplanned mission that God has for you, which you will be released into in His perfect timing (see *Rendezvous*).

101. A Dam Full of Snakes Dream

Dam, Snakes, Farm

I was walking along the bank of a dam on a farm where I grew up. And I saw the dam was full of snakes.

Interpretation:

The farm is representative of the harvest field (see *Farm*). Seeing a dam full of snakes is prophetically seeing a place where there was once the Holy Spirit (water), but which now has been replaced with sin and hypocrisy (see *Water* and *Snake*).

The Metaphor Dictionary

Dictionary Preface

It is important to read chapters 1-10 before attempting to use the dictionary. The dictionary contains possible interpretations for individual dream and vision elements. It includes material that we have found relevant to dreams interpreted up until the time of printing. The work is ever expanding, and as such, there will be interpretations for dream and vision elements beyond that of the material presented here. Therefore, the dictionary is set forth only as a guide to be confirmed by the witness of the Holy Spirit.

The authors take no responsibility for inappropriate actions taken based on this material.

Bible Book Abbreviations

Gen. = Genesis	Isa. = Isaiah	Rom. = Romans
Exod.= Exodus	Jer. = Jeremiah	1 Cor. = 1 Corinthians
Lev. = Leviticus	Lam. = Lamentations	2 Cor. = 2 Corinthians
Num. = Numbers	Ezek. = Ezekiel	Gal. = Galatians
Deut. = Deuteronomy	Dan. = Daniel	Eph. = Ephesians
Josh. = Joshua	Hos. = Hosea	Phil. = Philippians
Judg. = Judges	Joel	Col. = Colossians
Ruth	Amos	1 Thess. = 1 Thessalonians
1 Sam. = 1 Samuel	Obad. = Obadiah	2 Thess. = 2 Thessalonians
2 Sam. = 2 Samuel	Jon. = Jonah	1 Tim. = 1 Timothy
1 Kings	Mic. = Micah	2 Tim. = 2 Timothy
2 Kings	Nah. = Nahum	Tit. = Titus
1 Chron. = 1 Chronicles	Hab. = Habakkuk	Philem. = Philemon
2 Chron. = 2 Chronicles	Zeph. = Zephaniah	Heb. = Hebrews
Ezra	Hag. = Haggai	James
Neh. = Nehemiah	Zech. = Zechariah	1 Pet. = 1 Peter
Esther	Mal. = Malachi	2 Pet. = 2 Peter
Job	Matt. = Matthew	1 John
Ps. = Psalms	Mark	2 John
Prov. = Proverbs	Luke	3 John
Eccl. = Ecclesiastes	John	Jude
Song. = Song of Solomon	Acts	Rev. = Revelation

Understanding the Dictionary

Element (a dream is made up of several elements)

Curtains: (1) The fleshly veil; (2) The heart (beyond a curtain); (3) Heaven; (4) Cover; (5) Ending (closing curtain); (6) Death.
Also see entries under Veil.
(1) Heb. 10:20; (2) 2 Cor. 3:15; (3) Ps. 104:2; Isa. 40:22; (6) As in, 'its curtains!'

- The numbered interpretations (1), (2), (3), etc. are assembled in order of greatest to least likelihood of suitability.
- The brackets after an interpretation further refine the use of the element in it's context or help convey meaning.
- Cross-references to similar dictionary entries that may provide further interpretive options.

Life Raft: (1) Needing salvation; (2) Lost; (3) In danger of losing salvation; (4) Ark (Christ).
Also see entries under Adrift, Boat and Sea.
(1-2) Matt. 18:11; (2) Lk. 15:3-32; (3) Lk. 9:25; Acts 27:30-31; (4) Gen. 6:13-16; Matt. 24:37-39; (cf. Lk. 17:26ff.) Heb. 11:7.

- Underlined scriptures generally display the key meaning of an element.
- cf. means to compare the scriptures quoted.
- ff. means to look at this verse and the following verses.

Mouse/Mice: (1) Hidden unclean spirit; (2) Indicator of a spiritual maintenance; (3) Unbeliever (unclean); (4) Small: (5) Plague; (6) Judgment.
Also see entries under Rat.
(1) Matt. 10:1; (cf. Rev. 16:13); (2) Lk. 11:24-25; (3-4) Lev. 11:29; (5-6) (cf. 1 Sam. 5:12 & 1 Sam. 6:5(KJV)).

'&' means to combine the scriptures to gain the interpretation.

Aardvark: (1) Ant-eater (destroyer of the diligent); (2) Nosey.

(1) Prov. 6:6-8; (2) As a physical attribute.

Abominable Snow Man: (1) Abuse (horrible cold-hearted person).

Also see *Bigfoot.*

(1) Exod. 1:22; 7:14.

Aboriginal/s: See *Black Man, First Nations Peoples, Foreigner,* and *Native/s.*

Abortion: (1) Warning of an attempt to kill the promise (Herod spirit); (2) Actual abortion.

Also see *Birth* and *Child.*

(1) Exod. 1:16; Matt. 2:16; Rev. 12:4.

Above and Below: (1) Heaven and earth; (2) Spiritual and earthly (worldly); (3) Heaven and hell; (4) Head and feet; (5) Head and tail; (6) Heaven and the Deep; (7) Victorious and defeated.

Also see *Under* and *Underwater.*

(1-2) Exod. 20:4; Deut. 4:39; 5:8; 28:23; Josh. 2:11; John 8:23; Acts 2:19; (3) Job 11:8; Ps. 139:8; Amos 9:2; Matt. 11:23; (4) Eph. 1:22; (5) Deut. 28:13; (6) Gen. 49:25; (7) Deut. 28:13.

Accelerator Pedal: (1) Need to get in the Spirit (be quickened); (2) Need to speed up; (3) Go for it!

(1) John 6:63; Rom. 8:11; 1 Cor. 15:45; (2) 1 Sam. 20:38; 2 Sam. 15:14; (3) Rev. 3:8.

Acid: (1) Cutting or corrosive words; (2) Bitter; (3) Revenge (as in carrying an offense).

(1) Ps. 64:3; Prov. 25:18; (2-3) Acts 8:23; Heb. 12:15.

Acorn: See Seed.

Actions: See Individual Movement and Directions.

Adder: See Snake.

Adding: (1) Spiritual growth; (2) Salvations.

(1) 2 Pet. 1:5; (2) Gen. 50:20 (Joseph's name means "adding").

Adorn: See Wearing.

Adrift: (1) Aimless; (2) Without direction; (3) Doubting; (4) Needing power; (5) Driven by circumstance/troubles.

Also see *Boat, Life Raft, Sea,* and *Ship.*

(1) Prov. 29:18; 2 Pet. 2:17; Jude 1:12-13; (2) Isa. 2:3; Mark 6:34; (3) James 1:6; (4) Acts 1:4, 8; (5) Acts 27:15.

Adultery: (1) Intimately sharing your heart with another who is not your spouse; (2) Worldliness; (3) Spiritual adultery (worship of other gods); (4) Lacking judgment; (5) Snare or trap; (6) Literal adultery; (7) Lust issue; (8) Heart stronghold; (9) Work of the flesh.

Also see *Fornication* and *Sex.*

(1) Prov. 6:32; <u>Matt. 5:28</u>; (2) <u>James 4:4</u>; (3) Jer. 3:8-9, 7:9; Ezek. 16:31-32; Hos. 4:13; Rev. 2:22; (4) Prov. 6:32; (5) Prov. 7:23; (6) Exod. 20:14; Jer. 29:23; (7) Matt. 5:28; (8) Matt. 15:19; 2 Pet. 2:14; (9) Gal. 5:19.

Adversary/ies: (1) devil; (2) Human opposition; (3) demon spirits; (4) Religious leaders; (5) Self (the flesh); (6) the world.

(1) <u>1 Pet. 5:8</u>; (2) Matt. 5:25; Luke 12:58; 18:3; 21:15-16; Phil. 1:28; (3) <u>1 Cor. 16:9</u>; (4) Luke 13:14-17; (5) Acts 18:6 (KJV); 2 Tim. 2:25-26 (KJV); (6) John 16:33; 2 Pet. 2:20; 1 John 5:4-5.

Adversity: (1) Test/trial; (2) Tribulation; (3) Trouble; (4) Suffering.

(1) Prov. 17:17; (2) 1 Sam. 10:19; 2 Chron. 15:6; Ps. 10:6; (3) Ps. 31:7; <u>Prov. 24:10</u>; (4) <u>Heb. 13:3</u>.

Advisor: (1) The Holy Spirit.

(1) John 14:26.

Advocate: (1) Holy Spirit; (2) One who comes alongside; (3) Jesus Christ; (4) Someone who speaks for another/representation; (5) A positive witness.

(1-2) "Helper" <u>John 14:16</u>; (3-4) Heb. 7:25, 9:24; 1 John 2:1.

Aeroplane: (1) New heights; (2) Spiritual ministry or church; (3) High profile ministry (or high flyer); (4) Freedom in the Spirit; (5) Human-made imitation of the spiritual/spiritual things/church; (6) Travel; (7) Human-made structure.

(1) Isa. 40:31; (2) Isa. 60:8-9; <u>Ezek.</u> 3:14; <u>8:3</u>; 11:1, 24; <u>Acts 8:39</u>; (3) Gal. 2:9; (4) Ps. 51:12; Rom. 8:2; 1 Cor. 2:12; 2 Cor. 3:17; (5) Eph. 6:12b & Mark 8:33; (6) Acts 8:39-40; (7) Mark 14:58.

Aeroplane Landing: (1) Descending spiritually; (2) From Heaven; (3) Coming to town.

(1) 2 Sam. 1:4, 19; Rom. 11:12; (2) Isa. 14:12; (3) Luke 8:1; 10:38.

Aeroplane (Large Passenger Plane): (1) Church; (2) Big ministry.

(1-2) Ezek. 11:1 & Acts 11:26.

Aeroplane (Fighter Plane): (1) Spiritual warfare; (2) Evangelist; (3) Evangelistic ministry; (4) Literal war plane.

(1) Isa. 31:5; (2-3) Acts 8:5-6, 12, 39; (4) Hab. 1:8.

Aeroplane (Freight Plane): See Freight.

Affair: (1) Person or church seduced by the world; (1) Sharing your spouse with work, church, or a hobby.

Also see *Adultery.*

(1) Hos. 2:5; (2) 1 Pet. 2:14-15.

African: See Black Man and First Nations Peoples.

After (Behind): (1) Past; (2) Following; (3) Later; (4) Seeking after.

Also see *Back, Backward,* and *Behind.*

(1) Phil. 3:13; (2) Matt. 10:38; 16:24; (3) John 13:36; (4) Rom. 9:31; 1 Cor. 14:1.

Age: (1) Literal years; (2) Generational association; (3) Age may also indicate a characteristic portrayed by the number of years (i.e. 15 may portray innocence; 18 may mean complete putting off of the old self; 92 may mean judgment and separation); (4) A woman's age could be the age of a person or church.

Also see *Baby, Grey, Individual Numbers, Old, Young,* and *Youth.*

(2) 1 John 2:12-14.

Ahead: See Before.

Air-conditioner: (1) Holy Spirit; (2) Full Gospel ministry.

(1) Acts 2:2, 4a; (2) John 3:8.

Faulty air-conditioner: (1) Hindering the Holy Spirit.

(1) John 3:8; Acts 7:51.

Air Force: (1) Ministering angel/s; (2) Spirit (good or evil); (3) Heaven.
(1-3) Rev. 8:13; 14:6; 19:17.

Air Force One: (1) Ministry with Christ on board.
(1) Matt. 28:18-20.

Air Freshener: (1) The anointing of the Holy Spirit.
(1) Isa. 61:1-3.

Air Mattress (Airbed): (1) Holy Spirit.
(1) John 3:5, 8; Rom. 8:16; 1 John 5:6b.

Airplane: See Aeroplane.

Airport: (1) Waiting for destiny or ministry; (2) Transfer of ministries; (3) Spiritual grounding; (4) Spiritual refueling; (5) Waiting on the Holy Spirit.
Also see *Railway Station.*
(1) Isa. 40:31; Luke 2:25; (2) Acts 15:35-37, 40; (3) Acts 2:42; 2 Tim. 3:16-17;
(4) Acts 4:31; 6:3; 7:55; 11:24; 13:2-3, 9; (5) Acts 2:1.

Alarm: (1) Warning; (2) Warning of spiritual attack (smoke alarm); (3) Warning of judgment (fire alarm); (4) Conscience.
Also see *Fire, Smoke,* and *Trumpet.*
(1) Amos 3:6; (2) Rev. 9:2-3; (3) Ezek. 16:41; 2 Pet. 3:7; (4) Rom. 2:15; 13:4-5.

Alcohol: (1) False anointing; (2) Getting drunk on the spirit of the world; (3) Getting drunk with worldly power.
Also see *Drunk* and *Wine.*
(1) Eph. 5:18; (2) John 14:17; 1 Cor. 2:12; Eph. 2:2; 1 John 4:1; (3) Rev. 14:8; 18:3.

Aliens: (1) Unbelievers; (2) Fallen angels or familiar spirits; (3) Christians; (4) Angels or messengers from Heaven; (5) Outcast or scorned person; (6) Lying spirit (alien imitating a person); (7) Antichrist.
Also see *Foreigner* and *Stranger.*
(1) Eph. 2:12; 4:18; Heb. 11:34; (2) Gen. 6:2; Gal. 1:8; Heb. 11:34; (3) Heb. 11:13 (NIV); (4) Heb. 13:2; (5) Job 19:15; Ps. 69:8; (6) 1 Kings 22:22; (7) 1 John 4:1-3.

Alley: (1) Going through tough times; (2) Not on God's path or not yet on God's path; (3) Unprepared heart; (4) Sidelined; (5) Backslidden; (6) Low profile path; (7) Having something to hide; (8) Backstreet; (9) demonic path.

Also see *Back Door.*

(1) 1 Sam. 22:1; (2) Ps. 119:105; (3) Isa. 40:3; (4) Acts 15:37-38; (5) Prov. 14:14; (6) Luke 14:23; (7-8) Judg. 5:6; (9) Ps. 23:4.

Alligator: See Crocodile.

Allowance: (1) Deposit of faith.

(1) Luke 12:42; Rom. 12:3b; Eph. 2:8.

Almond: (1) Fruitfulness; (2) Chosen; (3) Watching (almond tree).

(1) Num. 17:8; (2) Num. 17:5; (3) Jer. 1:11-12.

Alms: (1) Good deeds; (2) Gifts God takes note of; (3) Gifts.

(1) Matt. 6:1; (2) Acts 10:4; (3) Acts 24:17.

Aloes: (1) Fragrance.

(1) Ps. 45:8; Song. 4:14.

Aloe Vera: (1) Healing; (2) Holy Spirit anointing (healing balm).

(1-2) Jer. 8:22; 51:8.

Alpha: (1) First; (2) Beginning; (3) Jesus Christ.

(1-3) Rev. 1:8, 11; 21:6; 22:13.

Altar: (1) Place of sacrifice and incense; (2) A place with God; (3) The human heart.

(1-2) Gen. 12:7; 2 Chron. 20:7b; (3) Jer. 17:1.

Altered: (1) Changed or exchanged; (2) Glorified.

Also see *Changed.*

(1) Lev. 27:10; Ezra 6:11; (2) Luke 9:29.

Alternative Therapist: (1) Faith ministry/church.

(1) Prov. 13:17b (NKJV); Matt. 9:22; Luke 17:19; Acts 14:9.

Aluminum: (1) Powerful Spirit-led ministry (quick and maneuverable); (2) Sensitive ministry/person.

(1) Rom. 8:14; (2) Acts 13:13.

Aluminum Foil: (1) Insulated.

Also see *Bake and Baker.*

(1) Prov. 1:30.

Ambassador: (1) A representative of God, satan, or a nation; (2) Peace-seeker; (3) Messenger; (4) Trouble or health; (5) Spy; (6) Deception.

(1) Ezek. 17:15; 2 Cor. 5:20; (2) Isa. 33:7; Luke 14:32; (3) Isa. 18:2; (4) Prov. 13:17; (5) 2 Chron. 32:31; (6) Josh. 9:4.

Amber: (1) Glory of God; (2) Caution; (3) Slow down or stop; (4) Fading glory.

Also see *Orange.*

(1) Ezek. 1:4; 8:2; (2-3) As with traffic lights; (4) 1 Sam. 4:21-22; Ezek. 10:4; (cf. Matt. 17:2).

Ambulance: (1) Warning of sickness; (2) Warning of serious accident; (3) Warning of death; (4) Someone who brings sinners to meet Christ; (5) Need of prayer help; (6) Emergency (ambulance with siren); (7) Urgency.

Also see *Paramedic.*

(1) Ezek. 33:5; Mark 6:55; (2) 1 Kings 22:34b; Ezek. 33:5; (3) 1 Kings 22:35; Ezek. 33:5; (4) Mark 2:4-5; (5) James 5:13-16; (6) Amos 3:6; (7) Exod. 12:33 (KJV).

Ambush: (1) Surprise demonic attack; (2) Going down wrong thought pathways can lead to the enemy ambushing your thought life.

Also see *Hijack.*

(1) Luke 10:30 & John 10:10; (2) John 13:27; 2 Cor. 10:3-5.

Amen: (1) Truly; (2) So be it; (3) Yes; (4) Conclusion.

(1) John 1:51; 3:3, 5, 11; (2-3) 1 Cor. 14:16; 2 Cor. 1:20; (4) Matt. 28:28; Mark 16:20.

America: (1) In the Spirit (eagle); (2) Babylon.

(1) Isa. 40:31; (2) Rev. 17:5.

Amethyst: This stone which is blue (heavenly) in color relates to the tribe of Issachar (partnership). Therefore this stone means: (1) Heavenly partnership; (2) Python or divination spirit.

Also see *Python* and *Precious Stones.*

(1) Exod. 28:19; 39:12; Rev. 21:20; (2) As in the "amethyst python."

Amphetamines: (1) Hype (false excitement); (2) Speed.

Also see *Drugs.*

(1) Rom. 10:2; (2) 2 Kings 9:20.

Amphibious Vehicle: (1) Evangelistic ministry; (2) Ministry in the Spirit.

Also see *Hovercraft* and *Sea.*

(1) Matt. 4:19; (2) Rom. 8:14; Rev. 1:10.

Amplifier: (1) *The Divinity Code to Understanding Your Dreams and Visions* (makes the message clearer); (2) Revelation (voice of God).

(1) Num. 12:6; Deut. 4:36; (2) Exod. 19:16; Rev. 10:3; 14:7.

Anaconda: See Python.

Anchor: (1) Jesus Christ; (2) Security; (3) Hope; (4) Brake; (5) Slow down.

(1-3) Heb. 6:19-20; (4) Acts 27:29; (5) As a "sea anchor" is used to slow a vessel.

Anchovy/ies: (1) School child/ren (small school fish); (2) Something that puts a bad taste in your mouth; (3) Someone who hasn't lost their saltiness.

(1) Matt. 4:19, 19:14; (2) 2 Kings 4:40-41; (3) Matt. 5:13.

Ancient: (1) Very old; (2) Lasting; (3) Forefather; (4) Long ago; (5) Wisdom.

Also see *Antique* and *Old.*

(1-2) Deut. 33:15; Judg. 5:21; Ps. 119:100; (3) 1 Sam. 24:13; Ezra 3:12; (4) 2 Kings 19:25; Ps. 77:5; (5) Job 12:12.

Angel/s: (1) Messenger of God; (2) Guardian; (3) Minister; (4) God's Presence; (5) God's servants; (6) Spirits (good); (7) Reapers; (8) Assistant; (9) Spiritual warriors; (10) Worshippers; (11) Familiar spirit (morphing angel); (12) Jesus (Angel of the Lord).

Also see *Feather/s* and *Wings.*

(1) Dan. 10:11, 14; Luke 2:19-20; (2) Ps. 91:11; Matt. 18:10; (3) Matt. 4:11; Luke 22:43; (4) Luke 9:26; 15:10; (5) Matt. 13:41; (6) Ps. 104:4; Matt. 25:41; Heb. 1:7, 14; Rev. 12:9; (7) Matt. 13:39; (8) Heb. 1:14; (9) Dan. 10:13; (10) Heb. 1:6; (11) 1 Sam. 28:7; (12) Exod. 3:2-5, 14.

Angels Ascending and Descending: (1) Portal/open Heaven; (2) Establishing the Kingdom on earth.

(1) Gen. 28:12; (2) Matt. 6:10.

Anger: (1) Literal anger; (2) Fear; (3) Frustration; (4) Insecurity; (5) Blocked goal; (6) Jealousy; (7) Grief; (8) Provocation.

(1) Matt. 5:22; (2) Ps. 20:2; (3) Luke 14:21; (4) 1 Sam. 18:8; (5) 1 Sam. 20:30; (6) Luke 15:28; Rom. 10:19; (7) Mark 3:5; (8) Col. 3:21.

Angler: See Fisherman.

Animals: As a very general rule, domestic animals may represent: (1) Christ; (2) Believers; (3) Israel.

Wild animals may represent: (4) Gentile nations; (5) Unbelievers; (6) People who return to the ways of the world; (7) Demon powers.

Also see entries under individual animal names.

(1) Lev. 4:3, 14, 23; (2) Isa. 53:6; (3-4) Jer. 50:17; (4-5) Dan. 7:3ff; 8:3, 20; (6) 2 Pet. 2:12-15; Jude 10-11; (7) Scripturally unclean animals may represent demonic powers.

Ankle: (1) Walk; (2) Support; (3) Base/foundation; (4) New standing; (5) Preaching the Gospel with strength; (6) Strained relationship (sprained ankle); (7) Ineffective preaching (sprained ankle); (8) Unfaithful person (sprained ankle); (9) Relationship; (10) Broken relationship (broken ankle).

(1) Ezek. 47:3; (2-4) Acts 3:7; (5) Ps. 147:10 & Rom. 10:15; 1 Cor. 4:20; (6) Eph. 4:16; (7) 1 Sam. 3:19; (8) Prov. 25:19; (9-10) Eph. 4:16.

Ankle-deep: (1) First-steps; (2) Shallow; (3) Uncommitted.

(1) Ezek. 47:3.

Anniversary: (1) Revival; (2) Revival of memories; (3) Memorial or reminder.

(1) Ps. 85:6; (2-3) Exod. 12:14; Lev. 23:24; Num. 10:10.

Anointing: (1) The Holy Spirit; (2) Consecration; (3) Spiritual Coronation; (4) Divine equipping; (5) Leadership.

Also see *Perfume* and *Spray.*

(1) Acts 10:38; (2) Exod. 28:41; 29:29; 30:30; (3) 1 Sam. 15:1 & (1 Sam. 10:1 & 11:15); (1 Sam. 16:13 & 2 Sam. 2); (4) Exod. 28:41; 2 Cor. 1:21; (5) 1 Sam. 10:1.

Anorexia: (1) Without spiritual revelation; (2) Depleted spiritually (no anointing/fat); (3) Lying spirit; (4) Selfish heart; (5) Possible sign of abuse (verbal, emotional, sexual); (6) Stress; (7) Actual anorexia.

(1-2) Prov. 28:25; Isa. 58:11; (3) 1 Kings 22:22; (4) Prov.11:25; 28:25; (5-6) Dan. 6:18.

Ant: (1) Diligence; (2) Wise one; (3) Small; (4) Insignificant.
Also see *Termites*.
(1) Prov. 6:6; (2-3) Prov. 30:24-25; (4) Prov. 30:25.

Antenna: (1) Spiritual sensitivity or senses; (2) Prophetic gifting.
(1) Matt. 11:15; (2) Jer. 29:19; Zech. 7:12.

Ant Hill: (1) Lowest mountain; (2) Works of the flesh.
(1) Isa. 40:4; (2) Gal. 5:19-21.

Antique: (1) Very old; (2) Valuable; (3) Collection; (4) Out of date; (5) Respect.
Also see *Ancient* and *Old*.
(1) Job 12:12; Ps. 77:5; (2) Matt. 13:52; (3) Luke 12:33; (4) 1 Sam. 2:22 &
4:18; (5) Job 32:6.

Antlers: See Horns.

Anus: (1) Seeing someone's anus may mean that you have been offended by
them; (2) Abomination.
(1) Gen. 20:9b; (2) Lev. 18:22; 1 Cor. 6:9; Rom. 1:27.

Ape: See Monkey.

Apostle: (1) Christ; (2) A "sent-out one"; (3) Church-planter; (4) Miracle-worker.
(1) Heb. 3:1; (2) From the Greek: *Apostolos* means "sent forth, one sent"; (3) 1 Cor.
9:1; (4) Acts 5:12; 2 Cor. 12:12.

Apple: (1) Love; (2) Temptation; (3) Fruit; (4) Health; (5) Precious (apple of the
eye); (6) Prized possession (apple of the eye); (7) New York.
(1) Ps. 17:8; Song. 2:5; Zech. 2:8; (2-3) Gen. 3:6 (loosely portrayed as an apple); (4) As in, "an apple a day keeps the doctor away"; (5) Deut. 32:10; Ps. 17:8;
Prov. 7:2; Lam. 2:18; (6) Zech 2:8; (7) Known as the "Big Apple."

Apple Tree: (1) Young man; (2) Lover; (3) Christ; (4) One who bears good or
bad fruit.
(1-3) Song. 2:3; (4) Matt. 7:17.

Apron: (1) Slave; (2) Serving; (3) Lay person.
(1-2) John 13:4; (3) Acts 6:1-7.

Aqua: As aqua is Latin for "water," see Water.

Archer: (1) Hateful person who uses piercing words; (2) User of hurtful words; (3) Wounder; (4) Man or woman of the flesh/world.

Also see *Arrows* and *Bow.*

(1-2) <u>Gen. 49:23</u>; (2) Ps. 64:3; (3) 1 Sam. 31:3; <u>2 Chron. 35:23</u>; Job 16:13; (4) Gen. 25:27 & 27:3.

Architect: (1) God.

Also see *Plan/s.*

(1) Ps. 127:1; 1 Cor. 3:9, 16.

Archway: (1) Godly opportunity; (2) Open Heaven.

Also see *Circle* and *Domed Roof.*

(1-2) Gen. 9:13.

Arena: See Spotlight and Stage.

Ark: (1) Christ; (2) Presence of God; (3) Throne; (4) Vessel of Salvation; (5) Mercy seat.

(1) Exod. 25:10; Josh. 3:13, 16; <u>Col. 2:9</u>; (2) <u>2 Sam. 6:11-12</u>; (3) Ps. 80:1; Rev. 11:19; (4) Gen. 6; (5) Heb. 9:4.

Arm: (1) Christ; (2) God; (3) Ministry assistant; (4) Church member; (5) Arms impaired indicates works affected; (6) Unable to assist (arms tied); (7) Strength or influence; (8) God's judgment (broken arm).

Also see *Left and Right, Limbs,* and *Legs.*

(1) <u>Isa. 40:10</u>; 59:16; 63:5; (2) Jer. 32:17-18; (3) As in, "my right hand man"; Matt. 5:30; (4) 1 Cor. 12:14-15; (5) Isa. 44:12a; (6) Dan. 6:14-16; as in, "my hands are tied"; (7-8) Ps. 18:34; <u>Ezek. 30:21</u>; Zech. 11:17.

Armchair: (1) God (as a place of rest); (2) You as God's resting place; (3) The throne of God; (4) Lazy know-all (armchair expert).

Also see *Chair* and *Sofa.*

(1) Deut. 12:9; 2 Chron. 14:11; Isa. 30:15; Heb. 4:10; (2) 2 Chron. 6:41; Acts 7:49; (3) 1 Kings 10:19; (4) Prov. 26:16.

Armor: (1) Christ; (2) Divine protection; (3) Natural reasoning (non-faith); (4) Protection; (5) Insurance; (6) Rejecting individual talents (forcing conformity); (7) Human intervention; (8) Arguments; (9) Right standing with God.

(1) <u>Rom. 13:12-14</u>; (2) Rom. 13:12; Eph 6:10-18; (3-6) 1 Sam. 17:38-39; (7) Isa. 22:8; (8) Luke 11:22; (9) <u>2 Cor. 6:7</u>.

Army: (1) Spiritual force; (2) God's people; (3) Spiritual warfare; (4) Those spiritually in step (who keep rank, same heart).

(1) 2 Kings 6:16-17; (1-3) Eph. 6:12; (4) 1 Chron. 12:33, 38; Joel 2:7.

Arriving: (1) Entering your destiny/Promised Land (arriving in vehicle).

(1) Josh. 1:11.

Arrow/s: (1) Piercing words; (2) False witness; (3) Evil words; (4) Children; (5) An individual as a ministry; (6) Conviction; (7) Judgment; (8) Adversity; (9) Deliverance; (10) Stay or depart; (11) Prophetic words (victory arrows); (12) On earth as in Heaven

Also see *Darts* and *Archer.*

(1) Ps. 38:2; 64:3; Prov. 25:18; (2) Prov. 25:18; Jer. 9:8; (3) Ps. 11:2; 91:5; (4) Ps. 127:4-5; (5) Isa. 49:2; (6) Job 6:4; (7) Deut. 32:23; Ps. 64:7; (8) Ezek. 5:16; Job 6:4; (9) 2 Kings 13:17; (10) 1 Sam. 20:20-22; (11-12) 2 Kings 13: 17-18; Matt. 6:10.

Art Class: (1) Prophetic school.

(1) 2 Kings 2:5; 6:1.

Art Gallery: (1) Prophetic conference; (2) Recognized prophetic ministry; (3) Recognized creative anointing; (4) Anointed to be creative.

(1) 2 Kings 2:3; (2) Gen. 37:3; 41:12; Dan. 5:11-12; (3) 1 Sam. 13:14 & 16:13; (4) Exod. 31:2-4.

Arthritis: (1) Sin; (2) Inflamed within; (3) Incapacitated; (4) Stiff/rigid/religious; (5) Bitterness/unforgiveness; (6) Bondage; (7) Need for the Word of God (medicine).

(1) Lev. 21:17-19 (NIV); (2) Eccl. 7:26; Jer. 4:18; James 3:14; (3) Eph. 4:16 (contrasted with); Col. 2:19; (5) Acts 8:23; (6) Matt. 22:13; John 11:44; Acts 21:11; (7) Heb. 4:12.

Artifacts (Ancient): (1) Foundational Bible truths; (2) Things that tell of ancient ways of life; (3) Made by skilled artificers (inventors).

(1-3) 2 Chron. 34:11-14 (craftsmen = artificers), note that when they set about faithfully (v. 12) rebuilding the temple, God gave them the spiritual flooring, pillars, and roofing (v. 14) to truly rebuild: the Word of God!

(Also see 2 Kings 22:8-11; 1 Chron. 29:5; Neh. 3:6 [Old Gate]).

Artist: (1) Creatively anointed; (2) Seer prophet (expressing what is seen in a vision or painting pictures with words).

(1) Exod. 31:3; 35:31; (2) Dan. 7:1; 8:26; <u>Matt. 17:9</u>.

Ascend/ing: (1) Rising spiritually; (2) Turning to God; (3) New position/authority; (4) Progress; (5) Rising with self-effort/religion; (6) Spiritual gift.

(1) <u>Gen. 12:10–13:1</u>; (2) Opposite of Jon. 1:3, 5; (3) Eph. 2:6; (4) <u>Ps. 24:3</u>; (5) Gen. 11:4; Gal. 1:13-14; (6) Eph. 4:8.

Ash/es: (1) Worthlessness; (2) Judgment; (3) Shame; (4) Repentance and sorrow; (5) Contrasted with prosperity; (6) Tread down.

(1) <u>Gen. 18:27</u>; (2) Exod. 9:8-9; 2 Pet. 2:6; (3) 2 Sam. 13:19; (4) Jon. 3:6-10; (5) Job 13:12; <u>Isa. 61:3</u>; (6) Mal. 4:3.

Ashtray: (1) Dealing with sorrow; (2) Disposing of oppression; (3) Odorous (bitter); (4) Spiritually devastated.

Also see *Smoking*.

(1) <u>Esther 4:1</u>; Isa. 61:3; Jer. 6:26; Ezek. 27:30; (2) Deut. 4:20 & 26:7-8; (3) Gen. 27:34 (burned by his brother); Exod. 1:14; 15:23-24 (murmuring); Dan. 3:27b; (4) Neh. 4:2b.

Asian: See Indigenous.

Asleep: See Sleeping.

Asp: See Snake.

Ass: See Donkey.

Assassin: (1) Spirit of death; (2) False witness (character assassin).

Also see *Contract Killer, Kill/ing, Mafia, Murder,* and *Sniper*.

(1) Ps. 10:8, 94:6 & John 10:10; (2) 1 Kings 21:10; Ps. 27:12; 35:11.

Assistant: (1) Ministering angel; (2) One's partner; (3) The Holy Spirit.

(1) <u>Heb. 1:14</u>; (2) Gen. 2:18, 20; (3) John 14:16-17.

Asthma: (1) Dying for want of the Spirit; (2) Dying spiritually; (3) Needing God.

(1) Job 33:4; Isa. 42:5; (3) <u>Ps. 104:29</u>; Isa. 42:5; (2) Job 15:30b.

Asteroid: (1) Message from Heaven; (2) Message of destruction/judgment; (3) Christ's return.

Also see *Meteor*.

(1) <u>Rev. 8:10a</u>, 9:1; (2-3) Matt. 24:29; Rev. 6:13.

Astray: (1) Sin; (2) Without God; (3) Lawless or unrighteousness; (4) Wrong teaching; (5) Off the path of life; (6) Lies; (7) Lost.

(1) Isa. 53:6; (2) Ps. 119:67; Jer. 50:6; Ezek. 14:11; (3) Ps. 119:176; Prov. 28:10; (4) Jer. 50:6; (5) Ps. 119:67; Prov. 5:21-23; (6) Ps. 58:3; (7) Ps. 119:176.

Astronaut: (1) Jesus; (2) Spiritual person raised up; (3) In the place of authority; (4) Abounding in spiritual blessings; (5) Enemy principalities or powers (foreign or threatening astronaut).

Also see *Space Suit.*

(1-4) Acts 1:11; Eph. 1:3, 20; 2:6; (5) Eph. 6:12b.

Atomic Bomb: (1) Power of the Spirit; (2) Consuming fire; (3) Outpouring; (4) The Day of the Lord/Judgment day; (5) Sudden destruction.

(1) Luke 3:16-17; Acts 4:31; (2) Lev. 9:24; Num. 16:35; Mic. 1:4; Heb. 12:29; (3) Rev. 14:10; 16:1-9; (4) Joel 2:30-31; Rev. 16:8; (5) Zech. 14:12; Jer. 4:20; 1 Thess. 5:3.

Atonement: (1) Covering; (2) Make peace; (3) To make "at-one."

(1) Gen. 6:14 (the word *pitch* means "atonement"); (2) Lev. 4:26, 31, 35; (3) As in, "At-one-ment."

Attic: (1) Head/mind; (2) Remembered (memories); (3) Heaven; (4) Place where old things are stored away.

(1) 2 Cor. 5:1 & Gen. 40:17, 19; (2) Acts 10:4; 2 Cor. 10:5; (3) Gen. 28:12; Matt. 6:20; (4) Matt. 6:20.

Audit: (1) Test; (2) Financial test; (3) Being examined; (4) Being assessed; (5) Weighed in the balance; (6) Judgment; (7) Need to put your affairs in order.

(1-2) Acts 5:8; (3) Luke 13:9; 1 Pet. 5:8; (4) Heb. 4:13; (5) Dan. 5:27; (6) Dan. 5:28; (7) Luke 12:20.

Aunt: (1) Married Christian sister; (2) Actual aunt; (3) An aunt could speak about her character, name, or profession.

(1) Lev. 18:14 (Father's brother's wife).

Aura: See Halo.

Author: (1) Originator; (2) Jesus Christ; (3) Writer; (4) God.

(1-2) Heb. 12:2; (3) Job 19:23; Ps. 45:1b; (4) Gen. 1:1.

Automobile: (1) Ministry or ministry gift; (2) Person (an individual); (3) Church; (4) Business; (5) Powerful ministry (sports pack); (6) Authority issue (auto with no roof); (7) Family unit; (8) The "old self" (vintage car); (9) The ministry of God's Generals (1940-50s car); (10) Not conforming to the religious system (unregistered auto).

Also see *Auto Accident and Auto Stolen, Bus, Driver, Parked Auto, Reversing Vehicle, Stalled Vehicle,* and *Taxi.*

(1) Prov. 18:16 & Eph. 4:8, 11; Eph. 3:6-7; (2) Acts 20:24; Rom. 1:1 (Paul is a servant and bearer of the Gospel); (3) Heb. 11:7; (4) Jer. 18:3 (KJV); (6) Matt. 8:8-9; (7) Gen. 45:19; (8) Matt. 9:17; Rom. 6:6; (9) Isa. 61:4; Heb. 11:32-33; (10) Acts 4:13, 19.

Auto Accident: (1) Warning; (2) Ministry threat, mistake, or catastrophe; (3) Potential clash of ministries; (4) Confrontation or conflict; (4) An attack on the destiny of a ministry.

Also see *Overtaking* and *Shipwreck.*

(1-2) Acts 20:23-24; 21:11; (3-4) Acts 15:36-40; (4) 1 Kings 19:2-3.

Auto Engine (Under the Hood): (1) Heart.

Also see *Engine.*

(1) Lam. 1:20 (KJV); Luke 1:17a.

Auto Interior: (1) Heart of the ministry; (2) The type of interior determines what type of ministry. i.e. if the interior is worn out, it means the ministry is old, needing renewal.

(1) Acts 13:22; Eph. 3:16-17; 1 Pet 3:4 (KJV).

Auto Stolen: (1) Robbed by the devil; (2) Promise or destiny stolen; (3) Ministry stolen.

(1-3) Gen. 27:36; Matt. 16:22-23; John 10:10.

Auto Trunk: (1) Heart; (2) Baggage.

(1) Deut. 9:5; Prov. 14:14; 22:15; Heb. 13:9 (KJV); (2) Matt. 23:4; Luke 11:46; Acts 15:28.

Autumn: (1) End; (2) Fading; (3) Carried away; (4) Sin; (5) Moving toward winter.

(1) Jer. 8:20; (2-4) Isa. 64:6.

Aviary: (1) Stronghold of the enemy; (2) Restricted in the things of the Spirit.

(1) Ps. 91:3a; 124:7; (2) Isa. 40:31.

Awake: (1) Alert; (2) Watchful; (3) Resurrection; (4) Salvation; (5) Stirred spiritually.

(1) Isa. 52:1; 1 Cor. 15:34; Eph. 5:14; (2) Matt. 26:40; Rev. 16:15; (3) John 11:11; (4) Eph. 5:8-14; (5) Hag. 1:14; Acts 17:16.

Awl: (1) Piercing; (2) Earmark; (3) Having loving (hearing) ears for.

Also see *Earrings*.

(1-3) Exod. 21:1-6.

Axe: (1) Weighty/heavy/impacting word of warning; (2) Repentance; (3) Forgiveness; (4) Judgment; (5) Instrument of judgment; (6) Chopper; (7) The Word of God.

(1) Dan. 4:14; Matt. 3:7-12; (2-5) Matt. 3:10-11; (5) Matt. 3:10-11 & Acts 8:22; Luke 17:3-4; (there is a link between repentance and forgiveness); (6) 1 Chron. 20:3; Isa. 10:15; (7) Matt. 3:10-11.

Baboon: See Monkey.

Baby: (1) God's promise; (2) Holy Spirit (God's Promise); (3) New ministry; (4) Immature; (5) New/young Christian; (6) Immature church; (7) New/young church; (8) Birth or fulfillment of promise by faith (unexpected baby); (9) Future; (10) Blessing (newborn baby); (11) The promise has arrived, but immature in the things of the Spirit (premature baby).

Also see *Birthing, Boy, Girl, Pregnancy,* and *Twins*.

(1) Acts 1:4, 7:5, 17; (2) Luke 24:49; (3) Rev. 12:2-4; (4) 1 John 2:12-14; Heb. 5:12-13; (5-7) Matt. 1:25; 21:16; Luke 2:12 & Acts 1:1; (8) 1 Sam. 1:17; Heb. 11:11; Gal. 4:23b; (9) Isa. 7:14; Acts 7:19; (10) Deut. 7:13; (11) Gal. 4:4-6.

Babylon: (1) Place of captivity; (2) Place of fornication/harlotry; (3) Habitation of devils and foul spirits; (4) Speaks of abundance, luxury, and riches; (5) Facing the wrath of God; (6) Facing torment; (7) Symbolizes rebellion; (8) The world system and false church; (9) Enticement; (10) Prostitution/ prostitute.

(1) Matt. 1:17; (2) Rev. 14:8; 17:5; (3) Rev. 18:2; (4) Rev. 18:3, 12-14; (5) Rev. 16:19; 18:9; (6) Rev. 18:10; (7) Isa. 13:1-22; (8) Rev. 17:5; Isa. 13:11; (9) Josh. 7:21; (10) Rev. 17:5.

Babysitting: (1) Holding on to a promise; (2) Nurturing a new church/ministry; (3) Caretaking a young church.

(1) Heb. 10:23; (2) Exod. 2:2; 1 Sam. 1:23; (3) 1 Tim. 1:3; 6:20a.

Back: (1) Past; (2) Reverse; (3) Behind; (4) Secret exit; (5) Burden; (6) Return; (7) Trying to steer you (on your back); (8) Persistent (on your back); (9) Ignoring/ignorant to (back to someone/thing); (10) Moving away (back to you); (11) Not able/wanting to face you (back to you).

Also see *Backpack, Backwards, Before,* and *Behind.*

(1) Phil. 3:13; (2) Gen. 9:23; (3) Phil. 3:13; (4) Acts 27:30-32; (5) Matt. 23:4; Acts 15:28; (6) 1 Kings 13:16, 19; (7) Matt. 16:22; (8) As in, "on your back about something"; (9) 1 Sam. 15:11; 1 Kings 14:9; (10) Exod. 23:27; Josh. 7:8, 12; (11) Exod. 33:23; Judg. 18:26.

Back Door: (1) Past; (2) Doubt/unbelief; (3) Undercover (hidden) entry/exit; (4) Not coming in the recognized way; (5) Backsliding; (6) Low profile entry/ exit; (7) Desertion; (8) Secret sin.

(1-2) Gen. 18:10, 12-13; (3) Gen. 31:27; Jer. 39:4; (4) John 10:1; (5) Jer. 2:19; 5:6b; John 16:32; (6) Matt. 1:19; (7) John 10:12; (8) Luke 12:2.

Back Massage/Rub: (1) Nurturing; (2) Care; (3) Serving the needs of another; (4) Imparting the anointing and breaking yokes.

(1-3) Isa. 9:4; 10:27; Matt. 11:30; (4) Isa. 10:27.

Backpack: (1) Carrying baggage; (2) Burden; (3) Heart; (4) Burden on your heart.

Also see *Bag.*

(1) Job 14:17a; (2) Matt. 11:29-30; (3) Matt. 16:9 (understanding is a heart issue); (4) Isa. 19:1 (The word *burden* in Hebrew has a double meaning: a burden that is carried and the oracle of a prophet.)

Backpackers Hostel: (1) People coming and going with burdens or issues.

Also see *Youth Hostel.*

(1) Luke 11:46.

Backstage: (1) What is happening in the inner self (behind the scenes); (2) Giving Christ the glory.

Also see *Spotlight* and *Stage.*

(1) 1 Pet. 3:4; (2) Col. 3:3.

Backward: (1) Past; (2) Backslidden; (3) Turned away from God; (4) Not ready/ preparation needed; (5) Retreat; (6) Need for introspection; (7) Not knowing where you are going.

(1) Gen. 9:23 (covering the past); Phil. 3:12; (2) Isa. 1:4; (3) Jer. 7:24; 15:6; Lam. 1:8; (4-5) Josh. 7:5, 10-11.

Backyard (Garden): (1) That which is private; (2) Concerning you or your own family; (3) Past issues; (4) Hidden.

Also see *Front Yard* and *Garden*.

(1) Acts 5:2; (2) As in, "take a look in your own backyard"; Mark 9:28; 13:3; (3) Phil. 3:13; (4) Gen. 3:8, 10; Song. 6:2.

Bacon: (1) Flesh.

Also see *Pig*.

(1) Isa. 65:4.

Bag: (1) Carrying baggage/burdens; (2) Heart; (3) Money; (4) Security; (5) Treasure; (6) Business; (7) Treasurer; (8) Thief; (9) Carrying; (10) Fashion accessory; (11) Putting yourself before God (bag with holes); (12) Carrying oppression or issues; (13) Carrying the anointing/mantle (a blue bag); (14) Heart full of faith (bag of money).

Also see *Backpack*.

(1) Job 14:17; Luke 11:46; Acts 8:18-20, 22-23; (2) Matt. 6:21; (3) 2 Kings 5:23; 12:10; Prov. 7:20; Isa. 46:6; (4-5) Luke 12:33; (6) Deut. 25:13; Mic. 6:11; (7) John 13:29; (8) John 12:6; 13:29; (9) 1 Sam. 17:40, 49; (10) Josh. 9:4-5; (11) Hag. 1:6; (12) Isa. 9:4 (NIV); (13) 1 Sam. 16:1; (14) 1 Sam. 2:35; Neh. 9:7-8; Rom. 10:8.

Bait: (1) Temptation; (2) Trap/snare; (3) Potential offense; (4) Wrongly using the Word of God; (5) Word of God; (6) Signs and wonders; (7) Revelation; (8) The Gospel.

Also see *Fishing, Poison,* and *Worm/s*.

(1) Luke 4:1b-2a, 13; 1 Cor. 10:13; (2-3) Isa. 8:14; 29:21; Matt. 13:57; 18:6; (4) 2 Cor. 2:17; 1 Pet. 1:23; 2 Pet. 2:1; (5-6) Heb. 2:3-4; (7) Matt. 16:15-18; (8) Matt. 4:19b.

Bake: (1) Something of your own making; (2) Concocting or scheming something.

Also see *Baker* and *Cook*.

(1) Gen. 40:16-18; Jer. 17:9; Hos. 7:6a; (2) 2 Sam. 15:3-6; 1 Cor. 4:5; 2 Cor. 2:11.

Baked Beans: (1) Revelation (seed in sauce).

(1) Exod. 29:7 & Luke 8:11.

Baker: (1) devil; (2) Someone who causes things to rise by sowing sin; (3) Schemer; (4) Someone who appeals to the senses, but has something else in the heart (oven); (5) Craftsman of own heart; (6) One who has something to hide; (7) Angry person.

Also see *Bake, Bakery,* and *Oven.*

(1-2) Gen. 3:1; Hos. 7:4; (3) Gen. 40:22; (4) Gen. 40:1ff; (5) Hos. 7:6; (6) <u>Gen. 40:16</u>; (7) <u>Hos. 7:6</u>.

Bakery: (1) Your heart.

(1) Hos. 7:6.

Balaclava: (1) Spirit of fear; (2) Thief; (3) Unaware of the devil's schemes (unknown assailant).

Also see *Terrorist.*

(1) Rom. 8:15; (2) John 10:10; (3) 2 Cor. 2:11; Eph. 6:11.

Balances (Scales): (1) Judgment (weighed); (2) Justice; (3) Business; (4) Integrity; (5) Divide; (6) Deceit; (7) Falsehood; (8) Purchase; (9) Considered; (10) Vanity.

(1) <u>Dan. 5:27</u>; Rev. 6:5; (2) Lev. 19:36; <u>Prov. 16:11</u>; Ezek. 45:10; (3) Isa. 46:6; Hos. 12:7; (4) Job 31:6; (5) Ezek. 5:1; (6) Hos. 12:7; Amos 8:5; Mic. 6:11; (7) Prov. 11:1; 20:23; Hos. 12:7; (8) Jer. 32:10; (9) Job 6:2; (10) Ps. 62:9.

Balcony: (1) Prophetic vision; (2) Position of a prophet.

(1) Num. 22:41; (2) Num. 22:41; <u>1 Sam. 9:19</u>.

Baldness: Appears to have two predominant lines of thought, based on: (1) Humbling and humility; (+) (2) A sign of the cutting away of the flesh; (-) (4) Shame or humiliation; (5) Judgment; (6) Mourning; (7) Fully bald man, like a vulture, could be a demon if unfriendly.

It may be that naturally occurring baldness signifies the former (+), and shaved baldness the latter (-).

Also see *Hair, Hair Cut Off, Head, Razor, Shave, Skinhead,* and *Vulture.*

(1) Isa. 22:12; Mic. 1:16; (2) Lev. 13:40-41; 2 Kings 2:23; (4) Lev. 21:5; Ezek. 7:18; (5) Isa. 15:2; <u>Jer. 47:5</u>; (6) Amos 8:10; (7) Mic. 1:16.

Ball: (1) Words; (2) Prophetic words.

Also see *Football, Golf Course, Golfer,* and *Tennis.*

(1) See entries below; (2) John 6:63.

Ball (Catching Ball): (1) Listening; (2) Taking hold of someone's words; (3) Trying to catch you out in your words.

Also see *Catcher's Mitt.*

(1) Matt. 13:19; Mark 12:13; (2) Luke 20:20, 26 (KJV); (3) Mark 12:13.

Ball (Deflated Ball): (1) Words without power; (2) Words without the Spirit; (3) Losing the Spirit.

(1-2) Job 33:4; 1 Cor. 2:4; 4:20; 1 Thess. 1:5; Heb. 1:3; (cf. Luke 4:32); (3) Judg. 16:20.

Ball (Hitting Ball): (1) Effective speaking; (2) Authoritative speaking.

(1) 1 Sam. 3:19; (2) Acts 5:40; 16:22.

Ball (Kicking Ball): (1) Passing on the message; (2) Going for goal; (3) Persecution; (4) Going against God; (5) Being proud and forgetting God.

(1) Judg. 11:17; 19; 2 Tim. 2:2; (3-4) Acts 9:5; 26:14; (5) Deut 32:15, 18; 1 Sam. 2:29.

Ball (Passing Ball): (1) Teaching (passing on knowledge).

(1) John 8:20; Acts 15:35.

Ball (Rolling Ball): (1) Writing words; (2) Written words.

(1-2) Ezra 6:1-2; Isa. 8:1; 34:4; Jer. 36:2ff; Ezek. 3:1-3; Zech. 5:1-2.

Ball (Scoring): (1) Winning souls.

(1) Acts 2:41.

Ball (Spinning Ball): (1) Lying; (2) Deceptive words; (3) Spinning yarns (story-telling).

(1) Prov. 6:19, 10:18, 12:19, 22, 14:5, 25, 19:5, 9, 21:6, 26:28, 30:6.

Ball (Throwing Ball): (1) Speaking; (2) Passing on to others; (3) Casting away.

(1) Ps. 50:17; (2) 2 Tim. 2:2; (3) Isa. 22:18; Mark 12:13.

Ball (Transparent Ball): (1) Words without substance (no heart or spirit).

(1) 1 Sam. 3:19.

Ballet: (1) Full of grace (graceful); (2) Love.

(1) Gen. 6:8; John 1:14b; (2) 2 Cor. 8:7; 13:14.

Balloon/s: (1) Celebration; (2) Words; (3) Prophecy: as words that lift (helium balloons); (4) In the Spirit; (5) Filled with the Holy Spirit; (6) Childlike faith; (7) Relief, freedom.

Also see *Ball*.

(1) Luke 15:23-24; (2) Ps. 33:6 (words are carried on one's breath); Prov. 1:23; John 6:63; (3) 1 Cor. 14:3; (4) Rev. 17:3a; (5) Luke 4:1; (6) Matt. 18:3; (7) Matt. 11:30.

Bamboo: (1) Young Christian; (2) Hollow Christian (no heart); (3) China; (4) Discipline.

(1) Prov. 11:28; Isa. 60:21; (2) Isa. 29:13; <u>Matt. 15:8</u>; (3) As in "the Bamboo Curtain"; (4) Prov. 23:13 (the rod or cane).

Bananas: (1) Fruit; (2) Wages (fruit of the hands).

Also see *Fruit* and *Yellow*.

(1) Deut. 1:25; (2) Prov. 31:16, 31 (KJV).

Banana Skin: (1) Watch your step.

(1) Ps. 73:2.

Band Aid: See Plaster.

Band (Rock): (1) Powerful worship; (2) False worship; (3) Rejoicing; (4) Revival.

Also see *Rock 'n' Roll*.

(1) <u>1 Chron</u>. 6:31-32; <u>15:16</u>; (2) Exod. 32:17-19; (3) 1 Sam. 18:6; (4) 2 Chron. 5:13-14.

Bank: (1) Your heart; (2) Heaven (God's treasury); (3) Jesus; (4) Reserve; (5) Sure thing; (6) Wealth/money; (7) Storehouse; (8) Interest; (9) Your place of employment (where you receive financially).

Also see *Riverbank*.

(1) <u>Matt. 12:35</u>; Luke 6:45; 12:34; 21:1-4; Rom. 2:5; 2 Cor. 4:7; (2) Matt. 6:19-20; Mark 10:21; Luke 12:33; 18:22; (3) Col. 2:2-3; Heb. 11:26; (4) Acts 5:3; (5) As in, "You can bank on that"; (6) <u>Luke 19:23</u>; (7) 2 Chron. 32:27; (8) Luke 19:23; (9) Matt. 20:2.

Banner: (1) Flag; (2) The protection of God; (3) Love; (4) Fearsome army; (5) A warning; (6) Memorial; (7) Victory.

(1-2) Ps. 20:5; 60:4; (3) <u>Song. 2:4;</u> (4) Song. 6:4, 10; (5) <u>Isa. 13:2</u>; (6) Exod. 17:14-15; (7) <u>Ps. 20:5</u> (NIV).

Banqueting: (1) Intimate communion; (2) Sumptuous feast; (3) Joy; (4) To feed on; (5) Fleshly indulgence (drinking parties).

Also see *Party.*

(1) Song. 2:4; (2) Esther 5:4-6; (3) Esther 5:6; 7:2, 7 (wine = joy); (4) Job 41:6; (5) 1 Pet. 4:3.

Baptise/d: (1) Burial of old life; (2) Death and resurrection; (3) Death to sin; (4) Burial of a sinful aspect of one's life.

(1-4) Rom. 6:1-11; Col. 2:12-13.

Bar (Nightclub): (1) Church/altar (as the communal place where we drink of the Spirit); (2) The world; (3) Haunt of the workers of the flesh; (4) Gathering place for lovers of darkness.

Also see *Nightclub.*

(1) Eph. 5:18; (2) 1 John 2:16; (3) Gal. 5:19-21; (4) 1 Thess. 5:5-7.

Barbed Wire: (1) Prisoner; (2) Captive; (3) Bondage or stronghold; (4) Legalism; (5) Prohibited area; (6) Boundary of the spiritual realm (should be entered through the cross).

(1-2) 2 Tim. 2:25-26; (3) Luke 13:16; (4) Rom. 7:2; 1 Cor. 7:39; (5) John 10:1-2; (6) Luke 16:26; John10:1-2 (cf. Matt. 27:29).

Barbeque: (1) Heart; (2) Independent spirit (cooking something up outside); (3) Solid Bible teaching (meatfest); (4) Outdoor preaching.

(1) Hos. 7:6a; as in "what's cooking?"; (2) Prov. 18:1 (cf. KJV); (3) Heb. 5:12; (4) Mark 6:12.

Barber: (1) Enemy; (2) Deceiver; (3) Seducer; (4) Groomer; (5) Cleaner.

(1) 2 Sam. 10:3; Isa. 7:20; (2-3) Judg. 16:19; (5) Lev. 14:8-9.

Barbershop: (1) Enemy's camp.

Also see *Hairdressers.*

(1) 2 Sam. 10:4; Ezek. 5:1.

Barefooted: See Shoes.

Barley: (1) Inferior grain; (2) Harvest.

(1) Judg. 7:13-14; (2) Ruth 1:22; 2:23; 2 Sam. 21:9.

Barn: (1) Church; (2) Storehouse of riches; (3) Increase; (4) Greed; (5) Call to trust God without a bank of resources behind you; (6) Judgment; (7) Harvest.

Also see *Building, House,* and *Stable.*

(1-2) Job 39:12; <u>Mal. 3:10</u>; Matt. 6:26; (3) 2 Chron. 32:28; Prov. 3:10; (4) Luke 12:18; (5) Matt. 6:25-33; Luke 12:22-24; (6) Joel 1:17 (broken down barns); (7) <u>Matt. 13:30</u>.

Barrel: (1) Heart (and therefore a person); (2) Storage place; (3) Vessel; (4) Fleshly vessel (individual).

Also see *Pans, Pots, Rifle,* and *Vessel.*

(1) A barrel holds water and wine; (2-3) 1 Kings 17:12, 14, 16; (4) As barrels are made of wood and wood is representative of the works of the flesh (see 1 Cor. 3:12-15).

Baseball: (1) Trying to get you out with words (pitching or catching); (2) Words with power (batting); (3) Spiritual warfare (batting and pitching); (4) Hitting hearts with your words (home runs); (5) The enemy getting at you or getting one past you (strike); (6) Lie (curve ball); (7) Making history (hitting the most home runs).

Also see *Ball, Bat, Cricket, Football Game, Sport, Umpire,* and *Winning.*

(1) <u>Mark 12:13</u>; (2) Eccl. 8:4; <u>Luke 4:32</u>; (3) Rom. 7:23 (internally: spirit vs. flesh); 2 Cor. 10:3; Eph. 6:12 (in the second heaven against evil spirits); 1 Tim. 1:18; (4) 1 Sam. 3:19; (5) Gen. 3:1; 1 Cor. 10:13; (6) Gen. 24:49; Ps. 33:4; Luke 20:21; (7) Esther 8:5, 8 (it is recorded).

Baseball Bat: See Bat.

Basement: (1) Hell; (2) Person's heart; (3) Hiding place; (4) Depression; (5) A place of the flesh.

Also see *Upper Room.*

(1) <u>Prov. 5:5</u>; Matt. 11:23; Ps. 55:15; (2) Prov. 22:17; (3) Jon. 1:5; (5) As in, "opposite of the upper room."

Basket: (1) Heart; (2) First-fruits; (3) Blessed fruitfulness; (4) A day's work or provisions; (5) Overflow from faith; (6) Group of people (family, church, nation); (7) Cursed fruit; (8) Escape pod.

(1) <u>Gen. 40:16-17</u>; Deut. 28:5; (2) Deut. 26:2-9; (3) Deut. 28:4-5; Jer. 24:1; (4) Gen. 40:16-18; (5) <u>Matt. 14:20</u>; 15:37; 16:9-10; (6) Jer. 24:1-10; (7) Deut. 28:17; Amos 8:1-2; Jer. 24:1; (8) <u>Acts 9:25</u>; 2 Cor. 11:33.

Basketball Ring (Hoop): (1) Sinking heavenly goals; (2) Reaching forward to what lies ahead.

(1-2) Phil 3:13-14.

Bat/s (Animal): (1) Evil spirits; (2) Unclean spirits; (3) Idolatry; (4) Children of darkness; (5) Blind spirit that develops and uses occultic/demonic senses to "see."

Also see *Vampire*.

(1-2) Lev. 11:13a, 19b; Deut. 14:18; (3) Isa. 2:20; (4) 1 Thess. 5:5; (5) 1 Sam. 28:8.

Bat (Baseball/Cricket): (1) The rhema word of God; (2) Your turn or innings; (3) Heart; (4) Discipline (rod of correction); (5) Verbal leverage (tongue).

Also see *Ball, Cricket, Sport,* and *Umpire*.

(1) Heb. 4:12; (2) Esther 4:14; Gal. 1:15-16; (3) Matt. 12:34-35; (4) Prov. 13:24; (5) Eccl. 8:4; Luke 4:32.

Bat without a Handle: (1) Position of no real leverage (influence); (2) Disempowered.

(1) 2 Kings 24:1, 17; (2) Gen. 49:6b.

Bath/ing: (1) Cleansing; (2) Purification; (3) Applying the Word; (4) Needing conversion (all of body washed); (5) Daily confession (washing parts of the body i.e. feet/hands); (6) Baptism (immersion in a bath).

(1) Lev. 15:5; (2) Num. 19:9, 17; (3) Eph. 5:26; (4-5) John 13:4-15; (6) Acts 8:38-39.

Bathroom: (1) Cleansing; (2) Heart (the mirror of God's Word reveals your heart); (3) Grooming; (4) Conviction/repentance; (5) Secret lust/sin; (6) Refreshing; (7) Old issue (old bathroom).

Also see *Faeces; Dung, Toilet,* and *Urination*.

(1) Eph. 5:26; (2) James 1:23-26; (3) Isa. 1:16; (4) Matt. 3:11; (5) Ps. 38:9; 51:6; Isa. 29:15; John. 7:4; (5) Acts 3:19; (6) Rom. 6:6; 2 Pet. 1:9.

Battery: (1) Holy Spirit (power source); (2) Power; (3) Reserve power; (4) Life.

(1) Luke 1:35; Acts 1:8; Rom. 15:13; (2) Acts 10:38; (3) Matt. 25:3-4; (4) 2 Cor. 13:4.

Battery Charge: (1) Fresh infilling of the Spirit.

(1) Acts 1:8; 2:3-4; 4:8, 31, 33; 9:17; 13:9.

Battle: (1) Spiritual warfare; (2) Attack; (3) Conflict.

Also see entry under *Fight*.

(1) Judg. 3:10; Eph. 6:10-12; 1 Tim. 1:18; (2) Josh. 10:19; Ps. 27:2; (3) Ps 13:2; 80:6.

Battleship: (1) Powerful evangelistic ministry.

Also see *Ship*.

(1) Acts 27:31; 2 Cor. 2:4.

Beach: (1) Limit; (2) Boundary; (3) Boundary of the Kingdom of Heaven (where souls are won and lost); (4) Recreation; (5) Earth; (6) No foundation in the Word (standing on sand); (7) Safety; (8) Battleground.

Also see *Coastline* and *Sand*.

(1-2) Josh. 15:2; Prov. 8:29; (3) Exod. 23:31; Num. 34:12; Job 38:11; Ps. 93:4; (4) Exod. 32:6; 1 Cor. 10:7; (5) Matt. 13:2; (6) Matt. 7:26-27; (7) Acts 28:1-2; (8) As in, "trying to get a beachhead."

Beach Ball: (1) Words said in jest/fun.

(1) Eccl. 2:1.

Beacon: (1) Sign; (2) Signal; (3) Warning; (4) Call for assistance; (5) Drawing your attention; (6) The Gospel; (7) Believer; (8) Christ.

Also see *Lighthouse* and *Torch*.

(1) Isa. 30:17; John 1:5; Acts 2:19; (2) Gen. 1:14; Judg. 20:38; Ps. 19:1; Jer. 6:1; (3) Prov. 6:23; Isa. 8:20b; John 1:7; (4) Luke 5:7; Acts 9:3, 6, 15; (5) Matt. 5:16; John 5:35; Acts 12:7; (6) 2 Cor. 4:4; (7) Phil. 2:15; (8) 2 Cor. 4:6; 1 John 2:8b; Rev. 21:23.

Beads: (1) Superficial adornment; (2) Worldly adornment.

(1-2) 1 Pet. 3:3; 1 Tim. 2:9.

Bean Bag: (1) Apathy; (2) Lethargy.

(1-2) Prov. 26:13-14; Heb. 6:12.

Bear: (1) Enemy; (2) Stealer of young Christians; (3) Powerful spiritual force; (4) Fierce anger; (5) Oppressive leader; (6) Russia; (7) Anti-Christ; (8) Religious spirit; (9) Iran; (10) Territorial spirit.

(1-2) 1 Sam. 17:34-37; (3) Rev. 13:2; (4) Prov. 17:12; (5) Prov. 28:15; (6) Ezek. 38:16, 18; (7) Rev. 13:2; (8-9) Dan. 7:5 (cf. Dan. 2:39, 8:20-21, 10:20); (10) 1 Sam. 17:36.

Beard: (1) Full manhood or spiritual maturity; (2) God's statutes and judgments; (3) Holy.

Also see *Hair*.

(1) 1 Chron. 19:5; (2) Ezek. 5:1-6; (3) Lev. 21:5-6.

Beard (Untrimmed beard): (1) Law/Legalism; (2) A person who has made an oath.

(1) Lev. 19:27; 21:5; (2) 2 Sam. 19:24.

Beard (Shaved beard): (1) Shame; (2) Grief/mourning; (3) Humbled; (4) Sign of coming destruction.

(1) 2 Sam. 10:4-5; Isa. 15:2; (2) Ezra 9:3-6; (3) Jer. 41:5; 49:37; (4) Ezek. 5:1.

Beard (Grabbed by the beard): (1) Warning of danger/death.

(1) 1 Sam. 17:35; 2 Sam. 20:9.

Beard (Spittle (saliva) in beard): (1) Madness.

(1) 1 Sam. 21:13.

Beast: (1) Antichrist; (2) Godly or ungodly being; (3) King/doms (nations); (4) Principalities and powers.

Also see entries under individual animals.

(1) Rev. 13:11-18; 14:9-11; (2) Rev. 4:6-8; 11:7; 13:1-4; (3) Dan. 7:17, 23; (4) Eph. 6:12; Dan. 10:13, 20.

Beastiality: (1) Reprobate mind; (2) Darkened heart; (3) Willful denial of God; (4) Diseased soul; (5) Abomination; (6) Demonic harassment; (7) Cursed.

(1-3) Rom. 1:21-31; (4) 1 Thess. 4:5; (5) Exod. 22:19; Lev. 18:23; 20:15-16; (7) Deut. 27:21.

Beaten Up: (1) Verbal abuse; (2) Verbal onslaught; (3) Warning of physical harm.

(1-2) Luke 22:64-65.

Beating Time: (1) Synchronization with God; (2) Slow down (slowing to get in synchronization; (3) Time is short (speeding up); (4) Lagging behind and need to push in (others beating faster than you).

(1) Gen. 5:22; (2) Eccl. 3:1; (3) 1 Cor. 7:29; (4) Mark 5:27.

Beautiful: (1) Warning of inner corruption; (2) Gospel preacher; (3) Well-favored; (4) Holy garments; (5) Holiness; (6) Seeing facets of God; (7) Salvation (upon the meek); (8) Desirable; (9) Reflects the heart; (10) Temptation; (11) Vanity; (12) Speaks of the timing of God; (13) At the right place at the right time; (14) Reflective of Christ's love relationship with you (or the Church); (15) Christ; (16) Temporary outward show; (17) In danger of pride.

Also see *Ugly.*

(1) Matt. 23:27; Prov. 6:25; (2) Isa. 52:7; Rom. 10:15; (3) Gen. 29:17; Ps. 90:17; (4) Exod. 28:2, 40; (5) 1 Chron. 16:29; 2 Chron. 20:21; Ps. 29:2; 96:9; 110:3; (6) Ps. 27:4; 50:2; 90:17; (7) Ps. 149:4; (8) Deut. 21:11; Isa. 53:2b; (9) 1 Sam. 16:12 & Acts 13:22; (10) 2 Sam. 11:2; (11) 2 Sam. 14:25; Ps. 39:11; Prov. 31:30; (12-13) Eccl. 3:11; (14) Song. 6:4; 7:1; (15) Isa. 4:2; (16) Isa. 28:1, 4; (17) Ezek. 28:17.

Beauty Shop: (1) Grooming; (2) Getting ready; (3) Call for inward beauty rather than outward; (4) Vanity.

(1-3) 1 Pet. 3:3-4; Rev. 21:2; (4) 2 Sam. 14:25.

Beaver: (1) Busy; (2) Diligent/hard working; (3) Banking up (saving) the Word/ Spirit.

Also see *Dam.*

(1) As in "busy as a beaver"; Luke 10:40-42; (2) Prov. 4:23; 10:4; 12:24; 22:29; 27:23; (3) Matt. 7:2; Mark 4:24.

Bed: (1) God (as the place of our rest); (2) Heart (as the place of God's rest); (3) Agreement (sharing bed); (4) Alignment with (double bed); (5) Rest; (6) Sickness; (7) Intimacy; (8) Laziness; (9) Adultery; (10) Asleep; (11) Warmth; (12) Sexual issue; (13) Suffering; (14) Thoughts; (15) Meditation; (16) In the Spirit (water bed); (17) Heart; (18) Association (bunk bed); (19) Position; (20) Death; (21) Single person (single or bunk bed as opposed to a double bed).

Also see *Bedroom, Sex,* and *Sheets.*

(1) Jer. 50:6; Matt. 11:29; Heb. 4:9-11; (2) Isa. 66:1; Prov. 14:33a; Acts 7:49; (3) Isa. 57:8; Rev. 2:22; (4) 1 Kings 17:19, 21; 2 Kings 4:34; (5) Isa. 57:2; (6) Gen. 47:31-48:1; Matt. 9:2; (7) Heb. 13:4; (8) Prov. 26:14; (9) Prov. 7:16-18; (10) Luke 11:7; (11) Eccl. 4:11; (12-13) Rev. 2:21-22; (14) Dan. 2:29; 4:5; As in, "the place where you lay your head"; (15) Ps. 4:4; (16) Dan. 2:29; (17) Ps. 4:4; Eccl. 2:23; Hos. 7:14; (18) Eph. 4:16; (19) Jer. 35:4 (chambers are bedrooms); Position as in "births/bunks" on a battleship; (20) Gen. 49:33 (death bed); (21) 1 Cor. 9:5.

Bed (Under Bed): (1) Hidden; (2) Secret; (3) Cover up; (4) Foundation.

(1-3) Mark 4:21-22; (4) 1 Cor. 3:11.

Bedhead: (1) Lazy authority; (2) Leadership spiritually asleep.

(1) Matt. 23:4; (2) Matt. 23:16.

Bedroom: (1) Private; (2) Intimacy or union; (3) Inner circle (confide in); (4) The place of heart communion.

Also see *Bed.*

(1) Matt. 6:6; (2) 2 Sam. 11:2-4; (3) Mark 9:2-9 (the mountain was Jesus' "secret place"); (4) Ps. 4:4; 63:6.

Bedside Table: (1) Storage of things close to you.

(1) 1 Sam. 26:7.

Bee/s: (1) Spiritual force/evil spirits; (2) Surrounded; (3) Busy; (4) People who sting; (5) People who make honey; (6) Laborers; (7) Angels; (8) Angels ascending/descending (bee flight path).

Also see *Ants, Honey, Sting,* and *Wasp.*

(1) Deut. 1:44; Isa. 7:18; (2) Ps. 118:12; (3) "Busy as a bee"; (4) Deut. 1:44; Ps. 118:12; (5) Matt. 3:4 & John 4:34; (7) Exod. 25:20 (mercy seat covered in gold like honey); Heb. 1:14; (8) Gen. 28:12; John 1:51.

Beehive: (1) Busy (a hive of activity); (2) Heaven; (3) The Church; (4) Enemy stronghold.

(1-2) John 1:51; (3) Num. 13:16; Acts 13:4; (4) Deut. 1:44; Ps. 118:12.

Before (In Front of): (1) Future; (2) Next (in time).

Also see *Ahead, Back,* and *Behind.*

(1-2) Luke 10:1; Phil. 3:13.

Beggar: (1) Recognizing one's spiritual state without God; (2) This is a good sign as it is the first step in coming to know God; (3) Petition; (4) Desperate; (5) Prayer.

(1-2) Matt. 5:3; Luke 16:23; (3) Ps. 38; Jer. 42:2; Dan. 9:3; (4) Prov. 30:7; (5) Judg. 13:8 (NIV).

Beheaded: See Decapitation.

Behind: (1) Past; (1) After; (2) To follow; (3) Something that will happen in time; (4) Later; (5) Moving on from.

Also see *Ahead, Back,* and *Before.*

(1) Phil. 3:13; (1) Matt. 10:38; (2) Mark 8:34; (3-4) Joel 2:28; (5) Gen. 19:26 (Lot's wife failed to move on).

Belch: (1) Offense; (2) Moving on before you have digested what God has said (eating too fast); (3) Digesting words coming with a wrong spirit (sodas are full of CO_2); (4) Bringing up the past.

Also see *Breath* and *Vomit.*

(1) <u>Ps. 73:15</u> (KJV); Prov. 18:19; (2) Josh. 1:8; (3) Prov. 14:15; 23:1-3; (4) Eccl. 3:15.

Bell: (1) Warning; (2) Proclamation of glory; (3) Attention gatherer.

Also see *Doorbell.*

(1) Matt. 24:3b; Mark 13:24-26; (2) <u>Exod.</u> 28:33-34; <u>39:25-26</u>; Zech. 14:20; (3) Isa. 40:3; Matt. 3:1-5; John 1:8.

Belly: (1) Person's spirit (core of the person); (2) Heart; (3) Gut feeling; (4) Womb; (5) Meditating (spiritually digesting); (6) Intestinal system.

(1) <u>Prov. 20:27</u>; (2) Matt. 12:40; (3) Job 34:4; (4) Job 3:11; (5) <u>Ps. 19:14</u>; (6) Mark 7:19.

Belly Button Pierced: (1) Conviction or obedience of heart; (2) Penetrated by the Word of God.

(1) Acts 2:37; (2) Luke 2:35.

Below: See Above and Below.

Belt: (1) Truth; (2) The Word; (3) Prophecy; (4) Prophet; (5) Office (ministry/role).

(1) <u>Eph. 6:14</u>; (2) John 17:17; (3) Acts 21:11; (4) 2 Kings 1:8; (5) 2 Sam. 18:11.

Bench: (1) Not being used or not wanted (sitting on the bench); (2) Sidelined; (3) Rest; (4) Team.

Also see *Sit/ting.*

(1-2) <u>1 Sam. 4:13</u>; (3) 2 Sam. 7:1; Zech. 1:11b; (4) Eph. 2:6.

Bench Top: (1) Heart; (2) Pulpit.

Also see *Chopping Board.*

(1) As an altar: Judg. 6:26; As a table: Exod. 34:28 & 2 Cor. 3:3; (2) Ps. 104:15b; Matt. 4:4.

Bend (noun): (1) Change; (2) Transition; (3) Deviation from God's path; (4) Ungodliness (bent); (5) Perversion (bent).

Also see *Bend* (verb), *Corner,* and *Curve.*

(1) <u>Exod. 13:17-18</u> (via an indirect route); Prov. 24:21; (2) Gen. 11:31 (at Haran, on way to Canaan); Exod. 13:17-18; (3) Deut. 5:32; Ps. 5:8; Isa. 40:3; (4) Acts 13:10; Jude 1:4; (5) Num. 22:32; Deut. 32:5; Acts 13:10.

Bend (verb): (1) Humbled/ing; (2) Readying an attack (of words); (3) Determined (bent on doing something); (4) Backsliding (no longer upright); (5) Being kept bound.

Also see *Arrow, Bend* (noun), *Bowing,* and *Knee.*

(1) Isa. 60:14; (2) Ps. 64:3; Jer. 9:3; (3-4) Hos. 11:7; (5) Luke 13:11-16.

Beneath: See Above and Below and Under.

Bent: See Bend, Bowing, Curved, and Crooked.

Berries: (1) Fruitfulness; (2) Resurrection.

Also see *Blueberries, Fruit,* and *Strawberries.*

(1-2) Isa. 17:6 (KJV); James 3:12 (KJV) (cf. Gen. 40:10, 13).

Best Man: (1) Jesus; (2) John the Baptist (friend of groom); (3) Spirit of Elijah (friend of groom).

Also see *Bride, Groom,* and *Marriage.*

(1) Heb. 7:22, 12:24; (2-3) John 3:28-29; Song. 5:1.

Bible: (1) Word of God; (2) Jesus Christ; (3) Christian walk; (4) What you believe to be truth; (5) Operating procedures;

(1) Josh. 1:8; (2) John 1:1; (3) Ps. 119:1, 105; (4) John 17:17; (5) 2 Tim. 3:16.

Bible Character: (1) Mantle of the Bible character coming to or on the dreamer; (2) Parallel incident happening in the life of the dreamer as happened for the Bible character; (3) An incident in the life of the character that springs to mind.

(1-3) Ezek. 34:23-24; Matt. 11:14; 17:10-12.

Bicycle: (1) Individual on a humble/ing journey (no horse-power); (2) Self-propelled ministry (doing things in your own strength); (3) Inferior ministry; (4) Denying or without the power of the Holy Spirit; (5) Self-employed; (6) Spiritual framework linking God's Spirit with our spirit; (7) Wrong spirit (riding in wrong direction).

Also see *Handlebars, Inner Tube, Tandem Bicycle, Unicycle,* and *Wheel/s.*

(1) Gen. 44:3; Dan. 5:21; Mark 11:2; (2) Zech. 4:6; (3-4) 1 Cor. 2:4; 4:20; 1 Thess. 1:5; (5) John 12:6; (6) Ezek. 1:20-21; (7) 1 Kings 16:31; Hos. 4:12; 2 Pet. 2:15; Jude 1:11; Num. 14:23-24.

Big/Bigger: See Tall, Taller, and Smaller.

Big Brother: (1) Government; (2) Leadership; (3) Jesus.

(1-2) 1 Sam. 9:2; (3) Heb. 2:11.

Bigfoot: (1) Spirit of antichrist (as in so-called "missing link") (2) Fear or torment of something that is not real (a hoax); (3) Threat (demon); (4) Authority putting its foot down (with threats).

Also see *Abominable Snow Man.*

(1) 1 John 2:22; 4:2-3, 5-6; (2) Num. 13:33; (3) 1 Sam. 17:44; Acts 13:8-10; (4) Acts 9:1; Dan. 3:13-15.

Biker/Bikie: (1) Rebels/rebellion; (2) Intimidation; (3) Strongman; (4) Evil spirit (hell's angel); (5) Gangster (underworld figures).

(1) Mark 15:7; (2) Rom. 8:15; 2 Tim. 1:7; (3) Matt. 12:29; Luke 11:21-22; (4) Matt. 25:41; Jude 1:6; (5) Neh. 4:7-8; Phil 2:10b.

Bikini: (1) Revealing; (2) In the flesh; (3) Carnal; (4) Enticing temptation.

(1) Gen. 3:7; (2) Gen. 2:25 & 3:7; 1 Pet. 4:2; (3) Rom. 8:5; Gal. 6:8; (4) 2 Sam. 11:2-4.

Billiards: See entries under Pool Hall, Pool Cue, and Pool Table.

Bingo: (1) Casting lots; (2) Idol; (3) False gods of luck and chance.

(1) Matt. 27:35; Mark 15:24; Luke 23:34; (3) 1 Sam. 6:9b.

Binoculars: (1) Distant; (2) Spiritual vision; (3) Seeing Heaven or seeing from Heaven; (4) Fearful; (5) Distant in time; (6) Prophet; (7) Foreseeing; (8) Focusing; (9) Faith (not seen with the naked eye).

Also see *Horizon.*

(1) Gen. 37:18; Jer. 4:16; Matt. 26:58; (2) 2 Kings 4:25-27; Mark 5:6; Luke 16:23; (3) Mark 11:13; 13:34; (4) Mark 15:40; Exod. 20:18b; (5) Gen. 22:4; 37:18; Ezek. 12:27; Heb. 11:13; (6) 2 Kings 2:7; (7) Ezek. 12:27; (8) Matt. 7:5; (9) Heb. 11:1.

Bird/s: (1) Good or evil spirits (heavenly beings); (2) The Holy Spirit; (3) A church or the Church; (4) Angel; (5) Black birds = generally evil; (6) A curse (may be seen as a pale or yellow bird landing on someone/thing); (7) Spirit of death (black bird).

Also see individual bird names, *Dove, Raven,* and *Wings.*

(1) Gen. 40:17-19; Lev. 14:4-7 (Jesus and the Holy Spirit); Matt. 13:31-32; (2) Luke 3:22; (3) Acts 14:27 & Matt. 23:37; Ruth 2:12; (4) Rev. 8:13; 14:6;

(5) Gen. 8:7-11 (the raven found no rest = no rest for the wicked); (6) Gen. 40: 17-19; Prov. 26:2; (7) Jer. 9:21.

Birds (Swooping): (1) Demonic harassment; (2) Divine protection.

(1) Gen. 40:17; (2) Isa. 31:5.

Bird Bath: (1) Heart; (2) The Word of God.

(1) Ps. 73:13; Jer. 4:14; Heb. 10:22; (2) Exod. 30:18-19 & Eph. 5:26.

Birth/ing: (1) Birthing a new ministry/church/venture; (2) Beginning of something new; (3) Bringing forward God's promises through prayer; (4) Travailing intercession; (5) Being born again; (6) Lost hope or promise (stillborn); (7) Judgment (stillborn); (8) Stopping God's promise (stillborn).

Also see *Baby, Caesarean Birth,* and *Pregnancy.*

(1) Rev. 12:2, 4-5; John 16:20-21; (2) Jer. 31:8; Mic. 4:10; (3) 1 Kings 18:1, 41-45; (4) 1 Sam. 1:10-18; Rom. 8:25-29; (5) John 3:3; (6-7) Isa. 47:9; (8) Matt. 2:16.

Birthday: (1) Born again; (2) Start of something new; (3) Celebration; (4) Memorial; (5) Death (a woman goes through a death before birth).

(1) John 3:3; (2) Exod. 12:2; 2 Cor. 5:17; (3-4) Exod. 12:2-14; (5) John 12:24; 19:34; Rom. 6:4; 8:22; 1 Cor. 15:21-22.

Biscuit: See Bread.

Bishop: (1) Overseer (to watch over); (2) Covering; (3) Spiritual authority.

Also see *Pastor* and *Priest.*

(1-3) 1 Tim. 3:1-2; 1 Pet. 5:2.

Bite/Bitten: (1) Infected (affected) by words; (2) Poisoned by words; (3) Destructive (devouring) words; (4) Falling to temptation; (5) Addicted (as in bitten by the gambling bug); (6) Test of faith; (7) Back-biting or slander (bite on back).

Also see *Eating, Snake,* and *Spider.*

(1) Matt. 27:20; (2) Gen. 3:1-6; Acts 13:8-10; (3) Ps. 52:4; (4) Gen. 3:1-6; (5) Prov. 23:2-3; (6) Mark 16:17-18 & Acts 28:3-6; (7) Num. 21:5-6.

Bitter: See Lemon.

Bitumen: (1) Hard; (2) Traffic or commerce; (3) Busyness; (4) Sealant; (5) Preventing growth.

(1-3) Matt. 13: 4, 19; (4) Gen. 6:14; (5) Deut. 29:23.

Black: (1) Without light or life; (2) Without the Spirit (operating in the soul); (3) Wicked; (4) Sin; (5) Deceitful; (6) Mourning; (7) Dead or unclean; (8) Burned; (9) Famine; (10) Hell; (11) Death; (11) Financially sound (in the "black")

Also see *Black Man, Black and White,* and *Woman* (black widow).

(1) Gen. 1:2-3; Lam. 4:8; (2) John 13:30b; James 2:26a; Matt. 25:8; (1 John 1:5b & Rom. 8:9); 1 Cor. 2:14; (3) Song. 5:11 & Gen 8:7 & Isa. 48:22; (4) Lam. 4:8; (5) Prov. 7:9; (6) Jer. 8:21 (cf. NKJV & KJV); (7) Lam. 4:8; Matt. 23:27 (contrasted with white); (8) Jer. 14:2, 8; (9) Rev. 6:5-6; (10) 2 Pet. 2:17; (11) Job 3:5.

Black Eye: (1) Persecuted prophet; (2) Domestic violence; (3) Abuse (physical, emotional, or spiritual); (4) Darkness around the heart; (5) Wounded heart.

(1) 1 Kings 19; (2) 1 Sam. 22:19; Jer. 4:31; (3) Luke 22:63-64; (4) Rom. 1:21; Eph. 4:18; (5) Ps. 109:22; 147:3.

Black Man: Note: The meaning of an African-American/First Nations (indigenous) person or Caucasian person in a dream may change dependent on the ethnicity (racial/cultural background) of the dreamer. An African-American/First Nations person may see Caucasians as the fleshly self (due to their past inclination to exploit, enslave, and be soulish). To a Caucasian, a First Nations person may represent the fleshly self due to their color or order in the land (see 1 Cor. 15:46). A person of a different race is generally interpreted as "Foreign." (Also see First Nations Peoples, Foreign, Foreigner, and Native/s).

Black and White: (1) Judgment/al; (2) Double-minded; (3) Religious; (4) Lukewarm.

(1) John 8:5-6; Acts 23:3; (2) James 1:6-8; (3) Matt. 23:5-7; (4) Rev. 3:16.

Blanket: (1) Covering; (2) Authority; (3) Smothering (wet blanket).

(1) 1 Kings 19:13; (2) 2 Kings 2:14; (3) Ezek. 32:7.

Bleeding: (1) Losing spiritual life; (2) Hurting; (3) Suffering; (4) Wounded; (5) Dying; (6) Purification; (7) Atonement; (8) Martyr.

Also see *Blood.*

(1) Acts 22:20; Lev. 17:11; (2-3) Isa. 53:4-5, 7; (4) 1 Kings 22:35; Ezek. 28:23; (6) Lev. 12:4; (7) Lev. 17:11; (8) Acts 2:20; Gen. 4:10.

Blimp: (1) High profiled Holy Spirit ministry; (2) Very discerning prophetic ministry.

Also see *Hot Air Balloon.*

(1) Ezek. 8:3; Acts 8:39; (2) Num. 22:41 (by virtue of the view).

Blind: (1) Spiritually blind; (2) In the dark spiritually or spiritually ignorant; (3) Unbeliever; (4) Received a bribe; (5) Hardened heart; (6) Lacking faith or love; (7) Hatred.

(1) Isa. 42:18; 56:10; Matt. 15:14; Luke 4:18; John 9:39; (2) 1 Cor. 12;1; Isa. 42:7, 16; Matt. 23:16-17; 23:26; Rev. 3:17; (3) Isa. 29:18; (4) 1 Sam. 12:3: Deut. 16:19; (5) John 12:40; 2 Cor. 3:14-15; 4:4; (6) 2 Pet. 1:9; (7) 1 John 2:11.

Blindfold: See Blind and Veil.

Blinds (Awning): See Shutters.

Blister: (1) Experiencing friction because of the Gospel; (2) Friction affecting your work (hand blister) or walk (foot blister); (3) Trouble adjusting to a new role (filling someone else's shoes).

Also see *Pimple*.

(1) Matt. 5:10; (Matt. 10:35 & Eph. 6:15); (2) Matt. 13:20-21; (3) Mark 9:33-34.

Block of Units (Flats/Apartments): (1) Sub-culture or group; (2) Spiritually undeveloped individual (one unit/flat).

(1) Acts 16:3 (KJV); (2) 2 Cor. 5:1.

Blood: (1) Life (of the flesh); (2) Spirit (spirit parallels blood); (3) Family; (4) Atonement; (5) Redemption or redeemed; (6) Judgment; (7) Strife; (8) Guilt/blame; (9) Money; (10) Sacrifice; (11) Murder; (12) Drunk; (13) Earnest search for repentance (tears of blood); (14) Anxiety (sweating blood); (15) Christ or His offspring (bloody husband); (16) Martyrdom (bloody bride).

Also see *Bleeding*.

(1) Lev. 17:11; (2) Job 33:4; Ezek. 37:14; 1 Pet. 4:6; Rev. 11:11 (the Life of God is the Spirit); (3) Num. 35:21; Deut. 19:6; Josh. 20:5 (avenger of blood = kinsman); (4) Lev. 17:11; (5) 1 Pet. 1:18-19; (6) Gen. 4:10; Exod. 4:9; (7) Prov. 30:33; (8) Matt. 27:24; (9) Matt. 27:6 (blood-money); (10) Exod. 34:25; Ps. 106:38; Isa. 1:11; Ezek. 39:19; (11) Gen. 4:10; (12) Jer. 46:10; (13) Heb. 12:17; (14) Luke 22:44; (15) Exod. 4:26 & 1 Cor. 10:16; (16) Rev. 17:6.

Blood Bank: (1) Church.

(1) John 6:53-56; Lev. 17:11; As in, the place where Spiritual life is renewed.

Blood Pressure: (1) Resistance to the Holy Spirit (high b.p.); (2) Lacking spiritual intimacy (low b.p.); (3) Lacking spiritual fortitude (low b.p.).

(1) Lev. 17:11 & (Job 33:4; Ezek. 37:14); Acts 6:10; (2) Isa. 40:30-31; (3) Heb. 12:3-4.

Bloody Nose: See Nose Bleed.

Blood Transfusion: (1) Salvation/conversion; (2) Spiritual life renewed.
(1) Heb. 9:14; 1 Pet. 1:18-19; 1 John 1:7; (2) Lev. 17:11.

Blossom: (1) Potential fruitfulness; (2) Chosen by God; (3) Abundance; (4) Joy and rejoicing; (5) Beauty; (6) Pride; (7) Associated with spring (summer is harvest time).
(1) Gen. 40:10; Num. 17:8; (2) Num. 17:5; (3) Isa. 27:6, 35:2; (4) Isa. 35:2; Hab. 3:17-18; (5) Isa. 35:1; (6) Ezek. 7:10; (7) Song. 2:11-12.

Blowing: (1) Opposition; (2) Testing; (3) Spirit; (4) Assisting a fire.
Also see *Hit, Trumpet,* and *Wind.*
(1-2) Matt. 7:25, 17; John 6:18; (3) Isa. 40:7; John 3:8; (4) Job 20:26; Isa. 54:16.

Blue: (1) Heaven/ly; (2) Spirit/ual; (3) Royalty (king); (4) Jesus; (5) Holy Spirit (dark blue); (6) Human spirit (light blue); (7) Healing (as a heavenly reality); (8) Complete; (9) Reminder of seeking the Kingdom first (if looking at blue).
(1-2) Exod. 28:31; 36:8, 35; 39:1; Num. 4:7; 15:38; (3-4) Esther 8:15; (5) John 1:32; (6) Rev. 1:6; 5:10; (7-9) (cf. Exod. 39:24; Num. 15:38-39 & Matt. 9:20-21).

Blueberries: (1) Fruit of the Spirit.
Also see *Berries, Blue,* and *Strawberries.*
(1) Gal. 5:22-23.

Blues Music: (1) Depression; (2) Cultural association with oppressed peoples.
(1-2) Ps. 137:1-3.

Blunt: (1) A blunt weapon means ineffective words; (2) Rude, outspoken, or tactless; (3) Dull; (4) Blunt words often require raised volume.
(1) Ps. 58:6; Isa. 54:17; (2) Eph. 5:4; (3) Isa. 59:1; (4) Eccl. 10:10.

Blushing: (1) Embarrassment; (2) Anger; (3) Shame; (4) Stress; (5) Guilty.
(1) Ezra 9:6; (2) Gen. 39:19 (NIV); (3) Ezra 9:6; Jer. 6:15; (4) Job 16:16 (5) Ezek. 16:63.

Board: (1) Secular leadership; (2) Religious council; (3) Elders.

(1) Acts 4:8; (2) Matt. 5:22; 10:17; 12:14; 26:59; (3) Acts 11:30; 14:23.

Boarding School: See Private School.

Board Meeting: (1) Communing over business matters; (2) Running a business; (3) Business plans and agenda; (4) Ambition; (5) Council; (6) Accountability.

(1) Acts 4:15; (2) Acts 4:16-21, 5:27, 29; (3) Matt. 26:59; Luke 22:66-67; (4) 2 Sam. 15:12; John 11:47-48; (5) Matt. 5:22; 10:17, 12:14; 26:59; (6) Acts 15:6, 22.

Boardwalk: See Jetty.

Boat: (1) Ministry; (2) Life's journey; (3) Person; (4) Holy Spirit transport; (5) Church.

Also see *Battleship, Canoe, Rowing, Ship, Shipwreck,* and *Speedboat.*

(1) Luke 5:3-10; (2) Mark 4:35; (3) John 3:8; Acts 18:21b; (4) 2 Sam. 19:18; (5) 1 Pet. 3:20; Matt. 14:22.

Boat Trailer: See Trailer (Boat).

Body: (1) Death (dead body); (2) The Body of Christ; (3) The temple of God; (4) Sacrifice; (5) Spiritual body; (6) Organization; (7) The flesh.

(1) Ps. 79:2; 110:6; (2) Rom. 12:5; 1 Cor. 6:15; Eph. 5:30; (3) 1 Cor. 6:19 (individually); 2 Cor. 6:16 (corporately); (4) Rom. 12:1; (5) 1 Cor. 15:44; (6) 1 Cor. 12:25; (7) Rom. 8:13; 1 Cor. 6:16; Col. 1:22a.

Body Odor: (1) Offense/ive; (2) Works of the flesh.

(1) Gen. 3:19 & Gen. 4:2-5; (2) Ezek. 44:18.

Bogey/Boogie (Dried Nasal Mucus): (1) Person offended by the things of the Spirit; (2) If another person has the bogey, it may be that they have offended you; (3) Wrong spirit (resistance to the Spirit of God); (4) Evil spirit; (5) "Bogey man": under Demon.

(1) Matt. 13:57; John 6:61-63; (2) Matt. 16:23; (3) Acts 7:51; (4) Acts 13:8-10.

Boiling: (1) Anger; (2) Purification; (3) Enlivening.

Also see *Pressure Cooker.*

(1) Gen. 44:18; Num. 11:1; Isa. 42:25; (2) Num. 31:23; (3) Jer. 20:9.

Boils: (1) Test; (2) Anger; (3) Plague.

(1) Job 2:7; (2) Lev. 13:23 (burning boil); (3) Lev. 13:22 (spreading).

Bolts: (1) Assurance; (2) Sure words; (3) Immovable; (4) Build/ing; (5) Tie together or unite; (6) Foundation; (7) Lock.

Also see *Nails, Nuts,* and *Bolts.*

(1) Ezra 9:8; Isa. 22:23; (2) Eccl. 12:11; (3) Isa. 41:7; Jer. 10:4; (4-6) Ezra 4:12; Neh. 4:6; Eph. 2:21; (7) 2 Sam. 13:17-18.

Bomb: (1) Words of sudden detrimental impact (dropped bomb); (2) Explosive or shocking words; (3) Sudden destructive event; (4) Shocking announcement (i.e. resignation); (5) Empowered by the Holy Spirit (loading a bombshell); (6) Words that burn (positive or negative); (7) Unresolved issue that will blow up in the future (time bomb); (8) Explosive outburst.

Also see *Arrow, Missile, Rocket,* and *Terrorism.*

(1) 1 Sam. 3:19 & Prov. 18:21; (2) Matt. 26:21; Luke 22:21; (3) Jer. 51:8; 1 Thess. 5:3; (4) As in, "she dropped a bombshell"; (5) Acts 1:8; (6) Jer. 20:8; Luke 24:32; (7) Gen. 4:2-3; (8) Prov. 18:21.

Bonds: See Bound.

Bones: (1) Dead; (2) Without spiritual life; (3) Broken-spirited; (4) Having sorrow of heart; (5) Hopelessness; (6) Feeling cut off from God; (7) Envy (rotten bones).

(1-2) Ezek. 37:4, 11; (3) Prov. 17:22; (4) Prov. 15:13; (5-6) Ezek. 37:11; (7) Prov. 14:30.

Book: (1) Bible; (2) Judgment (Lamb's book of Life); (3) Literal book; (4) Words; (5) Law; (6) Go by the book; (7) Contract; (8) Meditate; (9) Life plan; (10) An individual (a heart).

Also see *Bookcase, Library,* and *Scroll.*

(1) Josh. 1:8; (2) Rev. 13:8; 21:27; (3) Luke 4:17; (4) Luke 3:4; (5) Josh. 1:8; (6-7) Exod. 24:7; (8) Josh. 1:8; (9) Ps. 40:7; Heb. 10:7; (10) Prov. 3:3; 2 Cor. 3:3.

Bookcase: (1) Mindset; (2) Ideals and beliefs; (3) Church full of head knowledge.

Also see *Book.*

(1-2) Josh. 1:8a; Col. 3:2; (3) 1 Cor. 8:1-2.

Bookmark: (1) Revelation; (2) Verse for meditation.

Also see *Highlighter* and *Tassels.*

(1-2) Josh. 1:8.

Boomerang: (1) What goes around comes around (positive or negative); (2) Something that the Spirit brings back to you; (3) Australia.

(1) Isa. 55:11; Gal. 6:7; (2) Gen. 41:9-14 (cf. Gen. 40:23); (3) By association.

Boom Gate: (1) Waiting on God.

(1) Ps. 62:5.

Boots: (1) External or outward walk (what you do out of the home); (2) Work; (3) Military/warfare.

Also see *Cowboy, Shoes,* and *Ball-Kicking.*

(3) 2 Cor. 10:3.

Boss: (1) Jesus; (2) God; (3) Natural leadership; (4) Spiritual leadership; (5) Father.

(1) Matt. 10:24-25; John 13:13-14; (2) Ps. 123:2; Gen. 24:12; Isa. 40:22; (3) Gen. 39:2; 1 Sam. 24:6; (4) 2 Kings 2:3, 5; (5) Mal. 1:6.

Bottle/s: (1) Heart (as a vessel of the Spirit); (2) Old bottles may speak about the old self; new bottles the new self; new bottles (wine skins) are adjustable/flexible/stretchable; (3) Local church; (4) Wineskins need to be able to vent (that is, speak out or they will burst); (5) Old bottles may speak about deception; (6) Sharing a bottle speaks of friendship/communion/covenant meal; (7) Welcome; (8) Sucking the life out of people (emptying bottles and laying them down).

Also see *Vessels* and *Wine.*

(1-2) Jer. 13:12-13; Matt. 9:17; John 2:6-10; (3) Matt. 9:17; (4) Job 32:19; (5) Josh. 9:4, 13; (6) 1 Sam. 1:24; 10:3; 16:20; (7) 2 Sam. 16:1; (8) Jer. 48:12.

Bottle Cap/Top: (1) Stopping words coming out (+/-) (capping a bottle).

Also see *Bottle.*

(1) Matt. 9:17 (KJV) & Prov. 30:32 (cf. Eccl. 10:12). As in, "put a lid on it!"

Bought: See Buy/ing.

Bound: (1) Spiritually bound with words; (2) Under control; (3) Captive or confined; (4) Opposite of freedom; (5) To be dead spiritually.

A person can be bound: (6) By religion; (7) By the world; (8) By an unclean spirit; (9) By satan; (10) By iniquity; (11) In the Spirit; (12) By the state; (13) By people pleasing.

Also see *Cord, Loosing,* and *Rope.*

(1) Acts 23:12, 14, 21; <u>Matt.</u> 16:19; <u>18:18</u>; (2) Mark 5:3-4; (3) Mark 6:17-20; John 18:12; (4) John 8:33; (5) John 11:44; (6) John 18:12; Acts 9:2, 14, 21; 21:11; (7) Acts 7:7; (8) <u>Luke 8:29</u>; (9) Luke 13:16; (10) Acts 8:23; (11) Acts 20:22-23; (12) Acts 22:29; (13) Acts 24:27.

Boundary: (1) Covering; (2) Kingdom of God; (3) Decision; (4) Heaven and hell; (5) Righteous and sinner; (6) Blessed and cursed; (7) Dividing God's Word or God's Word dividing.

(1) Gen. 19:8b; (2) Deut. 17:14; (3) Num. 13:30–14:1; (4-6) Matt. 25:33-34; Luke 16:26; (7) 2 Tim. 2:15; Heb. 4:12.

Bow (As in, Bow and Arrow): (1) Heart (that which shoots words); (2) Words launched at a distance; (3) Deceitful heart (distorted bow); (4) Ready (bent bow).

Also see *Arrows* and *Left.*

(1) <u>Ps. 64:3</u>; Hab. 3:9; (2) <u>1 Sam. 20:20-22</u>; (3) Ps. 78:57; Hos. 7:16; (4) Ps. 11:2.

Bowing: (1) Humbling oneself; (2) Greeting; (3) Worship; (4) Paying homage.

Also see *Bending, Duck,* and *Knee.*

(1) Isa. 2:11; (2) Eastern culturally-accepted greeting; (3) Matt. 28:9; (4) Acts 10:25-26.

Bowl: (1) Heart.

Also see *Vessels.*

(1) Eccl. 12:6.

Box: (1) Heart; (2) Righteous/ness (white box); (3) Innocence (white box); (4) Insincere heart (plastic box); (5) Confined or restricted; (6) Spiritual gift or present; (7) Not unpacked or not in use (something boxed up).

(1) Matt. 26:7 (KJV); (2) 1 Kings 3:6; <u>Rom. 10:10</u>; (3) Ps. 106:38; (4) Isa. 29:13; (5) As in, "put in a box"; (6) <u>Mark 14:3</u> (as does the alabaster box, which was broken that the fragrance of the Holy Spirit may fill the house); (7) Luke 7:37 (KJV).

Boxing: (1) Spiritual Warfare; (2) Under attack; (3) Adversity; (4) Need for discipline.

(1-2) <u>2 Cor. 10:3-4</u>; Eph. 6:12; (3) Isa. 30:20; Heb. 13:3; (4) 1 Cor. 9:26-27.

Boy: (1) The world; (2) Actual boy; (3) Legacy or heritage; (4) Inheritance; (5) Heir; (6) Future; (7) Young generation; (8) Promise.

Also see *Baby, Girl,* and *Son.*

(1) Luke 9:41; John 16:21; Gal. 4:3; (3-5) Matt. 21:38; Gal. 4:1, 7, 30; Heb. 1:2; Rev. 21:7; (6) Job 21:8; (7) Gen. 48:19b; Amos 2:11; (8) Gal. 4:28.

Bra: (1) Righteousness; (2) Integrity of heart; (3) Support; (4) Brazen (no bra); (5) Loose woman (no bra); (6) Feral (no bra); (7) Whore (no bra); (8) Nurture (bra as care and support).

Also see *Breast.*

(1) Eph. 6:14; (2) 1 Kings 9:4; (3) Rev. 1:13 (KJV); (4-6) Hos. 2:2; Prov. 5:19, 6:29; (7) Prov. 5:19-20; (8) Isa. 60:4.

Braces (teeth): (1) Bound (restricted) by your words; (2) Ineffective bite/no power; (3) Speaking other than what God has directed you to say; (4) Legalism; (5) Hypocrisy; (6) Need for corrective speech.

Also see *Teeth.*

(1) Num. 21:5-6; Matt. 16:18; (2-3) Num. 22:38; (3) 1 Cor. 2:4; 1 Thess. 1:5; Heb. 4:12; (4) Matt. 23:4; (5) Matt. 23:2-3.

Brake/s: (1) Stop or slow down; (2) Stop speaking; (3) Stop hearing; (4) Slow down; (5) Feeling out of control (no brakes); (6) Feeling like you started something that you cannot stop (no brakes); (7) No limits (no brakes).

(1) Exod. 14:13; (2) Rom. 3:19; 2 Cor. 11:10; Tit. 1:11; Heb. 11:33; (3) Acts 7:57; (4) Ps. 103:8; 145:8; Prov. 14:29; 15:18; 16:32; Joel 2:13; Acts 27:7; James 1:19; (5) Prov. 25:28; (6) James 3:5; (7) Matt. 9:17 (the new wineskin has no breaks!).

Branch: (1) Jesus; (2) Channel of the Holy Spirit (anointed one); (3) Believer/ Christian; (4) Fruit bearer; (5) Honorable elder; (6) Influence (long branch = long reach); (7) Day; (8) Pride (endangered branches); (9) Union with God (flourishing branch); (10) The king (the highest branch).

(1) Isa. 4:2; 11:1; Jer. 23:5; 33:15; Zech. 3:8; 6:12; (2) Exod. 25:31-37; Zech. 4:12-14; (3) Matt. 13:31-32; John 15:5; (4) Num. 13:23; Isa. 4:2; 17:6; Ezek. 17:8; 19:10; John 15:2, 4; (5) Isa. 9:14-15; 19:15; (6) Ezek. 31:5; Dan. 4:14; (7) Gen. 40:10-12; (8) Rom. 11:17-22; (9) Prov. 11:28; (10) Ezek. 17:22.

Brass: (1) Judgment; (2) Financial Hardship; (3) Without love; (4) Third place.

(1) Exod. 27:1-2; Rev. 1:15; (2) Matt. 10:9; (3) 1 Cor. 13:1; (4) Mark 12:42.

Breach: (1) Break through/forth; (2) Fracture; (3) Break; (4) Spiritual gap; (5) Repair needed; (6) Wound; (7) Broken wall; (8) Hole.

(1) <u>Gen. 38:29</u>; 2 Sam. 5:20; 6:8; (2) <u>Lev. 24:20</u>; (3) Num. 14:34; (4) Judg. 21:15; 1 Kings 11:27; Ps. 106:23; Prov. 15:4; Isa. 22:9; (5) 2 Kings 12:5-7; 22:5; Isa. 58:12; (6) Job 16:14; Isa. 30:26; Jer. 14:17; Lam. 2:13; (7) Isa. 30:13; Ezek. 26:10; (8) Amos 6:11.

Bread: (1) Christ; (2) The Word of God; (3) Broken body (breaking bread); (4) Communion (breaking bread); (5) Death; (6) Words (our hearts feed on words); (7) Affliction (unleavened bread); (8) Life (bread sustains life).

Also see *Crumbs, Crusty Bread* (directly below), *Loaf, Toast,* and *Wine.*

(1) 1 Cor. 10:16; 11:27; (2) Deut. 8:3; Amos 8:11; <u>Matt. 4:4</u>; Luke 4:4; (3) Matt. 26:26; Luke 24:35; Acts 2:42; (4-5) Mark 14:1; <u>1 Cor. 11:26</u>; (6) Amos 8:11; Matt. 4:4; (7) Deut. 16:3; (8) John 6:33, 35, 48, 51, 58.

Bread (Crusty Bread): (1) Old words; (2) Deception; (3) Thoughts and words from a fleshly heart (wood oven loaves).

(1-3) Josh. 9:4-6, 12.

Bread (Moldy Bread): (1) Old manna/revelation; (2) Not exercising faith; (3) Need for daily bread.

(1-2) <u>Exod. 16:20-21</u>, 26; (3) Matt. 6:11.

Breakfast: (1) It's a new day; (2) New beginning; (3) Breaking your fast.

(1-2) John 21:12; (3) 2 Sam. 12:21.

Breaking: (1) Violating; (2) Stealing; (3) Destroying; (4) Brokenness; (5) Dying to self; (6) Repenting; (7) Desperate faith; (8) Cut short/nullified/without effect; (9) Physically broken; (10) Dispersing; (11) Pruning; (12) Giving the heart expression vocally (breaking forth).

(1) Matt. 5:19; John 5:18; 7:23; Rom. 2:23; (2) Matt. 6:19-20; 24:43; (3) Matt. 12:20; Mark 5:4; Luke 5:6; John 21:11; Acts 27:41; Eph. 2:14; Rev. 2:27; (4) <u>Matt. 21:44</u>; Luke 20:18; Acts 2:42, 46; <u>21:13</u>; 1 Cor. 10:16; 11:24; (5) Matt. 14:19; 15:36-37; 26:26; Mark 14:3; Luke 24:35; (6) Judg. 21:15; Joel 2:13; (7) Mark 2:4-5; (8) John 10:35; (9) John 19:31-32, 36; (10) Acts 13:43; (11) Rom. 11:17, 19; (12) Gal. 4:27.

Breast: (1) Nurtured; (2) Spiritual pioneer (i.e. Martin Luther); (3) Repentance (beating breast); (4) Embrace; (5) Sexually perverse spirit or spirit of lust (grabbing breast); (6) Close to the heart (love).

Also see *Bra, Harlot, Jezebel* (in Name and Place Dictionary), *Naked,* and *Woman.*

(1) Job 3:12; Song. 8:1; Isa. 60:16; (2) Someone who distributes the milk of the Word that the Body may grow thereby; (3) Jer. 31:19; Luke 18:13; (4) Ruth 4:16; Prov. 5:20; (5) Matt. 5:28; (6) John 13:23; 21:20.

Breath: (1) Spirit; (2) Spiritual life; (3) Offensive (bad breath); (4) Unclean spirit (bad breath); (5) God's Spoken Word (rhema).

Also see *Belch.*

(1-2) Gen. 2:7; (3) Job 19:17; (4) Mark 1:26; (5) Ps. 33:6.

Breath Analysis/Testing: (1) Testing/measuring the Spirit.

(1) 1 John 4:1.

Breathing: (1) Impartation of life; (2) Spiritual infilling; (3) Breath of life.

Also see *Blowing.*

(1-3) Gen. 2:7; Ezek. 37:9.

Brewery: (1) Because it utilizes fermentation, it infers a process of corruption and evil; (2) Worldly church.

Also see *Yeast.*

(1) Exod. 34:25; Lev. 2:11 (leaven and honey were excluded from offerings because they symbolize people seeking their own glory, i.e. corrupt worship); (2) 1 Pet. 1:23-25; Rev. 2:15-18; 18:2.

Bricks: The Scriptural use of the word portrays: (1) people's attempt to reach Heaven; (2) People attempting to make a name for themselves; (3) Human-made empires; (4) Rebellion against God; (5) Bondage of the world (Egypt); (6) A works-based service of people; (7) Keeping people busy so that they do not have time to truly worship God; (8) Pride; (9) Human-made altars; (10) Human-made words (bricks instead of stone).

Also see *Stone/s.*

(1-3) Gen. 11:3-4; (4) Gen. 9:1 & 11:4; (5-6) Exod. 1:14; (7) Exod. 5:7-8ff; (8) Isa. 9:9-11; (9) Isa. 65:3; (10) Gen. 11:3-4.

Bride: (1) Church; (2) Heavenly Jerusalem; (3) Israel; (4) United with (union); (5) Relationship; (6) Spotless and ready for Christ's return (bride in white dress); (7) Martyrdom (bloody bride).

Also see *Best Man, Blood, Groom,* and *Marriage.*

(1) <u>Eph. 5:25</u>; (2) <u>Rev. 21:9b-10</u>; (3) Isa. 54:5; (4-5) Gen. 2:24; (6) Rev. 19:7; (7) Rev. 17:6.

Bridegroom: See Groom.

Bridesmaid: (1) Loss of first love (should be the bride); (2) Getting others ready to meet Christ; (3) Pastor/leader.

(1) Rom. 7:4; Rev. 2:4; (2) Matt. 25:10; Rev. 21:2; (3) Matt. 23:11; Eph. 5:26-27.

Bridle: (1) Control the tongue.

(1) Job 30:11; Ps. 32:9; 39:1; <u>James 1:26</u>; 3:2.

Bridge: (1) The Cross; (2) Jesus Christ; (3) The Church; (4) Filling the gap; (5) Means to an end; (6) Human-made destiny; (7) Human-made efforts; (8) Life's passage or journey; (9) A link; (10) Salvation ministry (working on bridge); (11) Relationship or communication; (12) Human-made structure.

(1) 2 Sam. 18:9 (see *Oak*); (2) John 1:51; 1 Pet. 3:18; (3) John 1:41-42; 2 Cor. 5:20; (4) <u>Ezek. 22:30</u>; (10) By virtue of the fact that the bridge is the cross of Christ; (11) Ps. 133:1; Also, as in, "building bridges"; (12) Gen. 11:4.

Briefcase: (1) Business; (2) Financial management; (3) Business transaction; (4) Teacher or teaching.

(1) <u>John 12:6 & Acts 1:18a</u>; (2-3) <u>Prov. 7:20</u>; John 12:6; (4) Eph. 4:11.

Broad: (1) Destruction (road/gate); (2) All encompassing; (3) Easy (road/gate); (4) Made to impress; (5) Deep (river).

(1-3) <u>Matt. 7:13-14</u>; (4) Matt. 23:5 (adornments); (5) Eph. 3:18; Ezek. 47:3-5.

Broken: (1) Broken spirit; (2) Broken heart; (3) Ineffective work (broken hand); (4) Bad walk (broken foot); (5) Interrupted walk (broken feet).

(1) Job 17:1; (2) Prov. 15:13; (3) Job 22:9 (KJV); (4) Heb. 12:13; (5) 2 Sam. 4:4.

Broken Glass: (1) Disappointment; (2) Reproach; (3) Illegal entry into your spirit (breaking your spiritual window); (4) Cutting words.

Also see *Glass, Water* (water reflects like glass), and *Window.*

(1) Job 17:11; Ps. 38:8 (cf. Prov. 27:19 & 20:5); also as in "shattered dreams"; (2) Ps. 69:20; (3) Matt. 6:19; (4) Ps. 22:13a.

Bronze: (1) Strength; (2) Righteousness; (3) Boldness; (4) Third place.

Also see *Brass, Gold, Pewter,* and *Silver.*

(1-3) Rev. 1:15; 2:18 (NIV); (4) Num. 31:22 (NIV); also as in Olympic medals.

Brook: (1) Resting place; (2) A defining moment; (3) A dividing place; (4) Hiding place; (5) A place of trees; (6) A place of harvest; (7) A place of blessing; (8) The Word of God; (9) A place of sustenance; (10) A place of judgment; (11) A place of passage; (12) Deceitful; (13) A place of stones; (14) A place of refreshing and honor; (15) The human spirit; (16) A place of mourning; (17) Defense; (18) Border; (19) The words from a person's mouth.

Also see *River* and *Stream.*

(1) 1 Kings 17:4-6; (2-3) Gen. 32:23; Num. 21:14-15; Deut. 2:13-14; 1 Sam. 30:9-10, 21; 2 Sam. 15:23; 17:20; 1 Kings 2:37; (4) 1 Kings 17:3; Job 40:22; (5) Lev. 23:40; (6) Num. 13:23-24; (7) Deut. 8:7; Job 20:17; (8) 1 Sam. 17:40; Ps. 42:1; (9) 1 Kings 18:5; (10) 1 Kings 18:40; 2 Kings 23:6; (11) Neh. 2:15; (12) Job 6:15; (13) Job 22:24; (14) Ps. 110:7; (15) Prov. 18:4; (16) Isa. 15:7; (17) Isa. 19:6; (18) Jer. 31:40; (19) Prov. 18:4.

Broom: (1) Cleaning up; (2) Putting things in order; (2) Destruction.

Also see *Sweeping.*

(1-2) Luke 15:8; (3) Isa. 14:23.

Brothel: (1) Church whose members are selling themselves to the world or making money illegitimately; (2) House of sin; (3) Lust issue.

(1) Rev. 17:3-4; (2) Prov. 5:20-22; (3) Matt. 5:28.

Brother: (1) Fellow believer (male or female); (2) Jesus Christ; (3) Guardian; (4) Natural brother; (5) Brother in nationality.

(1) Rom. 14:13; 1 Cor. 5:11; 6:6; Matt. 22:30; 1 Pet. 3:1-4; (2) Matt. 28:10; John 20:17; Rom. 8:29; Heb. 2:11; (3) Eph. 6:21-22; Col. 4:7; (4) Gal. 1:19; (5) Rom. 9:3.

Brother-in-law: (1) Legalistic believer; (2) Someone who negates the Word through religious tradition; (3) Religious adversary; (4) Fellow believer wanting to impose their ways/culture opposing the flow of the Spirit; (5) New converts coming out of worldly ways.

Also see *Father-in-Law* and *Son-in-Law.*

(1) Gal. 2:16, 21; 5:10; (2) Matt. 15:1-3; (3) Matt. 16:21; 26:57; (4) Gal. 2:12-13; 3:3; (5) Acts 11:3, 18.

Brown: (1) Earthly or earthen (contrasted to heavenly); (2) Sin; (3) The imperfections of the flesh; (4) Marred, unwanted; (5) Dark-skinned.

(1) 2 Cor. 4:7; (2) Ps. 104:35; Eccl. 7:20; Matt. 9:6; (3) Gen. 6:12; 2 Cor. 4:7; (4) Gen. 30:32-40; (5) Song. 1:5-6.

Bruise: (1) Strike and injure (or injured); (2) Have victory over; (3) To crush or bind a heart; (4) Wounded; (5) Been ill-spoken of.

(1) Gen. 3:15; (2) Gen. 3:15; Rom. 16:20; (3) Matt. 12:20; Luke 4:18; 9:39; (4) Isa. 1:6; 53:5; (5) Prov. 25:18.

Brush: See Broom and Comb.

Bubble: (1) Spirit being; (2) Life (the Spirit bubbling up); (3) Protection (surrounded by a bubble); (4) Thought or revelation (as in thought bubble); (5) Anger (as in boiling); (6) Speaks of an episode in one's life or time period; (7) Fragile; (8) Separation or difference.

Also see *Balloon* and *Effervescence*.

(1) Ezek. 1:21; (2) John 4:14; (3) Job 1:10; Ps. 5:12; 32:7, 10; (4) 2 Cor. 10:5; (5) Job 30:27 (KJV); (6) 1 Sam. 10:2-9; Heb. 1:1; (7) Ps. 80:12; 89:40; Isa. 5:5; (8) Eph. 2:14.

Bubblegum: (1) Childish.

(1) 1 Cor. 13:11.

Bucket: (1) Unsaved person (wooden pail); (2) Insignificant; (3) Human vessel; (4) Preacher; (5) Superficial person (plastic bucket).

Also see *Plastic, Vessel,* and *Wood.*

(1) Exod. 7:19; (2) Isa. 40:15 (as in "drop in a bucket"); (3) Num. 24:7; (4) Num. 24:7 & Luke 8:11 & Eph. 5:26; (5) Matt. 15:8-9; Col. 2:18a.

Bud: (1) Resurrection life; (2) New life.

(1-2) Gen. 40:10; Num. 17:8; Job 14:7-9; Isa. 27:6; 55:10; Heb. 9:4.

Buddhist Monk: (1) Religious spirit; (2) Idolatry.

(1) Mark 7:3, 5, 8a; (2) Exod. 20:4.

Buddy: (1) Jesus Christ; (2) The Holy Spirit; (3) Close associate.

(1) John 15:15; (2) John 14:16.

Budgie: See Parrot.

Bugs: (1) Annoyance; (2) Religious spirit (bug in the ear).

Also see *Insects*.

(1) Isa. 1:14; Luke 18:5; Also, as in, "stop bugging me!"; (2) John 7:12b (bad-mouthing those moving in the Spirit).

Building (noun): (1) The individual; (2) Strong individual; (3) The Church; (4) Prayer tower (watch tower); (5) A business; (6) The glorified person; (7) Greed (barns); (8) Heavenly mansion; (9) Establishment.

Also see *Barn* and *House*.

(1) 1 Cor. 3:9; 6:19; John 2:21; Matt. 7:24, 26; (2) 1 Cor. 3:9; Gal. 2:9; (3) 2 Cor. 6:16 (corporate temple); Eph. 2:21-22; 1 Pet. 2:5; (4) Matt. 21:33; Mark 12:1; Luke 14:28; (5) Matt. 24:1 & John 2:16; Mark 13:2; (6) Mark 14:58; 1 Cor. 5:1; (7) Luke 12:18; (8) John 14:2; (9) Ezra 3:10; Isa. 44:28.

Building (verb): (1) Preaching the Gospel; (2) Building the Church; (3) Building the individual; (4) Christian works; (5) Putting together; (6) Association.

(1) Rom. 15:20; (2) Matt. 16:18; (3) Jude 1:20; Prov. 24:3-4; (4) 1 Cor. 3:14; (5-6) Eph. 4:16.

Builder: (1) God; (2) Gospel preachers/believers; (3) False builders; (4) You; (5) Church builder; (6) Businessman (trying to make a name for oneself).

Also see *Workman*.

(1) Ps. 127:1; Heb. 3:4; 11:10; (2) 1 Cor. 3:10; (3) Matt. 21:42; (4) Jude 1:20; 1 Cor. 3:10b; (5) Matt. 16:18; Acts 8:5-6, 14-15; (6) Gen. 11:4-5.

Building Blocks (ABC): (1) A call for child-like faith; (2) A message spelled out; (3) If the blocks are moved and the message unread, it may mean lacking spiritual insight/sensitivity; (4) Playing with building blocks with no message speaks of immaturity and entertainment-only value; (5) Early stage of building faith.

(1) Matt. 18:3-4; (2) Dan. 5:24-25; (3) Matt. 13:16-17; (4) 1 Cor. 13:11; (5) Jude 1:20.

Building Frame: (1) The Holy Spirit; (2) Understanding; (3) Structure.

(1) Eph. 2:21-22; (2) Prov. 24:3; (3) Isa. 61:4.

Bull: (1) Idol; (2) Danger; (3) Strong evil spirit; (4) Bellower (loud speaker); (5) Offering; (6) Financial predator.

Also see *Ox* and *Calf*.

(1) Exod. 32:4ff; 1 Kings 12:28, 32; 2 Kings 10:29; (2) Exod. 21:29; (3) Ps. 22:12-13; (4) Jer. 50:11; (5) Lev. 9:2; (6) (Red rag to a bull, being in the red); financial bull/Wall St.

Bulldog: (1) Determined; (2) Tenacious.

Also see *Dog.*

(1-2) Jer. 15:3.

Bulldozer: (1) Very powerful ministry (generally: constructive = good; destructive = evil); (2) Apostle, prophet, or evangelist; (3) Preparation ministry; (4) Heavy-handed leader; (5) Powerful trailblazing/groundbreaking ministry (pioneering).

Also see *Earthmover, Road Grader,* and *Truck.*

(1) Acts 8:5-6, 9-10; (2-3) Isa. 40:3-4; Matt. 3:3; Acts 8:5-6; (4) 1 Sam. 22:11-18; (5) Matt. 3:1-3.

Bullet/s: (1) Words against you; (2) Piercing words; (3) God's Word; (4) Wounds (used slugs); (5) Words lodged in your heart (used slugs).

(1) Ps. 64:3; Jer. 9:8; (2) Ps. 45:5; (3) Heb. 4:12; (4-5) Prov. 18:8; 26:22.

Bulrushes: (1) Lying prophet.

(1) Isa. 9:14-15.

Bum (Buttocks): (1) Curse of disobedience (tail).

Also see *Homeless Person* and *Sitting.*

(1) Deut. 28:44.

Bundle: (1) Life; (2) Treasure; (3) A gathered group.

(1) 1 Sam. 25:29; (2) Gen. 42:35; Song. 1:13; (3) Matt. 13:30; Acts 28:3.

Burden: See Backpack.

Burn/ing: (1) Judgment; (2) Holy; (3) Torment; (4) Not being able to hold back; (5) Being consumed by; (6) Dealing with potential gossip (back-burning); (7) Dealing with past issues (back-burning); (8) Lust.

Also see *Fire.*

(1) Ezek. 38:22; Mal. 4:1; (2) Isa. 10:17; (3) Rev. 14:10; (4-5) Jer. 20:9; (6) James 3:5; (8) Rom. 1:27.

Burnt: (1) Betrayed or let down by another; (2) Sacrificed; (3) Heart seared from abuse; (4) Needs to be healed by the love of God.

(1) Luke 21:16; (2) 1 Pet. 2:5; (3) Neh. 4:2; (4) Mark 12:33.

Burp: See Belch.

Burrow: (1) Resting place; (2) Hiding place.

(1-2) Ps. 104:18; Prov. 30:26.

Burst: (1) Trying to put things of the Spirit into the unsaved; (2) Not yet capable of containing the truth shared; (3) Unable to stop the flow of the Spirit.

(1) Mark 2:22; Luke 5:37; (2) John 16:12; (3) Jer. 20:9.

Burying: (1) Dying to self; (2) Baptism; (3) Being overcome by sin (being buried); (4) Hiding.

Also see *Underground*.

(1-2) Rom. 6:4; (3) Rom. 6:23; (4) Gen. 35:4; Josh. 7:19-21.

Bus: (1) Large ministry; (2) Church; (3) Commercial vehicle; (4) Vehicle to your destiny; (5) Prophetic teaching/ministry (double-decker bus).

Also see *Bus Queue, Bus Station, School Bus, Tourist Bus,* and *Missing the Bus*.

(1) Acts 9:15-16; (2) Acts 15:3; 3 John 1:6b-7; (3) John 2:16; (4) Acts 1:8; (5) 2 Kings 6:1.

Bus Queue: (1) Waiting for ministry.

Also see *Bus Station/Stop*.

(1) 2 Chron. 7:6; Rom. 12:7.

Bus Station/Stop: (1) Waiting for ministry; (2) Waiting for direction; (3) Awaiting the timing of God.

Also see *Bus Queue*.

(1-2) Acts 13:1-3; (3) Gal. 4:4; Luke 2:51a; 3:23.

Bush: (1) God's manifest Presence; (2) May speak of turning aside; (3) God wants to talk to you; (4) Hiding place; (5) Growing believer; (6) Unbelieving person of the flesh; (7) Humble person; (8) Person trusting in people.

Also see *Tree*.

(1) Exod. 3:2; Deut. 33:16; Acts 7:30, 35; (2) Exod. 3:3; (3) Mark 12:26; (4) Gen. 3:8; (5) Ps. 1:1, 3; (6) Jer. 17:5-6; (7) Exod. 3:2; (8) Jer. 17:5-6.

Bush Fire: See Wild Fire.

Business: (1) God's work; (2) Secular work.

(1) 1 Cor. 15:58; Luke 2:49; Acts 6:3; Rom. 12:11; (2) 1 Thess. 4:11.

Business Card: (1) New venture; (2) New association; (3) Identity.

(1-2) Acts 13:2-3; (3) Rev. 2:17.

Blank Business Card: (1) New name; (2) New beginning; (3) Favor of God; (4) Losing identity; (5) God about to do something new with you.

(1-2) Isa. 62:2; Zeph. 3:20 (NLT); Rev. 2:17; (3) 1 Sam. 10:7; 2 Sam. 7:3; (4) Ps. 9:5; (5) Isa. 42:9; 43:19a.

Busy: (1) Other agendas; (2) Commerce; (3) Hardened hearts.

(1) Luke 10:31-32, 41; (2) John 2:14-16; (3) Matt. 13:4, 19 (the wayside is hardened by much traffic).

Butcher's Shop: (1) Place of solid Bible teaching; (2) Place of judgment.

(1) 1 Cor. 3:2; Heb. 5:12-14 (KJV); (2) James 5:5.

Butler: (1) Faithful servant; (2) Fruitful servant.

(1-2) Gen. 40:9-13.

Butter: (1) Prosperity; (2) Smooth talker; (3) Charming words; (4) Strife because of the Word; (5) Growth through the Word; (6) Provision; (7) Change (melted butter).

(1) Deut. 32:14; Job 29:6; (2-3) Ps. 55:21; (4) Prov. 30:33; (5) Isa. 7:15, 22; 1 Cor. 3:2 (Moving beyond milk); (6) Judg. 5:25; 2 Sam. 17:29; (7) Ps. 97:5.

Butterfly: (1) New creation; (2) Believer; (3) Glorified body (heavenly); (4) In the Spirit; (5) Changed (no longer a caterpillar); (6) No longer earthbound; (7) Glorified through death; (8) A person who flits from church to church (spiritual butterfly); (9) Israel (from Jacob [worm] to Israel [butterfly]).

(1-2) 2 Cor. 5:17; Eph. 4:22-24; 1 Pet. 3:18; (3) 1 Cor. 15:40; (4) Rev. 1:10; (5) 2 Cor. 5:17; (6) Ezek. 3:14; 8:3b; 11:1; (7) 1 Cor. 15:53-55; (8) cf. 1 Cor. 12:18, 25; (9) Isa. 41:14a (cf. Gen. 32:28).

Button (Pushing): (1) Employing an emotional trigger; (2) Touching a sore spot; (3) Arousing interest; (4) Invoking a response; (5) Ready to explode (anger).

Also see *Remote Control.*

(1) 1 Sam. 18:7-9; Ps. 106:32-33 (KJV); (2) Acts 23:6; (3) John 4:17-19; (4) John 6:60-61, 66; (5) Acts 7:54.

Buy/ing: (1) Soul winning; (2) Caught up in money-making; (3) Anchoring oneself to the world (giving second-place to the salvation of souls); (4) Laying down your life (giving your all); (5) Commercial transaction; (6) Life as usual before judgment; (7) Seeing things from an earthly perspective; (8) Redeemed by God; (9) Commitment; (10) Believing; (11) Grabbing hold of (purchasing); (12) Taking something on board.

Also see *Sale* and *Shop.*

(1) 1 Cor. 6:20; (2) Matt. 21:12-13; James 4:13; (3) Luke 14:18-19, 21-24; (4) Matt. 25:9-12; 13:44-46; Rev. 3:18; (5) Matt. 14:15; 27:7; John 4:8; Acts 7:16; Rev. 13:17; (6) Luke 17:28; (7) John 6:5-7; (8) 1 Cor. 6:20; 7:23; (9) As in, "buying into"; (10) As in, "I just don't buy it!"; (11) 1 Chron. 21:24; (12) Prov. 18:17.

Cab: (1) Driven by money; (2) Money-driven ministry or person (hireling); (3) The road you are traveling down is costing you (you as passenger); (4) Business opportunity to your destiny (you as driver).

(1) John 12:5-6; (2) John 10:12-13; (3) Matt. 16:26; (4) Matt. 26:15.

Cabin (Holiday): (1) Rest; (2) Relaxed; (3) Holiday or break; (4) Intimacy.

Also see *Hut* and *Shack.*

(1-2) Ruth 1:9; 2 Sam. 7:1; 1 Chron. 28:2; Isa. 66:1; Ezek. 44:30b; Dan. 4:4; (3) Luke 9:10b; (4) Matt. 14:13.

Cabin (Ship's): (1) Heart.

(1) Jon. 1:2-3, 5b.

Caesar: (1) Allegiance to world system; (2) Conqueror; (3) Tyrant; (4) Deceitful temptation; (5) Worldly (money-focused) leader.

(1) Matt. 22:17-21; (2) Luke 2:1; 3:1; John 19:12, 15; (3) Acts 12:1-2; (4-5) Matt. 22:17-21.

Caesarean Birth: (1) Releasing the inner child; (2) Breaking a generational curse; (3) Deliverance; (4) Supernatural, pain-free birth (birthing either spiritually a promise or normal child-bearing).

Also see *Birth* and *Pregnancy.*

(1) Num. 15:25-26; 1 Kings 8:38-39; 1 John 2:12; (2) Exod. 34:7; Num. 14:18; (3) Luke 9:42; John 16:21; Rev. 12:2; (4) Luke 1:36.

Cage: (1) Stronghold; (2) Being treated like an animal; (3) Bondage; (4) Being confined; (5) Restrictions; (6) Unclean spirits (bird cage); (7) Choking the Spirit.

Also see *Aviary.*

(1) 2 Cor. 10:4-5; (2) Jer. 37:15; (3-5) Gen. 40:5a; (6) Rev. 18:2; <u>Jer. 5:27</u>; (7) Acts 5:18-19.

Cake: (1) Something of your own making (flesh); (2) Divine provision or sustenance; (3) The Word; (4) Communion with God (particularly if there is also a drink involved).

Also see *Bread.*

(1) 1 Kings 17:12-13; (2) <u>1 Kings 19:5-8</u>; (3-4) 2 Sam. 6:19 (KJV) (cf. NKJV).

Calculation: (1) Trying to work it out; (2) Trying to work it out in your head (mental calculation).

Also see *Calculator.*

(1-2) Prov. 3:5-6.

Calculator: (1) Trying to work it out in the natural; (2) Financial focus.

Also see *Calculation* and *Slide Rule.*

(1) <u>John 6:7</u>; (2) Matt. 9:9.

Calendar: (1) Planning; (2) Appointment; (3) Date with destiny.

Also see *Day* and look up individual numbers.

(1-2) 1 Kings 20:22, 25-26; (3) Dan. 9:25 & Matt. 21:4-5.

Calf: (1) Increased wealth; (2) Sacrifice/offering; (3) Idol; (4) Celebration; (5) Fellowship.

(1) <u>Ps. 50:10</u>; (2) Heb. 9:12, 19; (3) <u>Acts 7:41</u>; (4) Luke 15:23; (5) Gen. 18:7-8.

Calling (Your Name): (1) A calling to ministry; (2) Attention required; (3) A friend or family member calling your name could be God; (4) Hearing an unknown voice is possibly God calling you to deeper relationship; (5) A scary, threatening, or uncomfortable voice calling your name may represent demonic powers; (6) A voice may also be providing direction; (7) Temptation (a voice calling you to fulfill the flesh).

Also see *Knocking* and *Doorbell.*

(1) 1 Sam. 3:4-10; <u>Exod. 3:4</u>; (2) <u>Gen. 22:11</u>; (3-4) 1 Sam. 3:4-10; (5) Matt. 8:28-29; (6) Acts 16:9; (7) Matt. 4:3, 6-7, 9.

Calm: (1) Peace; (2) Still; (3) Sign of the Presence of God; (4) Removal of threat. (1-4) Ps. 23:2; Mark 4:39; Luke 8:24.

Calm Feelings: (1) Good Sign; (2) Means God's in control. (1-2) Mark 4:39; Ps. 107:29.

Camel: (1) Servant; (2) Endurance; (3) Speaks of being well-resourced; (4) Beast of burden; (5) Bearer of treasures; (6) Caravan; (7) Journey.
Also see *Camel's Hair* and *Caravan*.
(1) Gen. 24:10; Matt. 3:4; Mark 1:6; (2) Gen. 24; (3) Matt. 19:24; (4) Gen. 24:61; 2 Kings 8:9; Isa. 30:6; (5) Isa. 30:6; Matt. 2:11; (6-7) Gen. 24:10.

Camel's Hair: (1) Prophet's mantle or calling of a prophet (as burden-bearer).
Also see *Camel*.
(1) 2 Kings 8:9 (shows camels as burden-bearers); Matt. 3:4 & 11:9.

Camera: (1) Focusing; (2) Publicity; (3) Memories; (4) Fame; (5) Revealed (made public); (6) Seeking recognition (posing in front of camera); (7) Mind (as the place of memories); (8) Heart (as the place of the promises of God); (9) Seeing in the Spirit.
Also see *Cameraman, Movie Camera,* and *Photograph*.
(1) Acts 3:4; Heb. 12:2; (2) Mark 1:45; 5:20; 7:36; (3) Matt. 26:13; Mark 14:9; (4) Matt. 9:26, 31; 14:1; (5) Dan. 2:19; (6) Matt. 20:21; Mark 10:37; (7) Rom. 12:2; (8) 1 Cor. 2:9; (9) See *Window*.

Cameraman: (1) Seer; (2) Prophet; (3) Focused individual.
(1-2) Num. 24:4, 16; (3) 2 Sam. 18:24.

Camp: (1) Temporary location; (2) The army of God; (3) Army of angels; (4) Church (multiple tents); (5) Gathering of spiritual forces (good or evil); (6) Wilderness experience (refugee camp); (7) Church led by the Spirit.
(1) Exod. 19:2; Josh. 10:15; (2) Exod. 14:19-20; Josh. 6:18; Ps. 34:7; (3) Gen. 32:1-2. (4) Exod. 33:7; Num. 2:16-17 (KJV); 15:35-36; (5) Gen. 32:1-2; Joel 2:11; Judg. 7:11; (6) As a place of refuge from persecution in your own land, but not yet having moved into a new homeland (like Israel); (7) Exod. 13:21; John 3:8.

Canaan: (1) The Promised Land; (2) The land of God's promises; (3) The Kingdom of God within (the infilling of the Holy Spirit).
(1) Exod. 13:5, 11; (2) Luke 24:49; (3) Luke 17:21.

Canaanites: (1) Spiritual principalities/powers/spirits; (2) Bring low by traffic or trade (convenience, greed, materialism, and possessions); (3) They also remove spiritual uprightness (they "unwall" you).

(1) Exod. 3:8; (2) This is the meaning of the root of the name; Gen. 13:7; (3) Ps. 51:10; 2 Sam 12:1-7.

Cancer: (1) Sin; (2) Sin within the Church (Body of Christ); (3) Destructive self-consuming words; (4) Literal cancer/disease; (5) Doubt (eats away faith in one's heart); (6) Fear (eats away faith); (7) Bitterness; (8) Unforgiveness; (9) Stress.

Also see *Tumor.*

(1) Isa. 1:4; Hos. 9:9; (2-3) 2 Tim. 2:16-17; (5) Matt. 14:30-31; 21:21; (6) Matt. 8:26; Mark 4:40; (7) Job 21:25; (8) Num. 12:11-12; (9) Job 2:4-5.

Candle/stick: (1) Believer; (2) The Holy Spirit; (3) God's Word; (4) Church; (5) Wickedness (lamp put out).

Also see *Lampstand, Light,* and *Wax.*

(1) Matt. 5:14-15; (2) Rev. 4:5; (3) Ps. 119:105; (4) Rev. 1:20; (5) Prov. 24:20.

Candy (Sweets): (1) Words (often God's Words); (2) Treat; (3) Pleasurable to the flesh, but without spiritual nutrition; (4) Appealing to children or immature believers; (5) Temptation (tempting treats); (6) Without substance.

(1) Ps. 119:103; 141:6; Prov. 16:24; (2) Prov. 27:7b; (3) 1 Cor. 14:20; 2 Tim. 4:3-4; Rev. 10:9-10; (4) Rom. 16:18; (5) Eph. 4:14; (6) Heb. 5:14.

Cane Toad: (1) Plague/curse; (2) Plague of false religion; (3) Solution that becomes a bigger problem (in Australia);

Also see *Frog* and *Toad.*

(1-2) Exod. 8:2; (3) Gen. 16:1-2.

Cankerworm: (1) Subtle destruction; (2) Gangrene; (3) Rotting; (4) Corrosion.

Also see *Locust.*

(1) Joel 1:4; James 5:3.

Cannibals: (1) Something eating at you (issue not dealt with); (2) Church devouring one another; (3) Partaking/communing with Christ; (4) Communing with demons.

(1) Matt. 18:34; (2) Lev. 26:27-29; Gal. 5:15; (3) John 6:53; (4) Lev. 26:28; 1 Cor. 10:20-21.

Cannon: (1) Powerful voice; (2) Impacting words (unrelenting heart); (3) Very persuasive words; (4) Leader; (5) Anger; (6) Unbridled tongue/heart.

(1) Luke 4:32; Acts 7:22; Heb. 12:26; (2) 1 Kings 19:2-3; (3) Rom. 16:18; Col. 2:4; (4) Eccl. 8:4; (5) Dan. 2:12-13; (6) Ps. 32:9; James 3:5-6 (loose cannon).

Canoe: (1) Undeveloped (primitive) ministry or person; (2) The flesh (our "self"-propelled old vessel); (3) Ministry in own strength (paddling canoe); (4) Ministry without the Holy Spirit; (5) Holy Spirit-led individual (canoe/kayak moving without paddle in running water).

Also see *Boat, Rowing,* and *Underwater.*

(1) Acts 19:2b; (2) Deut. 12:8; Judg. 21:25 (doing your own thing); (3-5) Zech. 4:6.

Canteen: See Restaurant.

Cap: (1) Casual or familiar authority; (2) Weak authority.

Also see *Hat.*

(1) 1 Cor. 11:10.

Cape: See Mantle.

Captain: (1) Jesus; (2) Authority gained through suffering; (3) Leader; (4) Pastor.

(1-2) Heb. 2:10; (3) Rev. 6:15; (4) Jer. 51:23; Acts 20:28; 1 Pet. 5:2.

Captive: (1) Fallen into sin; (2) Bound by iniquity; (3) Under demonic oppression; (4) Under the influence of a dominant personality.

Also see *Chains, Prisoners,* and *Yoke.*

(1) Lam. 1:5; Amos 1:6; (2) Acts 8:23; (3) Matt. 12:29; Mark. 3:22-27; (4) Matt. 20:25.

Car: See Automobile.

Caravan (Camel): (1) Gifts; (2) Enduring trip; (3) Gathering the Church (bride).

Also see *Camel.*

(1-3) Gen. 24:10.

Caravan: See Trailer.

Carburetor: (1) Door to the heart; (2) Fueling the heart/ministry. Also see *Automobile*.

(1) Prov. 4:23; Matt. 6:6; Rev. 3:20; (2) Gen. 4:7; 1 Kings 10:24; Ezra 7:27; Neh. 2:12.

Car-Carrier/Transport: (1) Riding on someone else's ministry; (2) Big ministry about to release other ministries (new cars).

(1) 2 Kings 5:20; (2) Matt.28:19-20; Luke 9:1-2.

Carcass: (1) Unclean; (2) Dead to self.

(1) Lev. 5:2; (2) Matt. 24:28.

Cards (Playing): (1) Gambling; (2) Bluffing; (3) Partnership; (4) Entertainment; (5) Deception; (6) Chance; (7) Time-filler; (8) Patience; (9) Playing games and not revealing what's in your heart (hand); (10) Not telling you everything (keeping things close to your chest).

(9) Matt. 19:3; 22:17-18; (10) As in, "having not laid all your cards on the table"; Acts 5:8-9.

Cards (Pack of Cards): (1) Flimsy (as in, "the whole thing fell over like a pack of cards").

Cards (Patience): (1) Time-filler; (2) Boredom; (3) Needing patience.

Cards (Poker): (1) Gambling; (2) Bluffing; (3) Chance; (4) Deception.

Cards (Whist, etc): (1) Entertainment.

Cards (Bridge, Canasta, etc): (1) Partnership.

Cards (Birthday/Christmas): (1) Gift; (2) Celebration.

(1) Matt. 2:11b; (2) Matt. 2:10.

Cards (Tarot): (1) Familiar spirits; (2) Searching for hope (the wrong way); (3) Deception; (4) Shrouded in uncertainty; (5) Desire for destiny or answers; (6) By-passing God for answers.

(1) 1 Sam. 28:8; Acts 16:16; (2) 1 Chron. 10:13-14a; (5) 1 Sam. 28:7; (6) Mic. 5:12.

Care: (1) Concern for God, people, or the world; (2) Chokes the Word (worldly care); (3) Practical concern; (4) True heart for people.

(1) 1 Cor. 7:32-33; (2) Matt. 13:22; Mark 4:19; Luke 8:14; 10:40-41; 21:34; (3) Luke 10:34-35; (4) John 10:13; 12:6.

Caretaker: (1) God; (2) Pastor/leader.

Also see *Janitor.*

(1) Ps. 23:1; 1 Pet. 5:7; (2) Acts 20:28.

Cargo Plane: (1) Large spiritual ministry bearing and releasing international ministries.

(1) Acts 13:1-2.

Carnal: (1) In the Flesh; (2) Sinful; (3) Death.

(1) 1 Cor. 3:1, 3; 2 Cor. 10:4; (2) Rom. 7:14; (3) Rom. 8:6.

Carnival: (1) Showy church; (2) Entertaining church; (3) The world; (4) Pleasure.

(1) Rev. 3:1; (2) 2 Tim. 4:3-4; 3:4b-5; (3) Heb. 11:25; James 5:5a; (4) 1 Cor. 10:7.

Carpark: (1) Ministry rest; (2) Church; (3) Going nowhere; (4) Stuck in the wilderness (no destiny); (5) Wilderness; (6) Transition.

(1) Car = ministry, park = rest; (2) Acts 14:28; (3) Exod. 14:15; Luke 4:42; (4) Num. 26:65; (5) Luke 1:80; (6) Mark 14:34.

Carpenter: (1) Jesus; (2) Creator; (3) Builder.

(1) Matt. 13:55; (2) Matt. 13:55a; (3) 2 Sam. 5:11; 2 Kings 12:11.

Carpet: (1) Foundation; (2) Purging (carpet cleaning); (3) Covering/hiding issues; (4) Moving into a new spiritual home (carpet rolled up); (5) Changing on the inside (new carpet).

Also see *Rug* and *Vacuum Cleaner.*

(1) Eph. 6:11-18 (we are to stand on foundational truth); (2) 1 Cor. 5:7a; (3) As in, "sweeping under the carpet"; (4-5) Matt. 9:17; 2 Cor. 5:1.

Carport: (1) Exposed ministry going nowhere.

Also see *Carpark* and *Garage.*

(1) 1 Sam. 4:13.

Carrots: (1) Deposits to help someone see in the dark (sliced carrots); (2) Spiritual eyes opening.

Also see *Vegetables.*

(1) Ps. 112:4; Isa. 9:2; 42:16; (2) Dan. 1:12, 17.

Carry/ing: (1) Burden (of the Cross); (2) Heavy load; (3) Guilt; (4) Sickness; (5) Oppression; (6) Captive; (7) Extras; (8) Under the influence of the Spirit (being carried); (9) Dependent; (10) Dead.

Also see *Heavy* and *Weight*.

(1) Matt. 10:38; 16:24; (2) Matt. 23:4; (3) Lev. 5:17; Num. 5:31; (4) Matt. 6:55; (5) Acts 10:38; James 2:6; Ps. 106:42; (6) Matt. 1:11, 17; Mark 15:1; 1 Cor. 12:2; Gal. 2:13; Eph. 4:14; Heb. 13:9; Jude 1:12; (7) Luke 10:4; (8) John 21:18; Rev. 17:3; 21:10; (9) Acts 3:2; (10) Luke 7:12 (physically); Luke 16:22 (spirit-carried); Luke 24:51; Acts 5:6; 8:2; 1 Tim. 6:7.

Cart: (1) Traditional or human-designed ministry; (2) Old ministry; (3) Repeating history; (4) If cart is full, it means fruitfulness or abundance; (5) Heritage.

(1) 1 Sam. 6:7-8; 2 Sam. 6:3; (2) Gen. 45:27-28 (NKJV); (3) 1 Cor. 10:6-11; (4) Ps. 65:11; (5) Ps. 61:5; 111:6; 119:111; 127:3.

Cartoon Character: (1) Superficial person (not real); (2) Fable/myth; (3) Animated; (4) Relate the nature, personality, color of clothing, and the sayings of the character to ascertain the inferred meaning; (5) There may also be an automatic association between a known person and a cartoon character.

(1-2) 2 Tim. 4:7.

Carved: (1) Mark; (2) Ownership; (3) Deeply committed; (4) Costly; (5) Skilled workmanship; (6) Idolatry; (7) Permanent; (8) Identified.

(1) As in, "he made his mark"; (2-3) Isa. 49:16; (4) Prov. 7:16; (5) Exod. 35:30-33; (6) Judg. 18:18; (7) Isa. 49:16; (8) Gen. 4:15; Exod. 28:11.

Cashier: See Store Clerk and Salesman.

Castaway: (1) Lacking discipline; (2) Losing the battle with the flesh; (3) Backslider; (4) Reject.

(1-2) 1 Cor. 9:27; (3) Jer. 2:19; 3:8; (4) 1 Cor. 9:27.

Casting (Fishing): (1) Prophetic ministry; (2) Prophesying; (3) Stepping out in faith.

(1-2) Gen. 22:4-13; Casting, as in, "lifting one's eyes"; (3) Eccl. 11:1.

Castle: (1) Beautiful Christian; (2) Eternal house in glory; (3) Human-made kingdom or church; (4) Stronghold; (5) Safe refuge; (6) Name of the Lord;

(7) Heaven or heavenly home; (8) The kingdom of evil (haunted castle/s); (9) Demon possession (haunted castle).

(1) 2 Cor. 5:1; (2) John 14:2; (3) Gen. 25:16 (KJV); (4) Acts 21:37; 23:10; 1 Chron. 11:5, 7; (5-6) Prov. 18:10; (7) John 14:2; Heb. 12:22; (8) Luke 11:21-22; Eph. 6:12; (9) Mark 1:23 & 2 Cor. 5:1.

Cat (Domestic): (1) Vicious attack; (2) Witchcraft (black cat); (3) Independence; (4) Independent spirit; (5) Rebellious spirit; (6) Unteachable heart; (7) Rich person (fat cat); (8) Laziness (fat cat); (9) High ranking public servant (fat cat); (10) Curiosity; (11) Beginning, start, or young version of the above (kitten); (12) Innocence.

Also see *Dog, Mascot,* and *Pet.*

(1) Dan. 6:12, 24 (This was a vicious attack that was judged with a vicious attack); (2-5) 1 Sam. 15:23; (6) 2 Tim. 3:7; (7-9) Rev. 3:17; (10) As in, "curiosity killed the cat"; (11) Ezek. 19:3.

Catapult: See Slingshot.

Catcher's Mitt: (1) Sensitive or spiritual hearing; (2) Your spirit.

Also see *Ball.*

(1-2) 1 Kings 19:12; Matt. 11: 7-15.

Catching: (1) Listening; (2) Trying to catch you out in your words.

Also see *Ball, Baseball, Catcher's Mitt,* and *Cricket.*

(1) Matt. 13:19; Mark 12:13; (2) Mark 12:13.

Caterpillar: (1) Unsaved individual (not yet a butterfly); (2) Progressive destruction; (3) Judgment or plague; (4) Restoration.

(1) 2 Cor. 5:17; (2) Joel 1:4; (3) 1 Kings 8:37; Ps. 78:46; 105:34; Isa. 33:4; (4) Joel 2:25.

Cat Food: (1) Feeding independence; (2) Independent teaching; (3) Feeding witchcraft.

(1) Gal. 2:12; (2) Acts 18:26; (3) Acts 8:10-11.

Cathedral: (1) High profile church.

(1) Acts 11:26.

Catheter: (1) Secretly offended; (2) Secretly uncomfortable about a situation/person.

See *Urination.*

(1) <u>Matt. 15:12</u>; (2) John 13:27-30.

Cattle: (1) Prosperity; (2) Wealth.

Also see *Calf* and *Cow.*

(1) <u>Ps. 50:10</u>; 107:38; (2) Gen. 13:2 (KJV), 30:43 (KJV).

Caucasian: Note: The meaning of an African-American/First Nations (indigenous) person or Caucasian person in a dream may change dependent on the ethnicity (racial/cultural background) of the dreamer. An African-American/First Nations person may see Caucasians as the fleshly self (due to their past inclination to exploit, enslave, and be soulish). To a Caucasian, a First Nations person may represent the fleshly self due to their color or order in the land (1 Cor. 15:46). A person of a different race is generally interpreted as "Foreign" (Also see First Nations Peoples, Foreign, Foreigner, and Native/s).

Cauldron: (1) Witchcraft; (2) Mixing up trouble; (3) Spell casting; (4) Boiling; (5) Flesh; (6) City or location.

Also see *Cookbook* and *Pot.*

(1) Gal. 5:19-20; (4) Job 41:20; (5-6) Ezek.11:3, 7.

Cauliflower: (1) Glory of God (in the shape of clouds).

(1) 2 Chron. 5:14.

Cave: (1) Hiding place; (2) Stronghold; (3) Refuge or shelter; (4) Grave (place of burial); (5) What is going on inside of you; (6) Recluse; (7) Secret place; (8) Temporary home; (9) Underground; (10) Hell.

Also see *Tunnel* and *Underground.*

(1) Gen. 1:30; <u>1 Kings 18:13</u>; <u>19:9</u>, 13; (2) Judg. 6:2; 1 Chron. 11:15-16; (3) Ps. 142:5; 57:1; (4) Gen. 25:9; 49:29-32; 50:13; John 11:38; (5) 1 Pet. 3:4; (6) 1 Kings 19:9; Prov. 18:1; (7) Song. 2:14; (8) 1 Kings 18:4; (9) Gen. 19:30; (10) 2 Pet. 2:4; Jude 1:6.

Cedar: (1) Royalty; (2) Mighty person; (3) Spiritual; (4) Evergreen.

(1) This tree is tall and upright and was used extensively for the royal residence and temple <u>2 Sam. 5:11</u>; 1 Kings 9:10-11; (cf. 2 Chron.1:15, 9:27); (2) <u>Zech. 11:2</u>; (3) Jer. 17:8.

Ceiling: (1) In rule or dominating; (2) Limitation; (3) Covering; (4) Authority; (5) Heaven; (6) Spiritual heights.

Also see *Roof.*

(1) Deut. 28:13; Matt. 25:21; Rom. 6:14; Heb. 13:7; (2) 1 Kings 6:15; (3) Gen. 19:8; Matt. 8:8-9; 24:45; (4) Matt. 8:8-9; (5) Acts 10:4; Rev. 4:1 (attic door in ceiling); (6) Isa. 57:15; Eph. 6:12; Rev. 21:10.

Cell Phone: See Telephone.

Cement: See Concrete.

Cemetery: (1) Death; (2) Without life (Spirit of God); (3) Superficiality; (4) No faith (open grave); (5) The end of something; (6) Putting something to rest or death.

Also see *Grave* and *Graveyard.*

(1) Matt. 8:22; Luke 9:60; Acts 2:29; (2) Ezek. 37:1-10; (3) Matt. 23:27-28; (4) Ps. 5:9; James 2:26; (5) John 19:30; (6) Gen. 35:2-4.

Censer: (1) Relates to prayer; (2) Judgment of the prayers of the saints.

(1-2) Rev. 8:3-5.

Censor: (1) Gag; (2) Edit; (3) Cut.

(1) Ps. 63:11.

Center: If something or someone is in the center it infers that they are: (1) In control; (2) Center of God's will; (3) Divine order; (4) Deeply involved; (5) In plain view; (6) The main culprit; (7) Heart; (8) Dividing; (9) Identifying with who or whatever they are with; (10) Being, seeking, or needing attention.

Also see *Corner, Heart, Middle, Left,* and *Right.*

(1) Mark 14:60; Acts 1:15; (2) Rom. 12:2b; (3) Prov. 11:1; (4) Luke 2:46; (5) John 8:3, 9; Acts 17:22; (6) John 19:18; (7) Ps. 22:14; Prov. 14:33; Isa. 19:1; (8) Exod. 14:16, 22; (9) Luke 24:36; (10) As in "center of attention."

Cents: (1) Small amount of money; (2) May represent a large heart; (3) Don't look at the outward; (4) Unforgiveness issue.

(1-3) Mark 12:42; Luke 21:2-4; (4) Luke 12:58-59.

Chaff: (1) Waste; (2) Without heart (no substance); (3) Little weight (insignificant); (4) Easily blown away; (5) Momentary/quickly pass; (6) Separation of the unrighteous; (7) Judgment.

(1-4) Job 21:18; Ps. 1:4; Isa. 17:13; 33:11; 41:15; (5) Hos. 13:3; Zeph. 2:2; (6-7) <u>Matt. 3:12</u>; Luke 3:17; Isa. 5:24; Jer. 23:28b.

Chains: (1) Captivity or confinement test; (2) Pride; (3) Bound/bonds; (4) Spiritual warfare; (5) Oppression; (6) Joined in the Spirit (between people); (7) Negative soul tie (between people); (8) Allurement (neck chain); (9) Sign of wealth or opulence (golden chain around neck).

Also see *Captive, Cord, Prison,* and *Prisoners.*

(1<u>) Ps. 105:17-19</u>; (2) Ps. 73:6; (3) Ps. 68:6; Jer. 39:7; Mark 5:4; Luke 8:29; (4) Ps. 149:6-9; (5) Isa. 58:6; (6) Acts 20:22; <u>Eph. 4:3</u>; (7) 1 Cor. 6:16; (8) Song. 4:9; (9) Prov. 1:9; Song. 1:10; Ezek. 16:11.

Chair: See Sit/ting.

Chamber: (1) Place of torment; (2) Part of hell; (3) Old English term for bedroom.

(1-2) <u>Prov. 7:27</u>; (3) Jer. 35:4.

Champagne: (1) Celebration; (2) Victory; (3) Breakthrough.

(1-3) <u>Zech. 10:7</u>.

Change/d: (1) Change of heart (clothes); (2) Liberated (clothes); (3) Change of ownership; (4) Conversion; (5) Role and authority (changed name); (6) Allegiance (changed name); (7) Glorification; (8) Moving to next stage of glory; (9) Glory to shame or vice versa; (10) Change of attitude (facial expression); (11) Unreliable (given to change); (12) Disobedience; (13) Change of destiny (times and laws); (14) Deception and greed (wages); (15) Just feigning; (16) To turn; (17) God is in control of all change.

Also see *Altered* and *No Change* (directly below).

(1) Gen. 35:2; <u>2 Sam. 12:20</u>; Dan. 4:16; (2) Gen. 41:14 (no longer a prisoner); 2 Kings 25:2; Jer. 52:33; (3) Ruth 4:7; (4) <u>2 Cor. 5:17</u>; (5) 2 Kings 24:17; (6) Num. 32:38; (7) Job 14:14; Ps. 106:20; 1 Cor. 15:51-52; (8) 2 Cor. 3:18; (9) Jer. 2:11; <u>Hos. 4:7</u>; Rom. 1:23; (10) Dan. 3:19; 5:6-10; 7:28; (11) Prov. 24:21; (12) Ezek. 5:6; (13) Dan. 7:25; (14) Gen. 31:7, 41; (15) 1 Sam. 21:13; (16) Lev. 13:16; (17) Dan. 2:21.

No Change: (1) God does not change; (2) Lacking a fear of God; (3) Not having been emptied out; (4) Religious traditions (fight against change); (5) Stubbornness or hardened heart; (6) Not converted.

Also see *Change* (directly above).

(1) Mal. 3:6; (2) Ps. 55:19; (3) Jer. 48:11; (4) Acts 6:14; (5) Ps. 78:8; Heb. 3:8, 15; (6) Matt. 18:3.

Charge: (1) Accusation; (2) Condemnation; (3) Enemy attack; (4) Govern; (5) Suing.

(1) Job 13:19; (2) Ps. 69:27; (3) Prov. 28:15; (4) Zech. 3:6; (5) Matt. 5:40.

Charging (Electrical): See Battery Charging.

Chariot: See Automobile and Chariot of Fire.

Chariot of Fire: (1) Angelic vehicle; (2) Rapture; (3) Passionate vehicle.

(1) Ps. 104:4; 2 Kings 6:15-17; (2) 2 Kings 2:11; (3) Ps. 39:3; Jer. 20:9.

Chasing: (1) Threatening (chasing someone); (2) Being threatened (being chased); (3) Call to prayer (being chased); (4) Obsessed with (whatever you are chasing).

Also see *Hiding* and *Running*.

(1) Lev. 26:7; (2-3) Deut. 1:44 (*Hormah* means "devotion"); (4) 2 Kings 5:20 (chasing the dollar).

Check/ing: (1) Testing; (2) Inspecting; (3) Confirming; (4) Ensuring.

Also see *Exam*.

(1-2) Gen. 22:1, 12; (3-4) Prov. 22:21; Luke 24:24.

Check ($): (1) Faith (the currency of the Kingdom); (2) Finances; (3) Prosperity (receiving a check).

(1) Matt. 6:24; Luke 16:13; Acts 8:20; Rom 1:17; Heb. 11:4; (2) 2 Cor. 8:9; Phil. 4:12; (3) 1 Cor. 16:2.

Cheek: (1) Preparing for persecution; (2) Physical abuse; (3) Criticism/blame; (4) Responding to persecution with love; (5) Grief (tears on cheek); (6) Back chat.

Also see *Tears* and *Teeth*.

(1) Lam. 3:30; Matt. 5:39; (2) 1 Kings 22:24; (3) Job 16:10; (4) Isa. 50:6; (5) Lam. 1:2; (6) Job 15:6; Ps. 31:18; Lam. 3:62.

Cheek bone: (1) Making the enemies of God eat their words.

(1) Ps. 3:7.

Cheerleader: (1) Worshipper (including praise); (2) Believer; (3) Encourager.
(1-2) John 4:23-24; (3) 1 Sam. 18:7; Matt. 21:8-9.

Cheese: (1) Spiritual growth (maturing); (2) Words that sour or have soured (cheese is curdled milk); (3) Something has holes in it (Swiss); (4) Not real; (5) Gift of sustenance; (6) Neutral or non-committal words (Swiss cheese).
(1) 1 John 2:13-14; Rev. 12:11; (2) Job 10:10; (3) 2 Tim. 4:3-4; (4) Matt. 15:8; Mark 7:6; *cheesy* as in, "cheesy grin"; (5) 1 Sam. 17:18; 2 Sam. 17:29; (6) Rev. 3:15.

Cheeseburger: (1) Palatable teaching (seeker friendly message); (2) Fable; (3) Childish, ill-prepared words.
Also see *Hamburger.*
(1-3) 2 Tim. 4:2-4.

Cheesecake: (1) Temptation.
(1) Gen. 3:6.

Cheezels (Cheese-Balls): (1) Hollow/empty words.
(1) Esther 3:10; Prov. 23:1-3.

Chef: (1) Christ; (2) Pastor.
(1) 1 Pet. 5:2-4; (2) Acts 20:28.

Chemist Shop (Drug Store): (1) The Church as a dispenser of God's Word; (2) The Word of God; (3) Jesus Christ (healing dispensary); (4) A church without feeling (drugged-up).
Also see *Shop.*
(1-2) Prov. 4:20-22 (the right script); (3) Matt. 4:23; (4) Rev. 3:1-2, 15-17.

Chest (Torso): (1) Heart; (2) Righteousness; (3) Faith and love.
(1) Exod. 28:29; (2) Isa. 59:17; Eph. 6:14; (3) 1 Thess. 5:8.

Cheque: See Check ($).

Chew/ing: (1) Meditating; (2) Thinking about.
(1) Josh. 1:8; (2) As in, "chewing things over."

Chicken: (1) Church; (2) God; (3) Jesus Christ; (4) Gatherer; (5) Protector; (6) Scared; (7) Unclean spirit; (8) Revelation (chicken nuggets); (9) Criticism of the Church (fried chicken).

Also see *Hen.*

(1) Ps. 17:8 & 50:5 & 91:4; Isa. 49:5; Matt. 23:37; Acts 14:27; (2) Ps. 91:1, 3-4; (3) Matt. 23:37; Luke 13:34; (4-5) Matt. 23:37; Luke 13:34; Ps. 17:8; (6) As in, "He's nothing but a chicken"; (7) Lev. 20:25; (8) Matt. 23:37 & John 6:51; (9) Acts 8:1; 3 John 1:10.

Chicks (Baby Chickens): (1) Children of God; (2) Your offspring.

(1-2) Matt. 23:37.

Chief: (1) Jesus Christ; (2) Best of or the strongest; (3) Main; (4) Leader.

(1) Eph. 2:20; 1 Pet. 5:4; (2) Prov. 16:28b; Dan. 10:13; (3) Ps. 137:6.

Child/ren: (1) Future of oneself or Church (children of God); (2) Innocence; (3) Inner child; (4) Immaturity; (5) Past childhood; (6) Humility; (7) Receiving, trusting, believing; (8) Young converts; (9) Followers of Christ or satan; (10) Undisciplined child (illegitimate children); (11) Children of the devil (illegitimate children); (12) Children of wrath (disobedient).

Also see *Younger* and *Youth.*

(1) Jer. 31:17; John 1:12; (2) Matt. 18:6; (3) Deut. 29:29; 2 Kings 17:9; 2 Chron. 28:11-12; (4) Luke 7:32; 1 Cor. 13:11; (5) 1 Sam. 12:2; (6) Matt. 18:4; Luke 9:46-48; (7) Matt. 18:3; (8) 1 John 2:12-14; (9) Acts 13:10; 1 John 3:10; (10) Heb. 12:8; (11) John 8:44; (12) Eph. 2:3; 5:6; Col. 3:6.

Children's Book/s: (1) Children's Bible (childlike faith); (2) Belief and trust; (3) Innocence; (4) Humble dependence.

(1-4) Matt. 18:3-6.

Chilies: (1) Hot; (2) India; (3) Mexico.

(1-3) 1 Kings 10:2, 10, 15.

Chimney: (1) Soul-tie or opening for the enemy.

(1) Eph. 4:27.

China/Chinese: (1) Foreign; (2) Diligent; (3) Literally Chinese; (4) Low cost; (5) Populous; (6) Demonic (dragon); (7) Honorable; (8) Atheistic (communism); (9) Antichrist (dragon); (10) Integrity; (11) "Take away"; (12) "Plastic"; (13) Huge, dominant commercial entity.

Also see *Foreign.*

(1) Isa. 49:12; (2-12) Other characteristic perceptions.

Chips (Potato): See French Fries.

Chiropractor: (1) Manipulation and adjustment; (2) Getting the body in alignment.

(1-2) Eph. 4:12.

Chocolate: (1) Money hungry; (2) Hungry for pleasure; (3) Self-indulgence; (4) Sweet, deceptive words; (5) Palatable; (6) God's Word; (7) Words spoken in love (chocolates); (8) Gratitude (thanksgiving).

Also see *Junk Food.*

(1) Matt. 6:24; Luke 16:8b-9, 13; (2-3) 2 Tim. 3:4b; (4) Prov. 23:1-3, 6-8; (5-6) Ps. 119:103; 141:6; (7-8) Song. 2:14; 4:11.

Choice: (1) Options; (2) Decision; (3) Prepared; (4) Best; (5) Refined.

(1) 1 Sam. 6:7-9; 1 Kings 18:21; (2) Josh. 24:15; (3) Matt. 20:16; 22:14; (4) Gen. 49:11; 1 Sam. 9:2; 2 Sam. 10:9; (5) Prov. 10:20.

Choir: (1) Worship.

(1) 2 Chron. 29:28; Ps. 66:4.

Choke/ing: (1) Gagging communication (stopping words); (2) Stopping the life flow; (3) Demon oppression or possession; (4) Stifling the Spirit; (5) Attack; (6) Threat; (7) Incapable; (8) Care of the world and deceitfulness of riches; (9) Fear/anxiety; (10) Lust for things; (11) Pleasures of life; (12) Drowning; (13) Injustice; (14) Speaking lies; (15) Iniquity; (16) Dishonest gain; (17) Failing through nerves (choking under pressure).

Also see *Strangle/d.*

(1) 2 Kings 2:3; (2) John 5:24; 7:38; (3) Mark 9:17-18; (4) 1 Cor. 14:39b; (5) (cf. Matt. 17:15 & Mark 9:17-18); (6) Acts 4:18, 21; (7) Matt. 13:7, 22; (8) Matt. 6:25; (9) Mark 4:7, 19; (10) Luke 8:7, 14; (11) Mark 5:13; Luke 8:33; (13) Job 5:16; (14) Ps. 63:11; (15) Ps. 107:42; Rom. 3:19; (16) Tit. 1:11; (17) Matt. 27:22-26.

Chopping Block/Board: (1) Judgment/al; (2) Harsh words; (3) Dealing with the flesh (cutting the fat); (4) Sermon preparation.

(1-2) Matt. 3:10; (3) Rom. 8:13; (4) Heb. 4:12.

Christmas: (1) Celebration; (2) Gifts; (3) Self-indulgence; (4) Revival (Christmas day).

Also see *Santa.*

(1) Luke 2:10-11, 13-14, 20; (2) 1 Cor. 12:1, 9-11; (3) Luke 6:32-33; (4) Luke 2:9-11.

Christmas Tree: (1) Traditional person/church; (2) Glamorous ministry; (3) High profile ministry (the Christmas tree takes center stage at Christmastime); (4) A person or ministry that looks outwardly attractive, but has no spiritual life; (5) Spiritual gifts; (6) Celebration; (7) Paganism/idolatry.

(1) Col. 2:8; (2-3) Matt. 13:32; (4) Matt. 23:27-28; (5) 1 Cor. 2:12; 12:1, 4, 7, 9-11; (6) Luke 2:10-11, 13-14, 20; (7) 2 Kings 16:4; 17:10-11.

Chrome: (1) Hard/ened; (2) Cold-hearted (hardened heart).

Also see *Biker/Bikie.*

(1) Zech. 7:12; (2) Matt. 24:12.

Church Building: (1) May refer to a particular congregation; (2) The reference may also be general; (3) Often a church will appear as a house in a dream or vision; (4) May represent the individual; (5) Place of worship.

Also see *Congregation.*

(1) Rev. 2:1, 8, 12, 18; (2) 1 Tim 3:15; (3) Rom. 16:15; 1 Cor. 16:19; 1 Tim. 3:15; (4) 1 Cor. 3:16; 6:19; (5) Acts 24:11; 1 Sam. 1:3.

Church Service: (1) Worship; (2) Praise; (3) Fellowship.

Also see *Congregation* and *Temple.*

(1) 2 Chron. 29:28; (2) Heb. 2:12b; (3) Acts 2:42.

Cigar: (1) Big offense; (2) Celebration; (3) Lucrative business; (4) Thinking big (Mr. Big [positive (+) or negative (-)]).

(1) Job 19:17; (2) Prov. 13:9; (3) 1 Tim. 6:9; (4) Gen. 15:5 (+); Luke 12:18 (-).

Cigarette/s: (1) Offensive; (2) Odorous; (3) Taking up offensive words and language; (4) Temptation to return to an addictive lifestyle; (5) Stronghold; (6) Foul spirit.

Also see *Drugs* and *Smoking.*

(1) Job 19:17; (2) Joel 2:20; (3) Eph. 5:4; 4:29; Isa. 29:21; (4) Judg. 8:33; 1 Cor. 10:13; (5) Ps. 78:61; Ezek. 30:18b; (6) Mark 9:25 (stopping someone from hearing/speaking truth); Rev. 14:11; 18:2.

Cinema: See Picture Theater.

Circle: (1) God; (2) Eternally/eternity (as in a never-ending loop); (3) Covenant; (4) Earth; (5) Completion; (6) Repeating same mistake (going in circles); (7) Repeat relationship scenario (circle of friends).

Also see *Wheel.*

(1-2) Deut. 33:27; Jer. 10:10 (NIV); Eccl. 3:11; (3) Circumcision, which is the sign of covenant with God (Gen. 17:10-11), is a circle of flesh cut away; (4) Isa. 40:22; (5) As in, "I saw the project through full circle"; (6) Ps. 78:41, 57; (7) Deut. 2:3.

Circumcision: (1) Cutting away of the desires of the flesh; (2) Heart; (3) Believer; (4) Obedience.

(1) Jer. 4:4; Col. 2:11; (2) Rom. 2:29; Deut. 10:16; 30:6; Jer. 4:4; (3) Rom. 3:30; 4:9-12; Gal. 5:6; (4) Josh. 5:4-9.

Circus: (1) World; (2) Incompetent organization; (3) In the spotlight; (4) Circle of influence; (5) Entertainment; (6) Performance; (7) Itinerant flamboyant miracle evangelist (tent crusades).

Also see *Lion* and *Spotlight.*

(1) 1 John 2:16; (2) As in, "The place is a circus!"; (3) Acts 9:3; (4) 1 Kings 12:8-13; Matt. 17:1; (5) Luke 7:32a; (6) Matt. 16:1; (7) Acts 13:2-3.

Cistern: (1) Heart (storage/supply); (2) Marital faithfulness; (3) Ease (reservoir); (4) Two evils; (5) Confinement or prison.

Also see *Deep, Reservoir, Swimming Pool, Water,* and *Well.*

(1) Prov. 5:15; Eccl. 12:6; (2) Prov. 5:15-20; (3) 2 Kings 18:31; Isa. 36:16; (4) Jer. 2:13; (5) Jer. 38:6.

City: (1) The world; (2) Populous; (3) Preaching place; (4) Pride; (5) Each city to be judged; (6) Place of persecution; (7) May speak of the spiritual authorities over the city; (8) Represents life; (9) Busy; (10) Note type or name of city; (11) International influence (if cities in different countries); (12) New Jerusalem (modern city); (13) Kingdom of Heaven; (14) Becoming well-known (going to a big city).

Also see *Bricks* and *Tower.*

(1) Gen. 11:4; Isa. 14:21b; Matt. 5:14; (2) Matt. 8:34; 21:10; Mark. 1:33; (3) Matt. 11:1; (4) Matt. 4:5-6; (5) Matt. 10:15 (cf. 10:11, 14); 11:20-24; (6) Matt. 10:23; 23:34b; Luke 4:29; (7) Luke 19:17, 19; (9) Luke 17:28-29; (11) 1 Kings 10:24; (12) Isa. 62:1-4; Rev. 3:12; (13) Ps. 103:19; Dan. 2:44; Matt. 3:2; Rev. 12:10; (14) Gen. 13:12; 14:12; John 7:3-4.

Clap/ping: (1) Victory or triumph; (2) Approval; (3) Mocking; (4) Faith from revelation (heart and head in agreement); (5) Celebration.

Also see *Left* and *Right* (left hand [heart] and right hand [mouth])

(1) Ps. 47:1; (2) 2 Kings 11:12; Isa. 55:12; (3) Job 27:23; Lam. 2:15; (4) Rom. 10:9-10; (5) 2 Kings 11:12.

Classroom: (1) Heart; (2) Teachable heart; (3) Place of training; (4) Equipping and preparation.

Also see *School.*

(1) Job 8:10; Ps. 90:12; Prov. 4:4; 16:23; Isa. 29:13; Col. 3:16; (2) Matt. 26:55; Mark 12:35a; 14:49; 20:1; 21:37; John 7:14, 28; (3) 1 John 2:13-14; (4) Mark 10:39, 42; 2 Tim. 3:16-17.

Claw: (1) Aggression; (2) If a claw is grabbing you or someone else, it could be a spirit of death; (3) In the grip of satan; (4) Torment (tearing claw); (5) Stronghold.

(1) Ps. 7:2; Jer. 5:6; Hos. 5:14; (2) Ps. 18:4 (AMP); Ps. 116:3; (3) 1 Sam. 17:34; Isa. 5:29; (Amos 3:4 & 1 Pet. 5:8); (4) Matt. 18:34 (KJV); 1 John 4:18; (5) 2 Cor. 10:4-5.

Clay: (1) Human/kind or humanity; (2) Being molded; (3) Weakness; (4) Fragile; (5) From the earth.

(1) Job 10:9; Isa. 64:8; Rom. 9:20-21; (2) Jer. 18:4-6; (3-4) 2 Cor. 4:7; Lev. 14:5; 15:12; (5) Job 4:19.

Clean: (1) Redemption; (2) Possibly speaks of an outward appearance versus inward reality; (3) Unused; (4) Readiness; (5) Under the Blood.

Also see *Leprosy.*

(1) Tit. 2:14; Matt. 8:2-3; Mark 1:40-42; (2) Matt. 23:25-28; (3) Matt. 27:59; (4) Rev. 21:2; (5) 1 John 1:7.

Cleaning: (1) Confession and repentance; (2) Fasting.

(1) 1 John 1:9; Heb. 6:1; (2) Matt. 6:17.

Clear water: (1) Holy Spirit; (2) Life; (3) Cleansing; (4) God's Word.

Also see *Water.*

(1) John 7:38; James 3:11; Rev. 21:6; (2) Rev. 22:1; (3) Ezek. 36:25; Heb. 10:22; (4) Eph. 5:26.

Cleave: (1) Join; (2) Split; (3) Embrace; (4) Cling.

All (KJV) Refs: (1) <u>Gen. 2:24</u>; Luke 10:11; Acts 11:23; (2) Ps. 78:15; 141:7; Eccl. 10:9.

Cliff: (1) On the edge; (2) On the edge of destruction; (3) Place where natural resources run out; (4) Place of decision; (5) Place of launching into the Spirit; (6) A leap of faith; (7) The place where earth meets Heaven; (8) Place of refuge (in God); (9) Prophetic insight (overlooking from a cliff).

Also see *Edge*.

(1-2) Luke 4:29; (3) 1 Kings 17:11-14; 2 Kings 4:1-7; John 6:5-7; (4) 1 Sam. 14:9-10; 1 Kings 18:21; (5) <u>1 Sam. 14:10, 13</u>; <u>Luke 4</u>:29-<u>30</u>; 5:4-6; 8:22; Acts 27:4; (6) Matt. 14:29; 2 Cor. 5:7; (7) Matt. 27:33, 42; (8) Exod. 33:22; <u>Ps. 104:18</u>; (cf. Prov. 30:26); (9) Num. 22:41; 23:28.

Climbing: (1) Overcoming; (2) Overpowering; (3) Human effort; (4) Preparing for an encounter with Jesus; (5) Theft (climbing into); (6) Growing in the Spirit (climbing up); (7) Making spiritual progress (climbing up); (8) Growing up (children climbing up).

Also *Climbing Over, Down, Ladder,* and *Up*.

(1) 1 Sam. 14:13; (2) Joel 2:7, 9; (3) Amos 9:2; (4) Luke 19:4; (5) John 10:1; (6-7) <u>Isa. 40:31</u>; (8) Hos. 9:12; Matt. 22:24.

Climbing Over: (1) Lack of sensitivity; (2) No longer an issue; (3) Self-aggrandizement; (4) Skipping a level; (5) Lacking humility; (6) Ambition; (7) Overcoming.

Also see *Overtaking*.

(1) Mark 9:33-37; (2) Matt. 9:10-13; As in, "get over it!" (3) Isa. 14:13-14; Rom. 10:6; (4-5) Luke 14:8-11; (6) 1 Kings 1:5; (7) Rev. 12:11.

Cloak: See Coat.

Clock: (1) Time; (2) Waiting in (or on) God; (3) God appointed lifespan; (4) Hour is nearer; (5) End is near (5 minutes to 12); (6) Last hour; (7) Divine appointment; (8) Opportunity; (9) Timing is important; (10) Harvest; (11) Fullness of time; (12) Time to awaken; (13) Awaiting the timing of God to release a situation or ministry; (14) Note the time and look up individual meanings of the numbers.

Also see *Time* and *Watch*.

(2) 1 Sam. 13:8; (3) John 7:8; 8:20 (reference to His death); (4) Rom. 13:11; (5) Matt. 20:9; (6) 1 John 2:18; (7) Hab. 2:3; (8) Acts 16:25-26; (9) Eccl. 3:1; (10) Num. 13:20; (11) Luke 1:57; (12) Rom. 13:11; (13) Ps. 105:17-19; Dan. 4:16, 33-34; Jer. 29:10.

Closet: (1) Private; (2) Secret; (3) Place of prayer; (4) Hidden sins from past.

Also see *Cupboard.*

(1) Joel 2:16; Matt. 6:6; (2-3) Matt. 6:6; Luke 12:3; (4) Ps. 32:5; 69:5.

Cloth: (1) Speaks of the need to be born again; (2) Speaks of a superficial patch-up job; (3) Death (wrapped in cloth); (4) Nakedness (clothes taken); (5) Cast away (unclean cloth); (6) Mourning (sackcloth).

(1-2) Matt. 9:16; Mark 2:21; (3) Matt. 27:59; (4) Mark 14:51-52; (5) Isa. 30:22; (6) Gen. 37:34.

Clothe: (1) God's Glory; (2) Armor of God; (3) Armor of light; (4) Righteousness or salvation; (5) Speaks of growing up.

(1) Gen. 3:7; Rev. 16:15; (2) Eph. 6:11; (3) Rom. 13:12; (4) Isa. 61:10; Zech. 3:5; (5) 1 Sam. 2:19.

Clothes Dryer: (1) Losing the anointing; (2) Preparing a new anointing.

(1) Judg. 16:19-20; (2) Zech. 3:4.

Clothesline: (1) Being left out to dry; (2) Restored ministry.

Also see *Clothes Dryer.*

(1) Gen. 40:23; (2) Ps. 51:7.

Clothing: (1) God's glory; (2) Human-made cover up; (3) Adultery (burning clothes); (4) Guarantor issue (taken clothing); (5) A change of clothes is a change of role and authority; (6) Clothing depicts the state of our relationship with God (white = right); (7) Clothing may also be indicative of the state of one's heart; (8) Clean or new clothes may indicate conversion, separation, or preparation; (9) Something that doesn't fit (baggy clothes); (10) Warning of judgment/plague/death (wearing unbearably hot clothes); (11) Clothed with the zeal of God (non-tormenting fiery clothes).

Note also the color of the clothes and look up entries under individual colors.

Also see *Bra, Clothe, Coat, Inside Out, Pants, Shirt, Skirt,* and *Suit.*

(1) Gen. 2:25; (2) Gen. 3:7; James 2:2; Matt. 7:15; (3) Prov. 6:26-27; (4) Prov. 20:16; 27:13; (5) Gen. 41:14; Luke 15:22; 2 Kings 2:12-15; (6) Job 29:14; Isa. 61:10; Mark 16:5; Lam. 4:7-8; (7) John 19:23 (Jesus wore a seamless tunic because of his faultless heart); 2 Kings 22:19 (torn clothes = humbled heart); (8) Exod. 19:14-15; Matt. 9:17; Luke 15:22; (9) 1 Sam. 17:38-39; (10) Zech. 3:2-3; (11) Isa. 59:17; Jer. 20:9.

Cloud: (1) Presence of God; (2) God's glory; (3) Holy Spirit; (4) Guidance; (5) God's favor; (6) Coming shower; (7) Promise (of blessing or judgment).

Also see *Dust Cloud, Shower,* and *Storm.*

(1) Exod. 16:10; 24:16; Num. 16:42; (2) 1 Kings 8:11; 2 Chron. 5:14; (3) Num. 11:25; (4) Exod. 13:21; Neh. 9:12; (5) Prov. 16:15; (6) Luke 12:54; (7) Gen. 9:14; 1 Kings 18:44-45.

Dark Cloud/s: (1) Tribulation; (2) Trouble; (3) Judgment; (4) Testing/trial; (5) Oppression; (6) Depression (no hope).

(1) Joel 2:10; Acts 2:20; (3) Ps. 18:11; Jer. 23:19; 25:32; (2) Rev. 9:2; (4) Matt. 24:29; (5) As in, "under a cloud."; (6) Acts 27:20.

Cloudy: (1) Uncertainty; (2) Second coming; (3) Coming blessing (shower); (4) Heavenly witnesses; (5) Empty hearts (no rain).

Also see *Dark Clouds, Shower, Storm,* and *Rain.*

(1) Luke 9:34; (2) Mark 13:26; 14:62; 1 Thess. 4:17; Rev. 1:7; (3) Luke 12:54; (4) Heb. 12:1; (5) Jude 1:12.

Cloven-Hoofed: (1) Clean; (2) Divided; (3) Sure-footed; (4) Word-guided. (1-4) Deut. 14:6.

Clover: (1) Sports or fitness (three-leaf clover).

Also see *Grass* and *Mown Grass.*

(1) Ps. 147:10 (symbol of Adidas).

Clown: (1) Person always searching for laughs; (2) Entertainer; (3) Clumsy; (4) Attention grabber; (5) Fool or foolish; (6) Painted face; (7) Joker; (8) Playing with the things of God.

(1) Eccl. 2:2-3; (2) 2 Tim. 4:3-4; (3) 1 Sam. 25:25, 36; (4) Acts 8:9-11, 13, 18-24; 1 Pet. 3:3-4; (5) Eccl. 2:2-3; (6) 2 Kings 9:30; Jer. 4:30; Prov. 14:13; (7) Eph. 5:4; (8) John 6:66 (these were not serious or sincere in their search for truth).

Cluster: (1) Group of Believers; (2) Fruit (good [sweet] or bad [bitter]); (3) Harvest; (4) Revival; (5) Blessing; (6) Breasts.

(1) See *Congregation;* (2) Gen. 40:10; Num. 13:23; Deut. 32:32; 1 Sam. 25:18; (3) Rev. 14:18; Gen. 40:10; Num. 13:23-24; (4) 1 Sam. 30:12; (5) Isa. 65:8; Mic. 7:1; (6) Song. 7:7-8.

Coach (Sports): (1) Holy Spirit; (2) Jesus; (3) Five-fold ministry; (4) Mentor.

Also see *Pastor.*

(1) John 14:26; 1 John 2:27; (2) Luke 6:13-16; 9:10; (3) Eph. 4:11-12; (4) Exod. 18:19-22; 1 Tim. 1:18.

Coals: (1) Energy; (2) Cold (moving away); (3) Warm (moving closer); (4) Judgment or to condemn; (5) Angel (spirit); (6) Adultery (walking on coals).

Also see *Fire.*

(1) (2-3) John 18:18; 21:9; (4) Ps. 140:10; Prov. 25:21-22; Rom. 12:20; (5) Ezek. 1:13; (6) Prov. 6:28-29.

Coastline: (1) Represents a boundary; (2) Represents the interchange between the spiritual and natural realms; (3) Dominion on sea and earth (Heaven and earth).

Also see *Beach, Boundary, Rocks, Sand,* and *Sea.*

(1-3) Gen. 1:9; Rev. 10:2, 5-6, 8; (2) John 21:4, 15-17; also consider that the sea speaks of humanity and fishing of evangelism; (3) Rev. 10:5-6.

Coat: (1) Righteousness; (2) Salvation; (3) Authority or position; (4) Spiritual anointing (mantle); (5) Commitment; (6) Spiritual growth (new coat); (7) People's character and role are displayed in what they wear. For example: In First Samuel 15:27-28, Saul's robe represented his kingdom; in Matthew 3:4, John wore a prophet's clothes; in Mark 10:50, Bartimaeus had a beggar's cloak; in John 19:23, Jesus wore a seamless coat; in John 21:7, Peter had a fisherman's coat.

Also see *Mantle, Rainbow* (coat of many colors), and *Robe.*

(1) Job 29:14; Isa. 61:10; (2) Isa. 61:10; (3) Gen. 37:3; John 19:2; (4) 1 Sam. 28:14; Lev. 21:10; Matt. 9:20; 14:36; (5) Mark 10:50; (6) 1 Sam. 2:19.

Cobblestones: (1) Ancient paths.

(1) Jer. 18:15.

Cobweb: See Web.

Cockroach/es: (1) Sin; (2) Unclean; (3) In the dark spiritually; (4) Creeping infestation; (5) Areas of the heart not yet brought to the light; (6) Lies; (7) Defiling thoughts (roaches in your hair).

(1-2) <u>Lev. 5:2</u>; <u>11:31</u>, 43; 20:25b; (3) <u>1 John 1:6</u>-7; (4) 2 Tim. 3:6; Jude 1:4; (5) <u>1 Cor. 4:5</u>; 2 Cor. 4:6; 2 Pet. 1:19; (6) 1 John 1:6-7; (7) Tit. 1:15.

Coconut: (1) Purity/holiness (white of coconut).

(1) See *White*.

Codes: (1) Deposits of revelation from God; (2) Dreams; (3) Mysteries (requires code-breaker: the Holy Spirit).

(1) <u>Dan. 2:28a</u>, 47; <u>Prov. 25:2</u>; Matt. 16:15-17; (2) Num. 12:6-8; (3) Job 11:7; Dan. 4:9; 1 Cor. 13:2; 14:2.

Coffee: (1) Stain (spilt); (2) Sin (spilt); (3) Stimulant; (4) Fellowship or communion (having coffee with someone); (5) Ground (to powder); (6) Revelation.

(1-2) <u>Exod. 32:20-21</u>; (3) 2 Tim. 1:6; <u>2 Pet. 3:1</u>; (4) Rom. 14:17; 1 Cor. 10:21; (5) Exod. 32:20; Matt. 21:44; (6) Luke 8:11.

Coffin: (1) Death.

Also see *Grave* and *Graveyard*.

(1) <u>Gen. 50:26</u>.

Cogs: (1) Heart.

(1) As in, "heart of the operations."

Coins: (1) Money; (2) Provision; (3) Relatively small or interim amount of money; (4) Money from many nations (various multi-colored coins).

Also see *Gold* and *Money*.

(1-2) <u>Matt. 17:27</u>; (3) Mark 12:42; (4) 2 Sam. 8:11; 1 Chron. 18:11.

Cold: (1) Hardened; (2) Without Love; (3) Increase of wickedness; (4) Refreshing; (5) Resistant reception; (6) Alone; (7) Reluctance; (8) Away from God; (9) Dead/death; (10) Unforgiveness; (11) Evil presence.

Also see *Ice*.

(1) John 18:18; (2-3) <u>Matt. 24:12</u>; (4) Matt. 10:42; (5) Acts 28:2-6; (6) Eccl. 4:11 & 2 Cor. 11:27; (7) As in, "having cold feet"; (8) Matt. 24:12; (9) 2 Kings 4:34; (9) Matt. 24:9, 12; (10) Matt. 24:10, 12; (11) Job 4:15.

Cold Sore: (1) Sinning with the lips.

(1) Job 2:10b; Ps. 59:12; Prov. 10:19; Isa. 6:7.

Coles: See entries under Name and Place Dictionary.

Colors: The color of clothing and vehicles is a very important indicator of the meanings they carry. Color may communicate: (1) Newness; (2) Personality and character; (3) Splendor; (4) Honor; (5) Heavenly glory; (6) Promise (rainbow); (7) Favor (multi-colored covering); (8) Innocence/purity (multi-colored covering); (9) Glory (multi-colored); (10) May relate to a recent association of someone/something or someplace using that color; (11) Prophetic anointing (multi-colored).

Also see *Multi-Colored, Rainbow,* and individual colors.

(1) Matt. 9:16; Rom. 6:4; 2 Cor. 5:17; (2) Rev. 6:2-5; (3-4) 2 Sam. 13:18; 2 Tim. 2:20; 1 Pet. 1:7; (5) Rev. 4:3; (6) Gen. 9:13; (7) Gen. 37:3; (8) 2 Sam. 13:18; (9) Gen. 37:3 (prefigures his glory); 1 Chron. 29:2; Ezek. 17:3; 16:16; (10) By association; (11) Gen. 37:3.

Coloring Book: See Children's Book/s.

Colt: See Horse and Donkey.

Coma: (1) Spiritually dull; (2) Unreasonable; (3) Unresponsive; (4) Insensible; (5) Loss of God-consciousness (or ineffective conscience).

Also see *Sleep/ing.*

(1) Matt. 15:16; (2-4) Gen. 19:33; Jer. 51:39b, 57; (5) 1 Tim. 4:2.

Comb: (1) Vanity; (2) Grooming oneself for self-glory; (3) Examining (combing).

(1-2) 2 Sam. 14:25-26; (3) Gen. 13:10-11.

Comet: See Asteroid and Meteor.

Coming In: (1) Finishing a military campaign.

Also see *Going Out.*

(1) 1 Kings 3:7 (AMP); Judg. 3:10; 2 Sam. 3:25.

Commandments: (1) God is One, love God, love people (love, love, love); (2) Rules; (3) Instruction or guidance; (4) God's Word; (5) Law; (6) Tradition and ordinances of people (competing with).

(1) Mark 12:29-31; John 13:34; 14:21; 15:10, 12; 1 Tim. 1:5; (2) Matt. 15:9; (3) Matt. 8:18; John 10:18; 11:57; 12:49-50; 1 Thess. 4:2; Heb. 11:22; (4) Exod.

34:28; Num. 15:31; 1 John 2:7; (5) Rom. 7:9, 12; Eph. 2:15; 6:2; (6) Mark 7:8-9; Col. 2:21-22; Tit. 1:14.

Compass: (1) Bearings; (2) Direction; (3) God (God's habitation is known as the sides of the north).

Also see *North, South, East,* and *West.*

(1-2) Job 26:7; (3) Job 37:22; Ps. 48:1-2; Lev. 1:11.

Compass (Drawing): (1) Circle or circle of influence; (2) Growth rings (concentric circles).

(1-2) Acts 1:8.

Computer: (1) Heart (CPU); (2) Channel of communication; (3) Programmed.

Also see *Hard Drive, Hardware, Motherboard, Software,* and *Upgrade.*

(1) Prov. 4:23; (2) 2 Tim. 2:2; (3) Rom. 12:2.

Computer CD: (1) Impartation or teaching (loading a CD); (2) Programming (loading a CD); (3) Store of thoughts.

(1) 2 Tim. 2:2; (2) Prov. 22:6; (3) Rom. 12:2.

Computer Program: (1) A programmed way of thinking.

(1) Rom. 12:2.

Concealing: (1) Hiding; (2) Covering up; (3) Denying.

(1-2) Prov. 11:13; Judg. 3:16; (3) Matt. 26:70, 72.

Concordance: (1) Seeking deeper understanding; (2) Seeking God.

(1) Prov. 15:14; (2) Prov. 28:5.

Concrete: (1) Hard-hearted; (2) Stronghold; (3) human-made rock/stone; (4) Word foundation; (5) Solid as a rock; (6) City; (7) Foundation.

Also see *Brick, Rock, Stone,* and *Wall.*

(1) 1 Sam. 25:37; Job 41:24; Ezek. 11:19; 36:26; Zech. 7:12; 2 Cor. 3:3; (2-3) Nah. 3:14; (4-5) Luke 6:48; (6) As in, "concrete jungle"; (7) Isa. 28:16.

Condom: (1) Ineffective Gospel witness; (2) Not sowing the seed (the Gospel or the Word of God); (3) Sexual promiscuity; (4) Fornication.

Also see *Genitals.*

(1) Mark 14:56; 1 Cor. 15:15; (2) Gen. 38:9 & Luke 8:11; (3-4) Gal. 5:19.

Conference Room: (1) Prayer; (2) Spiritual dialogue; (3) Communion with God; (4) Fellowship; (5) Business decisions.

(1) Ps. 85:8; <u>Mark 12:26</u>; (2-4) Matt. 17:1; Luke 22:12; (5) 1 Kings 22:6; 2 Kings 6:11.

Coney: See Guinea Pig.

Conflict: (1) Warning; (2) Suffering for Christ; (3) Spiritual battle; (4) Inner battle.

Also see *Battle, Contend,* and *Fight.*

(2) <u>Phil. 1:30</u>; (3) Eph. 6:12; Col. 2:1; (4) Gal. 5:17.

Congregation: (1) Church (the Redeemed); (2) Gathering of good or evil; (3) Heavenly worshippers; (4) The Kingdom.

(1) <u>Ps.</u> 1:5, 26:12; <u>40:9-10</u>; 74:2; <u>89:5</u>; 149:1; (2) Acts 13:43; Ps. 22:22; 26:5; Prov. 21:16; (3) Ps. 22:25; (4) Isa. 14:13; Ps. 35:18.

Container: See Sack and Vessel.

Contend: (1) Argue; (2) Fight spiritually; (3) Compete against.

(1) Job 40:2; Prov. 29:9; Acts 11:2; (2) Deut. 2:9, 24; Isa. 41:12; 49:25; Jude 1:3, 9; (3) Jer. 12:5.

Continuous: (1) Without end; (2) Ongoing; (3) Consistent; (4) Persistent faith; (5) Abiding; (6) Eternity (Heaven).

(1) Acts 20:7; <u>Rom. 2:7</u>; <u>Heb. 7</u>:3b, <u>23-24</u>; 13:14; (2) Acts 1:14; 2:42, 46; Rom. 9:2; Heb. 13:15; 2 Pet. 3:4; (3) Acts 6:4; 18:11; (4) Luke 18:1-8; John 8:31; Acts 14:22; Col. 1:23; 1 Tim. 5:5b; James 1:25; (5) John 15:9-10; 1 John 2:24; (6) Isa. 57:15.

Contraceptive Pill: (1) Inability to reproduce spiritually; (2) Not sharing the Gospel (not reproducing your own kind); (3) Taking in a human-made contrivance that stops you from fruit-bearing.

(1) Acts 4:17-18; (2) <u>Rom. 10:14</u>; 1 Cor. 1:21; (3) 2 Cor. 11:4.

Contract Killer: (1) Angel of death; (2) The Law; (3) Legalism; (4) Judgment shown through grumbling; (5) The flesh; (6) Sin.

Also see *Assassin, Gunman, Rifle,* and *Sniper.*

(1) Exod. 12:23; 2 Sam. 24:16; (2-3) <u>2 Cor. 3:6-7a</u>; (4) James 5:9; (5) Gal. 5:19-23; (6) Rom. 7:5-6, 8-11.

Cook: (1) Scheming (concocting something); (2) Work of the flesh; (3) Poison. Also see *Bake, Baker, Cake,* and *Oven.*

(1-2) Gen. 25:29-34; (3) 2 Kings 4:39-40.

Cookbook: (1) Plan (recipe for disaster); (2) Witchcraft; (3) Ingredients; (4) Stirrer; (5) Formula; (6) Preparation; (7) Instructions; (8) *The Divinity Code to Understanding Your Dreams and Visions Dictionary.*

Also see *Baker* and *Cook.*

(1) Prov. 14:12; 16:25; (2-6) Acts 19:19; (7) 2 Tim. 3:16; (8) This interpretation suggests that you are not looking to the Holy Spirit enough and are looking more at dream interpretation as a formula.

Cooler/Cool Box: (1) Heart (preserving the Word); (2) Heart without love.

(1) Prov. 3:1; 4:4, 21, 23; Luke 8:15; Heb. 9:4; (2) Matt. 24:12.

Copper: See Bronze.

Cord: (1) Control; (2) Soul tie; (3) Generational curse; (4) Emotional attachment; (5) Stronghold; (6) Bondage; (7) Life (the tie between spirit and body); (8) The Blood of Jesus; (9) Protection or security; (10) Link; (11) Sin (or enslaved to sin); (12) Captivity; (13) Death; (14) Group of like-minded people.

Also see *Bound, Rope,* and *Umbilical Cord.*

(1) Ps. 2:3; (2) Gen. 44:30 (parent-child); 1 Sam. 18:1 (friends); 1 Cor. 6:16 (sexual partners); (3) Exod. 20:5; 34:7; Num. 14:18; Deut. 5:9; (4) Hos. 11:4; (5) Matt. 12:29; Mark 3:27; 2 Cor. 10:4; (6) Job 36:8; Ps. 118:27; Prov. 5:22; (7) Ps. 129:4; Eccl. 12:6; (8) Josh. 2:15, 18; (9) Eccl. 4:12; Ps. 129:4; Isa. 54:3; (10-11) Isa. 5:18; Prov. 5:22; (12) 1 Kings 20:31-32; (13) 2 Sam. 22:6; Ps. 116:3; (14) Ps. 119:61 (cf. KJV & NKJV); As in, "band of brothers."

Corn: (1) Word of God; (2) Believer; (3) Spiritual fruit; (4) Blessing.

Also see *Seed.*

(1) 1 Cor. 9:9-11; 1 Tim. 5:17-18; (2) John 12:24-25; (3) Mark 4:28; (4) Deut. 7:13; Prov. 11:26.

Corner (Building/Field/Room/etc) Dependent on context: (1) Legalism; (2) Grace; (3) Brawling wife/church; (4) Hidden (in a corner); (5) Whole/ly (4 corners); (6) Whole world (4 corners); (7) Foundational; (8) Insignificant; (9) Extremity; (10) Place of punishment; (11) Not in control; (12) Not central.

Also see *Center* and *Square.*

(1) Lev. 19:27; 21:5; (2) Lev. 19:9; 23:22; (3) Prov. 21:9; 25:24; (4) Isa. 30:20; Acts 26:26; (5) Job 1:19; Ezek. 7:2; Acts 11:5; (6) Isa. 11:12; Acts 10:11; Rev. 7:1; (7) Job 38:6; Isa. 28:16; Eph. 2:20; (8) (1 Sam. 10:22 & 15:17); Prov. 21:9; (9) Jer. 9:26; 25:23; (10) As in, "sit in the corner you naughty boy!"

Corner (Street): (1) Shortly or soon; (2) Decision; (3) Turn (change of direction or attitude); (4) Moving from worldly to spiritual or vice versa; (5) Worldly prominence (city corner); (6) Transition; (7) Turning point.

Also see *Crossroads, Left,* and *Right.*

(1) As in, "just around the corner"; (2) Prov. 7:8, 12, 22; (3) Matt. 2:22; 16:23; (4) Matt. 16:23; Luke 7:44; 9:54-55; John 20:16; Acts 9:35; (5) Matt. 6:5; (6) Mark 10:46; (7) 2 Chron. 26:9 (KJV); Neh. 3:24 (KJV).

It is very important that the direction—left or right—taken at the corner is noted.

Cornerstone: (1) Christ; (2) Chief; (3) Foundation.

(1-3) Ps. 118:22; Mark 12:10-11; Eph. 2:20.

Coroner: (1) Death confirmation; (2) The Lord declaring how a church has died; (3) Angel of the Lord investigating your death and possible judgment (get ready to meet the Lord); (4) Possible angel of death (if the subject is still alive, this is a warning of a predatory evil spirit).

(1-2) Rom. 6:11; (2) Rev. 3:1; (3-4) Job 4:15-17; Jude 1:9.

Correction Fluid (White Out): (1) Rewriting over a chapter in one's life; (2) Removing reproach.

(1-2) Gen. 30:22-23; Luke 1:24-25.

Corridor (Hallway): (1) Life journey; (2) Passage to and from the heart; (3) Past journey; (4) Future path; (5) Path to destiny; (6) Passing or passage of time; (7) Transition; (8) Pathway of the mind (soul-tie [godly or ungodly]).

Also see *Trench.*

(1, 3, 4) Exod. 14:22 (future), 29 (past); Num. 22:24; Also as in, "pass-age"; Ps. 23:4; (2) Job 31:7; Isa. 65:2; (5) Jer. 29:11; (6) Gen. 4:3; 21:22; (7) Num. 22:24; (8) Ps. 119:59; Isa. 55:7.

Corrugated Iron: (1) Roofing material; (2) Leadership or covering (poss. country church); (3) Strong faith; (4) Able to protect from and deflect storms, and at the same time, able to channel the flow of the Spirit; (5) No rust = Strong character.

Also see *Fence, Iron,* and *Roof.*

(1) Gen. 19:8; Josh. 2:6; Matt. 8:8; 10:27; Mark 2:4-5.

Corrupt: (1) Unsaved; (2) Evil (bad fruit); (3) Bad Company; (4) Mortal death; (5) Heart focused on earthly treasures; (6) The fleshly or old person; (7) Destructive or corrosive speech.

Also see *Corruption.*

(1) Eph. 4:22; 1 Tim. 6:5; 2 Tim. 3:8; (2) Matt. 7:17-18; 12:33; Luke 6:43-45; (3) 1 Cor. 15:33; (4) 1 Cor. 15:53-54; (5) Matt. 6:19-21; Luke 12:33-34; James 5:2; 1 Pet. 1:18; (6) Eph. 4:22; Jude 1:10; (7) Eph. 4:29.

Corruption: (1) Bad character; (2) Wickedness; (3) Deceitfulness; (4) Shortened life; (5) To be led astray; (6) Eternal death; (7) Weakness.

Also see *Corrupt, Decay,* and *Rust.*

(1) 1 Cor. 15:33; (2-4) Ps. 55:23; 2 Pet. 1:4; 2:19; (5) 2 Kings 23:13; Rev. 19:2; (6) Ps. 16:10; 49:9; Isa. 38:17; Jon. 2:6; Acts 2:27, 31; Rom. 8:21; Gal. 6:8; (7) 1 Cor. 15:42-43.

Costume Hire: (1) Wanting to be someone else; (2) Feeling like you need to be someone else; (3) False Christian (façade).

Also see *Mask.*

(1) 1 Sam. 21:13; Rom. 7:18-19; (2) Eph. 1:6; (3) Gen. 27:15; Prov. 6:19; Gal. 2:4.

Cotton: (1) Glory of God.

Also see *Wool.*

(1) Rev. 1:14.

Couch: (1) Heart (as the place of rest); (1) To lie down (lazy); (2) Reclining spiritually; (3) Sick; (4) Comfort/able; (5) Bed; (6) Somber place; (7) Seduction (woman lying on a couch).

Also see *Armchair* and *Sofa.*

(1) Prov. 14:33; Matt. 11:29; Acts 2:26; (2) Gen. 49:14; Job 7:13; 38:40; Also as in, "couch potato"; (3) Gen. 49:4; Luke 5:24; Acts 5:15; (4) Amos 6:4; Luke 5:19; Acts 5:15; (5) Amos 6:4; (6-7) Ps. 6:6.

Council: (1) Authority structure.

Also see *Government.*

(1) Matt. 5:22.

Counselor: (1) Holy Spirit; (2) Jesus Christ.

Also see *Teacher.*

(1) John 16:7; (2) Isa. 9:6.

Countenance: (1) Radiance; (2) Face; (3) Presence.

Also see *Face.*

(1) 2 Cor. 3:7; (2) Matt. 6:16; 28:3; Luke 9:29; Rev. 1:16; (3) Acts 2:28.

Counter (Shop): (1) Something on offer (something on the counter); (2) A deal; (3) Something deceitful (under the counter); (4) A bribe (under the counter); (5) The pulpit; (6) Hungry/searching for spiritual food (standing at a counter); (7) What you are having served up.

(1-2) Acts 24:26; (3) Ps. 26:10; Mark 12:13; (4) Prov. 21:14; (5) As the place where food is served up; (6) Ps. 78:19; Matt. 15:22-28; John 6:67-68; (7) John 12:2.

Country: (1) Offspring; (2) Consider what that country represents to you and the character of its people; (3) International (several countries); (4) Entering the Kingdom of God (entering another country).

Also see individual entries, i.e. *Chinese.*

(1) Gen. 10:20, 31; 12:7a; (4) Josh. 1:11b; John 3:5.

Country Road: (1) Country ministry; (2) Alone; (3) Off track; (4) Wilderness training.

Also see *Dirt Road, Road,* and *Winding Road.*

(1) Acts 8:26; (2) 1 Kings 19:4; (3) Luke 15:4; (4) Deut. 8:2-3.

Countryside: (1) Pleasant; (2) Peaceful; (3) Restful/leisurely; (4) Fresh; (5) Creation.

Also see *Grass, Green,* and individual tree names.

(1) Gen. 2:9; (2) Ps.23:2; Isa. 55:12; (3) Gen. 49:15; Deut. 3:20; 12:10; Josh. 1:13; Ps. 23:2; (4) Song. 7:13; (5) Gen. 1:12; 2:9.

Court (Law): (1) Tested; (2) Trial; (3) Judgment; (4) Salvation (judgment).

(1-3) John 18:28-38; 19:4-16; (3) Rom. 14:10; (3-4) John 3:17; James 4:12; Rom. 8:33-34; Rev. 20:12.

Courthouse: (1) Place of judgment; (2) Testing or trial; (3) Accusation; (4) Exposure of secrets of the heart; (5) Adjudication; (6) Brought before God/Christ.

(1) Rom. 14:10; 2 Cor. 5:10; (2) Matt. 22:35; Mark 10:25; (3) Acts 23:29; (4) Rom. 2:16; (5) John 19:10; (6) Acts 7:7; 10:42; Rom. 2:16; 2 Tim. 4:1; Heb. 12:23; 13:4.

Cousin: (1) Brother church (male cousin); (2) Sister church (female cousin); (3) Brother or sister in the faith (spiritual relative).

(1) Ps. 68:6; Jer. 31:1; Eph. 3:15; (2-3) Luke 1:36, 58; Rom. 16:1.

Cover: (1) Covering; (2) Hiding sin; (3) Protection; (4) Love.

(1) Ps. 32:1; 91:1; (2) Ps. 69:5; Prov. 28:13; Isa. 30:1; Luke 23:30; (3) Ps. 91:1; Matt. 23:37; (4) Song. 2:4; 1 Pet. 4:8.

Coveralls: (1) Self-righteous works; (2) Armor of God; (3) Manual labor/er; (4) Covering; (5) Redemption (taking off coveralls).

(1) Isa. 64:6; (2) Eph. 6:11; (3) Gen. 3:19; (4-5) Zech. 3:3-4.

Covert: (1) Hidden; (2) Secret; (3) Shelter; (4) Shadow/shade.

(1-2) 1 Kings 18:13; (3) Isa. 4:6; 16:4; 32:2; Jer. 25:38; (4) 1 Sam. 25:20; Job 38:40; 40:21; Ps. 61:4.

Cow: (1) Wealth; (2) Cash; (3) Blessing; (4) Idol.

(1) Ps. 50:10; (2) As in, "cash cow"; (3) Ps. 107:38; (4) Exod. 32:24; 1 Kings 12:28.

Cowboy: (1) Gung-ho believer; (2) Shady businessman; (3) Idolatry; (4) Jesus (as the Herdsman); (5) May describe a "driving" rather than a "leading" shepherd.

Also see *Cattle, Horse,* and *Whip.*

(1) Acts 19:14-16; (2) Gen. 31:7; (3) Exod. 32:24; (4) John 10:11; (5) Exod. 6:1; Num. 22:6; Luke 8:29.

Crab: (1) Believer with a tough exterior; (2) Believer with spiritual armor on; (3) Moody person; (4) Crabbing may represent evangelism amongst counter-culture groups; (5) Promise/s of God (as a living rock); (6) Believers in the armor of God; (7) Stronghold; (8) Partaking of an unclean thing (eating crab); (9) Spirit of cancer.

Also see *Fish, Lobster, Net,* and *Shrimp.*

(1) Matt. 4:19; As in, "shellfish"; (2) Eph. 6:12ff; (3) As in, "they were really crabby"; (5) 1 Pet. 2:4-5; (6) Eph. 6:11; 1 Pet. 2:4-5; (7) Job 21:6; Ps. 48:6; (8) Lev. 11:9-10.

Crack: (1) Old wineskin; (2) Flaw; (3) Lacking unity; (4) Barren ground (cracked ground).

(1) Josh. 9:4; Matt. 9:17; (2) Dan. 6:4; Hos. 10:2; (3) 1 Cor. 6:7; (4) 2 Kings 2:19.

Crackling: (1) Hot fire; (2) Fool's laughter.

(1-2) Eccl. 7:6.

Craftwork: (1) Witchcraft.

(1) 2 Kings 9:22; 2 Chron. 33:6; Mic. 5:12a; Gal. 5:19a-20a.

Crane (Bird): (1) Chatter; (2) Timely; (3) Honor and loyalty/fidelity (Japanese crane).

(1) Isa. 38:14; (2) Jer. 8:7; (3) Japanese tradition.

Crane (Machine): (1) Burden; (2) Burden lifting or lifted; (3) Made easy; (4) Powerful salvation ministry.

(1) Matt. 23:4; Luke 11:46; (2-3) Matt. 11:30; 27:32; (4) Isa. 49:22; 59:19b; Ps. 3:3; James 4:10.

Crash Dummy: (1) Test run; (2) Warning; (3) Observed impact; (4) Collision ahead.

(1-2) 1 Sam. 19:13-18; (3) Matt. 27:54; Mark 15:39; (4) Job 5:4; Isa. 8:9.

Crash Helmet: (1) Helmet of salvation; (2) Hardened heart (proud thoughts); (3) Fragmented/fragile mind.

(1) Eph. 6:17; (2) Dan. 5:20; Mark 6:52; 8:17; (3) James 1:8.

Crayfish: See Lobster.

Crazy: (1) Foolishness; (2) Anger/rage; (3) Fear; (4) Curse of disobedience; (5) Paranoia; (6) Obsession; (7) Demonic possession/oppression; (8) Person deep in the things of the Spirit (this looks like madness to the natural person).

(1) Hos. 9:7; (2) Luke 6:11; (3) 2 Tim. 1:7; (4) Deut. 28:28; (5) Matt. 2:16; (6) Prov. 19:13; 27:15; Luke 18:5; (7) Luke 8:35; (8) 1 Cor. 2:14.

Cream: (1) Best; (2) The Gospel.

Also see *Ice Cream.*

(1) Heb. 12:24; (2) Heb. 5:13 (the best part of the milk of the Word).

Cream (Color): (1) False holiness; (2) Self-righteousness.

Also see *White* and *Off-White*.

(1) Lev. 10:10 & Ps. 51:7; (2) Isa. 64:6 (cf. Rev. 19:8).

Creativity: (1) In the Spirit; (2) Using the gifts of the Spirit.

(1) Gen. 1:2ff; (2) John 9:6-7.

Credit Card: (1) Accounted as having faith; (2) Financial issue; (3) Having no spiritual credibility (wrong use of credit card).

(1) Gen. 15:6; Gal. 3:6; (2) Luke 14:28; (3) Acts 19:15.

Creek: (1) Creeks and rivers often depict boundaries.

Also see *Brook, Stream,* and *River.*

(1) Gen. 32:22-23; Josh. 1:11.

Creep/ing: (1) Warning; (2) Suspicious; (3) Secretive; (4) Outward form of godliness without the Spirit; (5) Abomination.

(1) 2 Tim. 3:6; (2-4) 2 Tim. 3:6; (5) Ezek. 8:10.

Crib: (1) New beginning; (2) Blessing started; (3) Nurturing; (4) Baby; (5) Pregnancy; (6) Feed tray; (7) The hand that feeds you.

(1-5) Luke 2:7, 12, 16; (6) Prov. 14:4; (7) Isa. 1:3.

Cricket (Insect): (1) Annoying person; (2) Deserted or empty.

(1) 2 Sam. 16:5-9; (2) Matt. 23:27; Isa. 34:13.

Cricket (Sport): (1) Noble; (2) Partnership; (2 batsmen); (3) Trying to get you out with words (bowling); (4) Words with power (batting); (5) Spiritual warfare (batting and bowling taking place); (6) Making history (hitting a hundred runs).

Also see *Ball, Bat, Football Game, Sport, Umpire,* and *Winning.*

(1) Supposedly a gentleman's game; Also as in, "that's just not cricket"; (2) Deut. 17:6; Matt. 18:19-20; (3) Mark 12:13; (4) Eccl. 8:4; Luke 4:32; (5) Rom. 7:23 (internally: spirit vs. flesh); 2 Cor. 10:3; Eph. 6:12 (in the second heaven: against evil spirits); 1 Tim. 1:18; (6) Esther 8:5, 8 (it is recorded).

Cricket bat: (1) Innings (as in your turn/or your time to bat).

Also see *Bat.*

(1) Esther 4:14; Eph. 1:4.

Crimson: (1) Sin; (2) Blood; (3) Opulence.

Also see *Blood* and *Red.*

(1-2) Isa. 1:18; (3) Jer. 4:30.

Crocodile: (1) Devourer; (2) Demon spirit; (3) The Devil; (4) Death; (5) Religious hypocrite; (6) One with biting remarks; (7) Predator; (8) Financial predator; (9) Faking or pretending (crocodile tears).

(1) By virtue of its teeth; (2) Matt. 13:4; (3) Isa. 27:1; Mal. 3:11; 1 Pet. 5:8; Rev. 12:4; (4) Prov. 5:5; Ezek. 28:8 (KJV); (5) Matt. 23:14; Mark 12:40; Luke 20:47; (6) Gal. 5:15; (7) 1 Pet. 5:8; (8) Mal. 3:10-11; (9) Mal. 2:13.

Crooked: (1) Faithless spiritual deviation; (2) Evil; (3) Ungodly; (4) Darkness; (5) Without peace.

Also see *Curved, Darkness, Straight,* and *Upright.*

(1) Prov. 3:4-5; Isa. 40:3-4; (2) Prov. 2:12-15; (3) Ps. 125:5; Isa. 40:4; Luke 3:5; (4) Isa. 42:16; Phil. 2:15; (5) Isa. 59:8.

Cross: (1) Jesus' cross; (2) Gospel of salvation; (3) Death; (4) Forgiveness (cancellation of debt); (5) Victory; (6) Healing; (7) Believer's cross; (8) Losing one's life for Christ.

Also see *Crucify.*

(1) John 19:17, 25; (2) 1 Cor. 1:17-18; Col. 1:20; (3) Phil. 2:8; (4) Col. 2:14; (5) Col. 2:15; Heb. 12:2; (6) Acts 4:10; (7-8) Matt. 10:38-39; 16:24; Mark 8:34; 10:21; Luke 9:23; 14:27.

Crossing (a bridge, lake, river, etc.): (1) Getting saved (entering Kingdom of Heaven); (2) Moving into the spiritual; (3) Journey of life; (4) Deliverance; (5) Exit from old; (6) Entry to new; (7) Double-mindedness (going backward and forward across); (8) The battle between the flesh and spirit (going backward and forward across).

Also see *Boom Gate* and *Railroad Tracks.*

(1) Exod. 14:16; 1 Pet. 3:20-21a; (2) 2 Kings 2:8-9, 14 (good); 2 Kings 21:6 (evil); (3) John 6:16-21; (4) Deut. 4:20; (5-6) Deut. 6:23; (7) James 1:6-8; (8) Gal. 5:17.

Crossroad: (1) Decision time; (2) Choice; (3) Vulnerable.

(1) Josh. 24:15; (2) Luke 22:42; (3) Matt. 25:36; 1 Cor. 4:11-13.

Crouching (1) Hiding; (2) Ready to attack.

Also see *Bending* and *Bowing.*

(1) Josh. 8:4; (2) Deut. 19:11.

Crow: See Raven.

Crowd: (1) Heavenly onlookers; (2) Busy; (3) Busyness; (4) Congregation; (5) Sheep without a shepherd; (6) Followers; (7) Public place; (8) Public opinion.

(1) Heb. 12:1; (2-3) Luke 9:10; (4) Matt. 5:1; (5) Matt. 9:36; (6) Mark 10:46; (7-8) Neh. 8:3; John 8:59.

Crown: (1) Victory; (2) Glory and honor; (3) Authority; (4) Life; (5) Righteousness; (6) Rejoicing; (7) Incorruptible; (8) Reward; (9) Pride.

Also see *Head.*

(1) 2 Tim. 2:5; Rev. 6:2; (2) Phil. 4:1; Heb. 2:7-9; 1 Pet. 5:4; Rev. 4:10; (3) Heb. 2:8; Rev. 4:10; (4) James 1:12; Rev. 2:10; (5) 2 Tim. 4:8; (6) 1 Thess. 2:19; (7) 1 Cor. 9:25; (8) Rev. 2:10; (9) Isa. 28:1, 3.

Crucify: (1) Lay down one's life (death to self); (2) Human weakness; God's wisdom and power; (3) Nailing the flesh with its affections and lust to live in the Spirit; (4) Torturous death.

Also see *Cross.*

(1) Gal. 2:20; (2) 1 Cor. 2:2-5; 2 Cor. 13:4; (3) Gal. 5:24-25; Rom. 6:6; (4) Matt. 27:31ff; Mark 15:25ff.

Cruise Ship: (1) Life's path or journey; (2) Journey, voyage, passage; (3) Can also represent a life without God or running from God; (4) Spiritual apathy.

Also see *Holiday, Houseboat, Suitcase, Tourist,* and *Yacht.*

(1) Prov. 5:6; 6:23; 10:17; 30:19; (2-3) Jon. 1:3; (4) Luke 12:19; Rev. 3:17-18.

Crumbs: (1) Insufficiency (lacking spiritual nourishment); (2) Spiritual pauper; (3) Great faith.

Also see *Bread.*

(1-2) Luke 16:21; (3) Matt. 15:27-28.

Crying: (1) Sorrow; (2) Grief; (3) Pain; (4) Pouring out one's heart; (5) Rejected; (6) Seeking repentance; (7) Disgraced; (8) Anguish of heart; (9) Due for blessing; (10) Tears do not ensure sincerity.

Also see *Tears*.

(1-3) Rev. 21:4; (4) Lam. 2:18-19; Heb. 5:7; (5-6) Heb. 12:17; (7) Matt. 26:75; (8) John 11:35; (9) Ps. 126:5-6; 84:6; (10) Mal. 2:13.

Cry Out: (1) Torment; (2) Fear; (3) Attention; (4) Uproar; (5) Unclean spirit; (6) Wilderness; (7) Anger; (8) Authoritative instructions; (9) Heartfelt supplication; (10) Declaration; (11) Inner conflict.

(1) Matt. 8:29; Mark 9:24; 15:34, 39; Luke 8:28; (2) Exod. 14:11; Matt. 14:26; Mark 6:49; (3) Matt. 20:30; 25:6; Mark 10:47; Luke 9:38; Acts 14:14; 21:28; 23:6; (4) Matt. 27:23-24; Mark 15:13-14; Acts 19:34; (5) Mark 1:23, 26; Luke 4:33, 41; 9:39; Acts 8:7; (6) Matt. 3:3; Mark 1:3; Luke 3:4; John 1:23; (7) Acts 7:57; 19:28; (8) Rev. 14:15, 18; (9) Exod. 8:12; Ps. 84:2; 3:4; 17:1; 18:6; Mark 9:24; (10) Matt. 21:15; Mark 11:9; (11) Mark 5:5-7.

Crystal/s: (1) Clear or pure; (2) Clarity; (3) Paganism; (4) New Age.

(1) Rev. 22:1; (2) Rev. 21:11; 22:1.

Crystal Ball: (1) Seeking direction; (2) Bypassing God (wrong entry into heavenlies); (3) Fortune telling; (4) Familiar spirit; (5) Occult practice; (6) Witchcraft. Also see *Cards (Tarot)* and *Witchcraft*.

(1-2) Lev. 20:6; 1 Sam. 28:3-8; (3) Acts 16:16-18; (4) Deut. 18:11-12; (5-6) Deut. 18:10.

Cucumber: (1) Symbol of world; (2) Turning back to the world; (3) Besieged.
(1-2) Num. 11:5; (3) Isa. 1:8.

Cud: (1) Meditation (chewing cud); (2) Needs outworking.
(1) Lev. 11:3; (2) Lev. 11:4.

Cummin (Cumin): (1) Small matter; (2) Taking care of miniscule issues while neglecting more important ones.
(1) Matt. 23:23.

Cup: (1) A person as a human vessel (heart); (2) Blessing; (3) Covenant; (4) Resurrection/life; (5) God's fury/wrath/judgment (also known as the cup of trembling); (6) Salvation or redemption; (7) Death/baptism; (8) Consolation; (9) Responsibility or calling; (10) God's will (the Father's cup); (11) Portion.
Also see *Platter.*

(1) Matt. 23:25-27; (2) Ps. 23:5; 1 Cor. 10:16; (3) Luke 22:20; 1 Cor. 11:25; (4) Gen. 40:9-13, 21; (5) Isa. 51:17, 22; Lam. 4:21; Ezek. 23:32; (6) Gen. 44:2, 12 (Silver = redemption); Ps. 116:13; (7) Mark 10:38-39; (8) Jer. 16:7; (9) Matt. 26:39-42; (10) Luke 22:42; John 18:11; (11) Ps. 11:6; 16:5.

Cupboard: (1) Heart; (2) Storage; (3) Thoughts (mind); (4) Delay; (5) Reserve or preserve; (6) Abundance: (7) Accumulated; (8) Hidden.

Also see *Closet.*

(1) Prov. 13:12; Amos 3:10; (2) 2 Chron. 11:11; 1 Cor. 16:2; (3) 1 Chron. 29:18; Ps. 31:12; (4) Exod. 22:29; (5) Gen. 41:36; (6) 1 Kings 10:10; 2 Chron. 31:10-12; (7) 2 Kings 20:17; Ezek. 4:9 (NIV).

Curb: See Kerb.

Currency Exchange: (1) Conversion to faith (place where your values change); (2) Receiving financial blessing from Heaven.

(1) Matt. 6:24; Luke 16:11, 13; (2) Exod. 12:35-36; Prov. 13:22; Phil 4:19.

Cursing: See Swearing.

Curtain: (1) The fleshly veil; (2) The heart (beyond a curtain); (3) Heaven; (4) Cover; (5) Ending (closing curtain); (6) Death.

Also see *Veil.*

(1) Heb. 10:20; (2) 2 Cor. 3:15; (3) Ps. 104:2; Isa. 40:22; (6) As in, "It's curtains!"

Curved: (1) Distorted or warped; (2) Leaning or having an inclination toward; (3) Deception; (4) Sin; (5) Bent on something; (6) Oppressed; (7) Bound; (8) Infirmity; (9) Mourning; (10) Not yet upright or straight; (11) Dismayed; (12) Flowing in the anointing; (13) Unrighteous.

Also see *Crooked, Straight,* and *Upright.*

(1) Ps. 62:3b; (2) Ezek. 17:7; (3) As in, "He threw me a curve ball"; Ps. 78:57; (4) Ps. 51:10; (5) Hos. 11:7; (6-8) Luke 13:11, 16; (9) Ps. 35:14; 38:6; (10) Luke 3:5; (11) Isa. 21:3; (12) John 3:8; (13) Ps. 125:4-5; Prov. 13:6.

Cushion: (1) Comfort; (2) Easy life ("cushy" job); (3) Desensitize/d (spiritually asleep).

(1) 2 Cor. 1:4, 7:4; (2) Luke 16:19; (3) Matt. 13:13.

Cussing: See Swearing.

Cut: (1) Harsh Words; (2) Using the Word of God; (3) Prune; (4) Edify; (5) Kill (cut off); (6) Cuts on the body can mean verbal abuse and/or wounded; (7) Cutting away the flesh.

(1) Luke 12:51; Acts 5:33; 7:54; (2) Eph. 6:17; Heb. 4:12; (3) John 15:2; (4) Heb. 12:11; (5) Dan. 9:26; Gen. 9:11; (6) Matt. 27:29-30; Mark 10:34; (7) Rom. 2:29.

Cutting Hair: (1) Breaking a vow; (2) Making a vow; (3) Shame; (4) Cutting away the flesh.

Also see *Hair, Razor,* and *Shave.*

(1) Num. 6:5; (2) Acts 18:18; (3) Jer. 7:29; Ezek. 5:1-2; (4) Lev. 14:8.

Cyclone: See Storm.

Cylinder: (1) 3-D object (spiritual); (2) Beyond the physical realm; (3) New dimensions.

Also see *Circle* and *Round.*

(1-3) Eph. 3:18 (multi-dimensional).

Cymbal: (1) All words no love; (2) Worship.

(1) 1 Cor. 13:1; (2) 1 Chron. 15:16, 19, 28.

Dad: See Father.

Dam: (1) Resisting or stopping the move of God; (2) Potential; (3) Controlled flow of the Spirit; (4) Holding back; (5) God's protection.

Also see *Deep, Lake, Pond, Reservoir,* and *Water.*

(1) Gen. 26:15; Deut. 2:30; Acts 2:17; 6:8-10; (2) Mal. 3:10; (3) 2 Chron. 32:3-5, 30; (4) Gen. 26:18; (5) Josh. 3:13; Isa. 59:19b.

Damnation: (1) Hell; (2) Doomed; (3) Cursed; (4) Unbelievers; (5) Eternal loss; (6) Judgment; (7) Result of unrighteous pleasure and denial of truth.

(1-7) Matt. 5:22; 10:28; Mark 16:16; 2 Thess. 2:12; (6) 2 Pet. 2:4.

Dancing: (1) Worship/praise; (2) Joyful celebration; (3) Being led by the Spirit (as in ballroom dancing); (4) Sensuous/fleshly; (5) Partner hunting; (6) Sign of positive change/deliverance; (7) Youthful/immaturity; (8) Spiritually immature; (9) Change (turning); (10) Performance; (11) Also consider that the music to which you are dancing may be indicative of its meaning; (12) Union/love.

Also see *Turning.*

(1) <u>2 Sam.6:14-16</u>; Ps. 149:3; 150:4 (2) Judg. 11:34; 1 Sam. 18:6; Ps. 30:11; Luke 15:25; (3) John 21:18; Rom. 8:14; (4) Exod. 32:19; 1 Sam. 30:16; Job 21:17; Matt. 14:6; (5) Judg. 21:21-23; (6) Ps. 30:11; cf. Lam. 5:15 (reversed); (7) Jer. 31:13; Job 21:11; (8) Matt. 11:16-19; (9) Ps. 30:11; Jer. 31:13; Lam. 5:15; Also as in "the dance of change" or "learning new steps"; (10) Matt. 14:6; Mark 6:22; (12) Amos 3:3.

Dandruff: (1) Renewing the mind (getting rid of the old wineskin); (2) Fragmented mind.

(1) <u>Rom. 12:2</u>; (2) Dan. 5:6; Luke 24:38; James 1:8.

Dark/ness: (1) Demonic presence; (2) Absence of Christ; (3) Separation from God; (4) Hell; (5) The kingdom of satan; (6) Spiritual blindness; (7) In sin; (8) Ungodliness; (9) Worldliness; (10) Lost; (11) Ignorant; (12) Judgment; (13) Secret/ly; (14) Lying; (15) Hatred; (16) Spiritually unaware or ignorant (in the dark); (17) Hidden Presence of God; (18) Death; (19) Subconscious.

Also see *Night* and *Shadow.*

(1) Ps. 22:12-13 & Matt. 27:45; Mark 15:33; Luke 23:44; (2) <u>John</u> 13:30; <u>8:12</u>; (3) Matt. 4:15-16; <u>1 John 1:5</u>; (4) Matt. 8:12; 22:13; 25:30; <u>2 Pet. 2:4</u>; Jude 1:13; (5) Luke 22:53; Acts 26:18; Eph. 6:12; Col. 1:13; (6) Matt. 6:23; <u>John 1:5</u>; Acts 13:11; (7) Eph. 5:11-12; (8) <u>John 3:19</u>; 8:12; 2 Cor. 6:14; 1 Thess. 5:5, 7b; (9) Rom. 13:12; Eph. 6:12; (10) John 12:35, 46; 1 John 2:11; (11) 1 Thess. 5:4; (12) Exod. 10:21; Acts 2:20; Jude 1:6; (13) Matt. 10:27; 1 Cor. 4:5; (14) 1 John 1:6; (15) 1 John 2:9, 11; (16) Exod. 10:22-23; Deut. 28:29; 2 Sam. 22:29; (17) Exod. 20:21; Num. 12:8; Deut. 5:23; 1 Kings 8:12; (18) Job 10:21-22, 12:22; (19) 2 Cor. 4:6.

Darkroom (Photography): (1) Private exposure and developing vision.
(1) Matt. 10:26; <u>1 Cor. 4:5</u>.

Darts: (1) Heart-piercing words; (2) Need for the shield of faith.
Also see *Arrows.*
(1) <u>2 Sam. 18:14; Prov. 7:23</u>; (2) Eph. 6:16.

Daughter: (1) Your future; (2) Natural daughter; (3) Fellow believer—female—daughters of faith; (4) May refer to a work, church, ministry, or city planted by God or another; (5) Female descendant.
(1) <u>Job 21:8</u>; Ps. 103:5b; Joel 2:28; 2 Cor. 4:16; (2) Acts 21:9; (3) Matt. 9:21; Luke 13:16; 2 Cor. 6:18; <u>1 Pet. 3:6</u>; (4) John 12:15; (5) Luke 1:5; 8:48.

Day: (1) Light; (2) Glory or honor; (3) Time to do the work of God; (4) Guidance; (5) In the Presence of Christ; (6) In Christ; (7) A day may equal a year.

Also see entries under individual numbers (one through seven) and individual days (Sunday through Saturday).

(1) Gen. 1:5; (2) Rev. 21:24-25; (3) John 9:4; (4) John 11:9; (5-6) John 8:12, 9:4; (7) Num. 14:34; Ezek. 4:6.

Dead: (1) Spiritually dead; (2) Unable to receive spiritual truth; (3) Literal, physical death; (4) An aspect of one's life laid down; (5) Death to self; (6) A dead person speaking to you may indicate soul-ties; (7) A dead person speaking to you may indicate demonic deception.

Also see *Death*.

(1) Matt. 8:22; (2) John 8:43, 47; (3) John 11:14; (4-5) Matt. 10:38; 16:24; Mark 8:34; 10:21; Luke 9:23; 1 Cor. 15:30-31 (5) Gal. 2:20; (6) Gen. 42:38; (7) 2 Cor. 11:14; Gal. 1:8.

Dead End: (1) No hope; (2) Bad decision; (3) Turn back; (4) Wrong way; (5) Not giving out; (6) Disobedience.

(1) Eph. 2:12; Heb. 3:10-12; (2) Gen. 12:10; Gal. 1:6; Jude 1:11; (3) Gen. 13:1, 3; James 5:20; (4) Gal. 2:18; (5) Mark 4:24; Luke 6:38; Matt. 10:8; (6) 1 Kings 13:9-22.

Deaf: (1) Lack of spiritual hearing; (2) Hardened heart; (3) Without spiritual understanding; (4) Unbeliever; (5) Deaf and dumb spirit.

Also see *Dumb*.

(1-3) Matt. 13:13-15; Mark 4:12; Luke 8:10; Matt. 13:15; Acts 28:27; Heb. 3:15; John 8:43; (4) Isa. 29:18; (5) Mark 9:25-26.

Dealer: (1) The authority figure; (2) The spiritually stronger one; (3) God; (4) Dominant one; (5) Rich with servants; (6) M.C. (Master of Ceremonies), host, or preacher.

(1) John 7:18-19; (2) John 4:9; (3) Luke 1:25; Rom. 12:3; Heb. 12:7; (4) 1 Sam. 17:4-10; (5) Prov. 22:7; (6) John 2:8-10.

Death: (1) Dying to self; (2) Literal death; (3) Spiritual death (result of sin); (4) Ending a relationship (with a known person); (5) Death of a ministry; (6) Separation; (7) Sin; (8) Martyrdom; (9) Condemned; (10) Judgment; (11) Conversion (salvation); (12) Crucifying the flesh; (11) If you know the name of the person, look up meaning (i.e. your friend Verity dies, means the death of truth).

Also see *Birth* and *Dead.*

(1) Matt. 10:38; 16:24; Mark 8:34; 10:21; Luke 9:23; 1 Cor. 15:30-31; (2) John 11:14; (3) Jer. 9:21; <u>Rom. 6:23</u>; (4) Rom. 16:17; 2 Cor. 6:14; Eph. 5:11; (6) Rom. 6:23 (spiritual death is separation from God); Physical death is separation of the spirit from the body; (7) Rom. 6:23; (8) Matt. 10:21; Acts 7:60; (9) Matt. 20:18; (10) 2 Sam. 12:19-23; (11) Rom. 6:4-8; (12) Gal. 5:24.

Debt: (1) Unforgiveness; (2) Offense taken; (3) Sin.

Also see *Payment.*

(1) Matt. 18:21-35; (2-3) <u>Luke 11:4</u>.

Decapitation: (1) In trouble with the law (capital punishment); (2) Punishment; (3) Martyr; (4) Defeated; (5) Loss of authority or authority figure; (6) Losing one's head (insanity, paranoia, psychosis); (7) Silenced.

Also see *Head* and *Throat (Cut).*

(1) 1 Sam. 5:4; <u>Isa. 9:14</u>; (2) 1 Sam. 17:51; 2 Sam. 16:9b; (3) Heb. 11:37a; (4) 1 Sam. 17:51; (5) 1 Cor. 11:3; Eph. 5:23; (6) John 10:20; Acts 12:15 (KJV), 26:24; (7) Mark 6:18-19, 24.

Decay: (1) Eternal death; (2) Perish.

(1) <u>Ps. 49:14</u>; Acts 2:27; (2) Isa. 1:28; Rom. 2:12.

Deck (Timber): (1) Foundation; (2) Platform.

(1) <u>2 Tim. 2:19a</u>; (2) Matt. 10:27.

Deed: (1) Contract; (2) Title (ownership); (3) Works of the flesh.

(1-2) Gen. 23:20; Jer. 32:44; (3) <u>Rom. 3:20, 28</u>.

Deep: (1) Heart; (2) Ocean/seas/waters; (3) Equivalent to death (deep sleep); (4) Well rooted/grounded; (5) Hell; (6) Profound; (7) Secrets; (8) The Heart of God (Word of God).

(1) Gen 1:2; 7:11; Lev. 13:3; Ps. 42:7; <u>64:6</u>; Prov. 18:4; 20:5; Dan. 2:22; John 4:11; (2) Gen. 1:2; Neh. 9:11; Job 38:30; 41:31; Ps. 104:5-6; 107:24; Isa. 51:10; 63:13; Zech. 10:11; Luke 5:4; 2 Cor. 11:25; (3) Gen. 15:12; Gen. 2:21 & John 19:34; Isa. 29:10; (4) Ps. 80:9; Luke 6:48; (5) Ps. 88:6; 140:10; Prov. 22:14; 23:27; Isa. 30:33; Jon. 2:3 & Matt. 12:40; <u>Luke 8:31</u>; Rom. 10:7; (6-7) Ps. 92:5; Dan. 2:22; 1 Cor. 2:10; (8) Gen. 1:2; Dan. 2:22; <u>John 4:11</u>.

Deeper: (1) Greater commitment; (2) Further on in spiritual walk; (3) Revelation (deeper in the things of God); (4) Caught or entrapped (going to hell).

(1-2) Ezek. 47:3-5; (3) Prov. 3:20; (4) Ps. 18:4; Jon. 2:5-6.

Deer: (1) Someone who thirsts after God; (2) Strong spiritual walk and reaching new heights; (3) Sure footedness.

(1) Ps. 42:1; (2) Ps. 18:33; (3) Song. 2:17; 8:14.

Deer Hunting: See Hunting.

De Facto Relationship: (1) Person or church with one foot in world, one foot in Christ; (2) No commitment; (3) Lukewarm person or church.

(1-3) Prov. 7:7-8; Hos. 2:5; John 4:18.

Deliverance: (1) Dealing with a controlling issue; (2) Getting something out in the open; (3) Cleansing the inner temple of the human heart; (4) Casting out a literal demon; (5) The Rapture; (6) Released through the Presence of God.

(1) Exod. 34:24; Deut. 7:1-5; Jon. 2:4, 10; (2) Lev. 18: 14-15, 28; Job 39:3; Prov. 22:10; Jer. 16:12-13; Matt. 5:13; (3) Gen. 21:10; Deut. 9:4; 1 Kings 14:24; 21:26; Ps. 80:8; (4) Matt. 8:16; 9:33; 10:1, 8; 12:28; (5) Isa. 26:19-21; (6) Ps. 44:2-3.

Demolition: See House.

Demon: (1) Fallen angel; (2) Evil spirit; (3) Unclean spirit; (4) Physical affliction; (5) Bondage; (6) Oppression; (7) Addiction; (8) Self-destruction; (9) Sickness; (10) Spirit of death; (11) Stronghold; (12) Issue (on which a demon might find ground to enter); (13) Spirit of infirmity; (14) Literal demon.

(1) Rev. 1:20 & Rev. 12:4; (2) 1 Sam. 16:14; (3) Matt. 10:1; Mark 5:8; (4) Acts 10:38; (4-5) Luke 13:12, 16; (6) 1 Sam. 16:14; (4-8) Matt. 17:15-18; (9) Matt. 8:16; Luke 8:2; (10) See *Reaper;* (11) Luke 8:29; (12) Matt. 18:34-35 & Eph. 4:27; (13) Matt. 4:24; Luke 8:2.

Den: (1) Dark hiding place for greedy predators; (2) Hiding place.

(1) Job 38:39-40; Ps. 104:21-22; Dan. 6:16; Matt. 21:13; Mark 11:17; Luke 19:46; (2) Ps. 10:9; Judg. 6:2; Rev. 6:15.

Dental Nurse/Assistant: (1) Church.

Also see *Dentist, Nurse,* and *Teeth.*

(1) Song. 4:2 & Isa. 40:11.

Dentist: (1) Christ; (2) Pastor.

Also see *Teeth*.

(1-2) This is by virtue of the fact that teeth are as sheep (Song. 4:2; 6:6), and the person who works on them would be their leader.

Deodorant: (1) Blessing (as a sweet fragrance); (2) Favor of God; (3) Covering up an offense; (4) Dealing with an offense.

Also see *Body Odor*.

(1-4) Song. 4:10; Prov. 27:9; Matt. 11:6; Luke 7:23; Phil. 4:18.

Deposit: See Credit Card, Currency Exchange, and Down Payment.

Descend: (1) Dropping away spiritually; (2) Death; (3) Bringing from Heaven to earth; (4) To humble; (5) Give up.

Also see *Dropping* and *Down*.

(1) Gen. 12:10; 26:2; 46:4; Jon. 1:3, 5; (2) Gen. 37:35; 44:29, 31; Josh. 3:11, 13, 16, (*Jordan* means "descender/death"); Job 7:9; (3-4) Ps 18:27; Phil 2:5-8; (5) Gen. 21:16.

Desert: (1) Testing place; (2) Place where heart is revealed; (3) Place of dependence on the Word; (4) Place of humbling; (5) Preparation for entry into Promised Land; (6) Without public profile; (7) Place of Spirit strengthening; (8) Barrenness; (9) Infertility; (10) Trials; (11) Place away from God.

(1-5) Deut. 8:2-3, 7-9; (6-7) Luke 1:80; (8) Job 39:6; (9) Gen. 29:31; Prov. 30:16; (10) Matt. 4:1; Acts 14:22; (11) Jer. 17:5-6.

Desk: (1) Speaks of a business or work situation/issue; (2) Schooling or learning; (3) Teaching.

(1) Matt. 9:9; (2-3) Deut. 6:7a; Matt. 26:55b.

Desktop Computer: See Computer, Hardware, Laptop, and Software.

Dessert: (1) Indulgence; (2) Inheritance/promise/blessing.

Also see *Ice Cream*.

(1) Prov. 25:16; (2) Lev. 20:24.

Destroy: (1) Ruin; (2) Kill; (3) Judgment; (4) Famine; (5) Devil.

(1) Jer. 4:7; (2) Esther 9:24; (3) Gen. 18:28; (4) Joel 1:10; (5) John 10:10.

Devil: (1) Chief of all evil; (2) Fallen angel; (3) Unclean spirit.

(1) Matt. 12:24; Mark 3:22; Luke 11:15; (2) Isa. 14:12-15; Ezek. 28:14-15; (3) Rev. 18:2.

Dew: (1) The favor of God; (2) A gift or blessing from God; (3) Eternal life; (4) Revelation from God; (5) That which comes from God because of prayer; (6) Replenishment/zest; (7) Judgment (no dew); (8) Guidance or confirmation.

(1) Prov. 19:12; (2) Ps. 133:3; Hos. 14:5; Mic. 5:7; (3) Ps. 133:3; (4) Exod. 16:13-15 (heavenly food); (5) Deut. 32:2; 1 Kings 17:1; (6) Ps. 110:3; (7) Hag. 1:10; (8) Judg. 6:38.

Diabetes: (1) Lack of sweetness of heart (as a measure of relationship with God); (2) Unsaved (unhealthy blood); (3) Doctrine of demons (faulty DNA); (4) Actual diabetes.

Also see *Insulin.*

(1) Ps. 16:8-11; (2) Lev. 17:11a; (3) 2 Cor. 11:4.

Diamond: (1) Jesus; (2) Precious work; (3) Permanent marker; (4) The word *diamond* comes from the Greek word *Adamas,* meaning "unconquerable"; (5) Resistance to abrasion; (6) Hardest natural substance known; (7) Excellent disperser of light; (8) Adamant/immovable/resolute; (9) Associated with the tribe of Gad.

Also see *Precious Stones.*

(1) 1 Pet. 2:4; (2) 1 Cor. 3:12; (3) Jer. 17:1; (4) Ezek. 3:8-9 (adamant); (9) Exod. 28:18.

Diaper: (1) Immaturity; (2) Spiritually unaware of offense.

(1-2) Eph. 4:14.

Diaper Soaking Solution: (1) Waiting on God (soaking) to remove stubborn fleshly characteristics.

(1) Ps. 69:2-3.

Diary (Personal): (1) Your heart (as the place where you record things of importance); (2) Agenda of your heart; (3) Date with destiny (Divine appointment); (4) Memory; (5) Record; (6) Memorable moment; (7) Anticipated event; (8) Personal secret.

(1) Deut. 11:18; (2) Num. 15:39; Prov. 19:21; Hab. 2:2; (3) Esther 4:14; Gal. 4:4; (4-6) 1 Sam. 30:6; Neh. 4:14; Ps. 78. (7) Tit. 2:13; (8) Matt. 13:35b.

Diary (Work): (1) Divine appointment; (2) Anticipated event; (3) Business event; (4) Schedule.

(1) Esther 4:14; John 15:16; 1 Pet. 2:9; (2) Dan. 9:24-27; Tit. 2:13; (3) John 21:3; (4) Gal. 4:4.

Dice: (1) Chance; (2) Gambling; (3) Trying to find God's will.

For particular numbers on dice, see entries under individual numbers. For example, if you threw a five, you might be gambling with God's grace.

(1) 1 Sam. 6:9; (2) Mark 15:24; (3) Exod. 28:30; Num. 27:21; 1 Sam. 28:6.

Digging: (1) Uncovering truth; (2) Fertilizing; (3) Digging a well; (4) Preparing for a protracted battle; (5) Seeking.

Also see *Dirt, Shovel, Spade, Earthmovers,* and *Excavate.*

(1) Matt. 13:44; (2) Luke 13:8; (3) Gen. 26:18-19; (4) As in, "digging in"; (5) Matt. 7:7; 13:45-46.

Dignity: See Formal.

Dim: (1) Lacking spiritual insight; (2) Calamity; (3) Sorrow or grief; (4) The Glory has departed; (5) Moving by faith; (6) Halfway between dark and light; (7) Compromise; (8) Lukewarm; (9) Lights are going out.

(1) Gen. 27:1; Deut. 34:7; 1 Sam. 3:2; 4:15; (2) Lam. 5:17; (3) Job 17:7; (4) Lam. 4:1; (5) Gen. 48:10, 13-20.

Dining Room: (1) Spiritual nourishment; (2) Intimacy; (3) Fellowship.

Also see *Bread, Restaurant,* and *Table.*

(1) Ps. 34:8; Heb. 5:12-14; (2-3) Ps. 23:5; Rev. 3:20.

Dinosaur: (1) Out of date (old); (2) Large predator; (3) Evil spirit/the devil; (4) Monster (wild); (5) Fierce (violent); (6) Untamable.

Also see *Monster.*

(1) Matt. 9:17; 2 Cor. 5:17; (2) Job 41:14; (3) Rev. 12:9; (4) Job 41:2-5; (5) Job 41:10; (6) Job 41:4.

Dirt: (1) Sin; (2) Finding someone's past sin; (3) Flesh; (4) Of humanity.

Also see *Dust* and *Earth.*

(1) Isa. 57:20; (2) As in, "digging up dirt on someone"; (3-4) Gen. 2:7.

Dirt Road: (1) Doing your own thing (uncleanness); (2) Heading toward uncleanness; (3) Off of God's highway; (4) A path of unwholesome talk; (5) Scandal; (6) Accusation; (7) Country ministry; (8) Wilderness path; (9) Path to Promised Land; (10) Path of humbling dependence on the Word of God.

Also see *Country Road, Dirt, Road,* and *Winding Road.*

(1) Ezek. 36:17; (2) 1 Cor. 15:33; (3) Prov. 16:17; Isa. 35:8; 40:3; (4-6) Ps. 73:8; (7) Judg. 5:6; (8-9) Exod. 13:18; Deut. 1:19, 31; (10) Deut. 8:2-3.

Dirty Water: See Water (Dirty Water).

Disability: (1) Unsaved (spiritually insensitive); (2) Not yet spiritually developed (spiritually dull); (3) Having a character flaw; (4) Curse (the result of sin); (5) Dependence on God (having been humbled).

Also see *Mentally Disabled Person/s.*

(1) 1 Cor. 2:14; (2) 2 Kings 6:17; Matt. 14:29-30; (3) Matt. 26:35 & 26:69-75; (4) John 5:5-14; (5) Gen. 32:25, 31.

Discount: (1) Disregard; (2) Favor.

(1) Mark 7:13; (2) Prov. 22:1; Matt. 18:27.

Disease: (1) Contagious sickness; (2) Common infirmity.

(1-2) Matt. 4:23-24; 9:20, 35; 10:1.

Dish: (1) Heart; (2) Preparing or cleansing hearts (washing dishes).

Also see *Plate* and *Spoon.*

(1-2) Matt. 23:25.

Dishwasher: (1) The Holy Spirit; (2) Holy Spirit evangelist (cleaning hearts).

Also see *Dish.*

(1) Ps. 51:10-12; (2) Matt. 10:8; Luke 4:18-19.

Distance: (1) Time; (2) Old; (3) Physically separated; (4) Trust issue (someone standing at a distance).

Also see *Horizon.*

(1) Acts 2:39; (2) Josh. 9:13; (3) Gal. 2:12; Jude 1:19; (4) 1 Sam. 26:13-25.

Distant: (1) Shutting off from someone; (2) Feeling unworthy; (3) Fearful; (4) Unsociable.

Also see *Horizon.*

(1) Luke 17:12; 23:49; (2) Luke 18:13; (3) Rev. 18:10, 15; (4) Prov. 18:24a.

Distributor (Auto): (1) Heart.

(1) Matt. 15:18-19.

Ditch: (1) Enemy hindrance; (2) Trap; (3) Whore (deep ditch); (4) Hell; (5) Place of refuse; (6) Human-made watercourse; (7) Depression.

(1-2) Ps. 7:15; 57:6; Isa. 42:22; (3) Prov. 23:27; (4) Matt. 15:14; (5) Job 9:31; (6) 2 Kings 3:16-17; Isa. 22:11; (7) 1 Sam. 28:20-21.

Dividing: (1) Separating: (2) Separating between soul and spirit; (3) Between truth and lies; (4) Between believer and unbeliever; (5) Between husband and wife (divorce); (6) Between family members; (7) About to fall over.

(1-2) Heb. 4:12; (3) 2 Tim. 4:4; Tit. 1:14; (4) Matt. 25:32-33; 2 Cor. 6:14; (5) Matt. 5:32; (6) Matt. 10:34-35; (7) Matt. 12:25.

Diving: (1) Boldly stepping out in faith (confidence in the Spirit); (2) Lack of support; (3) Hiding; (4) Descending spiritually; (5) Launching into the deep things of God.

Also see *Descending, Down,* and *Falling.*

(1) Acts 4:29-31 ("confidently diving in"); (2) Judg. 15:20b; (3) As in, "diving for cover"; (4) Ps. 107:12; (5) Ezek. 47:5.

Divorce: (1) Separation; (2) Hard-heartedness; (3) Disagreement; (4) Severance at workplace; (5) Adultery; (6) Actual divorce.

(1) Matt. 19:5-6; (2) Matt. 19:8; (3) Deut. 24:1; Amos 3:3; (4) Exod. 9:28b; Luke 16:2; (5) Matt. 5:32; 19:9.

Dizzy: (1) Busy; (2) Confusion; (3) Under the anointing (drunk in the Spirit); (4) Warning of intoxication with drugs or alcohol.

(1) Matt. 6:28; (2) Job 12:25; Ps. 70:2; (3) 2 Chron. 5:14; Jer. 23:9; (4) Job 12:25; 1 Cor. 5:11.

Dock: See Airport and Railway Station.

Doctor: (1) Jesus; (2) Authority; (3) Holy Spirit balm; (4) Sick; (5) Possible sin; (6) Need to seek God for healing; (7) Need of medication.

(1) Mal. 4:2; Mark 5:26; (2) Acts 5:34; (3) Jer. 8:22; James 5:14-16; (4) Matt. 9:12; Luke 5:31; (5) Mark 2:17; (6) 2 Chron. 16:12; James 5:14-16; (7) Jer. 8:22.

Dog: (1) Unbeliever/fool; (2) An attitude that rejects God's authority; (3) Symbolizes the world; (4) The flesh; (5) Someone who turns on you; (6) Turning on you with their mouths; (7) Turning back to old ways (self-willed, walking in flesh, despising authority); (8) Deceitful doers (under the table); (9) Those who tear apart with their mouth; (10) Stronghold; (11) Comforting friend; (12) Despised or insignificant; (13) Watchman (good or bad); (14) Lazy; (15) Not dealing with an issue (sleeping dog); (16) Religious spirit (blue heeler); (17) Liar; (18) Vicious (junk yard dog); (19) Spirit of condemnation (big vicious dog that attacks another dog [the flesh]); (20) Demon (evil spirit); (21) Demon of lust; (22) Depression (big dog); (23) Fear of discovery (hound/terrier on your trail).

Also see *Bulldog, Mascot, Pet,* and *Puppy.*

(1) Deut. 23:18; Prov. 26:11 (cf. Ps. 14:1); Matt. 16:26-27; Rev. 22:15; (2) Ps. 22:16; (3) Matt. 7:6a; 15:26; (4) Isa. 56:11 (appetite is a mark of the flesh); Phil. 3:2 (AMP); (5) Prov. 26:17; Matt. 7:6; (6) Ps. 59:6-7; Phil. 3:2; (7) 2 Pet. 2:10, 22; (8) Mark 7:27-28; Luke 16:21; (9) Exod. 11:7; Jer. 15:3; Matt. 7:6; (10) Luke 16:21; (11) As in, "A dog is man's best friend"; (12) 1 Sam. 17:43; 24:14; 2 Sam. 9:8; (13) Isa. 56:10-11; (14) "The quick brown fox… "; (15) Isa. 56:10; (16) Ps. 22:16; (Gen. 3:15 & John 11:47-48, 53); Phil 3:2; (17) Rev. 22:15; (18) Ps. 22:16; Jer. 15:3; (19) John 3:19; Rom. 5:16; 8:1; (20) Ps. 22:20; Phil. 3:2; (21) Isa. 56:11; (22) Isa. 56:10; (23) 1 Sam. 24:14.

Doggy Lodge (Kennels): (1) Live-in rehabilitation centre.

(1) 2 Sam. 9:4-5, 8.

Dog Poop: (1) Offense; (2) Taking on an offense (stepping in dog poop).

(1) Zeph. 1:17 (KJV); (2) Ps. 119:165 (KJV).

Dog Wash: (1) Rehabilitation ministry; (2) Ministry to the destitute or despised; (3) Secular rehabilitation.

(1) 2 Sam. 9:6-8; (2) 1 Sam. 17:43; 24:14; Luke 7:39; James 2:1-5; (3) Gen. 12:10.

Doll: (1) Woman's past childhood issues/memory; (2) Grooming for motherhood; (3) Childhood desire.

Also see *Mannequin* and *Toys.*

(1) 1 Cor. 13:11; Phil. 3:13; (2) Ruth 4:16; (3) Luke 2:49.

Dollar: See Money.

Dolphin: (1) Teacher; (2) Minor prophet;

Also see *Whale.*

(1) Job 12:7-8; 35:11; By virtue of the intelligence assigned to dolphins.

Domed Roof: (1) Religious stronghold (highly resistant mindset); (2) Church under law (mosque-type structure).

Also see *Archway* and *Circle.*

(1) Matt. 23:25, 27; (2) Matt. 23:23; Rom. 6:14-15; Gal. 3:23; 5:18.

Dominoes: (1) Spiritual momentum; (2) Others falling; (3) Sensitive balance; (4) Inter-connectedness; (5) Repercussions; (6) Shock wave.

Also see *Cards* and *Falling.*

(1-6) 1 Sam. 14:15-16, 20.

Donkey: (1) Humility; (2) Faithful burden-bearer; (3) Servant; (4) Judge (white donkey); (5) Hostile or stubborn person; (6) Determined individual or stubborn; (7) Unbeliever; (8) Needing guidance; (9) Without understanding.

(1) Zech. 9:9; Matt. 21:5; (2) Gen. 42:26; 49:14; Num. 22:30; Isa. 1:3; (3) Gen. 42:26; Exod. 23:5; (4) Judg. 5:10; (5) Gen. 16:12; (6) Prov. 26:3; Jer. 2:24; (7) Deut. 22:10 & 2 Cor. 6:14; Job 1:14; (8) Prov. 26:3; (9) Ps. 32:9.

Donut/s: (1) Sweet words without heart (false promises); (2) Spiritual meal.

Also see *Circle* and *Wheel.*

(1) Prov. 23:1-3, 7-8; Isa. 29:13; Matt. 15:8; (2) Ezek. 1:16.

Door: (1) Christ; (2) Opportunity; (3) Mouth; (4) Entrance; (5) Faith; (6) Heart; (7) The unstoppable work of God; (8) Imposition (door pushed in); (9) Going through transition; (10) Temptation (door ajar or at the door); (11) Destruction (broad door); (12) Gateway into the spirit realm (arched doorway); (13) Decision (several doors to choose from); (14) Violence (bullet holes in door); (15) Witnessing (going door to door); (16) Needing the anointing (squeaky door); (17) Rape (door kicked in).

Also see *Back Door, Front Door, Key, Next Door,* and *Sliding Door.*

(1) Gen. 6:16; John 10:7; (2) Col. 4:3; (3) Ps. 141:3; Col. 4:3; (4) Col. 4:3; (5) Acts 14:27; (6) Rev. 3:20; (7) Rev. 3:7-8; (8) Ps. 109:22; (9) Judg. 11:16; Ps. 23:4; (10) Gen. 4:7; (11) Matt. 7:13; (12) See *Circle;* (13) Josh. 24:15; (14) Ezek. 8:7-9; (15) Rev. 3:20; (16) Prov. 26:14 & Matt. 25:8-12; (17) Gen 19:9.

Doorbell: (1) Call to prayer and communion with Christ; (2) Loss of first love; (3) Calling; (4) Opportunity (hearing a bell); (5) Arrival (you ringing a bell); (6) Looking for opportunities (you ringing a bell); (7) Anticipation or expectation.

Also see *Calling* and *Knocking*.

(1) Rev. 3:20; (2) Matt. 7:21-23; Rev. 3:20; (3) Matt. 20:16 (KJV); 22:14; (4) Luke 11:9-13; Acts 14:27; 1 Cor. 16:9; 2 Cor. 2:12; (5) Acts 12:13; (6) 1 Cor. 16:9; Col. 4:3; (7) Matt. 24:33.

Doorpost (Threshold): (1) The cross; (2) Love slave.

(1) Exod. 12:6-7; (2) Exod. 21:6.

Door within a door: (1) A mouth within a mouth (someone speaking for another); (2) An opportunity within an opportunity; (3) Subculture; (4) Voice in a voice.

(1) Prov. 27:2; Isa. 28:11; John 5:43; 14:26; 18:34; Acts 8:34; (2) Neh. 7:3; Esther 2:21; Prov. 8:3, 34; (3) Job 38:17; Acts 12:13, 16 (door in a gate); (4) Matt. 10:20.

Dove: (1) Holy Spirit; (2) Innocent; (3) Poverty or poor; (4) See Jonah in Name and Place Dictionary.

Also see *Bird/s*.

(1) Matt. 3:10; (2) Matt. 10:16; (3) Lev. 12:8.

Down: (1) Fallen; (2) Rest; (3) Hell; (4) Spiritual decline; (5) Humbled; (6) Worship or homage (bow down); (7) Sleep (lay down); (8) Without hope or depressed (downcast or looking down); (9) Disapproval or unsuccessful.

Also see *Descend, Dropping, Laying Down, Up,* and *Upright*.

(1) Ps. 20:8; (2) Ps. 23:2; (3) Ps. 55:15; Prov. 5:5; (4) Isa. 59:14; Jer. 8:4; Luke 8:13; 2 Thess. 2:3; (5) Job 22:29; Isa. 2:11; 10:33b; Jer. 13:18; Luke 18:14; (6) Gen 24:26, 48; 43:28; Job 1:20; (7) Gen. 28:11; Ps. 3:5; 4:8; (8) Ps. 42:5, 11; 43:5; (9) As in "thumbs down."

Download: (1) Revelation.

(1) Matt. 16:17; James 1:17.

Down Payment: (1) Being Spirit-filled; (2) Guarantee of what was promised.

(1-2) 2 Cor. 1:22; 5:5.

Drag/ging: (1) Evangelism (net); (2) Subjection and capture; (3) Failure and defeat; (4) Idolatry; (5) Holding back.

(1) John 21:8; (2) Gen. 37:28; (3) 2 Kings 19:28; Isa. 37:29; Ezek. 29:4; 38:4; Amos 4:2; (4) Hab. 1:15-16; (5) As in, "Dragging your feet."

Dragon: (1) The devil; (2) China (foreign god); (3) Principalities (evil).

(1) Rev. 12:3-5, 7, 9, 13, 16-17; 13:2-4; 16:13; 20:2; (2) 1 Cor. 10:19-20; (3) Eph. 6:12; Rev. 12:7.

Drag Queen: (1) Façade, human-run church; (2) Church trying to be attractive to people (detestable Bride of Christ).

(1) Rev. 2:14-15; (2) Jer. 7:18; Rev. 3:17.

Drain: (1) Lifeless soakage pit; (2) Detoxing; (3) Loss (down the drain); (4) Feeling low or negative (looking down the drain).

Also see *Gutter/s, Overflow, Pipe,* and *Washbasin.*

(1) 2 Tim. 3:7; (2) Ps. 107:23; (3) Luke 15:8; Phil. 3:8; (4) Jon. 2:3-6.

Drawer: See Cupboard.

Dreadlocks: (1) Ungodliness (unclean); (2) Man or woman of the flesh; (3) Subcultural association; (4) Spiritually bound; (5) Unruly spirit (spiritually unkept).

(1) Dan. 4:33; (2) Gen. 25:25; (3) 1 Pet. 3:3; (4) Mark 5:2-5, 15; (5) Prov. 25:28.

Dream: (1) Message; (2) Word; (3) Direction; (4) Instruction; (5) Warning, (6) Prophecy.

(1) Gen. 37:8; Dan. 2:9; Matt. 2:13; (2) Ps. 105:17-19; (cf. Gen 37:5-10); Matt. 2:13, 19-20.

Interpreting a Dream (interpreting a dream in a dream): (1) Decoding the message.

(1) Gen. 41:25; Dan. 2:28.

Dreamer: (1) Prophet; (2) Your "old self" (fleshly person).

(1) Num. 12:6; Deut. 13:3; Jer. 23:28; (2) Acts 2:17.

Dregs: (1) The bottom of the cup of God's fury.

(1) Isa. 51:17, 22.

Dress: See Clothes.

Dressing: (1) Putting on Christ; (2) Preparation; (3) New anointing.

(1) Rom. 13:14; Gal. 3:27; (2) Matt. 22:11-12; Eph. 6:11; (3) Lev. 16:32, 21:10; 2 Kings 2:13.

Dressing Gown: (1) Relaxed; (2) Just cleansed (showered); (3) Old.

Also see *Pajamas.*

(1) Jer. 43:12b; (2) <u>Lev. 16</u>:4, <u>24</u>; (3) Cultural perception.

Dressing Room: (1) Heart; (2) Preparation for the King; (3) Preparation for self-glory.

(1) Rom. 13:14; Gal. 3:27; <u>1 Pet. 3:3-4</u>; (2) Matt. 3:3; (3) 1 Pet. 3:3-4; 1 Tim. 2:9.

Dribbling/Drooling: (1) Desire for something; (2) Uncontrolled emotion; (3) Anticipation; (4) Madness.

(1) 2 Sam. 23:15; (2) 1 Sam. 1:10-13; (3) Consider Pavlov's dog; (4) 1 Sam. 21:13.

Drinking: (1) Refreshing; (2) Drunkenness; (3) Partaking of the Spirit; (4) Uncovering the fleshly self (laying down the spiritual self); (5) Merriment; (6) Bitterness; (7) Revelry (excess); (8) Victory; (9) Revival; (10) Procrastination; (11) Satisfaction (often enjoying the fruit of one's labor); (12) Deception; (13) Adultery (drinking from another's cup); (14) Laying down one's life (living sacrifice); (15) A poured-out soul; (16) Prosperity; (17) Fellowship/alignment with another; (18) Disobedience; (19) Faith; (20) Arrogance; (21) Peace; (22) Desperation; (23) Pleasure; (24) The wrath of God; (25) Tears; (26) Brook; (27) Violence; (28) Partaking; (29) Wisdom; (30) Undeserved grace; (31) Receiving; (32) Heavy heart; (33) Perverted judgment; (34) Anesthetic; (35) Self-glory; (36) Non-satisfying; (37) Stupor/blindness/delusion; (38) Spiritual thirst; (39) Offerings; (40) Judgment; (41) Fouled water; (42) Defilement; (43) Hardened heart (lacking compassion); (44) Ease; (45) Redemption; (46) Celebration; (47) Provision; (48) Blood of New Testament; (49) Poison; (50) Old wine; (51) New wine; (52) Ease; (53) God's will; (54) Holy Spirit; (55) Spiritual Union; (56) Stumbling block; (57) Jesus Christ; (58) Fornication.

Also see *Brook, Cup,* and *Drinking Fountain.*

(1) Gen. 21:19; 25:34; Ruth 2:9; 2 Sam. 16:2; 1 Kings 19:6, 8; Matt. 10:42; (2) Gen. 9:21; 1 Kings 16:9; (3) John 4:14; (4) Gen. 9:21; 2 Sam. 12:3 & Ps. 51:10; (5) Gen. 43:34; Judg. 19:21-22; 1 Kings 18:41-42; Eccl. 8:15; 9:7; (6) Exod. 15:23-24; Num. 5:24; Isa. 24:9; Jer. 8:14; 9:15; 23:15; Hos. 4:18; Matt. 27:34, 48; (7) Exod. 32:6; 1 Sam. 30:16; Isa. 5:11; Eph. 5:18; (8) Num. 23:24; Ezek. 25:4; (9) Judg. 15:19; 1 Sam. 11:13; Isa. 43:20; (10) Judg. 19:4, 6; (11) Ruth 3:3; 1 Sam. 1:9; Eccl. 2:24; 3:13; 5:18; (12) 2 Sam. 11:13; Prov.

20:1; 23:7; Isa. 22:13 (self-deception); Hab. 2:15; (13) 2 Sam. 12:3; Prov. 5:15; Hos. 2:5; (14) 2 Sam. 23:15-17; Matt. 20:22-23; 26:42; Mark 10:38-39; (15) 1 Sam. 1:15; (16) 1 Kings 4:20-21; (17) 1 Kings 13:8; Job 1:4, 13; Mark 2:16; Luke 5:30; 13:26; 1 Cor. 10:21; 11:25-29; (18) 1 Kings 13:19-22; (19) 1 Kings 17:10; (20) 1 Kings 20:12; Dan. 5:1-3; (21) 2 Kings 6:22-23; Isa. 36:16; (22) 2 Kings 18:27; (23) Esther 1:8; Joel 3:3; (24) Job 21:20; Ps. 75:8; Isa. 51:17, 22; 63:6; Jer. 25:15; Rev. 14:8, 10; 18:3; (25) Ps. 80:5; 102:9; (26) 1 Kings 17:4, 6; Ps. 110:7; (27) Prov. 4:17; (28) Prov. 5:15; Song. 5:1; Jer. 2:18; 16:8; Ezek. 23:32-34; (29) Prov. 9:1-5; Matt. 11:18-19; (30) Prov. 25:21-22; Rom. 12:20; (31) Prov. 26:6; (32) Prov. 31:6; (33) Prov. 31:4-5; (34) Prov. 31:7; Mark 15:23; (35) Isa. 5:22; 37:25; Zech. 7:6; (36) Isa. 29:8; Amos 4:8; Hag. 1:6; (37) Isa. 29:9-10; 56:12; Jer. 51:57; Joel 1:5; (38) Isa. 32:6; John 7:37; (39) Jer. 7:18; 32:29; 44:17-19; (40) Jer. 25:17, 26-29; 46:10, 49:12; Ezek. 4:10-11; 23:32-34; 31:14; (41) Ezek. 34:18-19; (42) Dan. 1:8; (43) Amos 4:1; 6:6; (44) Matt. 24:49; (45) Matt. 26:27; (46) Matt. 26:29; Mark 14:25; Luke 22:18; (47) Matt. 6:25; Mark 9:41; (48) Mark 14:23-24; (49) Mark 16:18; (50) Luke 5:39; (51) John 2:10; (52) Luke 12:19, 45; 17:8, 27-28; (53) Luke 22:42; John 18:11; (54) John 4:14; 1 Cor. 12:13; (55) John 6:53-56; (56) Rom. 14:21; (57) 1 Cor. 10:4; (58) Rev. 18:3.

Drinking Fountain: (1) Flow of the Holy Spirit; (2) Church or ministry; (3) Everlasting life; (4) A move of God; (5) Fulfillment in God.

Also see *Drinking*.

(1-2) John 7:37-39; (3) John 4:14; Rev. 21:6; 22:1, 17; (4) John 4:39-42 (cf. context); (5) John 4:32-34 (cf. context).

Dripping Tap: (1) Contentious wife; (2) Contentious church that is quenching the Spirit.

(1) Prov. 19:13; 27:15; (2) 1 Thess. 5:19.

Driver: (1) If you are driving, you are steering your own destiny; (2) If you are in the passenger seat and someone unknown is driving, it means God is driving; (3) If the driver is corrupt, it means you are probably being manipulated/controlled; (4) If someone you know is driving a bus, it means they will head up a ministry; (5) Going in the wrong direction means wrong spirit.

(1-2) John 21:18; (3) 2 Tim. 3:5-6; (4) 2 Sam. 5:2; (5) Ps. 51:10 (KJV).

Drive Through: (1) Quick fix mentality.

(1) Matt. 14:15.

Driveway: (1) Entry; (2) Exit; (3) Awaiting ministry; (4) Parked ministry.

(1-2) Deut. 28:6; Ps. 121:8; (3-4) 1 Kings 3:7; Isa. 49:2b.

Drop/ping: (1) Heaven's provision; (2) Word of God (dew); (3) Teaching (rain); (4) Overflow; (5) Rain; (6) Enticement (lips); (7) Contentious wife/church; (8) Collapse; (9) A small and insignificant thing; (10) To fall away; (11) To let God's charge or promises go; (12) To let go of something.

Also see *Descend.*

(1) Judg. 5:4; Ps. 65:11; 68:8-9; Luke 22:44; (2) Ezek. 20:46; 21:2; Song. 5:2; (3) Deut. 32:2; (4) 1 Sam. 14:26; Song. 5:5; Joel 3:18; (5) 2 Sam. 21:10; Job 36:27-28; Ps. 65:11-12; 68:8-9; Prov. 3:20; (6) Prov. 5:3; (7) Prov. 19:13; 27:15; (8) Eccl. 10:18; (9) Isa. 40:15; (10) 1 Pet. 1:24-25; 2 Pet. 3:17; (11) Heb. 4:11; (12) Matt. 26:39; Acts 27:32.

Drought: (1) Tribulation and testing; (2) The grave; (3) Judgment; (4) Financial struggles; (5) Lacking the love of God; (6) Spiritual or natural famine; (7) Lack of the Spirit of God; (8) Lack of the Word of God.

Also see *Rain—No Rain.*

(1) Gen. 31:40; Deut. 8:15; Isa. 58:11; Jer. 2:6; 17:8; Hos. 13:5; (2) Job 24:19; (3) 1 Kings 17:1; Ps. 32:4; Jer. 50:38; Hag. 1:11; (4) 2 Cor. 8:9, 14; (5) Eph. 3:17-19 & Rev. 2:4; (6) Amos 8:11; (7) Ezek. 37:5-6, 9-10; (8) Amos 8:11.

Drowning: (1) Judgment; (2) Overcome by the words of one's enemies; (3) Beyond one's depth; (4) Catastrophe; (5) In need of salvation.

Also see *Underwater.*

(1) Gen. 6:17; Jon. 2:3, 5; (2) Ps. 42:7, 10; (3) Matt. 14:30-31; (4) Isa. 43:2; (5) Isa. 59:19b.

Drug Dealer: (1) Tempter; (2) The devil; (3) The world (drug dealer's wife); (4) Profiteer; (5) Manipulation and control; (6) Witchcraft; (7) Dependence; (8) Familiar spirits.

Also see *Drug Use.*

(1-2) Matt. 4:1; John 10:10; (3) Luke 4:5-6; Rev. 12:9; (5) Acts 13:8-10; (8) 2 Kings 21:6.

Drug Store: See Chemist Shop.

Drug Use: (1) Rebellion; (2) Defiance of authority; (3) Unmanageable; (4) Offense; (5) Speaks of the flesh; (6) Looking for a quick fix; (7) Looking for instant pleasure/

gratification; (8) Deceived; (9) Addiction; (10) Counterfeit fulfillment; (11) Searching for an anesthetic; (12) Actual drug use; (13) Manipulation; (14) Witchcraft; (15) Stronghold; (16) Sickness; (17) Dependence; (18) Medication.

Also see *Amphetamines, Needle, Pills,* and *Speed (Drug).*

(1-4) Consider that in <u>Rev. 9:21</u> the word *sorceries,* elsewhere translated "witchcraft," is the Greek word *pharmakeia,* from which we get the word *pharmacy,* and put this into <u>1 Sam. 15:23</u>; (5) Gal. 5:19-21; 2 Pet. 2:10; (6-7) 2 Tim. 3:1-4; (8) 2 Tim. 3:6-7; (10) Eph. 5:18.

Drum: (1) Spiritual warfare.

Also see *Beat, Drummer, Music,* and *Worship.*

(1) 2 Chron. 20:21-22; 2 Cor. 10:4.

Drummer: (1) God (as the One who is in charge of the timing); (2) Leader (pulse/heartbeat of the ministry).

Also see *Beat, Drum, Music,* and *Worship.*

(1) Gal. 4:4; Eph. 1:10; (2) John 13:25.

Drunk: (1) Spirit-filled; (2) Issue with alcohol; (3) Under the influence of religion; (4) Power trip; (5) Using the tongue against brothers in the Lord; (6) Disgraced; (7) Guaranteed woe, sorrow, contentions, complaints; (8) Intoxicated with the world.

(1) <u>Eph. 5:18</u>; Acts 2:4, 15; 1 Cor. 12:13; (2) Eph. 5:18; (3) Rev. 17:1-2; (4) As in, "drunk with power"; (5) Jer. 46:10; (6) Gen. 9:31; Lam. 4:21; (7) Prov. 23:29-35; (8) Rev. 17:2.

Dry: (1) Without the Spirit (dead); (2) Thirsting for God; (3) Barren place; (4) Wilderness; (5) Desert; (6) Valley.

(1) <u>Ezek. 37:2</u>, 9-10; (2) Ps. 42:1; (3) Job 15:34; (4) Isa. 50:2; Jer. 51:43; Ezek. 19:13; (5) Jer. 50:12; (6) Ezek. 37:1-2.

Duck (noun): (1) Unclean spirit; (2) Fleshly spirit being; (3) Migrating (in flight); (4) Unity (flying in formation); (5) Vulnerable (out of water); (6) Resisting the Spirit (water off a duck's back); (7) Easy target.

Also see *Birds* and *Mud.*

(1) Ps. 40:2; Isa. 57:20; duck's are muddy bottom-feeders with webbed feet; (2) <u>2 Kings 5:20</u>, 25-26; (3) Rev. 12:14; (4) Ps. 133:1; (5) As in, "sitting duck"; (6) Acts 7:51; (7) As in, "sitting duck."

Duck (verb): (1) Humble; (2) Hiding.

Also see *Bowing.*

(1) Isa. 2:11; (2) As in, "ducking for cover."

Dugong: (1) Worldly idol (sea cow).

Also see *Walrus.*

(1) Exod. 32:24; 1 Kings 12:28.

Dumb: (1) Silence because of confidence in God; (2) No reproof; (3) Ignorance; (4) Idolatry; (5) Influence of evil spirit (deaf and dumb); (6) The product of doubting God's Word; (7) Unbelief.

Also see *Deaf* and *Mute.*

(1) <u>Ps. 39:9</u> (NKJV); Isa. 53:7; (2) Ps. 38:13-14; (3) Isa. 56:10; (4) Hab. 2:18-19; 1 Cor. 12:2; (5) Matt. 9:32-33, 12:22; <u>Mark 9:</u>17-18, <u>25-26</u>; (6) Luke 18:21; (7) As in, "no confession of faith."

Dumb Waiter: (1) The Holy Spirit.

(1) John 16:13 (KJV).

Dune Buggy: (1) Powerful itinerant ministry.

(1) Luke 1:80.

Dung: (1) Works of the flesh that perish; (2) Offense; (3) Refuse, waste, garbage; (4) Fertilizer; (5) Dealing with, precedes the refreshing of the Holy Spirit.

Also see *Faeces, Rubbish,* and *Urination.*

(1) <u>Job 20:7</u>; Ps. 83:10; 113:7; Jer. 8:2; Ezek. 4:12; <u>Zeph. 1:17</u>; <u>Phil. 3:4-8</u>; (2) Matt. 16:23; Luke 14:23; Rom. 5:17; (3) 1 Kings 14:10; 2 Kings 9:37, 18:27; Lam. 4:5; Phil. 3:8; (4) Jer. 16:4; 25:33; Matt. 13:8; (5) Neh. 3:14-15.

Dusk: (1) End times; (2) Running out of time.

(1) Luke 24:29; (2) Matt. 20:6 & John 11:9.

Dust: (1) Human; (2) Humbled; (3) Numerous; (4) Under a cloud of controversy; (5) Under the feet; (6) Death; (7) Beginning and end of mortal humanity; (8) Dishonored; (9) Contempt or disapproval (throwing dust into air or dusting feet off).

Also see *Dust Storm* and *Earth.*

(1) <u>Gen. 2:7</u>; (2) Isa. 2:10-11; 47:1; (3) Gen. 13:16; 28:14; Num. 23:10; 2 Chron. 1:9; (4-5) <u>Nah. 1:3</u>; (6) Isa. 26:19; (7) Gen. 3:19; (8) Ps. 7:5; (9) 2 Sam. 16:13; Acts 22:23.

Dust Storm: (1) A declaration warning of pending judgment; (2) Earthly witness against a city or nation; (3) A call to come under the Blood; (4) If no repentance, then the strength of the city or nation will be struck down; (5) A sign preceding deliverance and revival.

Also see *Dust* and *Whirlwind.*

(1) Nah. 1:3 (cf. Exod. 8:16 & Matt. 10:14); (2) Exod. 8:16 & Matt. 10:14 (cf. Deut. 4:26; 19:15); (3-4) Exod. 12:7, 12-13 (cf. Gen. 49:3; Deut. 21:17; Ps. 78:51); (5) Exod. 12:31.

Dynamite: (1) Impact of the Holy Spirit.

(1) Acts 1:8; 8:19; 10:38; Rom. 15:13.

Eagle: (1) Spiritual self; (2) Prophet (seer); (3) God; (4) Strength; (5) Israel; (6) Swift; (7) Heavenly resting place (nest); (8) Lifted by the Spirit (not by effort); (9) Unsettled home/church (Time to move on); (10) Instrument of judgment; (11) Angel (white eagle); (12) Warring angel.

(1) Isa. 40:31; Matt. 24:28; (2) Exod. 19:4 & 1 Sam. 9:9; (3) Exod. 19:4; Deut. 32:11-12; the Book of John depicts Jesus as Divine (ie. the Eagle); (4) Ps. 103:5; Isa. 40:31; (5) Rev. 12:14; (6) Deut. 28:49; 2 Sam. 1:23; Job 9:26; Jer. 4:13; Lam. 4:19; Hab. 1:8; (7) Job 39:27; Prov. 23:5; Jer. 49:16; Obad. 1:4; (8) Prov. 30:19; (9) Deut. 32:11-12; (10) Prov. 30:17; Ezek. 17:3-20; (11) Luke 17:37 & John 20:12; (12) Dan. 10:6, 13.

Ear: (1) Heart; (2) Physical ear; (3) Turned to fables; (4) Hearing God's voice; (5) Eager to hear spiritually (cleaning ears).

Also see *Deaf, Hearing,* and *Itching.*

(1) Matt. 10:27; 11:15; 13:9, 15, 43; Luke 1:44; 9:44; Rev. 2:7, 11, 17, 29; 3:6, 13, 22; (2) Luke 22:50-51; Acts 7:51, 57; 11:22; 28:27; (3) 2 Tim. 4:4; (4) John 10:3; (5) Isa. 50:4; Matt. 11:15.

Early: (1) Quickly; (2) Eager; (3) Measure of your desire for God; (4) Time of revelation; (5) Beginning; (6) Straight away or soon; (7) Diligently.

(1) Hos. 5:15b; (2-3) Ps. 63:1; Prov. 8:17; 24:22; Mark 16:2; Luke 21:38; John 8:2; (4) Prov. 8:17; Luke 24:1-6 (5) Matt. 20:1; Mark 16:9; (6) Ps. 46:5; 78:34; 90:14; 101:8; (7) Ps. 63:1 (the word *early* [Hebrew: *shackar*] also means "diligently").

Earring/s: (1) Hearing; (2) Having ears (obedience) for false gods; (3) Love slave (ears for God); (4) Spiritual sensitivity (feathered earring); (5) Hearing heavenly glory (flower earring); (6) Hearing the voice of God (gold earring); (7) Hearing the words of redemption (silver earring); (8) Hearing a false gospel (brass/bronze earring).

Also see *Adorn, Awl,* and *Hearing.*

(1) Deut. 5:1; Mark 4:9; (2) Gen. 35:2-4; (3) Exod. 21:1-6; (4) Matt. 11:15; (5) Rev. 19:1; (6) Exod. 21:5-6 & Rev. 9:13; (7) Exod. 21:5-6 & Matt. 26:15; (8) Exod. 21:5-6 & 1 Kings 14:26-27.

Earth: (1) The non-faith realm; (2) Sight realm; (3) The natural non-spiritual realm; (4) Humanity; (5) God's footstool; (6) Land of our pilgrimage; (7) Physical domain.

Also see *Earthly, Four, Heaven, Sea,* and *Soil.*

(1) 1 Cor. 2:14; (2) Matt. 6:10; (3) 1 Cor. 15:46-47; (4) 2 Cor. 4:7; (5) Acts 7:49; (6) Heb. 11:13; (7) Matt. 6:10.

Earthly: (1) Human/flesh; (2) Worldly; (3) Without faith; (4) Secular; (5) Creation; (6) Worldly wisdom.

Also see *Earth, Orange,* and *Red.*

(1) Gen. 2:7; 1 Cor. 15:47; 2 Cor. 4:7; 5:1; (2) John 3:12, 31; Col. 3:2; (3) John 3:12; Phil. 3:19; Col. 3:2; (4) Phil. 3:19; (5) Matt. 13:35; Heb. 1:10; (6) James 3:15.

Earthmovers: (1) Leadership working in the flesh.

Also see *Digging.*

(1) 1 Cor. 15:47.

Earthquake: (1) Power of God; (2) Shaking; (3) Revival or eve of revival; (4) Voice of God; (5) Judgment; (6) Shock; (7) Opened heart/s; (8) Visitation by God.

(1) 1 Kings 19:11-12; (2-3) Acts 4:31, 16:26-34, 17:6; (4) Ps. 29:8; (5) Rev. 6:12, 8:5, 11:13, 19; (6) 1 Kings 19:11-12; (7) Matt. 27:54; Acts 16:26; (8) Isa. 29:6; Zech. 14:3-5; Matt. 28:2; Luke 21:11; Rev. 16:18.

East: (1) Place of God's glory; (2) Sun (Son) rising; (3) Expectancy; (4) Waiting on God; (5) Praise and worship; (6) Looking to God; (7) Receiving a gift/ message from someone noble from the east means it is God-given; (8) Receiving a gift from an unreliable source from the east may mean it is demonic (Eastern religion); (9) Consider aspects in your own environment relating to east.

Also see *West* and *Sun.*

(1-2) Ezek. 43:1-2; (3) The sun rises in the east; Mal. 4:1-2; (4) Jon. 4:5; (5) Num 2:3 (*Judah* means "praise").

Eating: (1) Reading or studying the Word (assimilating the Word); (2) Communing; (3) Agreement with (covenant); (4) Friendship; (5) Given to fleshly appetites; (6) The best the world has to offer without God; (7) Receiving; (8) Revelation; (9) Devouring; (10) Taking; (11) Consuming.

Also see *Biting, Cannibals, Eating (Satisfied),* and *Eating (Not Satisfied).*

(1) Isa. 55:1, 10-11; Jer. 15:16; Heb. 5:12-15; (2) Job 42:11; (3) Song. 4:16; (4) Ps. 41:9; (5) Prov. 23:2; (6) Eccl. 2:24; 3:13; 8:15; (8) Matt. 16:15-17; (9) 1 Pet. 5:8; (10-11) Gen. 41:20, 27-30.

Eating (Satisfied): All of these will be satisfied: (1) Tithers; (2) The meek; (3) The righteous; (4) The repentant.

(1) Deut. 14:28-29; (2) Ps. 22:26; (3) Prov. 13:25; (4) Joel 2:12, 26.

Eating (Not Satisfied): Causes of not being satisfied: (1) Walking contrary to God; (2) Wicked; (3) Not listening to God; (4) Sin; (5) Neglecting God's house.

(1) Lev. 26:26; (2) Prov. 13:25; Isa. 9:18-20; (3) Isa. 55:2-3; (4) Mic. 6:14; (5) Hag. 1:4, 6.

Echo: (1) Returning message; (2) Relayed message; (3) Bouncing words (hardened hearts); (4) Having your deeds/words return to you; (5) Not returning empty.

(1) Gen. 32:6; (2) Exod. 19:8; (3) Num. 13:26; (4) Ps. 7:16; (5) Isa. 55:11.

Ecstasy: (1) Speaking in tongues; (2) Bliss; (3) Revival; (4) Rapture; (5) Joy.

Also see *Drug Use.*

(1) 1 Sam. 10:4-6 (*prophesying* means literally "speaking in ecstasy"); (2) 2 Cor. 12:4; (3) Acts 2:4; (4) 1 Thess. 4:16-17; (5) John 16:24.

Edge: (1) Eve of something new; (2) On the forefront; (3) Upset or nervous; (4) Fringe; (5) Border.

Also see *Cliff.*

(1) Num. 33:37; (2) As in, "cutting edge" technology; (3) As in, "she was on edge all night"; (4) Exod. 26:4-5; (5) Num. 33:37.

Effervescence: (1) New spiritual life.

Also see *Soda.*

(1) John 4:14, 7:38-39.

Egg/s: (1) Promise/s; (2) New beginnings; (3) Gift; (4) Schemes/plans; (5) Eggs without yolks speaks of promises without heart (i.e. empty promises); (6) Potential; (7) Fertility.

(1-3) Luke 11:12-13 & 24:49; (4) Isa. 59:5.

Eggshells: (1) Sensitivity; (2) Fear of upset (walking on eggshells); (3) Proceed cautiously; (4) Vulnerable; (5) Empty promises.

Also see *Eggs*

(1-4) Job 39:14-15; (5) Prov. 23:7-8.

Egg Yolk/Yoke: (1) Promise; (2) The Holy Spirit; (3) Heart; (4) Life; (5) No egg yolk means no life or heart in a promise (empty promise).

(1-2) Luke 11:12-13 & 24:49; (3-5) Job 6:6; Jer. 17:11 (KJV).

Egypt: (1) The world; (2) The unspiritual, materialistic system; (3) The place of slavery to Pharaoh (satan); (4) That kingdom ruled by philosophy and the physical senses; (5) Anti-God; (6) Superpower.

(1) Exod. 3:8; John 15:19; (Acts 7:34 & Gal. 1:4); (2) Matt. 13:22; 16:26; 25:34; Mark 4:19; John 3:19; 8:23; Rom. 12:2; 2 Cor. 4:4; 2 Pet. 1:4; 1 John 2:16; (3) Gal. 4:3; (Exod. 6:5-6 & Eph. 2:2-3); John 12:31; 14:30; 16:11, 33; 17:15; 1 Cor. 2:12; 5:10; 1 John 4:4; (4) John 14:17, 19; Col. 2:8; (5) James 4:4; 1 John 2:15; (6) Ezek. 30:6.

Eiffel Tower: (1) The Cross; (2) Human achievement/ pride; (3) France.

(1) As the world's most recognizable landmark. Likewise many of Israel's memorials point to the Cross. Exod. 12:14 (Passover); Exod. 17:14 (victory over Amalek); Josh. 4:7 (crossing Jordan). (2) Gen. 11:4; (3) By association.

Eight: (1) New beginnings; (2) Superabundant and satiating; (3) Abounding in strength; (4) To make fat or cover with fat or oil; (5) Worship; (6) Resurrection or regeneration; (7) Circumcision of the heart (cutting off the sins of the flesh); (8) Eternity (eight sideways is an eternal loop).

(1) Matt. 28:1; Eight marks the start of a new week; (2-4) These meanings come from the root of the Hebrew word for eight, *Shah'meyn*; (5) Ezek. 40:26, 31; (Seven steps led to the outer court [rest], eight steps led into the inner court [worship]); (6) Matt. 28:1, 6 (first day of the week is the eighth day); 1 Pet. 3:20; 2 Pet. 2:5; (7) Gen. 17:12 & Rom. 2:29; Col. 2:11; (8) Mark 10:30 (two worlds now and future); Matt. 28:1 (eighth day); Rev. 21:6 (alpha and omega).

Eighteen: (1) 2 X 9 = 18; as such, 18 means: Judgment by the Word of God; or (2) Judgment by division (mutual destruction); or, (3) Fruitful association; Alternatively 18 may mean: (4) 10 + 8 = 18; As such 18 means: Complete new beginning; or (5) Complete putting off of the old self.

(1) Judg. 3:12, 14; 10:7-8; Luke 13:4-5; (2) Judg. 20:24-25, 42-44; (3) 2 Kings 22:3-10; (4-5) Luke 13:11-16 (v. 13, "made straight," i.e. upright in spirit cf. Ps. 51:10).

Electricity: (1) Power of God; (2) His Spirit witnessing with our spirits.

Also see *Lightning*.

(1) Luke 8:46; (2) Rom. 8:16.

Elephant: (1) God Almighty; (2) Prominent person (Christ); (3) Powerful ministry; (4) High profile ministry; (5) Large ministry; (6) Tough character; (7) Prophetic ministry; (8) Larger than life personality; (9) Insensitive (thick skinned); (10) Big issue; (11) A significant memory; (12) Great future (baby elephant); (13) Unwanted (white elephant); (14) Heavy-handed.

(1) Jer. 32:17; Rev. 11:17 (He is great and powerful as the largest land animal); (2) 1 Sam. 9:2b; (3) Acts 19:11; 1 John 4:4; (4) Luke 7:28; (5) John 6:10; (6) Exod. 11:3; Heb. 7:4; (7) Jer. 6:17; Ezek. 33:6; Amos 3:6-7; (elephants use their trunks as trumpets to sound alarm and have exceptional hearing and smell); (8) 1 Sam. 17:4; (11) Neh. 4:14.

Elephant Trunk: (1) Trumpet/voice; (2) Channel of the Spirit; (3) Arm of the Lord (strength).

(1) Rev. 4:1; (2) John 4:14; 7:38-39; (3) Isa. 51:9; 62:8.

Elevator: See Lift.

Eleven: (1) Disorder; (2) Disintegration; (3) Imperfection/incompleteness.

(1) Gen. 37:9; Eleven stars: Joseph's dream marked disorder in Jacob's household; (2) Matt. 26:56; Acts 1:16-17, 26; The 11 apostles speaks of disintegration of the 12; (3) Deut. 1:2 (11 days journey from Horeb to Kadesh Barnea)—one more day would have carried them into divine government; the 11 sons of Jacob—"one is not" (Gen 42:32) speaks of incompleteness.

Elite: (1) Apostle; (2) Choice or chosen; (2) Valiant warrior.

(1) 2 Cor. 12:12; (2) Matt. 20:16b; 22:14; (3) 1 Sam. 16:18.

Emaciated: (1) Something you are no longer feeding; (2) Losing its strength; (3) Anguish of soul; (4) Spiritually weak (lacking spiritual nourishment).

Also see *Skinny.*

(1) Job 19:20; (2) Ps. 102:5; (3) Lam. 4:7-8; (4) Lam. 4:9; Amos 8:11.

Embarrassment: (1) Shame/disgrace; (2) Nakedness (without God's glory); (3) People-conscious (fear of people); (4) Perceived failure.

(1) Gen. 9:22-23; 1 Sam. 20:34; 2 Sam. 19:5a; 2 Chron. 32:21; (2) Gen. 2:25; Exod. 32:25 (KJV); (3) Prov. 29:25; (4) Ps. 142:4

Embrace: (1) Taking to heart or opening one's heart; (2) Worship; (3) Love; (4) Showing affection; (5) False affection; (6) Taking teaching to heart; (7) Accept as your own.

(1) 1 Sam. 18:1; (2) Matt. 28:9; (3) 2 Kings 4:16; Song. 2:6; 8:3; Acts 20:10; (4) Gen. 33:4; Prov. 5:20; Acts 20:1; (5) Gen. 29:13 (cf. Gen. 24:29-31); (6) Prov. 4:8; Heb. 11:13; (7) Gen. 48:10.

Emerald: (1) Mercy; (2) Praise.

Also see *Green.*

(1) Rev. 4:3; (2) Exod. 28:18 (KJV) (Some associate this stone with Reuben, others with Judah).

Employee: (1) Servant of God; (2) Worker in the harvest; (3) Bad employee causing division may mean demonic force or rebellious person; (4) Helper; (5) Actual employee.

(1) Rom. 1:1; 6:18, 22; Phil. 1:1; 2 Tim. 2:24; (2) Col. 4:12; (3) Rom. 6:16; (5) Eph. 6:5-6; Col. 4:1; 1 Tim. 6:1; Tit. 2:9-10.

Empty: (1) Without the Spirit; (2) Without fruit.

(1) Matt. 12:44; Luke 1:53; (2) Mark 12:3; Luke 20:10-11.

Enemy: (1) Satan; (2) Evil spirits in the heavenly realms; (3) Child of the devil; (4) The world; (5) The flesh.

(1) Matt. 13:39; 1 Pet. 5:8; (2) Eph. 6:12; (3) Acts 13:10; (4) 1 John 2:15-16; (5) Gal. 5:17.

Engaged: (1) Busy; (2) Unavailable; (3) Awaiting union; (4) Focused.

(1-3) Luke 10:40-42; (4) Mark 10:46-52.

Engine: (1) Heart; (2) Victorious new beginning (V8 engine); (3) Working in the flesh (6 cylinder).

(1) Prov. 4:23; (2) 1 Cor. 15:54, 57; 1 John 5:4; (3) Exod. 20:9.

Entering a building via the rear entrance: (1) Not coming in via the system; (2) Secretly; (3) Keeping a low profile.

(1-3) John 7:10.

Entrapment: (1) Temptation; (2) Looking for legal ground to discredit; (3) Looking to catch in words.

(1) Matt. 4:3; (2) Matt. 19:3; (3) Matt. 22:15.

Envelope: (1) Communication; (2) Heart; (3) Person (vessel) carrying a message; (4) Consider color of envelope and stamp or title and address on envelope.

Also see *Colors, Letter, Mailbox, Name,* and *Postage Stamp.*

(1) 2 Cor. 3:1; 7:8; 10:9-10; (2) Prov. 3:3; Jer. 17:1; 2 Cor. 3:2-3; (3) 2 Sam. 18:20.

Eraser: (1) Starting again; (2) New beginning; (3) Cut off from God; (4) Redemption.

(1) Jon. 3:1; (2) John 21:15-17; (3) Deut. 9:14; (4) Isa. 43:25.

Escalator: See Lift (Elevator).

Escape Pod: (1) Deliverance; (2) Salvation; (3) Rescue.

(1-3) Gen. 7:1; Acts 9:25; 2 Cor. 11:33.

Esky: See Cooler/Cool Box.

Evening: (1) Departure/absence of Christ; (2) Represents the time when Christ is in Heaven; (3) Close of the day (4) Time of reckoning.

(1) Matt. 27:57; Mark 14:17; (2) Matt. 14:15, 23; Mark 1:32; 4:35; 6:47; 11:19; 13:35; 15:42-43; Luke 24:29; John 6:16; 20:19; (3) Matt. 20:8; Luke 24:29; (4) Matt. 20:8.

Evergreen: (1) Long life; (2) Feeding on the Word of God daily.
(1-2) Ps. 1:2-3.

Evidence: (1) Testimony (for or against); (2) Witness (for or against); (3) Substance of our faith.

(1-2) John 3:11; 1 Cor. 15:15; (3) Heb. 11:1.

Ewe: (1) Witness; (2) Wife; (3) Female believer; (4) Mother to young Christians.
(1) Gen. 21:28-30; (2) 2 Sam. 12:3; (3-4) Gen. 31:38; Ps. 78:71.

Exam: (1) Test; (2) Judgment; (3) A trial of life; (4) Temptation; (5) Searching the heart; (6) A look into the life and affairs of someone.
Also see *High School.*
(1) Matt. 4:1; (2) Rev. 20:12; (3) James 1:2-4; 1 Pet. 1:7; (4) Matt. 4:1ff; 26:41; Luke 4:13; (5) Ps. 26:2; 1 Cor. 11:28; 2 Cor. 13:5; (6) Acts 28:18; 1 Cor. 9:3.

Excavate: (1) Preparing foundations; (2) Opening your heart; (3) Searching your heart; (4) Uncovering the secrets of the heart; (5) Clearing your heart; (6) Enlarging your heart.
Also see *Digging, Dirt, Earthmovers, Shovel,* and *Spade.*
(1) Matt. 7:25; (2) Song. 5:2; Acts 16:14; (3) 1 Chron. 28:9; Ps. 139:23; Jer. 17:10; Rom. 8:27; (4) Ps. 44:21; (5-6) Gen. 26:18; (cf. 2 Cor. 4:7).

Exercise Bike: (1) Not spiritually fit; (2) Armchair expert (over-opinionated and under-achieving); (3) Busy, but going nowhere (laboring in vain).
(1) John 16:12; (2) Matt. 23:3-4; (3) Luke 10:40-42; 1 Cor. 15:58.

Exercise Equipment: (1) Personal well-being; (2) Working for personal well-being; (3) Physical fitness; (4) Spiritual fitness; (5) Self-concern; (6) Image or health concerns; (7) Spiritual strengthening.
(1) 3 John 1:2; (2) 1 Cor. 3:12; (3-4) 1 Tim. 4:8; (5) Eph. 5:29; (6) Phil. 3:4; (7) Luke 1:80a; Jude 1:20.

Experiment: (1) Test; (2) Testing time.
(1) Gen. 22:1; (2) Job 2:5-5; 1 Cor. 10:13.

Explosion: (1) Sudden destruction; (2) Warning of impending judgment; (3) Incident involving tempers flaring.
(1) Isa. 29:6; 1 Thess. 5:3; (2) Jer. 4:19-21; (3) Matt. 22:7.

Eye of the Storm: (1) Heart of the issue (what's in the center is the reason for the storm); (2) Protected; (3) Peace with God.
(1) Prov. 4:23; John 6:70; 13:21; (2) Isa. 43:2; Mark 4:39; (3) Ps. 46:10; Isa. 43:2.

Eyes: (1) Heart/spirit; (2) Eyes of the Lord; (3) Second sight (eyes of the spirit); (4) Seer; (5) Prophetic gift (eyes wide open); (6) Spiritual perception (heart receptivity); (7) May refer to the outward person (as different from the inner person of the heart); (8) Pride (looking down); (9) Waiting on God (looking up); (10) Closed to the things of God (shut eyes or no eyes); (11) Cherubim; (12) Spiritual sight/imagination (right eye); (13) Fleshly leader (damaged or blind right eye).

Also see *Tears* and *Winking*.

(1) (Prov. 20:27 & Matt. 6:22); Matt. 13:15; (2) Ps. 33:18; 34:15; 139:16; Prov. 5:21; 15:3; (3-5) Num. 24:4, 16; 1 Sam. 9:9; Isa. 1:1; (6) Eph. 1:18; (7) Ps. 36:1; 73:7; 131:1; Prov. 4:21; 21:2; 23:26, 33; Eccl. 2:10; 11:9; Isa. 44:18; Matt. 13:15; John 12:40; (8) Ps. 17:11; 131:1; Prov. 3:7; (9) Ps. 25:15; 121:1-2; 123:1-2; 141:8; 145:15; (10) Acts 28:27; (11) Ezek. 10:2; (12-13) Zech. 11:17.

Eyes (Seven or Many Eyes): (1) Spirit of prophecy (testimony of Jesus); (2) Perfect revelation; (3) Sign of prophetic anointing; (4) Spirit of God.

(1-3) Rev. 19:10; (4) Isa. 11:2; Rev. 5:6.

Eye Liner/Mascara : (1) Window dressing for appeal; (2) Vanity; (3) Beauty; (4) Applying mascara only to top eye lashes means to stop worrying about what the world thinks (people pleasing) and instead doing things to please God.

Also see *Above* and *Below*.

(1-4) 1 Cor. 7:33-34; 1 Pet. 3:3-4.

Fabric: (1) Life; (2) Life story; (3) The structure of a thing.

Also see *Cloth* and *Veil*, and see *Tucker* in Name and Place Dictionary.

(1) As in, "the fabric of life"; Isa. 49:18; Luke 7:25; 2 Cor. 5:4; (2) Rev. 3:5; Also as is depicted in some tapestries (i.e. Bayeux tapestry); Consider that fabric is made up of individual strands of material woven together; (3) Definition of fabric from which we get the word *fabrication*.

Face: (1) Heart; (2) Life; (3) Someone's identity.

(1) Prov. 15:13; 27:19; (2) Prov. 16:15; (3) Exod. 34:10; Acts 20:25.

Happy Face: (1) Cheerful heart.

(1) Prov. 15:13.

Hidden Face: (1) Afraid of God; (2) Fear of the Lord.

(1-2) Exod. 3:6.

Radiant Face: (1) God's Glory; (2) Wisdom.

(1) Exod. 34:30; 2 Cor. 3:7; (2) Eccl. 8:1.

Sad Face: (1) Sorrow; (2) Repentance (this can be a good thing).

(1) Eccl. 7:3; (2) 2 Cor. 7:10.

Factory: (1) Productive church; (2) Business (good or evil); (3) Manufactured (made up = lies); (4) human-made; (5) Work of a repetitive nature; (6) Church operating as a business (manufacturing for their own interest); (7) Church based on works.

(1) Acts 2:41-42, 47; (2) Ps. 127:1; 1 Tim. 3:3, 8; Jude 1:11; (3) Eph. 4:25; Col. 3:9; 1 Tim. 4:2; (4) Gen. 11:3-5; (5) Prov. 15:27a; 1 Tim. 6:5; (7) Rev. 3:15-17.

Fade: (1) Die; (2) Death; (3) Temporary; (4) Losing touch with eternal life; (5) Aged or old.

(1) Isa. 1:30; 24:40; 64:6; Jer. 8:13; James 1:11; 1 Pet. 5:4; (2) 1 Pet. 1:4; (3) Isa. 28:1; (4) Ezek. 47:12 (KJV); (5) Josh. 9:13.

Fail: (1) Cease or stop; (2) Sin.

(1) Ps. 12:1; 1 Cor. 13:8; (2) 1 Sam. 12:23; Ps. 31:10.

Fair: See Carnival.

Fake: (1) Not the genuine article; (2) Not real; (3) Façade; (4) Superficial.

(1-3) Mark 7:6; Luke 6:42; (4) Matt. 8:19-22.

Falling: (1) Taking eyes off God; (2) Losing God's protection/support; (3) Ungodly; (4) Opposite to standing/walking/uprightness.

Falling also indicates: (5) Out of control; (6) Sinning; (7) Death; (8) Worship (down); (9) War/argument/disagreement (falling out); (10) Attack (upon someone); (11) Embracing (upon someone); (12) Come under the influence of; (13) Talkative person who doesn't receive instruction; (14) Without counsel/support; (15) Person trusting in riches; (16) Pride/over confidence; (17) Having a bad tongue/ways; (18) Gloating over someone else's misfortune; (19) Troubled spirit; (20) Someone trying to trap another; (21) Hardened heart.

Also see *Diving, Dropping,* and *Lift (Elevator).*

(1-4) Ps. 20:8; 64:10; 91:7 (see all of psalm); 116:8-9; 118:13-14; Heb. 12:1-2; (5) Matt. 17:15; John 18:6; (6) Num. 11:4 (KJV); Acts 1:25; 1 Cor. 8:13

(AMP); (7) Gen. 14:10; Exod. 21:33-34; Acts 5:5, 10; (8) Gen. 17:3; John 11:32; (9) Gen. 45:24; Exod. 1:10; (10) Luke 10:30; (11) Gen. 33:4; (12) Lev. 19:29; (13) Prov. 10:8, 10; (14) Prov. 11:14; Eccl. 4:10; (15) Prov. 11:28; (16) Prov. 16:18; (17) Prov. 17:20; 28:18; (18) Prov. 24:17; (19) Prov. 25:26; (20) Prov. 26:27; 28:10; Eccl. 10:8; (21) Prov. 28:14.

Falling (Endless Falling): (1) The abyss; (2) The bottomless pit.

(1-2) Rev. 9:2; 11:7; 17:8; 20:1-3.

Falling Into Trouble: (1) Wicked messenger.

(1) Prov. 13:17.

Family: (1) Believers (those in the family of God); (2) The Church; (3) Those who speak the same language; (4) Spiritual fellowship; (5) Your own family.

(1) Eph. 3:15; (2) Ps. 107:41; (3) Gen. 10:5.

Famine: (1) Lack of the Word of God; (2) Poverty; (3) Actual famine.

(1) Amos 8:11; (2) Jer. 29:17.

Famous Person: (1) Jesus Christ; (2) Someone in your acquaintance who in some way relates as a parallel of a famous person; (3) The spirit of a famous person (if they are passed away and righteous); (4) Look up the meaning of the person's name (For example, if Mel Gibson was in your dream, Mel means "Chief," therefore, this may symbolize Christ); (5) That actual person; (6) The world's glory (as in Hollywood personality); (7) The job, role, character, or passion of the famous person.

Also see *Superhero.*

(1) Mark 1:28; Luke 4:14, 37; (2) Matt. 11:14; 17:12-13; (3) 1 Sam. 28:15; Matt. 17:3; 22:32; (6) Matt. 4:8; (7) Matt. 11:14.

Fan (verb): (1) Stirred by the Spirit; (2) Separate (winnow); (3) Judge; (4) Purge; (5) Increasing the heat; (6) Cooling.

(1) John 3:8; (2) Isa. 41:16; Jer. 4:11; (3) Jer. 15:7; 51:2; (4) Matt. 3:12; (5) Rev. 16:8-9; (6) Job 37:21b (KJV).

Fan (noun): (1) Spirit.

(1) John 3:8.

Fancy Dress: See Costume Hire.

Farm: (1) The harvest field; (2) Kingdom of Heaven; (3) God's Kingdom; (4) The World; (5) Israel; (6) The believer; (7) Evangelical ministry.

Also see entries under *Field* and *Harvest*.

(1) Matt. 9:36-37; 13:24-30; John 4:35; (2) Matt. 13:24-30; 20:1ff; (3) Matt. 21:28-32; John 10:9, 16; (4) Matt. 13:38-39; 21:33-43; Rev. 14:15; (5) Isa. 5:1ff; Luke 13:6-9; (6) 1 Cor. 3:9.

Farmer: (1) Spiritual leaders (good and bad); (2) God the Father; (3) Christ (Sower); (4) Preacher; (5) Evangelist; (6) Minister; (7) The believer; (8) Laborer; (9) Worker.

(1) Matt. 21:33-45; Mark 12:1ff; Luke 20:9ff; 2 Tim. 2:6; (2) John 15:1; 1 Cor. 3:9; (3) Matt. 13:37; (4-9) 1 Cor. 3:6.

Fast: See Fasting and Quick/ly.

Fast Food: See Junk Food.

Fasting: (1) Dying to self; (2) Cleansing of the vessel or garment; (3) Humbling oneself before God; (4) Cutting off the flesh; (5) Empowering; (6) Hungering for Christ; (7) Denying the flesh to sensitize the spirit; (8) Not swallowing what is being served up; (9) Separation from the world; (10) Literal fast;

(1) Matt. 6:16; Luke 2:37; Acts 13:2; (2) Matt. 9:14-17; (3) Ps. 35:13; (4) 1 Cor. 9:27; (5) Matt. 17:21; Luke 4:2, 14; (6) Mark 2:20; Luke 5:35; (7) Matt. 3:4 & Luke 1:80; (8) Prov. 23:1-3, 6-8; (9) Dan. 1:8.

Fat & Fatness: The meaning of fatness breaks into two main categories: (+) Well-favored; or, (-) One who has forsaken God and become desensitized to the things of the Spirit because of opulence and pride.

Fat & Fatness (+) Well-favored: (1) Well-favored; (2) The best; (3) Flourishing; (4) Generous; (5) Plentiful; (6) Influential (for good); (7) Anointing of the Holy Spirit.

(1) Gen. 41:4; (2) Gen. 4:4; 45:18; 1 Sam. 2:29; 2 Sam. 1:22; Luke 15:23, 30; (3) Num. 13:20; Ps. 92:14; (4) Prov. 11:25; (5) Isa. 30:23; (6) Ps. 92:14; Prov. 11:25; (7) Isa. 21:5; Acts 10:38 (anoint means "to smear with oil or fat").

Fat & Fatness (-) Proud/Desensitized: (1) Flesh; (2) Forsaken God; (3) Pride; (4) Desensitized; (5) Hired hands (in the ministry for money); (6) Living to fleshly appetites; (7) Influential (for bad); (8) Being spiritually lazy/resting in the flesh (fat backside); (9) This group are also being readied for judgment, as in, "fattened for the slaughter"; (10) Self-indulgent.

Also see *Cat.*

(1) <u>Deut. 32:15</u>; Jer. 50:11; (1 Sam. 2:15-16 & 4:18); (2) Deut. 31:20; 32:13-15; (3) Ps. 17:10; (4) Ps. 119:69-70 (fat heart = desensitized); Isa. 6:10; (5) John 10:13; (6) Ps. 78:29-31; (7) Ps. 78:31 (KJV); (8) Neh. 9:25-26; (9) <u>James 5:5</u>; (10) Judg. 3:17, 21-22; James 5:5.

Father: (1) God (Heavenly Father); (2) Spiritual authority/covering; (3) Jesus Christ; (4) Spiritual leader or mentor (father in the faith); (5) Natural father; (6) Spiritual ancestors; (7) The past; (8) The devil (unbeliever, sinner, or liar's father).

(1) <u>Matt. 6:9</u>; 2 Cor. 1:2-3; 6:8; (2) 1 Chron. 24:19 (KJV); 25:3, 6; (3) Isa. 9:6; (4) 1 Cor. 4:15; 1 Thess. 2:11; 1 Tim. 5:1; (5) Eph. 5:31; 6:2; (6) Heb. 1:1; (7) Job 21:8; (8) John 8:44; 1 John 3:8.

Father-in-Law: (1) Mentor; (2) Wise counsel; (3) Guide; (4) Mutual benefit; (5) Legalistic leader; (6) Actual father-in-law.

Also see *Brother-in-Law* and *Son-in-Law.*

(1-2) Exod. 18:18-24; (3-4) Num. 10:29, 31-32; (5) John 3:10.

Feathers: (1) Covering; (2) Protection; (3) Trust; (4) The Holy Spirit; (5) Glory; (6) Coward (white feather); (7) Evidence of angels.

Also see *Angel/s* and *Bird/s.*

(1-3) <u>Ps. 91:4</u>; (4) Isa. 40:31; (5) Ezek. 17:3, 7; (6) Rev.21:8; (7) Exod. 25:20; Isa. 6:2.

Feces: (1) Dirty (defiled); (2) Sin; (3) Self-righteousness; (4) Clean up required.

Also see *Dung, Sewage, Toilet,* and *Urination.*

(1-4) <u>Isa. 64:6;</u> Phil. 3:8.

Fear of Man: (1) People-pleasing; (2) Telling people what they want to hear.

(1) <u>Prov. 29:25</u>; (2) 2 Tim. 4:3.

Feeding: (1) Speaking or teaching; (2) Fueling; (3) Doing the will of God.

(1) <u>1 Cor.3:1-2</u>; (2) Prov. 26:20; (3) John 4:34.

Feeling: (1) Spiritual sensitivity. How a person feels in a dream or vision is a very strong indicator of meaning; (2) For example, a sense of peace while flying conveys we are comfortable in the Spirit. However, the same scene with a sense of impending danger is a warning about our spiritual state; (3) It should be noted that just as we have five physical senses, so we also have five spiritual senses: taste, touch, smell, sight, and hearing.

(1) Eph. 4:19; (3) Ps. 34:8; 1 Kings 18:44; 2 Kings 6:16-17.

Feet: (1) Messenger; (2) Bearer of good news; (3) Ministry; (4) Heart; (5) Walk; (6) Offense.

Also see *Broken* and *Shoes.*

(1) Rom. 10:15; (2 -3) Isa. 52:7; (4) Prov. 6:18; (5) Acts 14:8, 10; (6) Prov. 6:18; Matt. 18:8.

Feet (Dirty Feet): (1) Sinful nature; (2) Offense (wiping dust off).

(1) John 13:10; (2) Luke 10:11.

Feet Cut Off: (1) Unreliable witness (fool); (2) Unable to preach the Gospel.

(1) Prov. 26:6; (2) Rom. 10:15.

Feet On: (1) Defeat or oppression (someone's feet on you); (2) Victory (your feet on someone or something); (3) Being trampled on.

(1-2) Josh. 10:24; Matt. 5:13; Luke 10:19; (3) Matt. 5:13.

Feet (Stamping Feet): (1) Aggression; (2) Defiance; (3) Temper tantrum.

(1-3) Ezek. 25:6.

Feet (Webbed Feet): (1) Walking in the Spirit; (2) Seasoned in the things of the Spirit.

(1-2) Ezek. 47:5; Matt. 14:26; Gal. 5:16.

Female: See Woman.

Fence: (1) Barrier; (2) Boundary or demarcation; (3) Provides protection or rest; (4) Trust; (5) Garrison or army; (6) Fortified; (7) Blocked (fenced in); (8) Changing loyalties (jumping the fence); (9) Changing camps; (10) Control issue.

Also see *Hedge* and *Wall.*

(1-2) 2 Chron. 17:2; (3) Num. 32:17 (KJV); 2 Chron.14:6; Job 1:10; Isa. 5:2; (4) Deut. 28:52 (KJV); Jer. 5:17; (5) 2 Sam. 23:7; 2 Chron. 17:2; 32:5; (6) Deut. 9:1; Josh. 10:20; (7) Job 19:8; (8-9) 1 Sam. 29:4; (10) Num. 22:24, 26; 2 Kings 25:10; 2 Chron. 25:23; 2 Cor. 10:4-5.

Ferret/s: (1) Unclean spirit; (2) Someone who is mistakenly perceived as being inquisitive, playful, or innocent, but who is deadly and kills the Spirit (ferrets love blood, and the life [Spirit] is in the blood).

(1) Lev. 11:29-30 (KJV); (2) (Lev. 17:11 & Job 33:4).

Ferris Wheel: (1) Eternity; (2) God's will (bringing Heaven to earth); (3) Life (ups and downs); (4) Unsettling change (fast ferris wheel and struggling to hold on).

(1) Gen. 9:11 (note the "never again"); Ezek. 1:18-20 (spirit is eternal); (2) Matt. 6:10; (3) Eccl. 3:6; (4) Matt. 6:28.

Fertilizer: (1) Word of God; (2) Words of encouragement; (3) Edification; (4) Praying in the Spirit; (5) Prophecy; (6) Love; (7) Five-fold ministry gift; (8) Trials (testing of the Word); (9) Preparing for fruit.

(1) 1 Pet. 2:2; (2-3) Rom. 14:19; Eph. 4:29; (4) Jude 1:20; (5) 1 Cor. 14:4; (6) 1 Cor. 8:1; Eph. 4:16; (7) Eph. 4:11-12; (8-9) Luke 13:8-9.

Fever: (1) Curse for disobedience; (2) Plague; (3) Suffering or torment.

Fever (Healing from Fever): (4) Healed in the Atonement; (5) Jesus rebuked fever; (6) Healed through faith in the Word.

(1-2) Deut. 28:15, 22; (3) Luke 4:38-39; Acts 28:8; (4) Matt. 10:7-8 (the coming of the Kingdom); (5) Matt. 8:14-15; Mark 1:30-31; Luke 4:38-39; Acts 28:8; (6) John 4:47-52.

Field: (1) World; (2) The believer; (3) Harvest (someone in the field); (4) The Church or a church.

Also see *Farm* and *Harvest.*

(1) Matt. 13:38; (2) 1 Cor. 3:9; (3) Matt. 9:38; John 4:35; (4) Luke 15:25; 17:36.

Fifteen: (1) Acts of divine grace; (2) Resurrection.

(1) 3 (Spirit fullness) x 5 (Grace); (2) 2 Kings 20:6; Esther 9:18, 21; John 11:18 (KJV); Acts 27:28.

Fifty: (1) Jubilee; (2) Liberty/liberation; (3) Release/freedom; (4) Deliverance/rest; (5) Pentecost; (6) The perfect consummation of time; (7) Extreme grace.

(1-4) Lev. 25:10, 40, 54; Num. 8:25 (Levites freed from service at 50 years of age); (5) Lev. 23:16; Acts 2:1-4; (6) 7 x 7 +1 = 50; Acts 2:1; (7) 5 (grace) x 10 (complete).

Fig: (1) Represents political Israel; (2) False religion (fig leaves); (3) Prosperity; (4) Prayer (under the fig tree); (5) Judgment (falling fruit, no blossom); (6) Self-righteousness (fig leaves); (7) Dead religious system (bearing no fruit).

(1) Matt. 21:19; Hos. 9:10; (2) Gen. 3:7 (unable to cover sin); (3) 1 Kings 4:25; Song. 2:13; (4) John 1:48-50; (5) Isa. 34:4; Nah. 3:12; Joel 1:7; Hab. 3:17; Matt. 21:19 (pending judgment); (6) Gen. 3:7 (own covering); (7) Matt. 21:19-20.

Fight: (1) Fight of faith; (2) Spiritual battle/warfare; (3) Outward afflictions; (4) Worldly lusts; (5) Angelic battle; (6) Fight using the Word of God.

Also see *Battle*.

(1) 1 Cor. 9:26; 1 Tim. 6:12; (2) John 18:36; Eph. 6:12; (3) Heb. 10:32; (4) James 4:1-2; (5) Rev. 12:7; Dan. 10:13, 20; (6) Rev. 2:16.

Filing Cabinet: (1) Heart; (2) Memory.

(1) Prov. 3:1, 4:4b, 20-21; (2) 1 Chron. 28:9; Isa. 50:4.

Film: See Movies.

Filming: (1) Bringing focus to an issue or focusing on an issue; (2) Documenting (recording good/bad memories).

Also see *Camera* and *Movies*.

(1) 2 Sam. 12:1-7; Matt. 6:26; (2) Esther 1:19.

Filthiness: (1) Sinful; (2) Iniquity; (3) Self-righteousness; (4) The world's view of the Church; (5) Foul language; (6) Greed for gain.

(1) Job 15:16; Isa. 4:4; Ps. 14:3; 53:3; (2) Zech. 3:3-4; (3) Isa. 64:6; (4) 1 Cor. 4:13; (5) Col. 3:8; (6) 1 Tim. 3:3, 8; Tit. 1:7, 11; 1 Pet. 5:2.

Find: See *Lost* and *Found*.

Fine Print: (1) Details; (2) Instructions; (3) Contract; (4) Questionable content in a contract; (5) What is not said up front; (6) Revelation (mysteries revealed).

(1-3) Ezra 4:15, 21-23; Esther 1:22; (4-5) Matt. 22:15; Mark 12:13; Luke 20:20, 26; 1 Cor. 4:5; (6) Prov. 25:2; Rom. 16:25; Eph. 3:9.

Finger/s: (1) The Holy Spirit (The Finger of God); (2) Kingdom of God; (3) Ownership; (4) Recognition; (5) Speaks of looking for evidence through feelings; (6) Speaks of an amplification in intricacy and detail of what is being done (just as we use our fingers to amplify our touch); (7) Sensitivity; (8) God's government/rule (the finger of God).

(1-2) Matt.12:28 & Luke 11:20; (3) Lev. 4:6, 17, 25, 30, 34; Isa. 2:8; (4) Exod. 8:19; (5) John 20:25, 27; (6-7) Song. 5:5 (fragrance); Isa. 59:3 (sin); Dan. 5:5 (judgment); Ps. 144:1 (warfare); (8) Luke 11:20 (cf. Exod. 31:18).

Finger/s (Pointing Finger): (1) Accusation; (2) Blame-shifting; (3) Direction. (1-2) Prov. 6:13; Isa.58:9.

Finger/s (Tip of the Finger): (1) Amplifies the lesson; (2) Small amount; (3) Sensitivity.

(1-3) Luke 16:19-31 (note v. 24); Jesus teaches that even though the greatest faith (small amount of water [i.e. word]), be exercised after death, it is too late! (cf. Matt. 15:27-28). The small amount depicted in dipping the tip of the finger also amplifies the rich man's need/torment. Also note the great gulf between the believer and unbeliever. Therefore, Jesus amplifies here the need to outwork faith in love this side of eternity.

Fingernails: See Nails (Finger).

Fingerprints: (1) Identity (source of the evidence); (2) Ownership; (3) Recognition; (4) DNA; (5) Wrong motive; (6) Being exposed (fingerprints found); (7) Signs and wonders (marks of the Holy Spirit); (8) God's handiwork.

Also see *Finger* and *Hand.*

(1) Exod. 8:19; (2) Prov. 7:3; (3) Job 37:7; John 20:25; (5-6) Prov. 6:12-13; (7) Matt. 12:28 & Luke 11:20; (8) Exod. 31:18; Deut. 9:10; Luke 11:20.

Fire: (1) Presence of God; (2) Cleansing; (3) Judgment; (4) Strife; (5) Hell; (6) Affliction; (7) Tongue; (8) God's Word; (9) Gossip; (10) Passion; (11) Lust and adultery; (12) Anger or jealousy; (13) Glory of God; (14) Love.

Also see *Burn, Bush Fire, Flame, Forest Fire,* and *House Fire.*

(1) Deut. 4:24; (2) Num. 31:23; Luke 3:16-17; (3) Ps. 21:9; Ezek. 21:31; (4) Prov. 26:20-21; (5) Mark 9:43; (6) Deut. 4:20 & Ps. 66:12; (7) Acts 2:3; James 3:6; (8) Jer. 5:14; 23:29; (9) Prov. 26:20; James 3:5-6; (10) 1 Cor. 7:9; (11) Prov. 6:25-28; (12) Ps. 79:5; 89:46; (13) Exod. 24:17; (14) Song. 8:6-7.

Fire Engine: (1) Rescuer or deliverer; (2) Someone who tries to put out the fire of God; (3) Trouble (engine with siren); (4) Sign of fire out of control.

(1) Exod. 18:13-22; Zech. 3:2b; (2) Lev. 16:12; Ps. 39:3; Neh. 4:10, 12; 1 Tim. 5:12-13; James 1:6; (3) Prov. 12:13; 16:27; (4) James 3:5.

Fire Extinguisher: (1) Person who quenches the Spirit; (2) The Holy Spirit (right spirit/water); (3) Repentance.

Also see *Fire Engine, Fire Fighter,* and *Fire Warden.*

(1) Acts 2:3-4 & 1 Thess. 5:19 (the fire of the Spirit); (2) John 7:38-39 & Gal. 5:16, 20 (The fire of anger, strife, contention is put out by love); Num. 16:1-33 (fighting fire with fire); (3) Matt. 5:22, 25 (the fire of judgment).

Fire Fighter: (1) Revival police; (2) Opponents to the move of the Spirit; (3) Deliverer/Jesus/Angel of the Lord.

Also see *Fire Extinguisher, Fireman,* and *Fire Warden.*

(1-2) cf. Acts 2:3 & 4:17; (3) Gen. 19:13-15; Zech. 3:2; Luke 4:18-19.

Fireman: (1) Jesus; (2) Deliverer.

Also see *Fire Extinguisher* and *Fire Fighter.*

(1) Dan. 3:25; (2) Zech. 3:2b.

Fireplace: (1) Heart; (2) Anger or jealousy.

(1) Jer. 23:29; (2) Ps. 79:5; James 3:5-6.

Fire Warden: (1) Religious spirit/controlling spirit; (2) Quencher of the Spirit; (3) Peacemaker.

Also see *Fireman, Fire Extinguisher,* and *Fire Fighter.*

(1) Acts 5: 27-28a, 32; (2) 1 Thess. 5:19; (3) Matt. 5:9.

Firewood: (1) Deeds done in vain; (2) Covenant sacrifice or meal; (3) Gossip; (4) Contentious person; (5) Ready for judgment/hell; (6) People burning through God's Word; (7) Words that stir up anger (fuel for the fire).

(1) 1 Cor. 3:12-14; (2) Gen. 22:6-7; Lev. 1:7; (3) Prov. 26:20; (4) Prov. 26:21; (5) Isa. 30:33; (6) Jer. 5:14; (7) Acts 6:11-12.

Fireworks: (1) Celebration; (2) Conflict or trouble; (3) Spiritual warfare (clash of spirits).

(1) Lev. 23:32, 41; (2) Job 5:7; Acts 15:7; (3) Judg. 5:20; Rev. 12:7.

First Nations Peoples: (1) Innocence; (2) The old self (person of the flesh); (3) Ancestors; (4) Unsaved people.

Also see *Native/s, Old Man,* and note under *Black Man* or *Caucasian.*

(1) Gen. 2:25; (2) Rom. 6:6; 2 Cor. 5:17; Eph. 4:22; Col. 3:9; (3) Amos 2:4b (NIV); (4) 1 Cor. 15:46.

Fir Tree: (1) Choice individual; (2) Used in temple building; (3) Thanksgiving; (4) Joy; (5) Blessing; (6) Glory.

(1) 2 Kings 19:23 (KJV); Isa. 37:24 (KJV), As trees are a symbol of people, the upright fir tree is a picture of a choice individual; (2) 1 Kings 5:10; 2 Chron. 3:5; (3) 1 Kings 6:33-34 & Ps. 100:4; (4) Isa. 14:8; (5) Isa. 55:13; (6) Isa. 60:13.

Fish: (1) Believers; (2) Conversions (fish caught); (3) Humankind (potential believers); (4) Spiritual food (the Gospel); (5) Believers in the Spirit (flying fish); (6) Young believers (gold fish); (7) Financial blessing (money from fish's mouth); (8) Revival (fish jumping into boat); (9) Revelation of the truth (spiritual download); (10) A prospective spouse (a "catch").

(1-3) Eccl. 9:12; Hab. 1:14; Matt. 4:19; (4) John 6:11; 21:13; (5) Isa. 40:31; (6) 2 Cor. 3:18; (7) Matt. 17:27; (8) Luke 5:6-7; (9) John 21:10-19; (10) Prov. 18:22; Luke 5:7; 1 Cor. 7:28, 36, 38.

Fish and Chips: See French Fries.

Fish and Chip Shop: (1) Church feeding off battered fish (unhealthy believers); (2) Church/organization having a wrong spirit (dirty oil).

Also see *French Fries.*

(1) 1 Cor. 3:2-4; (2) 2 Cor. 11:4.

Fish Hooks: (1) Evangelistic ministries; (2) Taking the bait; (3) Messages from the Word of God; (4) Leading to Christ; (5) Dragged into or out of something against person's will.

Also see *Net.*

(1) Acts 8:5-7; (2) Gen. 3:6; (3) Matt. 17:27 & 1 Cor. 9:14; (4) Acts 8:12; (5) Ezek. 38:4; Isa. 37:29.

Fishing: (1) Evangelism; (2) Soul-winning; (3) Witnessing; (4) Investigating; (5) Looking for a partner; (6) Putting the Word out there (throwing a line); (7) Creative evangelism (fly tying).

(1-2) Matt. 4:19; (3) Acts 1:8, 22; 2:32; 3:15; (4) Luke 20:20; As in, "fishing around"; (5) Prov. 18:22; (6) Matt. 4:19; (7) 1 Cor. 9:22.

Fishing Line: (1) The means to catch fish; (2) The Gospel.

(1-2) Matt. 4:19; Rom. 1:16.

Fishing Pole: See Fishing Rod.

Fishing Rod: (1) Heart; (2) Tool of evangelism (person or thing used in evangelism); (3) Caught up in the world (black fishing rod).

(1) Jer. 9:8; Matt. 12:34b; (2) Matt. 4:19; John 21:6; (3) 1 John 2:16.

Fish Pond: (1) The world (sea of humanity); (2) Your fishing hole (evangelistic arena: workplace, school, town, etc.); (3) Church.

(1) Matt. 4:18-19; (2) Acts 8:5, 26, 29, 39-40; (4) As in, the place where fish are kept.

Fish Tank: (1) Church.

Also see *Fish Pond.*

(1) As the place where fish are kept.

Fist: (1) Threat of retribution; (2) Pending judgment; (3) Violence; (4) Grabbing; (5) Hitting/wickedness; (6) Aggression/contention.

Also see *Hand* and *Knuckles.*

(1-2) Isa. 10:32; (3) Exod. 21:18; (4) Prov. 30:4; (5-6) Isa. 58:4.

Five: (1) Grace; (2) Abundance; (3) Favor; (4) Redemption; (5) Multi-tasking (five-fold ministry).

(1) Gen. 45:11; (2) Gen. 1:20-23; (3) Gen. 43:34; Lev. 26:8; (4) Num. 18:16; (5) Eph. 4:11.

Fizzy Drink: See Soda.

Flag: (1) Surrender (white flag); (2) Nationality; (3) Spiritual warfare; (4) Praise; (5) Kingdom of God; (6) Love; (7) Covering/protection.

Also see *Banner.*

(1) Rom. 6:16 (KJV); (2-3) Ps. 20:5; Song. 6:4, 10; (4) Ps. 150:6; (5) Ps. 20:5, 60:4; (6-7) Song. 2:4.

Flame/s: (1) The Holy Spirit; (2) God; (3) The human spirit; (4) Judgment; (5) Light; (6) Torment; (7) Apostolic ministry; (8) Baptism in the Spirit; (9) Anger; (10) Jealousy.

Also see *Fire* and *Flamethrower.*

(1) Luke 3:16; Acts 2:3; 2 Cor. 4:6-7 & Judg. 7:20; (2) Isa. 10:17; (3) Prov. 20:27; Ps. 18:28; (4) Isa. 29:6; (5) Ps. 18:28; (6) Luke 16:24; (7) Acts 20:24 (fiery passion); Rom. 1:15; (8) Acts 2:3-4; (9) Ps. 21:9; (10) Ps. 79:5.

Flame Thrower: (1) Outburst of anger; (2) Imparting the fire of God.
Also see *Fire* and *Flame/s.*
(1) Ps. 78:21; 147:18a; Isa. 30:27, 30; (2) Acts 2:2-3.

Flashlight: See Torch.

Flat Tire/Tyre: (1) Spiritually flat (unable to go forward).
Also see *Tire* and *Wheel.*
(1) Job 27:3; 33:4; John 3:8.

Flea: (1) Parasite; (2) Itch; (3) Irritant; (4) Insignificant; (5) Hunted; (6) Secret, parasitic message that passes from person to person, stealing life.
Also see *Parasite.*
(1-3) See *Lice;* (4) 1 Sam. 24:14; (5) 1 Sam. 26:20; (6) John 7:12-13.

Flee: (1) Hide; (2) Fear; (3) Run away (move quickly); (4) Forsake; (5) Often associated with judgment; (6) Hired hands flee under threat.
(1) Matt. 2:13; 3:7; 24:16; (2) Matt. 8:33; (3) Matt. 10:23; 24:16; Mark 14:52; 16:8; (4) Matt. 26:56; (5) Luke 3:7; 21:21; (6) John 10:5.

Fleece: (1) Covering; (2) Stolen/stealing; (3) Looking for guidance (cut out rug entry); (4) Façade.
Also see *Cover* and *Rug.*
(1) Judg. 4:18; (2) John 12:6; (3) Judg. 6:37-40; (4) Matt. 7:15.

Flies: Beelzebub means "lord of the flies" and is a reference to the devil. Therefore flies represent: (1) Evil spirits; (2) satan; (3) Doctrine of demons (fly in drink).
Also see *Fly Spray, Frogs,* and *Odor (Bad).*
(1-2) Exod. 8:21-31; Matt. 12:24; (2) Matt. 12:24 & 1 Cor. 10:21a.

Flood: (1) Verbal onslaught of the enemy; (2) Overflow of sin; (3) Harvest time; (4) Divine assistance; (5) Test of foundations; (6) Sudden; (7) Floods destroy the unrighteous; (8) Judgment.
Also see *Water—Dirty Water.*
(1) Isa. 59:19b; Rev. 12:15; (2-3) Josh. 3:15; (4) Isa. 59:19b; (5) Matt. 7:25-27; (6) Matt. 24:38-39; (7-8) Gen. 6:13, 17; 2 Pet. 2:5.

Floor: (1) Foundation; (2) Place of sorting/purging (threshing floor); (3) Storage area; (4) Ground; (5) Humbling.

(2) Ruth 3:3, 6; Isa. 21:10; Matt. 3:12; Luke 3:17; (3) Deut. 15:14; Hos. 9:2, 13:3; Joel 2:24; Mic. 4:12; (4) Judg. 6:37; (5) Ruth 3:3.

Floorboards: (1) Foundation of the fleshly person (not of God).

(1) 1 Cor. 3:12.

Flour: (1) The Cross (crushed Christ); (2) Humility; (3) The laying down of individual fame for the Body of Christ (one grain dying for the benefit of making a loaf); (4) Contrite heart (crushed seed); (5) Prosperity.

Also see *Bake, Barley, Bread, Mill/stone, Seed, Self-Raising Flour, Wheat,* and *Yeast.*

(1) 2 Kings 4:40-41 (cf. Isa. 53:5 & John 12:24); (2) Exod. 11:5 (the lowest position); Lev. 5:11 (poor person's offering); cf. Num. 11:8 & John 6:32-33 & Phil. 2:7-8; (3) John 12:24; 1 Cor. 10:16-17; (4) Ps. 34:18; 51:17; (5) Ezek. 16:19; Rev. 18:13.

Flowers: (1) The righteous/upright; (2) Prosperity; (3) Brevity of life; (4) Offering praise (fragrance) to Christ; (5) Clothes; (6) Life; (7) Passing glory of people; (8) Glory.

(1) Prov. 14:11; (2) Ps. 12:12; 103:15; Isa. 27:6; (3) James 1:10-11; (4) 1 Kings 6:29, 32, 35; (5) Matt. 6:28, 30; (6) Isa. 35:1; (7) 1 Pet. 1:24; (8) Matt. 6:28-29.

Fluorescence: See Highlighter.

Fly: See Flies.

Flying: (1) Rising up out of the flesh into the Spirit (breaking physical laws); (2) In the Spirit; (3) Worship; (4) Moving in the gifts.

(1) Ps. 55:6; Prov. 23:5b; Isa. 40:31; (2) Matt. 3:16b; 4:1; Luke 23:46b; Acts 8:39; (3) Ezra 8:6; Isa. 6:2; (4) 1 Cor. 12:7 (flying as a manifestation of the Spirit).

Flying a Kite: (1) Beginning to grow in the things of the Spirit.

(1) 2 Kings 6:17a.

Flying Saucer/s: (1) Demonic deception.

(1) Matt. 24:24.

Fly Screen: (1) Covering; (2) Protection from the demonic.

Also see *Flies.*

(1-2) Eccl. 10:1.

Fly Spray: (1) The anointing/The Holy Spirit (demonic powers fleeing in His Presence).

Also see *Flies.*

(1) Matt. 12:28; Luke 11:20 (See *Fly*).

Foam: (1) Easily blown away; (2) Without substance; (3) Demonic oppression (mouth).

(1) Hos. 10:7; (2) Jude 1:13; (3) Matt. 9:18; Mark 9:20; Luke 9:39.

Fog: (1) Sin; (2) Life snippet; (3) In darkness; (4) Hell; (5) Hidden; (6) Secret.

(1) Isa. 44:22; (2) James 4:14; (3) Acts 13:11; (4) 2 Pet. 2:17; (5-6) Ps. 18:11.

Folding: (1) Putting away; (2) Preparation for storage or travel; (3) Protecting or hiding; (4) Humbling; (5) Sorting; (6) Corruption (wrinkle and creased/ crooked ways); (7) Giving up or quitting.

Also see *Spot* and *Wrinkles.*

(1) 1 Cor. 13:11 (childish things); Eph. 4:31 (evil speaking); Heb. 9:26 (sin); (2) Exod. 12:11 (KJV); (3) Josh. 7:11b-12a, 21; Acts 5:1-2; (4) Rom. 14:11; Phil 2:10-11; 2 Chron. 7:14; (5) Matt. 25:32-33; (6) Eph. 5:27; James 1:17; (7) Eph. 6:11, 14 (standing is the opposite of folding).

Food: (1) Word of God; (2) Jesus; (3) Will of God; (4) What you're feeding on.

Also see *Meal, Meat,* and *Refrigerator.*

(1) Heb. 5:13-14; Matt. 4:4; (2) John 6:54; (3) John 4: 34; (4) John 4:34.

Food Poisoning: (1) Tainted Gospel or ill-prepared preaching; (2) False promises; (3) Food of the world (newspapers, lies, gossip, false information, deceit); (4) Ungodly words that poison your spirit; (5) Curse.

(1) 2 Cor. 11:4; Gal. 1:6; 2 John 1:10; (2) Prov. 23:3, 6-8; (3) 1 John 2:15-17 (cf. John 4:34); (4) Ps. 58:3-4; 140:3; Rom. 3:13; (5) 2 Kings 40:4.

Fool: (1) Unbeliever; (2) Transgressor; (3) Despiser of wisdom and instruction.

(1) Ps. 14:1; 53:1; (2) Ps. 107:17; (3) Prov. 1:7b.

Foot: See Feet.

Football: (1) May represent the object of everyone's attention.

Also see *Ball, Goal,* and *Football Game.*

(1) 1 Sam. 9:20b.

Football Game: (1) Counterfeit worship/warfare; (2) False focus; (3) Idolatry; (4) May be representative of business (which for the most part is equally competitive and all about winning); (5) Life; (6) Spiritual warfare; (7) Ministry.

Also see *Goal, Sport,* and *Winning.*

(1-2) 1 Chron. 16:31-33; Ps. 74:4; 96:11-12; 98:7-9; (3) Exod. 20:3-4; (5) 2 Tim. 4:7; (6-7) See *Ball.*

Footpath: (1) Course of life (good or evil); (2) Hardened heart; (3) Busy heart; (4) Can be what lies ahead or in the past (behind you); (5) Child's path or journey; (6) Passage to hear the Gospel.

Also see *Pavement.*

(1) Ps. 17:5; 44:18; 119:101, 105; Prov. 1:16; 4:14, 26; (2-3) Matt. 13:4, 19; Luke 10:31-32; (4) Ps. 199:105; Phil. 3:12-13; (5) Gen. 18:19; (6) Rom. 10:15.

Footprints: (1) Angelic encounter; (2) Destiny; (3) Claiming the promise of God; (4) Evidence (proof of someone being there); (5) Evidence of strongholds (large footprints).

(1) Gen. 32:1-2; 2 Sam. 5:24; (2) Ps. 17:5; 18:33; (3) Josh. 1:3; (4) 1 Sam. 26:12, 16b; Job. 13:27 (KJV); (5) Num. 13:33.

Footsteps: (1) Following; (2) Someone's replacement (heir apparent); (3) Guidance; (4) Expectancy (getting louder); (5) Leaving (getting fainter).

Also see *Stepping* and *Walking.*

(1) Song. 1:8; John 21:19, 22; Rom. 4:12; Heb. 12:1-2; (2) 1 Kings 3:14; 8:25; As in, "walking in the footsteps of his father"; (3) Ps. 25:9; (the word *guide* here means "to tread"); (4) 1 Kings 14:6; 2 Kings 6:32; 2 Sam. 5:24; Isa. 52:7; (5) Isa. 40:31b.

Footsteps Inside Footsteps: (1) Same spirit; (2) Following someone's faith/example.

(1) 2 Cor. 12:18; (2) Rom. 4:12; 1 Pet. 2:21.

Forehead: (1) The mind/thinking; (2) Mental strongholds.

(1-2) 1 Sam. 17:49 (our biggest giants are likewise defeated with a stone (word) to the mind!); <u>2 Cor. 10:4-5</u>.

Foreign: (1) Non-believer; (2) Not operating in faith; (3) Christ (as not known by Him); (4) Made overseas; (5) Not familiar; (6) Not knowing a situation.

Also see *First Nations Peoples, Foreigner, Stranger, Unfamiliar,* and *Woman (Foreign Woman)*.

(1) Exod. 12:45; Obad. 1:11; Eph. 2:19; (2) Rom. 4:11-12; (3) <u>Luke 13:</u>25, <u>27</u>; (4) 1 Kings 10:6-7; (5) 1 Sam. 17:39; Acts 17:23; (6) <u>Heb. 11:9</u>-10.

Foreigner: (1) Possible warning of potential ungodly threat; (2) If you are the foreigner, it may mean you are set apart from the world; (3) A father-figure who is a foreigner may refer to the fact that your relationship with God as Father is foreign to you; (4) Liar; (5) False hand of friendship; (6) Religious worker who professes to know Christ, but in reality does not; (7) Person not understanding the voice of the Spirit.

Also see *Aliens, First Nations Peoples, Foreign, Indigenous, Woman (Foreign Woman),* and *Stranger*.

(1) Eph. 2:12; 4:18; Col. 1:21; Heb. 11:34; (2) Deut. 14:2; 26:18; Heb. 11:9; 1 Pet. 2:9; (3) (4) Ps. 144:11; (5) Ps. 144:11; (6) Matt. 7:22-23; (7) 1 Cor. 14:11.

Foreign Woman: See Woman (Foreign Woman).

Foreskin: See Circumcision.

Forest: (1) Lost/darkness; (2) Not out of the woods; (3) Harvest crop; (4) Church; (5) Multitude of people; (6) Army of mighty men; (7) Hiding place for predators; (8) Place of idolatry and works.

Also see *Beast, Cedar, Fir Tree, Forest Fire, Jungle, Park, Pine Tree, Rainforest,* and *Woods*.

(1) <u>Ps. 104:20</u>; (2) 1 Sam. 23:15; <u>2 Sam. 18:6-9</u>; (3) Isa. 32:15-20; (4) 1 Chron. 16:33; Ps. 96:12; Song. 2:3; Isa. 44:23; (5-6) <u>Isa. 7:2</u>, <u>10:18-19</u>, 34, 29:17-19; Jer. 46:23-24; Ezek. 20:47; Zech. 11:2; (7) 2 Kings 2:24; Ps. 50:10, 80:13, 104:20; Isa. 56:9; Jer. 5:6, 12:8; Amos 3:4; Mic. 5:8; (8) Isa. 44:13-15; Jer. 7:18, 10:3-5.

Forest Fire: (1) Judgment; (2) Gossip or rumor out of control.

Also see *Burn, Fire, Forest,* and *Wild Fire*.

(1) <u>Ezek. 20:47-48</u>; (2) James 3:6.

Fork: (1) Lying (forked-tongue); (2) Divided (paths/loyalties); (3) Choice (decision-making).

(1) Gen. 3:4 (serpent split-tongued); (2) Gen. 13:9-11; Mark 11:4 (KJV); (3) Mark 11:4 (KJV), (fork in the road).

Forklift: (1) Organizing (putting things in order); (2) Lying spirit (falsely raising hopes/left on the shelf); (3) Burden lifter.

(1) Neh. 12:44a; (2) 1 Kings 22:22; Mic. 2:11 (as in lifting with a forked-tongue); (3) Matt. 11:28.

Formal: (1) Religious; (2) Official/orderly (legitimate).

(1) Isa. 10:1 (a prescribed form); (2) 1 Cor. 14:40.

Fornication: (1) Actual fornication; (2) Defiled by other lovers; (3) Idolatry; (4) Communing with or friend of the world.

Also see *Adultery* and *Sex.*

(2) Isa. 23:17; (3) 2 Chron. 21:11; (4) 1 Cor. 6:16; James 4:4.

Forty: (1) A period of trial/testing/probation/proving which closes in victory or discipline; (2) 5 x 8 = 40, as such it means a period of grace [5] followed by revival or renewal [8]; (3) 4 x 10 = 40, as such it means extended or complete [10] dominion [4]; (4) Forty days may mean 40 years (and vice versa).

(1) Deut. 8:2; Num. 13:26 & 14:34; Luke 4:1-14; (2) 1 Sam. 17:16, 52; 1 Kings 19:4-7, 15-16; (3) 2 Sam. 5:4; (4) Num. 14:34; Ezek. 4:6; (cf. Matt. 4:1-2. Jesus passed the wilderness test that Israel failed).

Forty-Five: (1) Undergoing testing and trials with the grace of God followed by revival.

(1) See *Forty* and *Five.*

Forty-One: (1) New beginning after testing/trial; (2) Love after trial.

Also see *Forty* and *One.*

(1) Luke 4:14-15; (2) Song. 8:5.

Fossil: (1) Locked in the past.

(1) Gen. 19:26.

Found: See Lost and Found.

Foundation: (1) Christ; (2) Word of God; (3) Heart; (4) History; (5) Beginning; (6) Genesis; (7) Rock; (8) Love.

(1) 1 Cor. 3:11; (2) Matt. 5:18; 7:24-25; (3) Isa. 28:16; Matt. 13:23; Acts 13:22; Eph. 3:17; (4-5) Job 4:19; (7) Matt. 7:24-25; (8) Eph. 3:17.

Fountain: (1) Deep source; (2) Fountain of Life (Christ); (3) The Holy Spirit; (4) The human spirit/heart; (5) Abundant water supply; (6) Womb; (7) Cleansing; (8) Fear of the Lord; (9) Voice of the righteous; (10) Wisdom.

Also see *Waterfall.*

(1) Gen. 7:11; Lev. 20:18; Eccl. 12:6; (2) Ps. 36:7-9; Prov. 13:14; Jer. 2:13; Rev. 21:6; (3) John 7:38-39; (4) Matt. 12:34b & James 3:8-11; (5) Gen. 16:7; Num. 33:9; Ps. 114:8; Jer. 9:1; 17:13; (6) Lev. 20:18; Prov. 5:18; Song. 4:12; (7) Lev. 11:36; Zech. 13:1; (8) Prov. 14:27; (9) Prov. 10:11; (10) Prov. 18:4.

Four: (1) Rule or dominion; (2) Earth or the physical; (3) Creation or creative works; (4) Material or earthly completeness; (5) Earthly dominion; (6) Earthly effort or flesh; (7) World (especially city); (8) Division; (9) Not enough; (10) Not known; (11) Not bearable; (12) May say someone is not changing (four corners and four sides to square).

Also see *Earth* and *Earthly.*

(1) Gen 1:16; Prov. 30:31; (2) The fourth book of the Bible is Numbers; in Hebrew it is called *B'Midbar*, which means "the wilderness." This talks of the earth, which is a wilderness compared to Heaven; Prov. 30:24; Mark 13:27; (3-4) Fourth day saw material creation finished; Job 1:19 (Job's material completeness was taken that God may lead him into spiritual completeness); John 4:35; (5) John 11:17, 39, 19:23, Acts 10:11, 30; (6) Gen. 47:24; Acts 27:29; (7) Gen. 15:13; Acts 7:6 (Egypt is a picture of the world; [4x100; 100 = whole; 400 = complete earthly dominion or earthly dominion completed, beginning of spiritual dominion]); (8) Gen. 1:14-18; 2:10 (parted); (9) Prov. 30:15; (10) Prov. 30:18; (11) Prov. 30:22.

Fourteen: (1) Double measure of spiritual perfection; (2) Passover; (3) Deliverance and liberty.

(1) 2 x 7; (2) Exod. 12:6; Num. 9:5; (3) Gen. 31:41; Exod. 12:6, 31-33; Acts 27:27-44.

Four-Wheel Drive: (1) Powerful and independent ministry; (2) A ministry that does not have to stay on the road (traditional paths); (3) Full Gospel ministry; (4) Sign of opulence/wealth/prosperity (the "look" of success).

Also see *Jeep.*

(1) Luke 1:80; (2) Ps. 43:16; 77:19; (3) Mark 16:15-18, 20; (4) Matt. 23:5a.

Fox/es: (1) Little sins (apparently insignificant) that destroy fruitfulness; (2) Sly or cunning spirit/person; (3) Light-footedness (thief); (4) Vermin; (5) Cowardly (lacking spiritual fortitude); (6) Creature of the night; (7) Politician; (8) Stealer or attacker of sheep.

(1) Song. 2:15; (2) Luke 13:32; (3) Neh. 4:3; (4) Ps. 63:10 (KJV); (5-6) Ezek. 13:4-5; (7) Luke 13:32; (8) Ezek. 34:12; Acts 20:29.

Foyer: (1) Exposure (common place); (2) Entry; (3) Exit; (4) Place of welcoming, greeting, or arrival; (5) First impressions.

(1) Gen. 19:1; Exod. 38:8; Num. 10:3; 1 Sam. 2:22; Jer. 1:15; Mark 1:33; (2-3) Deut. 28:6; (4) 1 Cor. 16:20; 2 Cor. 13:12; (5) Isa. 53:2; Matt. 23:27.

Fragile: (1) Handle with care; (2) Vulnerable; (3) Sensitive.

(1) Gal. 6:1; (2) Gen. 4:7; Judg. 16:19-20; (3) 1 Sam. 18:8.

Frame: (1) The believer; (2) The Church; (3) A support; (4) A devised plan; (5) Something made or about to be made; (6) Something spoken or about to be spoken; (7) Treasuring a memory; (8) Set up.

(1) Ps. 103:14; 139:15; (2) Eph. 2:21 (KJV); (3) Ps. 139:15; (4) Jer. 18:11 (KJV); Ps. 94:20 (KJV); (5) Isa. 29:16 (KJV); (6) Judg. 12:6 (KJV); Ps. 50:19; (7) Phil. 3:13; Eph. 2:11a (KJV); (8) Gen. 39:14; 1 Kings 21:10.

Freezer: (1) Heart; (2) Long-term issue in the heart (long-term storage); (3) Love gone cold; (4) Hardened heart.

Also see *Frozen* and *Ice*.

(1) Luke 6:45; (2) Gen. 42:9; (3) Matt. 24:12; (4) Job 38:30.

Freight: (1) Business.

(1) 1 Kings 10:15.

French Fries: (1) Flesh (that which clogs the arteries and stops the flow of life).

Also see *Fish and Chip Shop* and *Junk Food*.

(1) Gal. 6:8.

Friday: (1) Six; (2) Human; (3) Double income; (4) Eve of rest; (5) Eve or victory; (6) Day of the flesh.

Also see *Day* and *Five* (the secular world sees Friday as the fifth day of the week).

(1-2) Gen. 1:26-31; (3) Exod. 16:5, 22, 26, 29; (4) Exod. 23:12; (5) Josh. 6:3; (6) As in, the world celebrates the end of the working week.

Fridge: See Refrigerator.

Friend: (1) Jesus; (2) Obedient disciple; (3) Literal friend; (4) Someone with whom you are familiar.

(1) Prov. 18:24; Matt. 11:19; Luke 12:4; <u>John 15:13, 15</u>; (2) John 15:14; (4) Job 19:14; Ps. 41:9.

Frill-Necked Lizard: (1) Spirit of fear; (2) Demon.

Also see *Lizard*.

(1-2) 2 Tim. 1:7.

Frog: (1) Unclean spirit; (2) Demonic powers; (3) Demon; (4) Deception; (5) Lying spirit.

(1-4) Exod. 8:2-13 (each plague pointed to the ineptitude of Egypt's gods, which in turn were empowered by demons, cf. 1 Cor. 10:19-20); Ps. 78:45; 105:30; Rev. 16:13; (4-5) 1 Kings 22:22; <u>Rev. 16:13</u>.

Front: (1) Future (as in front of you); (2) First appearance; (3) Seeing on the surface; (4) Exposed; (5) Leadership.

Also see *Front Door, Front Yard,* and *Before*.

(1) <u>Matt. 11:10</u>; Luke 9:52; 10:1; Acts 7:45 (as in, "what lies ahead or before me"); (3) As in, "It was all a front for the mafia"; (4) As in, "up front"; (5) Ps. 80:1; Isa. 40:11.

Front Door: (1) Entry to your heart; (2) Future (before you); (3) Face; (4) Mouth; (5) Meet; (6) Confront; (7) Seek, ask, knock; (8) Entrance; (9) Communication; (10) The door speaks for the household; (11) Spiritual sensitivity; (12) In secret (behind closed doors); (13) Not known (door shut); (14) Close/near/soon (at the door); (15) Jesus (The Door); (16) Salvation (open doors); (17) Hardened hearts; (18) Opportunity; (19) Opportunity to preach; (20) Door of Heaven; (21) Opening up to.

Also see *Door* and *Front*.

(1) Exod. 12:7; Ps. 24:7, 9; <u>Rev. 3:20</u>; (2) Ps. 5:8; (3) <u>Gen.</u> 1:2; <u>4:6-7</u>; (4) Judg. 11:31 (rash oath); Job 41:14; Ps. 141:3; Ezek. 33:30-31; (5) 2 Kings 14:8; (6) Gen. 19:6-7; 2 Kings 14:11; (7) 1 Chron. 16:11; Luke 11:7-13; (8) Gen. 6:16; Prov. 8:3; (9) Gen. 43:19; Exod. 33:9-11; (10) Exod. 12:22-23; <u>Josh. 2:19</u>; (11) Exod. 21:6; (12) Isa. 57:8; Matt. 6:6; (13) Matt. 25:12; Luke 13:25; (14) Matt. 24:33; Mark 1:33; 13:29; James 5:9; (15) <u>John 10:7</u>, 9; (16) <u>Acts 16:26</u>-28; (17) Acts 21:30 (doors shut); (18) 1 Cor. 16:9; 2 Cor. 2:12; Rev. 3:8; (19) Col. 4:3; (20) Ps. 78:23; Rev. 4:1.

Front Porch: See *Porch* and *Verandah*.

Front Yard (Garden): See *Yard (Front)*.

Frost: (1) Cold or hardship; (2) Judgment; (3) No love; (4) Wickedness.
Frost settles overnight, therefore also see *Night*.
(1) Gen. 31:40; Jer. 36:30; (2) Ps. 78:47; (3-4) Matt. 24:12.

Frown: (1) Disapproval; (2) Pride (looking down on you); (3) Troubled or burdened spirit.
(1) Gen. 31:5; (2) Isa. 2:11; (3) Dan. 7:28.

Frozen: (1) Love gone cold (cold-hearted); (2) Spiritually inactive; (3) Sexual issue of fear.
Also see *Freezer, Frost,* and *Ice*.
(1) Matt. 24:12; (2) Rev. 3:16; (3) 2 Sam. 13:20.

Fruit: (1) Produce of the Spirit; (2) Attributes of the heart (good or bad); (3) New believers; (4) An outward display of the heart; (5) Children or descendants; (6) Earnings (fruit in hand); (7) Laziness or resting on your laurels (rotten fruit).
(1) Gal. 5:22-23; (2-3) Jer. 17:10; Matt. 7:16-20; (3) Col. 1:6; (4) Matt. 12:33; (5) Acts 2:30; (6) Prov. 31:16; (7) Luke 12:16, 19.

Fruit Falling: (1) Untimely (too early/not ready/too late); (2) Ill-prepared; (3) Falling over in trials.
(1-3) Rev. 6:13.

Fruit Inspection: (1) Sampling for approval or quality; (2) Analyzing the heart.
(1) Matt. 3:8; 21:34-35; Luke 3:8; 13:6; John 15:5, 16; (2) Hos. 10:1-2.

Fruit Tree: (1) Believer.
Also see *Orchard, Plantation,* and *Vineyard*.
(1) Ps. 1:3.

Frying Pan: (1) Heart (as the place where meals are prepared); (2) Passion/zeal.
(1) Lev. 7:9; 1 Chron. 23:29; (2) Jer. 20:9.

Funeral: (1) Burying the past; (2) Death; (3) About to be resurrected; (4) Baptism.
Also see *Death* and *Mourning*.
(1-4) Rom. 6:4.

Furnace: (1) Hell; (2) Judgment; (3) Torment; (4) Affliction; (5) Purifying. Also see *Dross, Gold,* and *Iron.*

(1) Matt. 5:22b; Rev. 9:2; (2) 2 Pet. 2:4; (3) Luke 16:23; (4) Isa. 48:10b; (5) Ps. 12:6.

Furniture: (1) Past makeup/issues (old); (2) Gifts, riches, and promises of God (new); (3) May represent what is going on within you (God's house), e.g. a table may speak about communion; a chair, authority; a couch, perhaps laziness, etc. Also see *Chair, Couch, House, Sofa,* and *Table.*

(1-2) Prov. 24:3-4; 2 Cor. 5:17; (3) 2 Cor. 5:1.

Furniture Truck: See Removal Van.

Gambling: (1) Playing with your eternal destiny; (2) Flesh dominating the spirit (putting temporary fulfillment above eternity); (3) Addiction; (4) Stronghold; (5) Greed; (6) Deception; (7) Making decisions without God.

(1-2) Matt. 16:26; Luke 12:20; (3) Ps. 1:1 (*sinner* here is a habitual sinner); 1 Tim. 6:9; (4) Mark 10:21; (5) Prov. 1:19; 15:27; (6) Eccl. 5:10; 1 Tim. 6:10; (7) Gen. 16:2 (He didn't check with God); 2 Kings 1:3; 1 Chron. 10:14; Isa. 50:11.

Games: (1) Business (competitive sport); (2) Spiritually immature; (3) Toying with Christianity; (4) Missing the point (i.e. that it is about souls); (5) Life in the Kingdom of God. Also see *Ball, Cards, Playground, Playing,* and *Toys.*

(1) Mark. 9:33-34; (2) 1 Cor. 13:11; (3) As in, "They are just playing games"; (4) Matt. 11:16-19; (5) 2 Tim. 4:7.

Gang: (1) Fear; (2) Intimidation; (3) Spiritual warfare; (4) Anger and violence; (5) Unclean spirits; (6) Principality or power (gang leader); (6) Strongman (gang leader). Also see *Skinheads.*

(1-3) Josh. 1:4-9 (the word *Hittite* comes from a root word that means "affrighted with fear"); (4) Neh. 4:1-2; Ps. 22:16; (5) Mark 5:7-9, 13; (6) Matt. 12:27; Eph. 6:12.

Gap: (1) The connection between Heaven and earth; (2) Ministry of intercession; (3) Jesus Christ; (4) An opportunity or opening; (5) Hole needing filling; (6) Something missing; (7) Step, leap, or stand of faith.

(1-2) Ezek. 22:30; Heb. 7:25; Luke 16:26; (3) Heb. 7:25; John 1:51 (cf. Gen. 28:12, 17); (4-6) Ezek. 22:30; (7) Matt. 14:28-29.

Garage: (1) Parked or retired ministry; (2) In storage; (3) Church; (4) Undergoing a spiritual tune-up; (5) Going nowhere; (6) Restoration of a fallen ministry (workshop); (7) Repair shop (workshop).

Also see *Car Park* and *Parked Auto.*

(1) 1 Sam. 4:13-15; Luke 12:19; (2) Isa. 49:2; (4) Luke 1:80; (5) Gen. 42:16a; Luke 12:19; (3, 6-7) Rev. 3:2, 8; Gal. 6:1.

Garbage: (1) Sin; (2) Transgression; (3) The flesh; (4) Works of the flesh.

(1-2) Isa. 66:24 (garbage is taken to the dump!); Mark 9:43-45, 47; (3) Phil. 3:8; (4) Gal. 5:19-21.

Garbage Truck: (1) Large deliverance ministry (removes rubbish/sin); (2) Removing sin; (3) Unclean ministry/church; (4) Corrupt business; (5) Unholy destiny.

Also see *Flies* and *Rubbish.*

(1) Matt. 8:16; (2) Job 8:4; Isa. 31:7; Zeph. 1:17; (3) Isa. 64:6; John 2:14-16; Rev.17:4-6; 19:2-3; (4) Isa. 1:4; (5) Mark 9:43-44, 46, 48.

Garden: (1) The heart of the believer; (2) The human spirit; (3) The Church; (4) Growth; (5) Place of intimacy with God; (6) Workplace or that which is in your care; (7) Eternal life (evergreen garden); (8) Can be a place of death and burial; (9) Can represent sin (hiding in garden); (10) Can represent new life (fruitfulness); (11) Righteousness.

Also see *Park, Yard (Back),* and *Yard (Front).*

(1) Song. 4:16-5:1; Mark 4:7-8; (2) Song. 4:15; Jer. 31:12; (3) Song. 4:12; (4) Gen. 2:9; Luke 13:19; (5) Gen. 3:8; Song. 4:12, 15-16; 6:2, 11; John 18:26; (6) Gen. 2:15 (7) Isa. 51:3; 58:11; (8) John 19:41; 2 Kings 21:18, 26; (9) Gen. 3:10 (also consider that it was the place of the first sin); (10) Num. 24:6; Jer. 31:12 (joy); (11) Isa. 61:11.

Gardener: (1) Heavenly Father; (2) Earthly or spiritual caretaker.

(1) Gen. 2:8; Song. 5:1; 6:2; John 15:1; (2) Gen. 2:15; John 20:15; Also as the one who maintains and cares for the fruit-bearing trees.

Gardening: (1) Father's business; (2) Ministry; (3) Preparing the heart; (4) Working in the harvest.

(1) John 15:1; (2) Luke 13:7-9; (3) Jer. 4:3-4; Hos. 10:12.

Garment: See Clothes, Mantle, Robe, and Skirt.

Gas: (1) Spirit (Holy or evil); (2) Your life.

Also see *Poison.*

(1) Job 15:13; 27:3; (2) James 4:14.

Gasoline: (1) Fuel; (2) The Holy Spirit; (3) Power; (4) Ignition; (5) Anger; (6) Refuel; (7) Worldly wine or dependence; (8) Money.

Also see *Automobile* and *Motor.*

(1) Zech. 4:12; Matt. 25:8-9; (2-3) Mic. 3:8a; Zech. 4:12-14; Matt. 25:3-4; (cf. Matt. 25:1-12); Acts 1:8; (4) Ps. 104:4; (5) Isa. 9:19; (6) Acts 2:4; 4:31; 9:17; 11:24; 13:9, 52; 15:13; (7) Rev. 18:3; (8) Ezek. 27:17; Matt. 25:8-9.

Gas Station: (1) Church where you receive an infilling of the Holy Spirit; (2) An anointed ministry; (3) Place of refueling in the Spirit; (4) Place of restoration.

Also see *Gasoline, Mechanic,* and *Oil Rig.*

(1) Acts 2:4; (2) Luke 4:18; (3) Isa. 40:31; (4) Acts 9:17-19.

Gate: (1) Jesus Christ (The Gate of Heaven); (2) Heart; (3) Access; (4) Barrier (closed gate); (5) Opportunity (open gate); (6) Leadership (gatepost); (7) Not knowing Christ (shut gate); (8) Power; (9) Authority; (10) Narrow (life); (11) Broad (destruction); (12) Entry; (13) Separation; (14) Eldership; (15) Temple gate (beautiful); (16) The place of control; (17) The place of observation; (18) Exit; (19) Big entry; (20) Barred entry; (21) The place of sacrifice; (22) Protection; (23) The place of witness; (24) Locked up; (25) Death; (26) Thanksgiving; (27) The authority and strength of people (brass and iron); (28) Righteousness; (29) The place of wisdom; (30) The place of judgment; (31) The place of communication; (32) Worship (sheep gate); (33) Evangelism (fish gate); (34) Foundational teachings (old gate); (35) Death to self (valley gate); (36) Purging and refining (refuse gate); (37) Holy Spirit refreshing (fountain gate); (38) Word of God (water gate); (39) Intercession (horse gate); (40) Return of Christ (east gate); (41) Mustering or rapture (miphkad gate).

Also see *Door.*

(1) Gen. 28:12, 17 & John 1:51; Ps. 24:7, 9; 118:20; 2 Sam. 23:15; (2) Ps. 24:7, 9; (3) Ps. 100:4; (4) Neh. 7:3; 13:19; Rev. 21:25; (5) Prov. 1:21-22; 8:34; (6) Ruth 4:11; Prov. 31:23; Gal. 2:9; Rev. 3:12; (7) Luke 13:25; (8-9) Gen. 22:17; 24:60; Ps. 69:12; 127:5; Matt. 16:18; (10-11) Matt. 7:13-14; Luke 13:24; (12) Prov. 17:19; Luke 7:12; Acts 10:17; (13) Luke 16:20, 26; (14) Gen. 19:1; 23:10; 34:20; Ruth 4:1-2, 11; 1 Sam. 4:18; 9:18; Job 29:7; Prov. 31:23; (15) Acts 3:2, 10; (16-17) Acts 9:24; (18) Acts 12:10; (19) 1 Sam. 21:13; Acts

12:13; Rev. 21:12; (20) Deut. 3:5; Acts 12:14; (21) Acts 14:13; Heb. 13:12; (22) Exod. 20:10; Deut. 3:5; (23) Ruth 4:10-11; (24) 1 Sam. 23:7; (25) Job 38:17; Ps. 9:13; 107:18; Matt. 16:18; (26) Ps. 100:4; (27) Ps. 107:16; (28) Ps. 118:19; (29) Prov. 1:20-21; 8:1, 3, 34; 24:7; (30) Ruth 4:1-2, 10; Prov. 22:22; (31) Prov. 31:31; (32) Neh. 3:1; (33) Neh. 3:3; (34) Neh. 3:6; (35) Neh. 3:13; (36) Neh. 3:13; (37) Neh. 3:15; (38) Neh. 3:26; (39) Neh. 3:28; (40) Neh. 3:29; (41) Neh. 3:31.

Gather: (1) Harvest; (2) Revival; (3) Protect; (4) Church (a gathering).

(1) Luke 3:17; Rev. 14:15; (2) Mark 1:33; Luke 8:4; (3) Matt. 23:37; (4) Acts 14:27.

Gaunt: See Emaciated and Skinny.

Gear Lever: (1) Change or change agent; (2) Taking the ministry up or down a notch spiritually.

(1) Gen. 41:14; 2 Chron. 29:16; (2) 1 Kings 18:46, 19:3.

Gemstones: See Precious Stones.

General (Military): (1) Jesus Christ; (2) An archangel; (3) Apostolic ministry.

(1) Josh. 5:14-15; (2) Dan. 10:13; Jude 1:9; Rev. 12:7; (3) Acts 5:29; 6:2-7; 8:14-15.

Generator: (1) Power of God; (2) The Holy Spirit; (3) Powerful Spirit-filled ministry.

(1) Ps. 62:11; 68:35; 71:18; (2) Mic. 3:8; Luke 4:14; (3) Luke 1:17.

Genitals: (1) Evangelism or evangelist; (2) Sex/uality; (3) Sexual perversion; (4) Exposed; (5) Vulnerable; (6) Revealed secrets (possible sexual secrets).

Also see *Naked, Sex,* and *Sexual Abuse.*

Note: If the dreamer experiences an arousal or experiences an awareness of perversion in the dream, then it is very likely that there is a pornographic/sexual/lust/sex predator issue or evil spirit involved.

(1) Mark 4:14-20; As the reproductive organs of the Body of Christ (seed sowing); Lev. 15:16 (KJV); (2-3) Lev. 15:16-18 (KJV); (4) Gen. 3:7a; 9:22; (5-6) Deut. 25:11 (KJV).

Giant: (1) Big test; (2) Intimidation/fear; (3) Overwhelming; (4) Enemy resistance; (5) Large faith (if you are the giant); (6) Imposing obstacle; (7) Demons;

(8) Need for the anointing (not conventional battle cf. Eph. 6:12); (9) We are to look to God, not ourselves; (10) Giants need dispossessing; (11) Angel.

(1) 1 Sam. 17:4, 16; (2) Num. 13:32-33; 1 Sam. 17:11; (3) Job 16:14; (4) Deut. 3:1, 11; 2 Sam. 21:16-22; (5) Matt. 8:10; (6) Matt. 15:22-28; (7) Gen. 6:4; (8) 1 Sam. 17:33-47; (9) Num. 13:33; (10) Deut. 2:20-21; 3:13; Josh. 13:12; 17:15; (11) Rev. 7:1; 10:5, 8.

Gift: If your Father is giving you a gift, it can represent: (1) A spiritual gift; (2) The Holy Spirit; (3) The baptism in the Spirit (evidenced by speaking in tongues).

Alternatively, a gift could be: (4) A bribe.

(1) Heb. 2:4; (2) Eph. 1:17; Rom. 5:5; 2 Cor. 5:5; Gal. 3:5; (3) Luke 24:49; Acts 11:17; (4) Prov. 21:14.

Giraffe: (1) Pride; (2) Self-importance.

(1-2) Ps. 131:1; Isa. 2:11; 3:16.

Girl: (1) Young church; (2) Literal girl; (3) Young generation.

(1) Eph. 5:25; (3) Ruth 4:12b.

Glands: (1) Bitterness and unforgiveness [first sign of a spiritual infection] (swollen glands).

(1) Matt. 24:10 (note the progression: offense>betrayal>hatred).

Glass: (1) Heart; (2) Word of God; (3) Mirror; (4) Transparent and pure; (5) Seal; (6) Fragile (breakable); (7) Victory.

Also see *Broken Glass* and *Window.*

(1) Prov. 27:19; Matt. 5:8; John 2:25; (2-3) 1 Cor. 13:12; 2 Cor. 3:18 (KJV); James 1:23-25; (4) Rev. 21:18, 21; (5) Job 37:18; (6) Ps. 2:9; 31:12; Matt. 9:17; (7) Rev. 15:2.

Glass (Drinking): (1) Heart; (2) Pure heart (crystal glass); (3) Church (as a vessel of the Holy Spirit); (4) Anointed ministry.

Also see *Glass* and *Glass of Water.*

(1) Prov. 20:5; 21:1; Lam. 2:19; Matt. 5:8; (3) Ezek. 39:29; Acts 2:17-18; (4) Acts 28:8.

Glass Door: Prophetic opportunity (walking through glass door).

(1) 1 Kings 19:19-20; Rev. 4:1.

Glasses (Spectacles): See Reading.

Glass Office: (1) Office of a prophet.
(1) 1 Sam. 9:9; Prov. 7:6.

Glass of Water: (1) Installment of revelation from God's Word; (2) Partaker of God's Spirit (if drinking); (3) Eternal Life; (4) Unselfish deed (giving glass of water); (5) Returning good for evil (giving to your enemy).
Also see *Glass (Drinking)* and *Water.*
(1) Prov. 18:4; Amos 8:11; Eph. 5:26; (2) John 4:11; (3) John 4:14; (4) Matt. 10:42; (5) Prov. 25:21.

Glass Table: See Table (Glass Table).

Glitter: (1) Glamor; (2) Self-glory; (3) Apparent appeal; (4) Looking good.
(1-4) 2 Cor. 11:14; 2 Tim. 3:5; 1 Pet. 3:3-4.

Gloves: (1) Warm and loving help; (2) Warmth; (3) Protection; (4) Deed in secret; (5) With or without sensitivity.
(1) James 2:15-16; (2) John 18:18; (3) Ps. 44:3 (KJV); (4) Matt. 6:4; (5) Heb. 4:15 (KJV).

Glue: (1) Stuck (or stick); (2) Joined; (3) Soul-tie; (4) Stronghold.
(1) 2 Sam. 18:9; Isa. 5:13; (2) Gen. 2:24; 1 Cor. 6:17; (3) 1 Sam. 18:1; (4) Matt. 12:29.

Goal: (1) Success; (2) Achievement; (3) Overcoming the world.
Also see *Hole in One.*
(1-2) 2 Tim. 4:7; Phil 3:12; (3) Rev. 3:21.

Goalkeeper: (1) Defense of the Gospel.
(1) Phil. 1:7, 17.

Goat/s: (1) Unsaved; (2) Cursed; (3) One without compassion (heart); (4) Demon; (5) Hard-hearted.
Also see *Sheep.*
(1-4) Matt. 25:32, 41; (5) Matt. 9:34; 12:2, 24; 23:13 (full of "buts").

Go Cart: (1) Immature Christian walk; (2) Incomplete Christian walk.

Also see *Racing Driver.*

(1) 1 Cor. 13:11.

Going Out: (1) Beginning a spiritual military campaign; (2) Leaving.

Also see *Coming In* and *Outside/Outdoors.*

(1) 1 Kings 3:7 (AMP); Josh. 14:11; 2 Sam. 3:25; (2) John 13:30.

Gold/en: (1) Refined/pure/holy; (2) Glory; (3) Wealthy, great, or powerful; (4) Anointing (gold honey); (5) First place; (6) Money; (7) Beautiful or valuable; (8) Deeds done in the Holy Spirit; (9) Honor/able; (10) Rich or blessed; (11) Religious-glory.

Also see *Precious Stones* and *Yellow.*

(1) Job 23:10; Heb. 9:4; Rev. 21:15, 18-21; (2) Lam. 4:1; Isa. 60;9; 1 Pet. 1:7; (3) Ezek. 16:13; Dan. 2:38; (4) Zech 4:12; (5) 1 Kings 10:21; (6) 2 Kings 12:13; 2 Chron. 24:14; (7) Zech. 4:2-6; Rev. 5:8; (8) 1 Cor. 3:12; 2 Tim. 2:21; (9) 2 Tim. 2:20; (10) Rev. 3:18; (11) Rev.17:4.

Golden Gate Bridge: (1) Path to God's glory; (2) Path to riches.

(1-2) Rev. 21:21.

Golf Caddy: (1) Support role; (2) The Holy Spirit.

(1) 1 Sam. 14:6-7; (2) John 14:26.

Golf Course: (1) Progressing in faith (speaking the word and then following it).

Also see *Ball, Golfer, Golf Hole,* and *Hole in One.*

(1) Deut. 8:3; 30:14; Josh. 1:8; Ps. 119:105.

Golfer: (1) Someone walking by faith (following the Word).

Also see *Ball* and *Golf Course.*

(1) Ps. 119:133.

Golf Hole: (1) The goal or target God has for you; (2) The hole number may convey a message.

Also see *Golf Course* and *Golfer.*

(1) Phil. 3:14; (2) See individual number entries.

Golf Tee: (1) Preaching platform.

Also see *Ball, Trees,* and *Water.*

(1) As the launching place for words (the ball).

Gorilla: See King Kong.

Government: (1) Kingdom of God; (2) Church (government installation/dept.); (3) Authority.

(1-2) Eph. 1:20-23; (3) Rom. 13:1.

Governor: (1) Christ; (2) Ruler; (3) Authority and power; (4) Organizer and coordinator; (5) Judge; (6) Decision-maker; (7) Justice of the peace; (8) The Law; (9) Helmsman (the person steering the ship).

(1) Matt. 2:6; (2) Matt. 2:6; (3) Luke 20:20; Rom. 13:1; (4) John 2:8-9; (5) Acts 24:10; (6) Matt. 27:2, 11, 14, 21; (7) 2 Cor. 11:32; (8) Gal. 4:2; (9) James 3:4 (KJV).

Grader (Road): See Road Grader.

Grades: (1) Hot for God (A-grading); (2) Cold in my zeal for the things of God (F-grading); (3) Lukewarm (C-grading).

(1-3) Rev. 3:15-16.

Graffiti: (1) Spraying someone with words; (2) Self-promotion (graffiti initials); (3) Warning (The writing's on the wall).

(1) 2 Chron. 32:17; Mark 15:29; Luke 23:39; 1 Cor. 5:11; (2) 2 Sam. 15:4; (3) Dan. 5:25.

Grandchild: (1) The future or distant future; (2) The recipient—good and bad—of parental and grandparental influence; (3) Offspring; (4) Consider the meaning of their name.

(1) Exod. 2:9; Deut. 6:6-8; Ps. 34:11; 132:12; Prov. 13:22; (2) Exod. 34:7 & Prov. 13:22; 2 Kings 17:41 (idolatry); Ps. 78:5-6 (Word of God); Ps. 103:17 (righteousness); Ezek. 37:25 (land).

Grandfather Clock: (1) Unsaved people with time running out; (2) The past/history (time of old); (3) Living in the past.

(1) Ps. 89:47; Rev. 12:12; (2) Josh. 24:15.

Grandparent: (1) The past; (2) Heritage or generation; (3) Inheritance (good or bad); (4) Tradition (especially if depicted as a nationality rich in tradition); (5) Church history (grandmother); (6) May represent those that give up the call (retire); (7) God; (8) Patron.

(1) Heb. 1:1; (2) Gen. 50:24; (3) cf. Exod. 34:7 & Prov. 13:22; (4) Gal. 1:14; 1 Pet. 1:18; (5) 2 Tim. 1:5; (6) Deut. 4:25; (7) Dan. 7:9; (8) Prov. 17:6.

Grapes: (1) Good fruit; (2) Blood; (3) Sacrifice (crushed).

(1) John 15:16; (2) Gen. 49:11; (3) Gen. 40:11 (sacrificing the grape for its juice).

Grapes (Big Grape/s): (1) Blessing; (2) The time to act (harvest); (3) Possible resistance to move on in God due to insecurity and low self-worth.

(1) Num. 13:27; (2-3) Num. 13: 23, 33.

Grass: (1) Humanity or flesh; (2) Peace (tender grass); (3) The righteous; (4) Little faith; (5) A place to feed; (6) A dying rich person; (7) Judgment; (8) People of small power; (9) Numerous; (10) Spiritual food/provision; (11) Evildoers; (12) Flourishing; (13) A troubled heart (withered grass); (14) Speaks of the frailty and brevity of life; (15) Favor (dew on grass); (16) A time to be diligent; (17) Speaks of humbling; (18) Blessing.

(1) Isa. 40:6; James 1:10; 1 Pet. 1:24; (2) Ps. 23:2 (*green pastures* means literally "pastures of tender grass"); (3) Prov. 11:28; (4) Matt. 6:30; (5) Matt. 14:19; Mark 6:39 (green grass); John 6:10 (much grass); (6) James 1:10-11; (7) Isa. 15:6; 40:6-8; Jer. 14:5-6; Rev. 8:7; (8) 2 Kings 19:26; Isa. 37:27; (9) Job 5:25; (10) Job 6:5; Jer. 50:11; Zech. 10:1; (11) Ps. 37:1-2; 92:7; 129:6; (12) Ps. 72:16; (13) Ps. 102:4, 11; (14) Ps. 103:15; Isa. 51:12; (15) Prov. 19:12; (16) Prov. 27:23-27; (17) Dan. 4:15, 23, 25, 32-33; 5:21; (18) Deut. 11:13-15.

Grass (Mown Grass): (1) Humanity's mortality; (2) Sinful people; (3) Humbled person (cutting away the flesh); (4) Harvesting (mowing grass); (5) Death or destruction.

(1-2) Ps. 37:1-2; (3) Ps. 72:6 (KJV); (4) Ruth 1:22; John 4:35; (5) Ps. 37:1-2.

Grasshopper: (1) Little, small, or insignificant.

Also see entries under *Locust*.

(1) Num. 13:33.

Grave (Stone): (1) Death; (2) Darkness; (3) Grief; (4) A sure thing; (5) Resurrection for the righteous (an upright gravestone can represent resurrection); (6) Levels pride; (7) Hypocrite (whitewashed tomb); (8) Victory.

Also see *Cemetery, Coffin, Death,* and *Graveyard.*

(1) Exod. 14:11; Job 33:22-30; 38:17; (2) Ps. 88:6; (3) Gen. 50:10; 2 Sam. 3:32; John 11:31; (4) Ps. 89:48; Prov. 30:15b-16a; (5) Gen. 35:20 & 28:18; Ps. 49:15; Ezek. 37:12-14; Matt. 27:52-53; John 12:17; (6) Isa. 14:11; (7) Matt. 23:27; Luke 11:44; (8) 1 Cor. 15:55-57.

Gravel: (1) Deceit; (2) Shame.

Also see *Dirt, Dust, Gravel Road,* and *Rocks.*

(1) Prov. 20:17; (2) Lam. 3:16.

Gravel Road: (1) Ungodly path.

Also see *Dirt Road, Gravel,* and *Sandy Path/Trail.*

(1) Ps. 17:5.

Graveyard: (1) Valley of death; (2) Valley of dry bones; (3) Spiritually dead; (4) Religious or hypocritical.

Also see *Cemetery, Coffin, Grave,* and *Death.*

(1) Job 10:21-22; (2) Ezek. 37:1-14; (3) Ps. 107:10-11, 14; (4) Matt. 23:27-28.

Gravy: (1) The Anointing.

(1) Joel 2:28; Acts 2:17; Heb. 6:4;

Gray: See Grey and Grey Hair.

Green: (1) Righteousness; (2) Envy; (3) Peace; (4) Hypocritical; (5) Prosperous; (6) Productive; (7) Life; (8) Growth; (9) Zealous; (10) Youth; (11) Joy; (12) Fruitful; (13) Fruitless; (14) Work of the flesh/self; (15) Flesh; (16) Wickedness; (17) Idolatry; (18) Earth; (19) Mercy; (20) Anointing or anointed one (olive green); (21) Resurrection.

(1) Ps. 92:12; Prov. 11:30; (2) Prov. 14:30; Ezek. 31:9; Acts 7:9; 13:45; (3) Ps. 23:2; (4) Matt. 23:28-29; (5) Luke 23:31; (6) Song. 2:13; Isa. 15:6-7; (7) Exod. 10:15-17; (8-10) Isa. 53:2; (12) Jer. 11:16; 17:8; Hos. 14:8; (13) Mark 11:13; (14) Ps. 37:35; (15) Isa. 40:6-8; 1 Pet. 1:24; (16) Ps. 37:5; (17) Deut. 12:2; 1 Kings 14:23b; 2 Kings 16:4; 17:10; (18) Gen. 1:30; Exod. 10:15; Rev. 8:7; 9:4; (19) Gen. 9:12 (central color of rainbow); (20) Zech. 4:12-14; (21) Gen. 8:11.

Grey: (1) Depression; (2) Uncertainty or ill-defined; (grey area); (3) Double-minded (mixture of black and white); (4) Lukewarm; (5) Death; (6) Old or mature; (7) Loss of strength; (8) Honor.

Also see *Grey Hair.*

(1) Job 3:5; 16:16; (2) Matt. 4:16; Luke 1:79; (3) James 1:8 & Rev. 3:15-16; (4) Rev. 3:15-16; (5) Rev. 6:8 (pale horse); (6) Gen. 42:38; 44:29, 31; Deut. 32:25; (7) Hos. 7:9; (8) Lev. 19:32.

Grey Hair: (1) Old or mature; (2) Wisdom; (3) God; (4) Close to death; (5) Deserving honor and respect; (6) The devil (accusing, arrogant, proud, lying, or deceptive individual).

Also see *Hair.*

(1) Gen. 42:38; (2) Job 12:12; Prov. 16:31 & 20:29; (3) Dan. 7:9, 17, 22; (4) Gen. 42:38; 44:29, 31; Deut. 32:25; Hos. 7:9; (5) Lev. 19:32; (6) Rev. 12:9, 20:2.

Grief: See Mourning.

Griffin: (1) Commanding angel; (2) Powerful prophetic angel from God.

Also see *Lion* and *Eagle.*

(1) 2 Sam. 1:23b; Dan. 7:4; (2) Rev. 22:6.

Grim Reaper: See Death and Destroy.

Grind: (1) Proud person judged; (2) Judgment coming; (3) Sexual relations; (4) Harsh treatment; (5) Confinement and slavery.

(1) Matt. 21:42, 44; (2) Matt. 24:41; (3) Job 31:10; (4) Isa. 3:15; (5) Lam. 5:13; Judg. 16:21.

Groaning: (1) Symbolizes heartache and a desire for release or birth of the spirit; (2) Bondage or affliction; (3) Oppression; (4) Complaint; (5) Wounded or vexed soul; (6) Grief (heartache); (7) Bruised heart; (8) Pain; (9) Death; (10) Awaiting release.

(1) Rom. 8:26; 2 Cor. 5:2, 4; (2) Exod. 2:23-24; 6:5; Ps. 102:20; Acts 7:34; (3) Judg. 2:18b; (4) Job 23:2; (5) Job 24:12; Ps. 6:3, 6; 38:8-9; Jer. 51:52b; (6) Ps. 6:6-7; John 11:33, 38; (7) Ps. 102:4-5; (8) Rom. 8:22; (9) Ezek. 30:24b; Ps. 102:20; (10) Rom. 8:23.

Grocery Store: See Supermarket.

Groom: (1) Jesus; (2) You in union with someone or something; (3) Christ or His offspring (bloody groom).

Also see *Best Man.*

(1) Mark 2:19-20; John 3:29; (3) Exod. 4:26 & 1 Cor. 10:16.

Grotto: (1) Heart; (2) Earthly treasure; (3) Religious shrine.

Also see *Cave, Shrine,* and *Treasure.*

(1-3) Matt. 6:19-20.

Guarantee: (1) The Spirit; (2) Promise; (3) Assurance in Christ; (4) Faith.

(1) 2 Cor. 5:5; (2) Luke 24:49; (3) Acts 2:36; 17:31; (4) Heb. 11:1 (AMP).

Guide: (1) The Holy Spirit; (2) Jesus; (3) Mentor/leader; (4) An angel; (5) The Bible; (6) The rhema word (a word spoken in season).

Also see *Map* and *Pointing.*

(1) John 16:13; Rom. 8:14; (2) John 10:27; 21:19, 21; Heb. 12:2; (3) 1 Kings 19:21b; Acts 8:30-31; (4) Gen. 19:15-16; (5) Ps. 119:105; (6) Prov. 15:23b; Isa. 50:4; Acts 8:30-31.

Guinea Pig: (1) Feeble; (2) Fearful; (3) Wise; (4) Timid; (5) Pawn; (6) Experiment; (7) Sin that you want to keep (as a pet).

Also see *Pet.*

(1-4) Prov. 30:24-26 (conies KJV); (5) As in, "being used"; (6) As in, "They are just using me as a guinea pig"; (6) Heb. 12:1.

Guitar: (1) Praise and/or worship; (2) Freestyle worship (guitar with no neck); (3) May symbolize religious seduction (or false worship); (4) Performing/grandstanding.

Also see *Music, Musical Instrument,* and *Rock 'n' Roll.*

(1-2) Ps. 33:2; 92:3; 144:9; 150:4; Isa. 38:20; (3) 1 Tim. 4:1; 2 Tim. 3:13; 1 John 2:26; (4) 2 Sam. 6:5; John 7:18.

Gums: (1) Issue of the heart (bleeding gums).

(1) Matt. 15:18; Luke 6:45.

Gun: (1) Words; (2) Weapon; (3) Accusation; (4) Threatening words (loaded gun).

Also see *Bow* and *Bullets.*

(1-2) Isa. 54:17; (3-4) Ps. 22:13.

Gunman: (1) The accuser of the brethren; (2) Condemnation.

Also see *Assassin, Contract Killer, Gun, Sniper,* and *Rifle.*

(1) Rev. 12:10; (2) Matt. 12:37; John 5:24 (KJV); Rom. 8:1; 1 Tim. 3:6; James 3:1-9; 5:12.

Gutter/s: (1) Channel of the Spirit; (2) Lowest point (rock bottom); (3) Water catchment; (4) Humble soul recognition of being spiritually poor.

(1) Judg. 15:19; Isa. 44:3; John 7:38-39; (2) Mic. 7:10; (3-4) Matt. 5:3.

Also see *Drain, Kerb, Plumber,* and *Trench.*

Dirty Roof Gutters (1) not dealing with issues in your life/church/ministry (the run-off of wrong authority structures).

(1) Matt. 23:26.

Haemorrhoids: See Hemorrhoids.

Hail: (1) Judgment; (2) Wrath.

(1) Ps. 78:47; Isa. 30:30; Ezek. 13:13.

Hair: (1) Anointing; (2) Vanity or self-glory; (3) Sin; (4) Separation unto God; (5) Speaks of covering (woman); (6) Glory; (7) Strength; (8) Fine line (accurate); (9) Protection or care; (10) Prophet or recluse; (11) Innumerable; (12) Humbling love and devotion; (13) Speaks of shame (long hair on male); (14) Self-glory (long hair on male); (15) Set apart for God (long-haired boy);(16) Person in the world (ponytail); (17) Glory (curly hair like a lion's mane); (18) Stronghold of thoughts (caught in the hair); (19) Self-glory/pride (caught by the hair); (20) Renewal of the mind (+/-) (washing hair).

Also see *Baldness, Grey Hair,* and *Hairy.*

(1) Judg. 16:19-20; (2) 2 Sam. 14:26; 1 Tim. 2:9; 1 Pet. 3:3; (3) Lev. 13:3-4, 10ff; (4) Num. 6:5-8, 18-19; (5) 1 Cor. 11:15; (6) Prov. 16:31; Dan. 7:9; 1 Cor. 11:15; Rev. 1:14; (7) Judg. 16:22, 28-30; (8) Judg. 20:16; (9) 1 Sam. 14:45; 2 Sam. 14:11; 1 Kings 1:52; Matt. 10:30; Acts 27:34; (10) 2 Kings 1:8; (11) Ps. 69:4; (12) Luke 7:38, 44; John 11:2; 12:3; (13) 1 Cor. 11:14; (14) Judg. 16:17; 2 Sam. 14:26; (15) Judg. 13:5; (16) Isa. 31:1; (17) Song. 4:1; Dan. 7:9; Rev. 1:14; (18) Gen. 40:17; (19) 2 Sam. 18:9; (cf. 2 Sam. 14:26); (20) Tit. 3:5 & Rom. 12:2.

Haircut: (1) Cleansing from sin; (2) Rejection; (3) Loss of/or removing the anointing.

(1) Lev. 14:8; (2) Jer. 7:29; (3) Judg. 16:19-20.

Hair Cut Off: (1) Shame; (2) Subjection; (3) Judgment; (4) Humbling; (5) Breaking of a vow.

Also see *Baldness.*

(1-3) Isa. 3:24; 7:20; 15:2; Jer. 7:29; Ezek. 5:1; (4-5) Judg. 16:19-21.

Hairdressers: (1) Vanity; (2) Grooming (self-glory); (3) Church (as the place where hair [the flesh] is trimmed).

Also see *Barber Shop.*

(1-2) 2 Sam. 14:26; 1 Tim. 2:9; 1 Pet. 3:3; (3) Num. 6:19.

Hair Extensions: (1) Authority/covering; (2) Not happy with your covering (pulling out extensions).

(1-2) 1 Cor. 11:15.

Hair (Not Singed): (1) God's protection.

(1) Dan. 3:27.

Hair Pulled Out: (1) Abuse; (2) Ashamed; (3) Being taken advantage of (some/part of hair pulled out); (4) Frustration.

(1) Isa. 50:6; (2) Ezra 9:3; Neh. 13:25; (3) Isa. 50:6; (4) As in, "I'm pulling my hair out because nothing is being done about it!"

Hair (Wanting it white or black): (1) Warning to watch what is coming from your mouth; (2) Promises you can't keep.

(1-2) Matt. 5:36-37.

Hairy: (1) Fleshly person (hairy arms, legs, back).

Also see *Legs—Hairy Legs.*

(1) Gen. 25:25 & Rom. 9:13.

Hallway: See Corridor.

Halo: (1) Glory of God; (2) An angel.

(1) Matt. 17:2; Rev. 1:16; 10:1.

Hamburger: (1) Fast food; (2) Sermon; (3) Words or teaching quickly or ill-prepared; (4) Not balanced nutrition; (5) Words spoken without consideration of impact or consequences.

(1) Heb. 5:14; (2) Heb. 5:12-14; (3) 1 Tim. 3:15-16; 2 Tim. 4:3; (4) Mark 4:19; An example of this might be where someone says that fasting is no longer

applicable based on Isaiah 58, though Jesus plainly says that we are expected to fast in Matthew 6:16; (5) Eccl. 5:2.

Hammer: (1) God's Word; (2) Using the Word of God to bring thoughts captive and killing wrong (human-made) thoughts; (3) Speaks of human-made building; (4) Unholy efforts of people; (5) Idolatry; (6) Babylon (or warlike nation); (7) Communism.

Also see *Mark* in Name and Place Dictionary.

(1) Jer. 23:29; (2) Judg. 4:21; 5:26; (*Sisera* means "Binding in chains" and may speak of strongholds [attitudes of mind]) cf. 2 Cor. 10:3-5; (3) 1 Kings 6:7; (4-5) Ps. 74:6; Isa. 44:12; Jer. 10:2-5; (6) Jer. 50:23; (7) As in, "hammer and sickle" on flag.

Hand/s: (1) Heart; (2) Flesh; (3) Work of the flesh; (4) Works; (5) Crippled heart (withered or malformed hand); (6) The Church (God's hands); (7) God's provision or doing; (8) Taking; (9) Responsibility; (10) Dominion, control, or authority; (11) Oath or pledge; (12) Opposition; (13) Help; (14) Leading out; (15) Carrying; (16) Grabbing or grasping; (17) Gift or giving; (18) Payment; (19) Harm, hurt, or hit; (20) Readily available (at hand); (21) Within reach; (22) Custody or capture; (23) Reaching out; (24) Power or strength; (25) Invitation; (26) Direction; (27) Laziness (poor)/diligence (rich); (28) United; (29) Diligence (rule)/slothful (are ruled); (30) Doing (own); (31) Purchase; (32) Hidden (slothfulness); (33) Silence; (34) My side of the agreement (a hand); (35) Despondency and disappointment (hands hanging down).

Also see *Broken, Fingers, Fist, Handle, Hands Folded, Hands Laid On, Knuckles, Palm, Left and Right,* and *Shaking Hands.*

(1) Ps. 24:4; 58:2; Prov. 21:1; Eccl. 7:26; Song. 5:4; James 4:8; (2) Luke 24:39; Eph. 2:11b; (3) Exod. 32:3-4; Dan. 2:34; (4) Gen. 4:11; 5:29; 31:42; Deut. 3:24; Prov. 12:14; Eccl. 2:11; (5) Luke 6:6-11; (6) 1 Cor. 12:12; (7) Eccl. 2:24; 9:1; (8) Gen. 3:22; (9) Gen. 9:2; (10) Gen. 14:20; 16:6, 9; 24:10; 41:35; (11) Gen. 14:22; 21:30; 24:2; 38:20; 47:29; (12) Gen. 16:22; (13) Gen. 19:10; (14) Gen. 19:16; (15) Gen. 22:6; (16) Gen. 22:10; 25:26; Prov. 30:28; (17) Gen. 24:18; 33:10; Prov. 31:20; (18) Gen. 31:39; (19) Gen. 32:11; 37:21-22; Prov. 6:17; (20) Gen. 32:13; (21) Gen. 33:19; (22) Gen. 38:18; Prov. 6:5; (23) Gen. 38:28; (24) Gen. 49:24; Exod. 13:16; Prov. 3:27; (25) Prov. 1:24; (26) Prov. 4:27; (27) Prov. 10:4; (28) Prov. 11:21; 16:5; (29) Prov. 12:24; (30) Prov. 14:1; Eccl. 9:10; (31) Prov. 17:16; (32) Prov. 19:24; 26:15; (33) Prov. 30:32 (hand to mouth); (35) Heb. 12:12.

Handbag: See Bag.

Hand Grenade: (1) Anger needing/wanting release; (2) Carrying tension; (3) Wanting to throw cell phone (not being able to free oneself from people wanting you); (4) Fear of something erupting; (5) Wanting to get rid of—distance yourself from—a potential hazard (throwing hand grenade).

(1) Num. 24:10; Lam. 2:3; (2) Jer. 17:22; (3) Mark 3:7, 20; 7:33a; (4) Job 22:10b; (5) 2 Sam. 11:15.

Handkerchief: (1) Speaks of great faith and anointing; (2) Speaks of indirect acts of faith and healing; (3) Miracle; (4) Releasing the anointing for healing or deliverance (giving handkerchief); (5) Receiving the anointing for healing or deliverance (receiving handkerchief).

(1-5) Acts 19:12.

Handle: (1) To understand and gain control over something/someone; (2) Spiritual stranglehold; (3) No longer held captive (handle falling off); (4) No longer out of control; (5) Uncontrollable (too hot to handle); (6) Deceit and deception (secretive or wrong handling); (7) Truth (handling something openly).

(1) As in, "I've got a handle on my new position now"; (2-3) John 14:30 (NIV); (4-5) As in, "He's not able to handle it." (6-7) 2 Cor. 4:2.

Handlebars: (1) Leadership (steering the ministry); (2) Person getting in your way (someone on the handlebars); (3) Freeloader/burden to the ministry (someone on the handlebars); (4) Someone uncomfortable with the way things are going/or the way you are going about things (carrying someone on the handlebars).

(1) Ps. 23:2-4; (2) Gen. 13:1, 14; (blocking your vision); (3) Acts 15:36-39; (4) John 6:60, 66.

Hand Rail: (1) Barrier; (2) Support.

(1) Deut. 3:5 (KJV); Job 38:10-11; Ps. 107:16; (2) Job 40:18.

Hands Folded: (1) Laziness; (2) Famine; (3) Self-destruct.

(1) Prov. 6:10; 24:33; (2) Eccl. 4:5.

Hand Shaking: See Shaking Hands.

Hands Laid On: (1) Impartation; (2) Blessing; (3) Hurting; (4) Identifying with; (5) Death (hands on the eyes); (6) Healing; (7) Persecution.

(1-2) Gen. 48:13-20; (3) Gen. 22:12; (4) Gen 48:16; (5) Gen. 46:4; (6) Mark 6:5; 16:18b; (7) Luke 21:12; 22:53 (KJV).

Hand Writing on a Wall: (1) The future is determined; (2) Judgment; (3) Weighed and found wanting; (4) Rumor.

(1-3) Dan. 5:5, 27; (4) As in, hearsay.

Hanging: (1) Cursed; (2) The Cross; (3) Conversion; (4) Christ; (5) Despondency (hands hanging down); (6) Feeling regret and guilt; (7) In the second heaven (positive experience).

(1) Mark 9:42; <u>Gal. 3:13</u>; (2) Luke 23:39; (3) Gal. 2:20; (4) Acts 5:30; 10:39; (5) Heb. 12:12; (6) Matt. 27:4-5; (7) Ezek. 3:14, 8:3.

Hang Glider: (1) Ministry in the Spirit; (2) Waiting on God.

(1-2) <u>Isa. 40:31</u>; John 3:8.

Harbor: See Port.

Hard/Hardened Heart: (1) Pride; (2) Stubbornness; (3) Resistant to the will of God.

(1-2) Neh. 9:16; <u>Dan. 5:20</u>; (3) Exod. 7:14.

Hard Drive: (1) Intellect (mind of the flesh); (2) Mind of the Spirit (supernatural quick thinking without boundaries).

Also see *Hardware* and *USB*.

(1) <u>Rom. 8:5</u>; Col. 2:18; (2) 1 Cor. 2:16.

Hardware (Computer): (1) The body of flesh/temple.

Also see *Computer, Hard Drive, Laptop, Desktop,* and *Software*.

(1) <u>1 Cor. 6:19</u>; Col. 1:22.

Hardware Store: (1) Heaven; (2) Faith's storehouse (Faith is the substance . . .).

(1) Phil. 4:19; (2) Heb. 11:1.

Harlot: (1) Seducing spirit (sexual immorality); (2) An idolatrous or adulterous church; (3) A Christian dabbling with other gods; (4) A Christian dabbling in immoral sex; (4) Prostitute; (5) Church relying on enterprise; (6) Babylon; (7) Escort to hell (seducing harlot).

Also see *Woman*.

(1) Judg. 16:5; Prov. 7:10; (2) Jer. 3:1, 6; Ezek. 16:15-17, 32; Rev. 17:5; (3) Jer. 2:20; (4) 1 Cor. 6:15-18; (4) Prov. 29:3; (5-6) <u>Rev.</u> 16:19; <u>17:4-5</u>; 18:2-3; (7) Prov. 5:3-5; 7:10-27; 23:27.

Harvest: (1) Soul-winning; (2) The end of the world/final ingathering of souls. Also see *Farm* and *Field.*

(1) John 4:35-42; (2) <u>Matt. 13:39</u>.

Hash Brown: See French Fries.

Hat: (1) Identity; (2) Role or responsibility; (3) Covering; (4) Authority; (5) Honor; (6) Dishonor.

Also note the type of hat. For example: If you are wearing a captain's hat, it means you will steer a ministry. If you had a Captain Cook's hat, it may mean you are going to take a nation for Christ. A helmet means either salvation or spiritual warfare and the need to guard your thoughts (see Eph. 6:17).

Also see *Cap* and *Helmet.*

(1) Deut. 1:15; Judg. 11:11; <u>1 Sam. 10:1</u>; (2) As in, "I'm wearing so many hats"; (3-6) 1 Cor. 11:3-16.

Hatred: (1) Murderer.

(1) 1 John 3:15.

Hawk: (1) Sharp-eyed; (2) Under surveillance; (3) Soaring on spiritual thermals; (4) Spiritual predator.

(1-2) As in, "Hawk-eye"; (3) <u>Job 39:26</u>; (4) Hawks prey on other birds as well as small mammals.

Hay: (1) Carnal motives; (2) Carnal works.

(1-2) 1 Cor. 3:12-13.

Hay Fever: (1) Being spiritually shut-down by the works of the flesh; (2) Having been overcome and caught up in the world.

(1) 1 Cor. 3:12, 15; (2) 1 John 2:16.

Head: (1) Jesus Christ; (2) Authority; (3) Leadership; (4) Father; (5) Blessed; (6) Foundation (Dan. 2:31-33, note that this image starts at the head not the feet); (7) Disapproval or disgust (shaking of the head).

Also see *Decapitation* and *Platter.*

(1) <u>1 Cor. 11:3</u>; Eph. 4:15; 5:23; (2) Exod. 18:25; (3-4) Exod. 6:14; Num. 1:4; 1 Chron. 29:11; Ps. 133:2; (5) Deut. 28:13; (6) Ps. 133:1-3; Dan. 2:37-39; (7) Ps. 44:14; 109:25.

Head (Hitting Head): (1) Mocking Christ or leadership; (2) Mocking; (3) Scorned; (4) Sarcasm; (5) Disrespect; (6) Abuse; (7) Deadly blow; (8) Serious injury.

(1-6) Matt. 27:31; Mark 15:19; (7-8) Gen. 3:15.

Head (Over the Head): (1) Accusation (if sign over head); (2) Overwhelmed; (3) Subjection (if feet over head); (4) Transferring (if hands over head); (5) Deliverance; (6) Blinded or veiled; (7) Point missed.

(1) Matt. 27:37; (2) Ezra 9:6; Ps. 38:4; (3) Ps. 66:12; (4) Lev. 16:21; (5) Jon. 4:6; (6) As in, "That went over his head."

Headphones: (1) Hearing from God; (2) What someone is listening to (positive or negative).

(1) Mark 4:9; (2) Rom. 12:2; 2 Cor. 10:5.

Heal/ed/ing: (1) Heart conversion; (2) Through the Cross; (3) Literal healing; (4) Confirms that God's Kingdom is within and has now come; (5) A call to act by faith (on receiving a word [which can be a dream]); (6) A call to walk in the Spirit; (7) Demonic deliverance; (8) Counterfeit healing (e.g. through cultic or occultic religion).

(1) Matt. 13:15; Luke 4:18; John 12:40; (2) Isa. 53:5; (3) (4) Matt. 4:23; 9:35; Luke 9:2, 6, 11; 10:9; (5) Matt. 8:8; (cf. Mark 6:4-5; Luke 4:16, 22-23); (6) Mark 6:13; Luke 4:18; Acts 10:38; (7) Luke 8:2, 36; 9:42; (8) 2 Thess. 2:9.

Heap: (1) To amass or gather; (2) Witness; (3) Ruin; (4) Lots (heaps); (5) Do good to an enemy (heaping coals on his head).

(1) Gen. 31:46; Job 16:4; 27:16; Rom. 12:20; 2 Tim. 4:3; James 5:3; (2) Gen. 31:48, 51-52; (3) Isa. 17:1b; 25:2; Deut. 13:16; Josh. 8:28; 2 Kings 19:25; (4) Judg. 15:16 (KJV); (5) Prov. 25:21-22.

Hearing: (1) Receiving in your heart; (2) Obedience; (3) Understanding.

(1) Ezek. 3:10; Mark 4:9; 8:18b; (2) Ps. 49:1; The Hebrew word for hearing, *shama,* also carries with it the thought of obedience; (3) 1 Kings 3:9.

Hearse: (1) Death; (2) Burial/burial of an issue.

(1) 2 Kings 23:20; Luke 7:12; (2) Gen. 23:4; 49:29; Rom. 6:4; Col. 2:12-13.

Heart: (1) The real person; (2) The inner part of person; (3) The spirit; (4) God's measure of a person; (5) Innermost thoughts; (6) The mind; (7) The emotions; (8) The will; (9) The core or middle; (10) The place where wisdom is deposited; (11) The deep; (12) The real altar of God.

Also see *Hard/Hardened Heart.*

(1-2) Ps. 19:14; 24:4; 28:3; 55:21; (3) Rom. 2:29; 8:27; 2 Cor. 1:22; (4) 1 Sam. 15:7b; (5) Gen. 6:5; 27:42; (6) Gen. 24:45; Exod. 4:21; (7) Gen. 42:28; Exod. 4:14; Lev. 26:16; (8) Exod. 7:23; 25:2; 35:5, 21-22; (9) Exod. 15:8; (10) Exod. 35:25-26, 35 (KJV), 36:1-2; (11) Ps. 64:6; (12) Jer. 17:1.

Heat: (1) Adversity; (2) Pressure; (3) Anger; (4) Fire; (5) Wilting under pressure; (6) Judgment; (7) Noon (heat of the day); (8) Sun.

Also see *Fire.*

(1-2) Jer. 17:8; Luke 12:55; Rev. 16:9; (3) Deut. 29:24; Ezek. 3:14; (4) Acts 28:3; (5) James 1:11; (6) 2 Pet. 3:10, 12; Rev. 16:9; (7) 2 Sam. 4:5; 1 Sam. 11:11; Matt. 20:12; (8) Ps. 19:6.

Heater: (1) Turning up the heat (pressure, adversity).

Also see *Fire, Fireplace, Kitchen,* and *Oven.*

(1) Dan. 3:19.

Heaven: (1) The spiritual realm (second heaven); (2) The home of God (The Father); (3) Eternity; (4) The spiritual Kingdom; (5) The place of reward; (6) Permanent treasury; (7) The home of believers; (8) The angelic realm; (9) The throne of God (third Heaven); (10) Sky (first heaven); (11) God-given (from Heaven); (12) The place of unlimited blessings; (13) The place from which the Church is to exercise its dominion.

(1) Matt. 3:16; 6:10; Luke 10:18; Acts 10:11; (2) Matt. 3:17; 5:16, 34, 45, 48; 6:1, 9; (3) 2 Cor. 5:1; (4) Matt. 4:17; John 3:12; (5) Matt. 5:12; (6) Matt. 6:20; 19:21; (7) Matt. 8:11; Luke 10:20; 2 Cor. 5:1; (8) Matt. 18:10; 22:30; 24:36; 28:2; Luke 22:43; Gal. 1:8; (9) Matt. 23:22; Acts 7:49; 2 Cor. 12:2; (10) Matt. 24:30; Luke 4:25; James 5:18; (11) Luke 20:4; John 3:27; 6:51; (12) Eph. 1:3; (13) Eph. 3:10; 2:6.

Heavy: (1) Depression; (2) Grief; (3) Sorrow; (4) The glory of God; (5) Burden; (6) Responsibility; (7) Serious; (8) The big guns; (9) Physical thugs or spiritual giants; (10) Wealth/prosperity; (11) Honor/esteem; (12) Sin/guilt.

Also see *Carrying, Fat,* and *Weight.*

(1-3) Ps. 119:28; (4) 1 Kings 8:11; 2 Cor. 4:17; (5-6) Exod. 18:18; (7) As in, "Things were getting heavy"; (8-9) As in, "He sent in the heavies"; (10) Gen. 31:1 (cf. KJV & NKJV); (11) Mal. 1:6 (*Honor* is the Hebrew *kabod,* which carries the sense of weightiness); (12) Ps. 38:4; Heb. 12:1.

Hedge: (1) Protection; (2) Restricted or channeled; (3) Painful restriction; (4) A call to stand in the gap; (5) Wall.

Also see *Fence* and *Wall.*

(1) Job 1:10; Ps. 80:12; Matt. 21:33; Mark 12:1; (2) Job 3:23; (3) Prov. 15:19; (4) Ezek. 13:5; 22:30; (5) Hos. 2:6.

Heel: (1) Betrayal; (2) Strike from behind; (3) Past life; (4) Past revealed; (5) Trap/snare; (6) Hold back.

Also see *Wall.*

(1) Gen. 3:15; Ps. 41:9; John 13:18; (2) Gen. 49:17; (3) Ps. 49:5; (4) Jer. 13:22 (KJV); (5) Jer.18:9; (6) Gen. 25:26.

Height: (1) Measure of something; (2) Spiritual dimension; (3) The measure of a person (in human terms); (4) Heaven; (5) Spiritual high ground; (6) Pride; (7) Strength; (8) God's home; (9) Greatness and dominion.

Also see *High, Smaller, Tall,* and *Taller.*

(1) Rom. 8:39 (love); (2) Eph. 3:18; (3) 1 Sam. 17:4; Dan. 3:1; (cf. 1 Sam. 16:7b); (4) Job 22:12; Ps. 102:19; 148:1; Prov. 25:3; (5) Jer. 31:12; Ezek. 20:40; (6) Jer. 49:16; Ezek. 31:10; (7) Jer. 51:53; Amos 2:9; (8) Ezek. 20:40; (9) Dan. 4:20-22.

Helicopter: (1) Christ or a ministry of salvation (rescue); (2) Spiritual ministry; (3) Vertical lift; (4) Quick ascension; (5) In danger of pride (quick ascension); (6) Evil spirit (spying helicopter).

Also see *Helicopter Rotor Blades.*

(1-3) Ps. 91:12; Matt. 17:27; Luke 1:69; John 6:39; (4-5) 1 Tim. 3:1, 6; 1 Sam. 15:17; (6) 1 Pet. 5:8.

Helicopter Rotor Blades: (1) Leader's words that keep you ducking for cover; (2) Uplifting words.

Also see *Helicopter* and *Propeller.*

(1) Esther 7:6-7; Matt. 14:3-4, 8; (2) 1 Cor. 14:3.

Helmet: (1) Salvation; (2) Hope; (3) Protect your mind; (4) Keep your head down (watch pride); (5) Spiritual warfare.

Also see *Cap, Hat,* and *Motorcycle Helmet.*

(1) Isa. 59:17; Eph. 6:17; (2) 1 Thess. 5:8; (3) 2 Cor. 10:5; 1 Pet. 1:13; (4) Rom. 12:16; (5) 2 Cor. 10:3-5; Eph. 6:11.

Hem: (1) The place of overflow.

(1) Ps. 133:2; Matt. 9:20; 14:36.

Hemorrhoids: (1) Stress; (2) Straining to get rid of a burden/sin.

(1-2) 1 Sam. 6:11 (KJV).

Hen: (1) Christ; (2) Comfort, nurture, and protect; (3) Church.

Also see *Chicken.*

(1-2) Matt. 23:37; Luke 13:34; (3) Matt. 23:37 & Acts 14:27.

Herbs: (1) Bitterness.

Also see *Spices.*

(1) Exod. 12:8; Num. 9:11.

Hidden: (1) Dead to self; (2) Safe.

(1-2) Col. 3:3.

Hiding: (1) Guilt (awareness of sin); (2) Fear; (3) Shame; (4) Protection; (5) Ignoring an issue.

Also see *Chasing, Concealing,* and *Running.*

(1) Lev. 5:2-4 (*unaware* means "hidden from Him"); Prov. 28:1 (The Hebrew word for "wicked" here is *Rasha*—amongst its meanings is the thought of "guilty"); (2) Matt. 24:24-25; (3) Gen. 3:8, 10; (cf. Gen. 2:25); (4) Exod. 2:2-3; Job 5:21; Ps. 17:8; (5) Lev. 20:4; Deut. 22:1, 3.

Hiding (God Hiding Himself): (1) Sign of spiritual adultery.

(1) Deut. 31:17-18; 32:16-20.

High: (1) God; (2) Exalted; (3) Heaven; (4) Spiritual ground; (5) Secure (tower)/ Security; (6) Spiritually lifted; (7) Proud; (8) Praise; (9) Wisdom; (10) Abomination to God (that which is highly esteemed among men).

Also see *Height, Hills,* and *Mountains.*

(1) Gen. 14:18-20; Ps. 18:13; 78:35; 83:18; (2) Exod. 14:8; Num. 33:3; 2 Sam. 23:1; Job 5:11; Luke 14:8, 10; (3) Exod. 25:20; Job 11:8; 16:19; 22:12; Ps. 68:18; 103:11; Isa. 6:1; (4) 1 Sam. 9:12, 14; 10:5; 1 Kings 3:4; (5) 2 Sam. 22:3 (KJV); Ps. 18:2 (KJV); Ps. 61:2-3; 91:14; 144:2; (6) 2 Sam. 22:49; 23:1; (7) Job 21:22; Ps. 18:27; Ps. 62:9; 75:5; 101:5; Prov. 21:4 (KJV); (8) Ps. 149:6; (9) Prov. 8:1-2; 9:1, 3; 24:7; (10) Luke 16:15; 20:46.

High Heels: (1) Woman in authority; (2) Businesswoman; (3) Woman wanting more authority (to appear taller); (4) Gospel outreach to homosexuals (man in high heels); (5) Worldly woman.

(1) Judg. 4:4, 9; (2) Acts 16:14; (3) 1 Kings 21:7; (4) 1 Cor. 9:22; (5) Prov. 7:10.

Highlighter: (1) Illumination/revelation; (2) Outstanding; (3) Glory of God.

(1) Dan. 5:24-25; Rev. 19:16; (2) 1 Sam. 9:2; (3) Ps. 18:12; Isa. 60:19; Ezek. 1:28.

High Rise Apartment: (1) Sudden elevation; (2) Prophetic office; (3) Preoccupation with non-practical matters (ivory tower).

Also see *Tower*.

(1) Gen. 41:14; (2) Num. 22:41; (3) 2 Sam. 11:1-2.

High School: (1) Spirit training; (2) Place of higher learning; (4) Passing into eternity (exams/graduation); (5) Moving into spiritual adulthood (exams/graduation).

(1) Isa. 50:4; Luke 1:80; (2) Matt. 5:1-2; (4) Rev. 20:12; (5) Matt. 5:9 ("sons" are mature sons who have become like their Father).

Highway: (1) God's path (the "high" way); (2) Commercial path; (3) Broad, easy, or quick road (way of the world); (4) Highway to hell; (5) Unsafe; (6) The main route; (7) The path of life (faith); (8) Spiritual decline (empty highways); (9) A heart prepared for God; (10) The highway to Heaven; (11) Prayer (the "high" way).

Also see *Path*, *Road*, and *Street*.

(1) John 14:6; (2) Matt. 22:9-10; Mark 10:46; (3-4) Matt. 7:13; (5) Judg. 5:6; (6) Judg. 20:31-32; 21:19; Num. 20:19; (7) Prov. 16:17; Isa. 35:8; Jer. 31:21; (8) Isa. 33:8; (9) Isa. 40:3; (10) Isa. 62:10; John 1:51; (11) 2 Chron. 7:14; cf. John 14:6 & 14:13-14.

Highway Patrol: (1) Being assessed for ministry (road worthiness); (2) Angels.

Also see *Automobile*.

(1) 1 Tim. 3:1-7; (2) Heb. 1:14.

Hijacking: (1) Warning of potential derailed destiny; (2) Warning of diverted destiny; (3) Warning of a destroyed destiny; (4) Someone trying to influence you with a hidden agenda; (5) Interference in the second heaven.

Also see *Ambush*.

(1-2) Luke 10:30-34; (3) Num. 13:32-14:2; (4) Matt. 16:22-23; (5) Dan. 10:13.

Hill: (1) Strength; (2) Place of prosperity; (3) Exposed; (4) Proud person; (5) Pride; (6) Place of revelation; (7) Hiding place; (8) Spiritual high ground; (9) Home of God; (10) Place of idolatry; (11) Lasting; (12) Place to cut off the flesh; (13) Reference point; (14) Military high ground; (15) Rural land.

Also see *Mountain* and *Strength*.

(1) Ps. 95:4; (2) Ps. 50:10; (3) Isa. 30:17; Matt. 5:14; (4) Isa. 40:4; Luke 3:5; (5) Isa. 2:12-14; Jer. 49:16; Luke 4:25-29; (6) Num. 23:9; 2 Kings 1:9; 4:27; Luke 9:37; (7) 1 Sam. 23:19; 26:1; Ps. 104:18; Jer. 16:16; (8) Exod. 17:9-10; 1 Sam. 10:10; Ps. 2:6; 3:4; 15:1; 24:3; 43:3; (9) Ps. 68:15-16 (KJV); 99:9; 121:1; (10) Deut. 12:2; 1 Kings 11:7; 14:23; 16:4; 17:10; Jer. 2:20; Ezek. 6:3-4; Hos. 4:13; (11) Deut. 33:15; (12) Josh. 5:3; (13) Josh. 15:9; 18:13-14; 24:30; (14) 1 Sam. 9:11; 10:5; (15) Ps. 50:10; 65:12; Isa. 5:1.

Hippopotamus: (1) Horse.

Also see *Horse*.

(1) *Hippo* is a Greek name meaning "horse."

Hips: (1) Strength of the flesh; (2) Call to change from being self-reliant to rely more on the Spirit (hip replacement).

(1-2) Gen. 32:25, 28, 32.

Hit: (1) Judgment; (2) Death.

(1-2) Exod. 12:7, 22; Deut. 21:4-5; 2 Sam. 12:15; Isa. 53:4, 8.

Hole: (1) Hiding place; (2) Home, den, lair, or nest (resting place); (3) Snare; (4) Clay pit; (5) Spiritual portal; (6) Cave; (7) Flawed (in garment); (8) Empty; (9) Outlet; (10) Worn-out (in garment); (11) Not changed (garment); (12) Missing something (not complete); (13) Time to replace (in garment); (14) Your heart (hole in ground); (15) Covenant (a ring created by the rim).

(1) 1 Sam. 14:11; Isa. 2:19; 7:19; Jer. 13:4; 16:16; Mic. 7:17; (2) Isa. 11:8; Jer. 48:28; Matt. 8:20; Luke 9:58; (3) Isa. 42:22; (4) Isa. 51:1; (5) Ezek. 8:7-12; (6) Nah. 2:12; (7-9) Hag. 1:6; (10-11) Matt. 9:16; (13) Luke 5:36-38; (14) 2 Cor. 4:7; (15) Gen. 9:12-13.

Hole in One: (1) Accurate word that penetrates the heart; (2) Saying the right thing at the right time.

(1) Luke 2:35; Heb. 4:12; (2) Isa. 50:4.

Holiday: (1) Rest; (2) Celebration; (3) Caught up in religion/working your way to Heaven (holy day); (4) Letting down your guard.

Also see *Tourist*.

(1) Exod. 20:11; 31:17; (2) Exod. 12:14; (3) Gal. 4:9-10 (this is particularly true if the scene also pictures works); (4) 1 Pet. 5:8.

Hollow: (1) Empty (without substance); (2) Not solid; (3) Spirit.

(1-2) 1 Tim. 1:10; 4:3; 6:3-5; (3) Judg. 15:19.

Hollywood: (1) Fame (worldly glory); (2) Superficiality.

(1) Acts 8:9-10; 12:22-23; (2) Matt. 23:27; John 5:44.

Home: (1) Heaven; (2) On our way to Heaven (on our way home); (3) Home; (4) Comfort/rest.

Also see *House*.

(1-2) John 14:2-4; Heb. 11:10; (3) Literal home; (4) Ruth 1:9; Isa. 66:1; Dan. 4:4.

Homeless Person: (1) Christ; (2) True disciple; (3) Without a spiritual house; (4) Poverty; (5) Cursed.

Also see *Bum*.

(1) Matt. 8:20; (2) Mark 10:29; (3) Luke 13:35; (4-5) Gen. 4:12.

Homework: (1) Getting our hearts in order; (2) Understanding and studying the Word.

Also see *House*.

(1) 2 Kings 20:1; Isa. 38:1; (2) 2 Tim. 2:15.

Homosexuality: (1) Union of men with the inability to reproduce (non-evangelistic); (2) Boy's club; (3) Men run by fleshly lust; (4) Antichrist spirit.

Also see *Genitals* and *Sex*.

Note: If the dreamer experiences an arousal or experiences an awareness of perversion in the dream, then it is very likely that there is a pornographic/sexual/lust/sex predator issue or evil spirit involved.

(1) Mark 10:35-37; (cf. Mark 10:9; Eph. 5:31-32); (2) Matt. 14:15, 15:23; Mark 10:35-37; (3) Rom. 1:24, 27; (4) Dan. 11:37; Rom. 1:25.

Homosexual Acts: (1) Abomination; (2) Lust; (3) Abuse; (4) Violation; (5) Demonic harassment.

Also see *Genitals* and *Sex.*

(1-3) Rom. 1:24-28; 1 Cor. 6:9.

Honey: (1) God's Word; (2) Pleasant words; (3) Grace or mercy; (4) Flourishing fruitfulness; (5) Manna from Heaven; (6) Blessing and abundance; (7) Own glory; (8) The provision of God; (9) Sweet words; (10) Spiritually enlightening; (11) Money; (12) Unadulterated Word of God (wild honey); (13) Revelation; (14) Partaking of the Promised Land.

Also see *Bees.*

(1) Judg. 14:8; Ps. 19:9-10; 119:103; Prov. 24:13-14; Isa. 7:15; Ezek. 3:3; (2) Prov. 5:3; 16:24; Song. 4:11; (3) Matt. 3:4 (where locust speaks of judgment, and honey speaks of grace); (4) Exod. 3:8, 17; 33:3; Lev. 20:24; (5) Exod. 16:31; (6) Num. 13:27; 14:8; Deut. 8:8; (7) Lev. 2:11; Prov. 25:27; (8) Deut. 32:13; 2 Sam. 17:29; Ps. 81:16; (9) Prov. 5:3-4; 25:16; Rev. 10:9-10; (10) 1 Sam. 14:27, 29; (11) As in, "land of milk and honey"; (12) Matt. 3:4; Mark 1:6; (13) Exod. 16:31 & Deut. 8:2-3; (14) Exod. 13:5b.

Honeycomb: (1) Speaks of solid spiritual food; (2) Those who loathe it are full of other things.

(1) Song. 5:1; (2) Prov. 27:7.

Hooded: (1) Blinded mind/veiled heart; (2) Covering or hiding something; (3) Covered; (4) Dishonor or shame; (5) Needing Christ; (6) Fear; (7) Mischievous lips; (8) Mourning.

(1) 2 Cor. 3:13-15; (2) Gen. 38:15; (cf. Gen. 3:8); (3-4) Jer. 14:4; Ezek. 7:18; 1 Cor. 11:4; (5) 2 Cor. 3:16; Jer. 14:4; (6) Exod. 34:30; (7) Ps. 140:9; Prov. 10:6; (8) 2 Sam. 15:30; Esther 6:12.

Hook: (1) Promise; (2) The Gospel; (3) The Word with power; (4) Politically dragged by force into something (trap); (5) Snare of temptation.

(1) Acts 2:38-39; 7:17; Eph. 3:6; (2) Matt. 4:19; (3) 1 Cor. 2:4. (4) Ezek. 19:4; 38:4; (5) Gen. 4:7.

Horizon: (1) The foreseeable future; (2) Expectancy.

Also see *Binoculars, Distance,* and *Distant.*

(1) Matt. 24:33-34; (2) Luke 15:20.

Hornet: See Wasp.

Horn/s: (1) Strength; (2) Power; (3) Influence; (3) Voice; (4) Crown (king) or leader; (5) God's power (The Spirit); (6) Pride; (7) Strength of heart; (8) Christ (horn of salvation); (9) Appeal to God; (10) Human-made strength; (11) Dominion; (12) Alarm or warning (blowing "shofar" ram's horn); (13) Celebration; (14) Omnipotence, or full of power (seven horns); (15) Nations.

Also see *Anointing* (cf. 1 Sam. 16:1, 13) and *Shofar.*

(1-2) Gen. 22:13 (This is a prefigure of Christ laying down His strength); Ps. 89:17; 92:10; Lam. 2:17; Dan. 8:7-8; Amos 6:13 (KJV); Hab. 3:4 (KJV); (3) Josh. 6:4-8 (spiritual voice); Ezek. 29:21; Dan. 7:11, 24; (4) Ps. 75:10; Dan. 7:24; 8:20-21; Rev. 17:12; (5) 1 Sam. 16:13; (6) Ps. 75:4-5 (horn lifted up); (7) Jer. 17:1 (horns of the altar); (8) Ps. 18:2; 132:17; Luke 1:69; (9) 1 Kings 1:50-51; 2:28 (grabbing the horns of the altar); Ps. 118:27; Amos 3:14; (10) 1 Kings 22:11; 2 Chron. 18:10 (iron horns); (11) Zech. 1:21; (12) Num. 10:4, 9; (13) Lev. 23:24; (14) Rev. 5:6; (15) Zech. 1:21.

Horse: (1) Looking to the World; (2) The flesh; (3) Hiring the world; (4) Not looking to God; (5) Swiftness; (6) Strength; (7) Power; (8) Authority; (9) Famine (black horse); (10) Death (pale horse); (11) Warfare (red horse); (12) Worldly spirit (sea horse); (13) Divine (white horse); (14) Competitive spirit (race horse).

(1) Deut. 17:16; 1 Kings 10:28; 2 Chron. 9:28; Isa. 31:1; (2) Isa. 31:3; Rev. 19:18; (3) 2 Kings 7:6; (4) Deut. 17:16; Isa. 31:1; (5) Jer. 4:13; Hab. 1:8; (6) Isa. 31:1; Jer. 47:3; (7) Rev. 9:19; (8) Rev. 6:2; (9) Rev. 6:5; (10) Rev. 6:8; (11) Rev. 6:4; (12) Jer. 6:23; 50:42; (13) Rev. 6:2; (14) 2 Sam. 18:22; Ps. 147:10.

Horse (White Horse's Rider): (1) Jesus Christ; (2) Warrior; (3) Faithful & true; (4) Justice; (5) Judge.

(1-5) Rev. 19:11-13.

Hose (Garden): (1) The flow of the Spirit; (2) Outpouring of the Spirit.

Also see *Sponge.*

(1-2) Acts 2:17.

Hospital: (1) Church; (2) Healing & rebuilding ministry; (3) Sick church; (4) Heaven; (5) Needs healing (going to hospital).

(1) 1 Cor. 12:28; Eph. 4:12, 16; (2) Gal. 6:1-2; (3) 1 Cor. 1:10; Rev. 3:17; (4) Rev. 21:4; (5) Mark. 2:3-4.

Hostage: (1) Being held to ransom; (2) An area in your life not redeemed; (3) Stronghold; (4) Extortion.

(1) Job 33:24; Hos. 13:14; (2) Isa. 51:10-11 (KJV); Jer. 31:11; Matt. 20:28; 1 Tim. 2:6; (3) Jer. 38:6; (4) Prov. 6:1-3; Isa. 16:4.

Hot: (1) Anger; (2) Trouble; (3) On fire for God; (4) Passionate; (5) Confronting; (6) Fierce; (7) Purifying; (8) Judgment; (9) Devouring; (10) The latest.

Also see *Cold* and *Fire*.

(1) Exod. 32:19, 22; 22:24; Deut. 9:19; (2) As in, "They landed in hot water"; (3) Rev. 3:15-16; (4) Ps. 39:3; Jer. 20:9; (5) Mal. 4:1; (6) 2 Sam. 11:15; (7) Ezek. 24:11; (8) Dan. 3:22; (9) Hos. 7:7; (10) As in, "hot off the press."

Hot Air Balloon: (1) Ministry in the Spirit.

Also see *Blimp*.

(1) Ezek. 3:14; 8:3; 11:1.

Hot Chocolate: (1) Anointing.

(1) Ps. 23:5.

Hotel: (1) Temporary place; (2) Passing through; (3) A place to pause on the way; (4) In Scripture, staying overnight at an inn can be a place of revelation; (5) Church (as the place where we drink); (6) A church at rest; (7) Denomination (hotel chain); (8) Place of rest.

(1-3) Gen. 42:27; 43:21; Exod. 4:24; Luke 2:7; 10:35; (4) Luke 24:28-31; Gen. 28:11-15; (5) Eph. 5:18; (8) Heb. 4:1, 5, 9-11.

Hotel Reception: (1) New temporary ministry or venture (checking in); (2) Leaving temporary ministry or phase in one's life (checking out).

(1) Gen. 24:23b; (2) Gen. 24:56.

Hot Dogs: (1) Feeding you what you want to hear (convenient food); (2) Being spiritually lazy (wanting fast food).

(1) Isa. 30:10; Jer. 5:31; (2) Matt. 25:8-9.

Hot Rod: (1) Someone moving with anger; (2) Moving too quick; (3) Showing ministry without perseverance.

(1) Exod. 32:19; (2) 2 Sam. 18:19ff; (3) Heb. 10:38.

Hot Water: See Water (Hot).

House: (1) An individual; (2) Church; (3) Someone's home or household; (4) Yourself; (5) Covering; (6) Ministry; (7) Business; (8) Israel; (9) Glorious individual, church, or ministry (western red cedar house); (10) Death (demolition); (11) Spiritual renewal (interior renovation/decoration); (12) Superficial change (exterior renovation); (13) Delivered from a demon (clean house); (14) Demon-oppressed or -possessed (unclean home).

Also see *Building, Home, Interior of a House, Mansion, New House, Old House, Palace, Real Estate, Run-Down-House,* and *Temple.*

(1) 2 Cor. 5:1; Heb. 3:6; (2) 1 Tim. 3:15; 2 Tim. 2:20; Heb. 3:6; 1 Pet. 2:5; (3) 1 Tim. 3:4; 5:13; (5) Gen. 19:8; Matt. 8:8; Also as in, "under the head of the house"; (7) John 2:16; (8) Heb. 8:10; (9) 1 Kings 6:9; (10) John 2:19-21; (11) 2 Chron. 24:4; (12) Joel 2:13; Matt. 13:20-21; 1 Pet. 3:3; (13-14) Luke 11:24-25.

Houseboat: (1) Family; (2) Flowing in the anointing; (3) Taking things easy (cruising).

Also see *Cruise Ship* and *Yacht.*

(1) Gen. 7:1; (2) Ezek. 47:9; (3) See *Holiday.*

House Fire: (1) Judgment; (2) Words against your ministry; (3) Power of God, revival, or Pentecost (non-destructive fire); (4) Fire of God; (5) Angry individual.

Also see *Fire* and *House.*

(1) Rev. 18:8; (2) James 3:5-6; (3) Exod. 3:2-3; Acts 2:3; (4) Obad. 1:18; (5) Gen. 44:18.

House For Sale: (1) Soul in the balance; (2) Not yet purchased by Christ; (3) Selling out; (4) Vulnerable to exploitation.

(1) Joel 3:14; (2) 1 Cor. 6:19-20; (3) 2 Tim. 4:10a; (4) Matt. 26:14-16.

Hovercraft: (1) Spiritual vehicle or spirit; (2) (+) Angel; (3) (-) Demonic spirit (doing negative things or if the hovercraft is dark in color).

Also see *Amphibious Vehicle.*

(1) Job 4:15; Ezek. 10:17; (2) Mark 6:49; (3) Matt. 12:43.

Hundred: (1) Complete count (10x10 = complete completeness); (2) Whole; (3) Complete blessing; (4) Maximum blessing; (5) Financial wholeness ($100); (6) The debt of unforgiveness; (7) The glory of God (300); (8) The shame of people (300); (9) Full harvest.

(1-2) Luke 15:4-6 (the whole flock); (2) The tithe is 1/10 and means, as we have given the first 10th of our income, we acknowledge His right to the rest. It also means "as is the first round" (1-10), so the rest is likewise God-given; (3-4) Matt. 13:8; Mark 4:8; (6) Matt. 18:28; (7) Gen. 5:22; 45:22; Judg. 7:2, 6-7; 1 Kings 10:17; (8) Mark 14:4-5 (Mary was shamed); 2 Chron. 12:9-10; (9) Matt. 13:23.

Hunger: (1) Humbling; (2) Spiritual desire for God and His Word; (3) Judgment; (4) Desire for righteousness; (5) In need; (6) Denying the flesh; (7) Vulnerable to false doctrines.

Also see *Fasting* and *Thirsty*.

(1-2) Deut. 8:3; (3) Deut. 28:48; 32:24; Job 5:5; (4) Matt. 5:6; (5) Job 22:7; (6) Ps. 107:5; (7) Prov. 27:7; Matt. 4:6; Luke 4:10-11.

Hunter/Hunting: Everything about hunting in Scripture carries a negative or anti-Christian tone. Examples of meanings are: (1) The enemy; (2) The fleshly person; (3) A hunter of people or godly people; (4) Evil (hunts the violent person); (5) Surety for another; (6) Laziness (not roasting that which is caught); (7) Adultery (hunt for lives); (8) Being hunted may be a sign of iniquity/sin; (9) False prophets hunt for souls; (10) Corruption, disloyalty, or unfaithfulness.

(1) Prov. 6:5; 1 Pet. 5:8; (2) Gen. 25:27; 27:5; (3) Gen. 10:9; 1 Sam. 24:11; 26:20; (4) Ps. 140:11; (5) Prov. 6:1-5; (6) Prov. 12:27; (7) Prov. 6:26; (8) Jer. 16:16-18; (9) Ezek. 13:18-21; (10) Mic. 7:2.

Hurricane: See Storm.

Hurry (In a Hurry): (1) Get prepared (sense of urgency); (2) Quick departure; (3) Journey ahead; (4) Birth of a ministry; (5) Time running out (urgency); (6) Driven by the world; (7) God is not in a hurry; (8) Turning away from God; (9) Act quickly; (10) Escape; (11) Decisiveness required; (12) Eager to sin; (13) Not blessed; (14) Urgent repentance required.

Also see *Running* and *Urgency*.

(1-3) Gen. 19:15; Exod. 12:11; (4) Gen. 41:14; (5) Luke 14:21; 2 Pet. 3:12 (Christ is coming back); (6) Exod. 5:13; (7) Josh. 10:13; Isa. 28:16b; (8) Judg. 2:17; Ps. 16:4; (9) 1 Sam. 20:38; Acts 12:7; Rev. 2:5; (10) 1 Sam. 23:26; 2 Sam. 4:4; 17:16; Ps. 55:8; Acts 22:18; (11) 1 Sam. 25:17-18, 34; (12) Prov. 1:16, 7:23; 19:2; (13) Prov. 20:21; 28:20; 29:20; (14) Rev. 2:16.

Husband: (1) Jesus; (2) God; (3) Natural husband.

Also see *Groom.*

(1) Matt. 9:15; 25:1, 13; John 3:29a; (2) Isa. 54:5; (3) John 4:16.

Hut: (1) Spiritually impoverished individual.

Also see *Cabin* and *Shack.*

(1) 2 Sam. 9:4; (cf. 1 Cor. 6:19).

Hyena: (1) Warning of an attack upon a spiritual sleeper; (2) Call to stay awake spiritually.

(1-2) Isa. 52:1a; Luke 22:45-46.

Hysterectomy: (1) No longer able to win souls (unfertile church/person); (3) Barren church/person; (4) Robbed of the promises of God.

Also see *Birth.*

(1-2) Rev. 3:1; (4) Gen. 20:18.

Ice: (1) Cold; (2) Cold person; (3) No love (increase of wickedness); (4) Stopping the flow of the Spirit; (5) Deceitful heart; (6) Hardened hearts who melt under pressure.

Also see *Black* and *Cold.*

(1-2) Ps. 147:17 (KJV); (3) Matt. 24:12; (4) Job 38:30; Ps. 147:17-18; (5-6) Job 6:15-17.

Ice Cream: (1) Not sharing the Gospel; (2) Preaching the Gospel without love; (3) Promises of God; (4) Deceptive food (a sweetener).

Also see *Cream* and *Dessert.*

(1) Heb. 5:13 (cream is the best part of the milk); (2) Matt. 24:12; Phil. 1:17; (3) Exod. 3:8 (milk and honey); Lev. 20:24; (4) Prov. 20:17 & Prov. 23:1-3.

Ice Skating: (1) Gracious in a cold and hard environment; (2) In jeopardy (on thin ice); (3) At risk (thin ice); (4) Walking by faith in a cold-hearted environment (walking on water).

Also see *Slide* and *Slip.*

(1) Lam. 3:30a; Matt. 5:39; (2-3) 2 Sam. 23:17; Lam. 5:9; Rom. 16:4; 1 Cor. 15:30; Phil. 2:30; (4) Matt. 14:28-29.

Icing (Cake): (1) Sugar-coating the message.
(1) 2 Tim. 4:3-4.

Idol: (1) Devils; (2) False god; (3) Snare; (4) Silver and gold.
(1) 1 Cor. 10:19-20; (2) Ps. 96:5; (3) Ps. 106:36; (4) Ps. 115:4; 135:15.

Immigration: (1) Coming into the Kingdom; (2) Entering into the Promise.
(1) Matt. 12:28; Luke 17:21; John 3:5; (2) Deut. 27:3b.

Incense: (1) Prayers; (2) Worship; (3) Idol worship.
Also see *Perfume.*
(1) Ps. 141:2; Rev. 8:3-4; (2) Exod. 25:6; 30:7; 2 Chron. 32:12b; (3) Jer. 1:16; 44:19.

Indian (American): Explore associations held by the dreamer or visionary.
Also see *First Nations Peoples, Old Man,* and *Native/s.*

Indian (Asian): (1) Explore associations held by the dreamer or visionary; (2) See Foreign and Foreigner.
Also see *Black Man, Caucasian,* and *First Nations Peoples.*

Indigenous: See First Nations People and Native/s.

Industry/ial: (1) Big business; (2) Commercialization; (3) Mechanical.
Also see *Business, Busy,* and *Machines.*
(1-2) 1 Kings 10:14-15; 2 Chron. 1:17; (3) 2 Chron. 26:15a.

Information Desk: (1) Approaching God for guidance.
(1) Prov. 4:11; Jer. 29:11-14a.

In Front Of: See Before.

Ingrown Toenail: (1) Hurt leader that affects the Body's walk (big toe); (2) Self-inflicted problem that becomes painful and affects your walk; (3) Problems with your children/spiritual children (smallest members of your body); (4) Small issue that causes a lot of pain; (5) A nation's suffering which affects other nations around it.
Also see *Toes.*
(1) 1 Cor. 12:12; (2) 1 Sam. 2:29-30; Prov. 29:15; (3) 1 Cor. 12:12 & Gal. 6:10; cf. Matt. 10:35-36; (4) 1 Sam. 2:29-30; (5) Dan. 2:41-42.

Injection: See Needle.

Ink: (1) Writing; (2) Book (as in becoming an author); (3) The Spirit written on people's hearts; (4) May speak of coming face-to-face rather than writing; (5) An ink spot in a pocket speaks of writing that may offend.
(1-2) Jer. 36:18; (3) 2 Cor. 3:3; (4) 2 John 1:12; 3 John 1:13.

Inner Tube: (1) The Spirit; (2) The spiritual person.
Also see *Balloon, Bicycle,* and *Wheel.*
(1) Ezek. 1:20; John 3:8; (2) Eph. 3:16.

Insect: (1) Pest; (2) Plague; (3) Small.
Also see *Bugs.*
(1-2) Exod. 5:3 & Exod. 8:21; (3) Matt. 23:24.

Inside Out. Like back to front: (1) A person who has things reversed (i.e. money before Kingdom); (2) Revealing or perceiving the secrets of the heart.
(1-2) Matt. 6:33; 23:25-28.

Insincere: (1) Heart not in something.
(1) Prov. 23:7b; 1 Cor. 5:8; Phil. 1:16-17.

Institution: (1) Church.
(1) Acts 11:26; 15:5.

Insurance: (1) Covering; (2) The Holy Spirit; (3) Salvation (house insurance); (4) Mercy (goodness of God); (5) The grace of God.
(1) Exod. 12:7, 13; (2) 2 Cor. 1:22; 5:5; Eph. 1:13-14; (3) 1 Cor. 3:9; 2 Cor. 5:1; (4) Ps. 27:13; 103:4-5; Jon. 2:6-8; (5) Jer. 31:2; Acts 11:23; 15:11.

Intel (CPU): See Computer (CPU).

Interior Decoration: See House.

Interior of a House: (1) Within the believer; (2) A new interior suggests renewal; (3) A run-down interior suggests the old self in operation.
Also see *House.*
(1) 2 Cor. 5:1.

International Flight: (1) Multi-national ministry; (2) From earth to Heaven (entering Heaven); (3) Travelling from the earthly realm to the heavenly one.

Also see *Overseas*.

(1) Acts 19:26; (2) John 1:51; Rev. 4:1; (3) 2 Kings 2:11; Acts 1:9.

Intersection: See Crossroads, Road, and T-Junction.

Intestines: (1) Eating disorder (pulling intestines out of mouth); (2) Trials (pulling intestines out of mouth); (3) Wickedness (intestines spilling out); (4) Condemned to judgment (intestines spilling out).

Also see *Belly*.

(1) Matt. 15:17; (2) Prov. 18:14 (can't stomach or tolerate it anymore); (3) Acts 1:18; (4) 2 Sam. 20:10; Acts 1:18.

Investing: (1) Sowing into God's Kingdom/harvest.

(1) Prov. 31:16.

Iron: (1) Man; (2) Strong/Strength; (3) Dominion; (4) Strength of people; (5) Judgment; (6) Hard; (7) Hardened/Obstinate/Stubborn; (8) Bound; (9) Barrier; (10) Permanent; (11) Strong leadership; (12) Oppression (furnace of iron); (13) Works; (14) Earthly (from the earth).

(1) Prov. 27:17; (2) Josh. 17:16-18 (iron chariots symbolize the strength of people); Judg. 1:19; 1 Kings 22:11; Jer. 1:18; Dan. 2:40; (3) Deut. 33:25; Josh. 17:16-18; Judg. 4:3; 2 Sam. 12:31 (subjection); (4) 2 Sam. 23:7; Job 41:7 (KJV), 27; 1 Kings 22:11; 2 Chron. 18:10; Prov. 27:17; (5) Deut. 28:23; Ezek. 22:20-22; Amos 1:3; (6) Job 19:24; Jer. 17:1; (7) Lev. 26:19; Isa. 48:4; Jer. 6:28; (8) Ps. 105:18; 149:8; Jer. 28:13-14; (9) Lev. 26:19; Ps. 107:16; Acts 12:10; (10) Jer. 1:18; (11) Ps. 2:9; Rev. 2:27; 12:5; 18:12; 19:15; (12) Deut. 4:20; 1 Kings 8:51; (13) Deut. 27:5; Josh. 8:31; Job 41:27; (14) Job 28:2a.

Iron Furnace: (1) The world (Egypt).

(1) Deut. 4:20; 1 Kings 8:51.

Ironing: (1) Seared conscience; (2) Liar; (3) Hypocrisy; (4) Dealing with sin; (5) Spotless ready for Christ (ironing shirt or dress); (6) Starchiness (proud); (7) Rebellion.

(1-3) 1 Tim. 4:2; (4) Eph. 5:26-27; (5) Eph. 5:27; (6) Ps. 75:5; (7) Deut. 31:27.

IRS: (1) Giving grudgingly (feels like you are being taxed); (2) Money-hungry church; (3) Literal tax issue; (3) Sowing into the heavenly treasury; (4) Respecting/fearing God's financial right.

(1) 2 Cor. 9:7; (2) Rev. 3:17; (3) Mal. 3:10; 2 Cor. 9:6; (4) Deut. 8:18; Acts 5:3-4.

Islam: (1) "Submission to Allah"; (2) Legalistic church; (3) Militant church; (4) Counterfeit Christianity; (5) Antichrist spirit.

(1) Literal translation; (2) Gal. 3:7-11; (3) Matt. 26:52; (4) 2 Cor. 11:4; (5) 1 John 2:22.

Island: (1) Offshore; (2) Independent; (3) Remote; (4) Peaceful and serene; (5) An individual; (6) Independent culture.

(1) Rev. 1:9; (2) Gen. 10:5; (3) Ps. 72:10 & Jon. 1:3; (4) Rev. 1:9; (5) Job 22:30 (KJV); As in, "no man is an island"; (6) Gen. 10:5 (KJV).

Itching: (1) Judgment; (2) Hearing what you want to hear (itching ears).

(1) Deut. 28:27; (2) 2 Tim. 4:3.

Ivory: (1) Strong revelation (powerful word); (2) Righteousness; (3) Beauty and strength.

Also see *Elephant, High Rise Apartment,* and *Rhino.*

(1) Song. 5:14 (the heart of God); (2) 1 Kings 10:18 (cf. Ps. 96:10, Jer. 23:5); (3) Song. 7:4.

Jacket: (1) Mantle; (2) Authority; (3) Position or role; (4) Limited authority (short-sleeved jacket).

Also see *Coat, Mantle,* and *Robe.*

(1-3) 2 Kings 2:13-15; (4) 1 Sam. 15:27-28.

Janitor: (1) Minister content with the status quo; (2) Minister just doing a job; (3) Minister working to keep everybody happy.

Also see *Caretaker.*

(1) Ps. 55:19; Jer. 48:11 (maintenance person); (2) John 10:12-13; (3) Matt. 27:15-17, 22, 24; Acts 12:1-3.

Japanese: (1) Technology; (2) Technology-driven entertainment; (3) Strong traditional culture.

Also see *Foreign.*

(1) 2 Chron. 26:15; (2) Rev. 3:17-18; (3) Gal. 1:14; 1 Pet. 1:18.

Jaw/Jaws: (1) Mouth; (2) Words; (3) Greed (jaws); (4) Vicious attack of words (jaws).

Also see *Shark*.

(1) Judg. 15:16-19 (this passage prefigures Christ's victory and the outpouring of the Spirit); (3) Job 29:16; (4) Prov. 30:14.

Jazz: (1) Improvised or spontaneous worship; (2) Ad libbing.

Also see *Jazz* in Name and Place Dictionary.

(1-2) Josh. 5:14; 2 Sam. 6:16.

Jealousy: (1) Spiritually unfaithful; (2) Anger; (3) Displacement (Explore if you have in some way been replaced in the dream by those people about whom you experienced jealousy. This will need to be repented of, and soul-ties will need to be cut in the spirit).

(1) 2 Cor. 11:2, 4; 1 Cor. 10:21-22; (2) Rom. 10:19; Zech. 8:2; (3) 1 Sam. 18:7-8.

Jeep: (1) Spiritual warfare.

Also see *Four Wheel Drive*.

(1) Eph. 6:10-11.

Jello /Jelly: (1) Spiritual food without substance.

(1) 1 Cor. 3:2.

Jesus: (1) Literally Jesus (God); (2) A husband; (3) Your pastor.

Also see *Husband, Pastor,* and *Shepherd*.

(1) Exod. 3:13-14 & John 8:58; 2 Cor. 4:4; (2) Eph. 5:22-23; (3) John 10:11.

Jet Ski: (1) Thrill-seeker.

(1) Acts 8:18-19.

Jetty: (1) Church (as an outreach to the world [sea]); (2) Preaching platform.

Also see *Sea*.

(1) Acts 11:22; 13:1-3; (2) Matt. 4:19 & Rom. 10:14-15.

Jewelry: (1) Gifts of the Holy Spirit; (2) Worldly favor; (3) Willing heart; (4) Spoils of war; (5) Godly favor; (6) Discretion; (7) Lips of knowledge; (8) Over-emphasis on the outward; (9) Salvation, righteousness, and joy;

(10) Worldly allurements; (11) Those who bring glory to God; (12) The adornment of the harlot church.

(1) Gen. 24:53; (2) Exod. 3:22; 11:2-3; 12:36; Job 28:12-18 (cannot be compared to wisdom); (3) Exod. 35:22; (4) Num. 31:51, 53-54; 2 Chron. 20:25; (5) 2 Chron. 32:27-29; Ezek. 16:12; (6) Prov. 11:22; (7) Prov. 20:15; (8) Isa. 3:21; (9) Isa. 61:10; (10) Ezek. 23:26-27; Hos. 2:13-14; (11) Mal. 3:17; 1 Cor. 3:12; 1 Pet. 2:5; (12) Rev. 17:4-5; 18:12.

Jezebel: See Jezebel in Name and Place Dictionary.

Job Interview: (1) Date with destiny; (2) Test before service; (3) New job.
(1) Acts 9:6, 15; Gal. 1:15-16; (2) Luke 4:13-14.

Jogging: (1) Lukewarm (half-hearted); (1) Rev. 3:16. See Running.

Join: See Cleave.

Joking: (1) Not taking a situation seriously.
Also see *Laughter.*
(1) Eccl.2:1-2, 7:4b; Isa. 24:11.

Judge: (1) God; (2) Jesus Christ.
(1) Acts 7:7; Heb. 12:23; 13:4; Rev. 20:12; (2) Acts 10:42; Rom. 2:16; 2 Tim. 4:1.

Jugular Vein: (1) Poisoned thoughts (snake or spider bite on neck); (2) Spiritual life drained (blood sucked from neck).
Also see *Neck* and *Throat.*
(1) Ps. 58:4; Gal. 3:1; (2) Lev. 17:11.

Jumping: (1) Joining (jumping on something); (2) To assail someone (jumping on someone); (3) Overcoming; (4) Without patience or taking the shortcut; (5) Sudden discipline (being jumped on); (6) Sudden response to a command.
Also see *Leaping.*
(1) As in, "jumping on the band wagon"; (2) Luke 10:30; (3) Ps. 18:29; John 16:33; (4) As in, "jumping the queue"; (5) As in, "they jumped on her straight away"; (6) Matt. 8:9.

Junction (T or Y): See T-Junction.

Jungle: (1) World; (2) Trials; (3) Complicated journey; (4) Lush growth.

Also see *Forest* and *Rainforest.*

(1) John 13:31 & 1 Pet. 5:8; 16:11; (2) Jer. 6:21; (3) Isa. 57:14; (4) Prov. 11:28.

Junk Food: (1) Wrong doctrine; (2) Not doctrinally sound; (3) Convenient food.

(1) 1 Tim.1:3-4; 4:1, 6-7; 2 Tim. 4:3-4; (3) 2 Tim. 4:3.

Kaleidoscope: (1) Turmoil in relationship and emotions (possible nightmare as a child); (2) Receiving the glory of God as a child; (3) Confusion.

(1) Matt. 19:14; (2) Matt. 18:10; Rom. 8:17; (3) 1 Cor. 14:33; James 3:16.

Kangaroo: (1) Jump; (2) Bounce; (3) Boxing; (4) Australia; (5) Pouch; (6) Someone who has energy (bounce); (7) In the wilderness; (8) Someone who doesn't respect boundaries (fence jumper); (9) Australian church/es.

(3) 1 Cor. 9:26; (6) 1 Kings 18:44b-46; (7) Luke 1:80; (8) Exod. 20:17; Luke 12:39; John 10:1; (9) By association.

Kayak: See Canoe.

Kebab: (1) Mixed diet [God's Word and world's word inter-mixed] (i.e. meat, onions, capsicum, meat, etc).

(1) Job 12:11; Heb. 5:14; 13:9.

Kerb (Curb): (1) Boundary on God's path; (2) The Love of God; (3) The Fear of God.

Also see *Gutter/s.*

(1) Num. 22:24; (2) 2 Cor. 5:14a (The love of God keeps us from legalism); (3) Ps. 36:1 (The fear of God keeps us from lasciviousness [fleshly lifestyle]).

Key/s: (1) Authority; (2) Opportunity; (3) Access; (4) The rhema word (off your tongue); (5) Control; (6) Way out; (7) Heart; (8) God's will; (9) Prayer; (10) Faith; (11) Unity; (12) Praise; (13) Revelation; (14) Prophecy; (15) Knowledge; (16) Pivotal or indispensable person (i.e. "key player"); (17) Love; (18) The Gifts of the Spirit; (19) Signs and wonders; (20) *The Divinity Code to Understanding Your Dreams and Visions.*

Also see *Door.*

(1) Isa. 22:22; Matt. 16:19; (2) Luke 11:52; (3) Judg. 3:25; Rev. 9:1; 20:1; (4) Matt. 16:18-19 (tongue: small instrument that opens your destiny); (5) Matt. 16:19; Rev. 9:1; (6) Rev. 9:1-3; (7) Song. 5:2-6; Acts 16:14; Acts 13:22 & Rev.

3:7; (8) Isa. 22:22; 45:1; Luke 22:42; Col. 4:3; (9) Matt. 16:16-19; (cf. 1 Kings 18:1, 41-45); (10) Rom. 5:2a; 2 Cor. 5:7; Gal. 3:5; 5:6; Eph. 2:8; Heb. 11:5, 8, 29, 30; (11) Ps. 133: 1-3; 1 Pet. 3:7; (12) Ps. 100:4; (13-14) Matt. 16:16-19; (15) Luke 11:52; (16) Mark 12:28, 30; Rom. 2:4b; (17) John 3:16; (18) Matt. 16:19 (give = gift); (19) Deut. 6:22-23; (20) Prov. 25:2.

Kicking: (1) Resisting; (2) Aggression; (3) Using strength, power, or force.

Also see *Ball.*

(1) Acts 9:5; (2) Num. 22:23-25; Ps. 36:11; (3) Ps. 147:10.

Kidnap/ped: (1) Take/n away; (2) The devil holding someone for ransom.

(1) Gen. 30:15; (2) Tim. 2:25-26.

Kill/ed/ing: (1) Crucifying the flesh; (2) Stopping something; (3) Getting rid of; (4) Slandering or speaking against.

Also see *Assassin, Mafia, Murder,* and *Strangle/d.*

(1) Gal. 2:20; (2) John 19:30; (3) 2 Sam. 12:9; (4) Matt. 5:21-22.

Killer Whale: (1) Prophetic warrior; (2) Familiar spirit (appears friendly, but is dangerous); (3) Church leader who is a predator; (4) Spiritual predator.

Also see *Dolphin, Walrus,* and *Whale.*

(1) 1 Sam. 15:32-33; 1 Kings 18:40; (2) Matt. 7:15; (3) John 12:6; (4) Acts 8:18-19.

King: (1) Jesus Christ; (2) Authority; (3) Dominion.

(1-3) Rev. 1:5.

King Cobra: (1) The devil.

Also see *Snake.*

(1) Eph. 6:12 & Rev. 12:9.

King Kong: (1) Stronghold (defiant); (2) Strong person; (3) Stronghold of affluence; (4) Strength.

Also see *Monkey.*

(1) 1 Sam. 17:4, 23-25; (2) Matt. 12:29; (3) 1 Kings 10:22; 2 Chron. 9:21.

Kiss: (1) Empty promises; (2) Affection or embrace; (3) Seduction; (4) Betrayal; (5) Departure/farewell; (6) Welcome/greeting; (7) Deception; (8) Enticement; (9) Worship; (10) Union (joined).

(1) Ps. 12:2b; 55:21; (2) <u>Gen. 29:11</u>; 48:10; 1 Sam. 10:1; 1 Kings 19:18; Ps. 2:12; 85:10; Prov. 24:26; Hos. 13:2; Song. 1:2; 8:1; 1 Pet. 5:14; (3) 2 Sam. 15:5; Prov. 7:13; (4) 2 Sam. 15:5-6; <u>Matt. 26:48</u>-49; Mark 14:44-45; (5) Gen. 31:28, 55; 50:1; Ruth 1:9, 14; (6) Exod. 4:27; 18:7; 2 Sam. 14:33; 1 Kings 19:20; Luke 7:45; 15:20; Acts 20:37-38; <u>Rom. 16:16</u>; 1 Cor. 16:20; (7) Gen. 27:26-27; 2 Sam. 20:9; Prov. 27:6; (8) Job 31:27; (9) Luke 7:38; (10) Ps. 85:10.

Kitchen: (1) Heart; (2) The human spirit; (3) The place of preparation; (4) The Church (especially a commercial kitchen); (5) The place of storage; (5) Mind (upstairs kitchen); (7) Under pressure (turning up the heat).

Also see *House.*

(1) <u>Hos. 7:6</u>; Neh. 13:5; The kitchen is the heart of the house and the house is a temple; (3) Gen. 18:6; 27:17; Exod. 12:39; Judg. 6:19; 2 Kings 6:23; Neh. 5:18; Ps. 23:5; Matt. 22:4; 26:17-19; Luke 14:17; Acts 10:10; (4) Acts 6:1 (as a distribution center); (Matt. 16:18 & John 21:17b); (5) Neh. 13:5; (6) As the place where we "cook up" ideas; (7) Dan. 3:19; Luke 10:40.

Kite Flying: See Flying Kite.

Kitten: See Cat (Domestic).

Kiwi Fruit: (1) Fruit of new zeal in God (New Zeal-land); (2) Undergoing a spiritual clean-up.

(1) Ps. 69:9; 119:139; <u>Isa. 9:7</u>; 59:17; (2) John 2:14-17.

K-Mart: See Shop and K-Mart in Name and Place Dictionary.

Knee/s: (1) Relate to the heart; (2) Birthing; (3) Prayer/supplication; (4) Humbling submission/subjection; (5) Submission to Christ; (6) Devotion to God or false gods; (7) Fear (particularly knocking knees); (8) Weakness; (9) Being comforted (sitting on the knees); (10) To be blessed (kneeling).

(1) Rom. 10:9-10 & Phil. 2:10-11; Rom. 11:4; (2) Gen. 30:3; 1 Kings 18:42; Job 3:12; (3) 1 Kings 8:54; 2 Chron. 6:13; Ezra 9:5-6; Dan. 6:10-11; Eph. 3:14; (4) Gen. 41:43; 2 Kings 1:13; (5) <u>Phil. 2:10</u>; Rom. 14:11; (6) 1 Kings 19:18; Ezek. 47:4; Rom. 11:4; (7) Isa. 35:3-4; Ezek. 7:17; 21:7 (on the receipt of bad news); <u>Dan. 5:6</u>; Nah. 2:10; (fear indicates a melted heart); (8) Ps. 109:24; Heb. 12:12; (9) 2 Kings 4:20; Isa. 66:12-13; (10) Gen. 48:9, 12 (the Hebrew *barakh* means "to bend the knee and to bless").

Knife: (1) Words; (2) Person who causes division (good or bad); (3) Cut away the flesh (pocket knife); (4) Hold your tongue (knife to throat); (5) Threat; (6) Fear and intimidation; (7) Protection; (8) Dividing [judging] truth (butter knife); (9) Words of people.

(1) Prov. 30:14; Heb. 4:12; (2) Judg. 19:29; Luke 12:51-53; Heb. 4:12-13; (3) Josh. 5:2-3; (4) Prov. 23:2; (5-6) Isa. 54:17; (7) 2 Kings 11:8; (8) 2 Tim. 2:15; (9) Prov. 30:14.

Knit: (1) Joined; (2) United; (3) Woven; (4) Love; (5) Holding together.

(1) Acts 10:11; (2) Judg. 20:11; Col. 2:2; (3) Col. 2:19; (4) 1 Sam. 18:1; 1 Chron. 12:17; (5) Col. 1:17.

Knives: See Knife.

Knock/ing: (1) Desire; (2) Opportunity (if you are knocking, it may mean you are seeking opportunities; if you hear knocking, it may mean an opportunity opening to you); (3) Jesus' desire for intimacy; (4) Desire for answers/seeking God; (5) Heart asleep; (6) Need for readiness; (7) Seeking fellowship; (8) Not known by Christ (too late in entering into intimacy); (9) Call to wait on God; (10) God trying to get your attention (a sign).

Also see *Door, Doorbell,* and *Calling.*

(1) Matt. 7:7-8; (2-3) Rev. 3:20; (opportunity knocks) (3) Matt. 7:7-8; Luke 11:9-10; (4) Song. 5:2; (5) Luke 12:36; (6) Acts 12:13-16; (7) Luke 13:25; (9) Luke 12:36; (10) Rev. 3:20.

Knot: (1) Stronghold; (2) Secured; (3) Enigma or parable; (4) Tied up; (5) Having trouble finding release.

(1-2) Matt. 12:29; Mark 3:27; (3-4) Dan. 5:16 (*enigma* is literally "knot" [tied up]); (5) John 19:12.

Knuckles: (1) Fight or violence; (2) Disciplined; (3) Get serious and put in hard work.

(1) Exod. 21:18; Isa. 58:4; (2) As in, "wrapped over the knuckles"; (3) As in, "knuckle down."

Kombi Van: (1) Alternative or unconventional ministry.

(1) Matt. 9:33; Mark 2:12.

Kookaburra: (1) Mocking spirit.

(1) Prov. 1:26; Isa. 28:22.

Ladder: (1) The Cross; (2) Christ; (3) Entry into the spirit realm; (4) Salvation ministry.

Also see *Steps* and *Lift.*

(1) John 3:14; 8:28; 12:32-33; that which stands between Heaven and earth; (2-3) Gen. 28:12 & John 1:51; (4) John 12:32-33.

Lady: See Woman.

Lake: (1) Harvest field; (2) Place of testing; (3) May symbolize your life journey (crossing lake); (4) Place of final judgment (lake of fire); (5) Church (as a corporate reservoir of the Spirit); (6) The peace of God; (7) Restricting the move of the Spirit.

Also see *Dam, Pond,* and *Water.*

(1) Luke 5:2, 4; (2) Luke 8:23-26; (3) John 6:15-21; (4) Rev. 19:20; (5) John 7:38-39 & 2 Cor. 6:16 (corporate temple); (6) Ps. 23:2; (7) Acts 6:10; 7:51.

Lamb/s: (1) Young Christians; (2) Christ; (3) Sacrifice/offering; (4) Innocence; (5) Covenant witness; (6) Redemption price; (7) Poor man's wife.

(1) John 21:15; 1 Sam. 17:34; Isa. 40:11; (2) Isa. 53:7; John 1:29, 36; Acts 8:32; 1 Pet. 1:19; Rev. 5:6-13; (3) Gen. 22:7-8; Exod. 12:3; 29:38ff; Lev. 4:32; 12:6; 1 Sam. 7:9; (4) Luke 10:3; (5) Gen. 21:28-32; (6) Exod. 12:3-17; 13:13; (7) 2 Sam. 12:3-9.

Lamington: See Cake.

Lamp: (1) God's Word; (2) The believer's heart; (3) A church; (4) The Spirit of God (seven lamps).

Also see *Candle, Lampstand, Light, Flame,* and *Torch.*

(1) Ps. 119:105; (2) Prov. 20:27; Matt. 5:14; (3) Rev. 1:20; (4) Rev. 4:5.

Lampstand: (1) Church; (2) Revelation (enlightenment).

Also see *Lamp.*

(1-2) Rev. 1:20;

Land: (1) The promises of God; (2) The believer filled with the Holy Spirit; (3) The Kingdom of God; (4) This is our inheritance.

(1) Exod. 12:25; Deut. 6:3; 9:28; (2-3) Luke 11:20; 17:21; (cf. Luke 24:49 & Acts 2:1-4; This parallels Israel physically entering Canaan. Also note that Jesus

explains a two-fold fulfillment to the question of Acts 1:6-8. He says there is a future physical fulfillment and a present one through the indwelling of the Holy Spirit. Also note that it is the person who waits that inherits the land (see Ps. 37:9) and also is anointed (see Isa. 40:31)); (4) Gen. 12:7; Deut. 19:8.

Landlord: (1) The devil; (2) Lord Jesus

(1) John 14:30b; (2) Luke 12:45.

Landmark: (1) The Cross; (2) Point of reference for guidance or direction; (3) Memorial to faith; (4) Memorial to God's provision; (5) Point of remembrance.

Also see *Lighthouse* and *Monument*.

(1) Col. 2:14-15; Gal. 6:14; (2-4) Josh. 4:3-7; Matt. 26:13; (5) Exod. 17:14-15.

Laneway: (1) The narrow way; (2) Side-tracked to another Christ/Gospel; (3) The way of Balaam.

Also see *Alley*.

(1) Matt. 7:13-14; (2) John 14:6 & 2 Cor. 11:4; (3) Num. 22:26; 2 Pet. 2:15; Jude 1:11; Rev. 2:14.

Lap (noun): (1) Comfort; (2) Heart.

(1) 2 Kings 4:20; (2) 2 Kings 4:39; Neh. 5:13 (KJV); Prov. 6:27 (NIV); Eccl.7:9 (NIV).

Laptop Computer: (1) Heart; (2) Mind; (3) May represent whatever you use it for (work, writing, games, presentations, etc.); (4) Itinerant ministry.

Also see *Computer, Desktop, Hard Drive, Hardware, Motherboard,* and *Software*.

(1) Ps. 139:23 (KJV); Esther 1:20-22; (2) Eph. 4:23; (3) 1 Cor. 4:12a; (4) Neh. 2:7.

Laser: (1) Revelatory word (precise word); (2) Prophecy; (3) Judgment; (4) Word of judgment; (5) Alarm or warning; (6) Made a target in the spirit (laser dot on a person/item); (7) Study focus (laser pointer); (8) Measuring/analyzing levels (being measured up).

(1) Ps. 119:105, 130; Heb. 4:12; (2) 2 Pet. 1:19; (3) Hos. 6:5; (4) Isa. 51:4; Zeph. 3:5; (5) Joel 2:1; (6) 1 Kings 22:34; Job 2:5-6; (7) Isa. 50:4; (8) Amos 7:7.

Laundry: (1) Cleansing.

(1) Mal. 3:2b.

Laughter: (1) Rejoicing; (2) Ridicule and scorn; (3) Faith's receipt; (4) Can cover a heavy heart; (5) Fool (quickly spent); (6) Unbelief.

Also see *Joking*.

(1) Job 8:21; James 4:9; (2) 2 Kings 19:21; Ps. 2:4; 22:7 (KJV); Matt. 9:24 (KJV); Mark 5:40 (KJV); Luke 8:53 (KJV); (3) Gen. 21:6-7; Ps. 126:1-2; (4) Prov. 14:13; Eccl. 7:3; (5) Eccl. 7:6; (6) Gen. 17:17-18; 18:12-15.

Lava: (1) Wrath of God; (2) Sudden destruction; (3) Judgment; (4) Presence or glory of God.

Also see *Fire* and *Volcano*.

(1) Mic. 1:3a-5a; (2) 2 Pet. 3:10, 12; Num. 26:10; (3) Ezek. 22:20; (4) Ps. 46:6; 97:5; Nah. 1:5.

Law: (1) The Word of God; (2) Legalism; (3) Love; (4) The law of faith; (5) The law of the mind (that written on our hearts); (6) The law of the Spirit of Life; (7) Liberty; (8) The writings of Moses; (9) All the Old Testament; (10) The law of sin and death; (11) The civil legal system; (12) Brings sin to light.

(1) James 1:25; 2:12-13; (2) Matt. 12:2, 10; 22:17; 27:6; (3) Mark 12:29-31; Rom. 13:8, 10; Gal. 5:14; James 2:8; (4) Rom. 3:27-28; 4:13, 16; Gal. 3:23-24; (5) Rom. 7:23, 25; Heb. 8:10; (6) Rom. 8:2, 4; (7) James 1:25; (8) Luke 2:22; John 1:17, 45; 7:19, 23; 8:5; Acts 13:39; 15:5; 28:23; Rom. 2:12-13; 1 Cor. 9:9; (9) Ps. 82:6 & John 10:34; Micah 4:7 & John 12:34; John 15:25 & Ps. 35:19; Ps. 69:4; 109:3-5; Isa. 28:11-12 & 1 Cor. 14:21; (10) Rom. 7:7-9, 23; 8:2; 1 Cor. 15:56; (11) Matt. 5:40; Acts 22:25; 1 Cor. 6:1, 6-7; (12) Rom. 3:20.

Lawn: See Grass.

Lawnmower: (1) Ministry in the flesh; (2) Ministry keeping everybody under control (tall poppy syndrome); (3) Harvest ministry.

(1) Ps. 37:1-2; (2) Rev. 2:15 (hierarchy); (3) Joel 3:13a; John 4:35; Rev. 14:15.

Lawyer: (1) Someone giving counsel; (2) Holy Spirit as Counselor or Advocate; (3) Christ as Advocate; (4) Someone who is legalistic; (5) One who attempts to trap you with your words; (6) Tester; (7) Hypocritical believer who knows the Word, but not the Spirit; (8) Intercession.

(1) Rev. 3:18; (2) John 15:26; (3) 1 John 2:1; (4) Gal. 3:10; Tit. 3:9; (5-6) Matt. 22:35-36; Luke 10:25; (7) Luke 11:45-48, 52; Luke 14:3-5; (8) Rom. 8:26.

Lay-by (Shopping): (1) Promise of God held in Heaven.

(1) Matt. 6:20; Eph. 1:3; Phil. 4:19; <u>Col. 1:5</u>.

Laying Down: (1) Not standing in faith; (2) Spiritually dead; (3) Not upright; (4) Resting; (5) Evil; (6) Overcome by the glory of God; (7) Bound; (8) Not true to the Gospel; (9) Sinful.

Also see *Death, Down, Sleeping, Standing,* and *Upright.*

(1) Rom. 5:2; 11:20; 1 Cor. 2:5; 16:13; <u>2 Cor. 1:24b</u>; (2-3) Ps. 51:10-11 (KJV); (4) Jon. 1:5; (5) Prov. 16:17; (6) 1 Kings 8:11; Dan. 8:18; (7) Lev. 26:13 (opposite to upright); (8) Gal. 2:14; (9) 2 Sam. 22:24; Ps. 37:37-38 (opposite to upright).

Lead (Metal): (1) Heavy; (2) Shield.

Also see *Metal.*

(1) Zech. 5:7-8; (2) Lead is so dense that it is impenetrable by X-rays.

Leaf: (1) A life: (a) Righteous life; (b) New life; (c) Driven to and fro; (d) Evergreen life; (e) The temporary nature of; (f) Abundant life/prosperity; (g) Fearful life; (2) Words: (a) As in, "leaves of a book"; (b) Pages; (c) All words, no fruit (the fig tree is a picture of Israel); (d) Dead words/without fruit (dead leaves); (3) Covering up or hiding; (4) Healing.

(1a) <u>Prov. 11:28</u>; (1b) Gen. 8:11; (1c) Job 13:25; (1d) Ps. 1:3; Jer. 17:8; Ezek. 47:12; (1e) Isa. 64:6b; Jer. 8:13; (1f) Dan. 4:12, 21; (1g) Lev. 26:36; (2b) Jer. 36:23 (KJV); (2c) Matt. 21:19; (2d) Mark 11:13; (3) Gen. 3:7; Matt. 24:32; (4) <u>Rev. 22:2b</u>.

Leaning On: (1) Have faith in (trust); (2) Show affection (love); (3) Without physical strength; (4) Sign of old age; (5) Being supported; (6) Look to for support.

(1) <u>2 Kings 18:21</u>; Isa. 36:6; <u>Heb. 11:21</u>; cf. <u>Prov. 3:5</u>; (2) Song. 8:5; John 13:23; 21:20; (3) Judg. 16:26; Heb. 11:21; (4) 2 Sam. 3:29; (5) 2 Kings 5:18; (6) 2 Kings 7:2, 17; 2 Kings 18:21.

Leap/ing: (1) Joy; (2) Worship; (3) In the Spirit; (4) Overcoming an obstacle; (5) Revival; (6) Healing; (7) Being attacked (being leapt on).

Also see *Jumping.*

(1) <u>Luke 1:44</u>; 6:23; (2) 2 Sam. 6:16; 1 Kings 18:26; Acts 3:8; (3-4) 2 Sam. 22:30; Song. 2:8; (5) Isa. 35:6; Luke 1:41; (6) Acts 14:10; (7) Acts 19:16.

Lease: (1) Union or association; (2) Bond (tied to); (3) Contract.

(1-2) Matt. 26:14-16; (3) Gen. 23:15-20.

Leash: (1) Having control of; (2) Being controlled by.

(1-2) Isa. 10:27; (1) Lev. 26:13; Deut. 28:48; (2) Acts 15:10; 2 Cor. 6:14; Gal. 5:1; Isa. 9:4.

Leather Jacket: See Jacket.

Leaven: See Yeast.

Leaves: See Leaf.

Lectern: See Pulpit.

Leech: (1) Someone sucking the life out of you; (2) Soaking up your resources and strength; (3) Sponge; (4) Someone with an insatiable appetite to steal the life of others.

Also see *Mosquito* and *Parasite*.

(1-4) Prov. 30:15.

Left: (1) Weakness; (2) Flesh (natural), unbelief, cursed, death, goat, judgment; (3) Heart; (4) Below, after; (5) Riches and honor (left side of wisdom); (6) Foolishness; (7) Carefree and casual; (8) Intellect, soul, teaching.

Also see *Bow* and *Right*.

(1) Ps. 62:8; 80:17; Luke 22:69; (2) Matt. 25:41, (33-46); Luke 23:33-43; (3) Judg. 7:20 (see note in entry 3 under *Right*); Ezek. 39:3; (4) Gen. 48:13-22; (5) Prov. 3:16; (6) Eccl. 10:2; (7) Exod. 15:26; Prov. 15:19; (8) John 21:5-6 (right = faith).

Left (Turning Left and Right): (1) Searching elsewhere; (2) Distraction; (3) Taking eyes off God; (4) Without a goal/vision.

(1) Gen. 24:49; (2) 2 Sam.11:1-4; (3) Heb. 12:1-2; (4) Prov. 29:18.

Left (Not Turning Left or Right): (1) Obedience/blessing; (2) Long life; (3) Straight/narrow path; (4) Determined.

(1) Deut. 28:14; Josh. 1:7; (2) Deut. 5:33; 17:20; (3) Josh. 23:6; Matt. 7:13-14; (4) 2 Sam. 2:19-22.

Legs: (1) Strength/power; (2) Strength of humans; (3) Speaks of the walk; (4) Support; (5) Uncovered legs may speak of shame or uncovering of one's strength; (6) Hand under the leg (thigh) speaks of an oath; (7) Spiritual walk affected (legs impaired); (8) Long-term influence (long legs).

Also see *Broken Legs* (below), *Hairy Legs* (below), *Knees, Limbs, Shin, Thigh,* and *Tracksuit Pants.*

(1) Gen. 32:25; Ps. 147:10; Song. 5:15; (2) Ps. 147:10; Dan. 2:33-34; (3) Lev. 1:9, 13 (speaks of a cleansed walk); 2 Cor. 5:7; (4) Gen. 32:25; John 19:31-33; (5) Isa. 47:1-3; (6) Gen. 24:2-3, 9; 47:29; (7) 2 Sam. 4:4; 2 Cor. 5:7; (8) Gen. 6:4; (cf. Num. 13:33; 1 Sam. 17:4).

Legs (Broken Legs): (1) Broken strength; (2) Unable to stand and fight; (3) Laziness; (4) Death; (5) Wisdom spoken by a fool.

Also see *Knees* and *Legs.*

(1) Ps. 147:10; (2) Eph. 6:11, 13-14; (3) Prov. 22:13; 26:13; As in, "What's the matter with you?" "Are your legs broken or something?!" (4) John 19:31-33; (5) Prov. 26:7.

Legs (Hairy Legs): (1) Not walking in the Spirit (unattractive); (2) Walking in the flesh; (3) Person walking in own strength.

Also see *Hairy.*

(1-2) Gal. 5:16; (3) Gen. 25:25 (person of the flesh).

Leg Wax: (1) Freeing oneself from the flesh to walk in the Spirit; (2) Beautiful walk.

(1-2) Rom. 8:1, 4; Gal. 5:16.

Lemon: (1) Sour or bitter; (2) Sour (disagreeable/unpleasant) fruit; (3) Issue over which one has become bitter; (4) Complaint; (5) Fruit.

Also see *Fruit.*

(1-2) Ezek. 18:2; (3) Acts 8:23; (4) Job 7:11b; (5) Gal. 5:22.

Length: (1) Measurement of time; (2) Age.

Also see *Measure* and *Tall.*

(1-2) Deut. 25:15; 30:20; 1 Kings 3:14b; Job 12:12; Ps. 21:4; Prov. 3:2, 16.

Leopard: (1) Fast or swift; (2) Unchangeable; (3) Ambusher (lies in wait); (4) Predator that preys on the young/weak in faith; (5) Predator suddenly on the scene; (6) Evil principality in place over a city.

(1) Dan. 7:6; Hab. 1:8; (2) Jer. 13:23; (3) Jer. 5:6; Hos. 13:7; (4) Isa. 11:6; (5) Dan. 7:6; (6) Jer. 5:6 & Eph. 6:12.

Leper: (1) Sinner.

(1) Sin is spiritual leprosy (see Lev. 13:14-17). Lepers were not healed but cleansed (see Matt. 10:8); Note how they were declared clean in Lev. 14:2-8. Two birds were taken (heavenly beings = Jesus and the Holy Spirit). One is sacrificed in an earthen vessel (cf. 2 Cor. 4:7) over living water, while the other is dipped in his blood and released! The leper is to shave (cut off the flesh) and wash (apply the Word).

Also see Num. 5:2; 2 Kings 5:1ff, 7:8; 2 Chron. 26:16-21; Luke 17:12-19.

Lesbian: (1) Church with its eyes on another church instead of Christ (infatuated with the "successful" mega church); (2) Literal lesbian.

(1) Rev. 2:18, 20.

Letter: (1) Word; (2) Written instruction; (3) Written communication; (4) Reference to Bible Epistle; (5) Orders; (6) Authoritative word; (7) Important (large letter); (8) Invitation.

Also see *Envelope, Mailbox,* and *Postage Stamp.*

(1) Esther 9:26, 30; Jer. 29:1; 2 Cor. 10:11; Heb. 13:22; (2) Acts 15:23; (3) Acts 28:21; (4) 2 Cor. 7:8; (5-6) Acts 9:2; (7) Gal. 6:11; (8) Esther 5:8; Acts 7:14.

Letterbox: See Mailbox.

Levitating: (1) In the Spirit.

(1) Ezek. 3:12, 14; 8:3.

Liar: (1) The Devil; (2) Deception.

(1) John 8:44b; (2) Ps. 5:6; 101:7; 109:2.

Liberty Bell: (1) Proclamation of salvation; (2) The Gospel; (3) Eve or proclamation of revival (outbreak of the Spirit).

(1-2) Luke 4:18-19; (3) 2 Cor. 3:17.

Library: (1) Seeking of knowledge; (2) Seeking knowledge of God; (3) Heavenly wisdom or riches (upstairs library); (4) Books; (5) Study; (5) Reference or research; (6) History; (7) Be still and know.

Also see *School.*

(1) Rom. 15:4; (2) Prov. 2:3-5; 2 Tim. 3:16; (3) Rom. 11:33; James 3:17a; (4) Eccl. 12:12; (5-6) Ezra 4:15; Esther 6:1; (7) Ps. 46:10.

Lice: (1) If you have lice, it may mean you have been taken advantage of; (2) That someone has become a parasite; (3) It may also mean that someone is "in your hair"; Scriptural meanings include: (4) Plaque; (5) Curse; (6) Parasite; (7) Judgment; (8) Anger and frustration/annoyance (As in, "I'll get out of your hair").

Also see *Fleas* and *Parasite/s*.

(4-6) Exod. 8:16-17; Ps. 105:31; (7) Exod. 8:16-17; (8) Luke 18:5.

License: (1) Authority to minister; (2) Marriage covenant; (3) Permit.

Also see *Automobile*.

(1) Matt. 28:18-20; (2-3) 1 Cor. 7:39.

License Plate: (1) Identity.

(1) Rev. 13:18.

Lifeguard: (1) The Holy Spirit; (2) Jesus Christ; (3) Pastor (shepherd).

(1) Job 33:4; Isa. 59:19b; John 6:63; Tit. 3:5; (2) Gen. 45:5, 7 (Joseph is a type of Christ); Matt. 8:25-26; Luke 23:39; Acts 4:12; (3) Acts 20:28; 1 Pet. 5:2-4.

Life Raft: (1) Needing salvation; (2) Lost; (3) In danger of losing salvation; (4) Ark (Christ).

Also see *Adrift*, *Boat*, and *Sea*.

(1-2) Matt. 18:11; (2) Luke 15:3-32; (3) Luke 9:25; Acts 27:30-31; (4) Gen. 6:13-16; Matt. 24:37-39; (cf. Luke 17:26ff.); Heb. 11:7.

Lift (Elevator): (1) Entering the spiritual realm; (2) Moving in the Spirit; (3) Rapture; (4) Looking for spiritual growth; (5) Looking to get to God; (6) Praise; (7) Gateway to Heaven; (8) Heaven's Kingdom coming to earth (particularly like an escalator with people coming and going); (9) Suicide (falling lift); (10) On way to hell (lift to basement); (11) Church (as the vehicle to bring Heaven to earth); (12) For different floor levels see entries under individual numbers.

Also see *Angels*, *Ascending*, and *Steps*.

(1) 2 Cor. 12:2; (2) Isa. 40:31; John 3:8; Heb. 2:4; (3) 1 Thess. 4:17; (5) Isa. 14:13; (6) Ps. 68:4 (AMP); (7) Gen.28:12; (8) John 1:51; (9) Isa. 38:18; (10) Ps. 55:15; Prov. 7:27; (11) Matt. 16:18-19; Eph. 3:10; Heb. 12:22-24.

Lifting: (1) Bringing into the Spirit (lifting up); (2) Bringing into heavenly places; (3) Redeeming (lifting out); (4) Receiving spiritual vision (lifting eyes);

(5) Bringing into the Kingdom (lifting up); (6) Releasing captives (lifting up); (7) Looking unto the Father (lifting eyes); (8) Believing (lifting eyes); (9) Dying to self (lifted by cross); (10) Bruise (lifting heel); (11) Preaching (raising voice); (12) Resurrecting (lifting up); (13) Pride (lifting up).

Also see *Lifting Hands, Loosing,* and *Pit.*

(1) James 4:10; (2) Eph. 1:3; 2:6; (3) Matt. 12:11; (4) Matt. 17:8; Luke 16:23; John 4:35; 6:5; 8:7 (KJV), 10; (5) Mark 1:31; Acts 3:7-8; (6) Mark 9:27; (7) Luke 18:13; 21:28; John 11:41; 17:1; (8) John 3:14-15; (9) John 8:28; 12:32; (10) John 13:18; (11) Acts 2:14 (KJV); (12) Acts 9:41; (13) 1 Tim. 3:6 (KJV).

Lift/ed hands: (1) Worship or sacrifice; (2) Making an oath; (3) Surrender; (4) Exercising spiritual authority (moving in judgment); (5) Pronouncing a blessing; (6) Opposition or rebellion; (7) A claim to not have the means to help; (8) Prayer; (9) Healing or deliverance (lifting into the Kingdom); (10) Resurrection; (11) Encouragement; (12) Helping with a burden.

Also see *Lifting.*

(1) Neh. 8:6; Ps. 134:2; 141:2; (cf. Gen 22:5, 10 this is the first place worship is recorded in the Bible); (2) Gen. 14:22; Deut. 32:40; Ps. 106:26; Isa. 49:22; Ezek. 20:4-6, 15; 44:12; Rev. 10:5-6; (3) Universal signal of surrender; (4) Exod. 14:16; Num. 20:11; Isa. 26:11; Mic. 5:9; (5) Lev. 9:22; Ps. 63:4; Luke 24:50; (6) 2 Sam. 18:28; 20:21; 1 Kings 11:26 (KJV); (7) Job 31:21; (8) Ps. 28:2; Lam. 2:19; 3:41; 1 Tim. 2:8; (9) Mark 1:31; 9:27 (lifting someone else's hands); Acts 3:7; (10) Acts 9:41; (11) Heb. 12:12; (12) Matt. 23:4b.

Light: (1) Christ or God; (2) Revelation or illumination; (3) A righteous heart; (4) Life; (5) A guide to the right way; (6) The word as a guide; (7) God's glory; (8) Manifest/exposed; (9) Fellowship (walking in light); (10) Not walking in the Spirit (no lights on); (11) Without Christ (no lights on); (12) Lost (no lights on).

Also see *Black, Candle, Lamp, Spotlight,* and *Torch.*

(1) John 8:12; Acts 9:3-5; 1 John 1:5; (2) Dan. 2:22-23; Acts 26:18; (3) Ps. 97:11; 112:4-7; Prov. 13:9; (4) Isa. 8:20; John 1:4; 8:12; (5) Exod. 13:21; Luke 1:79; (6) Ps. 119:105, 130; 2 Pet. 1:19; (7) Acts 22:11; 2 Cor. 4:6; Rev. 18:1b; 21:11a; (8) John 3:21; 1 Cor. 4:5; Eph. 5:13; (9) 1 John 1:7; (10) John 8:12; (11) John 11:9-10; (12) John 12:35.

Light Fitting: (1) Heart.

(1) 2 Cor. 4:6; 2 Pet. 1:19.

Lighthouse: (1) Jesus Christ; (2) Church; (3) Powerful believer; (4) Landmark.
(1) Matt. 4:16; Luke 2:32; John 1:9; 8:12; 9:5; (2-3) Matt. 5:14, 16; Luke 16:8; John 12:36; (4) Matt. 5:14-16.

Lightning: (1) Powerful Word from God; (2) Power of God; (3) The Glory of God; (4) Instantly/quickly; (5) Judgment; (6) Destruction; (7) Fallen; (8) Angel.
(1) Exod. 19:16; 20:18; 2 Sam. 22:14-15; Job 37:2-4; Ps. 29:7 (NIV); Ps. 77:17-18 (see *Arrows*); (2-3) Ps. 97:4-6; Dan. 10:6; Matt. 28:3; Rev. 4:5; (4) Nah. 2:4; Matt. 24:27; Luke 10:18; (5) Ps. 144:6; Luke 10:18; (6) Rev. 8:5, 16:18; (7) Luke 10:18; (8) Ezek. 1:13-14.

Light Pole: (1) Jesus; (2) Believer.
(1) John 8:12; (2) Matt. 5:14-15.

Lily: (1) Jesus Christ; (2) Love; (3) Grows in the secret/hidden place (valley); (4) Lips (speaking sweet fragrant words); (5) Speaks of being clothed in spiritual glory.
Also see *Lips* and *Valley.*
(1) Song. 2:1; (2) Song. 2:1-2; [cf. 2:16 & 6:3 & 7:10 the progression of love]; (3) Song. 2:16; 6:3; Hos. 14:5; (4) Song. 5:13; 6:2; (5) Matt. 6:28-29; Luke 12:27.

Limbs: (1) Members; (2) Instruments of sin (flesh) or righteousness (Spirit); (3) The Body of Christ (the Church); (4) Loss of spiritual strength (limbs cut off); (5) Crucifying the flesh (you cutting your limb off).
Also see *Arms* and *Legs.*
(1) Matt. 5:30; (2) Rom. 6:13, 19; 7:5, 23; (3) Rom. 12:4-5; 1 Cor. 6:15; 12:12, 14, 26-27; (4) 1 Sam. 2:31; Jer. 48:25; (5) Matt. 5:29-30.

Limousine: (1) Glamour; (2) Opulence: (3) High profile.
(1-3) Song. 3:9-10.

Linen: (1) Symbolizes the robe of righteousness (white linen); (2) the garment of salvation; (3) Well-valued and expensive garments.
(1) Lev. 6:10; Rev. 15:6; 19:8, 14; (2) Isa. 61:10; (3) Luke 16:19; Rev. 18:12, 16.

Lion: (1) Symbolizes authority (king); (1) Jesus Christ; (2) The devil; (3) Powerful spiritual forces (good or evil); (4) Angels/servants/instruments of judgment; (5) Strong-mouthed individuals; (6) Strong or strength; (7) Brave/courageous/

valiant; (8) Enemy; (9) Fierce; (10) Lying in wait (ambush); (11) Bold believer (you as a lion); (12) Young believer or immature leader (lion without a mane); (13) Nation; (14) Anointing (lion's mane).

(1) 1 Kings 10:18-20; consider also the Gospel of Matthew shows Jesus as the Lion/King; (1) Rev. 5:5; (2) 1 Pet. 5:8; (3) Rev. 4:7-8 & Rev. 13:2; (4) 1 Kings 13:24-26; 20:36; 2 Kings 17:25-26; Rev. 9:8, 13-21; (5) Ps. 22:13; 57:4; 58:6-7; Heb. 11:33; (6) Num. 23:24; Judg. 14:14-18; 2 Sam. 1:23; (7) 2 Sam. 17:10; 23:20; (8) Judg. 14:5-6; 1 Sam. 17:34-37 (stealer of young Christians); (9) Job 10:16; 28:8; (10) Ps. 10:9; 17:12; (11-12) Prov. 28:1; (13) Num. 23:24; (14) Judg. 16:20 (Samson shaking himself is a picture of a lion shaking his mane).

Lips: (1) Voice/Words; (2) Flattery; (3) Praise; (4) Deceit; (5) Lying lips; (6) Seduction; (7) Wisdom; (8) Snare; (9) Destruction; (10) Call to depart (from lips of folly); (11) Digging up dirt on someone (burning lips); (12) Contention (fool's lips); (13) Perverse (fool's lips); (4) Precious jewel (lips of knowledge); (15) Hatred (disguised lips); (16) Fool (lips swallowing self); (17) Unrighteous (poisoned lips); (18) Saying something you regret (fat lip); (19) Double confession (split lip); (20) Doubt (split lip).

Also see *Kiss, Mouth,* and *Tongue.*

(1) Ps. 17:1; (2) Ps. 12:2; Prov. 20:19; (3-4) Ps. 17:1; (5) Ps. 31:18; Prov. 10:18; 12:22; 17:4; (6) Prov. 5:3; 7:21; (7) Prov. 10:13, 19 (can be restrained lips); 16:23; 17:28; (8) Prov. 12:13; 18:7; (9) Prov. 13:3 (wide lips); (10) Prov. 14:7; (11) Prov. 16:27; (12) Prov. 18:6; (13) Prov. 19:1; (14) Prov. 20:15; (15) Prov. 26:24; (16) Eccl. 10:12; (17) Rom. 3:13; (18) Prov. 18:6; Eccl. 10:12; (19-20) Ps. 12:2.

Lipstick: (1) Drawing attention to your words; (2) Being outspoken; (3) Sinful words (red lipstick); (4) Words of death (black lipstick); (5) Alluring; (6) Feminine/womanhood; (7) Love.

(1) Ps. 19:14; Prov. 12:6; (2) Num. 12:1; (3) Ps. 59:12; Prov. 10:19; Isa. 6:5; (4) Prov. 10:21; 16:30; 18:21; (5) Prov. 5:3; (6) 1 Sam. 25:3; (7) Song. 4:3.

Liquid Nails: (1) Stronghold; (2) Bondage. (3) Soul-tie.

(1-2) Matt. 12:29; Luke 13:16; (3) 1 Sam. 18:1.

Listening to: (1) Receptive heart; (2) Spiritual understanding; (3) Building faith.

(1-2) Matt. 13:18-23; (3) Rom. 10:17.

Little: (1) Child; (2) Beginning; (3) Seed; (4) Weak; (5) Insignificant; (6) Humble.

Also see *Short, Tall,* and *Smaller.*

(1) Exod. 10:24; Num. 14:31; (2) Job 8:7; Zech. 4:10; (3) 1 Kings 17:11:14; (4-5) Num. 13:33; (6) 1 Sam. 15:17 (cf. Acts 13:9).

Liver: (1) Heart.

(1) Prov. 7:23; Lam. 2:11.

Living Room: (1) Expose; (2) Public place; (3) Truth; (4) Revealed; (5) Flourishing; (6) Can be a place to relax.

(1-4) 2 Kings 9:2-3, 20:4-5; 2 Chron. 29:16; Esther 2:11; Jer. 26:2; (5) Ps. 92:13; (6) Isa. 32:18.

Lizard: (1) The devil; (2) Unclean spirit; (3) Tenacity (clinging on).

Also see *Frill-necked Lizard* and *Snake.*

(1) Isa. 27:1; (2) Lev. 11:30; (3) Prov. 30:28 (see marginal note).

Loaf: (1) Christ; (2) The Church; (3) Speaks about receiving and distributing that which is given; (4) Speaks about brokenness to create unity.

Also see *Bread* and *Table.*

(1) Matt.14:19-22 (speaks about Christ's death inexhaustibly providing for humanity); Matt. 26:26; 1 Cor. 10:16; 11:23-24; (2) 1 Cor. 10:17; (3) Matt. 14:19; (4) 1 Cor. 10:16-17.

Lobster: (1) Partaking in opulence.

Also see *Crab* and *Shrimp.*

(1) Dan. 1:8.

Locker: (1) Heart.

(1) Prov. 4:23.

Locust: (1) Judgment/plague/pestilence; (2) Speaks of curse of the Law; (3) Demons; (4) Possibly battle helicopters; (5) Devourer; (6) Death; (7) Call for humble prayer; (8) Individually weak; (9) Army (en masse); (10) Recovery possible; (11) Numerous (swarms); (12) Fickle (here today, gone tomorrow); (13) Prophet (as an instrument of judgment).

Also see *Grasshopper* and *Honey.*

(1) Exod. 10:3-4; Deut. 28:38, 42; 1 Kings 8:37; Ps. 78:46; 105:34; Joel 1:4; (2) Deut. 28:15, 38; Matt. 3:4; (3) Rev. 9:2-3, 7; (4) Rev. 9:7-10; (5) 2 Chron. 7:13; (6) Exod. 10:17-19; (7) 2 Chron. 7:13-14; (8) Ps. 109:22-23; (9) Prov. 30:27; (10) Joel 2:25; (11) Nah. 3:15; (12) Nah. 3:17; (13) Matt. 3:4 (cf. Matt. 5:17; 7:12; 11:13; 22:40).

Lodge: (1) Boy's club; (2) Religious and traditional church; (3) Occult (Masonic).

Also see *Holiday, Homosexuality,* and *Ski Lodge.*

(1) Mark 10:35-37; cf. Mark 10:9; Eph. 5:31-32; (2) Matt. 15:6b; Gal. 1:14; 1 Pet. 1:18; (3) Matt. 4:10; Luke 4:8.

Log/s: (1) Imperfection/s (faults, mistakes, or sin); (2) Flesh; (3) Unrighteous person (logs laying down).

(1) Matt. 7:3-4; (2) 1 Cor. 3:12-15; (3) Ps. 1:3 & 51:10 (steadfast = upright).

Lollies: See Candy.

Long: See Length.

Long-Legged: (1) Influential; (2) Tenacious; (3) Haughtiness or pride.

(1-2) Prov. 30:28 (As in, Jezebel); (3) Luke 20:46.

Looking: See Lookout.

Looking Back: (1) Not fully committed; (2) Disobedience/rejection of God; (3) Held by the world; (4) Desirous for past pleasure; (5) Looking at the past; (6) Not appreciating the grace of God.

(1) Luke 9:62; (2) Acts 7:39; (3) Heb. 10:38; (4) Gen. 19:26; (5-6) Num. 11:5-6.

Looking Through Window: (1) Prophet (godly person); (2) Perversion (ungodly person); (3) Demon/evil spirit (ungodly character).

Also see *Window.*

(1) 1 Sam. 9:9; Dan. 6:10; (2) Gen. 26:8; Jer. 9:21; Dan. 6:10-11; Joel 2:9; (3) Jer. 9:21.

Lookout: (1) Seeing prophetically; (2) Prophetic office.

Also see *Seeing* and *Window.*

(1-2) 1 Sam. 9:9b.

Loosing: (1) Operating with spiritual authority; (2) Healing (releasing those satan has bound); (3) Forgiving (releasing a debt); (4) Deliverance from demons; (5) Breaking a soul-tie; (6) Untying, releasing, opening, freeing, and bringing liberty; (7) Abiding in the Word of God.

Also see *Bound* and *Rope.*

(1) Matt. 16:19; 18:18; Rev. 5:2; (2) Mark 7:35; Luke 13:12-16; (cf. Rom. 7:2, 8:2) (3) Matt. 18:27 (KJV); (4) Luke 8:29; (5) Gen. 35:18-21 (after Rachel's death, Jacob becomes Israel); (6) Acts 13:25; 16:26; 22:30 (KJV); (7) John 8:31-33.

Losing Footing: See Falling.

Lost and Found (Lost): (1) Unsaved or sinner; (2) Spiritually dead (out of the Father's house); (3) Anxiety; (4) Through ignorance; (5) Through negligence; (6) Through greed, pleasure, or independence; (7) Through legalism or religion; (8) Losing one's destiny and calling; (9) Distracted (disoriented).

Lost and Found (Found): (1) Repentance or salvation; (2) Spiritually alive; (3) Revelation; (4-6) Joy and/or celebration (could symbolize Holy Spirit infilling); (7) Grace or Spirit.

(1) Luke 15:4-7; (2) Luke 15:32; (3) 1 Sam. 9:20; (4) Luke 15:4-7; (5) Luke 15:8-10; (6) Luke 15:11-24; (7) Luke 15:25-32; (8) Ps. 1:1; Prov. 10:17; (9) Prov. 9:15-18; Isa. 42:24; 1 John 2:11.

Lost and Found (Saying Something Is Lost When Found): (1) Deceitful gain; (2) Extortion; (3) Avoiding responsibility.

(1-2) Lev. 6:2-4; (3) Deut. 22:3-4.

Lottery: (1) Gambling; (2) Quick-fix mentality; (3) Looking for a financial breakthrough.

(1) See *Gambling;* (2) Isa. 28:16b; (3) Matt. 17:27.

Lounge Room: See Living Room.

Lowering Hands: (1) Lacking courage; (2) Despondency.

(1-2) Jer. 47:3 (cf. KJV & NKJV); Heb. 12:12.

Lunar Eclipse: (1) Religion (the flesh getting in the way of seeing the glory of God on the Church); (2) No witness; (3) Tribulation.

Also see *Moon.*

(1) Deut. 4:19; Job 25:5-6; 1 Cor. 15:41; (2) Ps. 89:37; (3) Matt. 24:29; Mark 13:24.

Machete: (1) Harsh/cutting words; (2) Trailblazing.

(1) Acts 5:33 (KJV); 7:54; (2) Matt. 3:2-3 (cf. Isa. 40:3; Mal. 3:1); Heb. 6:20.

Machines: (1) Human-made mechanisms; (2) Method or system; (3) Potential source of pride; (4) Sign of affluence; (5) Possible devices of warfare; (6) Reliance on people; (7) Representative of the strength of humanity; (8) human-made assistance; (9) Looking to the world; (10) Employing a method of greater efficiency and less effort.

(1-5) 2 Chron. 26:15-16; (6-10) 1 Kings 10:29; 2 Kings 18:24; Isa. 31:1.

Machine Gun: (1) Speaking in tongues; (2) Praying in the Holy Spirit; (3) Powerful preaching ministry.

(1-2) Acts 2:3-4; 10:46; 19:6; 1 Cor. 14:2, 4-5; Jude 1:20; (3) 1 Sam. 3:19.

Mafia: (1) Thug; (2) Racketeer; (3) Underground or subversive activity; (4) Mocker (hit man).

(1-3) John 12:5-6; (4) John 18:2-3.

Magazine: (1) Gossip; (2) Lies; (3) Renewing the mind (home magazines); (4) Sex issue; (5) Worldly influence; (6) Publication/publicity; (7) Glamor.

Note: a lot will depend on the type of magazine depicted in the dream.

(1) Prov. 6:19; 11:13; 20:19; (2) Prov. 6:19; 12:22; 14:5; (3) Rom. 12:2; (4) cf. Prov. 6:32 & Matt. 5:28; (5) 1 John 2:16; (6) 1 Sam. 31:9 (KJV); Ps. 68:11 (KJV); Isa. 52:7 (KJV); (7) 1 Pet. 3:3.

Maggot: (1) Disobedience; (2) Decay; (3) Judgment; (4) Death; (5) Corruption; (6) Despised person; (7) Eternal death; (8) Feeds on the flesh; (9) Someone who feeds off the Body (Church) grows wings and flies away (not really part of the Body).

Also see *Flies* and *Worm*.

(1-2) Exod. 16:20, 24; (3) Deut. 28:39; Isa. 66:24; Acts 12:23; (4) Jon. 4:7; Acts 12:23; (5) Job 17:14; (6) Job 25:6; Ps. 22:6; Isa. 41:14; Mic. 7:17 (KJV); (7) Mark 9:44, 46, 48; (8) Job 19:26 (KJV); 24:20; (9) Gen. 13:5-11; John 6:70; 12:6.

Mailbox: (1) Heart; (2) Invitation; (3) A letter may mean a dream or message is coming; (4) Wanting to hear from God (going to mailbox); (5) Written communication.

Also see *Envelope* and *Letter*.

(1) Ezek. 3:10; Matt. 13:19; (2) Mark 1:37; John 11:3; (3) 2 Sam. 18:20; (4) Exod. 33:13b; 1 Sam. 27:15b; (5) 2 Kings 5:7.

Main Road: See Highway.

Maintenance Man: See Janitor.

Makeup: (1) Trying to impress people; (2) Pretentious (false prophet); (3) Superficial or spiritually shallow person; (4) Marks those tainted with hypocrisy and sin (white-washed face).

(1-3) 2 Kings 9:30; Jer. 4:30; Acts 4:19; (4) Matt. 23:27-28.

Man: The colors worn by men in your dreams is a good indicator of who they represent: (1) Often seen in dreams is the old man (old self of the flesh), frequently seen in red or black; (2) Also prominent is Christ; (3) Your spirit self (often dressed in light blue); (4) The Holy Spirit (often dressed in white or dark blue); If colors are not evident, then the old self often appears as Jim, James, Jacob, or Jackie; (5) Another character seen is your will, identified by the name Bill or William. William comes from the German name Wilhelm, which stands for "will, desire and protection, helmet"; (6) If a man is unknown and kind, it may represent God, Jesus, or an angel; (7) An angel (messenger); (8) If unfriendly or tempting, it may represent the devil or a demon; (9) Spiritual or fleshly man; (10) Strongman (big and muscular man); (11) The flesh (strongman); (12) Spiritual principality or power (may appear as an intimidating figure); (13) Deceiving spirits keeping people from the truth/true Gospel (men in black/M.I.B./blues brothers); (14) The flesh/carnal ways; (15) Antichrist; (16) Sin; (17) Denomination of people; (18) Governing authority.

Also see *Name* and *Woman*.

(6) Gen. 1:26; Judg. 13:6; (7) Zech. 4:1; Heb. 13:2b; (8) Matt. 4:5-6; 8:28; 13:38-39; (9) Gen. 32:28; Gal. 5:17; (10) Matt. 12:29; (11) Matt. 12:25, 29; Mark 3:24-27; (12) Dan. 10:13, 20; Rom. 8:38; Eph. 1:21; 3:10; 6:12; Col. 1:16; 2:10, 15; (13) 1 John 4:6; 2 Tim. 3:5; (14) Matt. 16:23; (15) 2 Thess. 2:3; (16) Gen. 4:7 (KJV); Rom. 5:12; 6:6; 7:1; (17) 1 Cor. 1:12; 3:3; (18) Matt. 22:16-17.

Manhole (In Ceiling): (1) Trying to get into Heaven or God's presence in the flesh; (2) Self-righteously trying to get to Heaven.

(1) Luke 16:15; 18:10-14.

Manhole (In Ground): (1) Heart; (2) Gateway to hell (to the chambers of death).

(1) 2 Cor. 4:7; (2) Prov. 7:27.

Mannequin (Dummy): (1) No life or dead; (2) Superficial person; (3) New clothing; (4) Being fitted for new position; (5) Growing in God; (6) Special occasion; (7) A Christian who is into fashion, but not secure with God;

(1) Rom. 8:11b; (2) Luke 20:46; (3-5) 1 Sam. 2:19; (6) Matt. 22:11-12; (7) James 4:4.

Mansion: (1) Mature Christian; (2) Heavenly home; (3) Your current spiritual dwelling; (4) Church; (5) The household of faith/Christ/God; (6) Nation.

Also see *House* and *Palace.*

(1) 2 Cor. 5:1; (2) John 14:2; 2 Cor. 5:1-2; (3) 2 Cor. 5:1-2; (4) 1 Tim. 3:15; 2 Tim. 2:20; (5) Heb. 3:3, 6; 10:21; (6) Ezek. 27:14; 38:6; Heb. 8:10.

Mantle: (1) Spiritual authority; (2) Covering; (3) Spiritual position or office; (4) Anointing; (5) Mourning or humbling oneself before God (tearing one's mantle); (6) Reverting to the natural self (taking off the mantle); (7) Under the influence of evil (Dracula-like cape).

Also see *Coat* and *Robe.*

(1) 2 Kings 2:14; (2) 1 Sam. 28:14; Ps. 109:29; (3) 1 Sam. 15:27-28 (KJV); 1 Kings 19:19; 2 Kings 2:8, 13-14; (4) Exod. 29:21, 29; 40:13; Lev. 8:30; (5) Ezra 9:3 (KJV); Job 1:20 (KJV); 2:12 (KJV); (6) John 21:7; (7) John 8:44.

Manufacturer's Manual: (1) Bible; (2) Instructions; (3) Basics; (4) Step-by-step guide.

(1) Josh. 1:8; Ps. 40:7-8; 139:16; (2) Prov. 4:4b-6; 7:2-3; 22:17-21; (3-4) Isa. 28:10.

Map: (1) Seeking directions; (2) Guidance; (3) Life map; (4) Plan for your life; (5) Holy Spirit; (6) The Bible; (7) Wanting to know where we are at in the plan of God.

Also see *Guide.*

(1) Jer. 6:16; (2) Judg. 18:5; Song. 1:8; (3-4) Jer. 29:11; Luke 19:32; John 14:4-6; (5) John 16:13; Exod. 33:14; (6) Ps. 119:105; (7) Exod. 33:13a.

Marble: (1) Sign of opulence and wealth; (2) Solid and strong; (3) Spiritually dead (cold).

(1) Esther 1:6; Rev. 18:12; (2) Song. 5:15; (3) Luke 22:55-57; Rev. 3:15-16.

Marijuana: (1) Offense; (2) Spirit of deception; (3) Counterfeit spirit; (4) Entering into the things of the Spirit (getting high).

(1) Job 19:17; (2) 1 Kings 22:22; (3) Acts 8:9-10; (4) Acts 7:48 (no high like the Most High!) (cf. Eph.5:18); 1 John 1:4.

Mark: (1) Identification; (2) Ownership; (3) Note well; (4) Target; (5) Watch (gain understanding); (6) Measure; (7) Easily seen; (8) Open the heart to understand; (9) Noted; (10) Goal; (11) Impression.

Also see *Mark* in Names Dictionary and *Scar.*

(1) <u>Gen. 4:15</u>; Gal. 6:17; Rev. 13:16; (2) <u>Exod. 21:6</u>; (cf. Isa. 49:16 & Acts 20:28b); (3) Ruth 3:4 (KJV); 2 Sam. 13:28 (KJV); 1 Kings 20:7 (KJV); Ps. 37:37; Ezek. 44:5; <u>Rom. 16:17</u> (KJV); (4) 1 Sam. 20:20 (KJV); Job 7:20 (KJV); 10:14; 16:12 (KJV); Ps. 56:6; <u>Lam. 3:12</u> (KJV); (5) 1 Kings 20:22 (KJV); Job 18:2 (KJV); 33:11 (KJV); (6) Isa. 44:13; (7) Jer. 2:22; (8) Jer. 23:18; (9) Luke 14:7 (KJV); (10) Phil. 3:14; (11) Isa. 49:16.

Marketplace: (1) Corporate or commercial world; (2) Commercial church (profiteering); (3) The World (outside of Christ); (4) Babylon; (5) Trading place; (6) Gathering place; (7) Public place; (8) Those in position to buy or sell (entering the marketplace); (9) God's provision (bountiful market).

(1) <u>Luke</u> 12:18; <u>17:28</u>; James 4:13; (2) Matt. 21:12; <u>John 2:16</u>; (3) 1 John 2:16; (4) Rev. 18:2-3; (5) Ezek. 27:17; (6) Matt. 11:16; (7) Matt. 23:7; (8) Prov. 31:24; (9) Phil. 4:19.

Marquee: (1) Celebration/party; (2) Temporary home.

Also see *Tent.*

(1) 1 Kings 8:66; 2 Chron. 7:10; (2) 1 Chron. 21:29a; Acts 7:44.

Marriage: (1) Conversion (union with Christ); (2) Union or joined; (3) Partnership; (3) Soul tie; (4) Two being made one; (5) Christ & His Church; (6) Faith; (7) Christ's return; (8) Cares of the world; (9) Communion (reception); (10) Literal marriage.

Also see *Best Man, Bride,* and *Groom.*

(1) 1 Cor. 6:17; (2) Gen. 2:24; Matt. 19:4-6; (3) Gen. 26:26-28; 1 Sam. 18:3; (3) 1 Sam. 18:1 (friends); 1 Cor.6:16 (sexual partners); (4-5) Eph. 5:31-32; (6) 1 Tim. 5:11-12; (7) Rev. 19:7; (8) 1 Cor. 7:33; (9) Rev. 19:9.

Mars: (1) War/ hostility.

Also see *Planets.*

(1) Mars is the Roman god of war.

Marshmallow: (1) Without substance (not solid); (2) Sweet and pleasurable; (3) People-pleasing messages.

Also see *Rock* and *Sand.*

(1) Heb. 5:14; (2) 2 Tim. 4:3; (3) Gal. 1:10.

Mascot: (1) Represents the team, organization, or company associated with it.

(1) Num. 2:2-3.

Mashed Potatoes: (1) Baby food.

(1) Rom. 14:2; Heb. 5:14.

Mask: (1) Hypocrisy; (2) Falsehood/deception; (3) Hiding; (4) Two-faced.

Also see *Costume Hire.*

(1) Matt. 23:27; (2) Gen. 38:14-16; Prov.14:13; (3) Ps. 10:11; (4) Gal. 2:11-12.

Mast: (1) Upright; (2) Mighty person; (3) Sail; (4) Strength; (5) Drunk; (6) Speaks of being led by the Spirit (in contrast to chimney stacks); (7) Prophet (lookout or watchman).

Also see *Rowing, Sail,* and *Ship.*

(1-2) Ezek. 27:5 (See *Cedar*); (3-4) Isa. 33:23; (5) Prov. 23:34; (6) John 3:8; (7) 2 Kings 2:15; Ps. 74:9; Isa. 30:10.

Mathematics: (1) Finances; (2) Income.

(1-2) 1 Kings 10:14; Luke 16:4-8.

Material: See Fabric.

Maze: (1) Trying to find the heart of God (maze in a house); (2) Trying to find one's way through a situation that is not straightforward (has many turns); (3) Feeling lost because the path ahead looks complicated; (4) Need for a consistent series of godly decisions; (5) Need to walk closer with God to make it through.

Also see *Lost.*

(1) 1 Sam. 13:14; <u>Acts 13:22</u>; (2) <u>Exod.</u> 18:20; <u>33:13a</u>; (3) Matt. 10:39; 16:25; (4) Josh. 24:15; Luke 3:4-5; (5) Isa. 40:22 (He can see your way forward); Exod. 33:14-15; Ps. 37:5; Prov. 20:24; Jer. 10:23.

Meal: (1) Assimilating the Word; (2) Feeding on Christ; (3) Fellowship; (4) Intimate sharing; (5) Trust; (6) Provision; (7) Favor; (8) Healing; (9) Covenant.

Also see *Cup, Meat, Milk,* and *Table.*

(1) <u>Heb. 5:12-14</u>; 1 Cor. 3:1-3; (2) John 6:53-58; (3-5) Gen. 18:6-17; John 13:1b-2a; (6) Dan. 1:5a; (7) Ruth 2:14; (8) 2 Kings 4:41; 1 Cor. 11:24-25 (cf. Num. 21:8-9 & 1 Pet. 2:24); (9) Luke 22:20; 1 Cor. 11:24-25.

Measure/ing: (1) Faith; (2) Growing in God; (3) Duration or time (i.e. days or years); (4) Decision; (5) Distance; (6) Precision; (7) Judgment; (8) Reciprocity (as you use or do, so God measures to you); (9) Gauge of heart receptivity (hearing).

Also see *Length, Tape Measure, Time,* and *Weighing.*

(1) <u>Rom. 12:3</u>; (2) <u>Eph. 4:13</u>; (3) <u>Ps. 39:4</u>; (4) Deut. 21:2; (5) Josh. 3:4; (6) Job 28:25; Isa. 40:12; (7) Isa. 65:7; Dan. 5:27; Matt. 7:1-2; (8) Luke 6:38; (9) Mark 4:24.

Measure/ing (Different Measures): (1) Moral dishonesty.

(1) Prov. 20:10.

Measure/ing (Immeasurable): (1) God; (2) God's love; (3) The Holy Spirit; (4) Multitudes; (5) Multiplication; (6) Heaven; (7) Blessing; (8) Miracles; (9) Abundant/ce/ly; (10) Eternity.

(1) 2 Chron. 1:1; <u>Rom. 11:33</u>; 1 Tim. 1:17; (2) Eph. 3:18-19; (3) John 3:34; (4) Jer. 3:23; (5) Hos. 1:10a; (6) Gen. 49:26; Jer. 31:37; (7) Mal. 3:10; (8) Mark 6:51; 7:37; 10:26; (9) 2 Cor. 11:23; 12:7; Gal. 1:13; (10) Matt. 25:46.

Measure/ing (Increasing and Diminishing Measure): (1) Increasing = blessing; (2) Decreasing = judgment.

(1-2) Hag. 2:16-19.

Measure/ing (Precise Measurement): (1) Rightly dividing the Word (diligent study); (2) A precise set of measures may be a confirmation of a future event.

(1) <u>2 Tim. 2:15</u>; (2) Ezek. 40:2ff; Zech. 2:1-5.

Measure/ing (Same Measurement): (1) Balance; (2) Harmony; (3) Dividing.
(1) 1 Kings 6:25; (2) 1 Kings 7:37; (3) Heb. 4:12.

Measuring Self Against Others: (1) Comparing; (2) Foolishness.
(1-2) 2 Cor. 10:12.

Meat: (1) The Word of God; (2) Solid Bible teaching; (3) Doing the will of God.
(1) Job 12:11 (KJV), 34:3 (KJV); 1 Cor. 3:2; Heb. 5:12. (2) Heb. 5:14; (3) John 4:34 (KJV).

Meat Clever: (1) Word of God.
(1) Heb. 4:12.

Mechanic: (1) The Holy Spirit; (2) An angel; (3) Jesus Christ; (4) God; (5) Spiritual tune-up; (6) Helper correcting or helping your ministry; (7) Healer (evangelist); (8) One who maintains and repairs.
Also see *Automobile, Engine, Motor,* and *Oil.*
(1) John 14:16, 26; (2) Dan. 10:11; Heb.1:13a-14; (3) John 1:33 (The Holy Spirit also being symbolized by oil); (4) Ps. 51:10; (5) Acts 18:25-26; (6) Exod. 18:14; (7) Luke 4:18; (8) Isa. 58:12.

Mechanical: (1) Human-driven; (2) Works; (3) Strength of humanity.
(1-3) 2 Chron. 26:15-16.

Medal: (1) Honor; (2) Glory; (3) Rewards.
(1-2) Exod. 15:1; Ps. 8:5; 2 Cor. 2:14; Heb. 2:7; (3) Rev. 22:12.

Medicine: (1) Healing; (2) Prayer; (3) The Blood of Jesus; (4) The Word of God; (5) Holy Spirit joy; (6) Anointing oil; (7) Leaves (from Christ, the Tree of Life).
Also see *Doctor, Healed, Hospital,* and *Nurse.*
(1-2) James 5:14-15; (3) Isa. 53:5; John 6:53; (4) Prov. 4:20-22; (5) Prov. 17:22; (6) Jer. 46:11; James 5:14-15; (7) Ezek. 47:12b; Rev. 22:2.

Megaphone: (1) Make widely known; (2) Loud/ly.
(1) Matt. 10:27.

Memento: (1) Reminder; (2) Trophy (self-glory).
(1-2) 1 Sam. 17:54; (2) 1 Sam. 15:9, 12.

Men: See Man.

Mentor: (1) The Holy Spirit; (2) In need of a mentor.
(1) John 16:7, 13; 1 John 2:27; (2) 1 Kings 19:21.

Mentally Disabled Person/s: (1) Innocent child of God; (2) Evil spirit (aggressive and intimidating).
Also see *Disability.*
(1) 1 Cor. 1:27; (2) Mark 5:5, 15; Acts 19:16.

Message: (1) Word from God; (2) Letter; (3) Dream.
(1) 1 John 1:5; 3:11; (2) 2 Sam. 11:14; (3) Num. 12:6; Jer. 23:28; Matt. 2:13.

Messy: (1) Speaks of the works of people; (2) Not of God; (3) Busyness.
(1-2) 1 Cor. 14:33; (3) Mark 2:2, 4; Acts 6:1.

Metal: (1) Represents the strength of the natural human (human-made); (2) Strong; (3) Earthly treasure; (4) Prone to rust; (5) Valued by the world; (6) Trade or commerce; (7) Money.
Also see *Lead.*
(1) Josh. 17:16, 18; (2) Dan. 2:40; (3-4) Matt. 6:19; (5-7) Ezek. 27:12; Matt. 22:19-21; 25:16.

Meteor: (1) Message from Heaven; (2) Revival (meteor shower); (3) Judgment.
Also see *Asteroid.*
(1) Deut. 4:36; Isa. 55:10-11; Also consider that Christ (The Word of God) is our Rock from Heaven; (2) Ps. 72:6-7; (3) Isa. 30:30; Ezek. 38:22.

Meter: (1) Power supply; (2) Assessing the anointing; (3) Heart (like a parking meter); (4) Opportune time.
(1-2) Mark 5:30; Luke 6:19; 8:46; (3) Neh. 7:5; (4) Esther 4:14; Dan. 2:21.

Meter Man: (1) Measuring the strength of the Spirit/power of God.
(1) Acts 8:18-19; 1 Cor. 2:4.

Microphone: (1) Opportunity to speak or sing; (2) Speaking platform; (3) Amplifying the message.
(1-3) Matt. 10:27; Luke 12:3.

Microscope: (1) Nit-picking; (2) Under examination (detailed inspection); (3) Detail; (4) Science; (5) Biological, bacterial, or viral situation.

(1) Matt. 7:2-6; 23:24; (2) Ps. 26:2; Luke 23:14; Acts 22:24; 1 Cor. 11:28; 2 Cor. 13:5; (3) Heb. 4:15; 9:5; James 2:10; (4) The microscope is an accepted symbol for science; (5) Matt. 24:7; Luke 21:11.

Microwave Oven: (1) Heart; (2) Cooking on the inside; (3) Quick work; (4) Convenience; (5) Penetrating; (6) Sudden boil-over.

(1) Hos. 7:6; (2) Ps. 39:3; Jer. 20:9b; (3) Isa. 43:19; (4) Gen. 25:29-34 (consider the cost of convenience); (5) Luke 2:35; (6) 1 Sam. 18:8.

Middle: See Center.

Midnight: (1) The darkest hour; (2) Death; (3) Deliverance; (4) A turning of the situation; (5) End of the second watch; (6) Time to ask, seek, and knock; (7) Decision time; (8) The end of time.

(1) Ps. 119:62 (giving thanks at the darkest hour); Acts 16:25; (2) Exod. 11:4-5; 12:29; (3) Judg. 16:3; Acts 16:25-26; (4) Ruth 3:8; Matt. 25:6; (5) Mark 13:35; (6) Luke 11:5, 8-10; (7) Acts 16:25-26; 27:27; (8) Exod. 12:29 (judgment); Matt. 25:6-12.

Midwife: (1) The Holy Spirit; (2) An angel; (3) Intercessor; (4) Assistant or guide to help birth the promises of God.

(1) Rom. 8:22, 26; (2) Ps. 34:7; (3) Rom. 8:22, 26; (4) Gen. 35:17-18 (Here it is interesting to note the birth of Benjamin, meaning "son of my right hand", who is a type of Christ); Exod. 1:15-21; (cf. Gen. 50:24 & Acts 7:19-25).

Milk: (1) God's Word for young believers; (2) Foundational Bible teaching; (3) Immature Christian.

(1) 1 Pet. 2:2; (2-3) 1 Cor. 3:1-2; Heb. 5:12-14.

Millipede: (1) Annoyance; (2) Pest.

Also see *Worm.*

(1-2) Mark 10:41.

Mill/stone: (1) Judgment; (2) Place of humbling.

Also see *Flour.*

(1) Matt. 18:6; Mark 9:42; Luke 17:2; Rev. 18:21; (2) Acts 8:33 (cf. Isa. 53:5 & Phil. 2:8).

Mine: See Cave and Tunnel.

Mirror: (1) The Word of God; (2) The human heart; (3) Vanity; (4) Focus on self; (5) Deception (as in "smoke and mirrors"); (6) On reflection; (7) Past (looking behind you).

Also see *Broken Mirror.*

(1) 1 Cor. 13:12; James 1:23-24; (2) Prov. 27:19; (3-4) 2 Sam. 14:25-26; (5) Prov. 12:17, 20; 14:8, 25; 26:26; (6) Luke 15:17; John 14:9 (Jesus is in one sense a "reflection" of the Father); (7) Gen. 19:26 (looking back can paralyze you); Josh. 8:20 (looking back may disempower you); Phil. 3:13.

Mirror: (Broken Mirror): (1) Broken heart; (2) Broken focus/vision; (3) Letting go of the promises of God.

Also see *Mirror.*

(1) Prov. 27:19; 20:5 (the heart is a body of water that reflects); (2) Prov. 29:18; Lam. 2:9; Hab. 2:2; (3) Hab. 2:2; Matt. 14:29-30.

Miscarriage: (1) Lost promise; (2) Aborting the promise of God; (3) Promise robbed; (4) Death of a new ministry; (5) Judgment; (6) Curse; (7) Injustice; (8) Lacking spiritual strength.

(1-4) Matt. 2:16-18; Acts 7:19 (KJV); (5) Hos. 9:14; (6) Gen. 31:38; Exod. 23:26; (*Birth* means "blessed," therefore, *miscarriage* means "cursed"); (7) As in "a miscarriage of justice"; (8) Isa. 37:3.

Missile: (1) Powerful words; (2) Words of destruction; (3) Word of God (guided missile); (4) Sermon; (5) Attack; (6) Judgment; (7) Infliction.

Also see *Arrow, Bomb, Rocket,* and *Spear.*

(1) Isa. 54:17; Luke 4:32, 36; 1 Cor. 2:4; (2) 1 Sam. 18:11; 19:9-10; 20:33; (3) Heb. 4:12 & Isa. 55:11; (4) Matt. 3:1-2, 4:17; (launched or pointed words); (5) Ps. 109:3; Jer. 18:18; (6) Job 20:23-25; Ps. 64:7; Ezek. 39:3; (7) Job 34:6 (see alternative rendering).

Missing the Bus: (1) Missing opportunity; (2) Missing big ministry; (3) Doing things independently; (4) Waiting (not your time in God to go and minister).

(1-2) Luke 10:38-42; (3) Luke 9:49-50; (4) 1 Cor. 16:12.

Mobile Phone: See Telephone.

Mom: See Mother.

Monday: (1) Two; (2) Death; (3) New beginnings.

Also see *Day* and *One*.

(1-2) Gen. 1:6-8 (Note there is no mention that "it was good"). This is the death that precedes resurrection; (3) The secular world sees Monday as the first day of the week.

Money: The use of money seems to break into three groups. Positive: (1) Faith; (2) Income; (3) Blessing of putting God first in your life; (4) Representative of gifts or talents; (5) Purchase rights; (6) Redemption (to buy back); (7) Deposits of the glory of God (gold coins); (8) Making a sacrifice or offering; (9) Thanksgiving (currency); (10) The Word of God; (11) Seed. How you use it: (12) Decision between God or money; (13) Need to invest spiritually; (14) It is not the amount, but the heart that is important. Negative: (15) Root of evil (i.e. it has the power of manipulation and control); (16) Trading in church; (17) Greed (takes away the spiritual life); (18) Deceitfulness; (19) Possible betrayal; (20) Worldly power; (21) Bribe.

Also see *Currency Exchange, Riches, Seed,* and *Treasure.*

(1) cf. Prov. 23:23 & John 17:17 & Rom. 10:17 (as the currency of the Kingdom); 1 Pet. 1:7; (2) 2 Kings 12:11a; Prov. 10:4; (3) 2 Chron. 1:11-12; Matt. 6:33; Prov. 10:22; (4) Matt. 25:15; (5) Acts 7:16; (6) Lev. 25:51; Num. 3:49; Isa. 52:3; (7) Isa. 60:9; (8) Mark 12:41; (9) Ps. 100:4; (10) Gen. 44:2 (cf. Luke 8:11); (11) Mal. 3:10; (12) Mark 6:8; Luke 16:13; Acts 4:36-37; 8:18-20; (13) Matt. 25:27; Luke 19:23; (14) Mark 12:42-44; (15) 1 Tim. 6:10; (16) John 2:14-16; (17) Prov. 1:19; 15:27; Isa. 56:10-11; Acts 24:25-26; (18) Matt. 13:22; 28:12-13, 15; Acts 24:25-26; Rev. 3:17; (19) Mark 14:11; (20) Eccl. 10:19 (universal language); Matt. 22:17-21; (21) 1 Sam. 8:3; Ps. 26:10; Amos 5:12.

Mongoose: (1) Warring angel.

(1) Dan. 10:13.

Monkey: (1) Making you look like a fool; (2) Not serious; (3) Affluence; (4) Mischievous spirit; (5) Mood swings (depression [up one minute down the next]).

Also see *King Kong.*

(1) Someone "trying to make a monkey out of me"; (2) As in, "monkeying around"; (3) 1 Kings 10:22-23; (4) Ps. 38:12 (KJV); Prov. 24:8 (KJV); (5) James 1:8.

Monster: (1) Demon; (2) Evil spirit; (3) Fear.

Also see *Dinosaur.*

(1-2) Luke 4:33; Rev. 12:9; (3) 1 Sam. 17:11.

Month: January through December, see Name and Place Dictionary.

Monument: (1) The Cross; (2) Remembrance. In the Cross we see the fulfillment of the memorials in the Old Testament; (3) "I Am" (the name of God); (4) The sacrifice of the Passover Lamb; (5) The escape from Egypt (the world); (6) Victory under "The Lord our Banner"; (7) Judgment upon the High Priest for the children of Israel; (8) The Feast of Trumpets; (9) The Bread of Life; (10) Death defeated (Jordan cut off).

(1-2) 1 Cor. 11:24-25; 2 Tim. 2:8; (3) Exod. 3:15 & John 8:24; (4) Exod. 12:6-7, 13-14; (5) Exod. 13:3, 8; (6) Exod. 17:14-15; (7) Exod. 28:29-30; (8) Lev. 23:24; (9) Lev. 24:7; (10) Josh. 4:7.

Moon: (1) Wife or mother or woman or sister; (2) The Church; (3) Faithful witness; (4) The moon rules and has dominion in the night, and is a reflection of the sun (cf. Mal. 4:2); (5) God's Glory reflected; (6) Celebration; (7) Resurrection; (8) Satan.

Also see *Lunar Eclipse.*

(1) Gen. 37:9-10; 1 Cor. 11:7; (2) Song. 6:10; (3) Ps. 89:37; (4) Gen. 1:16; Ps. 136:9; (5) 1 Cor. 15:41; Rev. 21:23; (6-7) 1 Sam. 20:5 (the New Moon); (8) Matt. 17:15, where the word *epileptic* is literally "moonstruck" or "luna-tic"; here the moon symbolizes satan as the ruler of the darkness.

Mortgage: (1) Debt or curse; (2) Financial pledge; (3) The blood of Christ (frees us from the mortgage).

Also see *House.*

(1) Deut. 28:12; Rom. 13:8; (2) Gen. 28:20-22; (3) 1 Cor. 6:19-20; 1 Pet. 1:18-19.

Mosquito: (1) Little irritation that steals spiritual life; (2) Spiritual parasite; (3) Unseen attack that saps the life out of you (or poisons you); (4) Evil spirit; (5) Spirit stealing financially from you.

(1) Lev. 17:11; (2) John 12:6; (3) Deut. 25:18; (4) John 10:10; (5) Mic. 7:2-3; Matt. 27:6 (blood-money) (cf. Exod. 21:30 & Lev. 17:11).

Motel: (1) Stopover; (2) Place of refreshment and rest; (3) Speaks of a journey (or life path); (4) Place of encounter; (5) Place of discovery.

Also see *Bed.*

(1-3) Gen. 42:27; 43:21; Luke 10:34-35; (4) Exod. 4:24; (5) Luke 24:28-31.

Moth: (1) Corruption; (2) Decay; (3) Rotten; (4) Destruction; (5) Vulnerability; (6) Fleeting and brief existence (transient life); (7) Temporary shelter (cocoon); (8) Judgment; (9) Building earthly treasures.

(1-3) Job 13:28; Isa. 50:9; 51:8; Hos. 5:12; Luke 12:33; (3-4) Job 4:19; (5) Isa. 50:9; (6) Ps. 39:11; (7) Job 27:18; (8) Hos. 5:12; (9) Matt. 6:19-20; James 5:2.

Mother: (1) The Church; (2) The Holy Spirit; (3) Natural mother; (4) Spiritual mother; (5) Heavenly Jerusalem; (6) Israel; (7) The past; (8) Nurturer; (9) The law/legalism.

(1) Eph. 5:25, 31-32; (2) Gal. 4:29b; (3) 2 Tim. 1:5; (4) Gal. 4:19; (5) Rev. 21:2; (6) Rev. 12:1-2; (7) Job 21:8; (8) Song. 8:1; Isa. 49:23; (9) Prov. 1:8, 6:20.

Motherboard: (1) Mind; (2) Mother soul-tie; (3) Counsel of God.

Also see *Computer, Hard Drive, Laptop Computer,* and *Desktop.*

(1) Rom. 12:2; 1 Cor. 2:16; (2) Gen. 25:28; 27:6; (3) Col. 2:9-10.

Mother-in-Law: (1) Legalistic church; (2) Meddler; (3) Illegitimate church; (4) Counselor; (5) Church history (religious mother-in-law); (6) Actual mother-in-law.

(1) Gal. 3:23-25; (2) 1 Tim. 5:13; (3) Acts 19:2-5; (4) Ruth 3:1, 3-4; (5) Rev. 1:19-20.

Motor: (1) Power; (2) Holy Spirit; (3) Human-made power; (4) The human spirit; (5) Heart.

Also see *Ass, Automobile, Gasoline,* and *Ox.*

(1-2) Mic. 3:8a; Luke 1:17; 4:14; Rom. 15:19; (3) Zech. 4:6; Eph. 2:2; (4) Ps. 39:3; 104:4; Prov. 20:27; (5) As in, "The heart is the engine room."

Motorcycle: (1) Powerful and responsive individual ministry; (2) Independent ministry.

Also see *Trail Bike.*

(1) Acts 8:4-7, 26-39; (2) 1 Cor. 3:4-5; 12:15-16, 21.

Motorcycle Helmet: (1) Helmet of salvation; (2) Call to know and stand on what Christ achieved at Calvary; (3) Call to choose godly thoughts; (4) Guarding your mind from the enemy.

Also see *Helmet.*

(1-2) Eph. 6:17; (3) 1 Cor. 2:16; (4) Eph. 6:17.

Motor Scooter: (1) Individual ministry; (2) Young ministry.

(1-2) Acts 21:9.

Mountain: (1) Spiritual high place; (2) Heaven; (3) Impossibility; (4) Obstacle; (5) Refuge/hideaway; (6) Meeting place with God (God's Presence); (7) Triumph; (8) Place of prayer; (9) Place of worship; (10) Place of transformation; (11) Separation; (12) Ancient; (13) Apostolic calling (walking up mountain with Jesus); (14) Seeing God's Glory (top of mountain); (15) God; (16) Doubt and unbelief; (17) Pride.

(1) Luke 4:5; (2) Ezek. 28:16; Heb. 12:22; Rev. 21:10; (3-4) Song. 2:8; Mark 11:23; 1 Cor. 13:2; Luke 3:5; (5) Luke 21:21; Rev. 6:15; (6) John 6:3; 2 Pet 1:18; (7) 1 Kings 18:20-40; (8) Luke 6:12; 9:28; 22:39-40; (9) John 4:20-21; (10) Mark 9:2; (11) Song. 2:17 (*Bether* = separation); (12) Deut. 33:15; (13-14) Matt. 17:1ff; (15) Ps. 48:1; (cf. Deut. 33:15 & Ps. 90:2); (16) Deut. 1:20-26; Matt. 17:20; (17) Isa. 2:12-17; 40:4.

Mountain Bike: (1) Self exaltation.

Also see *Bike* and *Mountain.*

(1) Matt. 23:12; John 10:1.

Mourning: (1) Suffering loss.

Also see *Death.*

(1) 1 Sam. 25:1; Matt. 2:18.

Mouse/Mice: (1) Hidden unclean spirit; (2) Indicator of a lack of spiritual maintenance; (3) Unbeliever (unclean); (4) Small; (5) Plague; (6) Judgment; (7) Insignificant.

Also see *Rat.*

(1) Matt. 10:1; (cf. Rev. 16:13); (2) Luke 11:24-25; (3-4) Lev. 11:29; (5-6) (cf. 1 Sam. 5:12 & 1 Sam. 6:5 (KJV)); (7) Judg. 6:15.

Mouth: (1) Heart; (2) Word of faith; (3) Confession; (4) Silenced or mute (no mouth).

Also see *Dumb, Lips, Mute,* and *Teeth.*

(1) Matt. 12:34; 15:18; Luke 6:45; (2) Rom. 10:8; (3) Rom. 10:9-10; (4) Luke 14:5-6; 20:26.

Mouth (Hurt Mouth): (1) Pain in the heart; (2) Inability to open up (unable to speak freely); (3) Speaking out of hurt.

Also see *Gums.*

(1) 1 Sam. 1:12-14; (2) Matt. 12:34b; 15:18; (3) Gen. 4:23; 31:29; Ps. 38:12;

Movie: (1) Your life as a story (Book of Life); (2) The title or plot of a movie may reflect a past, present, or future episode in your life; (3) Entertainment.

Also see *Picture Theater.*

(1-2) Rev. 3:5; 20:12; 1 Tim. 6:12; (3) 1 Cor. 10:7.

Movie Camera: (1) Capturing the action; (2) Get ready for action; (3) Making history; (4) Documenting the past; (5) Becoming a person of renown.

Also see *Camera.*

(1-3) Acts 2:40-41; 3:6-10; 4:33; (4) Esther 6:2; (5) Num. 16:2b; Ezek. 23:23.

Moving House: (1) Salvation (moving from old to new house); (2) A call to get saved (get into God's house); (3) Changing allegiances (possibly a person easily moved by circumstance); (4) Changing churches; (5) Transition of God (growing or shrinking in God); (6) Not happy with or within yourself.

Also see *Removal Van.*

(1-2) Heb. 11:7; (3) Isa. 7:2; (4) 1 Cor. 16:19; (5) Matt. 9:17; Heb. 10:38; (6) Rom. 7:24.

Moving Offices: (1) Changing ministry roles.

(1) Eph. 4:11.

Moving Van: See Removal Van.

Mucky: (1) A slanderous accusation; (2) Muck raking.

(1) Jude 1:9-10, 13a; (2) Ezra 4:6; 2 Pet. 2:11.

Mud: (1) Stuck; (2) Backsliding (going back to the world); (3) Speaks of humanity; (4) Humbled; (5) Without solid footing (no foundation in God);

(6) Sinking; (7) Bad name (someone covered in mud); (8) Accusation (throwing mud at someone); (9) Trodden down; (10) Creating (wet clay); (11) Dungeon; (12) Working through issues (making your way through mud); (13) Not able to let go of the past; (14) Flesh; (15) Sin; (16) Defiled words.

Also see *Clay, Dirt, Earth, Mud Cake, Mudslide, Mud Slinging, Water,* and *Dirty Water.*

(1) As in, "stuck in the mud"; (2) Ezek. 47:11; 2 Pet. 2:22b; (3) Job 33:6; Dan. 2:43; John 9:6; (4) Job 30:19; (5) Ps. 40:2; (6) Ps. 69:2, 14; Jer. 38:6b, 22; (9) Isa. 10:6b; 41:25b; Mic. 7:10; Zech. 10:5; (10) John 9:6-7; (11) Jer. 38:6 (No water, but mud); (12) Luke 15:15-17; (13) 2 Pet. 2:22; (14) Ps. 40:2; (15-16) Isa. 57:20.

Mud Cake: (1) Indulgence in fleshly words.

Also see *Mud.*

(1) 1 Cor. 2:4.

Muddy Water: See Water (Dirty Water).

Mudslide: (1) Path into the world; (2) Falling back into the flesh.

Also see *Mud.*

(1-2) 2 Pet. 2:22.

Mud Slinging: (1) Slanderous words.

Also see entries under Mud.

(1) Ps. 69:14; Eccl. 7:21; Isa. 57:19-20.

Mule: (1) No longer in the world, but not yet humble (half way between a horse and a donkey); (2) Lukewarm; (3) Stubborn (no wisdom).

Also see *Donkey* and *Horse.*

(1) Deut. 8:2 (still in the wilderness); (2) Rev. 3:16; (3) Ps. 32:9.

Multi-Colored: (1) Glorious or clothed in glory; (2) Multi-faceted; (3) Having chameleon-like tendencies; (4) Covenanted.

Also see *Parrot/s* and *Rainbow.*

(1) Gen. 37:3; 2 Sam. 13:18-19; The coat of many colors prefigures the glorified Joseph and the glorious bride of Christ; (2) The Glory of God is made of a multitude of pure qualities, just as white light is a composite of the colors within; (3) 1 Cor. 9:22b; 10:33a; (4) Gen. 9:11-12.

Mum: See Mother.

Murder: (1) Hatred; (2) Self-hatred; (3) Anger; (4) Battle between fleshly (old) self and spirit (new) self; (5) Root of offense.

Also see *Assassin, Kill/Killing, Mafia,* and *Strangle/d.*

(1-2) 1 John 3:15; (3) Matt. 2:16; 5:21-22; (4) Gal. 5:17; Eph. 6:12; (5) Matt. 24:10 & 1 John 3:15.

Muscle-Building: (1) Praying in the Holy Spirit; (2) Literal muscle-building; (3) Muscling in; (4) Flexing muscle.

(1) Jude 1:20; (3) Gen. 27:36; (4) 1 Sam. 17:5-10.

Museum: (1) Old; (2) History; (3) Dead church; (4) A church that is honoring tradition and worshipping its history.

Also see *War Heroes/Museum.*

(1-3) Deut. 32:7; Ps. 44:1; (4) Matt. 23:29-30.

Mushroom: (1) Ignorant; (2) Willfully ignorant of God; (3) Deception; (4) Ignorant decisions (picking mushrooms); (5) Overnight sensation without foundation.

(1) Prov. 30:2; (2) Isa. 45:19; (3) As in, "kept in the dark and fed lies"; 2 Cor. 4:2a; (4) Gen. 16:2 (Abram made this decision without consultation with God, i.e. in the dark); (5) Matt. 7:26b; 13:5-6; 15:13;

Music: (1) Worship; (2) Praise; (3) Celebration; (4) Victory; (5) Joy.

Also see *Guitar* and *Musical Instrument.*

(1) Dan. 3:5, 7, 10; (2) 2 Chron. 5:13; 7:6; 23:13; (3) Luke 15:25; (4) Exod. 15:20-21; 1 Sam. 18:6; (5) 1 Chron. 15:16; Lam. 5:14-15.

Musical Instrument: (1) Ministry (particularly if you are a musician); (2) Ministry of worship; (3) Prophecy; (4) Entering the spirit realm/moving in the gifts (playing instrument); (5) Heart.

(1-2) 1 Chron. 6:32; 16:4; 2 Chron. 7:6; (3) 1 Chron. 25:1; (4) 2 Kings 3:15; (5) Ps. 9:1.

Mute: (1) Unable to speak; (2) Trauma; (3) Broken spirit; (4) Silenced; (5) Fear.

Also see *Dumb.*

(1) Luke 1:20; (2) Gen. 45:3; (3) Prov. 15:13; 17:22; (4) Ps. 32:3; 50:21; Eccl. 3:7; Amos 5:13; Luke 14:5-6; 20:26; (5) 2 Sam. 3:11.

Naked: (1) Seeing the person as they really are; (2) Shame or ashamed; (3) Clothed in Glory; (4) Demonic influence; (5) Death; (6) Unashamed Gospel-preaching; (7) Not spiritually clothed (heart revealed); (8) Not ready or ill-prepared; (9) Without the anointing; (10) Call to wait upon God; (11) Feeling vulnerable.

Also see *Dressing* and *Clothes*.

(1) Heb. 4:13; (2-3) Gen. 2:25; Rev. 3:18; (4) Luke 8:27; (5) Job 26:6 (AMP); (6) Rom. 1:16 (cf. Gen. 2:25); (7) Mark 14:52; (8) Mark 14:51-52; (9) Lev. 16:32; 21:10; (10) Ps. 69:6; Isa. 49:23b; (Isa. 25:9 & Isa. 61:10); (11) Rev. 3:17; 16:15.

Name: (1) A named person in a dream may refer to:

(a) Literally that person; (b) The meaning of the name, which displays its truth. Look up meaning in the name section of this book. If not listed, search in a comprehensive name book or on the Internet; (c) Someone with that same character/position (Ask yourself how you see that person); (d) An organization, business, church, or denomination that the person represents relating to their position (Ask yourself what that person represents); (e) The marking of a period of time when you were in association with a person or place with that name. The dream may show you what has happened between now and then or what lies ahead should you continue on this course; (f) Incidents between you and that person that are now being paralleled spiritually.

Name (Calling Someone by a Different Name): (1) Attack on a person's character or mistaken character; (2) Mistaken identity; (3) Offended person (Sometimes when we call someone by a different name, we may offend them); (4) Call to put on the spiritual self and change character; (5) Trying to force someone to be something they are not.

(1) 2 Sam. 16:7; (2) Gen. 27:24; (3) Gen. 20:2, 5, 9-10; (4) Gen. 32:28; (5) Dan. 1:7-8.

Nail Clippers: (1) Taking precautions not to hurt others.
(1) Eph. 6:12; 2 Cor. 10:3-4.

Nail Gun: (1) Penetrating words; (2) Harsh words.
(1-2) Eccl. 12:11.

Nails (Builder's): (1) God's Word; (2) Riveting words (words that engrave the heart and mind) that are God-given; (3) Permanent and secure fastening;

(4) Memory peg (not forgotten); (5) Debt paid in full; (6) Preparation; (7) Resistance (buckled nail).

Also see *Screw.*

(1) Isa. 22:23 (KJV); Col. 2:14; (2) Judg. 4:21-22; 5:26; Eccl. 12:11; Col. 2:14; (3) Ezra 9:8 (KJV); Isa. 22:23 (KJV); 41:7 (KJV); Jer. 10:4; Col 2:14; (4) Isa. 49:15-16 & John 20:25; (5) Col. 2:14; (6) 1 Chron. 22:3; (7) 2 Tim. 4:15.

Nails (Finger): (1) Female conflict; (2) Womanhood (painting fingernails); (3) Preparing to make an advance (flirting); (4) Disarming conflict (cutting nails).

Also see *Thumbnail.*

(1) Ps. 144:1b; Gal. 5:15; (2-3) Ezek. 23:40; (4) Ps. 46:9.

Nappy: See Diaper.

Narrow: (1) The path of life (often difficult); (2) Pressured situation; (3) Distress; (4) Restriction; (5) Too small; (6) Trap; (7) A call to live not by sight, but by faith (narrow windows); (8) God often leads those He wants to use into pressured situations to build a determination and resolve within them that breaks through to new spiritual levels. He achieves this through affliction, confinement, and relational pressure; (9) Inability to grab hold of new mental models (narrow-minded); or (10) Inability to absorb new information because of personal bias.

(1-2) Matt. 7:13-14; (3) 1 Sam. 13:6 & 14:4; (4) Num. 22:26; Job 13:27 (KJV); (5) Josh. 17:15 (KJV); Isa. 49:19 (cf. NKJV & KJV); (6) Prov. 23:27; (7) Gen. 6:16; Ezek. 40:16 (KJV); 41:16 (KJV), 26 (KJV); (8) 1 Sam. 1:6, 10, 11, 17; 1 Sam. 17:28; Matt. 11:12; (9-10) John 8:43, 47.

Nation: To determine the meaning of a country appearing in a vision or dream, ask the dreamer/visionary what that country means to them. What are the country's characteristics? Also explore whether there is an existing association between the country and the dreamer/visionary? Is there an immediate person of that nationality that comes to mind? If there is no existing association, it may be necessary to explore information on the country or wait for God to provide more information by being sensitive to future encounters with people or situations involving that country. (1) A country or countryman may appear in a dream or vision after a request for direction.

(1) Acts 16:9.

Nationality: See Indigenous and Nation.

Native/s: (1) People who are born and raised in a certain environment; (2) Spiritually aware (i.e. environmentally aware).

Also see *Alien, First Nations People, Foreign,* and *Foreigner.*

(1) Gen. 13:7b; (2) 2 Kings 6:16-17.

Navel: See Belly.

Neck: (1) Decision-making/maker; (2) Subjection (foot on neck); (3) Victory (foot on neck); (4) Dominion (yoke on neck); (5) Pride (stretched neck); (6) Death (broken neck); (7) Glory; (8) Strength/support; (9) Pride (stiff neck); (10) Stubborn (stiff neck).

Also see *Jugular Vein* and *Throat.*

(1) Ps. 73:6; Prov. 3:3-4; (2-3) Josh. 10:24; (4) Gen. 27:40; (5) Isa. 3:16; (6) 1 Sam. 4:18; (7) Song. 4:4; 7:4; (8) Job 41:22; Ps. 133:1-2; Song. 4:4; (9) 2 Chron. 36:13; Ps. 75:5; (10) Ps. 32:9; Jer. 17:23.

Necklace: (1) What's on the heart; (2) Condition of the heart; (3) Decision-maker/making; (4) Pride; (5) Yoke; (6) Subjection/service.

(1-2) Exod. 28:30; Isa. 59:17; Eph. 6:14; 1 Thess. 5:8; 1 Pet. 3:3-4; (3) Exod. 28:15, 22; (4) Ps. 73:6; (5) Deut. 28:48; (6) Jer. 28:14.

Necrophilia: (1) Soul-tie to dead relationships; (2) Contact with the dead (divination); (3) In relationship with an unbeliever; (4) Obsession.

(1) Rom. 7:24; (2) 1 Sam. 28:8; (3) Matt. 8:22; (4) Judg. 19:24-29.

Needle: (1) Looking for life; (2) Injection of life; (3) Accompanied with horror or fear may be a sign that the enemy is trying to corrupt you (as in poisoning your blood); (4) Taking on an offense (poisoning your heart).

Also see *Drug Use* and *Syringe.*

(1-2) Lev. 17:11; (3-4) 1 Sam. 15:23 & Rev. 9:21.

Neighbor: (1) Someone not in Christ (i.e. not in the household of faith); (2) Someone in close proximity, not a relative (a companion); (3) Someone needing compassion; (4) The person of the flesh in you (particularly if that person is at enmity with you); (5) Enemy; (6) Someone with whom you have experienced separation or division (i.e. a fence has been erected between you).

Also see *Next Door.*

(1) <u>Luke 10:29-37</u>; 1 John 3:1 (if sons, then in the household); (2) Mark 12:31; (3) <u>Luke 10:36-37</u>; (4) Rom. 8:1-5; Gal. 4:29 (cf. Rom. 7:14); (5) Matt. 5:43-44; (6) Gen. 13:11.

Nest: (1) Bed; (2) Home/house; (3) Forced growth (breaking up nest); (4) Security; (5) A place of security for the young; (6) Vulnerable (cast out of the nest); (7) Pride (high nest); (8) Sojourners (no nest).

(1) Matt. 8:20; (2) Num. 24:21; <u>Ps. 84:3</u>; 104:17; (3) Deut. 32:11-12; (4) Job 39:27; Jer. 22:23; 48:28; 49:16; (5) Ps. 84:3; (6) Prov. 27:8; <u>Isa. 16:2</u>; (7) Obad. 1:4; (8) Luke 9:58.

Net: (1) Evangelism for either Kingdom of God or the kingdom of darkness; (2) Kingdom of Heaven; (3) Ministry; (4) Trap; (5) Poetic justice (falling into your own net); (6) Seductive heart; (7) Death; (8) Trapped in the Internet.

Also see *Fishing, Hook,* and *Web.*

(1) Matt. 4:19; <u>23:15</u> (KJV); (2) Matt. 13:47; (3) Matt. 4:19; (4) <u>Ps.</u> 57:6; <u>140:5</u>; Prov. 29:5; (5) Ps. 141:10; (6) Eccl. 7:26; (7) Eccl. 9:12.

New: (1) Regenerated or born again (new vessel); (2) New level of Glory of God.

(1) Matt. 9:16; <u>2 Cor. 5:17</u>; <u>Tit. 3:5</u>; As in, "new wineskin"; (2) <u>2 Cor. 3:18</u>; 1 Sam. 2:19.

New House: (1) The new nature (the born-again believer in Christ).

Also see *House* and *Old House.*

(1) <u>2 Cor. 5:1 & 17</u>.

News: (1) The Gospel; (2) What God is doing; (3) A news report you need to see; (4) Reference to recent or up and coming events; (5) Something about to make headlines; (6) Mass exposure; (7) Sudden exposure (breaking news); (8) Sudden (newsflash).

Also see *Newspaper.*

(1) Isa. 61:1 (NASB); <u>Luke 2:10</u> (NASB); Rom. 10:15; (2) Luke 1:19b; 2:8-10; <u>Acts 11:20-22</u>; (3) Luke 19:2-5; (4) Amos 1:1; (5) <u>John</u> 13:19, <u>14:29</u>; (6) Isa. 52:7; Matt. 24:30; 26:64; (7) Gen. 45:13; 1 Sam. 4:14b; (8) Acts 22:17-18.

Newspaper: (1) God's Word; (2) Headlines; (3) Public Exposure; (4) Gossip; (5) Listening to the world.

Also see *News* and *Delivering Newspapers.*

(1) Ps. 68:11; <u>Isa. 52:7</u>; (2-3) <u>Acts 26:23, 26</u>; (4) Eccl. 10:20; (5) Matt. 16:13.

Newspaper (Delivering Newspapers): (1) Gospel-preaching; (2) Making something public; (3) Publishing; (4) Distributing Bibles.

(1) Isa. 61:1 (NASB); Matt. 3:1-2; 24:14; (2) Mark 1:45; Luke 5:15; (3) Ps. 68:11 (KJV); Isa. 52:7; (4) Ps. 68:11 (KJV); Acts 10:37-38 (KJV); 13:49 (KJV).

Next Door: (1) Signifies a parallel from your life of what is happening in the Spirit; (i.e. earthly to spiritual; business to spiritual); (2) Close in time or place; (3) Next opportunity; (4) Neighbor; (5) Associate or friend (someone close to you); (6) At hand.

Also see *Door* and *Neighbor.*

(1) 1 Sam. 15:27-28; Hos. 3:1; Jer.18:6; (2) John 4:46b-47, 49-53 (the miracle was performed at the same time, which means that there is no distance in prayer!); (3) 1 Cor. 16:9; (4) Luke 10:29; (5) Mark 12:31; (6) As in "nearby" in time or space (cf. Matt. 3:2).

Night: (1) Darkness; (2) Evil; (3) Betrayal; (4) Absence of Christ; (5) Stumbling (walking at night); (6) Secret or hidden (under cover of dark); (7) Walking at night is indicative of the old self (the unbelieving you); (8) Judgment; (9) Ignorance; (10) The realm of unbelief.

Also see *Darkness* and *Day.*

(1) Gen. 1:2, 5; 1 Thess. 5:5; (2-3) John 13:30; 1 Cor. 11:23; (4) John 8:12; 9:4; 11:10; (5) John 11:10; (6) John 3:2; 7:50; 19:39; (7) John 3:2; (Matt. 27:4 & John 13:30. Judas failed to see who Jesus was!); (8) Jude 1:6; (9) John 3:2 & 4; As in, "they are in the dark about…"; (10) John 3:2; 13:30.

Nightclub: (1) The world (place where those in the dark congregate); (2) Church without Christ.

Also see *Bar* and *Hotel.*

(1) Gen. 1:5 & 1 John 1:5-6; (2) John 8:12; 11:10; 13:30.

Nightmares: See Chapter Four: "Are all dreams from God?"

Nine: (1) Finality and judgment; (2) End or conclusion; (3) Fruitfulness; (4) Number of the Holy Spirit (The Fruitful One); (5) Not giving glory to God.

(1-2) The last digit nine marks the end and conclusion of a matter; (3) Gen. 17:1-2; Abraham was promised *exceeding fruitfulness* at 99 years of age; Matt. 7:16; John 15:8; Fruit is the final evidence of Christian growth and discipleship; (4) Gal. 5:22-23 (nine fruit); (5) Luke 17:17-18.

Nine O'Clock: (1) Time to be filled with the Spirit (Holy happy-hour).

(1) Acts 2:15.

Nineteen: As combinations of 9+10=19: (1) Complete judgment; (2) Certain finality; (3) Complete fruitfulness; (4) Fullness of the Spirit.

For Scriptures, see *Nine* and *Ten*.

Nineteen Seventy (1970): (1) A generation full of the Spirit.

For Scriptures, see *Nineteen* and *Seventy*.

Ninety: (1) Complete judgment; (2) Finality.

For Scriptures, see *Nine* and *Ten*.

Ninja: (1) Spiritual special agent (mighty people of valor); (2) Evil spirit/demon; (3) Spirit of death.

(1) 2 Sam. 23:8-12; (2-3) Jer. 9:21; Joel 2:9.

Nit: (1) Nit-picking; (2) Fault-finding; (3) Judgment (if someone is going through your hair).

Also see *Lice*.

(1) Matt. 7:2-6; 23:24; (2) Mark 3:2; (3) Matt. 22:15-17.

Noise: (1) Distraction; (2) Interference; (3) Busyness; (4) Annoying interference; (5) God's voice (loud trumpet noise); (6) A multitude.

(1) Matt. 13:22; Mark 10:21; Luke 9:59-62; Rev. 2:4; (2) Matt. 23:13; (3) Luke 10:40-42; (4) 1 John 2:15-17; (5) Exod. 19:19; (6) Isa. 13:4; 17:12.

Non-Deciduous: See Evergreen.

North: (1) Place of God's throne; (2) Place of judgment; (3) Location of the enemy; (4) Moving into your spiritual inheritance (turning northward); (5) Literally going somewhere north of your current location (turning northward); (6) Consider aspects in your own environment relating to north.

Also see *South*.

(1) Lev. 1:11; Ps. 75:6-7; Isa. 14:13-14; (2) Jer. 1:13-14; (3) Ezek. 38:6; (4-5) Deut. 2:3.

Nose: (1) Spiritual senses; (2) Spirit; (3) Led; (4) Insensitive; (5) Pride; (6) Offense (smoke in nostrils); (7) Offended; (8) Broken spirit (broken nose);

(9) Unrelenting (hard-nosed); (10) Proud and insensitive to the Spirit (hard-nosed); (11) Unapproachable (hard-nosed); (12) Spiritually insensitive (no nose).

Also see *Nosebleed.*

(1) Ezek. 23:25; Ps. 45:7-8; (2) Job 27:3 (KJV); (3) 2 Kings 19:28; Isa. 37:29; (4) Ps. 115:6; (5-6) Isa. 65:5; (7) As in, "who put their nose out of joint?"; (8) Ps. 51:17; (cf. Gen. 2:7 & Isa. 42:5); (9-10) Job 41:2; (11) Job 41:2; Ps. 115:6; (12) Ezek. 23:25.

Nosebleed: (1) Strife; (2) Possible family anger issue; (3) Damaged sensitivity.

Also see *Blood* and *Nose.*

(1-2) Prov. 30:33.

Nudity: See Naked.

Numbers: See individual entries.

Number Plate: See License Plate.

Nun: (1) Purity.

(1) 2 Tim. 5:2.

Nurse: (1) Christ; (2) Holy Spirit; (3) Caring church; (4) Gentle nurturer of young Christians; (5) Ministers who affectionately impart the Word; (6) Feeder and provider of the young; (7) Carer; (8) Male or female servants; (9) Angels; (10) Healing angel (messenger of God ushering in the healing power of God).

Also see *Doctor* and *Hospital.*

(1) Isa. 40:11; (2) John 14:26; 15:26 (KJV); (3) Acts 4:35; (4) Exod. 2:7, 9; 1 Thess. 2:7; (5) 1 Thess. 2:7-8; (4) Num. 11:12; (5) Ruth 4:16; (6) Isa. 49:23; (7) Matt. 18:10; Heb. 1:14; (10) John 5:4.

Nuts (Fruit): (1) God's Word; (2) Words of promise; (3) Someone distorting God's Word (sugar-coated nuts).

Also see *Seed.*

(1-2) Matt. 13:19-23; Luke 8:11; 1 Pet. 1:23; (3) Matt. 4:6.

Nuts and Bolts: (1) Underpinning truths.

Also see *Bolts.*

(1) Heb. 6:1-2.

Oak: (1) Longevity; (2) Stable (deeply rooted); (3) Kingdom pillar (landmark); (4) The Cross; (5) Place to shelter; (6) Place to bury the past; (7) Idolatry; (8) Represents a proud enemy; (9) Durable (used for oars); (10) Strong.

(1) Zech. 11:2 (KJV); (2) Amos 2:9; (3) Josh. 24:26; (4) 2 Sam. 18:9-10, 14 (KJV); (5) 1 Kings 13:14; (6) Gen. 35:4, 8 (KJV); 1 Chron. 10:12 (KJV); (7) Isa. 1:29 (KJV); 44:14-15; Ezek. 6:13; Hos. 4:13; (8) Isa. 2:12-13; (9) Ezek. 27:6; (10) Amos 2:9.

Oath: (1) Promise; (2) Pledge; (3) Allegiance; (4) Covenant.

(1-4) Gen. 21:22-31; 24:2-3, 8; Eccl. 8:2.

Ocean: See Sea.

Octopus: (1) Fleshly control or influence (tentacles); (2) Controlling spirit; (3) Soul-tie stronghold (octopus on head).

Also see *Eight* and *Squid.*

(1) Exod. 2:14; Prov. 6:5; Gal. 2:4; (2) 1 Kings 21:7-10; (3) 2 Cor. 10:4-5.

Odor (Bad): (1) Foolishness; (2) Monstrous deeds; (3) Demons; (4) Deception; (5) Wrong spirit; (6) Offensive.

Also see *Incense* and *Perfume.*

(1) Eccl. 10:1; (2) Joel 2:20; (3) Eccl. 10:1 (see *Flies*); (4) Mark 9:25; Eph. 4:14; Also as in, "something is off" or "I smell a rat"; (5) Ps. 32:2; Mark 1:23-24; (6) Matt. 13:21; 16:23.

Office: (1) Business; (2) Kingdom office or position; (3) Pastor, teacher, evangelist, prophet, and apostle; (4) The heart (as the place where we do business with God); (5) Heaven (place where God sits running everything).

(1) 1 Sam. 21:2; (2-3) Eph. 4:11-12; (4) Ps. 91:1; (5) Gen. 28:12; Heb. 12:22-23.

Offspring: (1) Future; (2) Fruits of faith.

(1) Job 21:8; (2) Rom. 4:13.

Oil (Dirty): (1) Unclean spirit; (2) Foolishness.

(1) Eccl. 10:1; (2) Eccl. 10:1.

Oil (Olive): (1) Anointing; (2) Crowned by God; (3) The Holy Spirit; (4) Light; (5) Spiritual strength; (6) The Glory of God.

Also see *Olive.*

(1) Exod. 29:7, 21; 30:24-31; Lev. 8:12; <u>Ps. 23:5</u>; 133:2; (2) <u>Lev. 21:12</u> (KJV); 1 Sam. 10:1; 16:13; <u>1 Kings 1:39</u>; 2 Kings 9:3; Ps. 45:7; 89:20; (3) <u>1 Sam. 16:13</u>; Isa. 61:3; Eph. 1:13; 4:30; (4) Exod. 25:6; 35:8, 28; (5) Ps. 92:10; (6) Zech. 4:12.

Oil Rig: (1) Church in the Spirit; (2) Anointed ministry.

Also see *Gasoline* and *Gas Station.*

(1-2) Matt. 25:9; 1 Sam. 16:13 & John 7:38-39.

Oil Slick: (1) Wrong spirit (slick on a road/path); (2) Someone causing others to backslide; (3) Slippery character; (4) Out of control (positive or negative).

Also see *Oil Spill.*

(1) Ps. 32:2; <u>Isa. 19:14</u>; (2) Prov. 14:14; Jer. 2:19; 3:6; 8:5; (3) Ps. 55:21; (4) John 21:18.

Oil Spill: (1) Stopping the flow of the Spirit; (2) Tragic environmental changes (Ecological disaster); (3) Anointing; (4) Outbreak of the Spirit, which is an offense to the world.

Also see *Oil Slick.*

(1) 1 Thess. 5:19; (2) Matt. 27:51, 54; (3) 1 Sam. 16:13; (4) Matt. 12:24, 28 (offended by the Spirit of God); Acts 2:15.

Old: (1) Past; (2) Unregenerate (not renewed by the Spirit); (3) Former life; (4) Memories.

(1-2) <u>2 Cor. 5:17</u>; (3) Isa. 43:18-19a; (4) <u>Isa. 65:17</u>.

Old House: (1) The old self (prior to Christ); (2) The past; (3) Grandfather/mother; (4) Heritage.

(1-2) <u>2 Cor. 5:1</u> (KJV); 1 Cor. 3:9b; Heb. 3:6; (cf. 2 Cor. 5:17); (3) 2 Sam. 8:3, 6; (4) Luke 1:27, 69; 2:4; (cf. Gen. 15:4 (spiritual lineage) & Luke 19:9).

Old Man: (1) Person of the flesh; (2) Unbeliever; (3) Past or history; (4) Grandfather; (5) Patriarch; (6) Wisdom; (7) God; (8) Stronghold; (9) The enemy (devil).

Also see *First Nations Peoples* and *Native/s.*

(1) <u>Rom. 6:6</u>; <u>Eph. 4:22</u>; <u>Col. 3:9</u>; 2 Cor. 5:17; Jude 1:4; Matt. 9:17; (2) <u>Luke 1:18</u>; John 3:4; (3) <u>2 Pet. 1:21</u> (KJV); (4) Prov. 17:6; 1 Sam. 2:31 & 4:18-19; (5) Gen. 25:8; 43:27; (6) Job 12:12; (7) <u>Dan. 7:9</u>, 13, 22; (8) Gen. 25:23; Lam. 1:7; <u>Hos. 7:9</u>; (9) Rev. 12:9.

Old Woman: (1) Person of the flesh; (2) Church history; (3) Grandmother; (4) Matriarch; (5) Wisdom; (6) Holy Spirit; (7) Past or history.

(1) Rom. 6:6; (2) Eph. 5:25, 27, 31-32; (3) 2 Tim. 1:5; (4) Gen. 18:11; 1 Pet. 3:5-6; (5) Prov. 8:1-2, 22-23; (6) Gen. 2:24 (cf. Eph. 5:31-32 & Phil. 2:7); (7) 2 Tim. 1:5.

Olive: (1) Fruit of the Spirit; (2) Depositing or birthing the anointing; (3) Spiritual offspring.

Also see *Oil (Olive)* and *Olive Tree.*

(1) Isa. 61:3; Gal. 5:22-23; (2) 1 Sam. 16:13; (3) Deut. 28:40-41.

Olive Tree: (1) Anointed person.

(1) Zech. 4:11-14; Rev. 11:3-4.

One: (1) God; (2) Literally one; (3) Beginning; (4) Source; (5) Commencement; (6) First in order, time, rank, or importance; (7) Compound unity; (8) Only; (9) Indivisible; (10) Love; (11) First heaven (the physical realm).

(1) Gen.1:1; (2) Literally one; (3) Gen. 1:1; 8:13; (4) God is the source of all that follows; (5) Genesis is the commencement of all that follows; (6) Isa. 44:6; 48:12-13; Rev. 1:11, 17; 2:8; 22:13; (7) Gen. 2:24; Num. 15:16; Mark 12:29; Acts 28:25; Gal. 3:28; (8-9) Isa. 43:10-11; (10) John 17:23; 2 Cor. 13:11; Phil. 2:2; (11) 2 Cor. 12:2.

One Hundred: See Hundred.

One Hundred and Twenty: (1) The end of the flesh (life in the Spirit); (2) A period of waiting; (3) One accord/Spirit utterance; (4) The Glory of God.

(1-2) Gen. 6:3, 13; (Deut. 34:7 & Matt. 17:3); (Luke 24:49 & Acts 1:15); (3) Acts 2:1-13; (4) Exod. 34:29-33 (Moses revealed the Glory of God); Deut. 34:7; Luke 9:30-31; Jude 1:9; (After 3 x 40 year periods Moses entered into Glory); Luke 2:22; [cf. Lev. 12:2, 4]; Matt. 4:2; Acts 1:3; John 17:5 (After 3 x 40 day periods Jesus ascended to the Father and was glorified).

Onion: (1) Represents the World (Egypt); (2) Dwelling in the past and getting upset over nothing (tears from peeling onions); (3) Focusing on the past, having murky vision; (4) Layers or levels; (5) New York; (6) Chicago; (7) Dealing with heartfelt issues (chopping onions); (8) Dealing with issues of the heart (removing layers of the onion).

(1-3) <u>Num. 11:5</u>; (4) As in, the rings of an onion; (5-6) These cities also known as the "Big Onion"; (7) Matt. 3:10; (8) Deut. 10:16; 30:6.

Open: (1) Opportunity (door); (2) Release; (3) Reveal/ed; (4) Manifest (tangibly seen); (5) Spiritual (in)sight; (6) In the Spirit; (7) Receive; (8) Freely; (9) Having a receptive heart; (10) Alive; (11) Released to speak; (12) Explain; (13) Bring to salvation; (14) Hear (open ears); (15) Opposite to secretly; (16) Opposite to shut.

Also see *Window (Open Window)*.

(1) 1 Cor. 16:9; <u>2 Cor. 2:12</u>; Col. 4:3; (2) Mark 7:34-35 (to speak); Acts 5:19; 12:10; 16:26; <u>Rev. 5:5</u>; 6:1; (3) Matt. 5:2; 9:30; 13:35; <u>Luke 24:27, 32</u>; Rom. 3:13; Eph. 6:19; Heb. 4:13; (4) Matt. 6:4, 6, 18; 27:52-53; Luke 4:17-21; John 7:4; Col. 2:15 (cf. NKJV & KJV); (5) Matt. 7:7-8; (6) Matt. 9:30; Luke 24:31-32; (7) Matt. 25:1-12; Luke 12:35-36; (8) Mark 1:45; 8:32; John 7:13; 11:54; 18:20; (9) Matt. 13:19 & Luke 24:45; Acts 16:14; 2 Cor. 3:17-18 (KJV); Rev. 3:20; (10) Acts 9:40; (11) Acts 10:34; (12) Acts 17:3 (cf. NKJV & KJV); Luke 24:31-32; (13) Acts 26:18 (bring to the light); (14) 1 Pet. 3:12; (15) John 7:10; (16) Rev. 3:7.

Open Heaven: (1) Revelation or vision; (2) Blessing; (3) Gift from God; (4) Abundance; (5) Righteousness comes down, and with open hearts, salvation is the response; (6) Easy to witness.

Also see *Windows of Heaven*.

(1) Ps. 78:23-24; <u>Ezek. 1:1b</u>; John 1:51; Acts 7:56; 10:11; Rev. 4:1; (2) Deut. 28:12; <u>Mal. 3:10</u>; Matt. 3:16; (3) Ps. 78:23-24; (4) Gen. 7:11; (5-6) Isa. 45:8.

Op Shop: (1) Looking for an opportunity; (2) Middle-aged person looking for a second-hand spouse; (3) Church full of old wineskins.

Also see *Secondhand Store*.

(1) Gal. 6:10; (2) Ruth 3:7-9 (wanting to be covered by another's clothes); (3) Matt. 9:17; Acts 21:30.

Optician: (1) God; (2) Jesus Christ; (3) The Holy Spirit; (4) Developing spiritual vision/faith (eye testing); (5) Prophet (as someone who helps you see).

Also see *Eyes, Window,* and *Windows of Heaven*.

(1) Gen. 21:19; 2 Kings 6:17; (2) John 9:6-7; (3) Ezek. 11:24; Joel 2:28; John 14:17; Acts 2:17; (4) Heb. 11:1, 3, 7, 27; (5) 1 Sam. 9:9; Eph. 4:11-12.

Orange (Color): (1) Warning; (2) Moving toward red (sin); (3) Human and flesh; (4) Transition/change or "given to change"; (5) The glory of God (amber). Also see *Amber*.

(1) As in when an amber traffic light signals a red light is about to be displayed; (2) <u>Gen. 4:6-7</u>; (3) Gen. 2:7; 25:25; 2 Cor. 4:7; (4) Prov. 24:21-22; (5) Ezek. 1:4, 27.

Orb: (1) Spirit; (2) Life.

Also see *Ball, Circle,* and *Wheel.*

(1-2) Ezek. 1:16, 19-21.

Orbit: (1) Life's path; (2) Being led by the Spirit.

Also see *Flying, Planet,* and *Satellite.*

(1) <u>Ps. 16:11</u>; 19:4; (2) Rom. 8:14.

Orchard: (1) Fruitfulness.

Also see *Fruit Tree, Plantation,* and *Vineyard.*

(1) <u>Eccl. 2:5</u>; Song. 4:13.

Ornament: (1) Something left on the shelf and forgotten about.

Also see *Trophy.*

(1) Gen. 40:23.

Ostrich: (1) Without wisdom and understanding.

(1) Job 39:13-17.

Other Side: (1) Opposite or opposed; (2) Enemy; (3) Separate; (4) Destiny or destination; (5) Heaven (spirit realm); (6) Avoidance or denial; (7) The believing or unbelieving side.

Also see *Passing Over Something* and *River.*

(1) John 8:44; 1 Sam. 17:3; (2) <u>1 Sam. 17:3</u>; (3) Matt. 8:18; (4) Matt. 14:22; (5) 1 Sam. 28:11; 2 Cor. 12:2-4; (6) Luke 10:32; (7) Matt. 25:33; John 19:18 (cf. Luke 23:39-43).

Otter: (1) Joy (fun/playful).

(1) Gal. 5:22-23.

Outboard Motor: (1) Power of the Spirit; (2) Evangelism.

(1) Mic. 3:8; Luke 4:14; 1 Cor. 4:20; (2) Mark 1:17.

Out-of-Body Experience: (1) In the Spirit; (2) Death.

(1) Ezek. 3:12, 14; 8:3; <u>1 Cor. 15:44b</u>; (2) John 19:30.

Outside/Outdoors: (1) Open or exposed; (2) Desire to make known; (3) Not intimate or not in fellowship (in contrast to inside); (4) Outside of Christ; (5) Independent or separate; (6) In the Spirit (heavenly places/eternity); (7) Interacting with the world; (8) Cut off from God.

Also see *Going Out.*

(1) 2 Sam. 11:11; (2) <u>John 7:4</u>; (3) John 13:30; (4) Eph. 2:12; (5) Acts 13:2; (6) 2 Cor. 12:2; Rev. 3:20; (7) Luke 15:12-13; John 13:30; (8) Matt. 25:10-12; Rev. 22:15.

Oven: (1) Heart; (2) Adulterer; (3) Place where sin develops (yeast rises); (4) Hot (devouring); (5) Place of judgment; (6) Black.

Also see *Black* and *Yeast.*

(1) Lev. 2:4; <u>Hos. 7:6</u>; (2-3) Hos. 7:4; (4) Hos. 7:7; (5) Ps. 21:8-9; Mal. 4:1; Matt. 6:30; (6) Lam. 5:10.

Overalls: See Coveralls.

Overflow/ing: (1) Fullness of the Spirit/power; (2) Building oneself up by speaking in tongues; (3) Overcoming; (4) Holy Spirit ministry; (5) Abundance.

Also see *Flood.*

(1) Ps. 23:5; <u>Mark 5:30</u>; Acts 2:4; 13:9; (2) John 7:38-39; 2 Tim. 1:6-7; Jude 1:20; (3) Gen. 49:22; (4) Ps. 133:2-3; (5) Ps. 115:13-14; Matt. 13:12; 24:12.

Overseas: (1) Different kingdom (kingdom of self or Kingdom of God); (2) Prior to conversion; (3) Journey to heaven (crossing sea); (4) Life's journey (crossing sea); (5) Going on a mission; (6) Ministering outside your domain.

Also see *International Flight.*

(1) Matt. 24:7; (2) Josh. 2:10; (3-4) Mark 6:45; (5-6) Acts 13:4-5; 28:1, 8.

Overtaking (Vehicle): (1) Decision necessary to go forward; (2) Decision necessary to get past perceived obstacle; (3) Ambition; (4) Jostling for position; (5) Spiritually blind decision (blind corner); (6) Impatience (not waiting); (7) Misuse of power (immaturity); (8) Presumption (without faith); (9) Moving to the expectation of others; (10) Call for humble obedience (being overtaken); (11) Call to beware of jealousy; (12) Disaster and judgment; (13) Won't wait; (14) Wanting leadership.

Also see *Automobile, Auto Accident,* and *Waiting.*

(1-2) 1 Kings 12:1-6; (3) 2 Sam. 15:4-6; (4) Matt. 20:21; Mark 9:34; (5) Prov. 3:5-6; (6) Gen. 16:1-4; 1 Sam. 13:5-13; (7) 1 Kings 12:8-10; (8) Gen. 16:1-2; (9) 1 Sam. 15:24; Prov. 29:25; (10) 1 Sam. 18:7; (11) Luke 15:28-30; (12) Gen. 19:19; (13) 2 Kings 18:19-23; (14) Mark 9:34.

Owe: See Debt.

Owl: (1) Loner; (2) Inhabits the desolate waste; (3) Astute unbeliever (creature of the night); (4) Wisdom; (5) Demon.

(1) Job 30:29 (KJV); Ps. 102:6-7; (2) Isa. 13:21; 34:10-15; Jer. 50:39 (KJV); (3) Lev. 11:13, 17; Deut. 14:12, 15; (cf. Isa. 34:14) (4) As in, "wise old owl"; (5) Isa. 34:14 (night creatures).

Owing: See entries under Debt.

Ox: (1) Strength; (2) Believer; (3) Time to plow; (4) Unknowingly following someone to your death.

Also see *Ass* and *Plowing.*

(1) Prov. 14:4; (2) Deut. 22:10; Job 1:14; (these verses contrast the ox and ass as believer and unbeliever); (cf. Deut. 25:4 & 1 Cor. 9:9-10); (3) Deut. 22:10; 1 Kings 19:19; Job 1:14; (4) Prov. 7:22.

Pad (Paper): (1) Heart.

Also see *Paper* and *Scroll.*

(1) Rom. 2:15; Heb. 8:10.

Paddock: See Field.

Padlock: (1) Security or secured; (2) Hard nut to crack; (3) Fear; (4) Shame; (5) Unforgiveness; (6) Yoke (or union); (7) Stronghold.

(1) Acts 5:23a; 16:23; (2) Josh. 6:1; (3-4) Prov. 29:25; (5) Matt. 18:30, 34; (6) 2 Cor. 6:14; (7) Ps. 89:40.

Paedophile: See Pedophile.

Pail: See Bucket.

Pain: (1) Spiritual childbirth; (2) A call to birth something in the Spirit; (3) Discipline; (4) Judgment against sin; (5) A heart pained; (6) Struggling to understand the prosperity of the wicked; (7) Pain of death; (8) Bad news.

(1) 1 Sam. 4:19; Ps. 48:6; Isa. 13:8; 66:7-8; Jer. 22:23; Mic. 4:10; Rom. 8:22 (KJV); Acts 2:24; Rev. 12:2; (2) 1 Sam. 1:12-17; 1 Kings 18:42-44; Rom. 8:26-27; (3) Job 33:19; Isa. 21:3; 26:16-18 (Note that God's chastening leads to birth); (4) Ps. 25:18; Jer. 15:18-19; 30:23 (KJV); 51:8-9; (5) Ps. 55:3-4 (by hateful words); Jer. 4:19; 6:24; (6) Ps. 73:16; (7) Ps. 116:3; Acts 2:24; (8) Isa. 23:5 (KJV).

Paintball Skirmish: (1) Playing church (not real warfare).

(1) Rev. 3:1.

Painting (noun): (1) Representation; (2) Image; (3) Illustration; (4) The likeness of something or someone; (5) Idol; (6) A conception; (7) View or vision; (8) Lacking the spiritual dimension (depth).

Also see *Painting (verb)* and *Photographs*.

(1-3) Matt. 13:3 (a word picture); (4) Gen. 5:3; (5) Num. 33:52 (KJV); (6-7) Hab. 2:2; (8) 1 Cor. 2:10.

Painting (verb): (1) Interior painting speaks of inner renewal or refurbishment; (2) Refreshing of the Spirit; (3) Exterior painting may refer to an outward show or hypocrisy; (4) Cover up; (5) Mere outward adornment; (6) Moving in faith (ad libbing); (7) Prophesying (inspired painting); (8) Preparation.

Also see *Artist* and *Painting (noun)*.

(1-2) 2 Kings 12:14; 2 Kings 22:5; 2 Chron. 24:4, 12; 29:3; 34:8-10; (3-4) Matt. 23:25-27; Luke 11:39; (5) 2 Kings 9:30; (6) Rom. 4:17; (7) 1 Sam. 9:9; Rom. 12:6; (8) Matt. 3:3 & Luke 7:28.

Pajamas: (1) Unprepared; (2) Spiritually unaware; (3) Sleeping on the job.

Also see *Dressing Gown* and *Sleeping*.

(1-3) Matt. 26:40-41; Luke 12:35-38.

Palace: (1) Spiritually rich Christian; (2) The place of the Presence of the King (God); (3) The place of the throne (authority); (4) The place of feasting; (5) The place of audience before the king; (6) The place of decrees; (7) The place of glories; (8) The place of rejoicing; (9) The place of prosperity; (10) The place to flourish; (11) The place of pride and judgment.

(1) 2 Cor. 5:1; (2) Ps. 45:8-9; 48:3; (3) Esther 1:2; (4) Esther 1:5; (5) Esther 2:3 (KJV); (6) Esther 3:15 (KJV); 8:14 (KJV); (7) Ps. 45:13-14; (8) Ps. 45:15; (9) Ps. 122:7; (10) Dan. 4:4; (11) Amos 6:8.

Palm (Hand): (1) Be buffeted; (2) Struck by words; (3) Heart (left palm); (4) Powerless (no hands); (5) Remembered (inscribed palms).

Also see *Hand*.

(1) Matt. 26:67; Mark 14:65 (struck by palm); (2) 2 Chron. 18:23; John 18:22; (3) Lev. 14:15-16, 26-27 (left palm represents the heart while the right finger its application, cf. Rom. 10:9-10); (4) 1 Sam. 5:4; (5) Isa. 49:16.

Palm (Tree): (1) Victory; (2) Salvation; (3) Believer; (4) Flourish; (5) Righteous (upright believer); (6) Leader (palm branch).

(1-2) Deut. 34:3; Judg. 4:5ff; John 12:13; Rev.7:9-10; (3-4) 1 Kings 6:29, 32; Ps. 92:12; (5) Song. 7:7 (upright); (cf. Jer. 10:5a); (6) Isa. 9:14-15.

Palsy: (1) Bedridden; (2) Spiritually lying down due to sin.

Also see *Bed*.

(1) Matt. 8:6 (KJV); 9:2 (KJV); (2) Ps. 51:9-10 (KJV); Mark 2:3-5 (KJV).

Pant: (1) Long for; (2) Birthing.

Also see *Birthing* and *Thirsty*.

(1) Ps. 42:1; (2) Ps. 48:6.

Pants (Underwear): (1) Self-righteous.

Also see *Genitals, Legs, Trousers,* and *Underwear*.

(1) Gen. 3:7.

Pantry: (1) Heart full of resources (The Word of God).

(1) 1 Kings 17:16; Matt. 14:14-21.

Paper/s: (1) Documents; (2) Record; (3) Certificate; (4) Deeds; (5) Account or debt; (6) Plans.

Also see *Pad (Paper)*.

(1-2) Ezra 4:15; Esther 2:23; 6:1; 10:2; (3) Jer. 3:8; (4) Gen. 23:17-18; (5) Matt. 18:23-24; (6) 1 Chron. 28:11-12.

Paper/s (Scrunched-Up Paper): (1) Debt or contract cancellation; (2) Failed plans.

(1-2) Col. 2:14-15.

Paper/s (Torn Paper): (1) Division; (2) Divorce; (3) Loss.

(1) Matt. 5:32; (3) 1 Sam. 15:27-28.

Paper Bag: (1) Temporary issue; (2) Hiding/cover up something.
(1) Matt. 5:25a; (2) Matt. 5:15.

Paper Cut: (1) Document, certificate, or deed that afflicts you.
(1) Ezra 4:18-19, 21.

Paper Plane: (1) Rhema word (words carried by the Spirit); (2) Words carried by a spirit (-); (3) Prayer requests (thrown into the air); (4) Someone trying to get your attention by sending you a message (someone throwing a paper plane at you).
Also see *Aeroplane* and *Paper*.
(1) 1 Sam. 3:19; 1 Cor. 2:4; (2) Eph. 6:16 (-); (3) Jon. 2:7; (4) 1 Kings 19:2; Luke 7:22.

Parachute: (1) Bringing Heaven to earth by the Spirit; (2) Leap of faith (no parachute); (3) Escape plan; (4) Way out; (5) Safety net; (6) Survival mentality; (7) Self-preservation; (8) Love.
(1) Matt. 6:10; John 5:36; (2) Matt. 14:29; (3) Josh. 2:15, 18; (4) Acts 9:25; (5) Acts 5:1-2; (6) Num. 13:31; Mark 14:50; (7) Luke 22:54-60; (8) Song. 2:4; 6:4; Rom. 8:38-39; 2 Cor. 5:14a (KJV).

Paramedic: (1) Evangelist (someone who brings people to meet the Physician/Healer [Christ]); (2) Ministering angels.
(1) Mark 2:3-11; John 1:40-42; (2) 1 Kings 19:5-6; Dan. 10:10-11; John 5:4.

Parasite/s: (1) Someone who lives by stealing the spiritual life of another; (2) Someone who is just along for the ride—for what they can get out of it.
Also see *Flea*, *Leech*, and *Maggot*.
(1) (Lev. 17:11 & Prov. 30:15); 2 Tim. 3:4-7; (2) John 12:6.

Parents: (1) Past; (2) Guardians; (3) Careers or guides; (4) Forebears; (5) Leadership or management; (6) Spiritual parents; (7) Jesus and the Church; (8) The Father and Holy Spirit; (9) Literal parents.
Also see *Father* and *Mother*.
(1) Luke 18:29-30; John 9:2; (cf. Exod. 20:5, 34:7); 2 Cor. 12:14b; (2) Luke 2:27; John 9:23; Heb. 11:23; (3) Rom. 1:30; (4) John 9:2; (5) Col. 3:20; (6) 1 Cor. 4:15; (7) 1 Cor. 4:15b; Eph. 5:25; (8) Ps. 68:5; Heb. 12:9; (Gen. 2:24 & Phil. 2:7).

Park (Noun): (1) Resting place; (2) Pleasure and recreation; (3) Informal; (4) Lush; (5) Appeals to the eyes; (6) Egypt (human-made park); (7) The Promised Land (natural park); (8) The Church; (9) The believer.

Also see *Garden.*

(1) Ps. 23:2; (2) Eccl. 2:5-6; (3) Esther 7:8; (4-5) Gen. 13:10; (6-7) Deut. 11:10-11; (8) Song. 4:12; 8:13; (9) Song. 4:12, 15.

Parked Auto: (1) Awaiting ministry; (2) Rest; (3) Being worked on (place of preparation); (4) Retirement.

Also see *Garage.*

(1) Luke 1:80; 2:51-52; (2) Ps. 23:2; Mark 6:31; (3) (cf. Deut. 6:23 & Deut. 8:2-3) Ps. 105:19; (4) Luke 16:2; 2 Tim. 4:7-8.

Park Ranger: (1) Informal Authority.

Also see *Gardener.*

(1) Matt. 11:29.

Parrot/s: (1) Repeater or gossip; (2) Angel/s.

Also see *Multi-colored.*

(1) Prov. 17:9; Eccl. 10:20; (2) Luke 2:9; 9:26; Rev. 18:1.

Party: (1) Revival; (2) Celebration; (3) The world.

Also see *Banqueting* and *Birthday.*

(1-2) Luke 15:23-24; (3) Gal. 5:21; 1 Pet. 4:3.

Passenger: Being a passenger is generally a good sign as it says: (1) I'm giving or handing my destiny/my ministry over to God; (2) God's in the driver's seat.

(1-2) Ps. 23:3; Prov. 3:5-6; 8:20 (KJV); John 21:18; Rom. 8:14.

Passing Over Something: (1) Deliverance; (2) Moving into possession of a promise; (3) Ownership (taking possession); (4) Victory; (5) Glory.

(1) Gen. 8:1; Exod. 12:27; Isa. 31:5 (and preservation); (2) Deut. 2:29 (KJV); 3:18; 27:3; Ps. 23:5; (3) Deut. 3:18; 9:1; 11:31; Josh. 1:11; (4) Deut. 2:24; 9:1-4; Josh. 5:1; Judg. 11:32 (KJV); 1 Sam. 14:6-14; 2 Sam. 10:17-19; (5) Prov. 19:11; Mark 4:35-41; Luke 8:22-25.

Passing Under Something: (1) Owned and counted; (2) Tested; (3) Judged; (4) Death; (5) In subjection.

(1-3) Lev. 27:32; Jer. 33:13; (4) 1 Cor. 10:1-2; (5) Neh. 2:14; Isa. 28:15; Jer. 27:8; Ezek. 20:37.

Past Friend/Acquaintance/Employer etc: (1) This may speak of someone similar in character; (2) Doing the same deeds in a spiritual setting; (3) God may be showing you they need prayer; (4) Them literally.

Also see *Aunt, Brother, Sister,* and *Uncle.*

(1) Matt. 11:14; (2) John 3:14; (3) Luke 22:31-32.

Pastor: (1) Jesus (as the head); (2) A shepherd; (3) Actual pastor; (4) Meaning of his/her name.

Also see *Priest.*

(1-2) John 10:11; Heb. 13:20.

Path: (1) What lies ahead; (2) The way of the righteous or the way of darkness; (3) Guidelines; (4) Pathways of your mind (wherever the path leads to is the way you are thinking); (5) The journey of life.

Also see *Cobblestones* and *Road.*

(1-2) Prov. 2:13; Isa. 42:16; Jer. 18:15 (ancient paths = righteous paths); (3) Ps. 17:4; 119:105; (4) Prov. 23:7a; James 1:8; 2 Pet. 3:1-2; (5) Ps. 119:105.

Pattern: (1) Example; (2) Spiritual blueprint; (3) Repeating issue.

(1) 1 Tim. 1:16; Tit. 2:7; Heb. 8:5; (2) Exod. 25:9, 40; Josh. 22:28 (KJV); 1 Chron. 28:11-12; Heb. 8:5; 9:23; (3) Num. 14:22.

Pavement: (1) Commercial pathway; (2) Busy pathway; (3) Judgment.

Also see *Footpath.*

(1-2) Matt. 13:4; (3) John 19:13.

Payment (Incoming): (1) Reaping a harvest (blessing); (2) Issuing forgiveness.

(1) Mark 10:29-30; Gal. 6:7; (2) Luke 11:4.

Payment (Outgoing): (1) Jesus' sacrifice for sin; (2) Cost; (3) Forsaking all to follow Christ; (4) Laying down one's life; (5) Debt cancellation; (6) Receiving forgiveness.

Also see *Debt*.

(1) 1 Cor. 6:20; Col. 2:14; (2) Luke 14:28; (3) Luke 14:33; (4) Matt. 16:24-25; (5-6) Matt. 18:30.

Peacock: (1) Vainglory (bringing attention to self); (2) Pride; (3) Clothed in glory of God.

(1) Prov. 25:27 (self-promotion); John 5:44; 7:18; 12:43; (2) 2 Tim. 3:2; (3) Gen. 37:3.

Peanut: (1) Word of God; (2) Fool (simpleton).

Also see *Seed*.

(1) Luke 8:11; (2) Ps. 14:1, 4.

Peanut Butter/Paste: (1) The Word simplified (smooth peanut paste); (2) Solid food (crunchy peanut paste); (3) Heart (a jar of peanut butter); (4) Deception (professing to be smooth, but actually crunchy).

(1-2) Heb. 5:12-14; (3) Prov. 14:14 (heart as a vessel); John 16:6; (4) Ps. 55:21.

Pearl/s: (1) Jesus Christ; (2) Revelations of God's Word (spiritual treasure); (3) The Kingdom; (4) Arrogance and pride; (5) Gate of the heavenly Jerusalem; (6) Faith; (7) Religious glory.

Also see *Precious Stones*.

(1) Matt. 13:46; (2) Matt. 7:6; (3) Matt. 13:45-46; (4) 1 Tim. 2:9; Rev. 17:4; 18:12, 16; (5) Rev. 21:21; (6) Rev. 21:21 (only entered by faith); (7) Rev. 17:4.

Pedestrian: (1) Sidelined ministry; (2) Spectator; (3) Not part of the race of faith.

Also see *Sidewalk*.

(1) Matt. 11:2-3; (2) Luke 6:7; (3) Acts 13:13; 15:38; Heb. 12:1.

Pedicure: (1) Preparation to preach the good news.

(1) Isa. 52:7.

Pedophile: (1) An authority figure abusing young Christians; (2) Warning of sex predator (evil spirit); (3) Cult leader that spiritually/psychologically over-powers the vulnerable; (4) Warning of an actual pedophile.

(1) 1 Sam. 2:22; (2) Gen. 19:5; (3) Acts 13:10; (4) Lev. 18:10.

Peel: (1) Cover; (2) Flesh; (3) Heart laid bare; (4) Judgment; (5) Labored (shoulders rubbed raw); (6) Affliction; (7) Aftermath of being burned (peeling skin).

(1) 2 Cor. 5:4; 2 Pet. 1:13-14; (2) Col. 1:22; (3) Luke 2:35; (4) Joel 1:7; (5) Ezek. 29:18; (6) Job 30:30; (7) Exod. 29:14.

Pelican: (1) Jesus Christ; (2) Prophetic evangelist (by virtue of the fact that this bird is white, soars, and fishes); (3) A person in the wrong environment (pelican in the wilderness); (4) Loner or alone; (5) Non-believer (unclean bird).

(1) Luke 5:4-5; (2) 1 Kings 18:21-22; Acts 2:40-41; (3-4) Ps. 102:6-7; (5) Lev. 11:13, 18 (KJV); Deut. 14:17 (KJV).

Pellet Gun: See Spud Gun.

Pen/Pencil: (1) Words; (2) Writing; (3) Written record; (4) Tongue; (5) Something written in pencil may indicate that it is temporary or not confirmed.

(1) Ps. 45:1b; (2-3) Job 19:23-24; (4) Ps. 45:1b; (5) James 4:14.

Penguin: (1) Legalistic church (black and white); (2) Religious spirit (flightless bird, feeds on fish).

(1) Rev. 2:2-4; (2) Matt. 23:15, 25.

Penis: See Genitals.

Pepper: Contrasted against salt, salt is white and pepper black. Pepper, therefore, may represent: (1) Decay; (2) Sin; (3) Death; (4) Bad; (5) Lacking character; (6) No peace (without God); (7) Speech without grace; (8) Anger (hot and spicy); (9) Flavoring things to your own liking.

Also see *Salt*.

(1-4) Matt. 5:13; Mark 9:50; (5) Mark 9:49; (6) Mark 9:50; (7) Col. 4:6 (8) Exod. 32:19; Judg. 2:14; (9) Deut. 4:2; Prov. 30:6; Rev. 22:18.

Perfume: (1) Anointing; (2) Presence of Christ; (3) Joyful heart; (4) Love/Intimacy; (5) Seduction; (6) Infidelity; (7) Love offering; (8) Womanhood (femininity).

Also see *Incense*.

(1) Exod. 30:25; 37:29; Ps. 45:8; (2) Ps. 45:6-8; (3) Prov. 27:9; (4) Exod. 30:35-38; Song. 3:6; (5) Prov. 7:17; (6) Isa. 57:8-9; (7) Matt. 26:7; (8) Esther 2:12.

Pergola: See Verandah.

Period: (1) No unity with partner; (2) Yearning for unity; (3) Loss of promise; (4) Grief; (5) Self-righteousness; (6) Embarrassment/shame (period exposed).

(1-4) Lev. 15:19, 25; Matt. 9:20-22; (5-6) Isa. 64:6.

Pet: (1) Something you are feeding (fueling); (2) Habit; (3) Companion or friend.

Also see *Cat, Guinea Pig, Mascot, Dog,* and *Veterinarian.*

(1) Rom. 13:14; 2 Cor. 10:5; Gal. 4:8-9; 5:16-21; (2) 2 Pet. 2:14b; (3) As in, "a dog is man's best friend."

Petrol: See Gasoline.

Petrol Station: See Gas Station.

Pewter: (1) Wickedness (dross); (2) Spiritually poor.

Also see *Tin* and *Tin Man.*

(1) Isa. 1:25; Ezek. 22:18 (pewter has approximately 90 percent tin content) & Ps. 119:119; Prov. 26:23; (2) Num. 31:22 (low on the scale of metals).

Pharmacy: See Chemist Shop.

Photocop/ier/ying: (1) Reproducing; (2) Spreading the Word; (3) Publishing; (4) Exaggerating (multiplying) the past.

(1) 1 Cor. 11:1; (2-3) Ps. 68:11 (KJV); Acts 10:37 (KJV); 13:49 (KJV); (4) 2 Sam. 1:8-10; (cf. 1 Sam. 31:4).

Photographer: See Cameraman.

Photographs: (1) Memories; (2) Identity; (3) A call to remember; (4) Nostalgic longing for the past.

Also see *Camera, Cameraman,* and *Painting (noun).*

(1) Exod. 17:14; (2) 1 Cor. 6:20; 7:23 (who you are is found in whose you are); Gal. 3:27; (3) Neh. 4:14; Ps. 78; (4) Num. 11:5; Ps. 137:1.

Piano: See Music.

Pickpocket: (1) Stealing your or other's hearts; (2) Stealer; (3) Being robbed unawares; (4) Loss of things close to you (husband, wife, or children taken unawares).

Also see *Pocket, Steal,* and *Thief.*

(1) 2 Sam. 15:6; Song. 4:9; Prov. 4:23; (2-3) John 10:10; (4) 1 Sam. 30:2.

Picnic: (1) Desiring casual and relaxed fellowship; (2) Pleasurable and personal communion; (3) Desire for your pleasure versus God's pleasure.

(1) 2 Sam. 11:1; (2) Luke 8:14; (3) Luke 12:29-34; 1 Tim. 5:6; 2 Tim.3:4.

Picture: See Camera, Painting, and Photographs.

Picture Theater: (1) Your life passing before you (before God on judgment day).

Also see *Movie.*

(1) Rev. 20:12.

Pie: (1) Works (something of your own making); (2) Something you desire; (3) Something from the heart; (4) Meddling or busy-body; (5) A heart (good or evil).

Also see *Bake, Baker,* and *Oven.*

(1) Gen. 40:16-17; (2) As in, "wanting a piece of the action"; (3) Hos. 7:6; (4) As in, "finger in the pie"; (5) 2 Cor. 4:7; (as contents enclosed).

Pier: See Jetty.

Pierce: (1) Sorrow and grief.

(1) Luke 2:35; 1 Tim. 6:10.

Pierced Ear: (1) Pledging love; (2) Pledging slavery; (3) Sensitivity to master's (God's) voice.

(1-3) Exod. 21:5-6.

Pig: (1) Unbeliever; (2) Sin; (3) Unclean spirit; (4) Devil/demon; (5) Woman without discretion.

(1-2) Matt. 7:6; Luke 15:13-18; (3-4) Matt. 8:30-32; Mark 5:16; (5) Prov. 11:22.

Pigeon: (1) Christ; (2) Spirit of poverty (poor person's sacrifice/offering).
Also see *Bird/s, Dove, Park,* and *Spirit of Poverty.*
(1) Lev. 1:14-17; 14:5-7; (2) Luke 2:24; (cf. Lev. 12:8).

Pillar: (1) Reliable and strong load-bearing (responsible) leadership; (2) Christ; (3) The Church; (4) The Holy Spirit; (5) Resurrection; (6) Stability and firmness; (7) Covenant witness; (8) Gravestone; (9) Corrosive person (salt); (10) Wisdom's seven pillars; (11) Warning of Christ's return (pillars of smoke).

(1) Gal. 2:9; Rev. 3:12; (2) Gen. 35:14-15; (3) Gen. 35:14-15; 1 Tim. 3:15; (4) Exod. 13:21-22 (fire and cloud); (5) Gen. 28:18 (a pillar erected); (6) Song. 5:15; (7) Gen. 31:51-52; (8) Gen. 35:20; (9) Gen. 19:26; (10) Prov. 9:1; (11) Joel 2:30.

Pillow: (1) Christ (He on whom we rest, and dream); (2) Resting in faith, regardless of circumstance; (3) Heart; (4) Covering that guards your heart (pillowcase).

(1) Gen. 28:11-18 (in setting the stone upright and anointing it Jacob prefigures the resurrection); (2) Mark 4:38, 40; (3) Matt. 11:29; (4) Prov. 4:23.

Pills: See Drug Use.

Pilot: (1) The Holy Spirit; (2) One who is steering; (3) Spiritual guidance.

(1) Ps. 43:3 (The light is fueled by oil); Luke 4:1; (2-3) Acts 13:2, 4.

Pimples: (1) Fleshly imperfections; (2) Adjust spiritual diet by being obedient; (3) Spiritual detoxification and heart revealed (facial pimples); (4) Spiritual immaturity; (5) Pimples on the body may indicate physical health issues relating to that part of the body.

Also see *Face* and *Spot.*

(1) 2 Cor.7:1; (cf. Gal. 5:19-21); (2) John 4:34; (3) 2 Tim. 2:21; (4) 1 Cor. 13:11.

Pin: (1) Word; (2) Tie/fastener; (3) Jesus Christ; (4) End of relationship/project (As in, "pulling the pin").

Also see *Nail* and *Pierce.*

(1) Eccl. 12:11; Col. 2:14; (2) Judg. 16:14; Isa. 22:23; (3) Isa. 22:23; (4) John 13:30.

Pinch: (1) Invitation of the flesh; (2) Fleshly seduction; (3) Offense.

(1-3) Gen. 4:7.

Pine (Tree): (1) Upright person.

(1) Isa. 60:13 (cf. Ps. 92:12).

Pink: (1) Flesh; (2) Sensual; (3) Immoral; (4) Sex; (5) Childhood innocence; (6) Feminine; (7) Young and delicate; (8) Calm.

(1) Rom. 2:28; (2-4) Deut. 22:15-17; (5) 1 Sam. 17:42; (6) As in, "pink for girls and blue for boys"; (7) 1 Sam. 17:42; (8) As in, "pink room."

Pipe (Smoking): See Smoking.

Pipe (Water): (1) Vessel (person or church) of the Word and Spirit; (2) Being led by the Spirit and Word of God.

(1) 2 Kings 20:20 (cf. 1 Kings 18:1, 6-7a); (2) 2 Sam. 5:8.

Pirate: (1) Immoral get-rich-quick lifestyle; (2) Gold-digger.

Also see *Thief.*

(1-2) John 12:4-6.

Pistol: (1) Close range attack of words/thoughts; (2) Someone close speaking against you; (3) Spirit of lust (9mm).

Also see *Bullets, Gun, Rifle,* and *Smoking.*

(1) Gen. 44:18; Mal. 3:5; (2) Matt. 26:14-16; (3) 2 Sam. 13:14-15.

Pit: (1) Hell; (2) Trap; (3) Prison; (4) Heart.

(1) Gen. 37:20; Prov. 1:12; Isa. 14:15; Ezek. 26:20; Rev. 9:1-2, 11; 11:7; (2) Prov. 22:14; 23:27; 26:27; 28:10; Jer. 18:22; (3) Jer. 38:10-13; (4) 2 Cor. 4:7.

Pitchfork: (1) Lies; (2) Devil.

Also see *Fork.*

(1-2) John 8:44; (2) By association.

Pizza: (1) Quick and easy fix for the flesh; (2) Temptation to doubt genuine revelation as a "pizza dream"; (3) Word of God (as bread).

(1) Luke 4:3; (2) Acts 26:24; (3) Deut. 8:3; Matt. 26:17.

Plague: (1) Curse; (2) Judgment; (3) Sin.

(1-3) Ps. 106:29.

Plain: The plain is contrasted against the mountain; therefore, plain represents: (1) Spiritual low place; (2) Place of the efforts of people; (3) Appealing to the natural eyes; (4) Lacking spiritual sight; (5) Place of vulnerability; (6) Place of preparation; (7) Straight or righteous (opposite of crooked).

Also see *Crooked* and *Mountain.*

(1) Gen. 19:17; (2) Gen. 11:2-4; (3) Gen. 13:10-12; (4) Deut. 34:1; (5) Gen. 19:17; (6) Num. 22:1-26:3, 63; 31:12; (7) Isa. 40:4 (KJV).

Plan/s: (1) God's destiny for you; (2) Blueprints of Heaven.

(1) Jer. 1:5; 29:11 (NIV); (2) Exod. 25:40; Luke 1:31-32.

Planet/s: (1) May represent people.

Also see *Mars, Orbit, Pluto,* and *Satellite.*

(1) Gen. 37:9-10; 1 Cor. 15:47.

Plank: (1) Fleshly issue of the heart.

(1) Matt. 7:3.

Plant (noun): (1) Individual or significant plants represent people, churches, or nations. (2) Small plants may represent children.

(1) Isa. 5:7 (Judah); Isa. 53:2 (Christ); Matt. 15:13 (individuals); Matt. 21:33ff; (2) Ps. 144:12, Isa. 53:2.

Plant (verb): (1) Established by God; (2) Burying the flesh; (3) Spreading the Gospel; (4) Be born again; (5) Flourish; (6) Leading to harvest; (7) Planting weeds.

Also see *Sowing.*

(1) Gen. 2:8; Matt. 15:13; Luke 20:9; (2) Rom. 6:5; (cf. John 12:24); (3) 1 Cor. 3:6; (4) Eccl. 3:2; Isa. 61:3; (5) Ps. 92:13; (6) Ps. 107:37; (7) Matt. 13:25; 15:13.

Plantation: (1) Church; (2) Kingdom of God.

Also see *Fruit Tree, Orchard,* and *Vineyard.*

(1) As a gathering of fruit trees (cf. Ps. 1:3); (2) Matt. 21:28-31.

Plaque: (1) Public declaration.

(1) Esther 8:13.

Plaster (Medical Strip): (1) Covering up the real issue; (2) Superficial patch-up job; (3) Placebo.

(1) Matt. 15:8; (2) Matt. 9:16; 2 Kings 12:2-3; 15:3-4, 34-35.

Plastic: (1) Superficial; (2) Not real; (3) Saying it, but not living it; (4) Cheap; (5) Not yet open to view (sealed plastic bag); (6) Not real; (7) Non-Christian hearts (plastic bags and bottles).

(1) Col. 2:18a; (2-3) Matt. 15:8-9; (4) Matt. 8:19-20; Luke 9:61-62 (looking for "easy believism"); (5) Isa. 29:11; Dan. 12:4, 9; (6) Rev. 3:1-2; (7) Matt. 5:29-30; 9:17 (these will perish!).

Plate: (1) Heart. (2) What is seen on a plate may be showing a heart's desire; (3) Someone's agenda; (4) Portion and serving; (5) Ration; (6) Resources and supply; (7) Workload and responsibility; (8) Food; (9) Provisions; (10) What someone deserves.

Also see *Platter, Pots and Pans,* and *Vessel.*

(1) Ps. 78:18; Prov. 3:3 (KJV); 23:7-8; (2) Ps. 73:25-26 (A *portion* is what you get on a plate); Eccl. 2:10 (KJV); Dan. 1:8; (3) Prov. 23:6-7; (4) Luke 12:42; (5) 1 Kings 17:12; (6) 2 Sam. 9:11 (What's on the plate speaks of the extent of resources available); (7) As in, "I have a lot on my plate at the moment"; (8-9) Prov. 23:1-3; (10) Luke 12:46.

Platform: (1) Pulpit.

Also see *Pulpit.*

(1) Gen. 23:3; Matt. 10:27.

Platter: (1) Represents the heart; (2) Too good to be true (silver platter); (3) Blessing; (4) Spoilt; (5) Martyr (head on a platter); (6) Influence of a Jezebel spirit (head on a platter).

Also see *Cup* and *Plate.*

(1) Matt. 23:25-28 (KJV); Luke 11:39 (KJV); (2) As in, "handed to him on a silver platter"; (3-4) As in, "handed to him on a platter"; (5-6) Matt. 14:8.

Playing: (1) Childlikeness; (2) Spiritual immaturity; (3) Spiritually deaf; (4) Looking for outward response; (5) Sexual defilement; (6) Spiritual idolatry; (7) Worship; (8) Foolishness; (9) Entering into the Spirit; (10) Innocence; (11) Sign of peace; (12) Not serious.

Also see *Toys.*

(1-4) Matt. 11:15-19; Luke 7:32; (5) Lev. 21:9; Judg. 19:2; Hos. 2:5; (6) Exod. 32:6; Jer. 2:20; 3:6; 1 Cor. 10:7; (7) 1 Sam. 16:16-18, 23; 2 Sam. 6:5; 1 Chron. 15:29; (8) 1 Sam. 26:21; (9) 2 Kings 3:15; (10) Isa. 11:8; (11) Zech. 8:5; (12) As in, "He's just playing around."

Playground: (1) Spiritually immature and idolatrous church.

(1) Exod. 32:6, 8.

Pliers: (1) Grabbing words (looking for leverage); (2) Gripping and tearing words (grabbing and pulling with pliers); (3) Can be looking for release from something (pulling out a nail).

(1) Mark 12:13; (2) Job 16:9; (3) Eccl. 12:11 (words); Isa. 22:23-25; Jer. 10:4 (idols).

Plowing: (1) Believer; (2) Preparation for harvest; (3) Call to seek God; (4) Hope; (5) Preparing or opening hearts; (6) Breaking up hardened hearts; (7) Working the heart with words (good or evil); (8) Questioning; (9) Whipping; (10) Wanting the past (looking back); (11) Looking forward; (12) Intercourse (seed sowing); (13) Worship.

Also see *Farmer* and *Plowman.*

(1) Luke 17:7, 10; (2) Job 4:8; Prov. 20:4; 21:4; Isa. 28:24-25; Hos. 10:11; 1 Cor. 9:10; (3) Hos. 10:11-12; (4) 1 Cor. 9:10; (5) (Isa. 28:24-25 & Matt. 13:18-19 cf. Luke 3:4-5); (6) Hos. 10:12; (7) Job 4:8; Prov. 21:4; Hos. 10:13; (8) Judg. 14:18; (9) Ps. 129:3; (10-11) Luke 9:62 (plowing requires that the plowman look forward, having two targets (the immediate and distant future) to keep his lines straight); (12) Deut. 22:10 (cf. 2 Cor. 6:14); Judg. 14:18 (social intercourse); (13) Hos. 10:11.

Plowman: (1) One who prepares the hearts; (2) God; (3) Pioneer; (4) Servant; (5) Believer.

See also *Farmer* and *Sower.*

(1) Isa. 28:24-25; Matt. 3:3; (2) Hos. 2:23; 1 Cor. 3:9; (3) 1 Cor. 3:6; (4) Luke 17:7; (5) Luke 9:62.

Plumber: (1) The Holy Spirit; (2) Anointed ministry connecting others to the life-giving Spirit; (3) God/Jesus Christ.

(1) Isa. 44:3; John 7:38-39; (2) Judg. 15:19; John 7:38-39; (3) John 1:33; 4:14; Acts 2:17-18.

Pluto: (1) Hell; (2) The devil; (3) Distant person.

(1-2) Pluto is an alternative name of hades; (3) Matt. 2:1.

Pocket: (1) Heart; (2) Profiting; (3) Stealing; (4) Hiding place; (5) Holding place; (6) Money.

Also see *Pick-Pocket.*

(1) 1 Cor. 4:5; 1 Pet. 3:4; (2-3) John 12:6; (4) Job 10:13; (5) 1 Sam. 25:29b; (6) John 12:6; As in "hip-pocket."

Pocketbook: See Wallet/Billfold.

Pointing: (1) The Finger of God (pointing to God's handiwork); (2) Accusation; (3) Giving direction (pointing the way).

Also see *Finger/s, Guide,* and *Poking.*

(1) Exod. 8:19; 31:18; Luke 11:20; (2) Isa. 58:9; (3) Exod. 14:16.

Poison: (1) Lies (something a person is being asked or forced to swallow); (2) Death; (3) Words against someone; (4) Sin; (5) Excessive alcohol.

Also see *Bait*.

(1) Ps. 140:3; Rom. 3:13; (2) 2 Kings 4:40; (3) Ps. 56:5; 140:1-3; (4) Rom. 6:23; (5) Prov. 23:30-32.

Pokemon: (1) Evil spirits; (2) Angels; (3) Spiritual warfare.

(1-2) Dan. 10:13.

Poker Machine (One-Armed Bandit): (1) Get-rich-quick scheme.

Also see *Gambling*.

(1) Prov. 28:20, 22.

Poking: (1) Accusation; (2) Offense; (3) Authority; (4) Correction; (5) Being stirred to action.

Also see *Pointing*.

(1-2) John 19:3; (3) Acts 9:5; (4) Eccl. 12:11; (5) Acts 12:7.

Polar Bear: (1) Religious spirit.

(1) Matt. 23:27; Mark 7:13.

Pole: (1) Cross; (2) Word of God.

Also see *Rod* and *Staff*.

(1) Num. 21:8-9; (cf. John 3:14); (2) Exod. 14:16 (the Word divides).

Police: (1) Authority; (2) Spiritual authority; (3) You exercising spiritual authority (you as policeman); (4) Angel/s; (5) God; (6) Protection; (7) Punishment of evil doers; (8) Point to legal implications; (9) Law; (10) Legalism/critical spirit.

Also see *Plainclothes Police* (below).

(1) Rom. 13:1; (2) 1 Cor. 6:1; 2 Tim. 4:1-2; (3) Luke 10:19; (4) Exod. 23:20; Ps. 91:11; Isa. 63:9; Luke 4:10; Acts 7:53; (5) Job 5:17; Heb. 12:23; Rev. 20:12; (6) Rom. 13:4; (7) 1 Pet. 2:13-14; (8-9) Acts 7:53; (10) Matt. 22:35-36; Acts 4:1-3a; 5:17-18.

Plainclothes Police: (1) Pastor; (2) Father or husband (unrecognized authority); (3) Angel in disguise; (4) God; (5) Unaware inspection; (6) Undercover; (7) Taxation (IRS); (8) Accountant.

Also see *Police.*

(1) 1 Cor. 6:1; 2 Tim. 4:1-2; (2) Eph. 5:23-24; (3) Gen. 19:1, 5; Heb. 13:2b; (4) Gen. 18:1-3, 20-21; (5) Prov. 24:12; (6) Josh. 2:1; (7) Matt. 17:24; (8) John 12:5-6.

Polio: (1) Spiritually impaired.

Also see *Legs* and *Wheelchair.*

(1) Matt. 14:29-31 (failing to walk by faith); John 5:6-7.

Polish: (1) To glorify; (2) Make shine; (3) Fine tune; (4) Make reflective.

(1) Lam. 4:7 (KJV); Dan. 10:6 (KJV); (2) Ps. 144:12 (KJV); (3) Isa. 49:2; (4) 1 Cor. 11:1.

Politics: (1) Denominationalism; (2) Buying votes; (3) Jobs for the boys; (4) Telling people what they want to hear; (5) Not being totally upfront with people; (6) Using people for personal gain.

(1) 1 Cor. 1:12, 3:3; (2) 2 Sam. 15:4; (3) 1 Sam. 22:7. (4) 2 Tim. 4:3; (5-6) 2 Sam. 15:4.

Pollution: (1) Defiling words; (2) Defiled heart; (3) Sin; (4) Oppression in the atmosphere (bad morale).

Also see *Mud, Sewage, Smoke,* and *Water—Dirty Water.*

(1) Job 16:4; Ps. 109:3; Matt. 12:32; (2) Exod. 15:23-25 (purified by the cross); (3) Isa. 1:4; Hos. 9:9; (4) 2 Cor. 10:3-5; Eph. 6:12.

Pomegranate: (1) Heart; (2) Joyful and fruitful (Fruit is round and full of seeds).

(1) Song. 8:2; (2) Exod. 28:33-35; Song. 4:3 (beautiful mind and fruitful thoughts).

Pond: (1) Church; (2) Local community; (3) Looking to or worshipping a past move of God; (4) Dam (old water not moving); (5) Place for fish.

Also see *Fish.*

(1-2) Isa. 19:10b & Matt. 4:19; (3) John 8:33; (4) 1 Sam. 3:1, 4:15.

Pool: See Lake, Pond, and Swimming Pool.

Pool Cue: (1) Powerfully impacting word (authoritative word); (2) Preparing to speak with authority (chalking cue).

(1) Exod. 14:16; Luke 4:36; (2) Isa. 49:2;

Pool Hall: (1) Group that is Christian by name only (no pool); (2) Cult group (haunt of underworld figures, plenty of words [balls], lots of gathering [tables], but no real Spirit [no pool]).

Also see *Swimming Pool.*

(1) Rev. 3:1. (2) 1 John 4:1-2.

Pool Table: (1) Communion; (2) Religious hearts (tables of stone); (3) Load of words around a table.

Also see *Sport* and *Winning.*

(1) 1 Cor. 10:21; (2) 2 Cor. 3:3 (KJV); (3) 1 Kings 13:20; Ps. 78:19; Dan. 11:27; John 13:28.

Porch (Front Verandah): (1) Out in the open; (2) Exposed; (3) Waiting or expectancy; (4) Could represent an extension of covering, as in missionaries.

(1) Mark 14: 68; Acts 3:11-12; (2) Matt. 26:71 (KJV); (3) Judg. 11:34; (4) Luke 9:1-2.

Pornography: See Chapter Four: "Are all dreams from God?"

Port: (1) Jesus Christ; (2) Place of departure (leaving); (3) Place of arrival; (4) Looking for a rest in a storm; (5) Haven.

Also see *Airport.*

(1) Ps. 107:28-30 (cf. John 6:18-21); (2) Acts 27:6-7; (3) Acts 28:12; (4-5) Acts 27:12.

Portal: (1) Open Heaven (portal in sky).

(1) Gen. 28:17; Ps. 78:23; Rev. 4:1.

Postage Stamp: (1) Coming communication; (2) Registered or authorized message; (3) Message bearer; (4) Small.

Also see *Envelope* and *Letter.*

(1-3) Esther 8:8, 10, 12b; 1 Kings 21:8.

Postman: (1) Angel (messenger); (2) Bearer of good news; (3) Courier; (4) Carrier of the Word; (5) Preacher.

(1) Gen. 22:11; Dan. 10:5, 11; (2) Rom. 10:15; (3) Esther 3:15; (4) Matt. 11:10-11; (5) Rom. 10:15.

Post Office: (1) Heavenly distribution centre; (2) Heart.

(1) Gen. 28:12; (2) Prov. 4:23; Matt. 12:34b.

Potatoes: (1) Works of the flesh (unwashed potatoes); (2) Heart full of earthly treasures (bag of potatoes).

(1) Gen. 3:17 & Jer. 17:5; (2) <u>Matt. 6:19</u>.

Potted Plant: (1) Believer's heart; (2) Young believer (with limited root structure); (3) The Church.

(1) Ps. 1:3; <u>Song. 4:12</u>; Isa. 61:3; Matt. 13:8; (2) Jer. 17:7-8; (3) Song. 4:12.

Potholes: (1) Faulty foundations; (2) Uncomfortable journey ahead; (3) Experiencing a shake-up; (4) Hardship; (5) Slowing down the ministry; (6) Downtrodden or issues in the heart; (7) Crooked ways.

Also see *Dirt Road*.

(1) Matt. 7:26-27; 1 Cor. 3:11-15; (2-3) Num. 22:32b; Prov. 28:10; Isa. 24:18; Luke 6:47-48; (4) <u>Prov. 13:15</u>; Jer. 2:6; (5) Judg. 16:4 & Prov. 23:27; (6) Prov. 22:14; Matt. 12:11; (7) Luke 3:5.

Pots and Pans: (1) Heart (a person as a vessel for the Holy Spirit to fill).

Also see *Barrel, Dish, Plate,* and *Vessel*.

(1) 2 Kings 4:3-7; 2 Cor. 4:7.

Potter: (1) God.

(1) <u>Jer. 18:6</u>.

Pottery: See Vessels.

Powder: (1) Judgment; (2) Ground.

Also see *Dust*.

(1-2) <u>Exod. 32:20</u>; Deut. 28:24; 2 Kings 23:6; <u>Matt. 21:44</u>; Luke 20:18.

Power: (1) Holy Spirit anointing; (2) Authority; (3) Miracle ability.

Also see *Strength*.

(1) <u>Acts 1:8</u>; (2) <u>Luke 4:36</u>; 9:1; Rev. 13:2; (3) Acts 10:38.

Power Lines: (1) Power of God's Word; (2) Flow of the Holy Spirit; (3) Principles of the Kingdom.

(1) Luke 4:32; <u>Heb. 1:3</u>; (2) <u>Luke 4:14</u>; Acts 10:38; (3) Mark 9:1; 1 Cor. 4:20.

Pram: (1) Someone carrying the promise of God; (2) Faith (that which carries the promise through to manifestation); (3) Beginning of a new ministry;

(4) Empty promise (empty pram); (5) Expecting something to be birthed (promise/church/ministry); (6) Someone in whom the promise of God has died (black pram).

(1-2) Rom. 4:20-21; Heb. 6:15; (3) Acts 13:9 (beginning of Paul's ministry); (4) Isa. 29:13; Matt. 15:8; (5) 1 Sam. 1:18; (16) Gen. 16:1-3; Prov. 13:12.

Prawn: See Shrimp.

Preacher: (1) Bearer of the Good News; (2) Anointed speaker; (3) Prophet; (4) Jesus; (5) Your spiritual oversight; (6) False teacher; (7) Your conduct (particularly under pressure).

(1) Rom. 10:14-15; (2) Isa. 61:1a; Mark 3:14-15; 16:15; 2 Tim. 1:11; (3) Jon. 3:2; Matt. 3:1; (4) Matt. 4:17; (5) Acts 20:28; 1 Pet. 5:2; (6) Gal. 1:8-9; (7) 1 Pet. 3:1.

Precious Stone/s: (1) Christ; (2) Believer/s; (3) Gift/s; (4) Spiritual gift/s; (5) Spiritual work/s; (6) Foundation/s; (7) Adornment of the harlot church; (8) The glory of God; (9) Something or someone of value or dear to you; (10) Wisdom.

Also see *Amethyst, Rubies, Stones,* and *Treasure.*

(1-2) 1 Pet. 2:4-7; (cf. Luke 21:5); (3) Prov. 17:8; (4) Prov. 2:3-4; 8:10-11; 20:15; 24:4; (cf. 1 Cor. 12:8); Rev. 2:17; (5) 1 Cor. 3:12-13; (6) Rev. 21:19; (7) Rev. 17:4; (8) Rev. 21:10-11; (9) Matt. 13:46; (10) Job 28:5-6, 12-18.

Pregnancy: (1) Expectancy; (2) Awaiting birth of a ministry; (3) Promise; (4) Warning of fornication (adolescent pregnant); (5) On the eve of revival (new life); (6) May show something ungodly/demonic is about to be unleashed (context and feeling will determine whether it is good or bad).

Also see *Baby.*

(1) Matt. 1:23; Luke 2:5; (2) Luke 1:13-17, 76, 80; (3) Judg. 13:3; (4) Matt. 1:18-19 (Joseph suspected fornication, v. 20); (5) Gen. 21:1-6; Prov. 13:12; Luke 1:57-58, 67-79; (6) Gen. 10:8-10 (Some suggest Nimrod was a hunter of people).

Premature Baby: See Baby.

President: (1) Jesus Christ; (2) Company boss; (3) Literally the president.

Also see *Air Force One* and *Prime Minister.*

(1) John 20:28; (2) Rom. 13:1.

Pressure Cooker: (1) Pending explosion (arguments, destruction, conflict).
Also see *Boiling* and *Bomb*.
(1) 1 Sam. 20:30-33.

Priest: (1) Religious or legalistic leader; (2) Believer; (3) Jesus Christ; (4) Holy man; (5) Religious spirit; (6) A father (priest of the home).
Also see *Pastor*.
(1) Heb. 8:4; 10:11; (2) 1 Pet. 2:9, 5; Rev. 1:6; 5:10; 20:6; (3) Heb. 7:17, 26; 8:1; 9:11; 10:19-21; (4) Exod. 31:10; (5) Num. 5:30b; (6) Judg. 18:19.

Prime Minister: (1) Jesus Christ; (2) Senior minister; (3) Literally the prime minister.
Also see *President*.
(1) Heb. 3:1; 1 Pet. 5:4; (2) Acts 20:28; 1 Tim. 1:12; 1 Pet. 5:1-2.

Prince: (1) Jesus Christ; (2) Satan; (3) Principality (ungodly); (4) Seated in heavenly places.
(1) Isa. 9:6b; (2) Matt. 12:24; Eph. 2:2; (3) Eph. 3:10; 6:12; (4) Eph. 2:6; Col. 3:1.

Printer (Computer): (1) Mouth; (2) Words.
(1) Job 15:13; Ps. 26:7; 68:11; (2) Ps. 19:14.

Prison: (1) The world; (2) Captivity and bondage; (3) Stronghold; (4) Place of confinement; (5) Place of heart refinement; (6) Place to develop truth; (7) Satan's kingdom; (8) Place of judgment/punishment; (9) Hell; (10) Taken captive; (11) Prisoner of Christ; (12) Constrained by the love of God; (13) Bound by your own thoughts/words.
(1) Col. 1:12-13; 2 Tim. 2:25-26; (2) Isa. 20:4; 61:1; (3) Zech. 9:12; (4-6) Gen. 42:16 (KJV); (cf. Ps. 105:17-19); (7) 2 Tim. 2:26; (8) 2 Pet. 2:4; (9) 2 Pet. 2:4 (NIV); Jude 1:6; (10) 2 Tim. 3:6; (11) Eph. 3:1; Philem. 1:1, 9; (12) 2 Cor. 5:14; (13) Prov. 23:7.

Prisoners: (1) Unbelievers; (2) Captives of satan; (3) Captive sinners; (4) Captives of false religion; (5) Oppression; (6) Addiction.
(1-2) Luke 4:18; 2 Tim. 2:26; (3) Rom. 7:23; (4) 2 Tim. 3:6; (5-6) Prov. 23:29-32.

Private School: (1) Holy Spirit schooling; (2) Mentoring (outside system); (3) Restricted or exclusive training; (4) Cult or religious church (boarding school).

(1) Luke 1:80; 1 John 2:27; (2) 1 Kings 19:19-21; Matt. 5:1-2; (3) Acts 4:13; (4) Matt. 5:20 (full of rules and you don't get to go home [Heaven])

Propeller: (1) Spirit-driven (good or evil).

Also see *Helicopter.*

(1) Mark 1:12 (KJV); Luke 8:29.

Prosthetic Limbs: (1) Not real; (2) Human-made; (3) False walk (legs); (4) False strength (legs or arm).

(1) 2 Sam. 20:9-10; Zech. 13:6a; (2) Ps. 147:10; (3) Num. 22:32b; Jer. 7:9; (4) Ps. 84:5a.

Prostitute: See Harlot.

Prostitution: (1) Exploited for money; (2) Selling yourself; (3) Sexual favors; (4) Unlawful trading; (5) Clandestine trading.

(1-5) Gen. 38:15-18.

Prune: (1) Discipline; (2) Judgment.

Also see *Purge* and *Trimming.*

(1) John 15:2; (2) Dan. 4:14; Matt. 3:10.

Psychiatrist: (1) Someone inside your head.

(1) Prov. 23:7a; Lam. 3:60-61 (cf. Ps. 119:95).

Public Toilet: (1) Slander; (2) Gossip; (3) Church that repeats a matter; (4) Church, ministry, business, or household whose sin is exposed publicly (possibly about to be exposed by media).

(1-2) Prov. 6:16-19; (3) Prov. 17:9; (4) Rev. 3:1.

Puddle: (1) Deposit of the Spirit.

(1) Acts 2:17-18.

Puffer Fish: (1) Proud Christian; (2) Wanting to appear more important/spiritual than they really are; (3) Christian filled with head knowledge; (4) Christian lacking love; (5) Religious spirit.

(1-2) 1 Cor. 4:18-19; 5:2; (3) 1 Cor. 8:1; (4) 1 Cor. 13:4; (5) Col. 2:18.

Pulley: (1) The Holy Spirit; (2) Encourager.

Also see *Crane*.

(1) Ezek. 3:14; 8:3; 11:1; (2) Prov. 12:25.

Pulling: (1) Saving (pulling into/out); (2) Redeeming (pulling in again); (3) Rescuing (pulling out); (4) Sheltering (pulling to you); (5) Destroying (pulling down); (6) Humbling (pulling down); (7) Selecting (pulling out); (8) Demolishing (pulling down); (9) Dismembering (pulling in pieces); (10) Uprooting (pulling up); (11) Stripping (pulling off); (12) Rebelling (pulling away); (13) Cleansing (pulling out); (14) Discouragement (pulling down).

Also see *Pushing* and *Towing*.

(1) Gen. 19:10; Jude 1:23; (2) 1 Kings 13:4; (3) Ps. 31:4; Luke 14:5; (4) Gen. 8:9; (5) Ezra 6:11; (6) Isa. 22:19; Jer.1:10; 18:7; (7) Jer. 12:3; (8) Jer. 24:6; 42:10; Luke 12:18; 2 Cor. 10:4; (9) Lam. 3:11 (KJV); Acts 23:10; (10) Ezek. 17:9; Amos 9:15; (11) Mic. 2:8; (12) Zech. 7:11 (KJV); (13) Matt. 7:4 (KJV); Luke 6:42 (KJV); (14) Deut. 1:28.

Pulpit: (1) Preaching ministry; (2) Church's teaching; (3) Pastor; (4) Sermon; (5) Invitation to speak.

(1-2) Matt. 4:23; 9:35; Luke 20:1; Acts 5:42; 15:35; (3) Eph. 4:11; Tit. 1:7a, 9; (4) 2 Tim. 4:2; (5) Acts 10:22.

Pulse: (1) Life.

(1) Lev. 17:11.

Pump: (1) Building up in the Holy Spirit; (2) Pressure; (3) Receiving spiritual life (pumping).

(1) John 7:38-39; Jude 1:20; (2) As in, "under the pump"; (3) Lev. 17:11; John 6:63.

Pumpkin: (1) Witchcraft; (2) Disappointment (something turns into a pumpkin); (3) Fruit of the world (pumpkin is the world's largest fruit).

Also see *Witchcraft*.

(1) 2 Chron. 33:6b-7a; (3) Num. 11:5.

Punch: (1) Spiritual warfare; (2) Exercising faith; (3) Impacting word; (4) Getting knocked around a bit.

Also see *Fist*.

(1) 1 Cor. 9:26; (2) 1 Tim. 6:12; 2 Tim. 4:7; (2) 1 Sam. 3:19; (4) Prov. 25:18.

Puppet: (1) Manipulative or controlling spirit; (2) Someone else is calling the moves; (3) Under someone's control; (4) Mouthing words without heart; (5) Not real.

Also see *Parrot* and *Remote Control.*

(1-3) 1 Kings 21:7-8; (4) Isa. 29:13; Matt. 15:8; (5) John 12:5-6.

Puppy: (1) Immature unbeliever; (2) Someone needing attention and support; (3) Uncommitted follower; (4) Someone who is going to grow into a dog.

Also see *Dog.*

(1) Rev. 22:15; (2) John 6:26 (someone following because they want their flesh satisfied); Also consider puppies are in need of constant care; (3) Matt. 8:19-22; 10:38; (cf. John 6:2 & 6:66); (4) Matt. 13:32 (just as seeds grow into trees).

Purchase: See Buying.

Purge: (1) Purify; (2) Cleansed; (3) Sort/separate; (4) Pruning.

(1) Heb. 1:3 (KJV); (2) Mark 7:19 (KJV); Heb. 9:14, 22 (KJV); 10:2 (KJV); 2 Pet. 1:9; (3) Matt. 3:12 (KJV); Luke 3:17 (KJV); 1 Cor. 5:7; 2 Tim. 2:21 (KJV); (4) John 15:2 (KJV).

Purple: (1) Royalty; (2) Kingship; (3) Luxurious and/or indulgent; (4) Righteousness.

(1-2) Judg. 8:26; Dan. 5:7; John 19:2; (3) Acts 16:14; Rev. 18:12; (4) Exod. 28:15 & Eph. 6:14.

Purse: See Wallet.

Pushing: (1) Doing things in own strength; (2) Without the Spirit; (3) Fleshly or immature leadership; (4) Struggling; (5) Forcing someone into something they don't want to do; (6) Working their/your agenda; (7) Forcing back; (8) To undermine; (9) Exerting dominance; (10) Expanding dominion and influence; (11) Exerting pressure upon; (12) Overflow (good measure pushed down).

Also see *Button Pushing* and *Pulling.*

(1-2) Rom. 8:14 (being led instead of pushing); (3) Ps. 80:1; Isa. 40:11; (4) As in, "I feel like I'm pushing uphill"; (5) As in, "She was pushed into it"; (6) As in, "pushing your own barrow"; (7) 1 Kings 22:11 (KJV); (8) Job 30:12; (9-10) Dan. 8:4; (11) Dan. 11:40 (KJV); (12) Luke 6:38.

Puzzle: (1) Confusion; (2) Test; (3) Riddle/parable; (4) Searching out mysteries.
(1) 2 Chron. 20:12; John 13:7; (2) Gen. 22:1; (3) Num. 12:8; (4) 1 Cor. 14:2.

Pyjamas: See Pajamas.

Python: (1) Divination; (2) Fortune-telling spirit (familiar spirit); (3) Forecasting spirit catering to the will of people; (4) Spirit that seeks to squeeze out the spiritual life by applying pressure.
Also see *Snake*.
(1-2) Acts 16:16; 1 Sam. 15:23 (*rebellion* means "divination" in Hebrew); (3) Matt. 16:21-23; (4) 1 Thess. 5:19.

Quarry: (1) Faith (moving mountains); (2) Removing major sin.
Also see *Rock/s*.
(1) Matt. 21:21; Mark 11:22-23; (2) Ezek. 11:19; 36:26; Zech. 7:12.

Queen: (1) The harlot of the false church; (2) Manipulation and control (Jezebel); (3) Queen of heaven (false god); (4) Brought forward for a time such as this (you as the queen); (5) Judgment.
(1) Rev. 17:1–18:7; 17:4; 18:7; (2) 1 Kings 19:1-2; 21:5-16; Rev. 2:20; (3) Jer. 7:18; 44:17-19; (4) Esther 4:14b; (5) Matt. 12:42; Luke 11:31.

Quench: (1) Smother; (2) Put out (fire or light); (3) Stop or restrict; (4) Satisfy their thirst.
(1) Matt. 12:20; (2) Num. 11:2; 2 Sam. 21:17; Mark 9:43-45; Eph. 6:16; Heb. 11:34; (3) 1 Thess. 5:19; 2 Kings 22:17; (4) Ps. 104:11.

Queue: (1) Waiting.
Also see *Ticket* and *Waiting*.
(1) Luke 8:40.

Quick/ly: (1) Holy Spirit upon; (2) Given spiritual life; (3) Importance; (4) Window of opportunity; (5) Time running out; (6) Salvation; (7) Suddenly; (8) Soon; (9) Can be a sign of unbelief.
(1) Rom. 8:11 (KJV); 1 Kings 18:46; 1 Cor. 15:45 (KJV); 1 Pet. 3:18 (KJV); (2) John 5:21 (KJV); 6:63 (KJV); Rom. 4:17 (KJV); Heb. 4:12; (3) Matt. 28:7-8; Luke 14:21; John 11:29; (4) Acts 12:7; Rev. 2:5, 16; (5) Matt.5:25; John 13:27; Rev. 3:11; (6) Eph. 2:1, 5 (KJV); Col. 2:13 (KJV); (7) Rev. 11:14; (8) Rev. 22:7, 12, 20; (9) Isa. 28:16; John 13:27.

Quiet: When people are quiet, it may indicate: (1) They are uncommitted; (2) They are showing prudence (cautiousness); (3) They have received correction; (4) They respect your wisdom; (5) They are fearful of reprisal; (6) They are meditating (thinking through the word); (7) They are waiting on God.

(1) 1 Kings 18:21; (2) Amos 5:13; (3) Job 6:24; (4) Job 29:10; (5) Esther 4:13-14; (6) Josh. 1:8; (7) Ps. 46:10.

Quilt: (1) Protected by God; (2) Covering (bed quilt); (3) Grand/mother's influence (ornate quilt); (4) Warmth.

Also see *Blanket*.

(1) Ps. 91:4-5; (2) Judg. 4:18; 1 Sam. 19:13; Prov. 7:16; (3) Gen. 24:67; (4) Job 31:20.

Quiver (noun): (1) Home; (2) Ready and waiting; (3) Spiritual warfare; (4) Threat of death; (5) Brace yourself with faith.

Also see *Arrows*.

(1) Ps. 127:4-5; (2) Isa. 49:2; (3) Gen. 27:3; Isa. 22:6; (4) Jer. 5:16; (5) Eph. 6:16.

Rabbit: (1) Unbeliever; (2) Sin; (3) Unclean spirit; (4) Multiplication; (5) Spirit of lust; (6) Pestilence (pestilent to farmers).

(1-2) Lev. 11:6; Deut. 14:7 (unclean and not dividing God's Word); (5) 2 Sam. 13:14. (as measured by the rabbit's prolific ability to reproduce); (6) Matt. 13:19.

Raccoon: (1) Ungodly, adaptive, and opportunistic thief.

(1) John 12:5-6.

Race: (1) The race of faith; (2) Christ's life; (3) The course of life.

(1) Gal. 2:2; 2 Tim. 4:7; Heb. 12:1-2; (2-3) Ps. 19:1-6.

Race Course: (1) Race of faith; (2) Church with a competitive spirit.

Also see *Race Horse*.

(1) Heb. 12:1; (2) Matt. 26:33; Mark 9:33-34.

Race Horse: (1) Competitive spirit (pride).

Also see *Horse*.

(1) Matt. 26:33; Mark 9:33-34.

Racing Driver: (1) Competitive spirit; (2) Fast life; (3) Ambition.

(1) Prov. 14:29b (KJV); 1 Tim. 6:5; (2) Prov. 19:2b (KJV); Isa. 28:16b; Acts 27:17; (3) Prov. 20:21; 28:20; Matt. 20:21.

Radio: (1) Prophet (receiver of the prophetic word); (2) Tuning in to God.

Also see *Stereo* and *Television.*

(1) Jer. 1:4, 9; (2) 2 Kings 3:15; Rev. 1:10.

Radio Station: (1) Spirit of the world; (2) Prophetic/evangelistic voice; (3) Declaring in the heavens/intercession (battling principalities in the heavenlies).

(1) Eph. 2:2; (2) Luke 8:39 (KJV); Acts 13:49; (3) Eph. 6:12.

Radio Tower: (1) Christ (The Word of God).

(1) John 1:1.

Rags: (1) Lethargy or drowsiness; (2) Self-righteousness; (3) Sin.

(1) Prov. 23:21b; (2-3) Isa. 64:6.

Railroad Crossing: See Boom Gate.

Railroad Platform: (1) Waiting place.

(1) Acts 1:4; Rom. 12:7 (KJV).

Railroad Track: (1) Particular job or ministry path; (2) Means of passage for powerful ministry; (3) The plans and purposes of God; (4) Holy Spirit ministry; (if the train is moving without tracks); (5) Guaranteed destiny (tracks can mean "no deviation").

Also see *Hand Rail.*

(1) Exod. 18:20b; Ps. 25:4; Isa. 2:3b; (2) Ps. 143:10 (KJV); Matt. 4:1; (3) Isa. 2:3; Mic. 4:2; (4) Rom. 8:14; John 3:8; (5) Num. 14:8; 1 Kings 11:38 (KJV).

Railway Station: (1) Awaiting release into ministry; (2) Coming and going; (3) Place of interchange; (4) Busy, outreaching church; (5) Base or foundation.

Also see *Airport* and *Train.*

(1) Isa. 49:2; Acts 12:25-13:1, 2-3; (2-4) Acts 11:26, 30; 12:25; 14:26-28; 15:2, 30, 35-36; 18:22; (5) Acts 1:8.

Rain: (1) Revival or resurrection; (2) Favor of God; (3) Judgment from on high; (4) Fruitfulness; (5) The Word of God; (6) Spiritual life; (7) Abundance; (8) Teaching; (9) Winter.

Also see *Shower.*

(1) James 5:18; 1 Kings 18:1; (2) Deut. 11:10-12; Prov. 16:15; (3) Gen. 7:4 (heavy); Exod. 9:18 (hail); Ps. 11:6 (coals); (4) Lev. 26:3-4; (5) Isa. 55:10-11; (6) Deut. 11:14; (7) Deut. 28:12; Job 36:27-28; Ps. 72:6-7; (8) Deut. 32:2; (9) Song. 2:11.

Rain (No Rain): (1) Sin; (2) Judgment.

Also see *Drought.*

(1) 1 Kings 8:35-36; 2 Chron. 6:26-27; (2) 2 Chron. 7:13-14; Isa. 5:6; Jer. 3:2b-3.

Rainbow: (1) Covenant promise; (3) Remembrance; (3) God's glory; (4) Heavenly vision; (5) Angel or heavenly being.

Also see *Multi-colored* and individual colors.

(1-2) Gen. 9:12-15; (3) Ezek. 1:28; (4) Rev. 4:2-3; (5) Rev. 10:1.

Rainforest: (1) Fruitfulness of the Spirit; (2) Revival.

Also see *Forest, Jungle,* and *Rain.*

(1) Ps. 147:8; (2) Isa. 35:1.

Rainwater Tank: See Cistern.

Raise: See Ascend and Lift.

Rake (Garden): (1) Gathering/gatherer.

Also see *Fork.*

(1) 1 Chron. 13:2.

Ram: (1) Christ; (2) Offering; (3) Compared to obedience; (4) Symbol of a strong person, city, or nation state.

(1) Gen. 22:13; (cf. Exod. 12:5 & 1 Cor. 5:7); (2) Lev. 5:15-18; 8:18-22; 9:2-4; (3) 1 Sam. 15:22; (4) Dan. 8:20.

Ransom: (1) Christ's life; (2) Redemption price; (3) Freed from hell; (4) Freed from slavery; (5) Wealth cannot redeem a soul; (6) Life for a life; (7) Adultery (unredeemable by ransom); (8) Price paid for an individual's atonement.

(1) Prov. 21:18; Matt. 20:28; Mark 10:45; 1 Tim. 2:5-6; (2) Exod. 21:30 (KJV); (3) Job 33:23, 24-28; Jer. 31:11; (4) Isa. 35:10; 51:10-11; Jer. 31:11; (5) Ps. 49:6-10; (6) Isa. 43:3-4; (7) Prov. 6:32-35 (KJV); (8) Exod. 30: 12-15.

Rape: (1) Overpowered and stolen from; (2) Forced theft; (3) Purity stolen; (4) Lust; (5) Spirit of lust; (6) Humbled; (7) Murder; (8) Morally violated; (9) Humiliation; (10) Taking on lies (unwelcome seeds sown).

(1-4) 2 Sam. 13:1-2, 11-14; (cf. Prov. 6:26-32; 2 Sam. 12:4, 7-9); (5) Gen. 19:5-9; Judg. 19:22-27; (6) Deut. 22:28-29; (7) Deut. 22:25-26; (8) Gen. 34:2, 5; (9) 2 Sam. 13:19; (10) Isa. 59:4, 13.

Rapture: (1) The snatching up of believers at the Lord's return; (2) Preparation or forewarning for this event.

(1-2) 1 Cor. 15:51-54; (demonstrated: Gen. 5:24; 2 Kings 2:11); 1 Thess. 4:15-17.

Rash (Bodily): (1) Sin; (2) Uncleanliness (away from God).

Also see *Leper*.

(1-2) Lev. 13:2-3 (NIV); Lev. 14:56-57 (NIV); As in, "cleanliness is next to godliness."

Rat: (1) Unbeliever (unclean animal); (2) Evil spirit; (3) Plague; (4) Someone who spreads disease by words.

Also see *Mouse/Mice* and *Teeth*.

(1) Lev. 11:29; (2) 1 Sam. 6:4 (idolatry) & 1 Cor. 10:20 (demons); (3) 1 Sam. 6:5a & 1 Sam. 5:12; (4) Ps. 22:13.

Raven: There are two main lines of interpretation: (1) Unbeliever: (2) Cared for by God; (3) Support from the world; (4) Evil spirit/demon: (5) Taker of spiritual sight.

Also see *Bird/s*.

(1) (Gen. 8:7 & Isa. 57:21); Lev. 11:13, 15 (unclean bird); (2) Job 38:41; Ps. 147:9; Luke 12:24; (3) 1 Kings 17:4, 6; (4) Birds are heavenly beings, ravens are black and, therefore, carry the emphasis of being without light/life. (5) Prov. 30:17; (cf. Matt. 13:4).

Rave Party: (1) Counterfeit revival.

(1) 1 Cor. 4:20 (words without power); 2 Thess. 2:9; 2 Tim. 3:5.

Razor: (1) Deceitful tongue; (2) Instrument of judgment.

Also see *Hair* and *Shave.*

(1) Ps. 52:2-4; (2) Isa. 7:20; Ezek. 5:1ff.

Reading: (1) Washing (in what is being read); (2) Hearing; (3) Learning/ teaching; (4) Understanding; (5) Spiritual conviction; (6) Receiving revelation; (7) Meditating (rereading).

Also see *Unable to Read* (Directly Below).

(1) Eph. 5:26; (2) Deut. 21:11; (3) Deut. 17:19; Josh. 8:35; (4) Neh. 8:8; (5) 2 Kings 22:10-11; Neh. 13:1-3; (6) Rom. 10:17; (7) Ps.1:2.

Reading (Unable to Read): (1) Unsaved and therefore unable to understand sealed truth; (2) Being superficial (mouth and heart different) before God; (3) Unworthy (not under the blood); (4) Hardened heart (without understanding); (5) Spiritual blindness; (6) Unbelieving.

Also see *Reading.*

(1) Hos. 4:6; Matt. 13:11; (2) Isa. 29:9-16; (3) Rev. 5:2, 9; (4) Matt. 13:4, 19; (5-6) Matt. 17:17-21.

Real Estate: (1) The Kingdom of God; (2) Soul-winning; (3) Building wealth (positive or negative); (4) Promise of investment.

Also see *House.*

(1-2) 2 Cor. 5:1; (3) Deut. 8:12-13; Luke 12:18; (4) Jer. 32:44.

Reaper: (1) Spirit of death; (2) Harvest; (3) Angel; (4) Preacher or evangelist; (5) Sower; (6) Person with perseverance.

Also see *Sower* and *Seed.*

(1) Joel 3:13; Rev. 6:8; Rev. 14:19; (2) Lev. 19:9a; 23:22; Matt.13:30; Rev. 14:15; (3) Matt. 13:39; (4) John 4:35-38; Acts 2:40-41; (5) 2 Cor. 9:6; Gal. 6:7-8 (reaping what you sow); (6) Gal. 6:9.

Rear: (1) Past; (2) Unseen; (3) Not in authority; (4) Humbly or in subservience; (5) Less.

Also see *Back, Back Door,* and *Back Yard.*

(1) Phil. 3:12-13, 14; Luke 9:62; (2) Matt. 9:20; (3) Deut. 28:13, 44; Matt. 16:23; (4) Luke 7:38; (5) 2 Cor. 12:11.

Rearview Mirror: (1) Past; (2) Looking back; (3) Back up; (4) Reverse. Also see *Mirror.*

(1-2) Gen. 19:26; Luke 9:62; (3) Gen. 9:23; (4) 2 Kings 20:10-11.

Receipt: (1) Faith; (2) The Holy Spirit; (3) Guarantee; (4) Proof of purchase or service.

(1) Heb. 11:1 (AMP); (2) Eph. 1:13-14; (3) 2 Cor. 1:22, 5:5; (4) Ruth 4:7.

Receptionist: (1) Someone who receives (the Word); (2) Prophet; (3) Preacher; (4) Writer; (5) Believer.

(1-4) Prov. 2:1; Jer. 9:20; Ezek. 3:10; (5) Matt. 10:14; 13:23; John 12:48; James 1:21.

Recognition: (1) Fruit; (2) Evidence; (3) Tell-tale signs; (4) Familiar person or surrounding; (5) Known; (6) Friend of the world (not recognized).

(1-3) Matt. 7:16-20; (4-5) Matt. 7:23; John 15:15; 18:2; (6) James 4:4.

Record (Vinyl): (1) Stuck in a rut (repeating record); (2) Old-fashioned worship; (3) Nostalgia.

(1) Deut. 2:3 (NIV); Ps. 78:41, 57; (2) Ps. 144:9; (3) Gen. 19:26;

Recycling: (1) Trying to repair the old nature (recycling in church); (2) Trying to reinvent the flesh (old nature); (3) Coming up with nothing new; (4) Working on superficial change; (5) Outward change, but no heart change; (6) Trying to bring change without God; (7) Equivalent to trying to change a caterpillar into a butterfly.

(1-7) Ps. 127:1a; Matt. 9:17; 1 Cor. 15:50; 2 Cor. 5:17; 10:3.

Red: (1) Sin; (2) Person of the flesh (red garments); (3) Blood shed for sin; (4) Wrath of God; (5) War; (6) Anger or provocation; (7) Redemption; (8) Rebellion; (9) Power; (10) Whore (false church); (11) Glorious individual, church, or ministry (western red cedar house); (12) Passion; (13) Babylon; (14) Holy Spirit fire; (15) In debt.

(1) Lev. 13:19-20; Prov. 23:31-32; Isa. 1:18; (2) Gen. 25:25, 30; (3) Exod. 25:5; 36:19 & Heb. 10:20; Num. 19:3-22; (4) Ps. 75:8; Isa. 63:2-3; (5) Rev. 6:4; 12:3-7; (6) Ps. 75:8; 106:7 (KJV); (7) Ps. 106:9 (8) Ps. 106:7 (NKJV); (9) Rev. 6:4 (KJV); (10) Rev. 17:1-4; (11) 1 Kings 6:9; (13) Rev. 17:4-5; (14) Acts 2:3; (15) As in, "in the red."

Redhead: (1) Evil spirit, often operating through: (2) A spiritually immature and lustful individual; (3) A powerful and influential fleshly church or individual (girl/woman); (4) Witch (girl/woman); (5) Fiery or passionate woman; (6) A fox; (7) Earthly man (man of the flesh).

Also see *Fox.*

(1) Gen. 25:25, 34 & Jude 1:6; (2) Gen. 25:25-34; (3-5) See combinations of *Red* and *Woman;* (6) Ezek. 13:3-4; (7) Gen. 25:25, 27 & Matt. 13:38.

Reed: (1) Someone easily shaken (double-minded person); (2) Symbol of Egypt/ the world; (3) A false support or trust; (4) Someone moved by circumstance; (5) Damaged people (bruised reed); (6) Mock scepter.

(1) 1 Kings 14:15a; Matt. 11:7; (2-3) 2 Kings 18:21; Isa. 36:6; Ezek. 29:6; (4) Matt. 11:7; (5) Isa. 42:3; Matt. 12:20; (6) Matt. 27:29-30.

Referee: See Umpire.

Refining: (1) Purifying; (2) Purging; (3) Trial of faith; (4) Passing through the fire of affliction to bring dross (scum, rubbish) to the surface; (5) Often the world is used to purify us; (6) God is with you through the fire; (7) God is refining you as gold.

(1) 1 Chron. 28:18; 29:4; (2) Mal. 3:3; (3) 1 Pet. 1:7 (KJV); Zech. 13:9; (4) Isa. 48:10; Mal. 3:2; (5) Deut. 4:20; (6) Isa. 43:2; (cf. Dan. 3:25); (7) Rev. 3:18.

Refrigerator: (1) Heart; (2) Cold person, church, or situation; (3) Feeding the flesh; (4) Sin; (5) No fire; (6) Without the Spirit; (7) Without love.

(1-2) Rev. 3:15; Matt. 24:12; (3) Phil. 3:19; 1 Cor. 6:13; (4) Matt. 24:12; (5) Lev. 6:13; (6) Matt. 25:8; (7) Matt. 24:12.

Refuge: (1) God; (2) Strong shelter from trouble/harm; (3) Place of security; (4) A fortress; (5) A place of trust; (6) A hiding place; (7) The fear of the Lord.

(1-2) Ps. 9:9; 14:6; 46:1; 59:16; 62:7-8; 71:7; 91:9-10; (3) Ps. 57:1; (4) Ps. 91:2; (5) Ps. 91:2; (6) Ps. 104:18; (7) Prov. 14:26.

Reluctance: (1) Guilt; (2) Sin; (3) Fear.

(1-3) Gen. 40:16.

Remote Control: (1) Laziness; (2) "Easy believism" without real works of service; (3) Someone else is calling the shots (puppet); (4) Non-committal/at a distance.

Also see *Button Pushing* and *Remote Control Car.*

(1) Judg. 18:9; <u>Prov.</u> 18:9; <u>21:25</u>; (2) James 2:13; (3) 2 Kings 24:17; (4) Mark 14:54.

Remote Control Car: (1) Spirit-led ministry (God steering you); (2) Someone else steering you (controlling or manipulative person).

Also see *Jezebel* in Name and Place Dictionary and *Remote Control.*

(1) John 3:8; Rom. 8:14; (2) John 19:10-11.

Removal Van (Moving Van): (1) Moving out of the fleshly home into the spiritual one; (2) Ready to be born again (changing homes); (3) God wanting you to grow spiritually (come into victory); (4) Possible preparation for death (going to a heavenly home); (5) Actual physical move of home or church.

(1) Eph. 4:22; <u>Col.</u> 2:11; <u>3:8-10</u> (cf. 2 Cor.5:1); (2) Deut. 21:13; John 6:56; 14:15-17; (3) Ps. 30:11; (4) John 14:2-3; 2 Pet. 1:14; (5) Gen. 45:27.

Rendezvous: (1) Preplanned appointment.

(1) <u>Esther 4:14b</u>; John 4:3-4, 6-7.

Repeated Dream: (1) Urgency required (soon to be evident); (2) Confirmation of message from God; (3) God attempting to get your attention; (4) Faith-filled determination required; (5) Possible soul-tie (repeatedly dreaming about same person); (6) Issue not dealt with; (7) Tied to a vow/oath (may be same character in dreams repeatedly).

(1) <u>Gen. 41:32</u>; (2) Gen. 41:32; Matt. 18:16; (3) Gen. 22:11; Exod. 3:4; (4) Josh. 1:6-7, 9; (5) Prov. 26:11; (6) Matt. 18:34-35; (7) Num. 30:2; Prov. 6:2-5.

Repeated Words: (1) Important need of attention—particularly if your name is repeated; this is a call to turn aside and listen to God.

(1) <u>Gen. 22:11</u>; Exod. 3:4; Acts 9:4.

Reporter: (1) History.

(1) Esther 2:23; 6:1.

Rerun: (1) Repeating or covering old ground; (2) Dealing with past issues (unforgiveness); (3) Not growing in God.

(1) Mark 11:15-18 & John 2:13-22 (2) Matt. 18:24, 28; (3) <u>Heb. 5:12</u>-14.

Reserved: (1) Set aside for a particular task; (2) A set aside blessing; (3) Set aside for judgment; (4) Protected; (5) Hold or keep back.

(1) Isa. 49:2; Acts 9:15; 2 Tim. 2:20-21; (2) Gen. 27:36; 1 Pet. 1:4; (3) 2 Pet. 2:4, 9, 17; 3:7; Jude 1:6; (4) Rom. 11:4; (5) 2 Sam. 8:4 (KJV); Jer. 3:5 (KJV).

Reservoir: (1) God; (2) Holy Spirit ministry; (3) Holy Spirit not flowing.

Also see *Cistern, Dam,* and *Pond.*

(1) Jer. 10:13; (2) John 7:37-39; (3) 1 Thess. 5:19.

Rest: (1) Faith in the finished work of Christ; (2) Entry into the Kingdom; (3) Eternal security in the Presence of God; (4) Release of burdens; (5) Peace; (6) Sleep; (7) Refreshment; (8) Finding a home (good and evil); (9) Heart of person; (10) Trust; (11) No longer laboring; (12) The true spiritual union of God and people.

Also see *Bed, Seven,* and *Sitting.*

(1) Heb. 4:1-11; (2) Exod. 33:14; Heb. 3:11, 18; (3) Acts 2:26-28; (4) Matt. 11:28; 2 Thess. 1:7; (5) Matt. 11:29; Acts 9:31 (cf. KJV & NKJV); 2 Cor. 2:13; 7:5; (6) John 11:13; (7) Mark 6:31; (8) Matt. 12:43; Luke 11:24; 2 Cor. 12:9; 1 Pet. 4:14; (9) Acts 7:49; (10) Rom. 2:17; (11) Rev. 14:13; (12) Acts 7:48-49.

Restaurant: (1) Heart (as the place of communion and fellowship with God); (2) Church; (3) Communion and fellowship; (4) In the confidence of someone; (5) Heaven.

See *Meal, Sitting,* and *Table.*

(1) Rev. 3:20; (2) 1 Cor. 11:20, 33-34; (3) Gen. 18:4-8; (4) Gen. 18:16-17; (5) Rev. 19:9.

Reunion: (1) Return to a former position; (2) Renewing an old association.

(1) John 6:66; Acts 7:39; Heb. 10:38; (2) Luke 15:20; Eph. 4:22.

Reverend: See Pastor and Priest.

Reversing Vehicle: (1) Backsliding; (2) Going over the past.

(1) Prov. 14:14; Jer. 2:19; Hos. 11:7; (2) Isa. 43:18; 65:17.

Revolver: See Pistol.

Rhino: (1) God (white rhino); (2) Africa.

Also see *Elephant* and *Ivory.*

(1) Ps. 18:2; (2) By association.

Rib: (1) Heart; (2) Spiritual birth; (3) Bloodshed; (4) Wife.

(1) As the place of spiritual birth and due to the rib's proximity to the heart; (2) (Gen. 2:21-23 & John 19:34); (3) 2 Sam. 2:23 (KJV); 3:27 (KJV); 4:6 (KJV); 20:10 (KJV); Dan. 7:5; (4) Gen. 2:21-23.

Ribbon: (1) Gift; (2) Finish line.

Also see *Bookmark, Silver Cord (Silver Ribbon),* and *Tassel.*

(1) Eph. 4:8; (2) 2 Tim. 4:7.

Rice: (1) The Word of God.

Also see *Seed.*

(1) Luke 8:11.

Rich/es: When you see riches in a dream or vision, it is important to understand: (1) There are two types of riches: heavenly and worldly. (2) The key is the state of the heart. Heavenly Riches include: (3) Fellowship with God; (4) God's Glory; (5) Faith; (6) The inestimable and inexhaustible riches of Christ; (7) Goodness, forbearance, and longsuffering; (8) Wisdom and knowledge; (9) The gifts of the Spirit; (10) Understanding; (11) Forgiveness; (12) Mercy/love; (13) Grace. Worldly Riches: (14) May focus the heart on materialism; (15) Create a crowded heart which chokes faith; (16) Tend to self-reliance (trusting riches) instead of faith in God (making it difficult to enter the Kingdom); (17) Blind the heart to the spiritual dimension and the needs of others; (18) Lead hearts to look for the rewards here and now; (19) Earthly riches decay; (20) Deceive us into thinking we are rich when we are actually spiritually poor.

Also see *Poor* and *Treasure.*

(1) Luke 16:11; (2) Mark 12:41-44; Luke 19:2-10; (3) Heb. 11:26; (4) Rom. 9:23; Eph. 1:18; 3:16; Phil. 4:19; Col. 1:27; Rev. 3:17-18; (5) James 2:5; (6) Eph. 3:8; (7) Rom. 2:4; (8) Rom. 11:33; (9) Rom. 11:33 & 1 Cor. 12:8; (10) Col. 2:2; Rev. 3:17-18; (11) Eph. 1:7; (12) Eph. 2:4; (13) Eph. 2:7. (14) Luke

1:53; 6:24; <u>18:23-25</u>; (15) Matt. 13:22; Mark 4:19; Luke 8:14; 1 Tim. 6:9; (16) Matt. 19:16, 23-24; Mark 10:23-25; <u>1 Tim. 6:17</u>; (17) Luke 12:16-21; 16:19-31; James 2:6; Rev. 6:15-18; (18) Luke 6:24; 14:12-14; 1 Tim. 6:18-19; James 1:10-11; (19) James 5:1-3; (20) Rev. 3:17 (cf. Rev. 2:9);

Rifle: See Bow, Shooting, and Sniper.

Right: (1) Strength; (2) Faith; (3) Spirit, blessed, or righteous direction; (4) Mouth; (5) Preferred, preeminence, above, before, double portion; (6) Authority; (7) Longevity; (8) Contentious woman; (9) Wisdom.

Also see *Left* and *Turning Left and Right* (under *Left*).

(1) <u>Ps. 20:6</u>; Isa. 41:10; 62:8; (2) John 21:6; Heb. 12:2; (3) <u>Matt. 25:33, 34</u>-46; Luke 23:33-43; (4) Judg. 7:20 (Right hand depicts the mouth while the left hand the heart); (5) Gen 48:12-22; (6) 1 Pet. 3:22; (7) Prov. 3:16; (8) Prov. 27:15-16 (oily right hand); (9) Eccl. 10:2.

Ring: (1) Identity and seal; (2) Authority and position; (3) Covenant; (4) Marriage or family; (5) Hands; (6) Wealth; (7) Pride; (8) Promise; (9) Independent spirit (worn on middle finger).

(1) Gen. 38:18; Esther 3:12; 8:8; <u>Dan. 6:17</u>; (2) <u>Gen. 41:42-43</u>; Esther 3:10; 8:2; Luke 15:22; (3) Gen. 9:13 (A rainbow is a ring from the sky); Gen. 17:11-14; (4) <u>1 Cor. 7:39</u>; (5) Song. 5:14 (KJV); (6) James 2:2; (7) Isa. 3:16, 21; (8) Gen. 9:10-13; (9) Esther 3:10-11.

Ripe: (1) Harvest time; (2) Ready; (3) Best; (4) Perfect or mature; (5) Good and edible.

(1) <u>Joel 3:13-14</u>; John 4:35; Rev. 14:15, 18; (2) Gen. 40:10; (3) Exod. 22:29; <u>Num. 18:12-13</u>; Isa. 18:5; (4) Isa. 18:5; (5) Jer. 24:2.

River: (1) Holy Spirit; (2) Move of the Spirit; (3) Word of God; (4) Life (River of Life); (5) Love; (6) Boundary or border; (7) Death to self (river crossing or dirty river); (8) Moving into Promised Land (river crossing); (9) Peace; (10) Eternity; (11) Prosperity.

Also see *Brook, Creek, Riverbank, River Bed (Dry),* and *Stream.*

(1-2) Ezek. 47:1-12; <u>John 7:38-39</u>; Acts 11:16; (3) Prov.18:4; Amos 8:11; Eph. 5:26; (4) Ezek. 47:9; Rev. 22:1; (5) Eph. 3:18-19 (Consider that this describes something that has length, width, and depth; its height depicts where it comes from!); (6) <u>Josh. 1:11</u>; (7-8) Deut. 27:3; Josh. 3; 2 Kings 5:12; (9) Isa. 48:18; (10) Dan. 12:7; (11) Ps. 1:3.

Riverbank: (1) Out of the Spirit; (2) Not entering in; (3) About to enter in; (4) Decision time (place of decision); (5) Place of prayer; (6) Fruitfulness and prosperity.

Also see *River*.

(1) Ezek. 47:6; John 7:37-38; (2-4) 2 Kings 5:10-14; (5) Acts 16:13; (6) Ps. 1:3.

River Bed (Dry): (1) Without the Spirit of God; (2) Making a path; (3) Judgment; (4) Grieving the Spirit; (5) Quenching the Spirit.

(1) Isa. 44:3; Luke 11:24-26; John 7:37-38; (2) Josh. 5:1; Rev. 16:12; (3) Isa. 19:4-6; 42:15; 44:27; 50:2b; Ezek. 30:12; (4) Eph. 4:30: (5) 1 Thess. 5:19.

Roach: See Cockroach.

Road (path): (1) Jesus Christ (Christianity); (2) The path of life (faith); (3) What lies ahead for you; (4) The path of the righteous; (5) Peace; (6) Decision (middle of road or intersection); (7) Following their path (someone you know driving you down the road); (8) Destruction (broad road); (9) Changing sides (crossing the road).

Also see *Country Road, Highway, Path, Roadblock, Roadwork, Rocky Road, Street, T-Junction,* and *Winding Road*.

(1) John 14:6 (The Way); (2) Ps. 16:11; Prov. 2:19; (3) Exod. 23:20; Prov. 5:21; 22:6; Luke 10:3; (4) Ps. 23:3; Prov. 2:13, 20; 4:11; (5) Isa. 59:8; (6) Josh. 24:15; (7) Ps. 1:1, 6; 18:21; 95:10; 119:3; 139:24; (8) Matt. 7:13; (9) Acts 9:11-15.

Road (Road Lighting Conditions): (1) Light = just; Darkness = wicked.

(1) Prov. 4:18-19.

Road (Turning Off the Road): (1) Evil; (2) Greed; (3) Adultery.

(1) Prov. 4:26-27; Rom. 3:12; (2) Jude 1:11; (3) Prov. 7:25.

Roadblock: (1) Delay (awaiting the timing of God); (2) Sin stopping destiny; (3) Inspection (being checked/tested); (4) Ambush; (5) Warning; (6) Alternative route required; (7) Go back from where you came; (8) A personal agenda that needs to be changed; (9) Potential physical heart or artery issue.

(1) Acts 16:6-7; (cf. Acts 19:10; 1 Pet. 1:1); Ps. 105:19; John 11:6; (Luke 19:38 & John 6:15); (2) Num. 14:22-24; (3) Gen. 42:16; Judg. 12:5-6; Ps. 105:19; Matt. 4:1; (4) Prov. 7:6-23; (5) Num. 22:22-35; (6) Acts 16:6-10; (7) Hos. 2:6-7; (8) Num. 22:22-35 (cf. Rev. 2:14); (9) Deut. 2:30.

Road Grader: (1) Restoration ministry; (2) Prophetic ministry.

Also see *Bulldozer* and *Earthmover.*

(1) Gal. 6:1; (2) Isa. 40:3-4.

Road Traffic Authority: See Highway Patrol.

Road Work/s: (1) Preparing one's destiny; (2) Improving one's destiny; (3) Building a path for others; (4) Preparing hearts for God; (5) Warning to slow down; (6) Detour; (7) Removing a barrier in your path; (8) Problems ahead; (9) Changed destiny; (10) Delay; (11) Diversion (detour).

(1) Exod. 23:20; Isa. 40:3-4; (2) 2 Chron. 27:6; Isa. 57:14; (3) Isa. 62:10; (4) Mal. 3:1; Matt. 3:3; 11:10; (5) Num. 22:22-35; (6) Exod. 3:2-4; John 4:3-4 (divine appointment); Matt. 2:13-15 (protection); Mark 6:31 (rest); Luke 4:1-2, 14 (testing); (7) Isa. 40:3-4; (8) Num. 22:22-33; (9) Acts 8:26-39; 9:3-6; (10) Gen. 11:31; (11) Deut. 5:32.

Roar: [A] Fearless authority making a declaration: (1) God's voice; (2) Loud voice; (3) A leader's anger; (4) Fearless (as a lion); (5) Territorial warfare (lion's roar).

[B] The spiritual enemies of God trying to paralyze their prey: (6) Voice of the spiritual enemies; (7) The adversary; (8) A wicked leader.

[C] The cry of a heart in anguish: (9) Heart cry; (10) The Second Coming; (11) The world (sea).

Also see *Lion* and *Sea.*

(1) Job 37:4-5; Isa. 42:13 (KJV); Jer. 25:30; Joel 3:16; Amos 1:2; (2) Job 3:24 (KJV); Rev. 10:3; (3) Prov. 19:12; 20:2; (4-5) Isa. 5:29; 31:4; (6) Judg. 14:5; Ps. 22:13; 74:4; 104:21; Jer. 2:15; 6:23; 50:42; Ezek. 22:25; Zech. 11:3; (7) 1 Pet. 5:8; (8) Prov. 28:15; (9) Ps. 22:1(KJV); 32:3 (KJV); 38:8 (KJV); (10) Luke 21:25; (11) Ps. 46:3; 96:11; 98:7; Isa. 5:30; 51:15; Luke 21:25.

Roast: (1) Purified (in fire); (2) Covenant memorial of deliverance; (3) Diligence; (4) Intimate fellowship.

Also see *Cooking.*

(1) Exod. 12:8-9; (2) Deut. 16:6-7; 2 Chron. 35:13; (3) Prov. 12:27; (4) 1 Cor. 10:21; (cf. Luke 22:8 & John 15:15).

Robe: (1) Righteousness; (2) Authority; (3) Spiritual equipping; (4) Covenant; (5) Pride; (6) Humbling oneself (taking off robe).

The length, fabric, and color of a robe may be indicators of its meaning.

Also see *Clothing, Coat,* and *Mantle.*

(1) Job 29:14; <u>Isa. 61:10</u>; Rev. 7:9 (see *White*); (2) 1 Kings 22:10; <u>Luke 15:22</u>; (3) Lev. 8:6-7; (4) 1 Sam. 18:3-4; (5) Jon. 3:6; Luke 20:46; (6) Jon. 3:6.

Robbery: (1) Devil; (2) The result of disobedience/sin; (3) Inviting demonic interference; (4) Failure to tithe; (5) Cursed; (6) Not having the right to something; (7) Denial of God; (8) Pending destruction; (9) Fornication; (10) Election rather than recognized godly appointment of leadership; (11) Robber's chance for redemption.

Also see *Steal* and *Thief.*

(1) <u>John 10:10</u>; (2) Lev. 26:21-22; <u>Isa. 42:24</u>; (3) Amos 3:10-11; Matt. 12:29; Mark 3:27; (4) Mal. 3:8-9; (5) Mal. 3:9; (6) <u>Phil. 2:6</u>; (7) Ps. 62:10, 12b; Prov. 28:24; (8) Prov. 21:7 (KJV); Isa. 17:14; (9) Hos. 6:9; (10) <u>John 10:1-2</u>; <u>Rom. 13:1</u>; (11) Ezek. 33:15-16; (cf. Luke 19:8-9).

Robot: (1) Programmed person; (2) Religious (mechanical) person; (3) Without heart (heartless); (4) Person with technological skills.

(1) <u>Matt. 16:22-23</u>; <u>Rom. 12:2</u>; (2) Mark 7:3-9; (3) <u>Matt. 15:8</u>; Mark 12:28-33; (4) 1 Chron. 22:15b; Song. 7:1b.

Robotics: (1) Technology; (2) Computing/internet; (3) Electronic gadgetry; (4) Human-made.

(1-4) <u>1 Chron. 22:15b</u>; <u>Song. 7:1b</u>.

Rock/s: (1) Christ; (2) God; (3) God's Word or revelation (rhema); (4) Human hearts as the natural place of worship (the true altar); (5) Hardened hearts; (6) Word-doer; (7) Christ as an offense or stumbling stone; (8) Hiding place, refuge, or fortress; (9) Foundation of the Church; (10) Salvation; (11) Hope; (12) Strong/strength; (13) A solid and secure foundation; (14) False gods; (15) Barren (as in the top of a rock); (16) Place of destruction for the children of Babylon.

(1) Exod.17:6; Num. 20:8, 10-11; (also see *Seven*); <u>1 Cor. 10:4</u>; (2) <u>Deut. 32:4</u>, 18, 30; <u>1 Sam. 2:2b</u>; 2 Sam. 22:2-3, 32; Job 29:6; 39:27-30; Ps. 18:2, 31; 28:1; 42:9; 61:2; 78:35; 92:15; Song. 2:14; Isa. 51:1; (3) <u>Matt. 7:24</u>; <u>16:18</u>; (4) Job 28:5-11; John 4:24; (1 Sam. 14:4; Bozez and Seneh possibly represent David and Saul; *Bozez* means "shining" and *Seneh* means "thorn"); (cf. Judg. 6:20-21,

26, 13:19); (5) Luke 8:6, 13; Jer. 5:3 (see *Face*); Jer. 23:29; (6) Matt. 7:24; (7) Isa. 8:14; Rom. 9:33; 1 Pet. 2:8; (8) Exod. 33:21-22; Num. 24:21; 1 Sam. 13:6; 1 Sam. 23:25; 24:2; Ps. 27:5; 31:3; 71:3; 94:22; Jer. 49:16; (9) Matt. 16:18; (10) Deut. 32:15; Ps. 18:46; 62:2a, 6; 89:26; 95:1; (11) Job 14:18-19; (12) Ps. 19:14b (see marginal note), 31:2 (KJV); 62:7; Isa. 17:10 (KJV); (13) Ps. 40:2; Matt. 7:24; (14) Deut. 32:31, 37; (15) Ezek. 26:14; (16) Ps. 137:8-9; (cf. Ps. 91:12).

Rocket: (1) Powerful ministry; (2) Quickly established; (3) Growing quickly. Also see *Bomb* and *Missile*.

(1-2) Gen. 41:14; (3) As in, "taking off like a rocket."

Rocking Chair: (1) Spiritual retirement.

(1) Gen. 27:1-4, 21 (cf. Gen. 35:28-29 & 48:10-21).

Rock 'n' Roll: (1) Rebellion; (2) Witchcraft; (3) Sexual fornication; (4) Anger; (5) Spiritual warfare (worship).

(1-2) 1 Sam. 15:23; (The foundation of rock 'n' roll is rebellion. See the DVD *Hells Bells 2* by Eric Holmberg if you want to explore rock's roots); (3) Prov. 30:19b; (5) Ps. 144:1; 2 Cor. 10:4.

Rocky Road: (1) Double-mindedness (unstable path); (2) On shaky ground (or going through shaking); (3) Going through a rough patch; (4) Journey with a hardened heart. Also see *Road*.

(1) James 1:8; (2) Ps. 18:7; (3) Prov. 13:15; Isa. 63:17; (4) Hos. 10:12.

Rod: (1) Discipline; (2) Judgment; (3) Dominion or rule; (4) Word of God (as a divider); (5) Jesus Christ; (6) Protection. Also see *Staff* and *Stick*.

(1) Ps. 23:4; Prov. 13:24 (NKJV); Rev. 2:27; (2) Exod. 7:19; 8:5, 16; 9:23; 10:13; Ps. 2:9; (3) Exod. 17:9-11; Rev. 12:5; 19:15; (4) Exod. 4:17; 7:10; 14:16; 17:6; (5) Exod. 7:10, 12 & John 3:14; (6) Ps. 23:4.

Roll (verb): (1) To have the heart moved; (2) To move or be moved; (3) Removing the heart's hardness; (4) Mourning (rolling on the ground); (5) Moving on in God (changing). Also see *Circle, Round, Square,* and *Wheel.*

(1) Matt. 28:2 (an earthquake); Mark 16:3-8; Luke 24:2; (2) Rev. 6:14 (KJV); (3) Gen. 29:3; (cf. Deut. 10:16 & Josh. 5:8-9; Jer. 4:4); (4) Mic. 1:10-11; (5) Josh. 5:8-9.

Roller Coaster: (1) Life out of control—up and down—carried by circumstance; (2) Unstable; (3) Emotionally-driven; (4) Trials; (5) A call for preparation of heart (repentance); (6) Lifting despair and humbling pride.

(1-3) Ps. 109:23 (KJV); (4) James 1:2, 6; (5) Isa. 40:3-4 & Mark 1:4; (cf. Acts 13:24); (6) Luke 3:4-6.

Roller Blades/Skates: (1) Free-spirited or in the Spirit; (2) Young Christian; (3) On a roll (when preaching); (4) Out of control.

Also see *Scooter* and *Wheels.*

(1-2) Ezek. 1:20; John 21:18; (3) Rom. 10:15; (4) James 1:8.

Roof: (1) Spiritual leadership; (2) Covering and protection (authority structure); (3) Preaching platform; (4) Reference to a household (those under one roof); (5) High profile; (6) Determined faith; (7) Peak of your ministry; (8) Refuge.

Also see *Ceiling.*

(1) Acts 20:28; 1 Pet. 5:2; (2) Gen. 19:8; (3) Matt. 8:8-9; Matt. 10:27; (4) Matt. 8:8; (5) Exod. 17:9; 1 Sam. 26:13; Prov. 8:2a (KJV); Ezek. 31:3; (6) Mark 2:4-5; (7) 2 Sam. 11:2a; (8) Prov. 21:9; 25:24; Isa. 22:1.

Roof (Leaking roof): (1) Indicates wrong authority structures; (2) Wrong covering.

(1-2) Luke 5:17-19.

Rooms: (1) Chambers of the heart; (2) Mental strongholds; (3) Position or place; (4) Storage areas (memory); (5) History or generations (compartments of time); (6) Periods of time (i.e. years); (7) Departments.

Also see *House, Mansion,* and *Upper Room.*

(1) 1 Kings 6:5; Neh. 10:37-39; 13:4-5, 7-9; (cf. 1 Cor. 6:19); (2) 2 Cor. 10:4-5; (3) 1 Kings 2:35 (KJV); Prov. 18:16; Matt. 23:6 (KJV); Luke 14:7-10 (KJV); (4) Luke 12:17; (5) 1 Kings 8:20; 19:16 (KJV); Walking backward through rooms is going back through generations or time; (6) Acts 24:27 (KJV); (7) 1 Kings 20:24 (KJV).

Rooms (Large Room): (1) Blessing or fruitfulness.

(1) Gen. 26:22; Ps. 31:8 (KJV); Mal. 3:10.

Rooms (No Room): (1) Difficulty or discomfort; (2) Poor; (3) Prosperity or abundance.

(1) Mark 2:2; (2) Luke 2:7; (3) Mal. 3:10.

Rooms (Spinning Room): (1) Turmoil; (2) Sickness; (3) Drunkenness.

(1) 2 Cor. 6:5 (tumult); (2) Luke 13:11; (3) Ps. 107:27.

Root: (1) Heart; (2) Foundation; (3) Jesus Christ; (4) Past ancestry/heritage; (5) Stronghold; (6) Evil heart; (7) Bitter heart; (8) The remnant; (9) Love; (10) That which is the foundation of fruit; (11) That which taps into God's Word; (12) The righteous; (13) Soul-tie.

Also see *Uprooted.*

(1-2) Job 29:19; Matt. 13:6; 15:8, 13; Eph. 3:17; (3) Isa. 53:2; Rev. 5:5; 22:16; (4) Isa. 11:1; (5) Heb. 12:15; (6) 1 Tim. 6:10 (love of money); (7) Deut. 29:18; Heb. 12:15; (8) 2 Kings 19:30; Isa. 27:6; (9) Eph. 3:17; (10) Prov. 12:12; Matt. 3:10; (11) Job 29:19; Jer. 17:8; Ezek. 31:7; (12) Prov. 12:3; (13) Exod. 20:5.

Rope: (1) Bound; (2) Influenced by (being pulled); (3) Influencing (pulling); (4) Noose; (5) Strength in unity (three-fold cord); (6) Being held back; (7) Being tied down; (8) Having a few "loose ends" (trailing rope); (9) Sin; (10) If you are tied to something or someone, it can refer to a soul-tie (positive or negative); (11) Renewing the mind (cutting a rope [soul-tie]); (12) Dependency.

Also see *Bound, Cord, Leash, Loosing,* and *Thread.*

(1) Judg. 16:11-12; (2-3) Isa. 5:18; Acts 27:30-32; (4) (5) Matt. 27:5; (6) Eccl. 4:12b; (7) Acts 24:27; Gen. 49:11; (9) Isa. 5:18b; (10) Gen. 44:30 (parent-child); 1 Sam. 18:1 (friends); 1 Cor. 6:16 (sexual partners); (11) Rom. 12:2; (12) Acts 27:32.

Rose/s: (1) Jesus; (2) The Church; (3) Love; (4) Beauty; (5) Death (black roses).

(1-3) Song. 2:1; (5) Isa. 9:2.

Rot: (1) Curse/d; (2) Wickedness; (3) Consume; (4) Diseased; (5) Cancer; (6) Hell.

(1) Num. 5:21-22, 27; Joel 1:17 (KJV); (2) Prov. 10:7; (3) Job 13:28 (KJV); (4-5) 1 Sam. 5:6 (NKJV); Job 13:28 (KJV); (6) As in, "Go rot in hell!"

Rough: (1) Unprepared or untilled heart; (2) Harsh; (3) Attire of a prophet.

(1) Luke 3:5 (cf. 3:9); Deut. 21:4; Isa. 40:4; (2) Gen. 42:7; 1 Sam. 20:10; 1 Kings 12:13; (3) Zech. 13:4 (KJV); Matt. 3:4; Mark 1:6; Rev. 11:3.

Round: (1) God; (2) Of God; (3) Speaks of cutting away the flesh; (4) Changed or changing.

Also see *Circle, Roll, Square,* and *Wheel.*

(1) Rev. 4:2-3; (2) Gen. 9:13; (3) Josh. 5:8-9; (4) Josh. 5:9.

Roundabout: (1) Experience a turnaround of the situation; (2) Turn from fleshly into spiritual or vice versa; (3) Repentance; (4) Change of direction; (5) Going around the mountain.

(1-2) Matt. 9:22; 16:23; (3) Luke 17:4; Acts 26:20; (4) Deut. 2:3; (5) Deut. 1:6.

Rowboat: (1) Ministry or life of self-effort; (2) Need for the Holy Spirit; (3) Going backward; (4) Old or limited thinking; (5) Not changing or adapting.

See *Rowing.*

Rowing: (1) Self-effort or doing things in your own strength; (2) Opposing the Holy Spirit (going against the wind).

Also see *Boat* and *Canoe.*

(1) Mark 6:48; (2) John 3:8.

Rubber Band: (1) Stretching the truth (exaggeration); (2) Not really letting go; (3) Bouncing back; (4) Falsely bound.

(1) Gen. 20:10-12; (2) Gen. 19:26; 30:25-27; (3) Luke 22:32; (4) Rom. 8:1-2.

Rubber Boots: (1) Protection from Sin.

(1) Ps. 18:36.

Rubbish: (1) Religious achievement (dead works); (2) Product of the world; (3) Fleshly build-up; (4) That which needs discarding; (5) That which putrefies if not emptied out; (6) That which gets in the way; (7) That which accompanies someone who has been burned.

Also see *Dung, Garbage,* and *Urination.*

(1-5) Phil. 3:4-8; (6) Neh. 4:10; (7) Neh. 4:2.

Rubbish Bag/Bin: (1) Heart filled with worldly/religious philosophies; (2) Sinful heart; (3) Removing sin (taking out the rubbish bag).

(1) Phil. 3:8; (2) (Matt. 12:34 & 15:18); (3) Phil. 3:8; 2 Pet. 1:9.

Rubbish Truck: See Garbage Truck.

Ruby: (1) Jesus Christ; (2) Heart; (3) Wisdom; (4) Virtuous wife; (5) Priceless; (6) Precious; (7) Incomparable; (8) Red.

Also see *Precious Stones, Red,* and *Treasure.*

(1) Prov. 31:10 (the price paid for the Church); (2) Prov. 31:10-11; (3) Job 28:18; Prov. 3:13, 15; 8:11; (4) Prov. 31:10; (5) Job 28:18; (6) Prov. 3:15; (7) Prov. 8:11; (8) Lam. 4:7.

Ruddy (facial skin): (1) Spiritually strong; (2) Healthy; (3) Young.

(1-2) Lam 4:7; Song. 5:10; (3) 1 Sam. 16:12; 17:42.

Rug: (1) Looking for guidance (a fleece); (2) Foundation; (3) Undermined; (4) Purging (rug cleaning).

(1) Judg. 6:37; (2) Eph. 6:11-14 (we are to stand on foundational truth); (3) As in, "having the rug pulled out from under you"; (4) Matt. 3:12a; Luke 3:17a.

Ruin: (1) Pride; (2) A flattering mouth; (3) Need to be born again; (4) Disobedient heart (not doing the Word); (5) Iniquity; (6) Judgment.

Also see *Run-Down House.*

(1) Prov. 16:18; Ezek. 31:9-13; Jer. 50:32a; Hos. 5:5 (KJV); 1 Tim. 3:6; (2) Prov. 26:28; (3) Acts 15:16; Amos 9:11; Gen. 12:8 & 13:3 (consider that *Ai* means "heap of ruins" and *Bethel* means "house of God"); (4) Luke 6:44-49; (5) Ezek. 18:30; (6) Isa. 23:13, 25:2.

Ruler (Measuring): (1) Someone or something used to bring order; (2) Judgment.

Also see *Measuring Tape.*

(1) 1 Cor. 11:34; 14:40; (2) Isa. 11:4.

Run-Down House (Collapsing): (1) Laziness; (2) Lazy Christian; (3) Sin; (4) Not looking after yourself; (5) No self-control.

(1-2) Eccl. 10:18; (3) Amos 9:10-11; (4) 1 Cor. 6:19-20; (5) Prov. 25:28.

Running: (1) The race of faith; (2) Hurry; (3) Fearful (running away); (4) Meet (run toward); (5) Engage (run toward); (6) Being self-willed/self-driven;

(7) Courage; (8) Showing eagerness/commitment; (9) Greed (running after); (10) Searching (running to and fro); (11) Attack; (12) Natural or spiritual strength; (13) Abundance/overflow (running over); (14) Sure-footedness; (15) To seek after; (16) Contend (a "run in with"); (17) Be unstoppable; (18) To gather (running together); (19) Disciplined; (20) Your mission; (21) Have an alliance with (to run with); (22) Outrun your enemies.

Also see *Chasing, Hiding, Hurry,* and *Runner.*

(1) Gal. 5:6-7; Heb. 12:1-2; (2) Gen. 18:7; Judg. 13:10a; (3) Judg. 7:21 (defeat); 9:21; (4) Gen. 18:2; 24:17; 2 Kings 4:26; (5) 1 Sam. 17:48; (6) 2 Sam. 18:23-24; Rom. 9:16; (7) 2 Sam. 22:30; Ps. 18:29; (8) 1 Kings 19:20; Luke 19:4; John 20:4; (9) 2 Kings 5:20-21; Jude 1:11; (10) 2 Chron. 16:9; (11) Job 16:14; Acts 7:57; (12) Ps. 19:5; Isa. 40:31; (13) Ps. 23:5; 78:15; 119:136; 133:2; Luke 6:38; (14) Prov. 4:12; (15) Song. 1:4; Isa. 55:5; (16) Job 15:26; Jer. 12:5; (17) Joel 2:7; (18) Acts 3:11; (19) 1 Cor. 9:24-27; (20) Gal 2:2; Isa. 40:31; Phil. 2:16; (21) 1 Pet. 4:4; (22) 1 Kings 18:46.

Running water: (1) Living water (The Holy Spirit).

Lev.14:5-6, 50-52 (two birds = two heavenly beings = Jesus and the Holy Spirit); Song. 4:12, 15; Isa. 44:3; Jer. 2:13; 17:13; John 4:10-11; 7:38-39; Rev. 7:17.

Runner: (1) Entrant in the race of faith; (2) Discipliner of the flesh; (3) Waiter on God (stamina); (4) Greed; (5) Sinner; (6) Messenger; (7) Herald.

Also see *Running.*

(1) Gal. 2:2; Heb. 12:1-2; (2) 1 Cor. 9:24-27; (3) Isa. 40:31; (4) Jude 1:11; (5) Prov. 1:16; 6:18; (6) 1 Sam. 4:12; 17:17; 2 Sam. 18:19-23; Jer. 51:31; (7) 1 Sam. 8:11.

Rust: (1) Decay; (2) Corruption; (3) Earthly treasures; (4) Need for heavenly treasure; (5) Without discipline (needing maintenance); (6) Lacking character; (7) Cancer; (8) Greed; (9) Old issue (rusty).

(1-4) Matt. 6:19-20; James 5:3 (KJV); (5) Eccl. 10:18; (7) James 5:3; (8) Matt. 6:19; James 5:3; (9) Matt. 6:19-20 & Heb. 8:13 (KJV).

RV: (1) Family unit (vehicle); (2) Recreation; (3) Holiday; (4) Relaxed.

Also see *Automobile* and *Trailer.*

(1-4) Mark 3:31-32; 6:31; Luke 9:10.

Sack: (1) Human body; (2) The flesh; (3) Human vessel; (4) Working container; (5) Burden (carrying sack); (6) Baggage (carrying sack).

(1-2) (cf. Gen. 43:23 & 2 Cor. 4:7); (3-4) Lev. 11:32; (5-6) Gen. 49:14; Josh. 9:4 & Isa. 30:6.

Sacrifice: (1) Life; (2) Praise; (3) Jesus; (4) You as a living sacrifice (His will, not yours); (5) A gift; (6) Doing good and sharing; (7) Idolatry; (8) Evil spirits; (9) Sin; (10) The Law.

(1) Heb. 11:4; (2) Heb. 13:15; (3) Eph. 5:2; Heb. 7:27; 9:26; (4) Luke 22:42-44; Rom. 12:1; Heb. 10:7; (5) Phil. 4:18; Heb. 8:3; 9:9; (6) Heb. 13:16; (7) Acts 7:41; 14:13, 18; Rev. 2:14, 20; (8) 1 Cor. 10:20; (9) Heb. 5:1; 10:3; (10) Luke 2:23-24.

Sadness: See Sorrow.

Safe (Bank): (1) Heart; (2) Stronghold; (3) Secure.

(1) Ps. 57:7; 112:7-8a; Prov. 31:11a; (2) 2 Cor. 10:4; (3) Ps. 91:1.

Sail: (1) Led by the Spirit; (2) Waiting on the Holy Spirit (unfurled or empty sail); (3) Journey; (4) Test of faith; (5) Broken spirit (torn sail or broken mast).

Also see *Mast* and *Ship*.

(1-2) John 3:8; Acts 13:4; (3) Acts 13:4; (4) Luke 8:23-25; (5) Prov. 15:13.

Sale: (1) Investment in one's destiny (good or evil); (2) Soul winning; (3) Moving in faith; (4) Redemption (purchase of used items); (5) Faithful service; (6) Preparation for ministry.

Also see *Buying*.

(1) Acts 1:18a; (2) Acts 20:28; 1 Cor. 6:20; 7:23; Eph. 1:14; (3) cf. Acts 8:20 & Acts 20:28; (4) Eph. 1:14; (5) 1 Tim. 3:13 (KJV); (6) Matt. 25:9-10; Rev. 3:18.

Salesman: (1) The Devil; (2) Profiteer; (3) Preacher.

Also see entries under *Buying*, *Sale*, and *Store Clerk*.

(1) Gen. 3:1-6; (2) John 2:14-16; Rev. 18:3; (3) Acts 8:12; Rom. 10:14 (Consider that "buying" can be the equivalent to "believing". As in, "I"m just not buying it!').

Salmon: (1) Real believer (dying to reproduce); (2) Swimming against the flow of the world.

(1) Matt. 4:19; John 12:24; 15:13; (2) Matt. 7:13-14; 1 John 2:15-17.

Salt: (1) Purity or purification; (2) Loyalty of covenant; (3) Barrenness (overdosing with salt); (4) Fertilizer (of spiritual growth); (5) Fruitfulness; (6) Believers; (7) Tasting or seeing the goodness of God; (8) Seasoning; (9) Healing; (10) Offering or sacrifice; (11) Bitter words; (12) Mariner; (13) Flavoring things to your own liking; (14) Salary.

Also see *Pepper, White,* and *Yeast* (salt's opposite).

(1) 2 Kings 2:19-22; Mark 9:49-50; (2) Lev. 2:13; Num. 18:19; 2 Chron. 13:5; (a covenant of salt refers to lifelong loyalty); (3) Deut. 29:23; Judg. 9:45 (In this context, sowing with salt was a symbolic action of cursing the land with barrenness); (4-5) Matt. 5:13; Col. 4:6; (Rock salt was used as a fertilizer in Jesus' day); (6) Matt. 5:13; (7) Job 6:6; Ps. 34:8; Mark 9:50; Col. 4:6; (8) Lev. 2:13; Mark 9:50; Col. 4:6; (9) 2 Kings 2:20-22; (10) Mark 9:49 (Salt was added to offerings as an anti-leavening agent); (11) James 3:10-12; (12) Ezek. 27:8-9; Jon. 1:5; As in, "He is an old salt"; (13) Rev. 22:18; (14) The word *salary* comes from the Roman practice of paying its army a *salarium* or allowance of salt.

Sand: (1) Believers; (2) Multiplication; (3) Innumerable; (4) Many or multitude; (5) Spiritual boundary (beach); (6) Faulty foundations; (7) Disobedience (hearing and not doing the Word of God); (8) God's thoughts toward you; (9) Getting bogged or weighed down; (10) Deceptive foundation or false security in God (compacted sand); (11) Long-standing issue (compacted sand).

Also see *Beach* and *Coastline.*

(1-2) Gen. 22:17; 32:12; (3) Gen. 41:49; Job 29:18; Jer. 33:22; (4) Josh. 11:4; Judg. 7:12; 1 Sam. 13:5; (5) Jer. 5:22; Rev. 13:1; (6-7) Matt. 7:26-27; (8) Ps. 139:17-18; (9) Exod. 14:25 (KJV); Job 6:3; Prov. 27:3.

Sand (Wet): (1) Heavy-hearted; (2) A fool's wrath.

(1) Job 6:2-4; (2) Prov. 27:3.

Sandal: (1) The Gospel of peace; (2) Preparation; (3) Sending out; (4) Humility; (5) Holy ground (taken off); (6) Deception (old); (7) Dominion; (8) Legal title (walking over land); (9) Transfer of title (sandal in hand); (10) Renunciation of title (removal of sandal); (11) Dishonor.

Also see *Shoes.*

(1) Rom. 10:15; Eph. 6:15; (2) Exod. 12:11; Eph. 6:15; (3) Mark 6:7-9; Acts 12:8; (4) John 1:27; (5) Exod. 3:5; Josh. 5:15; Acts 7:33; (6) Josh. 9:5; (7) Ps. 108:9; (8) Deut. 11:24; Josh. 1:3; (9) Ruth 4:7; (10-11) Deut. 25:7-10.

Sand Castle: (1) Unstable person (without foundations); (2) Individual who is hearing, but not doing the Word; (3) Church hearing only and not applying the Word (a people easily moved by the tide of public opinion/persecution).

(1-3) Matt. 7:26-27 (cf. 2 Cor. 5:1).

Sandpaper: (1) Preparation; (2) Affliction; (3) Judgment; (4) Abrasive person; (5) Having your rough edges knocked off.

(1) Isa. 49:2b; (2) Deut. 16:3; Job 2:8; Ps. 119:67; (3) Ezek. 26:4 (KJV) (4) Acts 8:3; (5) Isa. 49:2b.

Sandwich: (1) Spiritual meal; (2) Sermon; (3) Chicken sandwich is a church sermon.

(1-3) 1 Cor. 3:1-2; Heb. 5:12-14.

Sandy Path/Trail: (1) Paths taken without divine revelation; (2) Taking steps in your own strength.

Also see *Gravel Road.*

(1-2) Exod. 2:12; Matt. 7:26.

Santa: (1) Alternative to Christ; (2) Giver; (3) An imbalanced Christian leader preaching lifestyle (giving false hope without suffering or persecution).

Also see *Christmas.*

(1) 1 John 2:18, 22; 4:3; 2 John 1:7 (An antichrist can be either opposed to Christ or instead of Christ); (2) Acts 4:37; (3) Matt. 5:11; 1 Pet. 4:1.

Santa Hat: (1) Giving; (2) Traditional believer.

(1) Eph. 4:8; (2) Zech. 6:11.

Sap: (1) Life; (2) Anointing; (3) Human spirit (as the core of the tree).

Also see *Tree.*

(1-3) Ps. 104:16 (KJV); John 15:4-5.

Sapphire: (1) Foundation; (2) Throne of God; (3) Christ; (4) Some associate this stone with the tribe of Simeon (and others with the tribe of Reuben).

Also see *Blue.*

(1) Exod. 24:10; Isa. 54:11b; Rev. 21:19; (2) Ezek. 10:1; (3) Ezek. 1:26; (4) Exod. 28:18.

Satellite: (1) Worldwide prophetic evangelism; (2) Individual set apart; (3) Independent organization or church (led by the Spirit);

(1) Mark 16:15; (2) Gen. 49:26; (3) Acts 24:5.

Satellite Dish: (1) Communication with God.

Also see *Television.*

(1) Matt. 6:9.

Satin: See Silk.

Saturday: (1) Seven; (2) Rest.

Also see *Day* and *Six* (The secular world sees Saturday as the sixth day of the week).

(1-2) Gen. 2:2.

Saturn: (1) Godly person; (sixth planet with rings: person with halo).

Also see *Halo, Rainbow, Ring,* and *Six.*

Sauce: (1) The anointing; (2) Righteousness (through the blood); (3) Redemption.

(1) Exod. 29:7; Prov. 1:23; (2) Job 29:14; Isa.10:22; Amos 5:24; Rom. 3:21-26; Eph. 4:24; (3) Luke 22:20 (NIV); 1 Cor. 11:25.

Scaffold: (1) Superficial/temporary structure; (2) Preparatory structure; (3) Support.

Also see *Trellis.*

(1-2) Exod. 26:15 (NIV); 35:11 (NIV); Acts 7:47-48; 1 Cor. 15:46; (3) Acts 20:35; 1 Thess. 5:14.

Scales (Over Eyes): See Veil.

Scales (Lizard/Fish): (1) Protection (armor); (2) Pride; (3) Hardened heart.
(1-3) Job 41:15, 24.

Scales (Weight): (1) Heart (as the means of judgment); (2) Measuring the heart; (3) Judgment; (4) Weighed in the balance; (5) Balance (6) Deceit/deception (false balance); (7) Worth.

Also see *Weighing, Weight,* and *Weight Loss.*

(1) 1 Kings 3:9; Ps. 58:2; (2) Prov. 16:2; 25:20; 31:6; (3-4) Dan. 5:27; (5-6) Prov. 11:1; 20:23; Amos 8:5; (7) Zech. 11:12.

Scalp: See Bald, Hair, Head, and Razor.

Scalpel: (1) The Word of God.
(1) Heb. 4:12.

Scar: (1) Been hurt (scarred face = damaged heart); (2) Reminder (unable to forget); (3) Identity affected; (4) Walk affected.
(1) Ps. 35:12; (2) Isa. 49:16; (3-4) 2 Sam. 4:4; 9:4.

Scarf: (1) Growing cold (hardened heart); (2) Cold atmosphere; (3) Getting warmer (taking scarf off); (4) Insensitive (taking scarf off someone); (4) Enduring hardship for Christ; (5) Glory; (6) Hiding glory; (7) Covering.
(1-3) Matt. 24:12; (4) Prov. 25:20; (4) 2 Cor. 11:27; (5-6) Song. 4:4; 7:4; (7) Exod. 34:33 (see *Veil*).

Scarlet: See Red.

School: (1) Place of teaching or learning; (2) Church; (3) Bible college; (4) Discipleship.
Also see *Classroom, Library, Old School, Private School, School Master,* and *Teacher.*
(1) Matt. 5:1-2; Acts 20:20; (2) Matt. 4:23; 9:35; 13:54; Mark 1:21; 6:2; Luke 4:15; 6:6; (3) John 18:20 (church & temple); Acts 5:42; (4) Isa. 50:4.

School (Old School): (1) Old teaching; (2) Traditional church; (3) Pharisees.
(1) Matt. 16:6, 12.

School Bus: (1) Teaching ministry; (2) Itinerant preacher.
Also see *Bus* and *School.*
(1-2) Acts 13:1-4; 21:28a; 1 Cor. 4:17b.

School Master: (1) Authoritative teaching ministry; (2) Christ; (3) The Law; (4) The Holy Spirit; (5) Natural teacher.
(1-2) Matt. 7:29; John 3:2; 6:45; (2) Gal. 3:24-25; (3) John 14:26; 1 John 2:27.

Scientist: (1) Trying to work it out in your head; (2) Reasoning away the supernatural; (3) Trying to get to God through human wisdom (intellect); (4) Antichrist evolutionists; (5) Christian Scientists (wisdom of God).
(1) Matt. 16:7-10; (2) Isa. 10:12-13; John 20:25; Acts 2:15; (3) 1 Cor. 1:25; 2:5; 2 Tim. 3:5; (4) Rom. 1:25; 2 Pet. 3:4-7; (5) 1 Kings 4:29; Matt. 2:1.

Scissors: (1) Word of God.

(1) Heb. 4:12.

Scorpion: (1) Demonic power; (2) Stinging words; (3) Torment; (4) Betrayal; (5) Harsh discipline; (6) Deception (temptation); (7) Politics (attack when threatened); (8) Sin; (9) Legalistic person/church (grabs and paralyzes its prey); (10) Spirit of fear (as in paralyzed by fear); (11) Demon spirits (flying scorpions).

(1) Luke 10:19; 11:12; Rev. 9:5; (2) Ezek. 2:6; (3) Rev. 9:5; (4) Luke 11:11-12; (5) 1 Kings 12:11; (6) Deut. 8:15; (cf. Luke 4:1-13); (7) Rev. 9:3, 5; (8-9) 1 Cor. 15:56; (10) 2 Tim. 1:7; (11) Rev. 9:9-10.

Scooter: (1) Young Christian; (2) Undeveloped ministry or person; (3) May represent the youngest in the family.

Also see *Motor Scooter, Roller Blades,* and *Wheels.*

(1) Ezek. 1:20-21; (2-3) 1 Cor. 13:11.

Scratch: (1) Reciprocal favors (scratching someone's back); (2) Irritation; (3) Imperfection; (4) Wounded heart (scratched face).

(1) 1 Pet. 4:10; (2) Prov. 17:25; (3) Luke 23:4; John 18:38; (4) Ps. 109:22, 147:3.

Screw: (1) Secured in place; (2) Stronghold (screw in head); (3) The placement of the screw may indicate the area over which the stronghold operates (i.e. a screw in the jaw may indicate a problem of speech); (4) Intellectually challenged or crazy (loose screw).

Also see *Nail.*

(1) Isa. 22:23a; Col. 2:14; (2-3) 2 Cor. 10:4-5 (entrenched in wrong thought pattern); (4) As in, having "a screw loose."

Script: (1) Saying what you want to hear; (2) Someone speaking one thing with another thing in their heart; (3) Rehearsed lines.

(1) Matt. 21:30; Luke 22:71; (cf. Luke 18:23); (2) Prov. 23:7b; Jer. 23:16; (3) John 11:21, 32, It appears that Martha and Mary had said these words to each other while they waited in vain (as they thought) for Jesus.

Scroll: (1) The Word of God; (2) Ancient book; (3) Heaven; (4) Words typed on a computer.

Also see *Book* and *Library.*

(1) Jer. 36:2, 4, 6; Ezek. 2:9-3:3; (2) Ezra 6:1-2; (3) Isa. 34:4; Rev. 6:14; (4) Computer screens scroll.

Scum: (1) Rubbish that comes to the surface when heated (sin revealed); (2) That which is to be purged (filth).

Also see *Dross.*

(1-2) Ezek. 24:6, 11-13.

Sea: (1) The world (sea of humanity); (2) The unbelieving world; (3) Baptism; (4) Raised voices (rough sea).

Also see *Beach, Coastline, Sand,* and *Wave.*

(1) 1 Kings 18:44 (the cloud represented the prayers of Elijah!); Ps. 98:7; Isa. 17:12; Jer.50:42; Hab. 1:14a; Rev. 17:15; (2) Isa. 60:4-5; (cf. Ps. 2:1 & Ps. 89:9-10); (3) 1 Cor. 10:1-2; (4) Jer. 6:23a.

Séance: (1) Inviting unclean spirits (familiar spirits).

(1) 1 Sam. 28:7, 11.

Seat: See Sitting.

Seatbelt: (1) Exercising restraint; (2) Buckling up because of turbulence ahead; (3) Truth (protection against attack); (4) Protection from hindrance; (5) Secure in ministry or destiny.

Also see *Automobile* and *Auto Accident.*

(1) Exod. 19:12; (2) 1 Pet. 5:8; (3-4) Prov. 6:20-22a; Eph. 6:14; (5) Luke 10:42; Acts 21:11-13.

Second: (1) Spiritual; (2) Horizontal love; (3) Denial; (4) Servant (ox); (5) Made known; (6) Not first place or choice; (7) Not the best.

Also see *Two.*

(1) John 3:3-4; 1 Cor. 15:46-47; Heb. 8:7-8; 9:3, 7; 10:9; Rev. 2:11; 21:8; (2) Matt. 22:39; Mark 12:31; (3) Mark 14:72; (4) Rev. 4:7; Also second Book (Mark) of New Testament shows Christ as the tireless Servant; (5) Luke 13:34-35; Acts 7:13; (6) Matt. 22:25-26, 39; (7) As in, "second rate."

Second Place/Seat/Row: (1) Second best; (2) Inferiority; (3) Possibly feeling not worthy to take God's appointed position for you.

(1-3) Judg. 6:15; 1 Sam. 10:22; Matt. 22:25-26.

Secret: (1) Heart; (2) Private plans or counsel; (3) Revelation from God; (4) In the dark (darkness); (5) Brought to light; (6) Not open; (7) Private/ly; (8) Hidden; (9) God's Presence; (10) Personal issue; (11) Unknown; (12) Mystery.

(1) 2 Kings 4:27; Ps. 44:21; 139:15; Prov. 20:27; Matt. 6:6, 18; 1 Cor. 14:25; 1 Pet. 3:4; (2) Gen. 49:6 (KJV); Ps. 64:2, 4-5; Prov. 11:13; 20:19; (3) Deut. 29:29; Ps. 25:14; Prov. 3:32; Dan. 2:47; Amos 3:7; Matt. 13:35; (4-5) Ps. 18:11; Isa. 45:3; Dan. 2:22; Mark 4:22; Luke 8:17; Eph. 5:12-13; (6) John 7:10; 19:38; (7) Deut. 13:6; Jer. 38:16; John 11:28; (8) Ps. 10:9; 27:5; 31:20; Prov. 9:17-18; 27:5 (KJV); (9) Ps. 81:7; 91:1; (10) Prov. 25:9-10; (11) Dan. 2:18-19; (12) Rom. 16:25.

Secret Passage: (1) Entering in to spiritual mysteries; (2) Spiritual truth that leads to your destiny; (3) Walking in the Spirit.

(1) Isa. 45:3; Dan. 2:22; (2) John 8:31-32; (3) 1 Cor. 14:2.

Seed: (1) God's Word; (2) Words; (3) Potential; (4) Faith; (5) Christ; (6) Believer; (7) Children/offspring; (8) Money to sow (investment); (9) Multitudes; (10) Multiplication; (11) Death.

Also see *Nuts.*

(1) Matt. 13:19-23; Luke 8:11; 1 Pet. 1:23; (2) Luke 19:22; (cf. 2 Cor. 9:6); (3) Matt. 13:32; (4) Matt. 17:20; Luke 17:6; (5) Gen. 3:15; Gal. 3:16; John 7:42; (6) Matt. 13:38; John 12:24; (7) Matt. 22:24 (KJV); Mark 12:19-22 (KJV); John 8:37 (KJV); Heb. 11:11; (8) Matt. 6:19-20; 2 Cor. 9:5-6; (9) Rom. 4:18 (KJV); (10-11) John 12:24.

Seed Sower: (1) Christ; (2) The devil; (3) Pastoral leadership; (4) Believers; (5) Any or every person; (6) Worker in the harvest.

(1) Matt. 13:37; (2) Matt. 13:25, 28; (3) 1 Cor. 9:11; (4) 2 Cor. 9:6, 10; James 3:18; (5) Gal. 6:7-8 (good and evil); (6) 1 Cor. 3:6.

Seeing: (1) Being born again; (2) Prophetic insight.

Also see *Lookout* and *Window.*

(1) John 3:3; (2) 1 Sam. 9:9.

Self-Rising Flour: (1) Wrong teaching; (2) Treading on others to elevate yourself; (3) Religious works; (4) Self-righteous works.

Also see *Yeast.*

(1) Matt. 16:11-12; (2) Luke 11:53-12:1; (3-4) Matt. 12:2; Mark 2:16; 7:2-13; Luke 11:38;

Semi Trailer: See Truck.

Sequins: See Glitter.

Seven: (1) Divine perfection; (2) Rest; (3) Spiritual completion; (4) Blessed; (5) Full/satisfied/have enough of; (6) To swear an oath; (7) Seven items may = seven days or years.

(1) Gen. 2:2 (God rested because creation was full, complete, good, and perfect); Ps. 12:6; (2) Gen. 2:2; Ruth 3:15-18; (3) Rev. 1:4; 3:1; (4) Gen. 2:3; (5) The Hebrew for seven is *shevah*, from the root *savah*, which means "full/satisfied/have enough of"; (6) Gen. 21:29-31; (7) Gen. 41:26; Dan. 4:16; Josh 6:4.

Seventeen: (1) The perfection of spiritual order; (2) Walk with God.

Also see *Seven*.

(1) Seventeen is the seventh prime number (1, 3, 5, 7, 11, 13, 17), it therefore intensifies the meaning of number seven. Seventeen is the sum of 10 (complete order) + 7 (spiritual perfection); Gen. 8:4: The ark rested on the 17th day of the 7th month, likewise Christ's resurrection was on the 17th of Abib (Passover + 3 days) (cf. Exod. 12:6); Rom. 8:35-39, seventeen things as being impossible to separate us from the love of God; (2) Two who *"walked with God"*—Enoch (7th from Adam) and Noah (10th).

Seventy: (1) Perfect spiritual order; (2) Fullness of accomplishment; (3) Release from Babylon; (4) Set for increase; (5) A generation (years).

(1) As the product of 7 (perfect) x 10 (order); (2) Gen. 46:27; 50:3, 70 days mourning for Jacob; Exod. 1:5, 70 souls went into Egypt; <u>Ps. 90:10</u>, 70 years (life-span); <u>Dan. 9:24</u>, 70 weeks of Daniel; (3) <u>Jer. 29:10</u>; (4) Exod. 1:5; 15:27; Num. 11:25; Luke 10:1; (5) Ps. 90:10.

Sewage: (1) Flesh; (2) Shame and offense; (3) Cleansing or detoxing; (4) Manure; (5) Religious recognition or religious leverage; (6) Perishing; (7) Needy; (8) Despised; (9) Defiled/polluted.

Also see *Faeces* and *Urination*.

(1) <u>Zeph. 1:17 </u>(KJV); (2) Mal. 2:3 (KJV); (3) Neh. 3:13-14; The refuse gate was the gate through which refuse was taken; (4) 2 Kings 9:37 (KJV); Ps. 83:10 (KJV); Jer. 8:2 (KJV); 9:22 (KJV); Luke 13:8; (5) Phil. 3:7-8 (KJV); (6) Job 20:7 (KJV); Ps. 83:10 (KJV); (7) Ps. 113:7 (KJV); (8) Jer. 16:4 (KJV); (9) Ezek. 4:12-15.

Sewing: (1) Joining; (2) Uniting; (3) Sealing; (4) Mending; (5) Trying to put spiritual truth into the fleshly person;

(1-2) Gen. 3:7; (3) Job 14:17 (KJV); (4) Eccl. 3:7; (5) Mark 2:21.

Sewing Machine: (1) Joining or binding; (2) Manufacturing/fabricating; (3) Producing righteousness; (4) Repair or mend.

(1) Col. 3:14; (2) Judg. 16:13; (3) <u>Isa. 61:10</u>; John 19:23b; (4) Matt. 9:16.

Sex: (1) Union or agreement with someone (good or evil); (2) Lust; (3) Spirit of lust; (4) Adulterous heart; (5) Fleshly self; (6) Uncrucified Christian; (7) Feeding the flesh (you hunger for what you feed on!); (8) Stronghold of lust; (9) In love with the world; (10) Lover of pleasure; (11) Denial of the power of God; (12) Conceiving sin; (13) Contaminating or polluting the godly with the world.

Also see *Adultery, Fornication, Genitals,* and *Sexual Abuse.*

Note: If the dreamer experiences an arousal or experiences an awareness of perversion in the dream, then it is very likely that there is a pornographic/sexual/lust/sex predator issue or evil spirit involved.

(1) 1 Cor. 6:16; (2-3) Gen. 19:5; <u>Judg. 19:22, 25</u>; Ps. 81:12; <u>Prov. 6:25</u>; <u>Rom. 1:24-27</u>; (4) Matt. 5:28; James 4:2-4; (5) Gal. 5:16-17, 19; Eph. 4:22; (6) Gal. 5:24 (KJV); (7) Gal. 5:17; 2 Tim. 2:22; (8) 2 Tim. 2:22; (9) 1 John 2:16-17; (10-11) 2 Tim. 3:4b-6; (12) James 1:14-15; (13) 2 Pet. 2:10.

Sexual Abuse: (1) Perverted doctrine; (2) Literal abuse.

(1) Luke 20:47.

Shack: (1) Poor person; (2) Poor in spirit; (3) Actual spiritual state (while thinking you are rich).

Also see *Cabin* and *Hut.*

(1-2) 2 Sam. 9:5-6, 8; Matt. 5:3; (3) Rev. 3:17; (cf. 2 Cor. 5:1).

Shade: See Shadow and Under.

Shadow: (1) Darkness; (2) Sin; (3) Hiding or away from God; (4) Sickness; (5) Death; (6) Hiding place; (7) Under the influence of (positive or negative); (8) Preview; (9) Without real substance; (10) Under; (11) Protection (refuge); (12) Sign; (13) Brevity (of life); (14) Covered; (15) Trust; (16) Bound.

Also see *Darkness* and *Under.*

(1) Ps. 107:11, 14; Song. 2:17; 4:6; Isa. 9:2; (2-3) Gen. 3:8; <u>Job 34:22</u>; John 3:19-21; James 1:17; (4) (5) <u>Job 3:5</u>; <u>10:21-22</u>; 16:16; Ps. 23:4; 44:19; Matt. 4:16; Luke 1:79; (6) Ps. 17:8; Isa. 49:2; Mark 4:32; (7) Judg. 9:15; Acts 5:15; (8-9) Col. 2:17; Heb. 8:5; 10:1; (10) Song. 2:3; Heb. 9:5; (11) Gen. 19:8; Ps. 91:1; 63:7; Isa. 4:6; 25:4; 30:2; Dan. 4:12; (12) 2 Kings 20:9-11; (13) 1 Chron. 29:15; <u>Job 8:9</u>; 14:1-2; Ps. 102:11; 109:23; 144:4; Eccl. 6:12; (14) Job 40:22; Ps. 80:10; (15) Ps. 36:7; 57:1; (16) Ps. 107:10, 14.

Shake: (1) Fear; (2) Facing adversity; (3) Presence of God; (4) Easily moved by circumstances; (5) Sift or purge; (6) Taking responsibility for their own judgment (shaking shoes or clothes in front of someone); (7) Change; (8) Poor foundation; (9) Empowered by the Holy Spirit.

(1) Dan. 5:6; <u>Matt. 28:4</u>; (2) Ps. 10:6; (3) Isa. 19:1; (4) Matt. 11:7; (5) Luke 22:31; (6) Mark 6:11; Acts 18:6; (7) Luke 21:26; As in, "There was a shake-up of staff"; (8) Luke 6:48; (9) Acts 4:31.

Shaking Hands: (1) Pledge; (2) Agreement or unity; (3) Contract or covenant; (4) Surety (guarantor).

Also see *Fingers, Fist,* and *Hand.*

(1) Job 17:3; (2-4) <u>Prov.</u> 6:1; <u>17:18</u>; 22:26.

Shark: (1) Worldly predator; (2) Sex Predator; (3) Person greedy for gain (financial predator); (4) Devil; (5) Evil spirit.

Also see *Jaws* and *Wolf.*

(1) Ps. 17:9-14; 124:2-7; (2) Judg. 16:4-5; <u>Prov. 23:27-28a</u>; (3) <u>Ezek. 22:27</u>; (4) <u>1 Pet. 5:8</u>; (5) Mark 9:20 (KJV).

Shave/d: (1) Separation; (2) Cutting off the flesh; (3) Spiritual cleansing; (4) Near miss; (5) Expression of grief; (6) Shame; (7) Vow of consecration (keeping or breaking a vow); (8) Losing the anointing; (9) Mourning.

Also see *Cutting Hair, Hair,* and *Razor.*

(1) Num. 6:18-19; (2) Gen. 41:14; (3) Lev. 14:8-9; <u>Num.</u> 6:9; <u>8:7</u>; Deut. 21:12; Acts 21:24; (4) As in, "That was a close shave"; (5) Lev. 21:1-5; Job 1:20; Jer. 41:5; (6) 2 Sam. 10:4-5; 1 Chron. 19:4; <u>1 Cor. 11:5-6</u>; (7) Num. 6:18-19; (8) Judg. 16:17-20; (9) Mic. 1:16.

Shed: (1) Fleshly or immature Christian; (2) Person or organization built on greed (rusty shed); (2) Workshop business.

(1) 2 Cor. 5:1; (2) James 5:3; (3) 1 Sam. 13:19; Isa. 54:16.

Sheep: (1) Believers; (2) Christ; (3) Sinners (lost or astray); (4) Shepherdless (scattered sheep); (5) Church (flock of sheep).

Also see *Goat/s* and *Shepherd.*

(1) Matt. 10:16; 25:32; Luke 15:4-7; John 10:3-4, 7, 14; John 21:16-17; 1 Pet. 5:2-3; (2) Acts 8:32; (3) Isa. 53:6; (4) Matt. 9:36; (5) Acts 20:28; 1 Pet. 5:2.

Sheet: (1) Covering; (2) Garment; (3) Veil over the mind/mindset; (4) Thoughts; (5) Wrong thoughts (dirty sheets).

Also see *Bed.*

(1-2) Judg. 14:12-13 (KJV); (3-5) Acts 10:11-15; 1 Pet. 1:13.

Shells: (1) Protection; (2) Home or roof; (3) Currency; (4) Explosive projectile; (5) Cover; (6) Going into hiding; (7) Withdrawing; (8) Spiritual gifts.

(1) Job 41:7, 13, 15, 24, 26; (2) Gen. 19:8; (3) Matt. 13:45-46; (4) Acts 4:31; (5) Matt. 10:26; Luke 8:16; (6) 1 Kings 19:9; (7) As in, "going into his shell"; (8) Gen. 24:53; Prov. 17:8.

Shepherd: (1) Christ; (2) God; (3) Pastor; (4) Hireling; (5) Greedy pastors; (6) False shepherds.

Also see *Sheep.*

(1) Matt. 25:31-32; 26:31; John 10:2, 11, 14; Heb. 13:20; 1 Pet. 2:25; (2) Gen. 49:24; Ps. 23:1; 80:1; Isa. 40:10-11; (3) Gen. 46:34b; Acts 20:28; 1 Pet. 5:2; (4) John 10:12-13; (5) Isa. 56:11; Ezek. 34:2-5; (6) Jer. 50:6.

Shield: (1) Faith; (2) Word of God (truth); (3) Protector; (4) God; (5) Spiritual warfare/battle; (6) Spiritual warriors; (7) Righteous; (8) Ruler; (9) Grace; (10) Mighty person; (11) Salvation; (12) House.

(1) Ps. 28:7; 115:9-11; Prov. 30:5; Eph. 6:16; (2) Ps. 91:4; 119:114; (3) Gen 15:1; Ps. 33:20; (4) 2 Sam. 22:3; Ps. 3:3; 84:9 (KJV); 115:9-11; (5) 1 Chron. 12:8; Ps. 76:3; (6) 1 Chron. 12:24; (7) Ps. 5:12; (8) Ps. 47:9; (9) Ps. 84:11; (10) Song. 4:4; Nah. 2:3; (11) 2 Sam. 22:36; Ps. 18:35; (12) As in, a coat-of-arms or heraldic shield.

Shin: (1) Sensitivity affecting your walk or ability to stand; (2) Protection over a sensitive area (shin guard).

(1) Deut. 11:25; Josh. 10:8; 2 Chron. 20:17; Dan. 10:8; Hos. 4:14b; (2) Eph. 6:11.

Ship: (1) Big Ministry; (2) Big church (fellow-ship); (3) Christ; (4) Believer; (5) The church (the entire Body of Christ or individual congregations);

(6) Trade; (7) Business; (8) Wealth; (9) Strength; (10) Cargo; (11) Journey, voyage, or passage.

Also see *Battleship, Boat, Freight,* and *Shipwreck.*

(1) Gen. 6:14-15; (2) Matt. 14:22-33; Mark 6:45-54; Luke 5:3b, 10b; John 6:15-21; (Each incident describes Jesus' departure and the Church's subsequent opposition in the sea of humanity until His return); (3) Gen. 6:13-14 (Christ is God's vehicle of salvation today); Acts 27:31b; (4) James 3:4-5; (5) Gen. 6:13-16 & Matt. 24:37; (6) 2 Chron. 9:21; Prov. 31:14; Rev. 18:17; (7) 1 Kings 10:15; Ps. 107:23; (8) 1 Kings 9:26-28; Rev. 18:19; (9) Isa. 23:14; (10) Acts 21:3; (11) Matt. 9:1; Mark 5:21.

Shipwreck: (1) Not moving in faith; (2) Blasphemy; (3) Disobedience; (4) Listening to people; (5) Moved by wrong motives; (6) Seeking personal fulfillment and pleasure above work of the Kingdom (capsized boat); (7) This may also be a person or ministry that began OK, but has been lured into seeking fulfillment through finances; (8) Spiritual forces arrayed against the ministry.

Also see *Auto Accident, Storm,* and *Waves.*

(1-2) 1 Tim. 1:19-20; Matt. 8:25-26; Heb.11:29; (3) 1 Sam. 15:26-28; (4-5) Acts 27:10-11, 41; (6) Jude 1:11, 13 (cf. Matt. 6:33); (7) 1 Tim. 6:9-10; (8) Acts 27:14-18; Matt. 8:25-26.

Shirt: (1) Servanthood (taking shirt off); (2) Undue worry; (3) Little faith (overemphasis on); (4) Fleshly self (old shirt); (5) Color is a very important indicator of the meaning behind clothing, so check entries under individual colors.

Also see *Clothing* and *Robe.*

(1) John 13:4; (2-3) Matt. 6:28-30; (4) Matt. 9:16.

Shoe: (1) Gospel; (2) Word; (3) Walk; (4) Preparation; (5) Authority; (6) Ministry.

(1, 4) Eph. 6:15; (2) Ruth 4:7; (3) Deut. 25:4-10; (5) Luke 15:22 (Sons wore shoes; slaves did not); (6) Rom. 10:15.

Also see *Ballet Shoe, Sandal, Slippers,* and *Walking.*

Shoes Off: (1) Holy ground/God's Presence; (2) Not prepared; (3) Communion; (4) Affecting your work for God; (5) Walking in the flesh; (6) Disgraced; (7) Testimony; (8) Enslaved.

(1, 3) Exod. 3:5; Josh. 5:15; (2) Eph. 6:15; (4) Deut. 25:4-10; (5) Rom. 8:1, 4; 2 Cor. 10:2; 2 Pet. 2:10; (6) Deut. 25:9; (7) Ruth 4:7-8; (8) Isa. 20:2-4.

Shoes (Pair): (1) Witness (as in two words); (2) Balance; (3) Covenant.

(1) See *Two* and *Shoe;* (2) 2 Sam. 23:12; Prov. 3:3-4; (3) Amos 3:3; Ps. 86:11; Ruth 4:7-10.

Shoes (Two Pairs): (1) Two different aspects of the same walk (i.e. different person at home compared to outside).

(1) Ruth 1:15-16.

Shofar: (1) Prophet; (2) Prophetic voice.

Also see *Horn* and *Trumpet.*

(1) As one who has had the flesh cut out that the breath of God may flow through them; (2) Josh. 6:8.

Shooting: (1) Damaging words; (2) Rifle shooting means words spoken against you from afar; (3) Rifle can also mean words spoken against you distant in time (i.e. from your childhood); (4) Confronting or penetrating words to your face.

Also see *Arrows, Bullets, Gun,* and *Sniper.*

(1-3) Ps. 22:7-8; 64:3-4, 7-8; Isa. 54:17; (4) Ps. 22:7-8.

Shop: (1) Ministry; (2) Church; (3) Spiritual (food) supplier; (4) Materialistic church; (5) Commercial church; (6) Business.

Also see *Butcher's Shop, Hardware Store,* and *Shopping Center.*

(1-2) Jer. 3:15; Matt. 13:45; (3) Mal. 3:10; 1 Pet. 5:2; (4) John 2:16; (5) 1 Pet. 5:2; Rev. 18:3, 11; (6) Gen. 43:4.

Shoplifter: See Thief.

Shopping Cart: (1) Agenda (something you are trying to fulfill); (2) Provision; (3) Poverty/famine (empty cart); (4) Searching (shopping around);

(1) John 1:13 (will of people); (2) Deut. 26:2; 1 Kings 4:22ff; (3) Jer. 42:14; (4) Matt. 7:7.

Shopping Center: (1) Multi-faceted commercial church.

(1) Matt. 21:12-13.

Shopping Trolley: See Shopping Cart.

Short: (1) Little time; (2) Brief or briefly; (3) Soon (Lord's return); (4) Humble; (5) Sin; (6) Missing God's best; (7) Restless; (8) Insufficient; (9) Powerless (short arm or hand); (10) Soon angry (short-tempered).

Also see *Little* and *Tall.*

(1) <u>Rev. 12:12b</u>; (2) Ps. 89:47; (3) 1 Cor. 7:29; (4) 1 Sam. 15:17 (cf. Acts 13:9); (5-6) Rom. 3:23; (7) Heb. 4:1; (8) Isa. 28:20; (9) Num. 11:23; Isa. 50:2; 59:1; (10) Tit. 1:7; James 1:19.

Shoulder: (1) Burden; (2) Authority; (3) Responsibility; (4) Bearing or carrying (5) Rank (height); (6) Reminder (memorial); (7) Departure (worldly goods on shoulder); (8) Rebellion (turning or shrugging the shoulder); (9) Putting your back into it (commitment); (10) Hurt the fatherless (arm falls off); (11) Redeemed (laid on shoulder); (12) Ignoring someone (cold shoulder).

(1) Gen. 12:6 (*Shechem* means "burden"); 2 Chron. 35:3; Isa. 10:27; <u>Matt. 23:4</u>; (2) Isa. 9:6; (3) Gen. 9:23; 21:14; Num. 7:9; <u>Isa. 9:6</u>; (4) Gen. 24:15; Judg. 16:3; 1 Chron. 15:15; Isa. 46:7; (5) 1 Sam. 9:2; 10:23; (6) Exod. 28:12; Josh. 4:5-7; (7) Exod. 12:34; (8) Neh. 9:29 (KJV); Zech. 7:11; (9) Job 31:36; Luke 9:62; (10) Job 31:21-22; (11) Luke 15:5.

Shout: (1) Joy or rejoicing; (2) Triumph; (3) Battle (can be the shout of victory or defeat in battle); (4) Praise; (5) Associated with the presence of God or at the entrance of a king (praise or triumph).

(1) Ezra 3:11-13; <u>Ps.</u> 5:11; <u>35:27</u>; (2) Josh. 6:5, 16, 20; <u>Ps. 47:1</u>; (3) Exod. 32:17-18; Job 39:25; Amos 1:14; (4) Ezra 3:11; Isa. 44:23; (5) Num. 23:21; 2 Sam. 6:15; Ps. 47:5; Isa. 12:6; 1 Thess. 4:16.

Shovel: (1) Need to empty; (2) Labor or works; (3) Speaks of winnowing or separation; (4) Digging deeper in God (shoveling); (5) Faith.

Also see *Digging* and *Spade.*

(1) Exod. 38:3; (2-3) <u>Isa. 30:24</u>; (4) Gen. 26:15, 18; (5) Matt. 17:20; 21:21; <u>1 Cor. 13:2</u>.

Shower (Bathroom): (1) Cleansing; (2) Seeking cleansing in words (i.e. confession); (3) The Holy Spirit; (4) Human-constructed and controlled spiritual flow.

(1) John 13:10; (2) <u>John 15:3</u>; 17:17; 1 John 1:9; (3) Isa. 44:3; Joel 2:28; Acts 2:17; (4) Matt. 23:4, 15.

Shower (Rain): (1) Blessing; (2) God's favor; (3) God's strength; (4) Teaching; (5) Poor and needy (a wet person); (6) Softened hearts (soil); (7) God coming down; (8) Judgment for wickedness (withheld showers); (9) The remnant of Jacob; (10) Latter rain; (11) God's Word.

Also see *Cloud* and *Rain.*

(1) Ezek. 34:26; (2) Prov. 16:15; (3) Job 37:5-6; (4) Deut. 32:2; (5) Job 24:4, 8; (6) Ps. 65:10; (7) Ps. 72:6; (8) Jer. 3:1-3; (9) Mic. 5:7; (10) Zech. 10:1; (11) Isa. 55:10-11.

Showing Off: See entry 3 under Tricks.

Shrek: (1) Anger problem (ogre/tyrant); (2) Demon.

(1) 1 Sam. 20:30; (2) Mark 5:2ff.

Shrimp: See Crab and Lobster.

Shrine: (1) Place of idolatrous pilgrimage; (2) Place of false worship.

(1) 2 Kings 10:29; Ps. 97:7; (2) Deut. 8:19; Rom. 1:25.

Shrinking: See Smaller.

Shrub: See Bush.

Shutters: (1) Shutting out the glory; (2) Not prepared/able to receive the glory; (3) Spiritual blindness.

(1-2) Exod. 34:30, 33-35; 2 Cor. 3:15; (3) Rom. 1:21; 2 Cor. 3:14; Eph. 4:18.

Sick: (1) Sin; (2) Parts of the anatomy may refer to structures within a family, church, business, group, or nation (i.e. a head wound may indicate a sick leader, hands may relate to workers, etc); (3) Lacking spiritual well-being; (4) Actual physical ailment; (5) In need of healing; (6) Hope deferred; (7) Lovesick; (8) Lacking self-examination.

(1) Mark 2:17; Luke 5:20, 23-24, 31-32; John 5:14; James 5:14-15; (2-3) Isa. 1:5-6; (3) Matt. 10:7-8; (5) Matt. 4:24; 8:16; (6) Prov. 13:12; (7) Song. 2:5; 5:8; (8) 1 Cor. 11:28-30.

Side: (1) Heart (the birth place of faith); (2) God's side or the enemy's; (3) Wife/husband; (4) Next to; (5) Equal; (6) Support; (7) Strengthen; (8) Surrounded (every side); (9) Internal or external; (10) Choice; (11) This side or that of eternity (river sides); (12) Vexed (thorn in side); (13) Uncommitted (as in "beside" or "apart from"); (14) Out-of-body experience (beside yourself).

Also see *Other Side, Right and Left, North, South, East,* and *West.*

(1) Gen. 6:16; Exod. 32:27 (the sword comes from the heart); John 19:34; 20:20, 25, 27 (cf. Gen. 2:21-22); Acts 12:7; (2) Exod. 32:26; Josh. 24:15; Ps.

118:6; 124:2; <u>Eccl. 4:1</u>; (3) Ps. 128:3 (KJV); Gen. 2:21-22; (4) Matt. 13:1 (KJV); (5) (Ps. 110:1 & Phil. 2:6); (6) Exod. 17:12; (7) Acts 12:7; (8) Luke 19:43; (9) 2 Cor. 7:5; (10) Josh. 24:15; (11) Num. 32:32; Deut. 1:1; (12) Num. 33:55; (13) Rev. 3:15; (14) 2 Cor. 12:2.

Sideburns: (1) Heading toward maturity (not yet a beard).

(1) 1 Sam. 17:33; 1 John 2:13.

Sidewalk: See Footpath and Pavement.

Sieve: (1) Judgment; (2) Shake; (3) Test of the heart.

(1) Isa. 30:27-28; Amos 9:9-10; (2-3) <u>Luke 22:31-32</u>.

Signature: See Signed.

Signs: (1) Miracles; (2) Word/message/voice; (3) Confirmation/witness/evidence; (4) Divider; (5) Indicator; (6) Signal; (7) Directional pointer; (8) Warning; (9) Declaration; (10) Memorial/reminder; (11) End times/indication of His return.

(1) Deut. 7:19; 13:1-2; Matt. 12:38-39; Mark 8:11-12; Acts 2:43; 4:30; (2) Exod. 4:8-9, 17; Ezek. 12:6, 11; 24:24; <u>Luke 11:30</u>; John 20:30; (3) Exod. 4:28, 30; 13:9; 31:13-14; Num. 14:11; 1 Sam. 10:2-9; 1 Kings 13:3; 2 Kings 20:8-9; Isa. 7:11, 14; 19:20; <u>Mark 16</u>:17, <u>20</u>; John 2:18; 6:30; <u>Acts 2:22</u>; (4) Gen. 1:14; <u>Exod. 8:23</u>; 31:17; (5) Exod. 10:1-2; Judg. 6:17; <u>1 Sam. 14:10</u>; Matt. 16:1-4; 24:3; Mark 13:4; Luke 2:12; 21:7; (6) Judg. 20:38; Matt. 26:48; (7) Exod. 13:9; Deut. 6:8; 11:18; (8) Num. 26:10; Matt. 24:3; (9) Ezek. 24:24; John 19:19-22; (10) Josh. 4:6-7; Isa. 55:13; Ezek. 20:12, 20; (11) Matt. 16:3; 24:30; Mark 13:4.

Signed: (1) Sealed agreement; (2) Confirmed authority; (3) Ownership; (4) Miracle (signature of the Spirit); (5) Token (seal of authenticity); (6) Confirmation of God's Word.

(1-2) <u>Dan. 6:8</u>-12, <u>17</u>; (3) <u>1 Cor. 16:21</u>; Gal. 6:11; (4) Rom. 15:19; Heb. 2:4; (5) 2 Thess. 3:17; (6) Mark 16:20.

Also see *Shaking Hands.*

Silhouette: (1) Profile; (2) Exposure; (3) Eclipse; (4) Outline; (5) Icon.

(1) <u>1 Sam. 9:2</u>; Matt. 23:5; (2) Job 20:27; (3) Ezek. 32:7; (4) Matt. 23:5b; (5) Matt. 22:20-21.

Silk: (1) Honor; (2) Glory; (3) Opulence; (4) Seduction; (5) China. Also see *Fabric.*

(1-2) Gen. 41:42; (3) Luke 16:19; (4) Prov. 7:16-18; (5) By association (silk road/routes).

Silver: (1) Redemption; (2) Redemption money; (3) Second; (4) Secondary class.

(1-2) Exod. 30:11-16; 36:24 (Silver (redemption) is the foundation of the Christian); There is no record of silver in Heaven, we do not need redeeming in Heaven; Matt. 27:3-9; (3-4) 1 Kings 10:21.

Silver Cord: (1) Life and death; (2) Spinal column.

(1-2) Eccl. 12:6-7.

Sim Card: (1) Heart.

(1) Matt. 12:34.

Singing: See Music.

Sink (Bathroom/Kitchen): See Washbasin.

Sinking: (1) Death of a ministry/relationship/chapter in one's life; (2) Death; (3) Judgment; (4) Struggling in faith (fearful); (5) Overwhelmed (positive or negative); (6) Sometimes this can be a positive sign as it may mark the end of a facet of the old self.

(1-3) Gen. 7:20-22; Exod. 15:5, 10; 1 Sam. 17:49; 2 Kings 9:24; Ps. 9:15; (4) Matt. 8:24-26; 14:30-31; (5) Luke 5:7; (6) Rom. 6:3.

Sister: (1) The Church; (2) Kindred spirit (person, city, province, nation); (3) Fellow believer; (4) One's natural sister; (5) Wisdom; (6) Judah and Israel (sisters).

(1) Song. 4:9-10, 12; 5:1-2; (2) Jer. 3:8; Ezek. 16:45ff; 23:1-4; (3) Matt. 12:50; Rom. 16:1; 1 Cor. 7:15; 1 Tim. 5:2; James 2:15; (4) Mark 6:3; (5) Prov. 7:4; (6) Jer. 3:7-8, 10.

Sister-in-Law: (1) Legalistic or religious church; (2) Religious female; (3) One's natural sister-in-law.

See *Sister.*

Sit/ting: (1) Authority; (2) Finished work; (3) Rest; (4) Judgment; (5) Position; (6) Honor; (7) Doing business.

Also see *Bench.*

(1) Eph. 2:6; Rev. 2:13 (KJV); Rev. 13:2 (KJV); (2) Ps. 110:1; Heb. 10:11-14; (3) Ruth 3:18; 2 Sam. 7:1 (KJV); Zech. 1:11 (KJV); (4) Matt. 19:28; Rev. 4:2-3; (5) Eph. 2:6; (6) Matt. 23:6; (7) John 2:14 (cf. NKJV & KJV).

Six: (1) Human; (2) Humanity in independence and opposition to God (flesh or sin); (3) Human labor contrasted with God's rest; (4) Not of God; (5) Rest (six full days bring us to seven: rest); (6) Works.

(1) Gen. 1:26, 27, 31 (humanity created on sixth day); John 2:6; (2) John 19:14-15; (3) Exod. 20:9; 21:2; 23:10-12; 31:15; 34:21; 1 Kings 10:19; (4) Luke 23:44-45; (5) Ruth 3:15-18; (6) Luke 13:14.

Sixteen: This number is derived three ways: (1) 4 x 4 = 16, as such it means a double emphasis of the rule of humanity (abomination); (2) 2 x 8 = 16, as such it means renewal of relationship with God because of the Word of redemption, or association of resurrection; (3) 10 + 6 = 16, as such it means the complete order of humanity.

(1) 2 Kings 13:10-11; 16:2-3; (2) Exod. 26:25; 36:30; 2 Kings 14:21; 15:2-4, 33-34; 2 Chron. 26:1, 4; (3) Josh. 15:41; 19:22.

Sixty: (1) Completion of the flesh.

Also see *Six* and *Ten.*

(1) As the product of 6 and 10.

Skateboard: (1) Youth ministry; (2) Use of gifts (tricks); (3) Spirit (wheels); (4) Immature path.

(1) Isa. 40:30-31; (2) Ps. 71:17; (3) Ezek. 1:20; (4) 1 Cor. 13:11.

Skeleton: (1) Without the Spirit of God; (2) Dead/death; (3) Fear; (4) Framework; (5) Famine (black skeleton).

Also see *Skin* and *Skull.*

(1-2) Ezek. 37:7-9; (3) Ps. 64:1 & 1 Cor. 15:26; (cf. Deut. 20:3; Josh 10:25); (4) Ps. 139:15; (5) Lam. 4:8-10; 5:10 (KJV).

Transparent Skeleton: (1) Spirit being; (2) Evil spirit.

(1-2) Job 4:15-16.

Skiing: (1) In the Spirit (water skiing); (2) Moving by faith (water skiing); (3) Carried by the Glory of God (snow skiing).

Also see *Snowshoes.*

(1) John 6:19; 21:18b; (2) Matt. 14:29; (3) See entry 3 under *Snow.*

Ski Lodge: (1) Church in the Glory; (2) Heaven.

Also see *Snow.*

(1-2) Dan. 7:9; (Mark 9:3 & 2 Pet. 1:17); Rev. 1:14.

Skin: (1) Covering; (2) The flesh; (3) A life; (4) Clothing; (5) Narrowest margin (skin of the teeth); (6) Troubled heart (emaciated); (7) Indicative of the heart; (7) Wrath of God (old skin); (8) Famine (black skin).

Also see *Emaciated.*

(1) Gen. 3:21; Exod. 26:14; Ezek. 37:6, 8; (2) Lev. 13:2ff; (3) Job 2:4; 18:13; 19:26; (4) Job 10:11; (5) Job 19:20; (6) Job 19:20; Ps. 102:4-5; Lam. 4:8; (7) Jer. 13:23; (7) Lam. 3:4; (8) Lam. 5:10 (KJV).

Skinhead: (1) Rebellion; (2) Aggression; (3) Anarchy; (4) Anti-authority.

Also see *Baldness, Gang, Teenager,* and *Youth.*

(1-4) Num. 12:1-2; Prov. 30:11; Amos 3:10; Gal. 5:19-21.

Skinny: (1) Lacking the Word of God; (2) Spiritual poverty; (3) Poverty; (4) Famine; (5) Cursed (gaunt).

Also see *Emaciated, Fat,* and *Thin.*

(1-2) Amos 8:11; (3-4) Gen. 41:19; (5) Deut. 28:17-18.

Skip Bin: (1) Waste; (2) Clean up; (3) Demolition; (4) Refurbishment.

Also see *Garbage Truck, Rubbish,* and *Rubbish Bag.*

(1-4) Neh. 4:2.

Skip/ping: (1) Youthfulness; (2) Overcoming (impossibility); (3) Joy.

(1) Ps. 29:6; 114:4; (2) Song. 2:8; (3) Jer. 48:27 (KJV).

Skipping Rope: (1) Repetitive childhood issue/s; (2) Childlike joy.

(1) Gen. 42:24; (2) Ps. 29:6; 114:4, 6.

Skirt: (1) Area of influence (kingdom/domain); (2) Protection; (3) Impurity (dirty skirt); (4) Anointed servant (anointed skirt); (5) Shame or disgrace (lifted skirt); (6) Sin (dirty skirt); (7) Covered.

(1) <u>1 Sam. 15:27-28</u>; 24:5-6; (2) <u>Ruth 3:9</u> (KJV); (3) Lam. 1:9; (4) Ps. 133:2 (KJV); Matt. 9:20; 14:36; (5) Jer. 13:22, 26; Nah. 3:5; (6) Lam. 1:8-9; (7) Ezek. 16:8.

Skull: (1) Thoughts and plans; (2) The Cross; (3) Death or warning of death; (4) Warning of poison; (5) Curse/d; (6) Piracy.

Also see *Skeleton*.

(1) Judg. 9:52-53 (his thoughts and plans were dashed); (2-3) <u>John 19:17-18</u>; (5) 2 Kings 9:34-35; (6) Associated with skull and crossbones.

Sky: (1) Heaven; (2) Mirror; (3) Blessing; (4) Drought (clear sky); (5) Christ's return (blood-red moonlit sky); (6) Blessing (red sky at night); (7) Tribulation (red sky in morning).

Also see *Cloudy, Open Heaven,* and *Storm*.

(1) Deut. 33:26; 2 Sam. 22:12-14; Ps. 77:17; <u>Isa. 45:8</u>; Jer. 51:9; Matt. 16:1-3; Heb. 11:12; (2) Job 37:18; (3) Mal. 3:10; (4) 1 Kings 18:43-44; (5) Acts 2:20; (6-7) Matt. 16:1-3. It is possible that the red night sky symbolizes Christ's death and birth of the day of salvation and alternatively that the red morning sky symbolizes His return and pending tribulation.

Skyscraper: See Building and Tower.

Slate: (1) Heart; (2) Writing; (3) Record of a debt; (4) Give credit; (5) A list of candidates; (6) To criticize.

(1-2) <u>2 Cor. 3:3</u>; (3-5) From dictionary meanings; (6) As in, "to slate someone."

Clean slate: (1) Good record; (2) No debt; (3) Forgiveness of sins.

(1-3) Col. 2:13-14.

Sleep/ing: (1) Prayerlessness (spiritual death); (2) Death; (3) Rest and refreshment; (4) In the flesh (spiritually dead); (5) Spiritually naked; (6) Spirit willing, weak flesh; (7) Exhaustion; (8) Danger; (9) Warning of temptation; (10) Captive; (11) God-induced sleep; (12) Dormant or inactive; (13) Place of revelation; (14) Unaware; (15) Insensitive to the things of the Spirit.

Also see *Coma, Pajamas,* and *Television* (asleep in front of the television).

(1) <u>Matt. 26:40-41</u>; (2) <u>John 11:11, 14</u>; Acts 7:60; 1 Cor.15:6; Eph. 5:14; (3) Matt. 8:24; 26:45; Mark 4:36-40; <u>John 11:13</u>; Ps. 127:2; Song. 5:2; (4) Rom. 13:11-13; Eph. 5:14; (5) <u>Rev. 16:15</u>; (6) Matt. 26:40-41; (7) Mark 4:38; (8) Acts 20:9; (9) Matt. 26:40-41; (10) Isa. 52:1-2; (11) 1 Sam. 26:7, 23; (12) 1 Kings 18:26-27; (13) Dan. 7:1; 10:9; (14) 1 Sam. 26:12; (15) Judg. 16:20.

Sleeping Bag: (1) A heart that is spiritually unaware/insensitive; (2) Non-Christian; (3) Individual itinerant ministry.

(1) Judg. 16:20; Luke 21:34 (KJV); (2) John 3:3-5; (3) Luke 9:4; 2 Cor. 11:26-27.

Slide: (1) No integrity; (2) Not trusting God; (3) Word not in heart; (4) Deceit; (5) No repentance; (6) Spiritual adultery; (7) Backslide; (8) Judgment.

(1-2) Ps. 26:1; (3) Ps. 37:31; (4-5) Jer. 8:5; (6) Hos. 4:16 (KJV); (7) Jer. 8:5; Hos. 4:16 (KJV); (8) Deut. 32:35 (KJV).

Slide Rule: (1) Trying to work it out by yourself; (2) Precision; (3) Calculating.

Also see *Calculator.*

(1) Matt. 19:26; Eph. 2:9; (2) Matt. 10:30; (3) Luke 14:28.

Sliding Door: (1) Convenient way out; (2) Unannounced entrance; (3) Opportunity to backslide.

Also see *Door.*

(1) 1 Sam. 19:10; (2) John 10:1-2; 20:26; (3) Acts 7:39; Isa. 31:1.

Sling/Slingshot: (1) Faith (carries the stone to its target); (2) The heart (the pouch of the sling); (3) The Word of God (the stone that is slung).

(1) 1 Sam. 17:34-37 & Heb. 11:32; (2) 1 Sam. 25:29 (*Pocket* in Hebrew is *kaph,* which describes a concave vessel); (3) 1 Pet. 2:8 (KJV).

Slip: (1) Sin (Unrepentant); (2) At ease despising guidance; (3) Envious; (4) In danger of losing your salvation.

Also see *Slippery.*

(1) Ps. 38:16-18; (2) Job 12:5; (3) Ps. 73:2; (4) Heb. 2:1 (KJV).

Slippers: (1) Domestic walk (what you do at home).

(1) Matt. 11:8.

Slippery: (1) Without God; (2) Without the Word; (3) Plotting against the godly; (4) Ungodliness and wickedness; (5) Hard to handle; (6) Hard to grasp.

Also see *Slip.*

(1) 2 Sam. 22:37; (2) Ps. 17:4-5; 35:6 (in the dark); (3) Ps. 35:6; (4) Ps. 73:3, 18; Jer. 23:11-12; (5) Luke 20:26 (KJV); (6) 2 Pet. 3:16.

Slow Motion: (1) God appears to be taking His time; (2) Slow down; (3) Long-lasting.

(1) Gen. 15:2; Ps. 42:9; Prov. 20:21; Isa. 28:16b; Luke 18:6-7; 1 Pet. 3:8-9; (2) John 11:6; (3) 1 Tim. 1:16; 6:19.

Slug (Snail): (1) Lawlessness; (2) Unclean issue; (3) Abomination; (4) Eating away righteous truth.

(1) Hab. 1:14; (2-3) Lev. 11:41-45; 20:25; 22:5-6; (4) 2 Tim. 2:17.

Slug Gun: See Spud Gun.

Small: See Little and Smaller.

Smaller: If something is smaller than it was originally, it may mean that: (1) Its influence is diminishing; (2) You are getting stronger in relation to it; (3) People are leaving.

(1) Num. 33:54 (KJV); Ezek. 29:15b; (2) Exod. 1:9; (3) 1 Sam. 13:11.

Smell: (1) The Presence of Jesus (fragrant); (2) Love and adoration (fragrant perfume); (3) An acceptable sacrifice (sweet); (4) Fragrance of renewal (floral); (5) Deception/corruption; (6) Pride; (7) Battle; (8) Demons (bad or sulphur smell); (9) Offence/disfavor (bad smell); (10) Good or bad memory (reminder of an issue); (11) Discerning of spirits (smelling); (12) Spirit of death (bad smell); (13) Wrong spirit (bad smell); (14) Resurrection (scent of water); (15) Good counsel (sweet smell); (16) Royalty (smell of cedar); (17) Idolatry (inability to smell); (18) Love (smell of apples).

Also see *Nose, Odor,* and *Smelling Smoke.*

(1) Ps. 45:7-8; Song. 1:13; 3:6-7; (2) Song. 1:12; 4:10-11; 5:5, 13; (3) Gen. 8:20-21; Phil. 4:18; (4) Hos. 14:6; (5) Gen. 27:27; Isa. 34:3; As in, "I smell a rat"; (6) Isa. 3:16-24; (7) Job 39:25; (8) Eccl. 10:1; Rev. 9:2-4; (9) Gen. 34:30 (KJV); Exod. 7:21; 8:14; 16:20; 2 Sam. 10:6 (KJV); Eccl. 10:1; Isa. 3:24; (10) Num. 11:5; (11) 1 Cor. 12:17; (12) John 11:39; (13) Exod. 7:18; 8:14; (14) Job 14:9; (15) Prov. 27:9; (16) Song. 4:11; Hos. 14:6; (17) Deut. 4:28; Ps. 115:4-6; (18) Song. 7:8.

Smelling Smoke: (1) Serious warning of danger or emergency; (2) Judgment.

Also see *Smell* and *Smoke.*

(1) Judg. 20:40-41; Acts 2:19-21; (2) Dan. 3:27.

Smile: (1) Anointing and joy of the Holy Spirit upon someone; (2) Grace or favor upon someone; (3) A blessing imparted; (4) Pleased; (5) Glory of God upon someone; (6) Wisdom of God imparted (revelation); (7) Love.

(1) Ps. 104:15; (2-3) Ps. 67:1; 119:135; (4) Ps. 80:3-4, 7, 19; Luke 3:22; (5) Isa. 60:1; Matt. 17:2; (6) Eccl. 8:1; (7) Ps. 31:16.

Smoke: (1) Judgment and torment (wrath of God); (2) Presence of God or Glory of God; (3) Anger; (4) Signal (sign of trouble); (5) Vanish (like smoke); (6) Painful annoyance; (7) Consumed; (8) Prayers of the saints; (9) Evil spirits; (10) Wickedness.

Also see *Smoking* and *Toxic Vapors*.

(1) Gen. 19:28; 2 Sam. 22:9; Ps. 18:8; 74:1; Joel 2:30-31; Rev. 9:17; 14:11; 18:8-10; (2) Gen. 15:17; Exod. 19:18; Isa. 4:5; 6:1, 4; (3) Ps. 74:1; (4) Josh. 8:20; (5) Ps. 68:2; Isa. 51:6; Hos. 13:3; (6) Prov. 10:26; Isa. 65:5; (7) Ps. 102:3; (8) Rev. 8:4; (9) Rev. 9:2-3; (10) Isa. 9:18.

Smoking: (1) Offence (offended and/or offending); (2) Jealousy; (3) Consumed (in anger); (4) Worthless pursuit; (5) Bound by the world; (6) Evidence; (7) Shared or joint offense (passing pipe or bong).

Also see *Cigarettes* and *Smoke*.

(1) Job. 19:17a (NKJV); Isa. 65:5; (2) Deut. 29:20 (KJV); (3) Ps. 37:20 (KJV); Isa. 34:10; (4) Prov. 10:26; Matt. 16:23b (Smoking may well be filling our lungs with the devil's substitute for the Holy Spirit!); Ps. 102:3; Isa. 34:10; (5) Deut. 4:20; 1 Kings 8:51; Jer. 11:4; (6) As in, "We found no smoking gun"; (7) Matt. 13:57; 15:12.

Smooth: (1) Spiritual; (2) Spiritually effective (of God); (3) Deceitful words; (4) Preparation.

(1) Gen. 27:11 (Esau (hairy) speaks of the flesh, therefore, by comparison, here Jacob's skin speaks of the Spirit); (2) 1 Sam. 17:40 (These have had the edges knocked off in God's Word (the brook)); (3) Ps. 55:21 (sounded fantastic, but his heart was saying other things); Prov. 5:3; Isa. 30:10b; (4) Luke 3:5.

Smuggling: See Thief.

Snail: See Slug.

Snake: (1) Sin; (2) A person who speaks poisonous words; (3) Satan; (4) An evil spirit; (5) Curse; (6) A tempter; (7) A lying spirit; (8) Deception; (9) False teacher; (10) Jesus; (11) Hypocrisy; (12) Curse of poverty (skinny snake); (13) Deceptive person pretending to be righteous/false prophet (white snake); (14) False prophet (snake in a sock); (15) Seduction; (16) Fear; (17) A low-life full of deception (snake in the grass); (18) Strife in marriage (snake in bed); (19) White lies (white snake); (20) God/Jesus (white python); (21) Curse (yellow snake); (22) Revisiting an issue or spirit (double-headed snake); (23) Double-mindedness (double-headed snake); (24) Witchcraft; (25) Healing (snake on stick/pole).

Also see *Python, Spider, Snake—Bitten by a Snake,* and *Snakeskin.*

(1) John 3:14 & 2 Cor. 5:21; (cf. Num. 21:7-9); (2) Ps. 58:3-4a; James 3:8; Rom. 3:13b-14; (3) Rev. 20:2; (4) Luke 10:19; (5) Gen. 3:14; Gal. 3:13 & John 3:14; (6) Gen 3:1-15; (Ps. 91:9-13; cf. Matt 4:6-7); Rev. 12:9; (7) Gen. 3:4; John 8:44b; (8-9) 2 Cor. 11:3-4; Jude 1:4; (10) Exod. 7:12; Num. 21:8-9; John 3:14; (11) Matt. 3:7; 12:34; (12) See *Fat;* (13) Matt. 26:48-49; (14) Matt. 7:15; Acts 16:16; (15) Gen. 3:1-5, 13; 2 Cor. 11:3; (16) Gen. 3:15; 2 Cor. 11:3; (17) Gen. 3:1; Esther 3:6; Luke 22:47-48; (18) Gen. 3:1, 12 (unclean spirit causing division); (19) Gen. 12:13, 18; (20) Exod. 7:12 & John 3:14 (cf. Num. 21:8-9); (21) See *Yellow;* (22) Gen. 12:13 & 20:2; (23) James 1:8; (24) Exod. 7:11-12; (25) Num. 21:8-9.

Snake (Bitten by a Snake): (1) Disobedience; (2) Sin; (3) Breaking of protection; (4) Attack of the enemy; (5) Venomous words spoken against you; (6) Conflict; (7) Judgment.

(1-3) Num. 21:5-9; Eccl. 10:8; (4) Acts 28:3; (5) Num. 21:5-6; (6) Acts 28:3; Rev. 9:19; (7) Num. 21:7-9.

Snakeskin: (1) Satan now present in a different guise; (2) Deliverance and transformation; (3) Signs/evidence of demonic activity.

(1) Gen. 3:1 & 2 Cor. 11:14; (2) Acts 9:17-18; (3) Ezek. 28:17; Matt. 17:15; Luke 4:13.

Snare: (1) Trap; (2) Offense; (3) Unforgiveness; (4) Lust; (5) Suddenly/unawares; (6) Legalistic restriction; (7) Manipulative control; (8) Thought strongholds; (9) Idolatry; (10) Work of the proud, wicked, and devil; (11) God is the deliverer from snares; (12) Secretly conspired against; (13) Surety for others (particularly unbelievers); (14) Unwise and unbelieving words; (15) Death; (16) Anger; (17) Fear of people; (18) Harlot or bitter woman.

Also see *Trap.*

(1) Job 18:9-10; (Ps. 38:12 & Matt. 22:15-18); Ps. 69:22; (2) Isa. 8:14; 29:21; (3) 2 Cor. 2:10-11; (4) Prov. 7:10, 23; 1 Tim. 6:9; (5) Eccl. 9:12; Luke 21:34b-35; (6) 1 Cor. 7:35 (KJV); (7) 1 Tim. 3:7; (8) 2 Tim. 2:24-26; (9) Ps. 106:36; (10) Ps. 91:3; 119:110; 140:5; 141:9; (11) Ps. 124:7-8; (12) Ps. 142:3; (13) Prov. 6:1-2; (14) Prov. 12:13; 18:7; (15) Prov. 13:14; 14:27; (16) Prov. 22:24-25; (17) Prov. 29:25; (18) Prov. 7:10, 23; Eccl. 7:26.

Sneakers: (1) In the Spirit; (2) By faith.

(1) 1 Kings 18:46; (2) Heb. 12:1.

Sniper: (1) Words against you in secret; (2) Unexpected words against; (3) Intercessor; (4) The devil lining up to tempt you; (5) You are unaware that the enemy is focused on you to destroy you.

Also see *Assassin, Contract Killer,* and *Rifle.*

(1-2) Ps. 11:2; 64:3-4; (3) Neh. 4:9; (4) Luke 22:31; (5) Prov. 7:23.

Snorkeling: (1) Exploring things of the Spirit.

(1) 2 Kings 6:17; Matt. 7:7; Rom. 8:14.

Snow: (1) Pure (white); (2) Robe of righteousness (Snow on the earth is like a robe of righteousness on an earthen vessel); (3) Glory; (4) Refreshing; (5) God's Word; (6) Sin (Leprosy is the bodily equivalent of sin); (7) Inappropriate honor (snow in summer).

Also see *Snowballs* and *Snowman.*

(1) Job 9:30 (KJV); Ps. 51:7; Isa. 1:18; Lam. 4:7; (2) Matt. 28:3; (Job 37:6 & 2 Cor. 4:7); (3) Dan. 7:9; (Mark 9:3 & 2 Pet. 1:17); Rev. 1:14; (4) Prov. 25:13; (5) Isa. 55:10-11; (6) Exod. 4:6; Num. 12:10; 2 Kings 5:27; (7) Prov. 26:1.

Snowball/s: (1) Godly words without impact; (2) Words lacking power; (3) Words without love.

Also see *Snow* and *Snowman.*

(1) 1 Sam. 3:19; (2) 1 Cor. 2:4; (3) Matt. 24:12.

Snowman: (1) Cold-hearted person; (2) Righteous person.

(1) Matt. 24:12; (2) Ps. 51:7, 10.

Snowshoes: (1) Gospel ministry; (2) Shoes of peace; (3) Walking a righteous path.

Also see *Snow.*

(1) Eph. 6:15.

Soap: (1) Confession and repentance; (2) Cleansing; (3) Regular application of the Word of God.

(1-2) 1 John 1:9; (2-3) John 13:10.

Soccer: See Football Game and Sport.

Socks: (1) Little things that affect your walk; (2) Daily choice; (3) May speak about your past or your future walk; (4) Things that are held close to you (personal); (5) Clothing your feet to determine your path; (6) Preparation; (7) Walking in the flesh (no socks); (8) Unprepared (no socks); (9) Disorderly (odd socks); (10) The Gospel; (11) The old way of doing things (old socks).

Consider the color of the socks.

Also see *Feet, Shoes, Sole, Toes,* and *Walk.*

(1) John 11:9-10; 12:35; 1 John 1:6-7; (2) Josh. 24:15; (3) John 6:66; 7:1; (4) Acts 9:31; (5) John 8:12; 21:18; (6) Eph. 6:15; (7) 2 Cor. 10:3; (8) Eph. 6:15; (9) 2 Thess. 3:6, 11; (10) Eph. 6:15; (11) John 8:4-5.

Socket: (1) Leverage; (2) Support or strength; (3) Foundation.

(1-2) Gen. 32:25; (3) Exod. 26:19, 21; Song. 5:15 (KJV).

Soda: (1) The Holy Spirit (as a well of springing water); (2) Gaining spiritual insight.

Also see *Effervescence.*

(1) John 4:14; (2) Prov. 16:22.

Sofa: (1) Comfort; (2) God (as comfort); (3) Complacent.

Also see *Armchair, Couch,* and *Seat.*

(1-2) 2 Cor. 1:3; (3) Luke 12:18-19.

Software: (1) The human spirit; (2) The Holy Spirit.

Also see *Computer, Hard Drive, Hardware,* and *Laptop.*

(1) Gen. 2:7; John 6:63; (2) Col. 2:9.

Soil: (1) A heart or hearts.

Also see *Earth.*

(1) Matt. 13:19; Mark 4:15; Luke 8:15.

Soldier: (1) Spiritual warrior; (2) Spiritual warfare; (3) May speak of a battle in the mind; (4) Bringing your thoughts into line with God's Word in preparation for battle; (5) Angel; (6) Christ.

See *Battle* and *Weapon*.

(1) Judg. 6:12; (2) Eph. 6:12-18; (3) 2 Cor. 10:3-5; (4) 1 Pet. 1:13; (5) Dan. 10:13; (6) Josh. 5:13-15.

Sole (Foot): (1) Dominion; (2) Promise; (3) Step out in faith; (4) Resting place; (5) Lower extremity; (6) Dwelling place (home).

(1-2) Deut. 11:24; Josh. 1:3; 1 Kings 5:3; Mal. 4:3; (3) Josh. 3:13; (4) Gen. 8:9; Deut. 28:65; (5) 2 Sam. 14:25; Job 2:7; Isa. 1:6; (6) Ezek. 43:7.

Someone Giving Directions: (1) An angel.

(1) Matt. 1:20; 2:13, 19-20; Acts 10:3-6.

Somersault: (1) Being born again (turning things right-side-up); (2) Being upset (turbulence); (3) Being overturned; (4) Celebration.

(1) Acts 17:6; (2) Luke 23:28; John 16:20; (3) Ezek. 21:27; (4) Exod. 15:20-21; 2 Sam. 6:14.

Son: (1) Jesus Christ; (2) Mature believer; (3) Your future; (4) Natural son; (5) The meaning of your son's name (see Name and Place Dictionary).

(1) John 3:16; (2) Heb. 2:10; Rom. 8:14; (3) Job 21:8.

Son-in-Law: (1) Believer not free in the Spirit (bound by law).

Also see *Brother-in-Law* and *Father-in-Law*.

(1) 2 Cor. 3:17 & Heb. 2:10; Tit. 3:9-10.

Sore: See Spot.

Sorrow: (1) Repentance to life (godly sorrow); (2) Self-pity for being caught leads to death (worldly sorrow).

(1-2) 2 Cor. 7:10.

Soup: (1) Simple teaching of the Word; (2) Fleshly sell-out.

(1) Heb. 5:12-14; (2) Gen. 25:29-34.

Sour: (1) Not ripe; (2) Complaint (sour grapes); (3) Harlotry; (4) Rebellion; (5) Bitter.

(1) Isa. 18:5; (2) Ezek. 18:2; (3-4) Hos. 4:18 (NKJV & KJV); (5) Heb. 12:15.

South: (1) Place away from God; (2) Place of restoration; (3) Place of testing (source of hot wind); (4) Going back into the world (heading south); (5) Consider aspects in your own environment relating to south.

Also see *Down, North,* and *Steps (Going Down).*

(1) Ps. 48:2; 75:6; (2) Ps. 126:4 (Streams in the south fill suddenly after storms); (3) Song. 4:16 (The south wind in Israel is hot because it comes off the equator; in the southern hemisphere, the north wind will be hot); (4) Gen. 12:9-10; Num. 14:3-4; Josh. 15:4.

Sow (verb): (1) Speaking or preaching the Word of God; (2) What is sown to the flesh will reap flesh, what is sown to the Spirit will reap Spirit: (3) What you are putting into your life (investment); (4) Righteousness.

Also see *Investment, Plant,* and *Seed.*

(1) Matt. 13:3-4, 18-19; Mark 4:14; (2-3) Gal. 6:8; (4) James 3:18.

Sower: (1) God; (2) Jesus Christ; (3) Minister; (4) Believer; (5) Devil; (6) Person (good or evil).

(1) Matt. 13:3, 19, 24; (2) Matt. 13:37; (3-4) 1 Cor. 9:11; 2 Cor. 9:6; James 3:18; (5) Matt. 13:39; (6) Gal. 6:7-8.

Spa: (1) Refreshing in the Holy Spirit; (2) Refreshing Holy Spirit-led ministry.

(1) 1 Sam. 16:23; (2) 1 Cor. 16:17-18.

Space: (1) Eternity; (2) The heavenlies.

Also see *Spaceship* and *Space Suit.*

(1) Isa. 57:15; (2) Gen. 1:14-15.

Spaceship: (1) Rapture; (2) Heavenly encounter.

Also see *Starship Enterprise.*

(1-2) 2 Kings 2:11.

Space Suit: (1) In the Spirit; (2) Armor of God.

Also see *Astronaut* and *Space.*

(1-2) Eph. 6:11-18.

Spade: (1) Turning new ground; (2) New season in God; (3) Warning to remove the hardness of heart; (4) Open your heart; (5) Time to seek God (as in, "digging deep"); (6) Seed time; (7) Applying the Word of God to your heart (digging deep); (8) The Word of God.

Also see *Digging* and *Shovel*.

(1) Isa. 42:9; 43:19; (2) Song. 2:11; (3-4) <u>Jer. 4:3-4</u> (5) Gen. 26:18; <u>Hos. 10:12</u>; (6) Gen. 8:22; Hos. 10:12; (7) Luke 6:48; (8) Matt. 13:21; Mark 4:17 (unearthed by the Word); 2 Cor. 4:7; Heb. 4:12.

Spark/s: (1) Fiery dart; (2) A little word that ignites a fire of controversy; (3) Conflict; (4) Trouble or labor; (5) Trouble-maker; (6) The human spirit; (7) The beginning of judgment; (8) Self-destruction; (9) Anguish, torment, or sorrow; (10) Electrician; (11) The glory of God.

(1-2) Job 41:19; Eph. 6:16; <u>James 3:5-6</u>; (3) Exod. 11:7b; Lev. 10:10; 11:47a; <u>Acts 15:39</u>; (4-6) Job 5:7; (6) Job 18:5 (KJV); (7) Isa. 1:31; (8-9) Isa. 50:11; (10) Slang term for electrician; (11) Isa. 24:15 (KJV).

Sparrow: (1) Believer; (2) Cared for by God; (3) Someone who finds security in God's Presence; (4) Feelings of insignificance; (5) Alone, lonely, or loner; (6) Not at rest (flitting sparrow).

Also see *Birds*.

(1-2) Matt. 10:29, 31; (3) <u>Ps. 84:3</u>; (4) <u>Matt. 10:29</u> & <u>Luke 12:6-7</u>; (5) Ps. 102:7: (6) Prov. 26:2.

Spear: (1) Threat; (2) Word with piercing momentum; (2) Someone trying to nail you; (3) God's piercing Word.

(1) <u>1 Sam. 17:7-10</u>; 19:10-11; (2) Ps. 57:4 (teeth = spears); (Prov. 30:14 (teeth & Eph. 6:17)); 1 Sam. 17:7, 43-44; 1 Sam. 19:10-11; (3) Luke 2:35.

Speed: (1) Accelerating to destiny; (2) Carried in the Spirit; (3) Indicates power; (4) Indicative of a powerful ministry; (5) Soon (ASAP); (6) Quickly; (7) Without restraint; (8) Without delay; (9) At once (immediately); (10) Expulsion; (11) A salutation (greeting/farewell) of blessing a person with joyful health and happiness (Godspeed).

Also see *Speeding (Auto)*, *Time*, and *Urgency*.

(1) Exod. 12:11; Josh. 4:10; <u>1 Sam. 17:48</u>; (2-4) 1 Kings 18:46; <u>Acts 8:39-40</u>; (5) Acts 17:15; (6) Gen. 24:12 (KJV); Luke 18:8; (7) <u>Joel 3:4</u>; Isa. 5:26; (8-9) Eccl. 8:11; Zech. 8:21; (10) Exod. 12:33; (11) 2 John 1:10-11 (KJV).

Speedboat: (1) Accelerating the ministry (accelerating to destiny); (2) Powerful ministry; (3) Quickly or suddenly.

Also see *Boat*, *Ship*, and *Speed*.

(1) Gen. 41:14; 45:13b; (2) <u>Isa. 5:26-30a</u>; (3) <u>Job 9:26</u>.

Speed (Drug): (1) Offense; (2) Trying to jump ahead of the timing of God; (3) Counterfeit spirit.

Also see *Drug-Taking* and *Needle*.

(1) Isa. 28:16b; (2) 2 Sam. 18:19-23, 29-30; (3) John 6:63.

Speeding (Auto): (1) Trying to jump ahead of the timing of God.

Also see *Speed*.

(1) 2 Sam. 18:19-23, 29-30.

Spew: See Vomit.

Spice: (1) Fragrant anointing; (2) Fragrant prayer; (3) Romance; (4) Desire; (5) Oil; (6) Enliven (spice up); (7) Praise; (8) Heart (bed of spices); (9) Praise and adoration.

(1) Exod. 25:6; 30:23-25; Mark 16:1; (2) Exod. 30:34-37 (cf. Ps. 141:2a; Rev. 8:3-4); Exod. 35:8, 28; (3-4) Song. 4:16; Prov. 7:17; (5) In the 1700-1800s, spice was the commodity all the nations sought after; today oil has taken its place; (6) As in, "The team played woefully; we need to spice it up a bit in the next half" or "They need to spice up their love life"; (7) Song. 4:16; (8) Song. 6:2; (9) Song. 8:14 (mountain of spices).

Spider: (1) An issue or stronghold; (2) An issue that raises fear or has the potential to be messy to deal with; (3) Threat (with a danger of entanglement); (4) Deceiver (web = lies); (5) One who casts spells; (6) False trust; (7) Tenacious; (8) One from whom it is difficult to disentangle or extricate oneself; (9) A clever one; (10) Conflict; (11) A very big spider may mean death; (12) Death or danger (black widow); (13) Red (or red-backed) spider means sin; (14) Red spider can be the early stages of pregnancy (medical imaging); (15) Killing a red spider may refer to an abortion; (16) Influential deceiver (long-legged spider); (17) Long-standing issue (long-legged spider); (18) If bitten by a spider, it means venomous words against you; (19) Curse (yellow spider); (20) Spirit of fear (flying spider); (21) Conflict in the heavenlies (flying spider); (22) Religious spirit (white spider); (23) Evil spirit; (24) Predatory person/organization/church/issue (huntsman spider); (25) Condemning/blaming husband with words (black widow spider).

Also see *Bite/Bitten* and *Snake*.

(1) 2 Cor. 10:4-5; (2) (3) Acts 4:17, 21, 29; 1 Pet. 2:23; (4) Isa. 59:4-5; (5) 1 Kings 19:2; (6) Job 8:14-15; (7) Prov. 30:28; (8) Gen. 31:27; (9) Prov.

30:28; (13) Isa. 59:5-6; (16) Prov. 30:28 (as in Jezebel); (17) Mark 5:25; (18) 1 Kings 21:9-10, 13; (19) See *Yellow*; (20) 2 Tim. 1:7; (21) Eph. 6:12; (22) Matt. 23:27; (23) 1 Tim. 3:6; 2 Tim. 2:26; (24) Ps. 91:3; 124:7; Hos. 9:8; (25) Prov. 21:9.

Spine: (1) Boldness (backbone); (2) Will; (3) Controlling or in control; (4) Kundilini serpent spirit (associated with yoga).

(1) Acts 4:13, 29; (2) 1 Sam. 14:9; Ps. 94:16; (3) Gen. 37:7; (4) Luke 10:19; Rev. 9:19 (Kundilini is envisioned as a serpent coiled at the base of the spine).

Spinning: (1) About to collapse; (2) Drunk; (3) Lacking faith (trying to make it happen) (4) Not putting the Kingdom first; (5) Out of control (driven by circumstance); (6) Lying; (7) Laying a trap (spinning thread).

(1) Isa. 24:20; (2) Ps. 107:27; (3-4) Matt. 6:28-30; Luke 12:27-28; (5) James 1:6; (6) As in, "He's spinning you a yarn"; (7) Isa. 59:5-6; Mark 12:13.

Spirit of Poverty: (1) Withholding when things are tight and there is a call to bless; (2) Self-survival mentality; (3) Robbing your own blessing.

Also see *Pigeon*.

(1-3) Prov. 3:27-28; 11:24-25; (cf. 1 Kings 17:10-14; Matt: 14:15-21; 15:32-38).

Spit/ting: (1) Shame or contempt; (2) Dishonor; (3) Anointing; (4) Using the Word of God; (5) Rejection.

(1) Isa. 50:6; Matt. 26:67; Mark 14:65; (2) Deut. 25:9; (3) John 9:6; (4) Mark 7:33; 8:23; John 9:6; (5) Num. 12:14.

Splinter: (1) Something that gets under your flesh and is irritating you; (2) Fleshly Christian who gets under your skin.

(1) Job 2:7; 3:1; (2) Gen. 13:11; Matt.15:23.

Sponge: (1) Thirsting for God (thirsty heart); (2) Cleansing; (3) Soaking; (4) All word, no Spirit (watering plants using a sponge).

Also see *Hose*.

(1) Ps. 42:2; John 19:28; (2) John 13:3-4; (3) Joel 2:28; (4) Ps. 33:31b.

Spoon: (1) Heart; (2) A measure or amount; (3) Feeding (serving up); (4) Stirring (good or evil); (5) Someone who is used for a short time (plastic spoon); (6) Superficially or temporarily receiving (plastic spoon).

(1) Exod. 25:29; Num. 4:7 (Here the Hebrew word for spoon, *kaph,* describes a concave vessel); (2) Num. 7:14, 20, 26ff; (3) 1 Kings 17:11; (4) <u>Luke 23:5</u>; Acts 6:12; 13:50; (5) Matt. 11:7-10; (6) John 6:66; Acts 8:13.

Sport: (1) Moving in faith; (2) Spiritual warfare.

Also see *Ball, Bat, Cricket, Football Game, Sports Store, Umpire,* and *Winning.*

(1) Heb. 12:1; (2) Eph. 6:12.

Sports Store: (1) Church; (2) Place where the anointing is released.

(1-2) As the place of equipping the saints to run the race of faith; Eph. 4:11-12; Heb. 12:1-2.

Spot: (1) Moral blemish; (2) Defilement; (3) Irresponsible; (4) Blemish (sin); (5) Without godly fear; (6) Stain; (7) Works of the flesh; (8) Holding something back (not wholly given to God).

(1) <u>Eph. 5:27</u>; (2) Jude 1:23 (cf. KJV & NKJV); (3) 1 Tim. 6:14; (4) Heb. 9:14; 1 Pet. 1:19; 2 Pet. 2:13-14; (5-6) Jude 1:12; (7) Jude 1:23 (KJV); (8) Exod. 12:5 (The Hebrew word for "without blemish" means "entirely or whole").

Spotlight: (1) Bringing things from darkness into light (revealing issues/sin); (2) Salvation; (3) Your time to perform; (4) High profile; (5) All eyes are on you; (6) Caught unawares; (7) Suddenly exposed.

Also see *Light* and *Stage.*

(1) Rom. 13:12; 1 Cor. 4:5; 1 John 1:5-7; (2) <u>John 1:9</u>; 2 Cor. 4:6; Eph. 5:8; 1 Pet. 2:9; (3-4) <u>Acts 9:3</u>; (5) 1 Sam. 9:20b; 17:48; (6-7) Acts 9:3.

Spray: (1) Holy Spirit (Breath of God); (2) Evidence of a storm (enemy resistance); (3) Angry or emotional words.

Also see *Anointing* and *Perfume.*

(1) Gen.1:2; Job 33:4; John 3:8; Rev. 1:15; (2) Matt. 14:24; (3) 1 Sam. 20:30; Prov. 18:4.

Spring (noun): (1) Bouncing back or returning; (2) Comfort; (3) Young and enthusiastic (spring lamb); (4) Launching out.

(1) Ps. 78:34; <u>Luke 4:14</u>; (2) Job 7:13; Ps. 119:82; (3) Luke 1:41; (4) 2 Sam. 11:1a.

Spring (season): (1) Time to act; (2) Fruitfulness; (3) Time to fight spiritually; (4) Summer (harvest) at hand; (5) Jesus' return at hand.

(1-2) Song. 2:10-13; (3) <u>2 Sam.11:1</u>; 1 Kings 20:22; (4-5) Luke 21:29-30.

Spring Up: There are positive and negative aspects (+): (1) Spiritual enlivening/awakening; (2) Holy Spirit overflowing; (3) Grow; (4) A new thing; (5) Healing; (6) Truth; (-): (7) Lack of heart; (8) Choked by weeds; (9) Root of bitterness.

(1) Gen. 26:19 (KJV); 35:1-3; Isa. 45:8; Mark 4:8, 27; Luke 8:8; Acts 3:8; Heb. 11:11-12 (KJV); (2) Num. 21:17; John 4:14; (3) Job 38:27; Heb. 7:14 (KJV); (4) Isa. 42:9; 43:19; (5) Isa. 58:8; (6) Ps. 85:11; (7) Matt. 13:5; Mark 4:5; Luke 8:6; (8) Matt. 13:7, 26; Luke 8:7; (9) Heb. 12:15.

Sprinkle: (1) Cleansing; (2) Purification of the flesh; (3) Sanctification; (4) Forgiveness; (5) Covenant; (6) Salvation; (7) Clear conscience; (8) Call to exercise confident faith.

Also see *Shower, Rain,* and *Water.*

(1) Heb. 10:22; (2-3) Ezek. 36:25; Heb. 9:13; (3-4) Heb. 9:19-22; (5-6) Isa. 52:15; Heb.12:24; (7-8) Heb. 10:22; 11:28.

Sprout: (1) Resurrection; (2) New life; (3) Hope.

(1-3) Job 14:7-9.

Spud Bag: See Beanbag.

Spud Gun: (1) Words without power and effect.

(1) 1 Sam. 3:19b (this is the opposite).

Spy: (1) Prophet; (2) Seeing in the Spirit; (3) Gathering intelligence about the enemy.

Also see *Staring, U2,* and *View.*

(1-3) 2 Kings 6:8-12.

Square: (1) Unspiritual (not of God); (2) Legalism; (3) Religious; (4) Not changing; (5) Global; (6) All-encompassing (complete coverage); (7) Regulated or regulation.

Also see *Circle, Round,* and *Wheel.*

(1) Compare: Ezek. 1:20; Heb. 9:14 (in the sense that the eternal Spirit is never-ending like a circle); (2-3) Lev. 19:9; 23:22 (This is grace); Lev. 19:27; 21:5; (4) In the sense that a round object is capable of rolling whereas a square one is not; (5) Isa. 11:12; Rev. 7:1; As in, "the four corners of the globe"; (6) Ezek. 7:2; (7) A square has regular sides.

Squash (Racket Ball): (1) Indirect communication.

Also see *Ball, Bat,* and *Sport.*

(1) Prov.16:13.

Squid: (1) Spineless (not standing up for important issues).

Also see *Octopus.*

(1) Ps. 5:5; 106:23.

Stable (Horse): (1) House of an unbeliever/living as the unsaved; (2) Living in the world/flesh.

Also see *Barn.*

(1-2) Deut. 17:16; Isa. 31:1.

Staff: (1) The Word of God; (2) Strength or support; (3) Pledge; (4) Bread (The staff, Matteh in Hebrew, was used to walk, i.e. support life; therefore, figuratively it also meant "bread"); (5) Bearer of fruit; (6) Tool of discipline/judgment; (7) Shaft of an arrow or spear; (8) Authority or rule; (9) Care and comfort; (10) Person, church, or nation; (11) Tool or talent for the purposes of God; (12) Signifies readiness for journey (staff in hand); (13) May indicate agedness (i.e. need of support).

Also see *Rod* and *Sticks.*

(1) Exod. 14:16 (cf. Heb. 4:12); 1 Sam. 17:40, 43, 45 (cf. 2 Cor. 10:3-5); 2 Sam. 23:21; Mark 6:8; Heb. 11:21; (2) Exod. 21:19; Isa 36:6; Ps. 23:4; (3) Gen. 38:18, 25; (4) Lev. 26:26 (KJV); Ps. 105:16 (KJV); Ezek. 5:16 (KJV); 14:13 (KJV); (5) Num. 13:23; 17:8; (6) Num. 22:27; Isa. 10:5; (7) 1 Sam. 17:7; (8) 2 Kings 4:29, 31; Isa. 14:5; (9) Ps. 23:4; (10) Isa. 36:6 (whoever you lean on); (11) Exod. 4:2; 2 Kings 4:29; (12) Exod. 12:11; (13) Zech. 8:4.

Stage (Theater): (1) In the public eye; (2) Success; (3) Given a public profile (in the arena/under the spotlight); (4) Façade (being staged)

Also see *Pulpit* and *Spotlight.*

(1) Luke 1:80; (2) Josh. 1:8; (3) Gen. 37:9 & 42:6; Luke 1:80; (4) Matt. 2:4, 8.

Stain: (1) Offense; (2) Contempt; (3) Pollute; (4) Anger; (5) Sin.

(1) Matt. 15:11-12 (defile = unclean, pollute, make common); Jer. 16:18; (2-3) Isa. 23:9; (4) Isa. 63:3; (5) Zech. 3:3-4.

Stained Glass (Window): (1) Religious spirit; (2) Seeing the promises of God in the glory (refers to seeing through multi-colored glass).

(1) John 12:42-46 (having a tainted view of things); (2) Gen. 9:12-13 & 37:3; Rev. 4:3.

Stairs: See Steps.

Stakes (Tent Pegs): (1) Certainty; (2) Expansion (strengthening or moving stakes).

(1) Isa. 33:20; (2) Isa. 54:2-3.

Stalled Vehicle: (1) Ministry in limbo; (2) On hold; (3) Doing things your way, not God's way; (4) Stumbling; (5) Heart preparation (test); (6) Awaiting the timing of God; (7) Fear; (8) Not seeing in the Spirit (wrong perception); (9) A call to exercise faith/spiritual authority; (10) Something getting in the way, such as: (11) Religion; (12) Greater pressing needs; (13) Opposition; (14) Obstructed by the devil; (15) Problems in family relationships; (16) Emotional issues overriding obedience; (17) Loss of heart.

(1) 1 Kings 19:4; (2) Isa. 49:2; (3-4) 2 Sam. 6:3-10; (cf. 1 Chron. 15:11-13); (5) Gen. 42:16; (6) John 11:6; Isa. 49:2; (7) 1 Kings 19:2-3; (8) 1 Kings 19:9-10; (9) Exod. 14:13-16; (10) Any of the following: (11) Luke 11:52; (12) Rom. 15:22; (13) Mark 6:48; Gal. 5:7-12; (14) Neh. 4:1-18; 1 Thess. 2:18; (15) 1 Pet. 3:7; (16) Gen. 24:55-56; (17) Neh. 4:10-12.

Stamp: See Postage Stamp.

Stand/ing: (1) Ready to serve; (2) Standing one's ground in God's might; (3) Standing in faith; (4) Honoring; (5) Spiritual warfare; (6) Uprightness of spirit; (7) Being aligned with/rubbing shoulders with (positive or negative).

Also see *Laying Down* and *Upright.*

(1) Zech. 6:5 (KJV); (2) Eph. 6:13 (This is seen as the third of three progressive steps. [Sit>Walk>Stand]); (3) 2 Cor. 1:24b; (4) Acts 7:55-56; (5) Eph. 6:13; (6) Ps. 51:10 (KJV); (7) Ps. 1:1 (This verse shows the second of three progressively negative steps away from godliness. [Walking>Standing>Sitting]).

Star: (1) Believers or children of God; (2) Angels; (3) Satan; (4) Jesus Christ; (5) Evil spirits (fallen angels); (6) Someone who is a righteous and wise soul-winner; (7) Revival (seeing lots of stars); (8) Fame (stardom).

Also see *Shooting Star* and *Sun.*

(1) <u>Gen. 15:5-6</u>; Phil. 2:15; (2) Ps. 33:6; Rev. 1:20; (3) Isa. 14:12 (lucifer = day star); (4) Rev. 22:16 (The bright and morning star); (5) Rev. 12:4; (6) Dan. 12:3; (7) Gen. 15:5-6; (8) Rev. 22:16 & Matt. 14:1.

Staring: (1) Seeing in the Spirit; (2) Prophesying; (3) Seer; (4) Love; (5) May be a sign of an idolatrous heart; (6) Fleeting riches (staring at worldly goods); (7) Turning or looking to the world.

(1) Num. 24:3-4; Mark 10:21; <u>Acts 13:9-10</u>; (2) Ezek. 6:2; 13:17; 20:46; 21:2; (3) 1 Sam. 9:9; (4) Jer. 24:6; (5) Ezek. 14:4; (6) Prov. 23:4-5; (7) Jer. 42:15, 17.

Starship Enterprise: (1) Pioneering heavenly realities.

(1) Josh. 3:4b; Mission: "Boldly go where no man has gone before."

Station Wagon: (1) Family vehicle.

(1) <u>Gen. 46:5</u>.

Statue: (1) Memorial; (2) Person/event of past significance; (3) Someone once alive, but now dead; (4) Idol; (5) Pride (idolizing self); (6) Looking back at the world (pillar of salt).

(1-2) Josh. 4:7; (3) <u>1 Sam. 25:37</u>; (4) Dan. 3:1, 18; (5) 2 Sam. 18:18; (6) Gen. 19:26.

Statue of Liberty: (1) Freedom; (2) Spiritual deliverance.

(1-2) Isa. 61:1; Luke 4:18; <u>2 Cor. 3:17</u>.

Staying Somewhere: (1) Place of rest and refreshment; (2) Settling down (dwelling) instead of sojourning (pilgrimage); (3) Stopping short of God's intended destiny.

(1) Luke 24:29; (2) Heb. 11:9-10; (3) Num. 13:31.

Steak: See Meat.

Steal/Stealing: (1) The devil (thief); (2) Taking from or replacing God's Word; (3) Capturing hearts; (4) Deception; (5) Secretly leave (to "steal away"); (6) Take secretly; (7) Shame; (8) Adultery; (9) Hypocrisy; (10) Need to work; (11) Idolatry; (12) Taking the Lord's name in vain; (13) Earthly treasures (heart centered on earthly cares); (14) Not tithing to the work of God; (15) Not releasing sin at the Cross (you carrying something Jesus owns [paid for by the Blood]); (16) Doing your own thing on borrowed time (You are a love-slave owned by God).

Also see *Robbery* and *Thief.*

(1) <u>John 10:10</u>; (2) Deut.4:2; Prov. 30:6; Jer. 23:30; <u>Rev. 22:19</u>; (3) 2 Sam. 15:6; (4) Matt. 28:13; Gen. 31:20 (The word *unawares* means "to steal the mind of, deceive, outwit"); (5) Gen. 31:20; (6) Gen. 40:15; 2 Chron. 22:11; (7) 2 Sam. 19:3; (8) Prov. 9:17-18; (9) Rom. 2:21; (10) Eph. 4:28; (11) Gen. 31:19; (12) Prov. 30:9; (13) Matt. 6:19-21; (14) Mal. 3:8; (15-16) 1 Cor. 6:20; Gal. 2:20.

Steam: (1) Anger; (2) Power or powerful; (3) Venting.

(1) <u>Isa. 64:2, 5</u>; As in, "He was letting off steam"; (2) Job 41:20-22, 31-32; (3) As in, "letting off steam."

Steel: (1) Strong; (2) Powerful; (3) Strength of humanity; (4) Human strength. Also see *Bow* and *Iron*.

(1-4) <u>2 Sam. 22:35 </u>(KJV); Job 20:24; Ps.18:34.

Steering: (1) In control; (2) Leading; (3) The person steering is often God or the Holy Spirit (known noble character); (4) It may be wrong for us to be steering (i.e. not letting go); (5) If someone of questionable character is steering, it may mean that you are being manipulated, driven, or led.

(1) 1 Kings 19:19; <u>John 21:18</u>; (2) Ps, 23:2-3; (3) Ps. 5:8; 23:2-3; 31:3; John 14:6; 21:18; (4) Prov. 12:15; 14:12; 16:25; 21:2; John 21:18; (5) Prov. 7:25.

Stepping: (1) Moving into your inheritance (stepping through); (2) Overcoming (stepping through); (3) Boldness or courage (stepping out); (4) Stages of growth or development (stepping stones). Also see *Footsteps* and *Walking*.

(1) <u>Josh. 3:13</u>; (2) Num. 13:30; 1 John 4:4; (3) Acts 4:31; (4) 2 Cor. 3:18.

Stepping-stones: (1) Progressive revelatory words; (2) Moving in faith; (3) In transition; (4) Crossing over.

(1-2) Josh. 1:3; 1 Sam. 16:1 (God didn't tell him who he was to anoint); Heb. 11:8; (3) Isa. 40:3; Acts 22:21; (4) Josh. 4:7.

Steps (Going Down): (1) Stairway to death/hell; (2) Going away from God; (3) Self-indulgence; (4) Being seduced away from God; (5) Loss of heart; (6) Condemned (thrown down stairs/steps); (7) Becoming progressively more ungodly (steps becoming further apart as you go down).

Also see *South* and *Steps (Going Up)*.

(1) 1 Sam. 20:3; Prov. 5:5; (2) Ps. 44:18; 73:2; (3) Luke 12:16-21; (4) Prov. 7:25-27; (5) Judg. 20:42-43; (6) 2 Chron. 36:3; Isa. 54:17; Matt. 12:41-42; 2 Pet. 2:6; (7) Ps. 1:1; Prov. 5:3-5; Song. 2:15.

Steps (Going Up): (1) Stairway to Heaven/God; (2) Jesus Christ; (3) Flesh; (4) Established by God; (5) Discipleship (effort required); (6) God may be bringing you to a place of being mindful of the things of the Spirit; (7) Growing in the Spirit; (8) Praise; (9) Going from faith to faith/glory to glory; (10) A church.

Also see *Angels Ascending, Footsteps, Ladder, Lift, Steps (Going Down)*, and *Walking*.

(1-2) Gen. 28:12; John 1:51; (3) Exod. 20:26; (cf. 1 Kings 10:19-20 (six steps) with Ezek. 40:22 (seven steps)); (4) Ps. 37:23; (5) Matt. 5:1-2; (6-7) Isa. 40:31; Eph. 2:6; (8) Ps. 68:4 (AMP); (9) Rom. 1:17; 2 Cor. 3:18; (10) Matt. 16:18-19; John 1:51 (as the Body of Christ); Eph. 3:10.

Step-Sister: (1) Church on another level (positive or negative); (2) Church merger/transfer growth; (3) Fellow believer from another church.

Also see *Sister*.

(1) Rev. 3:8-10; (2) Judg. 21:21; Acts 15:22; (3) Acts 10:34-35.

Stereo: (1) Witness of the Spirit; (2) Witness.

See *Radio*.

(1) Mark 16:20; Rom. 8:16; (2) Matt. 18:16.

Sticks: (1) Discipline; (2) The Word of God; (3) An individual or group of people; (4) United (sticks bunched or tied together); (5) Turning the Word of God to their advantage (spinning sticks); (6) Firewood.

(1) Prov. 13:24; (2) 1 Sam. 17:40, 43 (Here the staff is called a stick); Exod. 14:16 (Here the rod or staff (Hebrew: *matteh*) divides); (3-4) Ezek. 37:16-22; (5) 1 Tim. 6:3-5; 2 Pet. 2:1, 3:16; (6) 1 Kings 17:10, 12; Acts 28:3.

Stilts: (1) Making yourself look more spiritual (higher); (2) Claiming to be more than you really are spiritually; (3) Elevating self; (4) Spiritual giant.

(1) 1 Sam. 15:17, 21; (2) 1 Sam. 9:2; 2 Chron. 26:16; Acts 8:9; (3) Acts 8:9, 19-20; (4) 1 Sam. 17:43-51.

Sting: (1) Painful consequences; (2) Deadly consequences; (3) Sin; (4) Hurt; (5) Rebuke; (6) Criticism.

Also see *Bees.*

(1) Prov. 23:32; (2-3) 1 Cor. 15:55-56; (4) Rev. 9:10; (5) Ezek. 5:15 (NIV) As in, "He gave them a stinging rebuke"; (6) Ps. 64:3-4.

Stink: See Odor and Smell.

Stolen: See Steal/Stealing and Thief.

Stomach: See Belly.

Stone/s: (1) Heart; (2) Words; (3) Believers; (4) People; (5) Jesus Christ or God; (6) Flesh; (7) Strong enough to build on; (8) Hardened heart or dead; (9) Blockage of heart (well); (10) Witness; (11) Memorial; (12) Law; (13) Death or dead; (14) Stumbling offense; (15) Judgment (throwing stones).

Also see *Brick, Foundation, Precious Stones,* and *Stony.*

(1) Prov. 3:3; 2 Cor. 3:3; (2) 1 Sam. 17:40, 49; Matt. 16:17-19; (3) Eph. 2:20; 1 Pet. 2:5-8; (4) Matt. 24:2; Luke 19:40, 43-44; John 2:6; Eccl. 3:5; (5) Gen. 28:11-18 & John 1:51 (Jacob's actions symbolize the death [sleep] and resurrection [pillar]); Gen. 49:24; Dan. 2:34-35; (6) Ezek. 11:19, 36:26; (7) John 1:42; (8) 1 Sam. 25:37-38; Job 41:24; Ezek. 11:19; 36:26; Zech. 7:12 (KJV); (9) Gen. 29:2-3, 8-10; (10) Gen. 31:46-49; Josh. 24:26-27; (11) Josh. 4:7-9; (12) Josh. 8:32; (13) John 8:59; 10:31; (14) Isa. 8:14; (15) Lev. 20:27; John 8:59; 10:31.

Stone/s (A Stone's Throw): (1) The distance a voice heard.

(1) Luke 22:41.

Stone/s (Cut & Uncut Stone): (1) Spirit ordained (uncut stone); (2) Human works (cut stone); (3) Idolatry (cut stone).

(1-2) Josh. 8:31; Isa. 37:19; Lam. 3:9; (3) Dan. 5:4, 23.

Stone/s (Falling on a Stone): (1) Brokenness.

(1) Matt. 21:44.

Stone/s (Stone Falling Upon): (1) Crushing; (2) Grinding; (3) Judgment.

(1-3) Matt. 21:44.

Stone/s (Throwing/Slinging Stones): (1) Words.

Judg. 20:16; 2 Sam. 16:6, 13.

Stone/s (White Stone): (1) Pure heart; (2) New name.

(1-2) Rev. 2:17.

Stoney: (1) Hardened heart; (2) No depth; (3) No heart experience; (4) Wilt under pressure; (5) Offended in affliction and persecution.

(1) Ezek.11:19; Zech. 7:11-12; (2-5) Matt. 13:5-6; Mark 4:5-6, 16-17.

Store: See Shop and Warehouse.

Store Clerk: (1) Pastor; (2) Hired shepherd.

Also see *Salesman*.

(1) Matt. 18:12-13 (keeping account of the stock); (2) John 10:12-13.

Stork: (1) Timing of God (sensitive to the seasons); (2) Revival (mass immigration); (3) Settled in righteousness.

Also see *Birds* and *Fir Tree*.

(1-2) Jer. 8:7; (3) Ps. 104:17.

Storm: (1) Trouble; (2) Test; (3) Adversity; (4) Judgment; (5) Purging or separating; (6) Words against you (opposition); (7) Spiritual opposition.

(1) Ps. 107:25-26, 28; (2) Mark 4:37, 40; Luke 8:23-25; (3) Isa. 25:4; (4) Ps. 83:14-15; Isa. 28:2; 29:6; Jer. 23:19-20; 25:32; Ezek. 13:13; (5) Job 21:18; (6) Ps. 55:3, 8; (7) Mark 4:35-37.

Storm Clouds: Forecasting and foreseeing of imminent: (1) Trouble; (2) Test; (3) Adversity; (4) Opposition; (5) Judgment.

Also see *Storm* for Scriptures.

Stove: See Oven.

Straight: (1) Of God; (2) Faithful spiritual progress; (3) Trusting God; (4) Prepared or open hearts; (5) Without deviation or detour; (6) Upright in spirit; (7) Resolve to go ahead; (8) Not turning aside; (9) Righteous; (10) Obedient.

Also see *Upright*.

(1) James 1:17; (2) Prov. 3:5-6; John 1:23; (3) Prov. 3:5-6 ("He shall direct your paths" = "make straight your paths"); (4) Isa. 40:3-4; Matt. 3:3; Mark 1:3; John 1:23; (5) Acts 16:11; 21:1; (6) Luke 13:11-13; (7) Heb. 12:12-13; (8) 1 Sam. 6:12; Prov. 4:25; (9) Ezek. 1:7; (10) Ezek. 1:12.

Straitjacket: (1) Unable to do anything about the situation (helpless); (2) Unable to do anything in your own strength; (3) Under control; (4) Disarmed or wounded; (5) No threat; (6) Controlling spirit; (7) Loss of strength and influence; (8) Wild and out of control; (9) Fool.

Also see *Arms.*

(1) Lam. 1:14; (2) Judg. 15:12-14; Dan. 3:21, 23-27; Eph. 6:10-11; (3-4) 2 Sam. 23:21; 1 Kings 22:34; (5) Judg. 15:12-14; (6) 1 Kings 21:7; Eccl. 7:26; (7) 1 Kings 13:4; (8) Mark 5:3-5; (9) Prov. 7:22b; 14:16-17a; 20:3.

Strange: (1) Foreign; (2) Unrecognized/not known/disguised; (3) Not of God; (4) Not home; (5) Worldly; (6) Profane; (7) False; (8) Wronged; (9) Offensive; (10) Liar; (11) Non-believing; (12) Unusual; (13) Homosexuality.

Also see *Foreign, Stranger,* and *Unfamiliar.*

(1) Gen. 35:2, 4 (KJV); Exod. 2:22; Ps. 137:4 (KJV); (2) Gen. 42:7 Josh. 24:23 (KJV); Ps. 114:1; Acts 17:20; (3) Gen. 35:2, 4 (KJV); Exod. 30:9; Lev. 10:1; Heb. 13:9; (4) Exod. 2:22; Heb. 11:9-10 (KJV); (5) Exod. 22:21; Deut. 32:12; Josh. 24:20 (KJV); (6) Lev. 10:1 (cf. KJV & NKJV); (7) Deut.32:16; (8) Job 19:3 (cf. KJV & NKJV); (9) Job 19:17 (cf. KJV & NKJV); (10) Ps. 144:7, 11; (11) Prov. 2:16-17; 6:23-24; 22:14; 27:13; (12) 1 Pet. 4:4, 12; (13) Jude 1:7.

Stranger: (1) Non-believer (not of the household of faith); (2) Not belonging; (3) Christ (If Christ appears as a stranger, it is either a test, as per the Scripture below, or a serious warning because it says you do not know Him); (4) Angel; (5) Sojourner or pilgrim; (6) Not of the family (alien); (7) Not at home; (8) An outcast; (9) One without their own provision; (10) Not yourself; (11) Not known or not knowing; (12) Not from the "in crowd."

Also see *Aliens, Foreign, Foreigner,* and *Strange.*

(1) Gen. 17:12 (KJV); Exod. 12:42-43, 48 (KJV); 29:33 (KJV); Lev. 22:25 (KJV); Deut. 17:15 (KJV); Ps. 18:45 (KJV); Ps.54:3; Prov. 2:16-17 (KJV); 6:1; 11:15; 27:13; Isa. 1:7; Luke 17:18 (KJV); Eph. 2:19; (2) Gen. 15:13; (3) Matt. 25:38, 40, 45; (4) Heb. 13:2; (5) Gen. 17:8; 23:4 (KJV); 28:4; 36:7; 37:1; Lev. 25:23; Exod. 6:4; Heb. 11:13; 1 Pet. 2:11; (6) Gen. 31:15; Exod. 18:3; Job 19:15; Ps. 69:8; Matt. 17:25; (7-8) Exod. 2:22; Ps. 119:19; (9) Lev. 19:10; 23:22; (10) Prov. 27:2; (11) Luke 24:18; John 10:5; (12) Matt. 25:35-36.

Strangle/d: (1) Having your spiritual life choked out of you; (2) Python spirit; (3) The cares of the world choking faith; (4) Stopping the flow of the Holy Spirit.

Also see *Choke/ing, Kill/Killing, Murder,* and *Python.*

(1) Job 7:15; (2) Acts 16:16-18; (3) Matt. 13:22; (4) 1 Thess. 5:19.

Strawberries: (1) Romance; (2) Love and friendship; (3) Good fruit; (4) Temptation.

Also see *Berries.*

(1) Song. 2:3b; (2) As a "heart-shaped" fruit with a sweet fragrance; (3) Matt. 7:17; (4) Gen. 3:6.

Stream: (1) A believer or church; (2) Outpouring of the Word or Spirit; (3) Place of refreshing; (4) Revival (streams in the desert); (5) Righteousness; (6) A flow of testing words; (7) Fickle person (changing stream); (8) Overwhelmed (overflowing stream); (9) Judgment (stream of fire).

Also see *Brook, Creek, River,* and *Water.*

(1) Song. 4:12-15; Isa. 66:12; (2) Ps. 46:4; 78:16, 20; (3) Ps. 126:4; (4) Isa. 35:6; (5) Amos 5:24; (6) Luke 6:48-49; (7) Job 6:15; (8) Ps. 124:4; (9) Isa. 30:28, 33; Dan. 7:10.

Street: (1) Exposed; (2) Bring out into the open (make public); (3) Public announcement or proclamation; (4) Well-known; (5) A person's path of life; (6) What lies ahead; (7) Gathering place; (8) Call to trust God (straight street); (9) Pure and without agenda (gold and transparent); (10) Destructive path (broad street); (11) The street may be a measure of a city's morality, prosperity, or spiritual condition; (12) The world (The street is contrasted with the house with the scarlet cord [the Church]); (13) The place of dirt (sin); (14) Uncared for (out on the street); (15) The place of busyness/diligence; (16) Place to be walked over.

Also see *Road, Walk, Path,* and *Highway.*

(1) Matt. 6:5; (2) 2 Sam. 21:12; Esther 6:9 (KJV); Prov. 1:20 (KJV); Eccl. 12:4; Song. 3:2; Isa. 15:3; Mark 6:56; Acts 5:15; 12:10; (3) 2 Sam. 1:20; Neh. 8:3 (KJV); Esther 6:11 (KJV); Prov. 1:20-21 (KJV); Eccl.12:5; Isa. 42:2; Jer. 11:6; Matt. 6:2; 12:19; Luke 10:10-11; (4) Luke 13:25b-26; (5) Prov. 7:8; 26:13; (6) Ps. 119:105; Prov. 4:18; Isa. 42:16 (God's path is lit); (7) Neh. 8:1 (KJV); Job 29:7; Luke 14:21; (8) Prov. 3:5-6 & Acts 9:11-15; (9) Rev. 21:21; (10) Song. 3:2 & Matt. 7:13-14; (11) Gen. 19:2; Judg. 19:15-27; Ps. 55:11; 144:13-14; Isa. 59:14; Jer. 5:1; 7:17; (12) Josh. 2:19; Prov. 7:12; (13) 2 Sam. 22:43; Ps. 18:42; Isa. 10:6; (14) Job 31:32; Jer. 14:16; As in, "on the streets"; (15) Prov. 22:13; 26:13; (16) Isa. 51:23.

Street Directory: (1) Lost; (2) Seeking directions; (3) Guidance; (4) Wanting to know the way; (5) Where someone is at.

(1-5) Exod. 33:13; Ps. 25:4; Jer. 42:3; Acts 16:17.

Street Light: See Light Pole.

Strength: (1) God; (2) Spiritual power; (3) Boldness; (4) Strength of heart, soul, or spirit; (5) Firstborn.

Also see *Hill* and *Power.*

(1) 1 Sam. 15:29; (2) Judg. 16:6, 19-20; Luke 1:80; (3) Ps. 138:3; (4) Ps. 27:14; 31:24; 73:26; 138:3; Luke 1:80; Eph. 3:16; (5) Gen. 49:3; Deut. 21:17; Ps. 78:51; 105:36.

Stretcher: (1) Casualty of spiritual warfare (because of ignorance).

(1) 1 Sam. 31:3.

Stretching: (1) Enlarging; (2) Exaggeration; (3) Preparing for ministry (stretching muscles); (4) Extending one's area of influence; (5) Exercising (or exerting) spiritual or physical power and dominion over (often forcibly); (6) Covering; (7) Waking up spiritually; (8) Being taken to the next spiritual level; (9) Reaching out (hand); (10) Embracing (hand); (11) Assisting (hand); (12) Exercising faith; (13) Displaying dominion; (14) Judgment (hand); (15) Forcibly; (16) Reaching out to (entreating); (17) Performing signs and wonders (exercising power); (18) Identifying with (body-to-body); (19) Entreating God (or a false god); (20) Defiance; (21) Expressing mercy or grace; (22) Haughtiness (necks).

Also see *Taller.*

(1) Isa. 54:2; (2) As in exaggerating the size of a fish with your hands; (3) Luke 1:80; (4) Isa. 8:8; (5) Exod. 14:16, 21, 26-27; 15:12; Deut. 4:34; 5:15; 9:29; Josh. 8:18-19; 1 Sam. 24:6; 26:9, 11; 2 Sam. 24:16; 1 Kings 8:42 (directed by prayer); Isa. 8:8; 23:11; (6) Exod. 25:20; 1 Kings 6:27; (7) Song. 5:2; Isa. 50:4; Zech. 4:1; (8) Rom. 1:17; 2 Cor. 3:18; (9) Matt. 12:13; 2 Cor. 10:14 (KJV); (10) Matt. 12:49; (11) Matt. 14:30-31; (12) Mark 3:5; (13) Acts 4:30; (14) Exod. 3:20; 6:6b; 7:5, 19; 8:5-6; 2 Kings 21:13 (measured and wanting); Isa. 5:25; 9:12, 17, 21; 10:4; (15) Exod. 6:6b; (16) Prov. 1:24; Rom. 10:21; (17) Deut. 7:19; Acts 4:30; (18) 1 Kings 17:21; 2 Kings 4:34-35; (19) Job 11:13; Ps. 44:20; 68:31; 88:9; 143:6; (20) Job 15:25; (21) Prov. 31:20; (22) Isa. 3:16.

Stripes: (1) Healing; (2) Iniquity; (3) Discipline; (4) Peace; (5) Purified; (6) Speaks of the bearing of one's cross (wearing stripes); (7) Speaks of double-mindedness (wearing stripes).

Also see individual colors.

(1) Isa. 53:5; 1 Pet. 2:24; (2-3) 2 Sam. 7:14; Ps. 89:32; (4) Isa. 53:5; (5) Lev. 8:15; (6) Col. 1:24; Matt. 16:24; (7) James 1:8; 4:8.

Stroke: (1) Bad blood; (2) Family relational problem; (3) Attack of the enemy; (4) Judgment.

(1) Judg. 5:26-27; (2) Isa. 1:5; (3) 2 Kings 4:17-37; (4) Jer. 30:23.

Stuffed Toy: (1) Not real/false (not truth); (2) False comfort; (3) Looking for comfort; (4) Harmless/innocent or looks harmless/innocent.

(1) Matt. 7:15; (2) Ps. 69:20; Zech. 10:2; (3) 2 Cor. 1:3-4; (4) Matt. 10:16; Acts 28:5.

Stumble: See Falling.

Stump: (1) A person cut down; (2) Judgment; (3) Humbling.

(1-3) Dan. 4:15-26.

Subdividing Land: (1) Moving into your inheritance.

(1) Josh. 1:6.

Submarine: (1) Not openly shown or not public; (2) Underground church; (3) Church in the Spirit; (4) Spiritual vessel not yet revealed; (5) The Spirit (submarine searching underwater).

(1) John 8:59; 12:36; (2) Acts 8:1, 3-4; (3) 1 Cor. 12:13; (4) John 14:22; 17:6; Rom. 16:25-26; (5) Prov. 20:27; Rom. 8:27.

Substitute: (1) Appointment; (2) Replacement.

(1) Gen. 4:25; (2) 1 Sam. 16:1.

Sucking: (1) Dependence; (2) Drawing from or being sustained by; (3) Nurturing and nursing (baby); (4) Emptying; (5) Sapping the life out of (parasite); (6) Providence; (7) Youngest and immature (baby); (8) Innocent; (9) Feeding (blood); (10) Milk-fed (baby); (11) Consolation; (12) Comfort;

Also see *Leech.*

(1) Deut. 32:13; 1 Sam. 1:23; (2) Deut. 32:13; Job 39:30; Isa. 60:16; (3) Num. 11:12; Matt. 24:19 (KJV); (4) Ezek. 23:34; (5) Prov. 30:15; (6) Deut. 33:19 (KJV); (7) Num. 11:12; Deut. 32:25; 1 Sam. 15:3; (8) 1 Sam. 7:9; Isa. 11:8; (9) Job 39:30; (10) 1 Sam. 1:23; 1 Kings 3:21 (KJV); (11) Isa. 66:11; (12) Isa. 66:12-13.

Sue/Suing: (1) Exercising your legal right spiritually over what has been stolen from you; (2) Claiming the wealth of the world; (3) Harboring unforgiveness (being sued); (4) A threat of real litigation.

(1) Prov. 6:30-31; (2) Exod. 3:22; 12:35-36; (3) Matt. 5:23-26; 18:32-35; Luke 12:58.

Sugar: See Honey.

Suicide: (1) Warning of pending suicidal thoughts; (2) Oppression and/or depression; (3) Hopelessness; (4) Spirit of heaviness; (5) Self-hatred; (6) Wanting to give up; (7) Self-pity; (8) Twisted form of revenge (getting back at someone).

(1) See below; (2) 1 Kings 19:4; Jon. 4:3, 8; (3) Num. 11:15; 1 Sam. 31:3-5; (4) Isa. 61:3; (5) 1 John 3:15; (6) 1 Kings 19:4; (7) 1 Kings 19:4; (8) Num. 35:31; Deut. 21:9 (trying to make them guilty).

The Bible appears to set forth three stages in the life of one contemplating suicide: (1) Impossiblity, loss, or failure; (2) Emotions dominating over sound decision making; (3) Lack of social support. If these seem evident, seek professional assistance immediately.

Suit: (1) Business; (2) Pastor; (3) Desire for prominence (expensive suit); (4) Pretense; (5) Renewed authority (best suit); (6) Mocking (stunning suit); (7) Angels (glorious suit); (8) Rottenness and decay (moth-eaten); (9) Garment of Christ (perfumed).

It is important to explore the understanding of what a suit represents to the person with the dream or vision; this will be of major significance in ascertaining its interpretation. The suit color may also be a major indicator of its meaning.

Also see *Clothing* and individual colors.

(1) Ezek.27:20-21, 24a; (3-4) Mark 12:38-40 (look for the other witnesses in this passage before proclaiming this interpretation); (5) Luke 15:22; (6) Luke 23:11; (7) Luke 24:4; (8) Job 13:28; (9) Ps. 45:8.

Suitcase: (1) Travel; (2) Departure; (3) Preparedness; (4) Baggage; (5) Giving you a burden (someone giving you a suitcase); (6) Helping with your burdens (someone carrying your suitcase).

Also see *Bag, Cruise Ship,* and *Holiday.*

(1) Josh. 9:3-6; (2-3) 1 Kings 10:2, 10; (4) Isa. 46:1-2; Jon. 1:5; (5) Luke 11:46; (6) Gal. 6:2.

Summer: (1) Harvest time (end of summer); (2) The prelude to the Second Coming of Christ; (3) Preparation time; (4) Time of drought (and heat); (5) Fruitfulness; (6) The end.

Also see *Drought, Fig,* and *Winter.*

(1) Prov. 10:5; Isa. 16:9b; 18:5-6; Jer. 8:20; Dan. 2:35; John 4:35; (2) Matt. 24:32-34; Mark 13:26-28; Luke 21:30; (3) Prov. 10:5; 30:25; (4) Ps. 32:4; (5) 2 Sam. 16:1-2; Isa. 28:4; Jer. 40:10; 48:32b; Mic. 7:1; (6) Amos 8:1-2; Jer. 8:20.

Sun: (1) Glory of God; (2) Father; (3) Jesus Christ.

(1) Ps. 19:1-6; 84:11; (2) Gen. 37:9-10; (3) Ps. 19:4b-6; Mal. 4:2a; Acts 26:13-15; Rev. 1:16-17.

Sun (Setting): (1) Setting sun means the Glory is departing; (2) End of an issue; (3) Time to settle accounts; (4) Followed by dark activity; (5) Death.

(1) Judg. 19:14-28; 1 Kings 22:36; 2 Chron. 18:34; (2) Exod. 17:12; Josh. 10:13; Eph. 4:26; (3) Deut. 24:13, 15; Josh. 10:27; Judg. 14:18; Ps. 50:1; Eph. 4:26; (4) Ps. 104:19-20; John 13:30; (5) Gen. 28:11; Sleep parallels death in Scripture (i.e. John 11:11-13); Dan. 6:14; Daniel's experience in the lion's den pre-pictures Jesus death, hell, and resurrection experience.

Sun (Rising): (1) New revelation; (2) Beginning or new beginning; (3) Eve of revival; (4) Resurrection.

(1) Gen. 32:31; (2-3) Matt. 28:1, 7-8; (4) Matt. 28:1, 7.

Sunburn: (1) The judgment of God; (2) Sin brought to the light; (3) Coming down out of the glory (only if the dream is positive).

Also see *Burn* and *Burnt.*

(1) Ezek. 16:41; Rev. 18:8; (cf. John 5:22 & Mal. 4:2); (2) John 3:20-21; (3) Exod. 34:29; Rev. 1:15; 2:18.

Sunday: (1) One; (2) God; (3) Resurrection; (4) New Beginnings; (5) Rest.

Also see *Day* and *Seven* (The secular world sees Sunday as the seventh day of the week).

(1-2) Gen. 1:1; (3-4) Matt. 28:1, 6; (5) Exod. 23:12.

Sunflowers: (1) Disciples (They follow the sun [Son] and are full of seeds [Word]).

(1) Mal. 4:2 & Matt. 8:23, (cf. Luke 8:11).

Sunglasses: (1) Christ's perspective; (2) Spiritual outlook; (3) Coping with God's glory; (4) Self-image issues (especially if sunglasses are worn inside); (5) Not able to handle the glory.

Also see *Sun.*

(1) Ps. 19:4b-5a; Mal. 4:2; (2) Num. 12:6-8; 1 Cor. 13:12; (3) 2 Cor. 3:7-8; (4) 1 Pet. 3:3; (5) Exod. 34:33, 35.

Suntan: (1) The glory of God (bronze suntan).

(1) Exod. 34:29; Rev. 1:15; 2:18.

Superhero: (1) Christ; (2) The Holy Spirit; (3) You empowered by the Holy Spirit (you as the superhero); (4) Powerful man or woman of God; (5) Demonic spirit (enemies); (6) Superman can be an antichrist (instead of Christ).

Also see *Famous Person.*

(1) Luke 24:19, 51; (2-3) Acts 10:38; (4) Acts 7:22; 2 Cor. 12:12; (5) Luke 4:6; 10:19; (6) 2 Thess. 2:9.

Supermarket: See Shop.

Supervisor: (1) The Holy Spirit; (2) Leader.

(1) John 14:26; Acts 16:6-7; (2) Acts 6:3.

Supper: (1) Marriage Supper of the Lamb (Great Feast); (2) Covenant meal; (3) Intimate fellowship; (4) Last Supper; (5) Remembrance of Jesus' death; (6) Celebration; (7) Call to heart fellowship with Christ.

Also see *Table.*

(1) Luke 14:16; Rev. 19:9a, 17; (2) Luke 22:20; (3) John 12:2; 21:20; Rev. 3:20; (4) John 13:2, 4; (5) 1 Cor. 11:20; (6) Mark 6:21; (7) Rev. 3:20.

Surf: (1) Wave of the Holy Spirit; (2) Flow of the Holy Spirit.

(1-2) 1 Kings 18:12; Isa. 44:3; Isa. 59:19 (Consider here that the comma is in the wrong place); Mark 1:8; Acts 2:17.

Surfer: (1) Prophet (waiting on the wave of the Spirit); (2) Worship leader (surfing the anointing); (3) Moving in the Spirit (operating in the gifts).

Also see *Surf, Surfing,* and *Waves.*

(1) Isa. 40:31; Hab. 2:1-2; (2) 1 Sam. 10:5-6; Matt. 14:29-30; (3) Rom. 5:15 (NIV).

Surfing: (1) Flowing in the Holy Spirit (standing surfer); (2) Negatively surfing the world wide web (surfer lying down, not upright).

Also see *Surf, Surfer,* and *Waves.*

(1) Acts 11:28; Rev. 11:11; (2) Ps. 51:10 (KJV).

Swallow (bird): (1) Type of true believer (heavenly being). Seen in the bird's attributes: (2) Brings up her young in God's courts; (3) Non-landing; (4) Non-stop prayer (chattering); (5) Aware of the times (seasons).

(2) Ps. 84:3; (3) Prov. 26:2 (cf. Heb. 11:9-10); (4) Isa. 38:14 (cf. 1 Thess. 5:17); (5) Jer. 8:7 (cf. 1 Thess. 5:1-2).

Swallow (verb): (1) Allow or embrace; (2) Engulf; (3) Consumed; (4) Caught and Killed; (5) Destroy; (6) Steal; (7) Smothered; (8) Partake; (9) Speed (swallow up the ground); (10) Devour; (11) Oppression; (12) Reproach; (13) Kill; (14) Abuse; (15) Envelope.

Also see *Drink, Eat,* and *Mouth.*

(1) Matt. 23:24; (2) Ezek. 36:3; 1 Cor. 15:54; (3) Num. 16:30, 32, 34; Deut. 11:6; Eccl. 10:12; Isa. 28:7; Lam. 2:5; (4) 2 Sam. 17:16; (5) 2 Sam. 20:19-20; (6) Job 5:5; (7) Job 6:3; (8) Job 20:18; (9) Job 39:24; (10) Ps. 21:9; (11) Ps. 56:1; (12) Ps. 57:3; (13) Ps. 124:3; Prov. 1:12; (14) Amos 8:4; (15) Jon. 1:17.

Swamp: (1) No flow of the Spirit; (2) No output; (3) Quenching the Spirit; (4) Stagnant water; (5) Bogged down.

(1) Matt. 13:58. & Acts 10:38; (2) Mark 4:24; (3) 1 Thess. 5:19; (4) Exod. 15:23; (5) Ps. 69:2, 14; Heb. 12:1.

Swan: (1) Gracefulness; (2) Love (two swans); (2) Sun; (3) Moon; (4) Unclean spirit.

(1-4) Historical, cultural, and mythological associations; (4) Lev. 11:18.

Swearing (Cussing): (1) Bitter water; (2) Speaking words of death; (3) Denial of Christ; (4) Putting a curse on someone or self; (5) To lose spiritual strength; (6) Corruption; (7) Ungodly discontent; (8) Covetousness; (9) Verbal violence; (10) Disputes; (11) Pride; (12) Jealousy; (13) Hatred; (14) Spirit of murder; (15) Frustration.

(1) Num. 5:18b; James 3:9-12; (2) Prov. 18:21; Mark 15:11-15; (3) Matt. 26:74-75; (4) Matt. 26:74; (cf. Matt. 27:23, Acts 5:30 & Gal. 3:13); (5-6) Eph. 4:26, 27, 29, 30; (7) Phil. 4:11; 3 John 1:10; (8) Heb. 13:5; (9) Luke 3:14; (10) Jude 1:8-9; (11) Prov. 21:24; 1 Tim. 6:3-6; (12) Prov. 6:34-35; (13-14) Mark 15:11-15; 1 John 3:15; (15) 3 John 1:10.

Sweat/ing: (1) Human works or self-effort; (2) Sin; (3) Anguish and distress (sweating blood); (4) Worry; (5) Poverty mindset.

(1) Gen. 3:19; Ezek. 44:18; (2) Gen. 3:17-19; (3) Luke 22:44; (4) As in, "don't sweat it"; (4-5) 2 Sam. 9:6-7; Matt. 6:31-33, 34; Luke 10:38-42.

Sweeping: (1) Cleaning out; (2) Searching; (3) Drastic reform; (4) Judgment.

Also see *Broom.*

(1-2) Luke 15:8; (3) As in, "sweeping changes"; (4) As in, "getting rid of sin and filth"; Gen. 18:23 (NIV).

Sweets: See Candy.

Swelling: (1) Flattery; (2) Sign of corruption or defilement; (3) Iniquity; (4) Poison or venomous; (5) Conceit.

Also see *Taller* and *Yeast.*

(1) 2 Pet. 2:18; Jude 1:16 (empty words); (2) Num. 5:21-22, 27; Deut. 8:4; (3) Isa. 30:13; (4) Acts 28:6; (5) 2 Cor. 12:20 (compare KJV & NKJV).

Swimming: (1) Moving in the Spirit; (2) River of Life; (3) Bringing to the surface; (4) Deep (suggests that the water is deep); (5) Having to let go and trust God; (6) Advancing in own strength; (7) Overcome with sorrow or grief.

Also see *Deep.*

(1-2) Ezek. 47:5; Isa. 25:11; (3) 2 Kings 6:6; (4) Ps. 42:7 (deep within); Ezek. 47:5; (5) Ezek. 47:5 (having to break reliance on the earth beneath your feet); (6) John 21:7 (cf. John 21:3, 18); (7) Ps. 6:6-7.

Swimming Pool: (1) Immersed in God (in pool); (2) Ready for baptism; (3) Purification or cleansing; (4) Church; (5) Church without love (pool with ice in it). Also see *Swimming*.

(1-3) Acts 8:38b-39a; Heb.10:22b; John 9:7; (4) John 5:2; (5) Matt. 24:12.

Swine: See Pig.

Swing: (1) Moved by circumstance/opposition; (2) Change of mind; (3) Doubt; (4) Double-mindedness. Also see *Shaking*.

(1) Matt. 11:7; 14:30; Luke 7:24; (2) 2 Thess. 2:2; (3) James 1:6; (4) James 1:8.

Swiss: See Switzerland in Name and Place Dictionary.

Sword: (1) Word of God; (2) Words; (3) Divides and separates; (4) Live by it, die by it; (5) Two-edged; (6) Tongue; (7) Judgment. Also see *Knife* and *Tongue*.

(1) Eph. 6:17; Heb. 4:12; (2) Ps. 55:21; 64:3a; (3) Matt. 10:34-35; Rom. 8:35; Heb. 4:12; (4) Matt. 26:52; Rev. 13:10; (5) Rev. 1:16; 2:12; (6) Rev. 1:16; 2:16; (7) 1 Chron. 21:16; Ezek. 21:3-5,9-17; Rom. 13:1-4; Rev. 19:15.

Syringe: (1) Inoculation; (2) Antidote (injection of life); (3) As they are used to inject into a vein, they speak of spiritual life or death (dependent on the contents). Also see *Drug-Taking* and *Needle*.

(1) Prov. 4:23; (2) Job 33:4; 2 Cor. 3:6; (3) Lev. 17:11a.

Table: (1) Communion or fellowship; (2) Alignment with someone; (3) In relationship; (4) Communion with God; (5) The King's or Father's provision; (6) Commerce or trade; (7) A writing place; (8) The heart; (9) Union with Christ; (10) Planning place; (11) Negotiation leading to agreement and treaty or contract signing; (12) Decision-making; (13) Serving the Body of Christ; (14) Indicative of your sphere of influence (big/small table). Also see *Glass Table*, *Kitchen*, *Meal*, *Sitting*, and *Under the Table*.

(1) 1 Cor. 10:20-21; (2) 1 Sam. 20:34; Luke 22:21; (3) John 12:2; 13:28; (4) 1 Cor. 10:20-21; (5) 2 Sam. 9:7-11; 19:28; Ps. 23:5; 78:19; Matt. 15:26-27; Luke 22:30; (6) Matt. 21:12; Mark 11:15; John 2:15; (7) 2 Cor. 3:3; (8) Lev. 24:6

(pure table); 2 Cor. 3:3; (9) John 13:28; (10) Dan. 11:27; (11) As in, "both parties came to the table"; (12) John 13:27, 30; (13) Acts 6:2; (14) 1 Kings 10:5.

Table (Glass): (1) Transparency of communion; (2) Seeing through to the heart; (3) Fragile relationship.

(1) 1 Cor. 10:21; (2) 2 Cor. 3:3 (KJV); (3) 1 Sam. 19:7-10; 20:32-34.

Table (Under the Table): (1) Deception; (2) Bribe; (3) Taxation.

(1) Prov. 23:7 (The heart is below the surface); (2) 1 Sam. 8:3; 12:3; Job 15:34; Ps. 26:10; Amos 5:12.

Table Tennis: See Tennis/Court.

Tail: (1) Subservient; (2) Second place; (3) Beneath; (4) Disobedience; (5) Cursed; (6) Troublemaker; (7) False prophet; (8) Powerful sting; (9) Influence or allegiance.

Also see *Head*.

(1-3) Deut. 28:13; (4) Deut. 28:44; (5) Gen. 3:14 (A snake is all tail!); (6) Isa. 7:4 (KJV); (7) Isa. 9:14-15; (8) Rev. 9:10, 19; (9) Rev. 12:3-4.

Tall: (1) Leader (tall person); (2) Authority (tall person); (3) Champion; (4) Proud or arrogant.

Also see *Length, Little, Short, Taller,* and *Tower* for *Tall Building*.

(1-2) 1 Sam. 9:2; (3) 1 Sam. 17:4; (4) Isa. 2:12; Jer. 48:29.

Taller: If something is taller than it was originally, it may mean that: (1) It is influence is increasing; (2) It is getting stronger; (3) It is taking more leadership; (4) It is becoming proud.

(1) Exod. 34:24; (2) Exod. 1:9; Ps. 119:32; (3) 1 Sam. 9:2; (4) 1 Sam. 15:17.

Tandem Bicycle: (1) Kindred spirits; (2) Working together.

Also see *Bicycle*.

(1-2) Phil. 1:27; 2:19-20.

Tank (Army): (1) Powerful ministry; (2) Impacting ministry; (3) Powerful deliverance ministry (breaks open enemy strongholds); (4) Spiritual warfare; (5) Heavy or weighty words.

(1-2) 1 Sam. 2:10; Deut. 20:1; Joel 2:5; Nah. 2:3; (3) Matt. 17:18; (4) Eph. 6:11; (5) Eccl. 8:4; Luke 4:32.

Tap: (1) Open portal; (2) Holy Spirit ministry; (3) Jesus.

Also see *Well*.

(1) Gen. 7:11b-12; (2-3) John 7:37-39.

Tape Measure: (1) Fitting preparation; (2) Being measured for service; (3) Small change of heart needed to enter in (small distance); (4) Expansion preparation.

Also see *Measure/measuring*.

(1) 1 Sam. 2:19; (2) Gen. 37:3; (3) Mark 12:34; (4) Isa. 54:2.

Tapestry: See Fabric.

Tar: (1) Atonement; (2) Protection against sinking; (3) Judgment; (4) Works of people.

Also see *Bricks* and *Salt*.

(1) Gen. 6:14 (The word *pitch* used here is the Hebrew word for "atonement"); (2) Exod. 2:3; (3) Gen. 14:10; Isa. 34:9; (4) Gen.11:3.

Target: (1) Place of vulnerability.

Also see *Goal* and see *Target* in the Name and Place Dictionary.

(1) 2 Kings 6:9.

Tasmanian Devil: (1) Evil spirit that attacks children; (2) Manifests in outbursts of anger; (3) Devil/demon.

(1-2) 1 Kings 4:32-33. These characteristics are seen in the size of the creature and its ferocity as well as experience; (3) Isa. 14:16; Matt. 17:18.

Tassels: (1) Mind of God (His laws, commandments).

Also see *Bookmark*.

(1) Num. 15:38-39.

Tasting: (1) Experiencing; (2) Testing and trying; (3) Partaking; (4) Strengthening; (5) Discerning; (6) Heart revelation; (7) Unchanged (bad taste); (8) Humbling (not eating).

Also see *Sweet, Sour,* and *Bitter*.

(1) Matt. 16:28; Luke 9:27; John 8:52; 1 Pet. 2:3; (2) Job 34:3; Matt. 27:34; John 2:9; (3) Luke 14:24; Heb. 6:4-5; (4) 1 Sam. 14:29; (5) Job 6:30; (6) Ps. 34:8; 119:103-104; Prov. 24:13-14; (7) Jer. 48:11; (8) Jon. 3:7.

Tattoo: (1) Tough; (2) Identity or Identifying mark; (3) Fleshly person; (4) Fugitive; (5) Vagabond; (6) Message; (7) The placement of a tattoo is important to its interpretation, i.e. a tattooed leg would mean corrupted strength; a tattooed face would mean a defiled or poisoned heart. (8) If the tattoo has recognizable figures or numbers within it, these of course will carry deep significance and must be interpreted individually.

Also see *Biker/Bikie* and *Scar.*

(1) Ps. 22:16; (2-5) Gen. 4:14-15; (6) Song. 8:6; Isa. 49:16.

Tax: See IRS.

Taxi: See Cab.

Tea Bag: (1) Healing.

(1) Rev. 22:2.

Teacher: (1) The Holy Spirit; (2) Mature disciple of Christ; (3) Fleshly (false, academic, money-hungry, demonic) teacher; (4) Nature; (5) Revelation; (6) Jesus; (7) Known teacher.

(1) Luke 12:12; John 14:26; 1 Cor. 2:13; 1 John 2:27; (2) Rom. 12:7; Eph. 4:11; Col. 1:28; 3:16; 1 Tim. 2:24; 2 Tim. 3:2; Heb. 5:12; (3) 2 Tim. 4:3; Tit. 1:11; 2 Pet. 2:1; Rev. 2:20; (4) 1 Kings 4:30-33; 1 Cor. 11:14; (5) Gal. 1:12; (6) Eph. 4:20-21; (7) Acts 13:1.

Team: (1) Family; (2) Church; (3) Business; (4) Christian (disciple); (5) Spiritual opposition.

(1) Eph. 5:22-27; (2) Eph. 4:16; (3) Neh. 4:6; (4) Mark 9:40; Rom. 8:31; (5) Eph. 6:12.

Tear (verb): (1) Loss; (2) Judgment; (3) Persecution; (4) Personal attack.

(1) 1 Sam. 15:27-28; (2) 1 Kings 13:26; Isa. 5:25 (KJV); (3) Ps. 7:1-2; (4) Ps. 35:15 (NKJV).

Tears: (1) Sadness or sorrow; (2) Grief (loss of expectation); (3) Trouble; (4) Affliction; (5) Joy; (6) Pain; (7) Repentance.

Also see *Crying* and *Sorrow.*

(1) John 16:20; Rev. 21:4; (2) Ps. 6:7; 31:9; (3) Ps.31:9; (4) Ps. 88:9; (5) Ps. 126:5; John 16:20; 2 Tim. 1:4; (6) John 16:20; Rev. 21:4; (7) Heb. 12:17.

Tea Towel: (1) Servanthood.

(1) John 13:4.

Teddy Bear: (1) Family-friendly false prophet; (2) Antichrist spirit that preys on immature believers; (3) False comforter.

(1-3) 2 Tim. 3:5-7; 2 Pet. 2:1-2.

Teenager: (1) Folly; (2) Rebellious; (3) Mocking; (4) Consider your perception of teenager/s.

Also see *Gang, Skinhead, Youth,* and *Younger.*

(1) Prov. 22:15; (2) Prov. 30:11; (3) 2 Kings 2:23.

Teeth: (1) Believer or congregation; (2) Words; (3) Wisdom; (4) Pride of appearance; (5) Maturity; (6) Unfaithful person (bad tooth); (7) Not the upfront person (bad teeth); (8) Biting; (9) Fierce (as in baring the fangs); (10) Instrument of judgment; (11) Decision making or discernment; (12) Mocking; (13) Lies (false teeth); (14) Predator (sharp teeth); (15) Power.

Also see *Braces, Cheek, Lips, Losing Teeth* (directly below), *Mouth, Tongue, Toothache, Toothbrush,* and *Toothpaste.*

(1) Song. 4:2; 6:6; (sheep); (2) Prov. 30:14; Ps. 35:16; 57:4; Jer. 2:16; (4) (5) Heb. 5:14; (6) Prov. 25:19; (7) Isa. 53:2-3; (8) (9-10) Isa. 41:15; Hab 1:8 (fierce = sharp); (11) Isa. 41:15 (Judgment carries the meaning of decision-making); (12) Ps. 35:16; (13) Ps 57:4 & 59:12; (14) Job 16:9; Ps. 57:4; (15) Dan. 7:7; Joel 1:6.

Teeth (Losing Teeth): (1) Losing face; (2) Shame; (3) Loss of words or lost for words; (4) Judgment of God (broken teeth); (5) Unfaithful or ungodly person (broken tooth); (6) Humbled (loss of pride); (7) Legalistic retribution; (8) Losing sheep; (9) Poor self-image; (10) Embarrassed to speak; (11) Hidden self-image problems (missing bottom teeth); (12) Hidden disability (missing bottom teeth); (13) Disarmed/no power (no teeth).

Also see *Arrows* and *Teeth.*

(1-3) Lam. 3:16; Eph. 5:12; Ps. 58:3-7; (4) Ps. 3:7; 58:6; (5) Ps. 3:7; Prov. 25:19; (6) Ezek. 28:17; (7) Exod. 21:24; Matt. 5:38; (8) Song. 6:6; (9) Isa. 41:14; (10) Exod. 6:30; (11) Nah. 2:10; (12) Prov. 25:19; (13) Dan. 7:7; Joel 1:6.

Teeth (New Teeth): (1) Dignity; (2) Glory.

(1) Lam. 3:16 (opposite of this); (2) Isa. 60:1.

Telephone: (1) Communication; (2) Heart/spirit (spiritual receiver); (3) Communication with God in prayer; (4) Heart sensitive to the Spirit of God (touchscreen cell phone).

(1) Gen. 23:8 (KJV); (2) Matt. 11:15; (3) <u>Ps. 4:1</u>; 17:6; 18:6; 1 Cor. 14:2; (4) Matt. 12:28 & Luke 11:30.

Telephone (Faulty Telephone): (1) Communication barrier; (2) Communication problems; (3) Hardened heart.

(1) <u>John 8:43</u>; (2) Eccl. 9:16; Jer. 22:5; (3) Heb. 3:15; 4:7b.

Telephone Message: (1) Message from God.

(1) Matt. 10:27.

Telescope: (1) Distant in space or time; (2) Long-term promise; (3) About to see visions of Heaven; (4) Turning to righteousness; (5) Prophet or seer; (6) Viewed from the second heaven (telescopic sight).

Also see *Sniper* and *Staring.*

(1-2) Gen. 3:15 & Gal. 4:4; <u>Gen. 15:5</u>; (3) Ezek. 1:1; Dan. 4:13; Acts 26:19; (4) Dan. 12:3; (5) 1 Sam. 9:9; (6) Ps. 14:2; 53:2 [The first heaven is the sky (see Deut. 4:19), the third Heaven is God's dwelling place (see 2 Cor. 12:2), and the second heaven the spirit realm (see Eph. 6:12)].

Television: (1) Vision/destiny; (2) Message; (3) News (media headlines good or bad); (4) Gift of reception (prophet); (5) Receiving visions and dreams; (6) Idol/idolatry; (7) Tuning/search/searching for God; (8) Mind-"set"; (9) Letting the world in; (10) Looking to the world.

Also see *Radio* and *Stereo.*

(1) Num. 24:4; Dan. 4:13; (2) <u>Num. 12:6</u>; (3) 2 Sam. 18:26; 1 King 14:6; Matt. 4:23-24; (4-5) Num. 12:6; (6) Dan. 3:5b; Rev. 16:2b; (7) Num. 23:3; (8) As in, "what you are watching"; (9-10) Isa. 31:1 (Egypt is the world); 1 John 2:16.

Television (Asleep in Front of Television): (1) Watchlessness or prayerlessness; (2) Spiritually insensitive; (3) Dulled by idolatry; (4) Not aware of idolatry in our lives.

Also see *Asleep* and *Sleeping.*

(1-2) Isa. 56:10-11; (3-4) <u>Matt. 13:15</u>.

Teller: (1) Author or authority.

(1) Heb. 12:2.

Temple: (1) Human body (individually); (2) Church body (corporately); (3) God's heavenly temple.

(1) <u>1 Cor. 6:19</u>; (2) 2 Cor. 6:16; (3) Rev. 11:19.

Ten: (1) Complete; (2) Completion of order/cycle; (3) Full.

(1-2) Gen. 16:3 (waiting); Gen. 31:7, 41 (deceit); Exod. 7–12 (plagues/judgment); Exod. 20:2-17 (instruction); Num 14:22 (rebellion); Matt. 25:1 (bride); Matt. 25:20, 28 (talents/investment); <u>Luke 15:8</u> (riches/redemption); 17:12-17 (cleansing); <u>Rev. 2:10</u> (tribulation/testing); (3) Num. 7:14ff.

Tennis/Tennis Court: (1) Verbal conflict; (2) Spiritual warfare.

Also see *Ball.*

(1-2) Matt. 4:1-10.

Ten Thousand: (1) Seems to express the maximum possible in earthly terms; (2) Extreme.

(1) Lev. 26:8 (enemies); <u>Matt. 18:24</u> (debt); 1 Cor. 4:15 (instructors); 1 Cor. 14:19 (words); Jude 1:14 (saints).

Tent: (1) Human body; (2) Temporary church; (3) Earthly dwelling place (contrasted with heavenly home).

(1) <u>2 Pet. 1:13-14</u> (NKJV); (2) Exod. 33:7-8; Num. 10:11-12; (3) Heb. 11:9-10; (cf. John 14:2).

Termites: (1) Heretic; (2) Undermining words (white-anting); (3) Unseen and Destructive; (4) Little unseen sins that bring down the house; (5) Cancer.

(1) 2 Tim. 2:17; Tit. 3:10-11; (2-3) Acts 15:24; <u>Tit. 1:11</u>; (4) Gal. 5:9; (5) 2 Tim. 2:17.

Terrorism: (1) Schemes of the devil.

Also see *Terrorist.*

(1) John 10:10; 2 Cor. 2:11.

Terrorist: (1) Children of the devil; (2) Distorter of the Gospel; (3) False believers; (4) Plotting in the shadows (5) Pending surprise attack.

Also see *Terrorism.*

(1-3) <u>John 8:44</u>; Acts 13:10; 1 John 3:10; (4) Prov. 6:14; (5) 1 Sam. 30:3.

Testicles: See Genitals.

Theater: See Stage (Theater).

Theft: See Thief.

Theme Park: (1) Representation of a believer's life; (2) Scenario or episode in one's life; (3) Entertainment; (4) Excitement; (5) The Kingdom of God.

(1) Deut. 32:13a; Rev. 20:12; (2) 2 Cor. 11:26; (3) Exod. 32:6b; Luke 8:14; 2 Tim. 3:4; (4) Ps. 68:4; (5) Mark 10:14.

Thick: (1) Fat; (2) Insensitive to God; (3) Insensitive; (4) Dull or insensitive heart.

Also see *Fat* and *Thin*.

(1-2) Deut. 32:15; (3) As in, "thick-skinned"; (4) Matt. 15:16 (Understanding relates to heart receptivity, Matt. 13:19).

Thief: (1) Warning; (2) Potential to have something—possession, virtue, spiritual gift, etc.—stolen; (3) Devil; (4) Destroyer; (5) Murderer; (6) Non-believer; (7) Doubt; (8) Sevenfold return (thief caught); (9) Dangerous partnership; (10) Shame; (11) Scorn; (12) Cursed; (13) A heart centered on earthly treasures; (14) Evil heart; (15) Profiteer in church; (16) Sign of prayerlessness; (17) Mocker; (18) Not caring; (19) Without warning; (20) Adulterer.

Also see *Robbery* and *Steal*.

(1-5) John 10:1, 10; (5) Job 24:14; (6) Ps. 50:17-18; 1 Cor. 6:9-10; (7) James 1:6; (8) Prov. 6:30-31; (9) Prov. 29:24; Isa. 1:23; (10) Jer. 2:26; (11) Jer. 48:27; (12) Zech. 5:3-4; (13) Matt. 6:19-21; (14) Matt. 15:19; Mark 7:21-22; (15) Matt. 21:12-13; (16) Matt. 24:43; Rev. 16:15; (17) Matt. 27:44; (18) John 12:6; (19) 1 Thess. 5:2-4; 2 Pet. 3:10; Rev. 3:3; 16:15; (20) 2 Sam. 12:4, 7-9; Prov. 6:26-32.

Thigh: (1) Oath; (2) Strength.

Also see *Leg* and *Shin*.

(1) Gen. 24: 2-3; 47:29; (2) Ps. 147:10.

Thin: (1) Famine; (2) Fine; (3) Lean.

Also see *Emaciated, Fat,* and *Skinny*.

(1) Gen. 41:6-7, 27; (2) Exod. 39:3; Lev. 13:30; 1 Kings 7:29 (KJV); (3) Isa. 17:4.

Thirsty: (1) Desire for God; (2) Desire for eternal fulfillment; (3) Dry and barren believer; (4) Desire to be filled; (5) In a wilderness; (6) It appears that thirst generally relates to a need for the Spirit whereas hunger relates to the Word.

Also see *Hunger* and *Throat.*

(1-3) <u>Ps. 42:1-2</u>; 69:3; (cf. Ps. 69:21; John 19:28); John 7:37-39; (4) Matt. 5:6; (5) Neh. 9:15; (6) Neh. 9:15; John 6:35; 7:38-39.

Thirteen: (1) Rebellion; (2) Sin; (3) Apostasy; (4) Defection; (5) Corruption; (6) Backsliding.

(1) Gen. 14:4; (2) The "sixth" prime number (1, 3, 5, 7, 11, 13); (3-6) Gen. 10:8, Nimrod 13th generation from Adam (beginning of Babylon); Gen 16:12, of Ishmael it was foretold he would be *"a wild man, his hand against every man"*; Gen. 17:25, Ishmael (son of the flesh) was circumcised at 13 years of age; 1 Kings 7:1, Solomon was 13 years building his own house, compared to seven building the Temple (1 Kings 6:38).

Thirty: (1) Right timing/moment to reign or minister; (2) 3 x 10 = 30 as such it carries the meaning of perfection or fullness [3] of Divine order [10] which marks the right moment.

(1-2) Gen. 41:46; 2 Sam. 5:4; Luke 3:23.

Thistle: See Thorn.

Thorns: (1) Sin; (2) Curse; (3) Deceitfulness of wealth/cares of the world; (4) Evil men; (5) Choker of the Word/Life; (6) Hedged in; (7) Fleshly weakness; (8) Face judgment.

Also see *Tree.*

(1-2) <u>Gen. 3:17-18</u>; (cf. Gen. 22:13; John 19:2); (3) Matt. 13:22; (4) Matt. 13:25 (false grain); Luke 6:44-45; (5) Luke 8:14; (6) Hos. 2:6; (7) 2 Cor. 12:7, 9; (8) Heb. 6:8.

Thousand: (1) Ever increasing (or More); (2) Amplification of the number; (3) Literal thousands; (4) Day; (5) Ankles (1,000); (6) Knees (2,000); (7) Waist (3,000); (8) Must swim (4,000); (9) Ever-increasing grace (5,000).

You may also use the meaning of the numbers 1-17 to interpret these thousands (With the exception of ten thousand, which is listed above).

If the number involves a figure such as 34,000, consider 30 (if there is an entry for the tens) and 4, e.g. Ever increasing dominion after the fullness of waiting.

You might also consider 3 and 4; in this case a possible meaning would be ever increasing fullness of dominion. If the number is a product (two numbers multiplied) or a sum (two numbers added) consider each number that make up these equations, e.g. 66,000 = 6 x 11 x 1000 = Ever increasing disorganization/disintegration of humanity. Another example might be 19,000 = 10 + 9 x 1,000 = Complete judgment for ever or ever increasing and complete fruitfulness. Allow the witness of the Spirit and the context of the dream to confirm which interpretation is more likely.

(1) Gen. 20:16 (Ever increasing redemption); Exod. 20:6, 34:7 (ever increasing mercy); (2) Exod. 32:28 (a full complement of humanity); (4) Ps. 90:4; 2 Pet. 3:8; (5) Ezek. 47:3; (7) Ezek. 47:4; (8) Ezek. 47:4; (9) Ezek. 47:5; (9) Matt. 14:21; John 6:10.

Thread (Scarlet Thread): (1) The story of redemption throughout God's Word; (2) Word of God; (3) The Blood of Jesus; (4) Thin or fine line; (5) Love.

(1-2) Song. 4:3a; (3-4) Josh. 2:18-19 (speaks of the Blood of Christ); (5) Song. 4:3a.

Three: (1) God/The Godhead (2) Complete; (3) Resurrection; (4) Perfect; (5) Divine fullness; (6) The Holy Spirit; (7) Three items may = three days or three years; (8) Witness; (9) Father, Son, and Holy Spirit; (10) Spirit, soul, and body; (11) Third Heaven.

Also see *Hundred* (i.e. 300), *Three Story Building,* and *Two.*

(1) Isa.6:3; Matt. 28:19; 1 John 5:7; (2) Exod. 5:3 (complete separation); Mark 14:30, 66-72 (complete denial); John 21:15-17 (complete confession); (3) Gen. 1:13; Josh. 1:11; Matt. 12:39-40; (4) Luke 13:32; (5) Eph. 3:19 (Father); 4:13 (Son), Col. 2:9 (Holy Spirit); (6) Matt. 28:19; (7) Gen. 40:10, 12, 16, 18; 41:1; (8) Deut. 19:15; Matt. 18:16; (9) Matt. 28:19; 1 John 5:7 (KJV); (10) 1 Thess. 5:23; (11) 2 Cor. 12:2.

Three Story Building: (1) Fullness of the Spirit; (2) Maturity in Christ; (3) Illustration of the first, second, and third heaven (which heaven [1-3] relates to the level in the building you are on).

Also see *House, Individual Numbers,* and *Three.*

(1-3) Col. 2:9-10; 1 John 5:8; Rev. 12:11; (cf. Gen. 6:16); 2 Cor. 12:2.

.357 Magnum: (1) Powerful words; (2) Threat; (3) Fear.

Also see *Bow* and *Bullets.*

(1) 1 Sam. 17:43-44; (2-3) 1 Sam. 17:7.

Throat: (1) Passage to the heart; (2) Open grave; (3) Infers that one's words reflect the state of the heart; (4) Threat of death (knife to throat); (5) Without God or missing God (thirsty or dry throat); (6) Heart unforgiveness (grabbed by the throat); (7) Threat.

Also see *Jugular Vein, Neck, Thirsty, Throat (Cut),* and *Tongue.*

(1-3) <u>Ps. 5:9</u>; Rom. 3:13; (4) Prov. 23:2; (5) Ps. 69:3 (cf. John 19:28); (6-7) Matt. 18:28.

Throat (Cut): (1) Death; (2) Ruthlessly killing someone with words; (3) Threat; (4) Warning; (5) Stop (as in "kill" what you are doing).

Also see *Decapitation, Kill/Killing, Murder, Neck, Jugular Vein,* and *Throat.*

(1) Isa. 1:11; (2) Ps. 57:4; (3-5) Prov. 23:2.

Thrombosis: (1) Lack of circulation; (2) Sitting down too long; (3) Lazy in the Lord; (4) Slowing the flow and hindering the walk.

Also see *Walking.*

(1) <u>Prov.</u> 6:9-11; <u>24:33-34</u>; (2-3) 1 Cor. 15:58; 2 Thess. 3:8; (4) <u>Ps. 44:18</u>.

Throne: (1) Authority; (2) Judgment; (3) Heaven; (4) Seat; (5) Christ's Glory; (6) Dominion; (7) The place of grace (mercy seat); (8) The place from which God rules.

(1) Luke 1:32-33; (2) Matt. 19:28; Luke 22:30; <u>Rev. 20</u>:4, <u>11-12</u>; (3-4) Matt. 5:34; 23:22; Acts 7:49; (5) Matt. 25:31; (6) Col. 1:16; (7) Heb. 4:16; (8) Heb. 12:2; <u>Rev.</u> 1:4; 3:21; <u>4:2-5</u>; 7:10; 19:4.

Throwing: (1) Launching Words; (2) Speaking; (3) Danger; (4) To pull down (throw down); (5) Condemning (thrown down).

Also see *Ball* and *Steps (Going Down).*

(1-2) 1 Sam. 17:40-49; <u>2 Sam. 16:13</u>; (3) 1 Sam. 18:11; (4) Jer. 1:10; (5) 2 Chron. 36:3.

Thumb: (1) Leverage; (2) Power; (3) Works; (4) Controlled by.

(1-2) <u>Judg. 1:6-7</u>; (3) <u>Exod. 29:20</u> (consecrated for service); Lev. 8:23-24; 14:14, 17, 25, 28; (4) As in, "under the thumb."

Thumbnail: (1) Miniature version of larger unfolding scene; (2) Embryonic view of the future; (3) Thumbnail sketch.

Also see *Nails (Finger).*

(1-2) Gen. 1:12; (3) See *Plan/s.*

Thunder: (1) Voice of God; (2) Judgment; (3) Power; (4) Powerful Voices.

(1) Job 37:4-5; John 12:28-30; (2) 1 Sam. 2:10; Rev. 6:1ff; (3) Job 26:14; (4) Rev. 10:4.

Thursday: (1) Five; (2) Grace or favor.

Also see *Day* and *Four* (The secular world sees Thursday as the fourth day of the week).

(1) Gen. 1:22-23; (2) Gen. 43:34; 45:11; Lev. 26:8.

Tick (noun): (1) Hidden parasite; (2) Life-sapping parasite.

Also see *Parasite.*

(1-2) Prov. 30:15a.

Tick (verb): (1) Approval of God; (2) Approval; (3) Correct; (4) Pass; (5) Right.

Also see *Mark.*

(1) Acts 2:22 (KJV); 2 Tim. 2:15; (2) Rom. 14:18; (3-4) Phil. 3:14, 17; (5) Luke 10:28.

Ticket: (1) Your ministry calling; (2); Salvation; (3) Entry authority; (4) Entry to the Promises of God (the Kingdom); (5) The Holy Spirit; (6) Something you have bought into; (7) Opening yourself up to something.

Also see *Buying* and *Queue.*

(1) Matt. 10:1; Luke 6:13; (2) Gen. 7:13; (3) Num. 14:24; (4) John 3:5; (5) 2 Cor. 1:22 (guarantee of entry); Rom. 8:16; (6-7) Prov. 18:17.

Tidal Wave: See Tide, Tsunami, and Waves.

Tide: (1) Public opinion (the pull of the world); (2) Flood of sin (high tide); (3) The Church's influence; (4) Flow of the Spirit leaving (tide going out); (5) Eve of destruction or revival (tide really out).

Also see *Flood, Moon,* and *Tsunami.*

(1) Matt. 16:14; John 7:12; As in, "the tide of public opinion"; (2) Josh. 3:15b; Isa. 59:19b; (3) 1 Cor. 11:7 & Mal. 4:2 & Eph. 5:23 (sun = Jesus, moon = Church, moon reflects the sun's glory); (4-5) Amos 8:11; Isa. 35:1.

Tie (noun): (1) Business; (2) Formal.

(1) Prov. 6:20-21; (2) As in, "black tie."

Tie (verb): (1) Secured; (2) Fastened; (3) Lead.

(1) Matt. 21:2; Mark 11:2; Luke 19:30; (2) Exod. 39:31; 1 Sam. 6:7; 2 Kings 7:10; (3) Prov. 6:21-22.

Tiger: (1) Strong evil force; (2) Satan; (3) Vicious religious spirit (white tiger).

Also see *Lion.*

(1) Mic. 3:1-3; (2) Mark 1:13; (3) Mic. 3:1-3.

Tightrope: (1) Walking a fine line; (2) In jeopardy of falling; (3) On a risky path; (4) Balance required; (5) Spiritually focused.

(1-2) Gen. 4:7; Ps. 56:13; Prov. 10:8; 11:5; (3) Num. 22:32; (4) Job 31:6; Prov. 11:1; 20:23; (5) Matt. 14:29-30.

Tiles: (1) Heart as a foundation (floor tiles); (2) Heart (shower tiles).

Also see *Stepping Stones.*

(1) Matt. 7:25; Luke 6:48; (2) Eccl. 12:6-7.

Time: (1) Life (As in, "life-time"); (2) An on-the-hour time (i.e. 6:00 A.M.) may refer to the meaning of the numbers 1 to 12. (3) Appreciate the timing of God; (4) Eve of Christ's return; (5 minutes to 12); (5) Time or part times may refer to years.

Also see individual numbers, *Before and After, Clock, Early, Late, Measure, Time Running Out, Timetable,* and *Urgency.*

(1) Gen. 18:10; Acts 17:26; James 4:14; 1 Pet. 4:2; (3) Acts 2:1; Gal. 4:4; Eph. 1:10; (4) Phil 4:5b; (5) Dan. 7:25b.

Time Running Out: (1) Endtimes; (2) Christ's return; (3) The brevity of life.

Also see *Urgency.*

(1) 1 Cor. 7:29; (2) 1 Cor. 7:29; Phil. 4:5; (3) Ps. 89:47-48.

Timetable: (1) Timing of God.

Also see *Clock, Diary (Personal), Diary (Work), Time,* and *Watch.*

(1) Esther 4:14b; Gal. 4:4; Eph. 1:10.

Tin: (1) Impurity; (2) Hypocrisy; (3) Refining.

Also see *Pewter.*

(1-2) Isa. 1:25 (KJV); Ezek. 22:18, 20; (3) Num. 31:22-23.

Tin Man: (1) Heartless man.

(1) Ezek. 11:19; Matt. 24:12.

Tire: (1) Where the rubber meets the road (where our faith is outworked); (2) The type of tires may indicate the nature of a ministry (i.e. chunky off-road tires may mean powerful, non-conventional ministry); (3) Fitting tires may be preparation for ministry; (4) Screeching tires may indicate: (a) In a hurry; (b) Powerful; (c) Immaturity; (d) Attention-seeking.

Also see *Automobile, Flat Tire, Four-Wheel-Drive, Tire (No Tread)* (directly below), and *Wheels*.

(1) Matt. 7:21; Luke 11:2b (KJV); Phil. 2:12 (obedience); (2) Ps. 18:33; (3) Eph. 6:15; (4a) Exod. 14:9; (4b) 1 Kings 18:46; (4c) Prov. 20:29; (4d) Prov. 25:27b; Jer. 9:23-24.

Tire (No Tread): (1) Unsafe ministry; (2) Worn out (spiritually tired); (3) Careless ministry.

(1) 1 Tim. 1:19-20; 2 Pet. 2:14-15; (2) Exod. 18:18 (not delegating); (3) Ps. 73:2.

Tissues: (1) Mourning or grieving; (2) Cleansing; (3) Repentance.

(1) Matt. 5:4; (2) Num. 8:7; Rev. 19:14; (3) Matt. 5:4; 2 Cor. 7:9-10.

T-Junction: (1) Decision; (2) Choice between God and the world (T-junction); (3) Lukewarm (standing at the intersection: indecision).

Also see *Crossroads* and *Road*.

(1) Josh. 24:15 & Matt. 25:33; (2) Josh 24:15; (3) Rev. 3:16.

Toad: (1) Poisonous individual.

Also see *Frog*.

(1) Rom. 3:13; James 3:8.

Toast (Bread): (1) Speaking in anger; (2) Getting angry about words; (3) If you are a regular toast eater, just see entries under Bread.

(1) 1 Sam. 17:28; Ezek. 5:13 (you're toast); (2) Judg. 9:30; Neh. 5:6; Prov. 15:1.

Toe/s: (1) The walk of the person; (2) Smallest division of a kingdom/body/church; (3) Spiritual offspring (smallest members); (4) Six toes symbolizes the ultimate of humanity's dominion; (6) Straining to reach or see (tippy-toes); (7) Secretly and quietly (tip-toe); (8) Dominant nation or superpower (big toe); (9) Leader or king; (10) Drive; (11) New spiritual vitality (running on toes).

Also see *Feet, Shoe,* and *Toe/s (Big Toe).*

(1) Exod. 29:20; Lev. 8:23; 14:14; (2) Dan. 2:41; (3) 1 Cor. 12:23-26; (4) 2 Sam. 21:20; (6) Luke 19:3; (7) 2 Tim. 3:6; Jude 1:4; (8-9) Dan. 2:41; (10) Judg. 1:6-7; (11) 1 Kings 18:46.

Toe/s (Big Toe): (1) Power and dominion; (2) Drive and influence; (3) Leverage; (4) Leadership.

Also see *Toes* and *Thumb.*

(1-3) Judg. 1:6-7.

Toilet: (1) Spiritual cleansing or detoxing; (2) Deliverance; (3) Confession and repentance; (4) Personal repentance; (5) Secret lust or sin; (6) Secret issues; (7) Dealing with sin apart from sexual immorality (outside toilet); (8) Heart (toilet cistern).

Also see *Bathroom* and *Dung.*

(1) Ps. 51:2; Mic. 7:19; Heb. 9:14; 1 John 1:7b; (2) Jer. 4:14; Ezek. 37:23; Tit. 3:5; (3) 1 John 1:9; (4) Ps. 22:14; (5-6) 2 Sam. 12:12; Ps. 64:4; Jer. 23:24; John 7:4; Eph. 5:12; (7) 1 Cor. 6:18; (8) Matt. 23:25, 27.

Toilet Paper: (1) Spiritual cleansing; (2) Putting off misdeeds of the body.

(1) Ps. 51:2; 1 John 1:9; (2) Rom. 8:13.

Tomorrow: (1) Future.

(1) James 4:14.

Tongue: (1) Words; (2) Spiritual language; (3) Confession; (4) Potential for good or evil (death and life); (5) Fire; (6) International languages; (7) Pain (gnawing the tongue); (8) Lying; (9) Flattery; (10) Justified/righteous (silver); (11) Perverse/crooked (cut out); (12) Health; (13) Wise; (14) Tree of life; (15) Wicked; (16) Need for control; (17) Soft; (18) Anger; (19) Deceit.

Also see *Lips, Mouth, Teeth,* and *Throat.*

(1) Rom. 3:13; 14:11; (2) 1 Cor. 12:10; 13:1; 14:2, 4, 14; (3) Phil. 2:11; (4) Prov. 18:21; James 3:5, 10; (5) James 3:6; (6) Rev. 5:9; 7:9; 9:11; 10:11; (7) Rev. 16:10; (8) Prov. 6:17; 12:19; 21:6; 26:28; (9) Prov. 6:24; 28:23; (10) Prov. 10:20; (11) Prov. 10:31; 17:20; (12) Prov. 12:18; (13) Prov. 15:2; (14) Prov. 15:4; (15) Prov. 17:4; (16) Prov. 21:23; (17) Prov. 25:15; (18) Prov. 25:23; (19) Rom. 3:13.

Tool/s: (1) Gifts of the Spirit; (2) Works of people; (3) Work of the flesh; (4) A work in progress; (5) Work needed; (6) Repairing; (7) Work of God (without tools); (8) Work of self-righteousness; (9) Ministry gift.

(1) 1 Cor. 12:11; (2-3) Exod. 20:25; Deut. 27:5; 1 Kings 6:7; Isa. 44:12; (3) Exod. 32:3-4 (cf. Gal. 5:19-20); (4) Neh. 4:17; (5) Jer. 18:3-4; 48:11; 2 Tim. 2:19-21; (6) 2 Kings 12:12; 2 Chron. 24:4, 12; (7) Exod. 20:25; Deut. 27:5; Dan. 2:34, 45; (8) Exod. 20:25; (cf. Eph. 2:8-9); (9) Eph. 4:11-12.

Tool Box: (1) Something that can be used against you; (2) Problem solver; (3) Maintenance.

(1) Mark 12:13; Luke 20:20-26; (2) Ruth 4:6; (3) 1 Chron. 26:27; Ps. 16:5.

Toothache: (1) Hurting believer; (2) Devouring words; (3) Painful messenger.

Also see *Teeth*.

(1) Song. 4:2; 6:6; (tooth = sheep); (2) Prov. 30:14; (3) Prov. 10:26.

Toothbrush: (1) The Word of God; (2) Pride of appearance (self-image); (3) Self-enhancement; (4) Tainted Bible (dirty toothbrush); (5) Ministry (as the vehicle delivering God's Word); (6) The means of delivering God's Word (dream, prophecy, etc).

Also see *Comb* and *Teeth*.

(1) Song. 4:2; 6:6 (tooth = sheep = believers); (cf. Ps. 119:9); John 15:3; Eph. 5:26; (That which cleans believers is the Word of God); (2-3) 2 Sam. 14:25-26; (4) 2 Cor. 2:17 (KJV); 2 Pet. 2:3 (KJV); (5-6) Ps. 119:9; John 15:3; Eph. 5:26.

Tooth Decay: (1) Sin; (2) Sinful words.

Also see *Teeth* and *Toothbrush*.

(1) Ps. 3:7; (2) Prov. 30:14.

Toothpaste: (1) The blood of Jesus; (1) The Word of God.

Also see *Teeth* and *Toothbrush*.

(1) 1 John 1:7; (2) Ps. 119:9; John 15:3.

Torch: (1) The Holy Spirit; (2) The human spirit; (3) The Word of God; (4) The Gospel of Christ (the glory of God); (5) A guide (pointing the way); (6) Deliverance and guidance; (7) Humanity's light (self-sufficiency); (8) Exposing something hidden (shining light onto something)

Also see *Beacon, Lampstand, Light, Lighthouse,* and *Spotlight.*

(1) Judg. 7:20 (cf. 2 Cor. 4:7); Matt. 25:3-4; (2) Job 18:5; Ps. 18:28; <u>Prov. 20:27</u>; (3) <u>Ps.119:105</u>; (4) 2 Cor. 4:4, 6; (5) Rom. 2:19-20; (6) John 5:35; Acts 12:7; (7) Isa. 50:11; (8) Job 12:22; 28:11; 33:30.

Tornado: (1) The devil; (2) Judgment against sin; (3) Unstoppable; (4) Trials and calamity; (5) Spirit of death.

Also see *Storm, Dust Storm, Whirlpool, Whirlwind,* and *Wind.*

(1) John 10:10; (2) <u>Jer. 30:23</u>; Zech. 9:14; (3) Dan. 11:40; (4) Acts 27:4; (5) Ps. 103:15-16; Prov. 10:25; Zech. 7:14.

Torpedo: See Bomb, Propeller, and Missile.

Tortoise: (1) Sluggish church; (2) Traditional religion; (3) Counterfeit gospel (false rock).

Also see *Turtle.*

(1-2) <u>Rev. 3:1-2</u>; (3) Gal. 1:6-7.

Touchdown: See Goal, Hole in One, and Winning.

Tour Guide: (1) Anointed international ministry (international ministry led by the Spirit); (2) Angel.

Also see *Tourist.*

(1) <u>Acts 16:6-9</u>; (2) Exod. 23:23; Zech. 1:9; Luke 1:19.

Tourist and Tourist Bus: (1) Searching from church to church; (2) Leisurely spiritual journey; (3) Looking for signs; (4) Ineffective mission; (5) Pleasure-seeker; (6) Learning the ropes; (7) Sight-seeing, but really going nowhere (non-productive); (8) Someone just passing through; (9) Sojourner.

Also see *Bus* and *Tour Guide.*

(1) 2 Kings 2:1-5; (2) Rev. 3:16; (3) Matt. 12:39; (4) Acts 13:13; (5) <u>James 4:3</u>; (6) Luke 8:1; (7) John 3:3, 5; (8) John 6:66; (9) Gen. 12:10; Acts 7:6.

Towel: (1) Servant ministry; (2) Ministry; (3) Cleansing (as in, cleaning the water off after a shower); (4) Drying; (5) Cover; (6) Giving up.

(1-5) <u>John 13:4-5</u>-16; Acts 3:19; (6) As in, "throwing in the towel."

Tower: (1) People's attempts to make a name for themselves; (2) Pride; (3) Christ; (4) The Church/Kingdom of God; (5) Salvation; (6) Refuge; (7) Security/

shelter/defense; (8) Watchtower (a prophet's place of prayer); (9) Place of the watchman (prophet); (10) Judgment (tower falling); (11) Spiritually strong person; (12) Jerusalem (Zion).

Also see *Brick, Tall,* and *Tornado.*

(1) Gen. 11:4; (2) Ezek. 30:6 (KJV); Isa. 3:16a; (3) Ps. 18:2; 144:1-2; Prov. 18:10; Isa. 5:2; (4) Luke 14:26-33; (5) 2 Sam. 22:51; Ps. 18:2; (6) 2 Sam. 22:3; (7) Judg. 8:9, 17; 9:46, 49, 51-53; 2 Chron. 14:7; 26:9-10, 15; Ps. 61:3; (8) 2 Kings 5:24-26; Hab. 2:1; (9) 2 Kings 17:9; 18:8; 2 Chron. 20:24; (10) Isa. 30:25; Luke 13:4; (11) Jer. 6:27; (12) Mic. 4:8; Matt. 21:33; Mark 12:1.

Towing (Being Towed): (1) Not in the main vehicle; (2) Along for the ride; (3) The one without strength; (4) Being brought into line.

Towing (Doing the Towing): (5) Helping a broken ministry; (6) The powerhouse; (7) The one with strength; (8) Showing the way.

Also see *Pulling, Tow Truck,* and *Trailer (Goods).*

(1-4) 1 Kings 19:19; (5) Gal. 6:2; (6-8) Ps. 23:1-2; Isa. 40:11.

Town: See City.

Tow Truck: (1) Five-fold ministry gift; (2) Strong ministry helping others; (3) Apostolic ministry.

(1) Eph. 4: 11-12; (2) Acts 18:26; (3) Acts 5:12; 2 Cor. 12:12.

Toxic Vapors: (1) Demonic strongholds.

Also see *Smoke.*

(1) Rev. 9:2-3.

Toys: (1) Playing games; (2) Childishness; (3) Childlikeness; (4) Spoilt (many toys); (5) Toying with; (6) Idolatry; (7) Immature ministry (toy car).

(1) Matt. 15:8; (2) 1 Cor. 13:11; (3) Matt. 18:2-4; (4) Ps. 78:29; Isa. 3:16-23; (5) Judg. 16:6-7, 10-11, 13, 15; (6) Exod. 32:6; 1 Cor. 10:7; (7) Matt. 9:33; Acts 13:13.

Tracksuit Pants: (1) Faith step (choosing track pants); (2) Preparing for the race of faith; (3) Call to walk by faith; (4) Being clothed with strength; (5) Youth ministry or fitness industry.

(1) Rom. 13:14; (2-3) 2 Cor. 5:7; Heb. 12:1; (4) Ps. 147:10; (5) 1 John 2:14.

Tractor: (1) Powerful; (2) Strength (parallels the ox as a strong servant); (3) Powerful harvest multiplier (plows in hope); (4) Powerful ministry/minister; (5) Earning potential; (6) Preparing the harvest; (7) Working the harvest; (8) Business interests/excuses; (9) Idol; (10) Business sowing into the Kingdom; (11) Breaking new ground.

(1-2) Ps. 144:14; Prov. 14:4; (3) 1 Cor. 9:9-10; (4) 1 Cor. 9:9; 1 Tim. 5:17-18; (5) Job 24:3 & Deut. 24:6; (The ox is someone's potential to earn or sustain themselves); (6) 1 Kings 19:19; (7) Ruth 2:3; (8) Luke 14:19; John 2:14; (9) Ps. 106:19-20; (10) 1 Kings 10:2; 1 Sam. 25:18; Acts 16:14-15; (11) Hos. 10:12.

Tradesman: See Workman.

Traffic: (1) Different walks of life (lanes of traffic); (2) Different ministries being busy; (3) Playing leap-frog in traffic means playing with life and death. This could point to having sexual relations without understanding the consequences.

Also see *Automobile, Bus,* and *Truck.*

(1) Prov. 14:12; Matt. 7:13-14; (2) Dan. 12:4; Eph. 4:11; 1 Cor. 12:28; (3) Deut. 30:15-16, 19.

Traffic Lights: (1) Waiting on God; (2) Guidance; (3) Timing of God; (4) Danger/stop (red light); (5) Warning (amber light); (6) Go into the world and preach the Gospel (green light).

(1) Ps. 27:14 & John 8:12; (2) Exod. 13:21b; Neh. 9:19b; Ps. 43:3; (3) Gal. 4:4; (4) Rev. 6:4; (5-6) See *Amber* and *Green.*

Trail Bike: (1) Independent ministry; (2) Pioneering spirit.

Also see *Motorcycle.*

(1-2) Ps. 18:33; Hab. 3:19.

Trailer (Boat): (1) Dependence on another ministry (not free to minister in your own right).

(1) Acts 15:40.

Trailer (Caravan): (1) Temporary home; (2) Itinerant ministry; (3) Mobile; (4) Holiday; (5) Contract work.

(1) 2 Cor. 5:1; 2 Pet. 1:14; (2-3) Gen. 13:18; Heb. 11:9.

Trailer: (Goods): (1) Burden (extra baggage you are carrying); (2) Something/one in tow; (3) Followers; (4) May represent a family, congregation, or ministry group; (5) Without leadership (no auto pulling the trailer); (6) Under the influence of the vehicle doing the towing.

(1) Isa. 46:1; Matt. 11:28; (2) See *Towing;* (3-4) Matt. 8:19, 23; 10:38; (5) Matt. 9:36b; 1 Pet. 2:25; (6) 2 Pet. 2:19.

Train: (1) Ministry with clout; (2) Large (continuous) ministry; (3) Vehicle to destiny; (4) The Church; (5) Vehicle of the flesh (ministry with an agenda. i.e. "rail-roading"); (6) Lucrative endeavor or money; (7) Nothing gets in its way; (8) Trying to stop the course of a train can be dangerous.

Also see *Freight, Railway Station, Railroad Platform, Railroad Tracks,* and *Train (Ride-on Model).*

(1) Acts 5:12; (2) Acts 2:42; (3) Jer. 29:11; (4) Acts 2:42; (5) John 3:8; (6) As in, "gravy train"; (7-8) 1 Kings 19:1-3.

Train (Ride-on Model): (1) Church playing games; (2) Not spiritually effective (Going around in circles); (3) Taking people for a ride; (4) Spiritually immature; (5) Small church.

Also see *Train.*

(1-2) Rev. 3:1; (3) Acts 5:37; (4) 1 Cor. 13:11; (5) Acts 2:46.

Train (Freight): See Freight.

Train (Off the Rails): (1) (any of the above) derailed; (2) Individual or church not on track for God's destiny.

(1) Job 12:24; Ps. 107:40; (2) Isa. 53:6.

Train Running Without Rails: (1) Holy Spirit led ministry.

(1) John 3:8.

Trample/d: (1) Taking authority over the enemy; (2) Sharing revelation with unbelievers; (3) Anger.

(1) Ps. 91:13; (cf. Luke 10:19); (2) Matt. 7:6; (3) Isa. 63:3.

Trampoline: (1) In the Spirit; (2) Launching in the Spirit.

(1-2) Isa. 40:31.

Transmission: (1) Spirit (good or evil).

(1) <u>Mark 1:12</u>; Luke 8:29; (Acts 27:15, 17; cf. John 3:8).

Transparent (Crystal): (1) River of life (water); (2) Glory of God (light); (3) Spirit; (4) Sea of glass before the throne; (5) Honest and open (revealing one's heart).

(1) <u>Rev. 22:1</u>; (2) Rev. 21:11; (3) Ezek. 1:22; (4) Rev. 4:6; (5) John 1:47.

Transparent: (1) The revealing of one's heart.

(1) John 1:47; Acts 1:24.

Trap: (1) Warning of danger; (2) Deceit and deception; (3) Sudden destruction; (4) Stronghold; (5) Sign of backsliding; (6) Sin.

Also see *Snare.*

(1) 2 Kings 6:9; 2 Cor. 2:11; 2 Tim. 2:26; (2) <u>Jer. 5:26-27</u>; (3) Eccl. 9:12; (4) Prov. 11:6, 12:13; (5) Josh. 23:13; (6) Prov. 5:22.

Trash: See Garbage, Garbage Truck, Rubbish, and Rubbish Bag/Bin.

Treasure: (1) Heart; (2) The Holy Spirit; (3) God's people; (4) God's (Heaven's) provision or storehouse; (5) Godly wisdom, understanding and knowledge; (6) Spiritual gifts; (7) Suffering reproach for Christ; (8) Earthly wealth; (9) Foolishness (bragging or showing all your treasure); (10) Intricate secrets; (11) May indicate a righteous or wise person; (12) May come with trouble; (13) Beware gaining it by lying; (14) Fear of the Lord; (15) Wickedness.

Also see *Precious Stones.*

(1) <u>Matt. 6:21</u>; Luke 2:19; (2) (1 Cor. 2:4-5 & 2 Cor. 4:7); (3) Exod. 19:5; Ps. 135:4; (4) <u>Deut. 28:12a</u>; Ps. 135:7; Isa. 45:3; Jer. 10:13; (5) Prov. 2:3-5; 8:21; Col. 2:3; (6) Prov. 8:10-11; 2:3-4; 20:15; 24:4; (cf. 1 Cor. 12:8); (7) Heb. 11:25-26; (8) James 5:3; (9) 2 Kings 20:15-18; (10) Job 38:22; (11) Prov. 15:6; 21:20; (12) Prov. 15:16; (13) Prov. 21:6; (14) Isa. 33:6b; (15) Prov. 10:2; Mic. 6:10.

Tree: (1) Person; (2) Righteous believer; (3) Jesus Christ; (4) Country or nation; (5) The Cross; (6) Life; (7) The Kingdom; (8) Family; (9) Company (of people); (10) If planted by a stream, it means prosperity; (11) Hanging on a tree means judgment or cursed; (12) Beside still waters means peace/rest; (13) Under a green tree can mean idolatry or spiritual adultery; (14) Cursed (stuck in a tree);

(15) Believer choked by cares of world/riches (tree of thorns); (16) People trusting in people, not in God (stunted tree).

Also see *Big Tree, Bush, Evergreen, Thorns,* and individual tree names.

(1-2) Ps. 1:3; Isa. 7:2; 61:3; Jer. 17:8; (3) See *Big Tree;* (4) 1 Kings 4:33; Ps. 29:5; (5) 1 Pet. 2:24; Acts 5:30; 10:39; Gal. 3:13; (6) Rev. 2:7; 22:2, 14; (7) Luke 13:18-19; (8) John 15:5 (cf. John 1:12); Rom. 11:17; As in, "family tree"; (9) Isa. 7:2; 24:13; 65:22; (10) Num. 24:6; Ps. 1:3; (11) Esther 2:23; Gal. 3:13; (12) Ps. 23:2; (13) Jer. 3:6; (14) Gal. 3:13; (15) Matt. 13:22; (16) Jer. 17:5-6.

Tree (Big Tree): (1) Jesus; (2) Church or leader; (3) Corporation; (4) Business or country leader; (5) Kingdom of God; (6) Longevity; (7) Pride and arrogance (tall tree); (8) Flourishing prosperity (tall tree); (9) Believer with strong foundation.

Also see *Oak* and *Tree.*

(1) Isa. 11:1; Jer. 23:5; 33:15-16; (2) Ps. 37:35; Luke 13:18-19; (3) As in, a hierarchy; (4) Dan. 4:10-11, 20-22; (5) Matt. 13:31-32; (6) Gen. 21:33; (7) Ezek. 31:3-10; (8) Ps. 92:12; (9) Isa. 61:3 (NIV).

Tree House: (1) Cursed individual; (2) You in Christ; (3) You in the Kingdom.

Also see *House* and *Tree.*

(1) Gal. 3:13; (2) Eph. 1:1; (3) Matt. 12:28; 13:31-32.

Tree Uprooted/Cut Down: (1) Warning of judgment; (2) Collapse of a ministry; (3) Not ordained of God; (4) Death or destruction.

(1) Dan. 4:14-15, 24-26; Luke 13:6-9; Matt. 3:10; (2) Dan. 4:14-15; (3) Matt. 15:13; (4) Luke 13:6-9.

Trellis: (1) Supportive framework; (2) The Word of God; (3) God.

Also see *Scaffold.*

(1) John 15:5 & 1 Thess. 5:14; (2) Job 4:4; Ps. 119:28; (3) Isa. 40:31 (the word *wait* can mean "to entwine").

Trench: (1) Heart; (2) Depression; (3) Path for the Holy Spirit; (4) Pathway of the mind (soul-tie [godly or ungodly]).

Also see *Gutter/s, Pipe, Plowing,* and *Plumber.*

(1) Matt. 13:19; Mark 4:15; (cf. Gen. 2:7 & 2 Cor. 4:7); (2) Ps. 42:5; (3) John 1:33; Acts 9:17; (4) Ps. 119:59; Isa. 55:7.

Trench Coat: (1) Someone stuck in a rut; (2) Stronghold (dug in); (3) Stronghold of depression.

Also see *Coat*.

(1) Ps. 40:2; 69:2; (2) 2 Chron. 11:11a; Ps. 89:40; 2 Cor. 10:4-5; (3) Ps. 43:5; Gal. 5:1.

Triangle: (1) Divine order; (2) Godhead; (3) Threesome.

(1-3) Matt. 28:19; 1 John 5:7-8.

Tribal: See Indigenous.

Trick: (1) Deception; (2) Mock or fool; (3) Self-glory (doing tricks to draw attention to oneself); (4) Moving in the gifts of the Holy Spirit; (5) Test; (6) Counterfeit signs and wonders.

(1) Prov. 10:23; 14:8b; Gal. 3:1; (2) Gal. 6:7-8; (3) Prov. 25:27b; 27:2; (4) Acts 10:44-45; Heb. 2:4; (5) Mark 12:13; (6) Exod. 7:11-12; Acts 8:9.

Trimming: (1) Short-cutting; (2) Fine-tuning; (3) Beautifying; (4) Cutting away that which is superfluous; (5) Trimming or not trimming may be a sign of allegiance, an oath, or respect; (6) Disciplining (as in pruning).

Also see *Pruning*.

(1, 3) Jer. 2:33 (KJV); (2) Matt. 25:7; (4) Acts 27:32; (5) 2 Sam. 19:24; (6) John 15:2.

Trip (noun): See Cruise Ship, Holiday, Suitcase, and Tourist.

Trip (verb): (1) Temptation (cause to sin).

Also see *Falling* and *Losing Footing*.

(1) Gen. 3:4-5; Matt. 4:6.

Tripod: (1) Stable; (2) God.

(1) Eccl. 4:12; (2) Matt. 28:19.

Trophy: (1) Victory; (2) Pride; (3) Self-glory; (4) The empty tomb (victory in Christ); (5) Heavenly rewards.

(1) 1 Sam. 17:54; (2) 1 Sam. 15:8, 17; Prov. 20:29; (3) Prov. 25:27; Jer. 9:23-24; Matt. 6:2; Rom. 1:23; 1 Cor. 3:21a; 2 Cor. 12:6; 1 Thess. 2:6a; 1 Pet. 1:24a; (4) 1 Cor. 15:57; (5) Luke 6:23.

Trousers: See Clothing.

Truck/Semi: (1) Powerful Ministry; (2) Big Ministry; (3) Deliverance ministry; (4) Leadership; (5) Business (freight truck); (6) Intimidation (relating to size: truck vs. car).

Also see *Automobile, Bulldozer, Earthmover,* and *Road Grader.*

(1) 1 Kings 10:2; 1 Sam. 14:6, 22; Acts 4:33; 6:8; (2) 2 Cor. 11:28; (3) Zech. 3:9b; As in, the removal of sin and iniquity; (4) Acts 13:43; (5) 1 Kings 10:15; (6) 1 Sam. 17:4-11; Isa. 37:10-11.

Trumpet: (1) Warning or alarm; (2) Gathering; (3) Gathering the elect; (4) Rapturous gathering; (5) Voice of God/Word of God; (6) Announcement/ self-glory/pronouncing own goodness; (7) Judgment; (8) Battle signal; (9) Memorial; (10) Jubilee; (11) Rejoicing.

Also see *Shofar* and *Thunder.*

(1) Num. 10:9; Jer. 4:19b; Amos 3:6; (2) Exod. 20:18-20; (3) Matt. 24:31; (4) 1 Cor. 15:52; 1 Thess. 4:16; (5) Exod. 19:16, 19; 1 Cor. 14:8; Rev. 1:10; 4:1; (6) Matt. 6:2; (7) Josh. 6:4; Rev. 8:2; (8) Num. 10:9; 31:6; 1 Cor. 14:8; (9) Lev. 23:24; (10) Lev. 25:9; (11) Ps. 81:3.

Tsunami: (1) Upheaval; (2) Destruction/judgment; (3) Carried away; (4) Holy Spirit outpouring/revival.

Also see *Wave.*

(1-3) Isa. 28:2-3; 59:19b; (4) Isa 59:19; Acts 2:17.

Tuesday: (1) Three; (2) Double Blessing; (3) Resurrection.

Also see *Day* and *Two* (The secular world sees Tuesday as the second day of the week).

(1-2) Gen. 1: 9-13 (Note v. 10, 12); (3) Matt. 20:19.

Tumor: (1) Judgment; (2) Corruption; (3) Self-destructive thoughts/words (brain tumor); (4) Literal tumor.

Also see *Cancer.*

(1) 1 Sam. 5:6; (2-3) 2 Cor. 10:5; 2 Tim. 2:16-17.

Tunnel: (1) Passage through; (2) Transition; (3) Way in or way out; (4) Entrance to your heart; (5) Way to the light (as in, "light at the end of the tunnel"); (6) What is going on inside of you; (7) Throat; (8) Going through dark times; (9) Uncertainty.

Also see *Cave.*

(1) 2 Sam. 5:8 (NKJV); (2) Exod. 14:22; Num. 22:24; (3-4) 2 Sam. 5:8; Ezek. 8:8; (5) Ps. 56:13; <u>Isa. 9:2</u>; Matt. 4:16; (6) 1 Pet. 3:4; (7) <u>Ps. 5:9</u>; (8-9) Matt. 4:16; Mark 15:33.

Turbulent: (1) Unsettling; (2) Rough; (3) Test or trial.

(1-2) Isa. 57:20; Matt. 14:25-26; (3) Josh. 3:15b; <u>Mark 6:48</u>.

Turkey: (1) Thanksgiving; (2) Christmas; (3) Contemptuously rich; (4) Foolish; (5) Pleasure-seeker; (6) Preparation for slaughter; (7) Waxen fat and forsaking God.

(1) <u>Ps. 107:22</u>; 116:17; (2) Esther 5:4; (3) Prov. 30:8-9; Luke 12:19-20; 16:19 (cf. v. 21) (4) Eccl. 9:12; (5) <u>James 5:5</u> (being fattened); (6) James 5:5; Jer. 12:3; (7) Deut. 32:15; Prov. 27:7.

Turning: (1) Altered course or change (of direction); (2) Denying or turning away; (3) Attacking you; (4) Repentance; (5) Moving into the Spirit; (6) Moving into the flesh (natural); (7) Coming to God; (8) To change the heart attitude; (9) To acknowledge or make your focus (turning to someone); (10) Unexpected opportunity (as in turning for the better); (11) Changing from sorrow to joy or vice versa; (12) Turning for the worse.

Also see *Corner, Dancing,* and *U-Turn.*

(1) <u>Matt. 2:22b</u>; Luke 1:17; Acts 13:46; (2) <u>Matt. 5:42</u>; (3) Matt. 7:6; (4) Luke 17:4; Acts 3:26; (5) Matt. 9:22; 16:23; Luke 2:45; 7:9; 9:55; 23:28; John 1:38; <u>16:20</u>; 20:16; (6) John 21:20-21; (7) <u>Luke 1:16</u>; 17:15; Acts 11:21; (8) Luke 1:17; Acts 7:39; 13:8; (9) Luke 7:44; (10) Luke 21:12-13; (11) John 16:20; Acts 2:20; (12) 1 Kings 17:18.

Turnstile: (1) Entry point; (2) Restricted entry (the narrow way).

(1) Acts 13:2; (2) Matt. 7:13.

Turtle: (1) Religious spirit (hardened hearts [shell]); (2) Traditional church (old covering); (3) Primarily concerned about protection/security; (4) Shy (not evangelistic); (5) Snake-like head (poisonous thinking); (6) Ducking for cover; (7) Believer; (8) Slow to change; (9) Withdrawn.

Also see *Shells* and *Tortoise.*

(1) Matt. 23:4; John 12:37-40; (2) <u>Matt. 15:1-3</u>; Mark 7:5; (3) 1 Thess. 5:3; (4) Joel 2:10 (cf. Gen. 15:5); (5) Rom. 3:13; (6) Matt. 26:56; Mark 14:50; (7) Isa. 28:16; (8) Jer. 48:11; (9) Gal. 2:12.

Tuxedo: (1) Special occasion; (2) Position of honor; (3) Ready for marriage supper; (4) Cleansed from sin.

(1) Gen. 41:14; (2) Luke 15:22; (3) Matt. 22:11-12; Rev. 19:9; (4) Zech. 3:4.

Tweezers: (1) Sensitivity; (2) Accuracy; (3) Carefully.

(1) 2 Sam. 18:5; (2) Matt. 7:5; (3) Luke 10:34; 1 Cor. 12:25.

Twelve: (1) Perfect government or rule; (2) Divine organization; (3) Apostolic fullness; (4) Literally 12.

(1-2) Gen. 49:28; Exod. 28:21 (12 sons of Jacob); Exod. 24:4 (12 pillars); Josh. 4:3, 9 (12 stones); Josh. 3:12-13 (12 priests bearing the ark); Job 38:32 (Sun and moon made to rule the day and night. To do this they pass through the 12 signs of the Zodiac. Hebrew: *Mazzaroth* completing 360 degrees); Luke 6:13 (12 apostles); John 11:9 (12 hours in a day); 12 months in a year; Rev. 21:10-21 (New Jerusalem (perfection of rule) 12 gates, 12 pearls, 12 angels, 12 foundations, 12 precious stones, 12 fruits); Exod. 15:27 (12 wells at Elim); (3) Exod. 24:4; Matt. 10:2-5; 19:28.

Twenty: (1) Expectancy; (2) Waiting; (3) Accountability; (4) Responsibility; (5) Service; (6) Literally 20.

(1-2) Gen. 31:38, 41; (Jacob waited 20 years to get his inheritance); Judg. 15:20; 16:31; (Israel waited for deliverance through Samson); 1 Sam. 7:2; (The Ark waited 20 years at Kirjath-jearim); 20 dreams recorded in Scripture; (3-5) Exod. 30:14; (Israel numbered from age 20 years and upward); Num. 1:3, 18-24; (Warfare at 20 years); 1 Chron. 23:24, 27; (Levites served from age 20 years).

Twenty-One: (1) The product of 3 x 7, it therefore means fullness or the completion [3] of spiritual perfection [7]; (2) Expecting God (20 + 1); (3) Serving God (20 + 1).

(1) Exod. 12:18; (2-3) Dan. 10:13; Hag. 2:1.

Twenty-Two: Carries the meaning of double eleven. (1) Disorganization; (2) Disintegration; (especially in regard to the Word of God); (3) Expecting testimony (20 + 2); (4) Expecting separation or division (20 + 2).

(1-2) 1 Kings 14:20; 1 Kings 16:29.

Twenty-Four: (1) Governmental perfection.

(1) Josh. 4:2-9, 20; 1 Kings 19:19; Rev. 4:4.

Twenty-Five: (1) Being brought to account by the grace of God; (2) Expecting grace or mercy (20+5).

(1-2) See *Twenty* and *Five.*

Twenty-Six: (1) Being brought to account because of the flesh.

(1) See *Twenty* and *Six.*

Twenty-Eight: (1) Awaiting or expecting a new beginning.

(1) See *Twenty* and *Eight.*

Twig: (1) Young and tender Christian; (2) The position of a twig on a plant may indicate its standing (i.e. high twig is royalty/leadership).

(1) Ezek. 17:4, 22.

Twins: (1) Contention; (2) Double-mindedness; (3) Unity/union; (4) Symmetry; (5) Double portion; (6) Double blessing; (7) A repeat experience.

The sex of the twins is important to their interpretation.

Also see *Baby, Boy, Girl,* and *Two.*

(1-2) Gen. 25:24, 27-28; Gen. 38:27 (the product of contention and different intent); (3-4) Song. 4:2, 5; 6:6; (5) Dan. 1:13; (6) Prov. 20:7; (1) Gen. 12:13 & 20:2; Ps. 85:8.

Twister: See Tornado.

Two: (1) Witness; (2) Testimony; (3) Division or separation; (4) Difference; (5) Association or agreement; (6) Reward: multiplication (7) Support; (8) Warmth; (9) Doubt (double-mindedness); (10) Death (precedes 3 [resurrection]); (11) Second heaven (spiritual realm); (12) Repeated situation.

Also see *Twins.*

(1) Matt. 18:16; (2) John 8:17; (3) Gen. 1:6-8; (4) Gen. 13:6-7; Exod. 8:23; Matt. 24:40-41; (5) Amos 3:3; (6) Eccl. 4:9; (7) Eccl. 4:10, 12; (8) Eccl. 4:11; (9) Matt. 14:30-31; 21:21; Mark 11:23; James 1:8; 4:8; (10) Gen. 1:6-8 (no blessing); (11) Eph. 6:12 (cf. 2 Cor. 12:2); (12) Mark 14:72.

Two Hundred: (1) Insufficient or insufficiency; (2) Double blessing/harvest (hundredfold x 2).

Also see *Hundred.*

(1) Josh. 7:21; (cf. Ps. 49:7-9; Mark 8:36-37) (insufficiency of money); Judg. 17:4-6; (insufficiency of religion); 2 Sam. 14:26; 18:9 (insufficiency of beauty); John 6:7 (KJV); (2) Matt. 13:23.

Tyre: See Tire.

UFO: (1) Spiritual principality; (2) Deceiving spirits; (3) Counterfeit portals. Also see *Alien* and *Spaceship.*
(1) Eph. 6:12; (2) Gal. 1:8; (3) 2 Cor. 11:3.

Ugly: (1) Ungodliness; (2) Sin; (3) Without the Spirit (no life). Also see *Beautiful.*
(1) 1 Sam. 16:13; (2) Isa. 64:6; (3) Gen. 41:3.

Umbilical Cord: (1) Soul-tie.
(1) Gen. 44:30.

Umbrella: (1) Covering; (2) Protection; (3) Authority structure; (4) Shield.
(1-2) Gen. 19:8b; Jon. 4:6; (3) Matt. 8:9; (4) Eph. 6:16.

Umpire: (1) God; (2) Authority.
(1) 1 Cor. 5:13; (2) Exod. 2:14; Deut. 21:2; 1 Chron. 17:10.

Uncertainty: (1) Double-mindedness; (2) Doubt (not operating in faith); (3) A call to draw near to God and humble the heart; (4) May indicate a person is avoiding the question; (5) Inner battle between flesh and spirit; (6) Awaiting confirmation or more revelation; (7) Time to look to God not circumstance.
(1-2) James 1:6-8; (3) James 4:8; (4) John 9:25; (5) Rom. 6:16; (6) Gen. 24:21; (7) Gen. 27:21; 1 Sam. 17:10-11.

Uncle: (1) Married Christian brother; (2) Actual uncle; (3) A relative who takes advantage of you; (4) An uncle could speak about his character, name, position, or profession.
(1-3) Gen. 28:2 & 29:25.

Uncooked: (1) Not ready for consumption; (2) Raw.
(1-2) Exod. 12:9; Acts 10:10; Heb. 5:12-14.

Under: (1) Inferior position; (2) In subjection to; (3) Influenced by; (4) Hidden; (5) In the shade; (6) In the shadow of; (7) Idolatry (green tree); (8) Spiritual adultery; (9) Protection and safety; (10) Living safely/prosperously; (11) Annoyance (under the skin); (12) Authority structure.

Also see *Above and Below*.

(1) Deut. 28:13; (2) 2 Sam. 12:31; (3) Luke 6:40; (4) Judg. 3:16; (5) Song. 2:3; (6) Ps. 91:1; (7) Deut. 12:2; (8) Jer. 2:20; 3:6, 13; (8) Ps. 91:1-4; (9) 1 Kings 4:25; Mic. 4:4; Zech. 3:10; (10) Neh. 4:1; Esther 5:9; (11) Matt. 8:9.

Underarm: See Body Odor and Hairy.

Underground: (1) Undercover (under authority); (2) Secretive or hidden; (3) Inside the heart; (4) Buried; (5) No hope (trapped underground).

Also see *Burying, Cave, Tunnel,* and *Under*.

(1) Exod. 33:22; Matt. 8:9; (2) Josh. 10:16; 1 Kings 18:13; (3) Song. 2:14; (4) Gen. 23:19; (5) Josh. 10:18.

Under the Hood: See Auto Engine and Engine.

Undertow: (1) Undercurrent; (2) Dissension; (3) Hidden pull (on hearts); (4) Lose position (pull down); (5) Destruction (pull down); (6) Division; (7) Sedition.

(1, 3) 2 Sam. 15:4-6; (2) Acts 23:10; (4) Isa. 22:19; Jer. 1:10; (5) Jer. 18:7; (6) Acts 13:8; (7) Num. 12:1-2; Gal. 5:19-20.

Underwater: (1) Death of the flesh; (2) Baptism; (3) Death or dead; (4) Cleaning the conscience; (5) Overwhelmed; (6) Going under (opposite of "keeping my head above water"); (7) In the Deep; (8) In the Spirit; (9) Sunk; (10) Not operating in faith.

Also see *Deep, Drowning,* and *Water*.

(1) Gen. 6:17; 2 Pet. 3:6; (2) Acts 8:38-39; 1 Cor. 10:1-2; (3) Job 26:5 (KJV); Rom. 6:3; (4) 1 Pet. 3:21; (5-6) Ps. 61:2; 77:3; 124:4; 142:3; 143:4; (7) Ps. 42:7; (8) Ezek. 47:5; (9) Exod. 15:5; Ps. 69:14; Jon. 2:3; (10) Matt. 14:30.

Underwear: (1) Spiritually vulnerable; (2) Coming to or from nakedness; (3) Not ready (ill-dressed); (4) Revealing someone's true spiritual state; (5) Not yet clothed with Christ; (6) Stripped of upper garments; (7) The bare essentials; (8) Shamed; (9) Deeply grieved; (10) Sexual perversion; (11) Self-atonement;

(12) Uncovered wickedness; (13) What you are wearing on the inside; (14) Unrighteousness (dirty underwear).

Also see *Breast, Genitals, Nakedness,* and *Pants*.

(1-4) <u>Mark 14:51-52</u>; John 21:7; (5) <u>Rom. 13:14</u>; Gal. 3:27; (6-7) John 21:7; (8) 2 Sam. 13:18-19; (9) Gen. 37:34; (10) Lev. 18:6-23; (11) Gen. 3:7; (12) Ezek. 16:57 (NKJV); (13) Eph. 3:16; (14) Isa. 64:6.

Undone: (1) Perishing (without protection); (2) Incomplete (not finished); (3) Revealed; (4) Without strength; (5) Destroyed or cut off; (6) Neglecting; (7) Loose or release.

(1) Num. 21:29; (2) Josh. 11:15; (3-5) <u>Isa. 6:5</u>; (6) Matt. 23:23; Luke 11:42; (7) Isa. 58:6.

Unfamiliar: (1) Not recognized; (2) Not known; (3) Dead to the world; (4) Spiritually insensitive.

Also see *Foreign, Foreigner, Strange,* and *Woman (Foreign Woman)*.

(1-2) <u>Matt. 25:12</u>; Acts 17:23; (3) 2 Cor. 6:9; (4) Matt. 17:12.

Unicorn: (1) God/Jesus; (2) Strength.

(1) Num. 23:22 (KJV); (2) Ps. 18:2; 89:17.

Unicycle: (1) Going it alone; (2) Moving in your own strength; (3) Without God.

Also see *Bicycle* and *Clown*.

(1) Gen. 2:18; Exod. 18:14; (2) <u>Num. 14:42</u>; Job 18:7; (3) Eph. 2:12.

Uniform: (1) Recognized authority. (2) Members; (3) All the same.

(1) <u>Rom. 13:3-4</u>. (2-3) Rom. 12:16; 1 Cor. 12:12; Phil. 2:2.

Unite: See Bound, Cleave, and Marriage.

University: (1) Education; (2) Study; (3) Intellect or human wisdom; (4) Degree or qualification; (5) Human authority; (6) Human wisdom; (7) Natural person; (8) School of the Spirit (higher learning).

(1-2) Acts 22:3; 2 Tim. 2:15; (3) <u>1 Cor. 1:19-20</u>-25; James 3:13-18; (4) John 7:15; Acts 7:22; (5-6) John 7:15-17; 1 Cor. 2:1-5; (7) 1 Cor. 2:14; (8) John 14:26.

Unprepared: (1) Prayerlessness; (2) Danger of falling into temptation; (3) Not willing to pay the price; (4) Need for a fresh anointing of the Holy Spirit; (5) Not praying in the Holy Spirit; (6) Not understanding the sign of the times.

Also see *Watch.*

(1) Matt. 24:42; 26:41; Luke 12:35-40; 21:36; 22:40; Eph. 6:18; Rev. 3:3; (2) Matt. 26:41; Mark 14:38; (3) Matt. 22:11-14; (4) Matt. 25:1-13; (5) Jude 1:19-20; (6) Matt. 16:3; Mark 13:33; 1 Pet. 4:7.

Unrecognized: (1) In the Spirit.

(1) Luke 24:16, 31; John 20:14; 1 Cor. 2:14.

Unseen Accomplice: (1) The Holy Spirit.

(1) John 16:13; 11:51.

Unstable: (1) Double-minded; (2) Heart trained in covetous practices; (3) Prone to fall back into sin; (4) Unlearned in the ways of God and likely to twist things to suit themselves; (5) Shall not excel.

(1) James 1:8; (2-3) 2 Pet. 2:14; (4) 2 Pet. 3:16; (5) Gen. 49:4.

Up: (1) God; (2) Heaven; (3) Spiritual ascension; (4) Approval or success; (5) Pride; (6) Positive; (7) Operating in faith (as in "nowhere to look but up"); (8) Spiritually strengthened.

Also see *Down, North,* and *Uphill.*

(1) Gen. 14:22; (2) Gen. 28:12; Deut. 4:19; (3) Isa. 2:3a; (4) As in, "thumbs up"; (5) Matt. 4:5-6 (appealing to "the pride of life"); (6) Ps. 24:7; (7) Heb. 12:2; (8) Ps. 110:7.

Upgrade: (1) Moving to another spiritual level; (2) Passing through death (spiritual promotion).

Also see *Computer.*

(1) 2 Cor. 3:18; (2) 2 Kings 2:11.

Uphill: (1) Spiritual ascension; (2) Battling, as in, "an uphill battle".

(1) Ps. 122:1; Isa. 2:3a; Mic. 4:1; (2) 1 Sam. 14:13.

Upper Room: (1) Spiritual place; (2) Heaven; (3) Spiritual thinking.

Also see *Upstairs.*

(1) Acts 1:13; 2:1-4; (2) John 14:2; (3) Isa. 55:9; Matt. 6:20.

Upright: (1) Righteous; (2) Standing in faith; (3) Truth; (4) Leadership; (5) Not in bondage; (6) Good; (7) Honest conduct; (8) God; (9) Integrity; (10) Understanding (spiritually in tune); (11) Blessed.

Also see *Crooked, Curved, Down, Straight, Standing,* and *Tall.*

(1) Prov. 11:6; (2) 2 Cor. 1:24b; (3) Eccl. 12:10; (4) Gen. 37:7; (5) Lev. 26:13; (6) 1 Sam. 29:6; (7) Ps. 37:14; (8) Ps. 92:15; (9) Ps. 11:3; (10) Prov. 15:21; (11) Ps. 112:2; Prov. 11:11.

Uproot/ed: (1) Judgment; (2) Idolatry; (3) Sin; (4) Deceitful and lying tongue; (5) Self-righteous, greedy, or rebellious heart; (6) The role of the prophet (to uproot sin).

Also see *Root.*

(1) Deut. 29:28; Zeph. 2:4; (2-3) 1 Kings 14:15-16; 2 Chron. 7:19-20; (3) Prov. 2:22; (4) Ps. 52:2-5; (5) Jude 1:11-12; (6) Jer. 1:10; Matt. 3:10; Luke 3:9.

Upside Down: (1) Overturned.

Also see *Somersault.*

(1) Acts 17:6.

Upstairs: (1) Heaven; (2) Presence of God; (3) Leading to spiritual blessing; (4) Going into heavenly places; (5) God's plans; (6) Thoughts; (7) Mind or thoughts; (8) Place of prayer or renewal (rest).

Also see *Upper Room.*

(1) Gen. 28:12; (2) Exod. 34:2; (Gen. 49:33 & Matt. 22:32); (3) Eph. 1:3; (4) Eph. 1:20; (5) Mark 14:15; Luke 1:76; Rom. 9:17; Col. 3:1; Heb. 8:5; (6) 1 Pet. 1:13; 2 Pet. 3:1-2; (7) 2 Cor. 10:5; Col. 2:18; (8) Mark 6:46; Luke 9:28-29.

Urgency: (1) Time running out; (2) Flesh (pushes whereas the Spirit leads); (3) Provocation; (4) Persecution (The devil's time is short and therefore he persecutes); (5) Rage; (6) Lacking foundation (Beware of being urged or rushed into something).

Also see *Hurry, Speed, Time,* and *Time Running Out.*

(1) 1 Cor. 7:29; Rev. 12:12-13; (2) Judg. 16:16; 2 Kings 2:17; (3) Luke 11:53-54. (4) Exod. 14:8-9; Rev. 12:12-13; (5) Dan. 3:19, 22; (6) Isa. 28:16.

Urination: (1) Insult or offense; (2) Offense needing to be dealt with; (3) Acts and words of defilement; (4) Foolishness; (5) Rubbish or refuse; (6) Cleansing (disposing of sin); (7) Unbelief; (8) Judgment; (9) Sin; (10) Disrespect (on someone); (11) Foul spirit.

Also see *Dung, Faeces, Rubbish,* and *Sewage.*

All KJV: (1-4) 1 Sam. 25:16, 21-22; 2 Kings 18:27 (urination literally: water of the feet); Isa. 36:12; (4) 1 Sam. 25:34; 1 Kings 14:10; (urination on your provider/protection); (5) 1 Kings 14:10; (6) 1 Kings 16:11-13; (7) 1 Kings 21:21; 2 Kings 9:8; (8) 2 Kings 18:27; (9) Deut. 28:20; Phil. 3:8; (11) Rev. 18:2.

USB: (1) Memories; (2) Thoughts.

Also see *Computer* and *Hard Drive.*

(1-2) Neh. 4:14; 1 Cor. 15:2; 2 Cor. 10:5.

U-Turn: (1) Repentance; (2) Return to idolatry; (3) Disobedience; (4) Changing your mind; (5) Going back on your word; (6) Drawn back to the world; (7) Double-minded.

(1) Luke 17:4; Acts 26:20b; (2) Josh. 23:12-13; (3) Job 23:12; (4) Matt. 21:29; (5) Matt. 26:33-35, 70-74; (6) Gen. 19:26; 2 Kings 5:20; (7) Luke 9:62.

Utility (Ute/Truck): (1) Working vehicle (i.e. business).

(1) Esther 3:9; Eccl. 5:3.

U2: (1) Secrets; (2) Heart secrets revealed; (3) Spiritual insight; (4) Prophetic ministry.

Also see *Spy.*

(1-2) Luke 10:21; 1 Cor. 4:5; 1 Pet. 3:4; (3-4) 1 Sam. 9:9. Isa. 45:2-3.

Vacuum Cleaner: (1) Deep cleansing work of the Holy Spirit; (2) Deliverance ministry (casting out unclean spirits).

(1) 1 Cor. 6:11; Tit. 3:5; (2) Matt. 12:28; Luke 11:14.

Vagina: See Genitals.

Valley: (1) Depression; (2) Hopelessness; (3) Discouragement; (4) Trouble; (5) Fear; (6) Separation; (7) The enemy's domain; (8) Mourning or grief; (9) Shadow of death or death; (10) Weeping; (11) Hell; (12) Pride or haughtiness (limiting spiritual vision); (13) Salt; (14) Humble person (to be exalted); (15) Fruitfulness; (16) Decision; (17) Tribulation; (18) Trial; (19) Hidden (in the secret place).

Also see *Hills.*

(1) By physical association; Isa. 7:19; (2) Ps. 23:4a; (3) Num. 32:9; (4) Josh. 7:24-25 (*Achor* = trouble); (5-6) 1 Sam. 17:3; (7) Judg. 1:19, 34; (8) Ezek. 7:16; Zech. 12:11; (9) Ps. 23:4a; Isa. 57:5; (10) Ps. 84:6 (*Baca* = weeping); (11) Prov. 30:17 (see *Raven*); (12) Isa. 22:1, 5; (13) 2 Sam. 8:13; 2 Kings 14:7; (14) Isa. 40:4; Luke 3:5; (15) Song. 6:11; Isa. 65:10; (16-18) Joel 3:14; (19) Song. 2:1 & 2:16.

Vampire: (1) Totally sold out to the devil; (2) Resurrection of something from the past (an issue) that sucks the life out of you; (3) Powerful evil spirit (principality) that seeks to take the life out of you; (4) Spirit behind chronic fatigue syndrome.

Also see *Bats (Animals)*.

(1) Num. 23:24b & 1 Pet.5:8; Jer. 46:10b; (2) 2 Sam. 14:21 & 15:6; (cf. Lev. 17:11a); (3) Isa. 2:20; Eph. 1:21; 6:12; (4) 1 Sam. 26:12; Isa. 61:3

Van: (1) Commercial vehicle; (2) Business outlook; (3) Courier; (4) Delivery/deliverer.

Also see *Automobile, Trailer,* and *Utility.*

(1-4) Gen. 45:27; 1 Sam. 6:7-8; Joel 3:5; Amos 2:13.

Vase: (1) Flesh; (2) Person/people (as human vessel/s).

(1-2) Mark 14:3; John 2:6-7.

Vegetables: (1) Weak; (2) Insufficient sermon; (3) Immature; (4) Avoiding offense; (5) Legalistic food laws; (6) Spiritual health (incorporating wisdom, knowledge, dreams, and visions); (6) Doing nothing ("vegging out"); (7) The Word of God (that which is sown).

(1) Rom. 14:2; (2-3) 1 Cor. 3:2; Heb. 5:12-14; (4) Rom. 14:15-21; (5) 1 Tim. 4:3; (6) Dan. 1:12, 15-17 (NKJV); (7) Dan. 1:12 (vegetables = that which is sown) & Luke 8:11.

Veil: (1) Spiritual blindness; (2) Deception; (3) Flesh; (4) Heart (behind the veil); (5) Secret (as in, "secret place"); (6) Covering; (7) Eternity/Heaven (behind the veil); (8) Authority (on head: marriage veil).

Also see *Curtain.*

(1) 2 Cor. 3:13-14; (2) 2 Cor. 4:4; (3) Matt. 27:50-51 & 2 Cor. 3:15; Heb. 10:20; (4) Heb. 6:19 (heart of the temple. (cf. 1 Cor. 6:19)); Heb. 9:3; (5) Gen. 24:65; Heb. 9:3; (6) Exod. 35:12; 34:33; 39:34; 40:3; (7) The root of the Hebrew word *olam* means "to be veiled from sight"; (8) 1 Cor. 11:10.

Velvet: (1) Royal; (2) Rich and sumptuous.

(1-2) Esther 1:6a; As in, "royal velvet."

Vending Machine: (1) Convenience (hearing what you want to hear); (2) Accessibility; (3) God (as accessed by prayer); (4) Wrong concept of God (quick fix).

Also see *Junk Food*.

(1) Mark 14:11; 2 Tim. 4:3; (2) John 6:5b; (3) Phil. 4:6; (4) James 4:3.

Venom: (1) Poisonous words.

(1) Job 6:4; 20:16; Ps. 58:3-7; <u>140:3</u>; <u>Rom. 3:13</u>; <u>James 3:8</u>.

Venus Fly Trap: (1) Authority over evil spirits; (2) Spiritual warfare; (3) Witch (partaking of demons).

Also see *Fly* and *Fly Spray*.

(1) Luke 10:19; (2) Matt. 16:19; 18:18; (3) 1 Cor. 10:21.

Verandah: (1) Covering; (2) Hidden; (3) Protected.

Also see *Porch*.

(1-2) Matt. 26:71-72; Gen. 19:8; (3) <u>Gen. 19:8</u>.

Vessels: (1) The human body; (2) The human heart; (3) An instrument of God; (4) The Church or a nation.

(1-3) <u>2 Cor. 4:7</u>; (4) Isa. 40:15; Jer. 18:6; 2 Cor. 6:16 (corporate temple).

Veterinarian: (1) Christ; (2) Pastoral leadership; (3) Leader working with unsaved people and on domestic issues.

Also see *Doctor* and individual animal types: *Cat, Dog,* etc.

(1) 1 Pet. 5:4; (2) 1 Pet. 5:2; (3) 1 Cor. 15:32 (cf. Acts 19:29-31).

Videoing: See Filming.

View: (1) Prophetic office; (2) Oversee (shepherd); (3) Watchman; (4) Reconnoiter; (5) Choosing; (6) Assess and plan.

Also see *Spy*.

(1) <u>1 Sam. 9:9</u>; 2 Kings 2:7, 15; (2) Acts 20:28; Heb. 13:17; <u>1 Pet. 5:2</u>; (3) 2 Sam. 18:24; Ezek. 3:17; (4) Josh. 2:1; 7:2; (5) Ezra 8:15; (6) Neh. 2:13, 15.

Vine: (1) Christ and His Church; (2) Life (A vine in relationship with God is prosperous, a vine in rebellion is unfruitful); (3) Israel; (4) Wife; (5) A vine speaks of fruit not works; (6) Peace (under a vine); (7) Poison (wild vine); (8) Reaping of godless wicked (vine of the earth).

Also see *Grapes.*

(1) John 15:1, 4-5; (2) Gen. 40:9-11; 49:22 (NIV); 2 Chron. 26:10 (also see vs. 4-5); Ps. 78:47; (3) Ps. 80:8-11; Isa. 5:2; Jer. 2:21; Hos. 10:1; Joel 1:7; (4) Ps. 128:3; (5) Gen. 40:9-11; Ezek. 15:2; (6) 1 Kings 4:25; 2 Kings 18:31; Mic. 4:4; Zech. 3:10; (7) 2 Kings 4:39; (8) Rev. 14:18.

Vinegar: (1) Sour/Bitterness; (2) Fruit of the vine; (3) Soliciting a negative reaction (vinegar on soda); (4) It is evident from both Jesus' and Judas' responses that bitterness is a choice.

(1) Ps. 69:21; Matt. 27:34, 48; Mark 15:36; Luke 23:36; (Exod. 12:8 & John 13:26-30); (2) Num. 6:3; John 19:29-30 (cf. Mark 14:25); (3) Prov. 25:20; (4) cf. Matt. 27:34 & John 13:26-30.

Vineyard: (1) Kingdom of Heaven; (2) Israel.

Also see *Fruit Tree.*

(1) Matt. 20:1-8; (2) Isa. 5:1-7.

Violin: (1) Instrument of love; (2) Heart (violin case); (3) Worship.

Also see *Music* and *Musical Instrument.*

(1) Ps. 18:1; (2) Eph. 5:19; (3) John 4:24; Phil 3:3.

Viper: (1) Small issue with potential for calamity; (2) Venomous words from son/daughter/children.

Also see *Snake.*

(1) Acts 28:3-6; (2) Prov. 30:14.

Virgin: (1) Church; (2) Pure; (3) Kingdom of Heaven; (4) Unmarried; (5) Jerusalem; (6) Israel.

(1-2) 2 Cor. 11:2; (3) Matt. 25:1-12; (4) 1 Cor. 7:25, 28, 34; (5) Isa. 62:5; Jer. 14:17; Lam. 2:13; (6) Amos 5:2.

Visit/ors: (1) Impartation (visitation); (2) Taking someone and their words in; (3) Brief ministry; (4) Angelic visitation; (5) Audience with God.

(1-2) Gen. 21:1; (3) Acts 10:33; (4) Gen. 19:1-2; Heb. 13:2; (5) Gen. 18:1-3.

Vitamins: (1) Spiritually healthy; (2) Strengthening in the Holy Spirit; (3) Communion.

(1-2) 1 Sam. 30:6b; 1 Tim. 4:8; Jude 1:20; (3) John 6:35, 48, 68.

Voice: (1) God (voice of father); (2) The Word of God; (3) Powerful witness; (4) Still small voice; (5) God (trumpet voice); (6) Evil or demon (disturbing voice).

(1) 1 Sam. 3:4-9; Ps. 29:3-4; (2) (Acts 9:4-5 & John 1:1); (3) Luke 3:4; (4) 1 Kings 19:12; Ps. 46:10a; (5) Exod. 19:16, 19; (6) Mark 1:26; 9:26.

Volcano: (1) Wrath of God; (2) Judgment; (3) Person who erupts; (4) Pressure within; (5) Unresolved anger; (6) Sudden destruction.

Also see *Lava.*

(1) Ezek. 22:20; Nah. 1:2b, 5-6; (2) Isa. 5:24-25; Mic. 1:4, 5a; (3-4) Ps. 39:3; (5) Ps. 4:4; (6) 1 Thess. 5:3.

Vomit: (1) Backsliding fool; (2) Expulsion or purging; (3) Empty promises; (4) Greed; (5) To go astray morally or spiritually; (6) Erring with wine; (7) Coughed up; (8) Self-destruction (drowning in vomit); (9) Lukewarm (God vomiting); (10) Rejection of something or someone; (11) Revival or resurrection.

Also see *Belch, Drunk,* and *Purge.*

(1) Prov. 26:11; 2 Pet. 2:22; (2) Lev. 18:25; (3) Prov. 23:6-8; (4) Prov. 25:16; (5) Isa. 19:14; Jer. 48:26; (6) Isa. 28:7-8; (7) Jon. 2:10; (8) (9-10) Rev. 3:16; (11) Jon. 2:10-3:1.

Voting: (1) Decision on who leads you; (2) A call to put that which is in the heart into action.

(1-2) Josh. 24:15.

Vulture: (1) Keen-eyed; (2) Bird of the wilderness; (3) Sign of death; (4) Demons taking souls to hell.

(1) Job 28:7; (2) Isa. 34:15; (3) Matt. 24:28; Luke 17:37; (4) Lev. 11:13-14.

Wages: (1) Harvest (reaping) wages; (2) Death; (3) Unrighteousness (greed); (4) Deception (changed wages); (5) Rewards.

(1) John 4:36; (2) Rom. 6:23; (3) 2 Pet. 2:15; Jude 1:11; (4) Gen. 31:7; Prov. 11:18; (6) Prov. 31:31 (NIV).

Waiter: (1) Faithful servant of God; (2) Filled and ready for service.

Also see *Waiting*.

(1-2) Luke 12:35-42.

Waiting: (1) Awaiting ministry; (2) Preparation time; (3) Awaiting God's timing; (4) A need to spend time with God.

Also see *Waiter*.

(1-2) Luke 1:80; (3) Isa. 49:2. (4) Ps. 27:14; Isa. 40:31.

Walking: (1) Living by faith; (2) In step with the Spirit; (3) Our pre-Christian lifestyle (worldly living); (4) Taking up God's ways; (5) Endurance; (6) Advancement (positive or negative); (7) Progress or forward movement; (8) Natural reasoning; (9) Brotherly hatred (walking in darkness).

Also see *Footsteps* and *Stepping*.

(1) Rom. 4:12; 6:4b; 2 Cor. 5:7; Gal. 2:14; (2) Rom. 8:1, 4, 14; Gal. 5:25; (3) Eph. 2:2; 1 Pet. 4:3; (4) Isa. 2:3; (5) Isa. 40:31; (6) Ps. 1:1; Eph. 5:2; (7) 1 John 1:7; (8) Eph. 4:17; (9) 1 John 2:11.

Walking together: (1) Agreement.

(1) Amos 3:3; Ps. 1:1.

Wall/s: (1) Protection; (2) Strength; (3) Barrier or blockade or blockage; (4) Partition; (5) Hardened hearts; (6) God; (7) Barrier to the things of the Spirit (no windows); (8) Security; (9) Body or flesh (wooden wall); (10) Phobia; (11) Protected or forced path (walls either side); (12) Boundary; (13) Defensive fortification; (14) Place from which words launched (vulnerability: close to the wall); (15) Vantage point; (16) Hiding or hidden; (17) A rich person's status and protection; (18) Salvation; (19) The believer; (20) Recluse.

Also see *Bricks, Fence, Hedge,* and *House*.

(1) 1 Sam. 25:16, 21; (2) 2 Chron. 32:5; Neh. 4:10; Prov. 18:11; Isa. 25:4; (3) Gen. 49:22; Num. 13:28; 2 Sam. 22:30; Isa. 5:5; Heb. 11:30; (4) Eph. 2:14; (5) Ps. 62:3; Eccl. 10:8; (6) Ps. 18:2; 144:2 (cf. Deut 28:52); (7) 2 Kings 2:10; (8) Num. 13:28; (9) 1 Kings 6:15 (The walls symbolize our earthly bodies) (cf. 1 Cor. 6:19); (10) Prov. 29:25; (11) Exod. 14:22, 29; Num. 22:24; (12) Num. 35:4; (13) Deut. 3:5; (14) 2 Sam. 11:20-24 (See *Arrows*); (15) 2 Sam. 18:24; (16) Ezek. 8:7-12; (17) Prov. 18:11; (18) Isa. 60:18; (19) Jer. 1:18; 15:20; (20) Prov. 18:1 (AMP) as in, "putting walls up."

Wall/s (Falling or Fallen Wall): (1) Judgment; (2) Loss of protection; (3) Spiritually unguarded; (4) Disgraced, naked, or vulnerable; (5) Spiritually lazy; (6) Spiritually undisciplined; (7) Revealing of the heart; (8) Rape (Forceful breaking down of a wall); (9) Breakthrough.

(1) 1 Kings 20:30; (Gen. 15:16 & Josh. 6:4-5); 2 Kings 14:13; Neh. 2:13; Jer. 1:15; Ezek. 13:14; (2) 2 Kings 25:10; Isa. 5:5; (3) Neh. 1:3-8; Jer. 39:8; Ezek. 38:11-12; (4) Neh. 2:17; Ps. 62:3; (5) Prov. 24:30-33; (6) Prov. 25:28; (7) Ezek. 13:14; (8) Ezek. 26:12; (9) 1 Chron. 14:11.

Wall/s (Measuring an Internal Wall): (1) Dividing between soul and spirit; (2) Rightly dividing the Word of truth; (3) Call for personal introspection.

(1) Heb. 4:12; (2) 2 Tim. 2:15; (3) 1 Cor. 11:28.

Wall/s (Repairing a Wall): (1) Renewing relationship with God; (2) Rebuilding; (3) Favor of God; (4) Diligence.

(1) 2 Chron. 33:12-16 (note v. 14); Ps. 51:17-18; (2-3) Neh. 2:5, 8; 6:16; (4) Neh. 4:6.

Wallet/Billfold: (1) Heart (as the place where values stored); (2) Identity; (3) Money or finances; (4) Credit; (5) Security; (6) Two masters; (7) Greed; (8) Faith; (9) Forgetting the house of God (wallet with holes).

Also see *Money.*

(1) Matt. 6:21, 24; (4) Eccl. 7:12; (5) Matt. 6:21; (6) John 12:6; (7) Mark 6:8 (no money in purse); Luke 9:3; (8) Hag. 1:6.

Wallpaper: (1) Build-up of heart issues (several layers); (2) Allowing issues to build up over time (several layers of wallpaper); (3) Façade that covers sin (dirty or faulty walls).

(1-2) Gen. 6:5; Neh. 13:6-8; John 13:10 (need for regular cleansing); Rom. 7:17; (3) Matt. 23:27.

Walrus: (1) If attacking you is an evil spirit (walrus is a pinniped [winged-feet] creature).

Also see *Dolphin, Dugong,* and *Whale.*

(1) Matt. 8:28; 1 Pet. 5:8 (walrus' roar).

Wardrobe: See Cupboard.

Warehouse: (1) Heaven; (2) Place of equipping; (3) Place of abundant supply; (4) Unconventional church; (5) Underground church. (6) Stopping the flow of the Spirit (mothballing the Spirit).

(1) Phil. 4:19; (2) 2 Chron. 2:9; (3) 1 Chron. 29:16; (4) Mal. 3:10a; (5) 1 Sam. 22:1-2. (6) 1 Thess. 5:19; Acts 7:51.

War Heroes/Museum: (1) Heroes of faith.

Also see *Museum*.

(1) Heb. 11.

Warrior: See Soldier.

Wash/ing: (1) Being born again (whole body wash); (2) Washing in the Word of God (part of body being washed); (3) Confession of sin; (4) Bible study and application; (5) Being born again or need to be born again (clothes washing); (6) Renewal.

Also see *Washbasin, Washcloth,* and *Washing Machine*.

(1-2) John 3:5; 13:10; Tit. 3:5; (3) 1 John 1:9; (4) John 15:3; 17:17; Eph. 5:26; (5) Joel 2:13; Matt. 23:25-28; Mark 7:21-23; 11:39-40; (6) Tit. 3:5.

Washbasin: (1) Heart; (2) The Word of God; (3) Cleansing.

(1) Matt. 23:27; 2 Cor. 4:7; (2) Exod. 30:18-19; Eph. 5:26 (that which holds the water of the Word); (3) John 13:10; Isa. 1:16.

Washcloth: (1) Cleansing; (2) Servanthood.

Also see *Towel.*

(1-2) John 13:4-5.

Washing Line: See Clothesline.

Washing Machine: (1) Need for regeneration; (2) Wanting to be right (clean/white) with God; (3) Wanting clean clothes (robes of salvation and righteousness); (4) Holy Spirit ministry used in cleaning others.

(1) Tit. 3:5; (2-3) Isa. 61:10; (4) Isa. 61:1, 10.

Wasp: (1) Evil spirits; (2) Used in God's clearance of enemy forces; (3) Sting/ing; (4) Painful scourge.

Also see *Bees.*

(1-2) Exod. 23:28; Deut. 7:20; Josh. 24:12; (3-4) Taken from the Hebrew word used in these passages and its root.

Watch (Timepiece): (1) Time; (2) Deadline (time's running out); (3) Timing of God; (4) Not wanting to be there (time to leave); (5) Glory that comes from waiting on God (gold watch); (6) Life; (7) Death (time to die); (8) Glorious calling (selecting a gold watch).

Also see *Time* and *Clock.*

(1) Mark 13:33; (2) 1 Cor. 7:29; Eph. 5:15-16; Col. 4:5; Rev. 12:12; (3) Esther 4:14; John 7:30; Gal. 4:4; (4) John 6:24; (5) Exod. 34:29; (6-7) Eccl. 3:2; John 7:6, 8; (8) Esther 4:14; 2 Thess. 2:14; 1 Pet. 5:10.

Water: (1) The Holy Spirit (flowing water); (2) The Word of God (still water); (3) Cleansing; (4) Heart; (5) Desire for God (thirsting); (6) Prayers; (7) Peoples; (8) Peace (still waters); (9) Calm (still water); (10) In the Spirit (in the water); (11) Deliverer (someone drawn out of water); (12) Spiritually dead believers (stinky water); (13) Judgment (stinky water); (14) Emotions (as in, "stirred up"); (15) Unstable.

Also see *Clear Water, Deep, Glass of Water, Water (Dirty Water), Watering,* and *Underwater.*

(1) Lev. 14:6 (*running water* means "living water" in the Hebrew); John 7:37-39; (2) Eph. 5:26; (3) John 13:5-10; (4) Lam. 2:19 (cf. Prov. 18:4 & Luke 6:45b); (4) Ps. 42:1-2; 63:1; 69:21; John 19:28; Note that in Exod. 17:3-6 the people thirsted and water came forth by striking the Lord who "stood before the Rock." Their natural thirst was to lead them to a spiritual revelation that God was the satisfier of the soul; (5) Ps. 126:5; Jer. 31:9; 50:4; (6) Rev. 17:15; (7) Ps. 23:2; Mark 4:39; (8) Ps. 107:29; (9) Ezek. 32:14; (10) Exod. 2:10; (11) Exod.15:23-24; (12-13) Exod. 7:18; Rev. 3:1; (14) Jer. 51:55; Matt. 14:30; Luke 8:24; (15) Gen. 49:4.

Water (Dirty Water): (1) Causing strife (muddying the waters); (2) Tainted words; (3) Sowing poisonous words (murmuring); (4) Having not applied Christ (salt) to the heart (source) of an issue; (5) Personal fleshly issues muddying the flow of God's Spirit; (6) Instability; (7) Deceitfulness (8) Lies; (9) Adding to the Word (tainted truth); (10) Wickedness; (11) Unappealing.

Also see *Clear Water, Flood, River, Water,* and *Underwater.*

(1) Isa. 57:20; Ezek. 32:2; 34:18-19; (2-3) Num. 20:24; Prov. 18:4; (4) Exod. 15:23-25; 2 Kings 2:19, 21; Prov. 18:4; James 3:10-11; (5) 2 Cor. 4:7; (6) Job

8:11; (7-8) Ps. 62:4 (mouth saying one thing, heart another); Ps. 78:36-37; 101:7; 120:2; Prov. 14:25; (9) Prov. 30:5-6; 2 Cor. 2:17; (10) Isa. 57:20; (11) 2 Kings 5:12.

Water (Hot): (1) A heart on fire for God; (2) Angry words; (3) Finding oneself in trouble.

(1) Jer. 20:9; (Lam. 2:19 & Matt. 24:12); (2) Ps. 79:5 & Eph. 5:26; (3) As in, "I found myself in hot water about. . .."

Waterfall: (1) Outpouring of the Spirit; (2) Baptism in the Holy Spirit.

Also see *Fountain*.

(1) Ps. 42:7; Prov. 1:23; Isa. 32:15a; 44:3; Ezek. 39:29; Joel 2:28-29; Acts 2:17-18; (2) Acts 10:45.

Watering: (1) Speaking under the anointing; (2) Sharing the Gospel (cleaning); (3) Speaking.

(1) John 6:63; 7:38-39; (2) Eph. 5:26; (3) Prov. 18:4.

Watermelon: (1) Word of God.

(1) Eph. 5:26.

Water Meter: (1) The human agency (church, pastor, father), by which the Word and Spirit of God is measured out; (2) The human heart; (3) Measuring the anointing.

Also see *Meter*.

(1) John 3:34; Eph. 5:26; (2) 2 Tim. 2:15; Heb. 4:12; (3) John 12:3; Acts 4:8; 6:5.

Water Pipe: (1) Holy Spirit minister or ministry; (2) Christ; (3) Mouth; (4) The avenue to breaking strongholds (through the water shaft).

(1-2) John 7:37-39; (3) Matt. 12:34; Luke 6:45; (4) 2 Sam. 5:6-9; 1 Chron. 11:6-9; (*Jebus* means "trodden down." Notice how the Jebusites put David down: 2 Sam. 5:6).

Water Pump: (1) Heart; (2) Sensitivity (understanding) to the Spirit of God; (3) Thirst for the Spirit of God; (4) Minister or ministry; (5) Full Gospel church.

(1) John 7:38; (2) Prov. 20:5; (3) Ps. 42:1; (3) John 7:37-39; 2 Tim. 4:2; (4) Matt. 28:18-20; Eph. 1:22-23 & Col. 1:18; (5)

Waterslide: (1) Flowing in the anointing; (2) Bringing things from Heaven to earth in the Spirit.

(1-2) Ezek. 47:5.

Waves: (1) Strong and emotive words or great voice; (2) Outpouring of the Holy Spirit (big wave); (3) Opposition; (4) Double-minded Christian; (5) Change of mind (given to change); (6) Complainers, grumblers, mockers; (7) Tests; (8) Circumstance; (9) Death; (10) Pride; (11) False/dangerous spirit (dumpers); (12) Heart in turmoil.

See *Beach, Deep,* and *Water.*

(1) Ps. 65:7; 42:7; 51:15; 93:3-4; Jer. 51:42, 55; Jon. 2:3; (Gen. 7:17 & John 12:48); (9) Isa. 59:19, *". . . When the enemy comes in, like a flood the Spirit of the Lord shall lift up a standard against him";* (2) Matt. 14:24; (3-4) James 1:6-8; (5) Jude 1:13, 16; (6) Matt. 8:24; Mark 4:37; (7) Matt. 14:24; (8) 2 Sam. 22:5; (9) Job 38:11; (11) 1 Kings 22:22; Mic. 2:11 (Dumpers only let you down hard); (12) As a body of water stirred; Ps. 42:7; Prov. 20:5; Lam. 2:19.

Wax: (1) Melted away; (2) Seal.

Also see *Candle.*

(1) Ps. 22:14; 68:2; 97:5; Mic. 1:4; (2) 1 Kings 21:8.

Weapon: (1) Words or cutting words; (2) Spiritual weapons: Obedience, Faith, the Word of God, Prayer, Truth, Righteousness, the name of Jesus, the Gospel of peace, Salvation.

Also see *Arrows, Guns,* and *Hands.*

(1) Eccl. 9:17-18; Isa. 54:17; (2) 2 Cor. 10:4-5; Eph. 6:10-18.

Wear/ing: (1) The heart shown outwardly; (2) Outward/ly; (3) Superficial/ly; (4) Praise; (5) Joy; (6) Honor bestowed upon; (7) Prepared or ready; (8) Pride (when showy); (9) Modesty or humility (when conservative); (10) Welcome.

Also see *Clothing, Hat, Robe,* and *Skirt.*

(2) Isa. 61:10; 1 Pet. 3:3-5; (2) 1 Pet. 3:3; (3) Luke 21:5; (4-5) Isa. 61:3; (6) Dan.5:29; (7) Rev. 21:2; (8-9); 1 Tim. 2:9; (10) As in, a Hawaiian lei.

Weasel: (1) Someone who reneges on their word; (2) Unclean animal.

(1) As in, "He weaseled his way out of it"; (2) Lev. 11:29.

Weaving/Woven: (1) Union (close connection); (2) Interlocking (strong and robust); (3) Creating; (4) Planning (good or evil); (5) Skilled work; (6) Expensive; (7) Trap.

(1) Ps. 133:1; Eph. 4:3; (2) Exod. 39:22, 27; (3-4) Isa. 59:5; (5) Exod. 35:35; (6) John 19:23; (7) Isa. 59:5.

Web: (1) Predator's trap; (2) Deception; (3) Schemes of iniquity; (4) False trust; (5) Place of old (end of an era [old wineskin]); (6) Not spiritually active (abandoned house); (7) Ensnared by the internet.

Also see *Spider, Net,* and *Trap.*

(1-3) Isa. 59:5-6; (4) Job 8:14; (5) Matt. 9:17; (6) Isa. 58:12; Hag. 1:4b; (7) Ps. 91:3; 124:7.

Wedding: See Marriage.

Wedding Dress: (1) Standing in righteousness (white dress).

(1) Rev. 19:8.

Wednesday: (1) Four; (2) Dominion or rule.

Also see *Day* and *Three* (the secular world sees Wednesday as the third day of the week).

(1-2) Gen. 1:18-19.

Weeds: (1) Curse; (2) Quick growing and energy-soaking issues/individuals that block out the light; (3) Enemy plant; (4) People that choke others; (5) The result of the enemy's words; (6) Sin.

(1) Gen. 3:18; (2-3) Matt. 13:25; (4) Matt. 13:7; (5) Matt. 13:25 (sowing = words); (6) Gal. 6:8.

Weevils: (1) Hidden destruction of the Word of God.

Also see *Wheat* and *Termites.*

(1) 2 Cor. 2:17a.

Weighing: (1) Thinking something through (weighing up); (2) Judging a prophetic word.

Also see *Scales (Weight)* and *Weight.*

(1) 2 Tim. 2:15; (2) 1 Cor. 14:29; 1 Thess. 5:20-21.

Weight: (1) Glory; (2) Power; (3) Sin (that which holds us back); (4) Hearts/spirits and actions are weighed; (5) Measured; (6) More important (weightier); (7) Responsibility.

Also see *Balances, Heavy, Weighing,* and *Weight Loss.*

(1) 2 Cor. 4:17; (2) 2 Cor. 10:10; (3) Heb. 12:1; (4) 1 Sam. 2:3; Ps. 58:2; Prov. 16:2; Isa. 26:7; Dan. 5:27; (5) Job 6:2; 31:6; (6) Matt. 23:23; (7) As in, "feeling the weight of responsibility."

Weightlifting: (1) Building your faith; (2) Burden-bearing; (3) Taking on someone's sin or burden (spotting weights for someone); (4) Sinning; (5) Taking on more than you can handle.

(1) Jude 1:20; (2) Matt. 11:30; (3) Matt. 11:30; Heb. 12:1; (4) Heb. 12:1; (5) Matt. 11:28; 17:16-17.

Weight Loss: (1) Sin dealt with; (2) Loss of glory/anointing; (3) Loss of importance.

Also see *Fat, Scales (Weight), Weighing,* and *Weight.*

(1) Heb. 12:1; (2) 2 Cor. 4:17; (3) As in, "Weightier matters are more important."

Welding: (1) Joining (strong bond); (2) Manufacturing/fabricating; (3) Repairing.

Also see *Steel.*

(1) Exod.28:7; 1 Chron. 22:3 (KJV); (2) 2 Kings 15:35; (3) Neh. 3:6.

Well: (1) God; (2) Heart; (3) God's Word; (4) Jesus Christ; (5) Salvation or eternal life; (6) The Holy Spirit.

Also see *Fountain.*

(1) Gen. 21:27-32 (well of covenant); Gen. 49:22; Num. 21:16-17 (They sang to the well!); (2 Sam. 17:17-19 & Col. 3:3); (2) Prov. 5:15; 18:4; John 7:37-38; (3) Gen. 29:2 (flock watered from this well); (4-5) Isa. 12:2-3; (6) John 7:37-38.

Stopped-up Well: (1) Things dumped on the spirit to spoil it; (2) Attempt to stop salvation.

(1-2) Gen 26:15, 18; 2 Kings 3:19, 25.

West: (1) Glory departing; (2) Departure from God or God departing; (3) Place of sunset; (4) A setting down or end; (5) From the west may mean ungodly/unbeliever; (6) Consider aspects in your own environment relating to west.

Also see *East.*

(1-2) The sun sets in the west. A setting sun ushers in night (ungodliness); John 9:4; 12:30; (3) Isa. 59:19; (4) Ps. 103:12; Matt. 8:11; (4) Dan. 8:5; John 3:2 (by night).

Wet: See Water.

Wet Suit: (1) An anointing/mantle (having put on Christ); (2) Protected by the Holy Spirit (wet suit); (3) The old self (coming out of sea and taking off the wet suit).

Also see *Surfing* and *Waves.*

(1) Exod. 29:7; Lev. 8:12; 1 Sam. 10:1; 2 Kings 2:8; (cf. Gal. 3:27 & 2 Cor.3:18 (AMP)); (2) 2 Kings 2:13-14; Isa. 61:1-2; (3) Col. 2:11-12; (Here a black wetsuit may represent putting off the old self).

Whale: (1) Prophetic ministry (leader who is sensitive to the Spirit); (2) Great fish; (3) Big fish; (4) Influential believer.

(1) As the whale is an extremely sensitive creature communicating over long distances, so is the prophet sensitive to the Spirit; (2-3) Matt. 12:40 (cf. KJ & NKJ); (4) As believers are as fish, a big fish is seen as one of significance.

Wheat: (1) The Word of God; (2) Believers; (3) Believers that lay down their lives (death to self); (4) Purified hearts (threshed/sifted); (5) Related to the main harvest (favor of God); (6) Fruitfulness and provision.

Also see *Barley, Chaff,* and *Seed.*

(1) Matt. 13:20; Mark 4:14; (2) Matt. 3:12 (contrasted with chaff); Matt. 13:25, 29-30 (contrasted with tares); Luke 3:17; (3) John 12:24-25; (4) 1 Chron. 21:20; Luke 22:31; (5) Exod. 34:22; Ruth 2:23 (wheat harvest followed barley harvest); 1 Sam. 6:13; (6) Deut. 8:8, 32:14; 2 Sam. 17:28; Ps. 81:16 147:14; Song. 7:2.

Wheel/s: (1) Holy Spirit; (2) Spirit; (3) Progress; (4) Movable; (5) Repeat; (6) Roll; (7) Transport.

Also see *Automobile, Bicycle, Circle, Rollerblades,* and *Scooter.*

(1) (Job 33:4 & Jer. 18:3); Heb. 9:14 (eternal = never ending); (2) Eccl. 12:6; Ezek.1:20; (3) Exod. 14:25; (4) 1 Kings 7:30-33; (5-6) The Hebrew for "wheel" is *ghalghal*; (7) Gen. 45:27.

Wheelbarrow: (1) Carrying burdens; (2) Sinful journey; (3) Deliverance; (4) Vessel of sin; (5) Carrying sinful burdens; (6) Walking in the flesh.

(1) Jer. 17:22; Matt. 11:28; (2) 1 Kings 15:26; Isa. 30:1 (NIV); (3) Zech. 3:9 (as in removing sin); (4) Luke 11:39; (5) Luke 11:46; (6) Gal. 5:16-21; Ps. 38:4.

Wheelchair: (1) Incapacitated/infirmity; (2) Not walking by faith; (3) Dependence (on the person pushing the chair); (4) Healing (coming out of the chair); (5) Wholeness (coming out of the chair).

Also see *Polio*.

(1) 2 Sam. 4:4; (2) 2 Cor. 5:7; (3) Acts 3:2; (4) Matt. 21:14; Acts 3:6-8; (5) Acts 4:10.

Whip: (1) Harsh chastisement, discipline, or punishment; (2) Correction; (3) Purging; (4) Authority (cracking the whip); (5) Being driven rather than led.

Also see *Cowboy*.

(1) 1 Kings 12:11, 14; 2 Chron. 10:11; (2) Prov. 26:3; (3) Prov. 20:30; Isa. 53:5; (4) John 2:15, 18 (NIV); (5) cf. Ps. 23:2-3.

Whirlpool: (1) Being drawn or sucked into something; (2) Path to hell; (3) Troubled heart.

Also see *Tornado*.

(1) Prov. 7:22-23; 9:13-18; (2) Ezek. 31:14b; Matt. 8:32; (3) Ps. 46:3; 77:16; Isa. 57:20.

Whirlwind: Open Heaven bringing: (1) Rapture; (2) Revelation (hearing the Word of God); (3) Resurrection; (4) Destruction; (5) Judgment.

Also see *Dust Storm* and *Tornado*.

(1) 2 Kings 2:1, 11; (2) Job 38:1; Ezek. 1:4ff; (3) Job 40:6–42:10; (4) Prov. 1:27; Jer. 23:19; (5) Isa. 66:15; Jer. 30:23.

Whispering: (1) Voice of the Holy Spirit; (2) Secret; (3) Plotting against; (4) Sowing strife (division); (5) Familiar spirit sowing deception; (6) No strength or spiritually dying.

Also see *Lips*.

(1) 1 Kings 19:12; (2) 2 Sam. 12:19; (3) Ps. 41:7; (4) Prov. 16:28; Rom. 1:29-30; 2 Cor. 12:20; (5) Isa. 29:4; (6) Gen. 21:16-17; 1 Sam. 30:11-13.

White: (1) Righteous; (2) Pure/holy(garments); (3) Believer; (4) Clean/ washed/purified; (5) Angel; (6) Worthy; (7) Portrayed innocence/purity/

righteousness; (8) Ready for harvest; (9) Sin (skin); (10) Glory (cloud); (11) Glory (whiter than white); (12) Tasteless (white of an egg); (13) Conquer/ing (horse); (14) Light.

(1) Rev. 19:8; (2) Lam. 4:7; Dan. 7:9; Matt. 17:2; Rev. 3:5; (3) Rev. 4:4; 6:11; 7:9; (4) Ps. 51:7; Isa. 1:18; Dan. 11:35; 12:10; Rev. 7:14; (5) Matt. 28:2-3; Mark 16:5; John 20:12; Rev. 15:6; (6) Rev. 3:4; (7) Gen. 40:16; Matt. 23:27 (outward white/inward black); (8) John 4:35; (9) Num. 12:10-11; 2 Kings 5:27; Joel 1:7; (10) 2 Chron. 5:12-14; (11) Mark 9:3; Rev. 14:14; (12) Job 6:6; (13) Rev. 6:2; 19:11; (14) Mark 9:3; Luke 9:29; Rev. 1:14; 3:18 (Glory is the opposite of shame).

White (Off White): (1) Not quite right; (2) False righteousness; (3) Not right with God.

(1-3) Isa. 64:6a; 2 Cor. 11:14-15; 2 Tim. 3:4b-5.

White Man: See Black Man, Foreigner, and Caucasian.

Widow: (1) Casting off the faith; (2) Naturally or spiritually without a husband; (3) Spiritual grief; (4) Cared for by God; (5) Gather gleanings; (6) Trusting in God; (7) Their oppression is a sign of ungodliness; (8) Their abuse will be judged by God; (9) Widowhood may be a sign of judgment; (10) Reproach; (11) Place from which God can become our Husband; (12) Spirit of death (black widow).

Also see *Woman.*

(1) Eph. 5:23-25 & 1 Tim. 5:11-12; (2) Exod. 22:22, 24; 2 Sam. 20:3; (3) Isa. 54:6; (4) Deut. 10:18; Ps. 68:5; 146:9; Prov. 15:25; (5) Deut. 24:19-21; (6) 1 Kings 17:9-15; 1 Tim. 5:5; (7) Ps. 94:6; Isa. 1:16-17, 23; 10:2; (8) Isa. 1:23-25; (9) Isa. 9:17; 47:8-10; (10-11) Isa. 54:4-6; (12) Isa. 59:5.

Wife: (1) The Church (Bride of Christ); (2) Actual wife; (3) Israel; (4) Business.
(1) Eph. 5:23-25; Rev. 19:7; (3) Jer. 3:1, 20; (4) 2 Cor. 6:14; (5) As in, "married to the business."

Wig: (1) False anointing/authority; (2) Without the Spirit; (3) Pretending to be something you are not; (4) High up in the hierarchy ("big wig"); (5) Pending court case (judge-type wigs).

(1) 2 Sam. 14:26 & 2 Sam. 15:10; (2) Judg. 16:19-20; (3) 1 Sam. 28:8; Rom. 1:21-22; (4-5) Acts 23:2-5.

Wilderness: See Desert.

Wild Fire: (1) Judgment; (2) Encounter with God; (3) Words that have gotten out of control (gossip, slander, lies, false promises, etc).

(1) Matt. 13:40; 2 Pet. 3:7; (2) Exod. 3:2; (3) James 3:6.

Willow: (1) Sadness; (2) Weeping.

(1-2) Ps. 137:1-2.

Wind: (1) Holy Spirit; (2) Affliction/adversity/trouble (windy); (3) False teaching; (4) Evil spirits; (5) Resurrection (second wind).

Also see *Dark Clouds* and *Storm.*

(1) John 3:8; Acts 2:2-4; (2) Matt. 7:25; 8:25-26; (3) Eph. 4:14; (4) Dan. 7:2-3; Matt. 14:24; Eph. 4:14 (These are behind false teaching); (5) Gen. 8:1; Judg. 15:19; Luke 8:55.

Wind Chimes: (1) Spirit of God moving; (2) Spontaneous worship.

(1-2) John 3:8.

Winding Road: (1) Inability to see what's ahead; (2) Difficult path ahead; (3) Sin or evil; (4) Self-reliance (not trusting God); (5) Double-minded; (6) Unstable; (7) Loss of peace.

Also see *Country Road, Crooked, Road,* and *Up and Down.*

(1) James 1:6 (without the eyes of faith); (2) Lam. 3:9; (3) Prov. 2:15; (4) Prov. 3:5-6 (NKJV alternative rending); (5-6) James 1:6-8; (7) Isa. 59:8.

Window: (1) Prophetic gifting (seeing through window); (2) Entrance to the soul; (3) Insight/revelation; (4) Escape; (5) Opportunity; (6) Thief; (7) Prophecy; (8) Lacking spiritual discernment (small window/s); (9) Spiritual discernment (large window); (10) Trying to get a spiritual breakthrough (trying to break window); (11) Broken heart or shattered hope (smashed window).

Also see *Lookout, Open Window,* and *Shutting Window.*

(1) 1 Sam. 9:9 (seer); Prov. 7:6; Isa. 6:1; (2) Matt. 6:22-23; (3) Gen. 26:8; 2 Sam. 6:16; Prov. 7:6-7; Song. 2:9; (4) Josh. 2:15; 1 Sam. 19:12; (5) As in, "window of opportunity"; (6) Joel 2:9; (7) 1 Sam. 9:9; (8) Prov. 7:7; Jon. 4:11; Luke 12:56; 1 Cor. 2:14; (9) 1 Cor. 2:14; 12:10; (10) Exod. 19:21, 24; (11) Ps. 69:20; Prov. 15:13; 27:19.

Window (Open Window): (1) Momentary opportunity; (2) Prayer/worship; (3) Investigation; (4) Calling for you to see in the Spirit (prophetic ministry); (5) Flow of the Spirit (air flow/fresh air); (6) Revelation; (2 Kings 13:17).

Also see *Shutting Window* (directly below).

(1) 2 Kings 13:17; (2) Dan. 6:10; (3) Gen. 8:6-9; (4) 1 Sam. 9:9; (5) Job 33:4.

Window (Shutting Window): (1) Opportunity closing; (2) Closing off the Spirit; (3) Shutting out the prophetic; (4) Closing the windows of Heaven.

(1) Heb. 11:15; (2) Ezek. 3:24; Acts 4:18-20; (3) Num. 11:27-28; 23:13; Isa. 30:10; (4) Gen. 8:2; Mal. 3:10.

Windows of Heaven: (1) Abundance; (2) The delivery of a promise from Heaven; (3) Blessing; (4) Revelation.

Also see *Open Heaven*.

(1-2) Gen. 7:11b-12; 2 Kings 7:2, 18-19; Mal. 3:10; (3) Mal. 3:10; (4) Matt. 3:16.

Window-shopping: (1) Desire of the heart; (2) Not yet entering in; (3) Meditating on the things of God.

(1) Ps. 10:3; 37:4; (2) John 3:3 (cf. John 3:5); (3) Gen. 24:63.

Wine: (1) Holy Spirit; (2) Joy; (3) Communion; (4) Resurrection; (5) Prosperity/Plenty; (6) Loud/Violent/Mocker; (7) Blessing; (8) Beguiled/Deceived; (9) Heavy-hearted/wanting to forget; (10) Blood; (11) Cup of wrath for fornication with the world; (12) Under the influence of the religious whore; (13) Substitute for God.

Also see *Bread*.

(1) Matt. 9:17; John 2:3-4; Eph. 5:18; (2) Ps. 4:7; 104:15; Eccl. 10:19; Isa. 16:10; (3) Gen. 14:18; (4) Gen. 40:10-13; (5) Deut. 33:28; Ps. 4:7; Prov. 3:10; Hos. 2:8; (6) Ps. 78:65; Prov. 4:17; 20:1; 23:29-35; (7) Prov. 9:2, 5; (8) Gen. 9:21; 19:32-35; 27:25; Isa. 28:7; Hos. 3:1; 4:11; (9) Prov. 31:4-7; (10) Gen. 49:11; (11) Ps. 75:8; Rev. 14:8, 10; 16:19; 18:3; (12) Rev. 17:2; (13) Ps. 42:2; 63:1; 69:21; Song. 1:2; John 19:28.

Wine Skins: See Bottles.

Wing/s: (1) Carried by the Spirit; (2) Covering; (3) Protection/trust; (4) Intimacy (under wings); (5) Warmth; (6) Hidden/refuge; (7) Worship & service;

(8) Heavenly; (9) Heavenly beings (good or bad); (10) Escape; (11) Joy (under wings); (12) Glory; (13) Lifted; (14) Riches that quickly disappear; (15) Come under the dominion of (stretched out); (16) Healing; (17) Spiritual judgment (plane wings on fire); (18) Angel imparting the fire of God (bird wings on fire).

Also see *Angel/s, Bird/s,* and *Feather/s.*

(1) Exod. 19:4; Deut. 32:11; Ps. 18:10; 139:9; Isa. 40:31; Rev. 12:14; (2) Exod. 25:20; 37:9; (3) Ruth 2:12; Ps. 36:7; 61:4; 91:4; (4) 1 Kings 8:6-7; (3-5) Matt. 23:37; Luke 13:34; (6) Ps. 17:8; 57:1; (7) Isa. 6:2; Rev. 4:8; (8-9) Eccl. 10:20; Ezek. 1:4ff, 10:5ff; Dan. 7:4ff; (10) Ps. 55:6-8; Jer. 48:9; (11) Ps. 63:7; (12) Ps. 68:13; (13) Zech. 5:9; (14) Prov. 23:5; (15) Isa. 8:8; Jer. 48:40; 49:22; Ezek. 17:3; (16) Mal. 4:2; (17) Lev. 1:17; (18) Isa. 6:6.

Wing Nut: (1) Tightening things up spiritually (tightening); (2) Putting something together; (3) Letting things slide spiritually (loosening and falling away).

(1-3) 1 Pet. 1:13; 2 Thess. 2:3.

Wink/ing: (1) Deception; (2) Wickedness; (3) Pending trouble.

(1) Ps. 35:19-20; (2) Prov. 6:12-13; (3) Prov. 10:10.

Winning: (1) Divine favor and blessing; (2) Victory; (3) Salvation; (4) Finishing the race; (5) Financial blessing (winning money).

(1) Deut. 28:6 ("going out" and "coming in" is reference to going to and returning from battle); Ps. 41:11; (2) 1 Chron. 26:27; (3) Prov. 11:30b; (4) 1 Cor. 9:24; 2 Tim. 4:7; Heb. 12:1; (5) Prov. 10:22; Eph. 2:7.

Winter: (1) Death; (2) Hardship/tribulation; (3) Little light (no revelation of Christ); (4) Difficulty in progress; (5) Time of rain; (6) Time of pruning; (7) Time of hibernation/rest; (8) Time of planning and preparation.

(1) Song. 2:11-14 (represents death to resurrection); (2) Mark 13:18-19; (3) John 10:22-24; (4) Acts 27:12; 2 Tim. 4:21; (5) Song. 2:11; (6) John 15:2; (7) Isa. 18:6; Acts 27:12; 28:11; (8) 1 Kings 20:22-26.

Wipe: (1) Cleanse; (2) Rub out/forget; (3) Replace; (4) Dry; (5) Judgment; (6) Comfort (as in wiping away tears).

(1) 2 Kings 21:13; Luke 7:38, 44; John 11:2; 12:3; (2) Neh. 13:14; Prov. 6:33, 30:20; (3) Isa. 25:8; Rev. 21:4; (4) John 13:5; (5) Luke 10:11; (6) Rev. 7:17; 21:4.

Wire: (1) Communication (telephone cord); (2) Snare; (3) Test or trap (trip wire); (4) Bomb (colored wires); (5) Conductor of power; (6) Someone as a connection or connector.

Also see *Barbed Wire* and *Fence.*

(1) Matt. 13:43b; (2-3) Heb. 12:1; (4) 1 Thess. 5:3; (5) Job 37:3; (6) 1 Cor. 1:10; 6:17.

Witch: (1) Demonic powers (a devil); (2) Manipulator and controller; (3) Spell-caster; (4) Deception; (5) Manipulating church.

These people enter the spirit realm outside of Christ (the Door) and, therefore, are an abomination to God.

Also see *Witchcraft, Witch Doctor,* and *Woman—Ungodly.*

(1-5) Exod. 22:18; 1 Sam. 28:3-25; Rev. 2:20.

Witchcraft: (1) Rebellion; (2) Illegitimate authority (= rebellion); (3) Manipulation and control; (4) Use of familiar spirits and spells; (5) Practice magic; (6) Work of the flesh; (7) Drug use.

Also see *Witch.*

(1) 1 Sam. 15:23; (2) 2 Kings 9:22 (cf.1 Kings 21:7); (3) 2 Kings 9:22 & 1 Kings 21:7, 10, 15; (4) 2 Chron. 33:6; (5) Mic. 5:12 (Soothsayers practiced magic); (6) Gal. 5:19-20; (7) Rev. 9:21 (The word *sorceries* is the Greek *pharmakeia,* from which we get the word *pharmacy*).

Witch Doctor: (1) Counterfeit healer; (2) Demonic powers; (3) One under the influence of familiar spirits; (4) Opposed to God/resisters of truth.

(1-4) Exod. 7:11, 22; 8:7; Deut. 18:9-12; Acts 13:8-11.

Wolf: (1) Satan; (2) Unregenerate predators; (3) Predatory ministers; (4) False prophets; (5) Those who ruthlessly destroy people for selfish gain; (6) Sexual or financial predator; (7) Fierce; (8) Deception; (9) Independent spirit (lone wolf).

(1) John 10:10-12; (2) Matt. 10:16; Luke 10:3; (3) 2 Pet. 2:15 (greed); Jude 1:11(greed); (4) Matt. 7:15; Acts 20:29; (5) Ezek. 22:27; (6) Judg. 16:4-5; (7) Hab. 1:8; (8) Matt. 7:15; (9) Gen. 49:27.

Woman: (1) Church; (2) The Holy Spirit; (3) Israel; (4) Spiritual mother; (5) Angel; (6) Literally a woman (possibly you).

The interpretation depends on your assessment of the person. How do you see that person?

Woman (Godly Woman): (2) The Holy Spirit; (5) An angel; (7) A godly example; (8) Wisdom; (9) Justice (legal system).

Woman (Foreign Woman): (1) Ungodly church/person; (2) The Holy Spirit (you do not know her); (3) Church or person from overseas/different denomination; (4) Seductive woman; (5) Idolatrous woman; (6) Corrupt woman; (7) Someone leading you astray; (8) Worldly church (Egyptian woman); (9) Unclean spirit.

Also see *Foreign, Foreigner,* and *Woman.*

(1) Rev. 3:1-3; (2) See *Woman;* (3) John 4:9; Acts 16:9; (4-7) 1 Kings 11:1a, 4; Prov. 5:3-10; (8) See *Egypt* and *Woman;* (9) Prov. 7:26-27.

Woman (Ungodly Woman): (10) Demonic powers; (11) Jezebel Spirit (controlling or in purple); (12) Religious spirit (seducing followers); (13) Sinful church; (14) Babylon (sexually seductive); (15) Spirit of death (black widow); (16) Independent spirit; (17) Fleshly or unattractive church (woman with facial hair). (18) Spirit of the world (uncouth woman).

Also see *Black, Woman (Foreign Woman), Jezebel, Red, Widow,* and for an enticing married woman in red, see *Harlot.* Finally, also see individual names in Name and Place Dictionary.

(1) Eph. 5:25; (2) (Gen. 8:9 & Matt. 3:16); Matt. 23:37; John 3:5; Rom. 8:14, 22, 26a (giving birth); Eph. 5:31-32; (3) Jer. 3:20; (4) 1 Tim. 5:2; Tit. 2:3-4; (7) 1 Pet. 3:5-6; (8) Prov. 9:1; 14:1; (9) As in, blindfolded woman with scales in her hand; (11) Rev. 2:20; 17:4; (12) Prov. 7:10-27; (13) 2 Cor. 6:16; 7:1; (14) Rev. 17:5; (15) Isa. 59:5; (16) 1 Sam. 20:30; Ezek. 36:17; 1 Cor. 11:6a; 1 Pet. 3:5; (17) Gen. 25:25 & Eph. 5:23; (18) 1 Cor. 2:12; 7:33.

Womb: (1) Heart or spirit; (2) Foundation; (3) Place of conception; (4) The place of faith; (5) The place from which one is sent out; (6) Fruit (offspring); (7) Place of unseen preparation.

(1) John 3:3-4; Heb. 11:11; (2) Jer. 1:5; Matt. 1:18; 13:23; John 18:37; (3) Luke 1:31; 2:21; Rom. 4:19-20; (4) Rom. 4:19-20; 1 John 5:4; (5) Gen. 25:23; Gal. 1:15; (6) Gen. 30:2; Deut. 7:13; Ps. 127:3; (7) Isa. 49:5; Ps. 139:15-16 (NKJV).

Wombat: (1) Underground church/person (not openly acknowledged).

(1) John 7:10.

Wood: (1) Fleshly works (earthly effort); (2) Coming from self rather than from the Spirit; (3) Dishonor; (4) Talebearer (gossip); (5) Contention.

Also see *Tree.*

(1-2) <u>1 Cor. 3:12-13, 15</u>; (3) 2 Tim. 2:20; (4) Prov. 26:20; (5) Prov. 26:21.

Woods: (1) Beginning of freedom, but not yet fully secured; (2) Group of people.

Also see *Forest.*

(1) As in "We're not yet out of the woods"; (2) <u>Isa. 7:2</u>.

Wooden Sword: (1) Carnal words; (2) Fighting in the flesh; (1) Naïve presumption; (4) Play fighting or training.

(1) 1 Cor. 3:12-15 & Eph. 6:17; (2-3) 1 Cor. 3:12-15 & Heb. 4:12; (4) 1 Sam. 17:42-43 (NKJV).

Wool: (1) Godly garment rather than human-made garment; (2) Glory; (3) Righteousness; (4) Fleece (test).

Also see *Clothes, Cotton, Snow,* and *White.*

(1) Lev. 19:19b; Deut. 22:11; (2) Dan. 7:9; <u>Rev. 1:14</u>; (3) <u>Isa. 1:18</u>; (4) Judg. 6:37.

Woolworths: See Name and Place Dictionary.

Work: (1) Work for God (faith in action); (2) Self-effort (as opposed to faith); (3) Flesh (as opposed to fruit of the Spirit).

(1) <u>1 Cor. 15:58</u>; Gal. 5:6 (the key); 1 Thess. 1:3; James 2:14, 17-18, 20, 26; (2) <u>Ps. 127:1a</u>; Gal. 2:16; Heb. 6:1; (3) <u>Gal. 5:19-21</u>.

Workman: (1) Believers in the harvest; (2) Healing angel (working on the house); (3) Jesus (fixing the body/temple); (4) Person of the flesh.

Also see *Builder.*

(1) Matt. 9:38; 2 Cor. 8:23; (2) Job 33:23-24; (3) Matt. 12:13; (4) Gal. 2:16.

Worm/s: (1) Old self (person of the flesh); (2) Stinking flesh; (3) Having no backbone or spineless (lacking spiritual fortitude); (4) Disobedience/transgression; (5) Decay/rottenness/corruption; (6) Despised and reproached; (7) The Gospel (as bait); (8) Opening up something that is complicated and may lead to chaos; (9) Bitterness (worms in wood).

(1) Isa. 41:14; (2) Exod. 16:20, 24; Isa. 66:24; (3) Isa. 41:14; Mic. 7:17; (4) Exod. 16:20; Isa. 66:24; (5) Deut. 28:39; Job 7:5; 17:14; (6) Ps. 22:6; (7) Matt. 4:19; (8) As in, "opening a can of worms"; (9) Prov. 5:4; Rev. 8:11.

Worry: (1) Spirit of fear; (2) Double-mindedness.

(1) 2 Tim. 1:7; (2) Matt. 6:25, 31, 34 (cf. NKJV & KJV).

Worship: (1) A life (sacrifice); (2) Service; (3) Activating the Kingdom of Heaven (releasing the lordship of Christ into a situation); (4) Divine warfare.

(1) Gen. 22:5, 10; (2) Matt. 4:10 (Whatever you worship you serve); (3-4) 2 Chron. 20:21-22; Ps. 22:3; 2 Cor. 10:4.

Wound/ed: (1) Damaged conscience; (2) Wounded heart/spirit; (3) Heart pierced by words; (4) Sin; (5) Judgment; (6) Hurts; (7) Troubled; (8) Grief; (9) Adultery; (10) Addict (innumerable wounds); (11) Friendly correction; (12) Victory over the enemy.

Also see *Healing.*

(1) Gen. 4:23; Job 24:12; Ps. 38:4-8; 1 Cor. 8:12; (2) Ps. 109:22; 147:3; Prov. 18:14; 20:30; (3) 1 Sam. 31:3; Ps. 64:7-8; Prov. 18:8; 26:22; (4) Ps. 38:4-5; 68:21; Isa. 1:6, 18; 53:5; Jer. 6:7; 30:14; 1 Cor. 8:12; (5) Jer. 51:52; Ezek. 28:23; (6) Jer. 10:19; (7) Ps. 38:4-8; ,(8) Jer. 6:7; 10:19; 30:12; Nah. 3:19; (9) Prov. 6:32-33; 7:26; (10) Prov. 23:29-30; (11) Prov. 27:6; (12) Isa. 51:9.

Wrap/ping: (1) Caring for; (2) Respect; (3) Preserving; (4) Nurturing; (5) Hiding or keeping secret; (6) Protecting; (7) Wrapping something may change its function; (8) Wrapping strengthens; (9) Be deeply enmeshed; (10) Preparing a gift.

(1-3) Matt. 27:59; Mark 15:46; Luke 23:53; (3) 1 Sam. 21:9; (4) Luke 2:7; (5) Gen. 38:14; (6) 1 Kings 19:13; (7) 2 Kings 2:8; (8) Job 40:17; (9) Jon. 2:5; (10) Matt. 2:11.

Wrecking Ball: (1) Heavy-handedness; (2) Demolish or demolition.

(1) 1 Kings 12:13-14, 19; (2) 2 Cor. 10:4.

Wrestling: (1) Spiritual warfare; (2) Coming to the point of admission/submission; (3) Internal battle between flesh and spirit; (4) Strongman.

(1) Eph. 6:12; (2-3) Gen. 32:24-28; (4) Luke 11:21-22.

Wrinkles: (1) Hardship; (2) Sign of age and decay; (3) Holy (without wrinkles); (4) Sin (as the opposite of holiness).

Also see *Folding* and *Shadow.*

(1) Job 16:8; (2) Eph. 5:27; (3-4) Eph. 5:27.

Wrist: (1) Relationship (particularly within the Body of Christ); (2) Broken relationship (broken wrist).

Also see *Ankle.*

(1-2) Eph. 4:16; Col. 2:19.

X-Box: (1) Playing games; (2) No heart for the things of God.

(1) Matt. 11:16-17; (2) X = No, and box = heart.

X- Ray: (1) Spiritual insight; (2) Actual X-ray required.

(1) Mark 1:10; John 1:32-33; 11:33, 14:17; Acts 2:17.

Yacht: (1) Holy Spirit ministry.

Also see *Boat, Cruise Ship,* and *Houseboat.*

(1) John 3:8.

Yard (Back): (1) Private; (2) Personal; (3) Closed; (4) Exit; (5) Works; (6) Past; (7) Return to idolatry; (8) Disobedience; (9) Your family.

Also see *Garden* and *Yard (Front).*

(1-2) (Matt. 24:3 & John 18:1); Luke 8:17; (3) Song. 4:12; (4) 2 Kings 9:27; 25:4; (5) Gen. 2:15; 3:23; (6) Ruth 1:15-16; 2 Sam. 12:23; (7) Josh. 23:12-13 (KJV); (8) Job 23:12; (9) As in, "You first need to deal with issues in your own backyard."

Yard (Front): (1) Public; (2) Widely known; (3) Open; (4) Entry; (5) Expectancy; (6) Faith; (7) Future; (8) Obedience.

Also see *Garden* and *Yard (Back).*

(1-2) John 18:20; (4) 2 Chron. 3:4; (5) Judg. 11:34; (8) As in, "coming in the right way."

Year: (1) A year may equal a time; (2) A year may equal a day.

Also see *Time* and individual numbers.

(1) Dan. 7:25; (2) Num. 14:34; Ezek. 4:6.

Yeast: (1) Pride; (2) Sin; (3) That which grows when heated/pressured/persecuted; (4) Teaching that puffs up/corrupts; (5) Hypocrisy/treading on others/legalism; (6) Skepticism and rationalism (denial of the supernatural); (7) Sensualism and materialism; (8) The Kingdom of Heaven; (9) Imposed legalism; (10) Unclean or unholy; (11) Causes double-mindedness; (12) Concentrating on knowledge.

Also see *Salt*.

(1) That which corrupts by puffing up; 1 Cor. 5:6; (2) 1 Cor. 5:6-8; (3) Matt. 13:33; (4) <u>Matt. 16:6 & 12</u>; Mark 8:15; <u>Gal. 5:9</u>; (5) Luke 12:1 (leaven of Pharisees); (6) Matt. 16:6 (leaven of Sadducees); (7) Mark 8:15 (leaven of Herod); (8) Matt. 13:33; (9) Matt. 16:6-11; (10) Lev. 10:12; <u>1 Cor. 5:7</u>; (11) Matt. 16:11-12; (12) 1 Cor. 8:1.

Yellow: (1) Welcoming (ribbon); (2) Fearful or cowardly; (3) Spirit of fear; (4) Sin (unclean); (5) Glory of God; (6) Attention-seeking (self-glory); (7) Judgment; (8) Curse/plague.

Also see *Gold*.

(1-3) Present day cultural associations; (4) Lev. 13:30-36 (Yellow hair associated with leprosy. Leprosy is bodily equivalent to sin, leprosy is cleansed, but never healed); (5) Ps. 68:13-14; 1 Pet. 1:7 (association between gold and glory); Isa. 60:9 (association between gold and glory); (6) <u>Prov. 25:27</u>b; 27:2; Isa. 42:8; 48:11b; <u>Jer. 9:23-24</u>a; Matt. 6:2; John 8:50; Acts 12:23; 2 Cor. 12:5-6; (7) Rev. 9:17; (8) Dan. 9:11 (cursed for sin) & Lev. 13:30 (Leprosy is a type of sin).

Yesterday: (1) The past.

(1) Ps. 90:4.

Y-Junction: See T-Junction.

Yoke: (1) Legalistic bondage; (2) Oppression; (3) Joined with; (4) Burden (heavy or light); (5) Under the control of; (6) Harnessed power; (7) Service; (8) Half an acre.

Also see *Bound* and *Egg*.

(1) Acts 15:10; <u>Gal. 5:1</u>; (2) Lev. 26:13; Deut. 28:48; 1 Kings 12:4; (3) <u>2 Cor. 6:14</u>; (4) <u>Isa.</u> 9:4; 10:27; <u>14:25</u>; <u>58:6</u>; Matt. 11:29-30; (5) Gen. 27:40; (6) Job 1:3; 42:12; (7) Jer. 27:2, 7; <u>1 Tim. 6:1</u>; (8) 1 Sam. 14:14.

Younger: If in a dream a person appears younger than they currently are, possible meanings include:

(1) You are looking at the spiritual person who is having youth renewed like the eagle; (2) This is the person of the future; (3) Can symbolize purity and humility; (4) Submissiveness (see 1 Pet. 5:5); (5) Spiritual dominion; (6) Immaturity; (7) You may be conversely looking at a person's past, where that person was independent, selfish, and living a life apart from the Father; (8) This is a person ruled by the lust of the eyes and the flesh; (9) Religious zealot; (10) Someone you haven't known long (If there are two and one younger you may not have known the younger person as long, i.e. it is a younger relationship).

Also see *Child/ren* and *Youth.*

(1) <u>Ps. 103:5</u>; (2) Acts 7:19 (where the babies were the future men of Israel); <u>2 Cor. 4:16</u>; (3) Luke 22:26; John 12:14; (4) 1 Pet. 5:5; (5) Rom. 9:12; (6) 1 Cor. 13:11; (7) Luke 15:12-13; (8) Eccl. 11:9; John 21:18; (9) Acts 7:58; (10) Acts 7:58.

Youth: (1) Redeemed individual; (2) Young person.

Also see *Teenager* and *Younger.*

(1) <u>Job 33:23-25</u>; Ps. 103:3-5.

Youth Hostel: (1) Vibrant young church.

Also see *Backpackers Hostel.*

(1) 1 John 2:13-14.

Yo-yo: (1) Something/issue that goes away and comes back again; (2) Idle hands.

(1) Prov. 26:11; (2) Eccl. 10:18.

Zebra: (1) Africa; (2) Double-mindedness (black and white); (3) Lukewarm and in the world (horse: not black, not white).

Also see *Horse.*

(1) Country of origin; (2) <u>Matt. 5:36-37</u>; (3) Rev. 3:16.

Zeppelin: See Blimp.

Zipper: (1) Opening or opportunity; (2) Not open (stuck zipper); (3) Undone (exposed, revealed, or shamed); (4) Door of your heart; (5) Window of Heaven; (6) Teeth (mouth: keep it "zipped").

Also see *Curtain, Door, Genitals,* and *Veil.*

(1-2) Col. 4:3; (3) Isa. 6:5; (4) Acts 16:14; (5) Luke 17:21 & Rev. 4:1; (6) Job 41:14; Prov. 25:19; Prov. 30:14.

Zombie: (1) A Christian who claims to be alive, but who is without true spiritual life; (2) Someone unable to think for themselves; (3) Someone bewitched and controlled by another.

(1) Rev. 3:1; (2-3) Gal. 3:1.

Zoo: (1) Mix of types/races; (2) Caged/frustrated; (3) On display; (4) Out of your environment; (5) Out of control; (6) The world.

(5) As in, "the place is a zoo"; (6) 1 John 2:16.

The Name and Place Dictionary

Aaron: (1) Elevated; (2) Stately; (3) Christ as High Priest; (4) High priest; (5) Spokesperson; (6) Intercessor.

(1-2) Name meaning; (3) Heb. 5:1-4; (4) Exod. 28:1-4; (5) Exod. 4:14; (6) Heb. 7:25-26.

Abba: (1) Father; (2) Papa.

(1) Mark 14:36.

Abbott: (1) Head priest of an abbey.

Abb/y/ey: (1) Her father rejoices.

Abel: (1) Vanity; (2) A meadow; (3) True believer; (4) Shepherd; (5) Martyr.

(3-5) Gen. 4:1-8; Heb. 12:24.

Abigail: (1) Father of exultation; (2) Her father rejoices.

(1) 1 Sam. 25:14.

Abraham: (1) God the Father; (2) Father of many nations; (3) Friend of God; (4) Patriarch.

(1) Gen 22:2ff; (2) Gen 17:4-5; (3) James 2:23; cf James 4:4; (4) Heb. 7:4.

Absalom: (1) Peaceful father; (2) Bodily perfection and outward beauty, but wicked heart; (3) Treasonous heart-stealer; (4) Infidelity.

(1) Name meaning; (2) 2 Sam. 14:25-26; (3-4) 2 Sam. 15:2-6.

Achan: (1) Misfortune or trouble; (2) A person who enriches themselves from God's work; (3) Remover of protection; (4) Thief; (5) Deceiver.
(1) Name meaning; (2-4) Josh. 7:1, 11; (5) Josh. 7:4-8.

Adam: (1) Red; (2) Earth colored (of the earth); (3) Human; (4) Humankind (5) Sin; (6) Christ.
(1-2) Name meaning; (3-4) One of four Hebrew words for "human"; 1 Cor. 15:22; (5) Gen. 3; (6) 1 Cor. 15:45.

Adan: See Aidan.

Adelaide: (1) Dignified; (2) Aristocrat; (3) May also carry the person's assessment of the city or a person by this name.

Adele: (1) Dignified aristocrat.

Adeline: (1) Amiable; (2) Pleasant.

Adrian: (1) Dark; (2) Dark-skinned.

Adullam: (1) Justice of the people; (2) Shelter.

Agnes: (1) Spotless and pure; (2) Chaste.

Aidan: (1) Fervent; (2) Fiery.

Akubra: (1) Lit. "head covering"; (2) Aussie drover's (one who drives cattle/sheep) hat.

Alabama: (1) Cleaners of thickets; (2) Thicket clearers.

Alamo: (1) Poplar tree.

Alan: (1) (Celtic) Good-looking; (2) (Gaelic) Rock; (3) (French) Noble.

Alana: See Alan.

Alba: (1) Dawn.

Albert/o: (1) Shining nobleman.

Alby: See Albert.

Alcatraz: (1) Pelican; (2) Prison.

Alexander: (1) Protector; (2) Defender of people.

Alex/Alexi/Alexia: See Alexander.

Alf: (1) (German) Noble and ready to fight; (2) (Swedish) Advised by elves.

Alfonso: (1) Noble and ready to fight.

Alfred: (1) Advised by elves (evil spirits).

Alice: (1) Dignified aristocrat.

Alicia: See Alice.

Alita: (1) Having wings.

Allison: (1) Honorable; (2) God-like fame.

Almund: (1) One who defends the temple.

Almunda: (1) Worships the Virgin Mary.

Althea: (1) Faultless.

Alvaro: (1) Guard of all; (2) Guards the truth.

Alvin: (1) Noble friend.

Amado: (1) Beloved.

Amalia: (1) Work; (2) Diligent.

Amanda: (1) Worthy of love.

Amato: See Amado.

Amerigo: See Henry.

Amos: (1) Courageous; (2) Carried; (3) A prophet of judgment; (3) Amos 1:1-3.

Amparo: (1) Protection; (2) Shelter.

Amy: (1) One who is dearly loved.

Ananias: (1) Liar; (2) Greed-driven deception; (3) Messenger; (1-2) Acts 5:3; (3) Acts 9:17.

Anarhlia: (1) Drink of water (as possible variant of nahla).

Andre: See Andrew.

Andrea: (1) Womanly.

Andrew: (1) Masculine; (2) Man; (3) Of a man; in Scripture the name is associated with; (4) Evangelism (It was Andrew who gathered Simon-Peter). (4) John 1:40-41.

Angelo: (1) Messenger; (2) Angel.

Angus: (1) Unique choice; (2) Only option.

Ani: (1) Good-looking.

Anita: See Hannah.

Ann: (1) Favored graciously.

Annabel/la: (1) Favored graciously; (2) Full of grace and beauty.

Annunziata/o: (1) Announces news; (2) Proclaims.

Anthea: (1) Flower lady.

Anthony: (1) Invaluable.

Antoinette: (1) Invaluable.

Anton: (1) Invaluable.

April: (1) To open; (2) When the buds open.

Ari: (1) (Greek) Great thinker; (2) (Norse) Strength of an eagle.

Ariel/e: (1) Lion of God.

Arizona: (1) Place of the small spring.

Arlene: (1) A sworn promise; (2) Oath.

Arnold: (1) Strength of an eagle. (Isa. 40:31).

Art: See Arthur.

Arthur: (1) Having the strength of a bear.

Asa: (1) One who heals.

Asher: (1) Joyful.

Ashley: (1) Grove of ash trees.

Ashlyn: (1) Grove of ash trees.

Ashton: (1) A farm of ash trees.

Aspen: (1) The poplar or aspen tree.

Atlanta: (1) Mighty huntress.

Audrey: (1) Has strength.

August: (1) (English) Born in the eighth month; (2) (Latin) Grand and magnificent (venerable).

Aurelio: (1) Golden; (2) Gilded.

Austin: (1) Renowned.

Austen: (1) Grand and magnificent.

Aymeric: (1) Diligent ruler.

Azam: (1) Greatest; (2) Biggest.

Balder: (1) Without hair.

Bali: (1) Jewel of the east.

Baltimore: (1) Settlement of the big house.

Bani: (1) Constructed.

Barack: (1) Blessed.

Barak: (1) Lightning flash.

Barbara: (1) Stranger; (2) Foreigner.

Barret: (1) Having the power of a bear.

Barrett: (1) At the head; (2) Chief.

Barry: (1) Lives near the border; (2) Having the strength of a bear; (3) Excellent marksman.

Bart: (1) Son of the furrows; (2) Son of the ridges; (3) Son of the plowman.

Barton: (1) Lives on a barley farm.

Baruch: (1) Exalted; (2) Blessed.

Bea: See Beatrice.

Beatrice: (1) One who brings joy.

Beena: (1) Comprehends; (2) Discerns.

Belinda: (1) One who comes with wisdom.

Benedict: (1) Blessed.

Benit/a/o: (1) Blessed; (2) Happy.

Benjamin: (1) Son of my right hand; (2) Son of my strength.

Ber: (1) A bear.

Bernadette: (1) As brave as a bear; (2) Burn a debt (play on words).

Bernice: (1) She brings victory.

Bernie/Bernard: (1) As brave as a bear.

Berri: (1) Bend in the river.

Bess: (1) My God is bountiful.

Betty: See Elizabeth.

Bethany: (1) House of dates.

Bethel: (1) House of God.

Bevan: (1) Young soldier.

Beverley: (1) Field where beavers live.

Beulah: (1) Married; (2) Joined in marriage.

Biju: (1) Victory; (2) Jewels.

Bill: See William.

Bina/h: (1) Comprehends; (2) Discerning.

Bing: (1) Cauldron-shaped hollow.

Blake: (1) Dark; (2) Dark-skinned.

Blair: (1) Child of the field; (2) From the plain.

Blaise: (1) One who lisps or speaks imperfectly.

Blayze: (1) Flaming fire.

Bo: (1) Pleasing appearance; (2) Respected; (3) Having the strength of a bow; (4) Cherished.

Boaz: (1) Fleetness; (2) In His strength.

Bob: (1) One whose fame shines brightly.

Bobby: (1) One whose fame shines brightly.

Boca Raton: (1) Mouth of the mouse; (2) Place where pirates hid.

Bolton: (1) From the main house on the farm.

Bondi: (1) The place of breaking water.

Bonnie: (1) Beautiful; (2) Good.

Boston: (1) Town by the woods.

Bosworth: (1) Lives near the cattle yards.

Boyle: (1) Money-making.

Brad: (1) Broad.

Bradley: (1) Large clearing; (2) Broad meadow.

Brazil: (1) Strength; (2) Conflict.

Brenda: (1) A sword or swordsman.

Brendon: (1) Lives by the beacon.

Brenton: (1) A steep hill.

Brett: (1) Old English tradition; (2) British; (3) Not changing; (4) Government;

Brewer: (1) Beer-maker.
Also see *Brewery* and *Drugs.*

Brian: (1) Strength; (2) Hill; (3) May represent Jesus as the arm or strength of God.
Also see *Hill* and *Strength* in Metaphor Dictionary.
(3) 2 Kings 9:24 & John 12:38.

Bridget: (1) Has strength.

Brock: (1) Lives beside the stream.

Bronwyn: (1) Fair-breasted; (2) May represent the Holy Spirit.

Brooke: (1) Lives beside the stream.

Bruce: (1) Forest.

Bruno: (1) Brown

Brunswick: (1) Bruno's village.

Bryce: (1) (Celtic) Quick; (2) Watchful; (3) Aspiring; (4) (Scottish) Marked with freckles.

Bubba: (1) Good fellow.

Buick: (1) (Irish) Outlying farm; (2) (Dutch) Fat man.

Burn: (1) Lives near the stream.

Cain: (1) Murderer; (2) Carnal believer; (3) Man of the flesh; (4) Self-righteous believer; (5) Sin at the door; (6) Religious.
(1-6) Gen. 4:1-16; Heb. 11:4.

Cairns: (1) Mound of rocks.

Caitlin: (1) Pure; (2) Spotless.

Caleb: (1) Dog; (2) Bold; (3) Impetuous.

Callum: (1) Dove-like.

Campbell: (1) Crooked mouth; (2) Bent mouth.

Camden: (1) Winding valley.

Cameron: (1) Has a bent nose; (2) From the place where the stream bends.

Camilla: (1) Temple attendant.

Canada: (1) Village; (2) Settlement.

Canberra: (1) Field for meeting; (2) Capital (place of decision-making).

Candace: (1) Radiant.

Cape Canaveral: (1) Cane break; (2) Place of rocket launches.

Cara: (1) One who is loved.

Carlo/s: (1) Manly; (2) Masculine.

Carlton: (1) Land between two creeks.

Carol: (1) Womanly; (2) Manly.

Carolyn: (1) Feminine; (2) Womanly; (3) May relate a woman's point of view; (4) Female influence in your life.

Carolina/e: (1) Womanly.

Carmel: (1) Fruitful pasture; (2) Place of victory.
(2) 1 Kings 18:20-40.

Carmen: (1) Crimson color.

Casey: (1) Attentive or alert; (2) Fragrant spice; (3) Small stream.

Cassandra: (1) She confuses.

Cassi: See Cassandra.

Catherine: (1) Spotless; (2) Pure.
(1-2) Eph. 5:27.

Cavan: (1) Born good-looking.

Ceduna: (1) A place to sit down and rest.

Chad: (1) Warrior.

Chandler: (1) Produces candles.

Chantal: (1) Nun who birthed an order to care for the sick; (2) Place of stones; (3) To sing.

Charles: (1) Manly; (2) Masculine.

Charlotte: (1) Man.

Chelsea: (1) Place to land on a river.

Cheryl: (1) One who is loved.

Chevy: (1) Skillful with horses; (2) Mounted soldier.

Chicago: (1) Onion place; (2) Bears (football team).

Chloe: (1) Lush green and blooming.

Christine: (1) One who believes in Christ.

Christopher: (1) Carries the Anointed One.

Christy: (1) One who believes in Christ.

Chrysler: (1) Veil; (2) Weaver of veils.

Chuck: See Charles.

Cienega: (1) Marsh; (2) Swamp.

Cilla: (1) Old; (2) Lived long.

Cinderella: (1) From cinders or ashes.

Cindi/a: (1) To illuminate.

Cindy: (1) Lofty; (2) From the mount.

Cindylou: (1) Fight from the ashes.

Clare: (1) Bright and clear.

Clarence: (1) Shining sword.

Clark/Clarke: (1) Keeper of records; (2) Scholarly.

Claude: (1) Crippled; (2) Lame.

Claudia: See Claude.

Cleveland: (1) Area full of cliffs.

Clinton: (1) Village on a hill.

Col: (1) Dove-like.

Colby: (1) Lives in the dark town.

Cole: (1) (Latin) Farms cabbages; (2) (Greek) Victory over the people; (3) (Irish) Immature cub.

Colin: (1) Victory of the people; (2) Vigorous masculine child.

Colleen: (1) A girl child; (2) Young woman.

Collette: (1) Victory of the people.

Colorado: (1) Reddish.

Con: See Constantine.

Concha: (1) Becoming pregnant.

Connecticut: (1) The long river; (2) Beside the long tidal river.

Connie: (1) Determined and wise; (2) Not changing or constant (Constance).

Constance: (1) Unchanging, constant; (2) Certainty.

Constantine: (1) Unchanging, constant; (2) Certainty.

Conway: (1) (Irish) Plains hound; (2) (Welsh) Consecrated water.

Copenhagen: (1) Merchants' harbor.

Cora: See Coralea.

Coral: (1) Sea-coral; (2) Salmon colored.

Coralea: (1) Young lady; (2) Virgin.

Coralee: See Coralea.

Corby: (1) Raven; (2) Black-bird.

Corbyn: See Corby.

Corcoran: (1) Having a reddish complexion.

Cordel: (1) Maker of rope.

Cordelia: (1) Jewel from the sea.

Coree: (1) Hollow or depression.

Corey: (1) (Irish) A rounded depression or hill; (2) (Scottish) Pool appearing to boil; (3) (English) Chosen one.

Corvette: (1) A fast, lightly armed warship, smaller than a destroyer, often armed for anti-submarine operations.

Cornelius: (1) Horn-shaped; (2) Animal horns.

Corrin: (1) A spear-bearer.

Corrinne: (1) Young lady; (2) Virgin.

Corry: (1) A round hill.

Costa: (1) Unchanging; (2) Constant.

Courtney: (1) Lives at the court.

Craig: (1) Rock; (2) Cliff or crag; (3) Steep rocky outcrop.

Croydon: (1) Saffron valley; (2) Spice valley.

Crystal: (1) Clear and sparkling gem.

Cunningham: (1) Milk bucket hamlet.

Cyndy: (1) Lofty; (2) From the mount.

Dakota: (1) Ally; (2) Friend.

Dale: (1) A valley.

Dallas: (1) From the waterfall.
(1) Ps. 42:7.

Damon: (1) Overcomes; (2) Tames.

Damian: (1) Overcomes; (2) Tames.

Daniel: (1) God is judge.

Danielle: See Daniel.

Dannika: (1) Star of the morning.

Danny: (1) Judging (evaluating).

Daphne: (1) Victory.

Darlene: (1) Darling; (2) Loved.

Darren: (1) Great; (2) Tiny; (3) Stony hill.

Darryl: (1) One who is loved.

Darryn: (1) Little and great.

Darwin: (1) Close friend.

David: (1) Dearly loved one; (2) Beloved; (3) Jesus (as the Beloved).
(3) Eph. 1:6.

Dawn: (1) Sunrise.

Dayna: (1) Judged by God.

Dayton: (1) From the sunlit village.

Dean: (1) From the sandhills (see Matt. 7:26-27).

Deborah: (1) Honey bee; (2) Religious spirit.

Debbie: See Deborah.

December: (1) Ten/th; (2) Tenth month from March, the beginning of first month of ancient Roman calendar.

Declan: (1) Man of prayer; (2) Saint of Ireland.

Deiter: (1) People's army.

Deitrich: (1) One who rules the people.

Deja: (1) Ahead of time; (2) Before.

Dejon: See Deja.

Delany: (1) Challenger; (2) Son of the competitor.

Delilah: (1) Wanted; (2) Desired (see Judg. 16).

Dell: (1) (English) A valley; (2) (German) Dignified aristocrat.

Delma: (1) Belonging to the sea.

Del Sur: (1) Of the south.

Demi: (1) Half of a whole.

Demiah: See Demi.

Demicah: (1) Overcomes.

Demingo: (1) Of the Lord.

Denise: (1) Follower of the wine god.

Dennis: (1) Follower of the wine god.

Denver: (1) Green or grassy valley.

Deion: (1) Plunderer.

Deon: (1) (m) The wine harvest god; (2) (f) The moon.

Derek: (1) One who rules the people; (2) The way (see Ps. 103:7).

Dermot/t: (1) Content; (2) Free from jealousy.

Detroit: (1) Strait; (2) Also see Automobile (auto capital).

Dharma: (1) Justice and duty.

Dianne: (1) Godly; (2) Divine.

Dick: (1) Powerful ruler; (2) Strong.

Diego: (1) See James.

Dierdre/Diedre: (1) Full of grief.

Dinah: (1) Judged as innocent.

Dixie: (1) Strong; (2) Powerful ruler.

Dixy: (1) Upright structure; (2) Wall; (3) Embankment.

Dolores: (1) Sorrowful.

Dominic: (1) Of the Lord.

Donald: (1) Rules over everything.

Donegal: (1) Stranger's fortress.

Donna: (1) Respected woman.

Doreen: (1) Changeable disposition; (2) Melancholy; (3) Good-looking.

Doris: (1) Gift; (2) Present.

Dorothy: (1) A gift from God.

Douglas: (1) Lives near the dark waters; (2) Dark or blood waters.

Drew: (1) Manly; (2) Masculine (i.e. man/kind); (3) Carrier; (4) Vigorous.

Duane: (1) Dark-skinned; (2) Black.

Dudley: (1) From the people's field.

Duncan: (1) Dark fighter; (2) Brown fighter.

Dusten: (1) Courageous soldier.

Dustin: (1) Quarry for brown rock.

Dutch: (1) From Germany.

Dwayne: (1) A song; (2) Little and dark.

Dwight: (1) White.

Dylan: (1) Son of the sea.

Dymock: (1) Swine enclosure.

Dymphna: (1) Poet; (2) Minstrel.

Dympna: (1) Suitable for the task.

Dyna: (1) Having authority.

Earl: (1) Aristocrat; (2) Earl. The fourth rank of nobility (prince, duke, marquis, earl).

Earn: (1) Falcon or eagle.

Edinburgh: (1) Secure; (2) Wealthy and content.

Edith: (1) Gives richly.

Edna: (1) Wealthy advisor.

Edward: (1) Affluent (rich) protector.

Edwin: (1) Wealthy companion.

Egor: (1) Farmer.

Eileen: (1) Of the light.

Elaine: (1) Of the light.

Eleazar: (1) Helper; (2) Whom God aids.

Eli: (1) My God; (2) Uplifted.

Elijah: (1) My God is Jehovah; (2) Preparatory prophet; (3) The Prophets.

Elim: (1) Palm Trees; (2) Oaks.

Eliot/t: (1) The Lord is God.

Elise: (1) Dignified aristocrat.

Elisha: (1) God is Savior; (2) To whom God is salvation.

Elizabeth: (1) To whom God is the oath; (2) My God is bountiful.

Ellen: (1) Of the light.

Ellie: (1) Of the light.

Elliot: (1) An old man from Wales.

Elliott: (1) The Lord is God.

Eloise: (1) Well-known in battle.

El Paso: (1) Passage.

Elton: (1) From the village given by elves.

Elvin: (1) Loved by everyone.

Emi: See Emily.

Emilio: (1) One who flatters.

Emily: (1) One who works hard.

Emma: (1) Great; (2) Universal.

Encino: (1) Oak.

England: (1) Angel-land; (2) The people who dwell by the narrow water.

Enoch: (1) Teaching; (2) Instructed; (3) Dedicated; (4) Experienced.

Enrica: (1) Commands the household.

Enrikos: (1) Commands the household.

Enya: (1) Kernel; (2) Seed.

Enyo: (1) Destroyer of cities.

Enz/o/io: (1) Commands the household.

Eric: (1) Will rule forever.

Erielle: (1) Lion of God.

Erin: (1) Peace; (2) From Ireland.

Esau: (1) Hairy; (2) Man of the flesh;
(1-2) Gen. 25:25, 34; Rom. 9:13; Heb. 12:16-17.

Estelle: (1) Star.

Esther: (1) Star.

Ethan: (1) Firmness.

Eugene: (1) Of good birth.

Eunice: (1) Joyfully triumphant; (2) Conquering well.

Eva: (1) Life-giving.

Evans: (1) Young soldier. (1) 1 John 2:14.

Eve: (1) Life; (2) Life-giving; (3) Womankind; (4) Mother; (5) Deceived; (6) Church.
(1-2) Name meaning; (3) As Eve was the first woman she may be representative of women; (4) Gen. 3:20; (5) 1 Tim. 2:14; (6) Adam and Eve can symbolize Christ and the Church.

Evin: (1) God has favored.

Ezekiel: (1) Whom God will strengthen.

Ezra: (1) Help; (2) Gives assistance.

Fabio: (1) A bean farmer.

Fatima: (1) Fascinating; (2) Weaned; (3) Daughter of the prophet.

Fausto: (1) Favoring.

Fay: (1) A fairy; (2) Demon.

February: (1) To purify by sacrifice.

Felicity: (1) Lucky; (2) Happy.

Ferdinand/o: (1) Bold travel; (2) Daring adventure.

Fernando: (1) One who dares adventure.

Ferrari: (1) Blacksmith; (2) Iron; (3) Recognized as fast, powerful, and expensive autos.

Findon: (1) Lit. "heap-hill"; (2) Church hill.

Fiona: (1) Fair complexioned.

Flabio: (1) Golden-haired.

Fletch/Fletcher: (1) One who makes arrows.

Fleur: (1) A flower.

Flint: (1) Hard stone that sparks when hit.

Florence: (1) Blooming.

Florida: (1) Blooming; (2) Flowering. (Song. 2:12-13; Matt. 24:32).

Floyd: (1) (Irish) God's will; (2) (Celtic) Grey-haired.

Fogerty: (1) Banished.

Fons/Fonsie/zie: (1) Noble and ready to fight.

Ford: (1) Shallow river crossing.

Forest: (1) One who guards the woods.

Forrest: (1) Tree-covered land.

Forrester: (1) One who guards the woods.

Fran/Francis: (1) From France; (2) A javelin; (3) Free.

Frank: (1) A javelin; (2) Free; (3) From France.

Franklin: (1) A landholder of free birth.

Fred: (1) Peace-making ruler.

Freda: See Fred.

Freeman: (1) At liberty.

Fremantle: (1) A poor man's thin coat.

Fremont: (1) Great guardian.

Fresno: (1) Ash tree.

Gabby: (1) See Gabriel.

Gabriel: (1) God-given strength.

Gad: (1) Fortunate; (2) Favorable.

Gail: (1) Full of joy; (2) Delighted.

Gareth: (1) Gentle; (2) Compassionate.

Garth: (1) Gardener.

Gary: (1) Spear-carrier; (2) Spear.

Gavin: (1) Hawk used in battle.

Gemima: (1) One of two; (2) A twin.

Gemini: (1) One of two; (2) A twin.

Gemma: (1) Precious stone.

Gena: (1) (French) White spirit; (2) (Russian) Of good birth.

Genna: (1) Springtime.

Geoff/rey: (1) Full of peace; (2) Has the peace of God.

George: (1) Farmer; (2) Ground-breaker; (3) Harvest worker.

Gerrald: (1) Commands with a spear.

Gerrard: (1) Strength like a spear.

Gideon: (1) One who cuts down; (2) May symbolize a great work done by a few. (1) Judg. 6:25; (2) Judg. 7:7.

Gilbert: (1) Bright pledge/promise; (2) Intelligent boy.

Gilchrist: (1) One who serves Christ.

Gilead: (1) Hill of witness.

Gillian: (1) Youthful.

Giovani: (1) God has favored.

Gisele/Giselle: (1) Promise.

Gladys: (1) Crippled.

Glen: (1) Lives in the valley.

Glenda: (1) Lives in the valley.

Glenelg: (1) In and out of a valley (viewed as a palindrome).

Glenice: (1) Lives in the valley.

Glynn: (1) Lives in the valley.

Godfrey: (1) The peace of God.

Godwin: (1) Friend of God.

Gold Coast: (1) Glorious living; (2) Money (expense or wealth); (3) Ritzy (up-market); (4) The world.

Goldie: (1) Finances; (2) Precious metal.

Goliath: (1) Exile; (2) Soothsayer; (3) Giant.
(1-4) 1 Sam. 17:4, 23.

Gomez: (1) Adult male.

Goran: (1) Farmer.

Gordon: (1) From the wetlands; (2) Marshy field.

Grace: (1) Favor; (2) Esteem; (3) Mercy; (4) Gift.
(1-4) John 1:14.

Graham: (1) From the gravelly farm.

Grant: (1) Bestow or give.

Greg/Gregory: (1) Watchful; (2) Alert; (3) Vigilant.

Gretel: (1) Pearl; (2) Sea jewel.

Grosvenor: (1) Mighty hunter.

Guenter: (1) Fighter; (2) Warrior.

Guido: (1) Escort; (2) Pilot.

Guiseppe: (1) My God will increase.

Guild: (1) Association of craftsmen.

Gunter: (1) Fighter; (2) Warrior.

Gus: (1) Sword or club of the Goths.

Guy: (1) (Celtic) Well-reasoned; (2) (Teutonic) Fighter; (3) Warrior.

Gwen: (1) Fair complexion; (2) White spirit.

Hal: (1) Ruler of the house.

Halifax: (1) Sacred field.

Ham: (1) Warm or hot/heat; (2) Burnt; (3) Dark.
(1) Gen. 9:18.

Hamish: (1) Replacement; (2) See James/Jacob.

Hank: (1) Commands the household.

Hannah: (1) Favored graciously; (2) Experienced anguish to break through to birth the promise in the Spirit.
(2) 1 Sam. 1:10-17 & Rom. 8:26 & Eph. 5:18.

Hans/el: (1) God has favored.

Harley: (1) Field of hares; (2) Doctor/specialist (Harley St.).

Harold: (1) Military commander.

Harris: (1) Son of the commander of the household.

Harry: (1) Commands the household; (2) Military commander.

Harvey: (1) Soldier; (2) Warrior.

Hawaii: (1) From the breath of God came the water of life.

Hayley: (1) Field of hay.

Hazel: (1) Under God's protection.

Heath: (1) Moorland; (2) Wilderness.

Heather: (1) Purple flowering shrub.

Heidi: (1) Dignified aristocrat.

Helen: (1) Of the light.

Henderson: (1) Son of the commander of the household.

Hendon: (1) Valley frequented by hinds.

Henry: (1) Commands the household; (2) Home ruler; (3) Home power.

Herbert: (1) Glorious soldier.

Hilary: (1) Joy; (2) Happiness.

Hilda: (1) Warrior; (2) Battle.

Hilton: (1) Lives at the farm on the hill.

Hobart: (1) Exalted brightness.

Holden: (1) Benevolent; (2) Courteous.

Holly: (1) Small woody plant with red berries; (2) Sacred.

Homer: (1) Security; (2) Held as a pledge; (3) Earnest down payment. (3) 2 Cor. 1:22.

Honda: (1) One from the base of the fields.

Honolulu: (1) Place of shelter; (2) Sheltered bay.

Horace: (1) Keeps account of time.

Houston: (1) Village on a hill.

Howard: (1) The chief watchman.

Hudson: (1) The hooded man's son.

Hugh: (1) Intelligent; (2) Clever.

Hume: (1) The river island.

Humphrey: (1) Guards the household.

Hyde: (1) Prepares hides.

Ian: (1) God has favored.

Illinois: (1) Tribe of superior men.

Imani: (1) Follower; (2) One who believes.

Imogen: (1) Daughter; (2) Girl child.

Impala: (1) Medium-sized African antelope.

Imran: (1) One who entertains guests.

India: (1) River; (2) Body of water.

Indiana: (1) Land of Indians.

Ingrid: (1) Beautiful one.

Innsbruck: (1) Bridge over the inn.

Iona: (1) (Greek) Amethyst; (2) (Aust. Aborigine) Flame.

Iowa: (1) Sleepy ones; (2) This is the place; (3) The beautiful land.

Iran: (1) Mountain.

Iraq: (1) The bank; (2) Between the rivers (from meaning of Mesopotamia).

Ireland: (1) Fat land; (2) Land of abundance.

Irene: (1) Peace; (2) At peace.

Iris: (1) Rainbow; (2) Message from God.

Irwin: (1) One who enjoys the ocean.

Isaac: (1) Laughter; (2) Promise.

Isabel: (1) My God is bountiful.

Isaiah: (1) Salvation of Jehovah; (2) Jehovah is Helper.

Ishmael: (1) Whom God hears; (2) Born of the flesh.
(1) Gen. 16:11; (2) Rom. 9:7-9.

Israel: (1) Prince with God (sitting in heavenly places); (2) Struggles with God; (3) Compared to Jacob, Israel is the spiritual man; (4) Compared to Judah, Israel is the backslidden church.

Issachar: (1) He is hired; (2) One who works for wages.

Italy: (1) Calf land.

Jabez: (1) Causing pain.

Jacinta: (1) Fragrant bell-shaped flowers.

Jack: (1) (English) God has favored; (2) (American) See Jacob.

Jackie/Jacquie: See Jacob.

Jackson: (1) Son of God's gift.

Jacob: (1) Man of the flesh; (2) The old man; (3) Grabber/swindler; (4) Opponent of the spiritual man; (5) Deceiver; (6) Spineless; (7) Worm.
(1-4) Gen. 32:28; (5) Gen. 27:36, 31:20; (6-7) Isa. 41:14.

Jamaal: (1) Beautiful; (2) Good-looking.

Jamahl: (1) Beautiful.

Jameel/a: (1) Beautiful.

James: (1) Replacement; (2) See Jacob.

Jamie: (1) See Jacob.

Jamin: (1) Right arm; (2) Strength.

Jan: (1) God has favored.

Jana: (1) God has favored.

Jane: (1) God has favored.

Janel: (1) Winner; (2) Champion.

Janelle: (1) God has favored.

Janet: (1) God has favored.

Janine: (1) God has favored.

Jannette: (1) God has favored.

Janson: (1) God has favored.

Janssen: (1) Son of God's gift.

January: (1) Beginning; (2) Entrance; (3) Passage; (4) Named after Janus, Roman god of gates and doorways.

Japan: (1) Land of the rising sun.

Japheth: (1) Extension; (2) Expanded; (3) Open.

Jarad: (1) Descending.

Jar/rad/red/rod: (1) (English) Strength like a spear; (2) (Hebrew) Descending.

Jason: (1) Healer.

Jasmine: (1) Fragrant shrub.

Jean: (1) God has favored.

Jeanette: (1) God has been gracious.

Jed: (1) Loved by God.

Jeffery: (1) Full of peace.

Jemimah: (1) Small dove; (2) Affectionate.

Jenna: (1) Tiny bird.

Jennifer: (1) Fair and smooth skinned; (2) White spirit.

Jeremiah: (1) Esteemed by God; (2) Uplifted by God.

Jeremy: (1) Esteemed by God; (2) Uplifted by God.

Jericho: (1) Moon city.

Jeriel: (1) God notices.

Jerusalem: (1) City of wholeness; (2) City of peace; (3) Hub of the kingdom.

Jess: (1) He exists.

Jesse: (1) God is.

Jessica: (1) God exists; (2) God sees.

Jesus: (1) The Lord is deliverance; (2) Savior.

Jezebel: (1) Unmarried (lit. "not at home"); (2) Controlling and manipulative spirit; (3) The spirit behind false or religious church.

Jill: (1) Youthful.

Jim: See James.

Joab: (1) God is my Father.

Joan: (1) God has favored; (2) The grace of God.

Joash: (1) On fire for God.

Job: (1) A desert; (2) One persecuted.

Jody: (1) God gives the ability to increase.

Jody-ann: (1) Celebrated.

Joe: (1) He (God) shall add; (2) May God increase.

Joel: (1) The Lord is God; (2) Jehovah is might.

John: (1) God has favored; (2) The grace of God; (3) Love.

Jonah: (1) Dove. See Dove in Metaphor Dictionary.

Jonathan: (1) A gift from God.

Jones: (1) Son of one God has favored.

Joni: (1) God has favored.

Joram: (1) The Lord is lifted up.

Jordan: (1) Descender; (2) Going down; (3) Death.

Joseph: (1) He (God) shall add; (2) May God increase; (3) God exceeds.

Joshua: (1) Jehovah is salvation; (2) Jesus.

Josiah: (1) Whom Jehovah heals; (2) The fire of the Lord.

Josilin: (1) Joy.

Josy/Josi: (1) God adds.

Joy: (1) Happy.

Joyce: (1) Joy.

Juan: (1) God has favored.

Juanita: (1) God has favored.

Judah: (1) Praise.

Judas: (1) A Jew from Judea.

Judith: (1) Praised; (2) Youthful; (3) From Judea.

Judson: (1) Celebrated.

Judy: (1) Celebrated.

Julia/Julie: (1) Young; (2) Youthful.

Julian: (1) Young; (2) Youthful.

Julie-anne: (1) Young; (2) Youthful; (3) Young by God's grace.

Juliette: (1) Young; (2) Youthful.

July: (1) Young; (2) Youthful.

June: (1) Protector of women; (2) Guardian.

Justin: (1) Unbiased; (2) Upright.

Kalisha: (1) Spotless; (2) Pure.

Kansas: (1) People of the south wind.
(1) Song. 4:16; Luke 12:55; Acts 27:13.

Kara: (1) Small marsupial; (2) Possum.

Karen: (1) Spotless; (2) Pure.

Karl: (1) Masculine; (2) Manly.

Karralee: (1) Spotless or pure-haven.

Kasey: (1) Attentive; (2) Alert.

Kasie: See Kasey.

Kate: (1) Spotless; (2) Pure.

Katherine: (1) Spotless; (2) Pure; (3) The Church.
(1-3) Eph. 5:27.

Kay: (1) Spotless; (2) Pure.

Kaylene: (1) Cares for the keys.

K.C.: (1) Courageous; (2) Brave.

Keith: (1) From the woodlands.

Keiler: (1) Maker of wooden pegs/wedges.

Keimer: Described by Ben Franklin as an: (1) Odd fish.

Keisha: (1) Great happiness.

Kelly: (1) Fighter; (2) Warrior.

Kelsie: (1) From island of ships.

Kemp/e: (1) Fighter; (2) Warrior.

Kenneth: (1) Handsome.

Kentucky: (1) Meadowland; (2) Land of tomorrow.

Kevin: (1) Born good-looking.

Kerry: (1) Dark; (2) Dark-skinned.

Kim: See Kimberley.

Kimberley: (1) From a royal town.

Kira: See Jacob.

Kirk: (1) Lives near the church.

Kirrily: (1) Leaf or bark of a gum tree.

Kirrin: See Kyrin.

Kirsten: (1) Christ follower.

Kirsty: (1) Christ follower.

K-Mart: From meaning of the founder's name Kresge: (1) Love; (2) Fish (believer); (3) Merchandising/greedy (business or church).

Korah: (1) Baldness; (2) Worship; (3) Rebellion.

Kristan: (1) One who believes in Christ.

Kristen: (1) Consecrated by anointing.

Krystal: (1) Sparking clear quartz gemstone.

Kurt: (1) Candid counselor.

Kyle: (1) Where the water narrows.

Kylie: (1) Boomerang; (2) Something that has to go ("take off" overseas) and return to be appreciated.

Kym: (1) Chief; (2) Ruler.

Kyrin: (1) Dark-skinned.

La Brea: (1) Tar; (2) Tar pits.

Lachlan: (1) Hostile; (2) War-like.

Lachlann: (1) Comes from Scandinavia (Denmark, Norway, or Sweden).

Lalor: (1) One with leprosy.

Lana: (1) Calmly floating.

Lancaster: (1) Castle on the Lune (pure) River.

Lance: (1) An attendant; (2) One who serves.

Lara: (1) Shining ones; (2) Full of joy.

Larissa: (1) Full of joy; (2) Laughing.

Las Cruces: (1) The crosses.

Las Vegas: (1) Meadows; (2) Gambling.

Latoya: (1) Achieved victory; (2) Triumphed.

Laura: (1) Victory.

Lauren: (1) Victory.

Laurence: (1) Victory.

Lavinia: (1) Cleansed; (2) Made pure.

Lazarus: (1) Whom God aids; (2) Protected by God.

Leane: (1) Favored willow tree.

Leann: (1) Young and beautiful.

Leanna: (1) Bound like a vine-covered tree.

Leanne: (1) Luminous; (2) Full of beauty.

Leah: (1) Weary; (2) Tired.

Lee: (1) On the sheltered side.

Leif: (1) Relative; (2) Descendant; (3) Heir.

Leisel: (1) Dedicated to God.

Leith: (1) Grassy land; (2) Broad.

Lenny: (1) Like a lion.

Leon/a: (1) Lion cub.

Leonard: (1) Lion-like.

Leroy: (1) Kingly; (2) Royal.

Lesley: (1) Lives by the grey fort/castle.

Lester: (1) Camp of the legion.

Levi: (1) United; (2) Joined; (3) Union.

Lewis: (1) Famed in battle.

Liam: (1) Determined to guard. See William.

Libby: (1) My God is bountiful.

Lillian: (1) Lily.

Lima: (1) Goddess of the entrance.

Linda: (1) Beautiful; (2) One who comes with wisdom; (3) Could be from Germanic lindi, which means serpent or dragon.

Lindley: (1) From the peaceful field.

Lindsay: (1) Island of linden trees.

Linley: (1) Pool of water in a field.

Lionel: (1) Lion cub.

Lisa: (1) My God is bountiful.

Lissie/Lissy: (1) My God is bountiful.

Liz: (1) My God is bountiful.

Lobethal: (1) Valley of praise.

Lois: (1) At liberty.

Lola: (1) Womanly.

London: (1) The moon's stronghold; (2) Church stronghold.

Lorenzo: (1) Victory; (2) Faith; (3) From the island of the bay trees.

Lorraine: (1) Known for war exploits.

Lorna: (1) From the place of the bay (laurel) trees; (2) Victory (laurel wreath).

Lorne: (1) Desolate; (2) Deserted.

Los Angeles: (1) The angels.

Los Gatos: (1) The cats.

Los Nietos: (1) The grandchildren.

Lou: (1) Famed in battle.

Louise: (1) Famed in battle.

Luba: (1) Delightfully affectionate.

Luca: (1) To illuminate.

Lucas: (1) Of the light.

Lucien: (1) To illuminate.

Lucille: (1) To illuminate.

Lucinda: (1) To illuminate.

Lucretia: (1) Gain; (2) Profit.

Lucy: (1) To illuminate.

Luigi: (1) Well-known in battle.

Luisa: (1) Famed in battle.

Luke: (1) Of the light.

Lulu: (1) Famed in battle.

Lynda: See Linda.

Lynne: (1) Water cascade or the pool beneath.

Mac: (1) The son of.

Macadam: (1) Son of the red earth.

Maddison: (1) (English) Child of courage; (2) (Hebrew) Gift of God.

Madeleine: (1) From the place of the tower.

Madison: (1) Child of courage.

Madonna: (1) My lady; (2) Religious church (Mary and child).

Magill: (1) Son of the lowlander; (2) Son of the foreigner.

Makala: (1) The myrtle tree.

Malachi: (1) Messenger of Jehovah.

Malcolm: (1) Dove servant.

Mandy: (1) Worthy of love.

Manel: (1) God is with us.

Mannum: (1) Unknown; (2) Camping ground.

Manoah: (1) Relaxed; (2) Tranquil place.

Manuel: (1) God is with us.

Mara: (1) Bitter.

Marcell/o: (1) Small hammer.

March: (1) Lives at the border; (2) The god of war; (3) March was originally the beginning of the year and marked the return to war.

Marcy: (1) A large hammer.

Marduk: (1) Chief god, champion against chaos.

Margaret: (1) Pearl; (2) Sea jewel.

Maria/h: (1) Beloved one.

Marilyn: (1) Descended from Mary.

Mario: (1) Hostile; (2) Warlike.

Marion: (1) Sea of bitterness; (2) Rebelliousness; (3) Beloved one.

Marjorie: (1) Pearl; (2) Sea jewel.

Mark: (1) A hammer.
(1) Jer. 23:29.

Marlane: (1) From the place of the tower.

Marlene: (1) Beloved one from Magdala (tower).

Marlon: (1) Small hawk or falcon.

Marlow: (1) Hill by the sea.

Marshall: (1) One who manages another's property.

Martin: (1) Hostile; (2) Warlike.

Marty: See Martin.

Marvel: (1) Miraculous.

Mary: (1) Beloved one.

Marylou: (1) Beloved one who is famed as a warrior.

Massachusetts: (1) At the range of hills; (2) At or about the great hill.

Makita: (1) Pet form of Matilda; (2) Sweet.

Matilda: (1) Strong battle maiden; (2) Stamina to fight.

Matsushita: (1) Below the pine.

Matthew: (1) Gift from God.

Maureen: (1) Beloved one.

Maurice: (1) One who has dark skin.

Maverick: (1) Self-confident; (2) Self-sufficient.

Max: (1) Most of all; (2) Greatest; (3) From maximum.

May: (1) (Old English) Grandmother; (2) Growth or increase.

McAllister: (1) Son of the one who protects men.

McArthur: (1) Son of a fearless father.

McBride: (1) Son of one who has strength.

McCallum: (1) Son of the dove.

McCauley: (1) Son of ancestors.

McCloud: (1) Unattractive man's son.

McCoy: (1) Bright; (2) Intelligent.

McCrea: (1) Son of mercy.

McDonald: (1) Son who rules over everything.

McDougall: (1) Lives near the dark waters.

McDuff: (1) Blackman's son.

McGuire: (1) Fair son.

McKenzie: (1) Good-looking.

McKinley: (1) Son of the wise chief.

McLaine: (1) Son of a lion.

McLean: (1) Son of a lion

McMahon: (1) Son of a bear.

McMurray: (1) Son of the sea lord.

McSorley: (1) Son of summer seafarer.

Megan: (1) Pearl; (2) Sea jewel.

Mel: (1) Chief.

Melanie: (1) Dark; (2) Dark-skinned.

Melbourne: (1) From the mill by the stream.

Melissa: (1) As sweet as honey; (2) Honey.

Merlin: (1) Hill by the sea.

Mervyn: (1) Seafarer; (2) One who enjoys the sea.

Mexico: (1) In the navel of the moon; (2) The rabbit's navel.

Miami: (1) People of the peninsula.

Michael: (1) Who is like God! (2) Who is like God? (3) Chief angel.

Michelle: See Michael.

Michigan: (1) Great or large lake.

Midian: (1) Judgment.

Miles: (1) (English) Tender (benevolent); (3) (Latin) Member of the army (soldier).

Millar: (1) Mill manager.

Miller: (1) Grinds grain at the mill.

Millicent: (1) Diligent; (2) Hard-working.

Milwaukee: (1) A rich beautiful land; (2) Fine land.

Minnesota: (1) Water that reflects the sky; (2) Sky-tinted water.

Miranda: (1) Fantastic; (2) Wonderful.

Miriam: (1) One who opposes authority.

Mississippi: (1) Large river; (2) Father of waters.

Missouri: (1) People with the dugout canoes; (2) Town of large canoes.

Mitsubishi: (1) Three water chestnuts.

Mitchell: (1) Who is like God! (2) Who is like God?

Mahogany: (1) Wealthy; (2) Powerful.

Molly: (1) Beloved one.

Mona: (1) (Greek) Alone; (2) (Irish) Honorable, noble.

Monaro: (1) High plateau or high plain.

Monica: (1) Advisor.

Montana: (1) Mountain.

Montecito: (1) Little woods.

Montreal: (1) Imperial mountain.

Monty: (1) A mountain.

Monro: (1) At the mouth of the river.

Monroe: (1) Red-colored marshland.

Moor/e: (1) One who has dark skin.

Mordecai: (1) Worshipper of Marduk/Merodach.

Moriah: (1) God educates.

Morocco: (1) Land of the setting sun; (2) Fortified.

Morris: (1) Son of dark skin.

Moses: (1) Delivered from water; (2) Drawn out of the water; (3) The Law.

Muncie: (1) People of the stony country.

Munro/e: (1) Red-colored marshlands.

Murial: (1) Perfume; (2) Aromatic ointment.

Muriel: (1) Ocean sparkle.

Murray: (1) Of the ocean.

Mustafa: (1) Chosen as king.

Mustang: (1) Wild and untamed.

Myer/s: (1) Illuminates.

Myra/n: (1) Aromatic ointment; (2) Perfume.

Nabal: (1) Fool.
(1) 1 Sam. 25:25; Ps. 14:1.

Nadia: (1) Hope.

Nadine: (1) Hope.

Nahbi: (1) Hidden. (1) Num. 13:14.

Nahum: (1) Comforter.

Nancy: (1) Favored graciously.

Naomi: (1) Pleasant; (2) Delightful.

Naphtali: (1) My wrestling. (1) Gen. 30:8.

Narelle: (1) Small one.

Natalie: (1) Born on Christmas day.

Natanya: (1) Gift of God; (2) What God gave.

Natasha: (1) Born on Christmas day.

Nathan: (1) Gift.
(1) 2 Sam. 7:2.

Nathaniel: (1) Gift of God; (2) God has given.

Nazareth: (1) Branch.

Neah: (1) Of a slope.

Nebai: (1) Fruitful.

Nebo: (1) A lofty pace; (2) Could relate to pride; (3) Place where Moses died. (1) Deut. 32:49.

Nebraska: (1) Flat or spreading water.

Nehemiah: (1) God comforts.

Nelly: (1) Of the light.

Nelson: (1) Son of Neil; (2) Champion; (3) Winner.

Neo: (1) Chosen one; (2) New.
(1) As in, *The Matrix;* Matt. 22:14.

Neil: (1) Winner; (2) Champion; (3) Cloud.

Nestle: (1) Bird's nest.

Nevada: (1) Snow-covered.

Neville: (1) From the new settlement.

New Zealand: (1) New zeal-land; (2) Land of the long white cloud.

Nick: (1) Victory; (2) Triumph.

Nicolas: (1) Victory of the people; (2) Conqueror of the people. (2) Acts 6:5.

Nicole: (1) Victory of the people.

Nigel: (1) Champion; (2) Winner.

Nike: (1) Victory.

Nikita: (1) Victory of the people.

Nintendo: (1) Entrusted to Heaven's store.

Noah: (1) Comfort; (2) Rest.

Nolly: (1) The olive tree.

Noni: (1) Highly esteemed; (2) Honored.

Nora: (1) Esteemed; (2) Honored.

Noreen: (1) Law; (2) Regulation.

Norelle: (1) Comes from the north.

Norm/an: (1) Man from the north.

Norr/ie/y: (1) Man from the north.

North Dakota: (1) Allies.

Norton: (1) Northern farm.

Norwood: (1) Northern forest.

November: (1) Nine.

Nun: (1) Fish.

Oakley: (1) Field of the oak tree.

O'Brien: (1) Son of a strong man.

October: (1) Eight/h; (2) Eighth month from March, the beginning of ancient Roman calendar.

Odette: (1) Prosperous.

Odin: (1) The chief god.

Ohio: (1) Beautiful river; (2) Great river.

Oklahoma: (1) Red people.

Olaf: (1) Relic; (2) Inherited from forbears.

Olive: (1) The fruit of the olive.

Oliver: (1) The olive tree.

Olivia: (1) Fruit of the olive tree.

Onkaparinga: (1) The women's river.

Onslow/e: (1) Hill of a zealous man.

Ony: (1) An eagle.

Oprah: (1) A young deer. (1) Ps. 42:1.

Orlando: (1) Well known in the land.

Orson: (1) Young bear.

Osborn/e: (1) One who fights for the gods.

Oscar: (1) Spear of the gods.

Oshea: (1) Son from the fairy palace.

Osmar: (1) Glory from God.

Osmund: (1) Security of God.

Ossie: (1) One who fights for God.

Oswald: (1) The power of God.

Oswego: (1) The outpouring.

Oswin: (1) Friend of God.

Owen: (1) Of good birth.

Pacoima: (1) Running water. (1) John 7:38.

Paige: (1) Attendant.

Pamela: (1) Sweetness of honey.

Parkhurst: (1) Dweller in the park house.

Parkins/on: (1) Son of stone.

Pasquale: (1) Born at Easter.

Patrice: (1) Noble; (2) Aristocrat.

Patricia: (1) Noble; (2) Aristocratic.

Patrick: (1) Noble; (2) Aristocratic.

Paul: (1) Small; (2) Little; (3) Humble.

Paris: (1) One who loves.

Paterson: (1) Father's son.

Payne: (1) Rural; (2) Villager; (3) Homely.

Pedro: See Peter.

Peggy: (1) Pearl.

Pennington: (1) Lit. "Penny town"; (2) i.e. Poorville.

Penny: (1) Plant with large, handsome flowers.

Penrith: (1) Main river crossing.

Percival: See Percy.

Percy: (1) Penetrates the valley.

Perri: (1) The tree bearing pears.

Perry: (1) (French) Rock; (2) (Latin) Roaming, travelling, wanderer; (3) (French) The tree bearing pears.

Persian: (1) Independent (as in cat).

Perth: (1) Shrubbery with prickles or spines.

Peta: (1) See Peter; (2) Golden-colored eagle.

Peter: (1) A rock; (2) A stone.

Petronella: See Peter.

Philadelphia: (1) Brotherly love.

Philip: (1) One who loves horses; (2) Lover of Egypt (turning to the world). (2) Isa. 31:1, 3.

Phoebe: (1) Radiant; (2) Glowing.

Phoenix: (1) Red as blood; (2) Mythological bird that was resurrected.

Phylis: (1) A leafy green branch.

Pierre: See Peter.

Pino: (1) My God will increase.

Pirie: (1) The son of Peter; (2) Dweller by the pear tree.

Pittsburgh: (1) Former steel producer; (2) Pirates (baseball team).

Polly: (1) Beloved one.

Porsche: (1) Portion or offering.

Port: (1) A door; (2) Doorkeeper.

Priscilla: (1) Old; (2) Lived long.

Prospect: (1) Positive future.

Pryor: (1) Officer in a monastic order.

Quade: (1) Powerful ruler.

Quaide: (1) Powerful fighter.

Quanesha: (1) Energetic or vivacious; (2) Woman.

Queens (NY): See Queen in Metaphor Dictionary.

Queensland: See Queen in Metaphor Dictionary.

Quigley: (1) Wild or unruly hair.

Quigly: (1) Of mother's side.

Quimby: (1) Lady's estate.

Quincy: (1) Fifth born.

Quinten: (1) Fifth born.

Quong: (1) A bright light.

Rachel: (1) Ewe; (2) Female sheep; (3) May represent one's wife; (4) Christ (as the lamb).
(2-3) 2 Sam. 12:3, 7-9.

Raelene: (1) A female sheep.

Rafael: See Raphael.

Rahab: (1) Broad; (2) Violence; (3) Proud; (4) Free; (5) Prostitute.
(1) Josh. 2:1; (2) Ps. 87:4.

Ralph: (1) Consults with wolves.

Randall: (1) Shield wolf; (2) Courage and strength.

Randy: (1) Shield wolf; (2) Courage and strength.

Raphael: (1) Healed by God. (1) 1 Chron. 26:7.

Raul: (1) Consults with wolves.

Ray-anne: (1) Friendly.

Raylena: (1) Ewe.

Raylene: (1) Deer by the cascades.

Raymond: (1) Mighty and wise protector.

Rea/h: (1) Poppy (graceful and delicate flower).

Reannan: (1) Favored graciously.

Rebecca: (1) Tied to; (2) Noose; (3) Secured.

Redondo: (1) Round.

Reese: (1) Keen; (2) Fervent; (3) Fiery.

Reg: (1) Judges with strength.

Regan: (1) Royal descendant.

Reinhart: (1) Judges with strength.

Renee: (1) Born again (see John 3:3).

Reuben: (1) Behold a son.

Rex: (1) A king.

Rhea: (1) Flowing stream.

Rhett: (1) Fervent; (2) Keen.

Rhonda: (1) Majestic; (2) Noisy.

Rhyanna: (1) A nymph or demon.

Rhys: (1) Fervent; (2) Keen.

Ria/h: (1) The river mouth; (2) The river.

Richard: (1) Strong; (2) Powerful ruler.

Richmond: (1) Powerful guardian.

Rick: See Richard.

Riddley: (1) Marshy land where reeds grow.

Ridley: (1) Red-colored fields.

Riki: See Richard.

Riley: (1) Courageous; (2) Field of rye.

Rita: (1) Pearl; (2) Sea jewel.

Robert: (1) One whose fame shines brightly.

Robin: (1) One whose fame shines brightly.

Rochelle: (1) Rock.

Rod: (1) See Rodney; (2) Word of God (as the Rod in Moses' hand).

Rodney: (1) Reedy island.

Roebuck: (1) Small deer.

Roger: (1) Famous spearman (see 1 Chron. 11:11).

Rohan: (1) Horse country; (2) Having red hair; (3) Fragrant wood.

Roland: (1) Well-known in the land; (2) lit. "Famous land."

Roma: (1) From Rome, Italy; (2) May be a symbol of the religious church.

Romeo: (1) A Roman pilgrim.

Ronald: (1) Judges with strength (see Ps. 54:1).

Rosalind: (1) Wisdom and strength.

Ross: (1) From the cape or peninsula.

Rowan: (1) Red.

Roweena: (1) Well-known friend.

Rowland: See Roland.

Roxanne: (1) Sunrise; (2) A bright light.

Roy: (1) Having red hair.

Rundle: (1) Spacious or roomy valley.

Rush: (1) Having red or fox-colored hair.

Russell: (1) A fox; (2) Red-haired.
(1) Luke 13:31-32; (2) Gen. 25:25.

Ruth: (1) Companion; (2) Friend.

Ryan: (1) Royal descendant.

Rylie: See Riley.

Salem: (1) Peace; (2) At peace.

Salisbury: (1) Fortress or stronghold near a pond.

Sally: (1) Princess.

Samantha: (1) God heard.

Samsung: (1) Three stars.

Samuel: (1) God has heard; (2) God hears.

San Francisco: (1) Saint Francis of Assisi.

San Diego: (1) Saint James.

Sandra: (1) Protector; (2) Defender of man.

Sangre de Cristo Mountains: (1) The blood of Christ mountains

San Pedro: (1) Saint Peter.

Santa Fe: (1) Holy faith.

Sarah: (1) Princess.

Sasha: (1) Protector; (2) Defender of men.

Saul: (1) Asked for; (2) Demanded.

Savannah: (1) Wide grasslands.

Sawyer: (1) Wood cutter.

Scott: (1) From Scotland; (2) Tattooed (from the blue faces of the Picts).

Sean: (1) God has favored.

Sears: (1) Carpenter.

Seaton: (1) Sea town.

Sebastian: (1) Revered or respected.

September: (1) Seven/th; (2) Seventh month from March which used to be the beginning of Roman calendar.

Sergio: (1) Assistant; (2) Aide.

Shalem: (1) Whole; (2) Peace.

Shane: (1) God has favored; (2) The grace of God.

Shanghai: (1) Lit. "Above sea"; (2) Heaven's river.

Shani: (1) Wonderful.

Shanna: See Shannon.

Shannon: (1) Small, but wise.

Shantelle: See Chantal.

Sharna/y: (1) Flat plain.

Sharpay: (1) Sand skin.

Sharon: (1) Flat plain.

Shaun: (1) God has favored.

Sheila: (1) Sight-impaired; (2) Blind.

Shelley: (1) From the field on the ridge.

Shemus: (1) Replacement; (2) See James.

Sherilyn: (1) One who is loved.

Shireen: (1) Sweet.

Shirley: (1) Sunlit meadow.

Shivon: (1) God has favored.

Shivonne: (1) Bowman/archer.

Shona/h: (1) God has favored.

Sibyl: (1) Fortune teller; (2) Sage.

Siegfried: (1) Peace from victory.

Silvana/o: (1) From the woodland.

Silvia: (1) From the woodland.

Silvio: (1) Made of silver.

Simeon: (1) Hearing; (2) Obedience.

Simon: (1) One who hears; (2) Reed (moved by the wind of circumstance).

Simone: See Simon.

Simmonds: See Simon.

Simpson: See Simon.

Singapore: (1) Lion city.

Siobhan: (1) God is gracious; (2) God has favored.

Slobodan: (1) Freedom.

Smith: (1) Iron worker; (2) Blacksmith; (3) Works.

Sommara: (1) One who calls a group together.

Sonya: (1) One who is wise.

Sony: (1) Sound.

Sophie/a: (1) One who is wise.

Spalding: (1) From a divided meadow.

Spencer: (1) Custodian of the provisions.

Sporting Team Names:
Aussie Rules Football

Adelaide Crows: See Raven.

Brisbane Lions: See Lion.

Carlton Blues: See Blue.

Collingwood Magpies: See Raven and Black and White.

Essendon Bombers: See Aeroplane and Bomb.

Footscray Bulldogs: See Dog.

Fremantle Dockers: See Fremantle.

Melbourne Demons: See Demon.

North Melbourne Kangaroos: See Kangaroos.

Port Adelaide Power: See Power.

Richmond Tigers: See Tiger.

Sydney Swans: See Sydney and Swan.

St. Kilda Saints: (1) Fellow believers; (2) Deceased fellow believers.

West Coast Eagles: See Coast, Eagle, and West.

Hawthorn Hawks: See Hawks.

Baseball

Anaheim Angels: See Angels.

Cleveland Indians: See Indigenous.

Detroit Tigers: See Tiger.

Houston Astros: See Astronaut and Flying.

Los Angeles Dodgers: See Jacob.

Milwaukee Brewers: See Brewer.

Minnesota Twins: See Thomas and Two.

Montreal Expos: See Carnival.

N.Y. Mets: See City.

Pittsburgh Pirates: See Thief.

San Francisco Giants: See Giant.

Basketball

Atlanta Hawks: See Hawk.

Denver Nuggets: See Gold.

Detroit Pistons: See Cog and Automobile.

Indiana Pacers: See Horse.

Los Angeles Clippers: See Sail and Ship.

Los Angeles Lakers: See Lake.

New Jersey Nets: See Net.

N.Y. Knickerbockers: See York.

Seattle Supersonics: See Aeroplane, Flying, and Speed.

Utah Jazz: See Jazz.

Football

Arizona Cardinals: See Priest.

Baltimore Ravens: See Raven.

Chicago Bears: See Bear.

Green Bay Packers: See Gift, Industry, and Moving House.

Philadelphia Eagles: See Eagles.

Kansas City Chiefs: See Chief.

Ice Hockey

Anaheim Mighty Ducks: See Duck.

Boston Bruins: See Boston and Bear (Bruin is Dutch for brown).

Calgary Flames: See Flame.

Detroit Red Wings: See combinations of entries under Red and Wings.

New Jersey Devils: See Demon.

New York Rangers: See Police.

Sri Lanka: (1) Resplendent land.

Stacey: (1) Restored to life.

Stanley: (1) From the rocky meadow.

Stavros: (1) The Cross.

Stefani: See Stephen.

Stella: (1) A star.

Stephanie: See Stephen.

Stephen: (1) Crowned with a laurel wreath; (2) Victorious; (3) May represent faith; (4) May represent Christ.
(3) Acts 6:5, 8; 1 John 5:4.

Steven: (1) See Stephen.

Stuart: (1) A caretaker of royal property.

Susan: (1) Lily

Suzuki: (1) Bell tree.

Switzerland: (1) Neutral; (2) Banking.
(1) Isa. 62:6; (2) Ob. 1:3; Jer. 17:3.

Sydney: (1) Wide meadow; (2) Wide island; (3) From the French town St. Denis near Paris.

Sylvester: (1) From the woodland.

Tabor: (1) Height; (2) Broken.

Tahiti: (1) Facing the sunrise; (2) East.

Tahlia: (1) (Hebrew) Small, gentle sheep; (2) (Greek) Blossoming or blooming.

Takahashi: (1) High bridge.

Talya: (1) Heaven dew; (2) Light rain.

Tamara: (1) A palm tree.

Tameka: (1) One of two; (2) A twin.

Tammy: (1) Palm tree.

Tampa: (1) Stick of fire.

Tamsin: (1) One of twins.

Tandy: (1) Masculine; (2) Male.

Tanicha: (1) Symbol.

Tanja: (1) Angel; (2) Messenger from God.

Tanya: (1) Fairy queen; (2) Queen.

Tara: (1) Rocky crag or hill; (2) Tower; (3) King's meeting place.

Target (Shop-Mart): (1) Targeted (vulnerable); (2) Goal.

Tarzana: (1) Tarzan.

Taylor: (1) Worker in cloth.

Teak: (1) Writer of poems.

Ted: (1) Affluent protector.

Teegan: (1) Attractive woman.

Teresa: See Theresa.

Terri: (1) One who harvests.

Terry: (1) Glossy; (2) Smooth.

Tess: (1) One who harvests.

Tessa: (1) Fourth born.

Tessie/Tessy: (1) One who harvests.

Texas: (1) Friendship; (2) Ally.

Thailand: (1) Land of the free.

Thampy: (1) Second son.

Theadora: (1) A gift from God.

Thelma: (1) Nurturing.

Theo: (1) God.

Theodore: (1) A gift from God.

Theresa: (1) One who harvests.

Thomas: (1) One of two; (2) A twin; (3) Doubt; (4) From which the surnames Thompson, Tomkin, and Tomlin come.

Thor: (1) The god of thunder.

Thorp: (1) One who looks after the fires.

Thorpe: (1) Lives in the small village.

Tiara: (1) Semi-circular crown.

Tiffany: (1) God is appearing.

Timothy: (1) Gives honor to God; (2) God-honoring.

Tina: (1) Small.

Tobias: (1) The Lord is good.

Toby: (1) The Lord is good.

Todd: (1) Fox hunter.

Tokyo: (1) Expressing hope.

Tom: See Thomas.

Toni/y: (1) Invaluable.

Topeka: (1) A good place to grow potatoes.

Toronto: (1) Place where trees stand in the water; (2) Meeting place.

Toula: (1) Light of God.

Toya: (1) Achieved victory; (2) Triumphed.

Toyota: (1) Lucky; (2) Eight.

Tracey: (1) One who harvests.

Travis: (1) Road junction.

Trent: (1) Fast flowing stream.

Trevor: (1) From the large village.

Tri: (1) Third child.

Troy: (1) (Irish) Foot soldier; (2) (French) Having curly hair; (3) From Troyes, France.

Truc: (1) Bamboo.

Trudy: (1) Having strength.

Tucker: (1) One who sews tucks in fabric.

Tujunga: (1) Mountain range.

Tyler: (1) Tiler of roofs; (2) Can be a reference to Christ as covering.

Tyrone: (1) Land of the youthful soldier.

Tyson: (1) Flaming torch.

Ulrich: (1) King of the wolves.

Una: (1) Number one; (2) Unity.

Ur: (1) Light; (2) Flaming fire.

Uri: (1) The Lord is my light.

Ursula: (1) A bear.

Utah: (1) High up; (2) Land of the sun; (3) People of the mountains.

Valentine: (1) Brave and strong.

Valerie: (1) Brave; (2) Courageous.

Valiant: (1) Brave and strong.

Valmai: (1) Hawthorn blossom; (2) May.

Valyermo: (1) Desert valley.

Vancouver: (1) Cow ford; (i.e. from the place where cows cross the river).

Vanessa: (1) A butterfly.

Vashti: (1) Good-looking.

Vasilis/Vasilii: (1) Kingly; (2) Royal.

Vaughan: (1) Small.

Vera: (1) Faith; (2) Belief.

Verity: (1) Truth.

Vermont: (1) Green mountain.

Veronica: (1) True image.

Vesna: (1) Messenger.

Vick: (1) One who looks after the fires.

Vicki: (1) Achieved victory or triumph.

Victoria: (1) Achieved victory or triumph.

Vietnam: (1) Great south.

Vincent: (1) Conqueror.

Violet: (1) Small blue-purple flower.

Virgil: (1) One who carries the staff.

Virginia: (1) Chaste; (2) Pure.

Vivien: (1) Lively; (2) Spritely.

Volker: (1) Protector of the people.

Vulcan: (1) The god of fire, metalwork, and craftwork.

Waikerie: (1) Many wings; (2) Things that fly.

Wakelin: (1) Foreigner.

Wallace: (1) Foreigner; (2) Stranger.

Wallie: See Wallace.

Wally: See Walter.

Walter: (1) Powerful fighter.

Wanda: (1) To wander.

Warren: (1) Guardian of wildlife.

Washington: (1) (English) Lives at the farm of the discerning; (2) (Teutonic) Spritely; (3) Active; (4) Capital (place of decision-making).

Wayne: (1) Maker of wagons.

Wendle: (1) A wanderer.

Wendy: (1) Friend.

Wesley: (1) Western field.

Westcott: (1) Cottage to the west.

Whitaker: (1) A white field.

Whitmore: (1) White grassy fields.

Whitney: (1) A white island.

Whittany: (1) White island.

Whoopie: (1) Enthusiastic merrymaking.

Whyalla: (1) Place with deep water.

Wilfred: (1) Steadfast tranquility.

William: (1) Your will acting as a guard of the thoughts of your mind (lit. "will-helmet"); (2) Strong-willed; (3) Determined to guard; (4) Speaks of choice.

Wilson: (1) Determined to guard; (2) See William.

Windsor: (1) Where the river bends.

Winifred: (1) Made peace; (2) Rewarded.

Winona: (1) First-born daughter.

Winston: (1) Wine's town.

Wisconsin: (1) Gathering of waters.

Wolfgang: (1) Wolf who moves forward.

Woolworths: (1) Sheep enclosure; (2) Sheep farm.

Wyoming: (1) Extensive plains; (2) Mountains and valleys alternating.

Yago: See Jacob.

Yale: (1) Fertile high ground.

Yamada: (1) Mountain rice field.

Yamamoto: (1) Base of the mountain.

Yan: (1) God has favored.

Yana: (1) (Slavic) God has favored; (2) (American Indian) A bear.

Yasmin: (1) Fragrant shrub.

Yisrael: (1) Rules with God.

York: (1) From the area of the yew trees; (2) Boar settlement.

Yorke/Yorkie: (1) Wild pig farm.

Yshua: (1) God is Savior.

Yukimura: (1) Snowy village.

Yvonne: (1) Bowman or archer.

Zac: (1) Remember; (2) Past.

Zachary: (1) God has remembered.

Zam Zam: (1) Well of Mecca; (2) Spring of Islam.

Zane: (1) God has favored.

Zara: (1) Daybreak.

Zebulun: (1) Dwelling.

Zechariah: (1) The Lord has remembered.

Zedekiah: (1) God is impartial; (2) Justice of Jehovah.

Zeeb: (1) A wolf.

Zeena: (1) A woman; (2) Feminine.

Zephaniah: (1) Hidden by God.

Zoe: (1) Spiritual Life.

Zoran: (1) Daybreak; (2) Dawn.

Zorka: (1) Star of the morning.

Appendix A

The Parallel of Joseph and Jesus

Adapted from A. W. Pink's, Gleanings in Genesis, 1922, Moody Press, USA.

No.	Joseph	Parallel	Jesus
1	Gen. 30:24 Gen. 41:45	Both share two names Joseph's name means "Adding" Christ adds to Heaven's inhabitants Zaphnath-paaneah: "Revealer of secrets" The thoughts of many hearts revealed He knew what was in people	John 12:24 Luke 2:34-35 John 2:25
2	Gen. 37:2	Occupation: shepherd	John 10:11
3	Gen. 37:2	Opposition to evil	John 7:7
4	Gen. 37:3	His father's love	Matt. 3:17
5	Gen. 37:3	Relation to his father's age	Mic. 5:2
6	Gen. 37:3	Coat of many colors	Titus 2:13
7	Gen. 37:4	Hated by his brethren	John 1:11
8	Gen. 37:4-5, 8	Hated because of his words	John 7:7
9	Gen. 37:11	Prophetic future	Isa. 9:6-7
10	Gen. 37:7, 9	Future sovereignty foretold Earthly and heavenly	Matt. 28:18
11	Gen. 37:4, 11	Envied by his brethren	Matt. 27:18
12	Gen. 37:13	Sent forth by his father	1 John 4:10
13	Gen. 37:14	Seeks the welfare of his brethren	John 1:11

No.	Joseph	Parallel	Jesus
14	Gen. 37:14	Sent forth from the vale of Hebron Hebron: "fellowship, communion"	Phil. 2:6-7
15	Gen. 37:14	Came to Shechem, meaning "shoulder" Jesus became our burden-bearer	Isa. 53:6b Phil. 2:7
16	Gen. 37:17	Became a wanderer in a field	Matt. 8:20
17	Gen. 37:17	Finds his brethren in Dothan Dothan means "law" or "custom"	Mark 7:8
18	Gen. 37:18	Conspired against	Matt. 12:14
19	Gen. 37:19-20	Words disbelieved	Matt. 27:39ff
20	Gen. 37:24	Stripped	Matt. 27:28
21	Gen. 37:24	Cast into a pit	Zech. 9:11 Matt. 12:40
22	Gen. 37:28	Bodily lifted from the pit	1 Cor. 15
23	Gen. 37:25, 27	Hypocrisy mixed with hatred	John 18:28
24	Gen. 37:28	Sold Judah=Judas	Matt. 26:14-16
25	Gen. 37:31-32	Blood presented to the father	Heb. 9:11-12
26	Gen. 39:1	Becomes a servant	Phil. 2:6-7
27	Gen. 39:2-3	Prospers as a servant	Isa. 52:13
28	Gen. 39:4	Master well pleased with him	John 8:29
29	Gen. 39:5	As a servant, made a blessing for others	Heb. 11:26
30	Gen. 39:6	A goodly person	Matt. 27:54
31	Gen. 39:7-12	Tempted, yet sinned not	Matt. 4:1-11
32	Gen. 39:16-19	Falsely accused	Matt. 26:59
33	Gen. 39:19	No defense offered	Isa. 53:7 Mark 15:3-5
34	Gen. 39:20	Cast into prison	Isa. 53:8 Mark 15:6, 9
35	Gen. 40:15	Suffered though innocent	2 Cor. 5:21
36	Gen. 39:20	Suffered at the hand of Gentiles	Acts 4:27-28
37	Gen. 39:21	Won respect of the jailer	Luke 23:47

No.	Joseph	Parallel	Jesus
38	Gen. 40:1-3	Numbered with the transgressors	Isa. 53:12 Matt. 27:38
39	Gen. 40:13, 19	Means of blessing and judgment	Luke 23:39-43
40	Gen. 40:8	Foretold the future from God	John 12:49
41	Gen. 40:20-22	Predictions came true	Matt. 26:31
42	Gen. 40:14	Desire to be remembered	Luke 22:19
43	Gen. 41:1	Resurrected on the third day (In Hebrew culture: a week of years)	1 Cor. 15:4
44	Gen. 45:7-9	Delivered by the hand of God	Acts 2:24-25
45	Gen. 41:45	Seen as a revealer of secrets Jesus knew what was in people's hearts	John 2:25 Matt. 19:21
46	Gen. 41:25-36	Warning of retribution	Matt. 24
47	Gen. 41:33-36	Wonderful Counselor	Isa. 9:6 Col. 2:3
48	Gen. 41:37-39	Counsel commended	Matt. 13:54
49	Gen. 41:39-41	Exalted and set over all Egypt	1 Pet. 3:22
50	Gen. 41:40-43	Seated on the throne of another	Rev. 3:21
51	Gen. 41:38	Exalted because of personal worthiness	Acts 2:24
52	Gen. 41:42	Given positional insignia	Heb. 2:9 Rev. 1:13
53	Gen. 41:43	Authority and glory publicly declared	Phil. 2:10-11
54	Gen. 41:45	Received a new name	Phil. 2:9 Rev. 3:21
55	Gen. 41:45	Given a Gentile bride	Rev. 19:7-9
56	Gen. 41:45	Marriage arranged by Pharaoh	Matt. 22:2
57	Gen. 41:46	Thirty years old when began work	Luke 3:23
58	Gen. 41:46	Went forth on his mission from Pharaoh's presence	John 17:8
59	Gen. 41:46	Service was active and itinerant	Matt. 4:23 Matt. 9:35
60	Gen. 41:47-49	Exaltation followed by season of plenty	John 12:24
61	Gen. 41:53-54	Exaltation followed by a season of famine	Rev. 11:25

No.	Joseph	Parallel	Jesus
62	Gen. 41:55	Dispensing to a perishing world	1 Cor. 7:31 1 John 2:17
63	Gen. 41:55	Alone dispenses the Bread of Life	Acts 4:12 John 6:26-59
64	Gen. 41:57	A Savior to all the world	John 3:16
65	Gen. 41:49	Unlimited resources	Eph. 2:7; 3:8
		Dispensationally Considered	
66	Gen. 42:1-5	Brethren driven out of own land	Deut. 28:63-68
67	Gen. 42:6-8	Unknown and unrecognized by brethren	John 1:11 Luke 19:42, 44
68	Gen. 42:7	Brethren seen and recognized	Luke 19:41
69	Gen. 42:7, 17	Brethren punished	Matt. 23:35-39
70	Gen. 42:17-19, 24	Made known to them a way of deliverance through substitution	Acts 2:21-41
71	Gen. 42:25	Made provision for his brethren while they were in a strange land	Jer. 30:11 Ezek. 11:16
72	Gen. 45:1 Acts 7:13	Made known to his brethren the second time	Matt. 23:39
73	Gen. 44:16	Brethren confess their guilt in the sight of God	Zech. 12;10
74	Gen. 45:3	Brethren initially troubled in his presence	Zech. 12:10
75	Gen. 45:4, 5, 15	Demonstrated marvelous grace	Zech. 13:1 Isa. 54:7-8
76	Gen. 45:1	Revealed as a man of compassion	John 11:35
77	Gen. 45:1	Revealed to Judah and brethren before rest of Jacob's household	Zech. 12:7
78	Gen. 45:18	Jacob then sent for	Isa. 66:20
79	Gen. 45:9, 13	Brethren go forth to proclaim his glory	Isa. 66:19
80	Gen. 46:29	Goes forth in his chariot to meet Jacob	Isa. 66:15
81	Gen. 47:6, 27	Settles brethren in best of land	Ezek. 48
82	Gen. 50:18-19	Brethren prostrate before him as a representative of God	Phil. 2:10-11
		Evangelistically Considered	
83	Gen. 42:5	Brethren dwelt in a land of famine	John 6:33, 35

No.	Joseph	Parallel	Jesus
84	Gen. 42:3	Brethren wanted to pay for what they received	Gal. 2:16
85	Gen. 42:7-11	Brethren assumed a self-righteous attitude before the lord of Egypt	John 8:39, 41
86	Gen. 42:17	Cast into prison three days	John 2:19 2 Pet. 3:8
87	Gen. 42:21	Smitten of conscience	John 8:9
88	Gen. 42:25	Makes known deliverance is by grace	Eph. 2:8-9
89	Gen. 42:26	Brethren enjoy a brief respite	
90	Gen. 42:27-28	Superficial peace disturbed	Heb. 12:6-11
91	Gen. 43:11, 15	Brethren continued to manifest legalistic spirit (doubled money)	Gal. 3:3
92	Gen. 43:16, 33-34	Brethren dine with him and make merry	Matt. 13:20-21
93	Gen. 44:1-2	Determined to bring his brethren into the light	John 1:4, 7-9
94	Gen. 44:4, 16	Brethren take their true place before God	1 John 1:7-9
95	Gen. 45:1	Makes himself known (alone)	1 Cor. 13:12
96	Gen. 45:4, 7	Invites brethren to come close to him	Matt. 11:28-30 John 20:27
97	Gen. 45:10-11	Brethren told of full provision for them	Phil. 4:19
98	Gen. 45:15	Gives proof that he is fully reconciled to them	Rom. 8:31-39
99	Gen. 45:16	Joy shared by others	Rev. 5:9-13
100	Gen. 45:9-13	Brethren go forth seeking others	Acts 1:8
101	Gen. 45:24	Instruction as they go forth	Matt. 28:19-20

Appendix B

Getting Right With God

If I am not a Christian, what must I do to get right with God?

God loves you and has been trying to get your attention through the dreams He has given you. If you now want to get right with Him, then you need to take the following steps:

1. Admit your insensitivity to His communication (the Bible calls this *having a hardened heart*).

2. Recognize and admit that in your life you have done wrong (the Bible calls this *sin*).

3. Turn away from doing your own thing and be prepared to let God lead you.

4. Understand that when Jesus Christ died upon the cross, He died as the penalty for your sin. He took your punishment. Jesus willingly laid down His life so that you could come into a relationship with God. This privilege is based solely on your faith in the worth of Jesus' blood shed for you. Jesus is the sinless and eternal Son of God. (Jesus was raised from the dead after three days as proof of God's acceptance of Jesus' blood as payment for your sin).

5. With this knowledge, now ask God with all of your heart for forgiveness for all your sins. By faith as you pray this prayer, your sin is placed upon Christ, and in return God has brought you into right standing with Himself. You are now born again and have eternal life. Hallelujah!

6. If you prayed that prayer, you have been cleansed from your sin and now need the Holy Spirit to fill you so that you have the power to live the Christian life. Simply ask Jesus to fill you with His Spirit right now.

7. Congratulations! You have just made the most important decision of your life!

8. Where do you go from here?

   - Get to know God by reading the Bible daily (The Gospel of Mark in the New Testament is a great place to start).

   - Set aside a time to speak with God in prayer on a daily basis.

   - Ask Him to lead you to a Spirit-filled church that you may be strengthened and encouraged by the faith of other believers.

Subject Index

Sample Dream and Vision Index

ABOUT THE AUTHORS

Adam F Thompson

Adam has a remarkable grace to interpret dreams, move in the word of knowledge, and demonstrate the prophetic. Supernatural signs and manifestations regularly accompany his ministry as he desires to see Jesus "magnified" through the moving of the Holy Spirit. He has ministered extensively in America, Pakistan, India, Africa, Indonesia, Papua New Guinea, Malaysia and the Philippines in crusades, feeding programs, and pastor's conferences. Adam has been instrumental in planting 'Field of Dreams' Church in South Australia.

Adrian Beale

Adrian is an international itinerant Bible-teacher with a consistent ability to open God's Word and bring supernatural revelation with impartation. He possesses more than 18 years pastoral experience and has a strong desire to see believers enter the Kingdom of God.